the CREATION *of the* AMERICAN STATES

the CREATION *of the* AMERICAN STATES

A. Ward Burian

NEW YORK

LONDON • NASHVILLE • MELBOURNE • VANCOUVER

the CREATION *of the* AMERICAN STATES

Published in New York, New York, by Morgan James Publishing. Morgan James is a trademark of Morgan James, LLC. www.MorganJamesPublishing.com

The Morgan James Speakers Group can bring authors to your live event. For more information or to book an event visit The Morgan James Speakers Group at www.TheMorganJamesSpeakersGroup.com.

ISBN 978-1-68350-909-7 paperback
ISBN 978-1-68350-910-3 eBook
Library of Congress Control Number: 2017919150

Cover Design by:
Rachel Lopez
www.r2cdesign.com

Interior Design by:
Bonnie Bushman
The Whole Caboodle Graphic Design

Dedication

This book is dedicated to the memory of my parents, Margaret Ward Burian and Arthur J. Burian. My father's parents were immigrants from Austria-Hungary, and my mother's came from Ireland in the late 1800's. My mother's ancestors left after the Great Famine devastated so many people in Ireland. My father's ancestors left Vienna to escape the political turmoil in their country. My parents started to work as teenagers in New York City when they graduated from high school. They lived in New York their entire lives with modest means and were dedicated to my receiving a good education. Having graduated from Friends Academy in Locust Valley, New York, Dartmouth College, and New York University Graduate School of Business, I fulfilled their goals. They represented the hopes and ambitions of so many Americans who lived through the Great Depression of the 1930's and the horrors and depravations of the Second World War. They were part of the continuing story of America whereby each generation aspired to a better life for their children, and I shall always be grateful for their sacrifices.

About the cover: *The front cover is an adaptation of the Great Seal of the United States with the addition of 50 stars representing the total number of states existing in 1959 down to the present day. In 1776, shortly after adopting the Declaration of Independence, Congress asked Benjamin Franklin, Thomas Jefferson and John Adams to form a committee to design a Great Seal. The project took four years for the design and two more years before gaining congressional approval in 1782. Francis Hopkinson, Chairman of the Continental Navy's Middle Department is credited with designing the "Stars and Stripes" American flag with its circle of 13 stars on a dark blue background as well as the Great Seal. The reverse side of the Seal appears on the United States dollar bill and consists of many significant symbols: the eagle clutches a 13-leaf olive branch symbolizing peace while also clutching 13 arrows symbolizing war to defend itself. The eagle holds a 13-word banner in its beak with the country's first motto "E Pluribus Unum" meaning "one from many." The shield has 13 vertical alternating red and white stripes symbolizing the valor and purity of the 13 colonies. Above the eagle is a hexagon of 13 stars which represent a new constellation in the heavens just as it does on the American flag. Using the amended seal is most appropriate for a book that discusses the American transition from 13 colonies to a nation of 50 states.*

Table of Contents

Preface

Every state has a unique history that deserves a separate book. However, this book attempts to give the reader essential information on how each of the fifty American states came into being from the time of the first explorers and settlers to becoming a state. It tells the story of how the United States was established over the course of four hundred years. I have chosen to concentrate on the time frame for each state's discovery, settlement, and consolidation into one country. The discovery phase is there to set the stage and give credit to those individuals who dared to put their life, fortune, and reputation on the line. In the Introduction, we start with what motivated these brave souls to venture into an unknown wilderness, whether to Massachusetts or Mississippi or the far west. Their personal privations were unimaginable, but their desires for fortune or simply a better life were even stronger. Many had come from countries where there were few, if any, personal rights or opportunities to realize their hopes, talents, or ambitions. Even after arriving, if conditions were bleak, they dared to move on in search of some place in North America promising better opportunities. Their spirit was best described in Thomas Jefferson's "Declaration of Independence" where he wrote that "…all men are created equal…they are endowed by their Creator with certain unalienable rights that among these are Life, Liberty and the pursuit of Happiness." To the early American settlers, the right to "happiness" was not the right to have everything one wanted. Instead, the key word was "pursuit" of a better life where established laws were adhered to and individual freedoms were protected.

Part One is presented in chronological order of establishment as colonies and not as states because all thirteen came into statehood shortly after the Constitutional Convention in 1787. All thirteen colonies had to ratify legislation, and their order of statehood was determined by fleet of foot (or horse) of whoever arrived in Congress to deliver their papers first. Part Two shows the order of all the territories achieving statehood. I have tried to encapsulate the major events that shaped their beginning. A number of states in many regions had similar explorers and early origins, so I have included some special events that were unique to each state. Also, I have added brief biographies of statesmen and heroes who were responsible for particular issues, decisions, or accomplishments. The purpose is to inject human interest into the narrative and give perspective to what was taking place during their lives. In many cases America's expansion victimized the Native Americans, and even though leaders like Washington and Lincoln had some success with native assimilation, issues on the frontiers were often decided by force and bloodshed that created deep-seated animosity.

It is my intent for readers to learn a great deal about the history of the United States with this one small book. They should gain a better understanding of how the North American continent was transformed from a wilderness into a powerful nation.

A. Ward Burian
Williamsburg, Virginia

Introduction

Migration Caused By Economic Conditions

Most stories of America's settlement focus on the hardships of those brave people who dared to start a new life in a strange and foreign land. However, we should also study what drove these hardy souls to sacrifice everything they possessed to make such a dangerous venture across uncharted and stormy seas. This is more easily understood if we examine what life was like in England in the early 17th century. Events in 16th century England set the stage for the momentous changes that were about to unfold in the next century. Chief among these was the emergence of England as a new world power during the reign of Queen Elizabeth and the religious upheaval caused by her father, King Henry VIII, in 1536 when he broke with the Roman Catholic Church and assumed sovereignty of the Anglican Church. Before the great migrations to North America started in the early 1600's, England experienced enormous migrations from its predominantly rural populations to its large cities of which London was the largest with an estimated 350,000 people. Young men and women flocked to Europe's largest city in search of betterment through domestic service jobs, professional careers, apprenticeships, navigation, and trading opportunities. Their search for adventure and fortune was extremely difficult because of the excess labor supply and limited availabilities. Other obstacles included poor sanitation and malnutrition, which led to poor health and poverty. The migration overwhelmed cities and even just parts of cities like East London where the population grew from 21,000 in 1600 to 91,000 in 1700. These conditions led to increased vagrancy at a time when England's textile industry was in collapse and plague spiked mortality rates to 24 percent. Conditions worsened causing Parliament and the monarchy to find ways of controlling migration which ultimately led to regulating travel, especially to overseas colonies. Navigation and trade with North America and the West Indies were seen as the best opportunities, and the government encouraged and supported these endeavors through the granting of charters throughout the North American and Caribbean plantations.

We should not overlook the important role played by investors who gathered in the key city of London from all over England and the continent. They were responsible for organizing and financing the many colonial trading companies which led to the birth of the English empire. This was also true of the well-established merchant guilds which invested heavily in colonial enterprises. Because many of these companies were structured as stock entities, this allowed even the small investor to participate in the burgeoning new trading opportunities. The wealthier investors usually purchased shares in several such companies in an effort to broaden their holdings and mitigate their risk. The result of these new-found business activities was a mixing of the investor class together with those who sought employment. Hundreds of ships carried crowds of adventurous people with differing means, social standing, and objectives which otherwise would never have happened in England's stratified society. One could make the argument that America's "melting pot" was started on the docks of England's ports. However, the sense of community aboard ship was not shared equally because of the varying purposes and destinations involved. New England bound passengers frequently travelled as an entire family seeking a new economic and religious life. Adventurers and merchants usually disembarked in Virginia or in Bermuda or Barbados where they sought work or investment opportunities. Those going to the West Indies were mostly single men seeking work as servants. This resulted from high mortality rates and the ever-increasing demand for labor.

The most critical resource necessary for the success of a colony was a constant supply of labor to clear land and cultivate the soil for planting crops for export. Also, colonies needed skilled labor which was more difficult to find.[1]

The most common form of labor was the use of indentured servants. This was a widespread practice in England where laws confirmed what servants were entitled to. The contract was for a stipulated term of years for which the servant was provided with clothing, room and board, and adequate training for the work to be performed as well as his passage. Masters sometimes mistreated their servants with physical abuse, but this was no different from their treatment in England. If planters did not adhere to their contractual responsibilities, servants had recourse to legal redress. Officers of the court would be appointed to investigate the complaint, and they could intervene to correct the situation. The courts realized that maintaining good relations between managers and labor was in the best interests of a successful colony. Upon the completion of the indentured term, the servant was granted his or her (women were also indentured) freedom together with promised monies and/or goods as well as 50 acres of land. It was the land that attracted most migrants to the colonies because of affordability or availability. This was what they had really worked for as land was an enormous commodity that was rarely available to them at home.[2] After adequate migratory controls were in place in the early part of the 17th century, it was Parliament's policy to settle the colonies as quickly and as prudently as possible. The distribution of land was a key element in achieving that goal. For every indentured servant transported to the colonies as much as 200 acres could be granted. The investor, the ship owner, the ship captain, and the passenger servant were each entitled to 50 acres of land with the stipulation that a minimum of 1 acre had to be planted and a house of any size must be constructed. A good example of this was the land acquired by George Washington's great-grandfather, John. After arriving penniless from England in 1656, following the sinking of his employer's cargo ship in the Potomac, he worked as a planter, married well, and served with distinction in the Virginia militia as well as in the House of Burgesses. He was granted land on the Potomac and proceeded to invest in transporting as many as 60 servants to the Tidewater area, thereby acquiring thousands of acres of land. This was easily done as the Crown "owned" the land in all Royal Colonies. When one considers the size of Virginia claimed by the Crown we should note that this first colony encompassed all of present Virginia, West Virginia, Maryland, Delaware, New Jersey, the western part of New York, most of Pennsylvania, Ohio, Indiana, Illinois, Michigan, and Wisconsin. The Charter granted to the Virginia Company in 1606, by King James I, describes the boundaries from the Virginia/North Carolina border northward to a point just below New York City, northwest along the eastern shores of the Great Lakes with everything encompassed from "sea to shining sea" meaning the Atlantic and Pacific Oceans. When the Crown took back that charter in 1624, it was free to parcel out vacant lands and plantations to form other emerging colonies.

Other forms of acquiring land involved purchasing it for hard currencies which were in short supply. It could also be inherited, and certainly large tracts were handed down by first- and second-generation settlers. It was also gifted as was the case with John Washington when he married Nathaniel Pope's daughter and received 700 acres on the Potomac as a wedding gift. However, the most prominent form of acquisition was through grants from wealthy owners, most of whom resided in England. Certainly, one of the largest gifts of land was a parcel of eight million square miles in Virginia known as the Northern Neck. It was bounded on the east by the Chesapeake Bay, on the south by the Rappahannock River, on the north by the Potomac River and on the west by the foothills of the Appalachian Mountains. The gift was from King Charles II to Lord Thomas Culpepper whose father had sheltered the young prince during the time of England's Parliamentary Period when Oliver Cromwell captured and then executed the prince's father, King Charles I. When Culpepper's daughter married Lord Thomas Fairfax, the land eventually passed to the Fairfax family. In 1670, John Washington applied to Fairfax for a grant of 4,800 acres on the Potomac side of the Northern Neck. He did this in partnership with one of his Virginia militia lieutenants, Nicholas Spencer, to be shared equally. The land was divided in 1690, and the 2,400 acres was passed down from John Washington's son, Lawrence, and then to his daughter, Mildred, who then sold it to her brother, Augustine, who then left it to his son, Lawrence, who then willed it to his wife, Ann Fairfax, and finally to his half-brother, George. It was Lawrence who named the property "Mount Vernon" in honor of his commanding English navy officer, Admiral Edward Vernon. When George inherited the original 2,400 acres in 1752 when his brother Lawrence died, he began his life-long acquisition of 5,500 contiguous acres and also enlarged and remodeled the small structure that his brother had built in the mid-1740's.

Migration Caused By Religious Conditions

Because the head of the Anglian Church was also the monarch, the church and state acted in concert. With his accession to the position of Archbishop of Canterbury in 1633, William Laud became the second most powerful man in England. Laud was of necessity a strong royalist, and he and Charles I promulgated many regulations over the migrating hordes eager to leave England for North America. They appointed commissioners to the various ports of embarkation and were required to record the names, addresses, place of birth, trade, vocation, and cause for leaving. In addition, they administered an oath of allegiance to the crown. Passengers had to prove they did not owe taxes and had to provide letters from their respective parishes that they were members in good standing. Laud was perceived as wanting a closer relationship with the Vatican. He introduced reforms in the Anglican ritual that were regarded as "popish" and which affected even the smallest parish. Those clerics who did not conform were relieved of their pulpits. Naturally, such tendencies toward church hierarchy and even the movement of communion tables to "altars" were not well received. Puritans were especially horrified at the decided shift to Catholicism which was deemed to be supported by Charles whose mother and wife were Roman Catholic. It should be noted that the Scottish Stuarts were Roman Catholic, and the acceptance of James I, Charles I, and Charles II as monarchs by the English Parliament was only due to their being raised and educated by protestants as well as their personal allegiance to the Church of England. However, Archbishop Laud's policies only served to unite the puritans in their determination to leave England. To better understand the intense anti-Catholic feelings of English citizens, one has to go back to 1536 when King Henry VIII caused Parliament to pass the Act of Supremacy making him the "Supreme Head" of the Church of England. Catholic churches, monasteries, abbeys as well as all objects of value were sold with proceeds going into the crown's treasury. Roman Catholic England became protestant overnight which caused major upheavals and discontent. The throne was soon inherited by Queen Mary in 1553. She was Henry VIII's first child by Catherine of Aragon. As the devout Catholic daughter of King Ferdinand and Queen Isabella of Spain, she persecuted all non-Catholics and earned the name "Bloody Mary" for her gruesome treatment of those who did not worship as devout Roman Catholics. Mary was succeeded by her half-sister, Elizabeth, in 1558. She was a staunch Anglican who declared herself as "Supreme Governor" of the Church of England. Any challenge to Church authority was a direct affront to the crown. All English subjects were required to attend weekly worship, and failure to attend worship or refusal to participate in the liturgy was regarded as a crime and a subversive act. Protestant sects and many Anglican members were deeply offended by Elizabeth's and Mary's Catholic practices. They wanted a purer worship based on Scripture. The offended Anglicans were known as "Puritans", and while they were tolerated by Elizabeth, she stated there could not be two religions in one state.[3] These dramatic changes from 1536 to Elizabeth's death in 1603, had a lasting effect on the English for many years and accounted for religious turmoil until Parliament resolved the issue in 1701 by law denying the throne to Roman Catholics. It is imperative to know the religious background of this period in order to understand the strong religious convictions of America's founders. These beliefs formed the basis for colonial attitudes toward religious tolerance and the founders' insistence on America's right to freedom of religion to be incorporated in its Constitution in 1790.

The Creation Of North American Colonies

Before actual "colonies" were created through the explorations of men like Walter Raleigh and John Cabot these new settlements were called "plantations." They included New England, Virginia, Bermuda, Barbados, and several smaller islands in the West Indies. Plantations is a most appropriate name inasmuch as these new-found lands were used as sources of raw material and specialty crops for export back to England. These ranged from iron ore in the mid-Atlantic area, tobacco in the Tidelands, lumber and hemp in the Carolina's, to fruits and vegetables in the Caribbean. There was practically no manufacturing at this early stage or for many years to come. In fact, almost all manufacturing was prohibited and restricted to England to protect their economy. This practice eventually became a major issue in America's fight for independence. One can think of the Plantation Period as a time of planting the seeds of a new nation as political and religious thinking germinated in the 17th century. As the seeds germinated and formed roots, these "plantings" developed into the flowering of new ideas and concepts in the fields of science and political philosophy. Such notables as Isaac Newton, Robert Boyle, Voltaire, John Locke, David Hume, Adam Smith, Immanuel Kant, James Watt, Jean-Jacques Rousseau, Richard Blackmore, Joseph Black, John Milton, and even America's Benjamin Franklin were born during 1650's to the early 1700's and became prominent in what is known as "The Enlightenment." Americans George Mason, John Adams, Thomas Jefferson, and James Madison, among many others, studied the writings of these men which had a great impact on the development of the American concepts of liberty and personal freedoms.

The British Bill of Rights was formed in 1688, and the Divine Rights of Kings was being challenged as England's Glorious Revolution succeeded in bloodlessly overthrowing King James II in 1689 and installing William of Orange as their new monarch. With the passing of King William III in 1701 and the last of the Stuarts, we see an emerging new element in political government in the form of a more powerful Parliament. With the ascendancy of the House of Hanover in 1714 and the non-English speaking English King George I residing in Germany, the political leadership vacuum was filled by Robert Walpole in the newly created unofficial position of Prime Minister. As the American colonies took hold and Parliament gained more power relative to the monarchy, we can begin to better understand the events that led to America's emergence as an independent nation.

The establishment of colonies in North America by England took three different forms. First was by corporate joint stock ownership by investors. However, that charter could be changed if conditions warranted as was the case with Virginia. The second was by Royal Charter directly from the monarch whereby the Crown owned and ruled that colony even though they all elected their own legislative bodies. The third was by a Proprietary contract to an individual or group of individuals allowing them to govern their colony themselves. Royal Charters granted to North American colonies were issued under the authority of England's monarchs. Each was ruled by a royal governor who was the king's appointed agent charged with executing the king's policies. The colonies elected their own legislatures. This included Virginia which was first granted a corporate charter from King James I to the Virginia Company in 1606 as a joint stock enterprise. After barely surviving from 1607 to 1624, the stock charter was revoked and replaced by a Royal Charter. This was followed by New York which was founded as a Dutch proprietary settlement in 1626 but was later acquired by England under a Royal Charter when they invaded and defeated the Dutch in 1664. Proprietary charters were issued to individuals who had the authority to govern themselves. The third colony was Massachusetts which received its Corporate Charter in 1630 which allowed it to govern itself. In 1633, Maryland was granted a proprietary charter by King Charles I to George Calvert, Lord Baltimore. The next colony of Rhode Island was founded by Roger Williams in 1636 under a Corporate Charter which was changed to a Royal Charter in 1663. Also in 1636, a Corporate Charter was granted to Connecticut. Another Proprietary Charter was issued to Delaware in 1638. That same year, New Hampshire gained a Corporate Charter which was changed to a Royal Charter in 1679. Another Proprietary Charter was given to North Carolina in 1653 and also one to New Jersey in 1660 which was changed to a Royal Charter in 1664 as a result of the English defeat of the Dutch. Two more colonies received a Proprietary Charter with South Carolina in 1670 and Pennsylvania in 1682. The 13th colony of Georgia was granted a Royal Charter in 1733. The two settlements of Roanoke and Plymouth never received charters because the first didn't survive from its initial founding in 1584, and the second was an unofficial pilgrimage and settlement without English government or church sanction or support.

The Appointment of William Laud to the position of Archbishop of Canterbury in 1633 marked the beginning of the first significant migrations to North America. In 1635 alone over 5,000 passengers left their English homeland for America. Major destinations were New England, Virginia, Bermuda, and Barbados. Other smaller plantations included St. Kitts and Providence Island in the Caribbean. All English colonies in the 1600's were known as "plantations." However, all were not settled by puritans, even though all plantations did receive them. There is no question that the persecution of puritans in England was the principal motivation for the large migrations in the 1630's and 1640's. It was the in-dominatable faith of the puritans that accounted for their survival in spite of the varied forms of worship from colony to colony and the differing political structures they adopted. Although disputes about certain practices arose in almost every parish, the newly arrived settlers realized that the most important part of their new environment was church membership. Without church affiliation, children could not be baptized, important sacraments could not be received, and they would not be eligible for political office. Oddly enough, it was the internal divisions among the puritans that led to the rapid founding of new towns because they could not resolve their differences. While external forces threatened their survival, it was the internal differences that would have dissolved their puritan mission if it wasn't for the fact that the settlers accepted the unified authority of their political and religious leaders. If religious practices within their respective towns or colonies changed to their disfavor, or if political policies became unbearable, settlers would migrate to another area in that colony or even to another colony.[4] This was particularly true for New Englanders who had a history of similar behavior in England. The whole process of colonization was something new to most settlers, but if conditions warranted, they were not averse to moving elsewhere in order to avoid conflict and find new opportunities.[5] Some of these internal migrations were due to changed business conditions or land possibilities, but most of the changes were a result of religious worship or political considerations. The close proximity of the New England colonies as well as few possessions made such moves quite easy. A good example of religious conflict causing migration was the departure of Thomas Hooker from Cambridge to Connecticut where he started a settlement in Hartford. Many of his Massachusetts parish followed Hooker to Connecticut even though that colony did not require church membership as did Massachusetts. Rhode Island had even greater freedoms because it had no established church and offered the greatest religious tolerance in all of New England. When Roger Williams was banished from Salem in 1636 because of his religious convictions and practices, he founded the Providence Plantation. Accordingly, many of his former parishioners followed him there.[6]

As the original 13 colonies grew over the years, they developed their own distinctive characteristics from the races, cultures, and religions of those settlers who sought people who shared similar backgrounds. One of the greatest distinctions was religion. Most notable were Puritans in New England who later were termed Congregationalists. Virginia was populated mostly by Anglicans who changed their name to Episcopalians after the Revolutionary War. Quakers occupied Pennsylvania, and Catholics settled in Maryland. All colonies, except Rhode Island, had so-called "established" churches which were charged with specific obligations among which was a responsibility to provide for the poor in their respective colony. Other denominations in each colony were required to contribute funds to their established church for that purpose. There was no central government to assume that role. The various colonies created their own currency, tariffs, militia, and laws. Each assumed sovereignty, resulting in 13 independent entities. The spirit of independence was extremely strong, and citizens identified themselves as Virginians or New Englanders rather than as Americans. This was the situation by the time that frictions developed between Massachusetts and England just after the French and Indian War ended in 1763. The causes of that friction were many, but it was mainly due to the British policy to tax the colonies to defray the cost of protecting them and to reimburse the Crown for the war just ended. The larger issue was the hegemony England was exerting over their colonial brethren. Parliament passed a "Proclamation of 1763," which drew a longitudinal line down the Appalachian Mountains which denied settlers from occupying any lands west of that line. In fact, existing title holders had their property taken by the Crown. Some viewed the Proclamation as invalid, among who were a number of important investors in the Ohio River Valley, including such figures as George Washington. Perhaps the greatest cause of conflict was the perception by colonial leaders of England's behavior in Canada. They had defeated France in the Seven Years' War which ran consecutively and slightly longer than the French and Indian War. In taking possession of Canada, the English invoked martial law following the Treaty of Paris of 1763, a condition which they never relinquished until passage of the Quebec Act in 1774.They also expanded the Canadian boundary line southward into present-day Indiana which was designated for the Native American Indians. Americans eyed these moves with great suspicion and assumed similar treatment would befall them as they witnessed more taxes, the closing of the Port of Boston, quartering of British troops in private houses, blockading of American shipping, revoking some colonial charters, and the realization that they were no longer protected as British-American subjects under England's Constitution. Actually, there was some serious support for American rights in Parliament, but their influence diminished under the reign of King George III. American leaders miscalculated the political situation in England by appealing for support from the king thinking that it was Parliament that opposed them. In fact, the young 23-year-old king who assumed the throne in 1760 had been advised by his grandfather George II to wrest control of his country back from a Parliament that had grown quite strong over the prior 50 years. It was an adamant king who insisted that the American colonials should be taught a lesson thereby preventing any chance of a rapprochement. The king didn't realize that the Americans were not fighting to gain independence, but rather they were asserting their rights as British subjects to retain the independence they had practiced for 170 years since Jamestown. It was a colossal mistake on the part of King George to risk the loss of such a valuable treasure, but he had never fully understood or appreciated the American society, and he was convinced by his military that England was invincible. As frictions developed in Massachusetts in 1774 and early 1775, it was becoming obvious that open hostilities were likely. The key issue was whether other colonies would act in sympathy with them considering how independent they had been for so long. When Virginia's House of Burgesses met to discuss the growing problems in Massachusetts, royal Governor Dunmore dismissed them whereupon they convened a Day of Prayer for the people of Boston whose port had been blockaded. From that point on it was agreed to convene a Continental Congress in Philadelphia to prepare for possible war. It should be remembered that Virginia was the largest and wealthiest colony and dominated the south. Massachusetts leaders knew very well that they needed the support of Virginia, and assured that support with their proposal of George Washington as their Commander-in-Chief. The Americans dared to confront the mightiest military in Europe, but with Washington's strong leadership, patience, and resolve, the "impossible" happened and independence was won.

The Treaty of Paris ending the war in 1783 did a lot more than assure American independence. Quite unexpectedly to the American negotiators, John Adams and Benjamin Franklin, it granted American rights to the enormous tract of land below the Great Lakes to the Ohio River and westward to the Mississippi River. Known as the Northwest Territory, the land was preserved for future growth and eventually became the states of Ohio, Indiana, Illinois, Michigan, and Wisconsin. This was soon followed by the Louisiana Purchase in 1803, when Napoleon needed funds to finance his conquest of Europe and initiated the sale of all French holdings from the Gulf of Mexico northwestward from the Mississippi River to the Rocky Mountains northward to the border of Canada. Without any negotiating, he offered to sell the 828,000 square miles for $15 million. President Jefferson immediately accepted the offer without consulting Congress which technically was an act beyond his authority. Congress signed the sale afterwards fully realizing that the price paid was $.18 per square mile which they knew was the greatest land deal imaginable. The size of the United States immediately doubled, and from these lands another 15 states were created. What is also interesting is that at that time, France owned more property in the United States than any other foreign power. It should be noted that prior to the loss of Canada to England in 1763, France had established towns and trading settlements below the Great Lakes southward along the Mississippi River to the Gulf of Mexico. Their ultimate goal was to develop the middle of North America west of the Allegheny Mountains and block England from expanding westward. Indeed, maps published in Paris in the early 1700's show this territory as "New France." If Napoleon hadn't intervened in his European conquests, it is plausible that the United States would have had quite a different development.

The Constitutional Convention

During the Revolutionary War the Continental Congress believed it was necessary to adopt a document outlining their new form of government. This was to be far different from the Declaration of Independence which was a philosophical document describing American beliefs in freedom and God-given rights to life, liberty and the pursuit of Happiness. The new Articles was intended to form a structure of governance among 13 very independent states. It called for a "league of friendship" between the 13 sovereign states. In Congress, each state was entitled to one vote and could send two to seven delegates. However, the Articles did not provide for an executive branch or a Federal Judiciary system. These were purposely excluded out of fear of government interference in personal matters and domination from a strong central government. Also, there were no means for Congress to raise revenues for the public good, again out of the strong opposition to the British taxes of the 1760's and 70's. During the post-war period of 1783-1788, the nation prospered economically, but it was suffering from growing divisiveness between the states, a breakdown in law and order, and international weakness. Leaders like Washington, Madison, Hamilton, Adams, and Jay shared a deep concern in this deteriorating situation and proposed to call a convention of all the states for June of 1787 in Philadelphia. It was supposed to strengthen the existing Articles, but it soon became obvious that an entirely new constitution should be established. The result was a representative government that included a chief executive, a two-chamber Congress with a House of Representatives and a Senate and a Judicial Branch with a Supreme Court designed to keep laws that did not violate the Constitution. Adoption of the Constitution required each state to hold a ratifying convention with approval from a minimum of two-thirds (9) of them. Passage was not assured because of the absence of individual freedoms. The document did allow for future amendments, and when a Bill of Rights was promised, ratification was assured. However, one should note that many state votes were surprisingly close.

The Northwest Ordinance of 1787

The Peace Treaty of Paris ending the American Revolution in 1783 produced an unexpected provision granting the new American government ownership of land west of Pennsylvania, northwest of the Ohio River, north to Canada, and west to the Mississippi River. This enormous tract of land encompassed all of present-day Ohio, Indiana, Illinois, Michigan, Wisconsin, and part of Minnesota. The Confederation Congress enacted several regulations on the new "Northwest Territories," but the one passed in 1787 was the most critical for future expansion of the United States. It was the first organized U.S. territory and established that the impending new federal government should have sovereign authority which would allow new states to be formed from it.[7] The Ordinance was subsequently confirmed as legal by the Supreme Court. Slavery was to be prohibited in all of the territory, and this set the stage for the future of all states as they debated their rights to be "slave" or "free" states—an issue that eventually would be resolved through the crucible of a civil war. The Northwest Territory had been taken by Great Britain following their defeat of France in the Seven Years' War and the 1763 Treaty of Paris. They then closed it to new European settlers with the Proclamation of 1763 which revoked claims of ownership by Massachusetts, Connecticut, New York, and Virginia dating from early colonial days. The new territory was to be administered by the Congress which divided it into gridded townships which were surveyed and then sold to individuals and land companies. This provided a precedent for new lands to be administered temporarily by the federal government as well as all navigable waters to be common highways. After the state reached a population of 60,000, it would be admitted to representation in the Congress on an equal basis with existing states. The first state admitted under the Enabling Act of 1802 was Ohio. Other states to follow from the Northwest Territory were Indiana, Illinois, Michigan, Wisconsin, and the eastern portion of the future Minnesota. Prior to then, during the 1790's, the Republic of Vermont and the Kentucky and Tennessee territories were admitted. It should be noted that the Ordinance provided "Natural Rights" that were soon to be voted into the U.S. Constitution and the Bill of Rights. These included religious toleration and public education: "religion, morality, and knowledge being necessary to good government and the happiness of mankind, schools and the means of education shall forever be encouraged." Other rights included: habeas corpus, religious worship, prohibiting excessive fines, cruel and unusual punishment, and trial by jury.[8]

Manifest Destiny

With the rapid economic expansion of the United States following the Louisiana Purchase, Americans viewed their destiny as obvious, and in 1845 the term "Manifest Destiny" was coined. England, Spain, and France had withdrawn from their North American settlements, and as the U.S. economy grew together with inventions and agricultural advancements, it was clear to most that growth was a strong American driving force. It therefore became obvious to many that the country would or even should continue its expansion to the Pacific and the southwest. This meant that geographical conflicts with existing natives, whether American Indians or Mexican Hispanics, would occur. Americans thought of themselves as a civilizing society that would bring order to otherwise undeveloped lands. After all, this is what other countries like England, France, and Spain had done although with somewhat differing results. The earlier settlers of the 17th century were hopeful of assimilation and peaceful co-existence with the Native Americans, and while that was a possibility, it proved to be very difficult due to a growing lack of trust by both the natives and the newcomers who were regarded as intruders who acquired land and established towns and laws unfamiliar to the natives. The two cultures seemed incompatible, and savage waring and expansion proceeded with more animosities and atrocities. There was some accommodation with certain tribes like the Creeks in the south and Mohicans in New England, but the real problems persisted in the Allegheny frontiers and then in the west following the Louisiana Purchase. Likewise, slavery was an even greater issue and almost prevented the formation of the United States. As the Constitutional Convention met in 1787, the first words spoken to Chairman George Washington were from the representatives of South Carolina and Georgia who advised him that if the subject of slavery was introduced they would leave the Convention. Some historians remain critical of Washington for not dealing with slavery at that time, but his highest priority was forming a central government in order to preserve what seemed to be a country suffering from internal frictions as neighboring states infringed on sovereign rights, Revolutionary War debts remained unpaid, the British remained in a series of frontier forts around all the Great Lakes, England and France hijacked American ships and seamen, and chaos was widespread. Perhaps the one man who understood the need for unity was Washington who fought for 8 years for American independence with very little support from 13 very independent colonies. The Articles of Confederation had been in effect since 1778 but did not provide a judicial or executive branch of government or means to gather revenue. He realized the need for international credit and fiscal responsibility. When he assumed the presidency in 1789, he expressed support for banning slavery once it was introduced by Congress, but such bills were never introduced. He also warned that the unresolved slavery issue would someday divide the country. A compromise was reached by shelving the issue for 20 years, and in 1808 Congress passed a law prohibiting the slave trade and declaring it illegal. Slavery itself was not prohibited, and history tells us that it festered until 1861 and was only resolved through the agony of a civil war. In the 1780's and 90's there was a belief by some that slavery would diminish over the years, and this was supported by some evidence of manumission by slave owners of the voluntary freeing of slaves. Demographic figures of the 1780's to 1810 show the slavery population declining from 17.8 percent to 16.5 percent of the population. However, the trend reversed itself afterwards with the introduction of the cotton gin and the explosion in cotton exports and need for more manual labor.

The Nation Prospers

With the devastation of the Civil War that claimed over 600,000 American casualties and the assassination of one of its greatest leaders, Americans got to work to build a mighty nation. Westward expansion through new railroads and homesteading proceeded apace while industrialization exploded in the east and Midwest. New states were created and the population grew from 38 million in 1870 to 132 million in 1940 and 317 million in 2013. The number of states increased from 37 in 1870 to 50 in 1959 when Alaska and Hawaii were admitted. The origins of the states tell unusual stories about American history. They all have their founders and leaders, and some were actually started through the effort of a single person. As we have discussed, few if anyone could have envisioned the growth of the original plantations from their solitary existence in the 1600's into their size and complexity today. Our towns and streets are filled with names of the earliest settlers, and it is only proper that we pay our respect and give thanks to these unsung heroes who sacrificed their lives in pursuit of building a better life for themselves, their families, and, eventually, our comfort and happiness. The stories of their hardships and perseverance should serve as an inspiration for us all in the greatest experiment of mankind known as the United States of America.

I would like to end this Introduction with the final paragraph of Alison Games' excellent book: *Migration and the Origins of the English Atlantic World.* I believe these words capture the essence of those people who dared to journey into an unknown wilderness armed with little more than their spiritual beliefs and confidence in themselves: "Although the process of migration and remigration gradually made different parts of the Atlantic world familiar to many travelers and adventurers, the integration of this Atlantic world by any number of measures would be slow. The English people who inhabited it and traveled within it provided a crucial commonality that connected and sustained this odd and uncertain world. But in the 17th century the English Atlantic world remained, above all, a wild and chaotic place, one where servants rocked alone in hammocks strung between cedar poles under palm branch roofs, where puritan saints reigned; where children were bartered with other trade goods and livestock measured secured wealth; where desperate, brave, and ambitious people clambered between a fragile ship's decks and ventured over 3,000 treacherous miles for something better than the pittance they found at home; and where, above all, new accommodations were essential for survival." [9]

PART ONE

THE ORIGINAL THIRTEEN COLONIES IN CHRONOLOGICAL ORDER

DISCOVERY
To
SETTLEMENT
To
COLONY
To
STATE

Chapter One

Virginia

Founded as a colony in 1607 by John Smith and John Rolfe
State on June 25, 1788

The First Colony

As England was becoming a world power under Queen Elizabeth in the last half of the 16th century, it increasingly explored new trade routes to the Far East and the Americas. They were not alone as Spain and France were doing the same in an effort to claim new found lands as their own. Sir Walter Raleigh organized (but did not participate in) an expedition to Roanoke in 1584. He reported to Queen Elizabeth I that he had founded land that was ruled over by a Native American king by the name of "Wingina." The queen supposedly modified the name to "Virginia" in recognition of her being known as the "Virgin Queen." In 1606, a group of investors in England formed a joint stock company to explore Virginia and obtained a corporate charter from King James I. The ships Susan Constant, Godspeed, and Discovery were led by John Smith, John Rolfe, and Christopher

Newport with 105 passengers and 39 crew. They entered the Chesapeake Bay in May of 1607 and sailed up a body of water they named James River to honor King James I. Selecting a protected location they built a fortified settlement and called it Jamestown. The venture was strictly a commercial one even though one of their first projects was to build a church. Jamestown was to become the first permanent English settlement in the Americas.

That summer Christopher Newport returned to England with two ships, and those remaining in Jamestown sustained hardships of hunger and illness and the fear of attack from local Algonquian tribes. Relations between the settlers and the Natives were tense at first but did improve when John Smith established trade guidelines between them. Algonquian chief, Powhatan, and Smith managed to control relations, but skirmishes still occurred. In 1609, Smith returned to England, but without his presence the settlers were in a precarious position and continued to suffer illness and mounting deaths. In the spring of 1610, just as the remaining settlers were preparing to abandon Jamestown, two ships arrived with supplies, 150 new immigrants, and a new governor, Lord De La Warr. The governor soon fell sick and had to return home but was replaced by Sir Thomas Gates and Sir Thomas Dale who introduced laws that were designed to improve relations with the Algonquians. However, more raids led to the burning of crops and houses which led to more killings. Conditions improved by 1614 when John Rolfe married Chief Powhatan's daughter, Pocahontas. It was Rolfe who saved the settlement when he developed a special blend of tobacco from seeds gathered in the West Indies. After a few years of experimentation, he created a tobacco that became wildly popular in England and Europe and soon became the most successful export from the colonies. At last, the settlers found the gold they were looking for, but it was in the form of a cured tobacco leaf.

In 1619, the colony organized the first representative government in America. A General Assembly was elected by male landowners. That same year around 50 men, women, and children were brought to Jamestown having come from a Portuguese slave ship that was captured in the West Indies. They were hired to work as indentured servants, but were not treated as slaves as the institution of slavery occurred around 1680.

Origin of the Tobacco Trade

The primary objective of the Virginia Company for its investment in the colony of Virginia was to develop a source for commodities that could replace the necessities England was buying from other countries. By importing goods from her colonies, England would be reducing her imports from abroad and improving her balance of trade in an age of competitive mercantilism. The Company hoped Virginia would produce lumber, wine, skins, fish and herbs, and other staples, but these could not be produced on a profitable scale so the Company faltered economically and came very close to dissolving within the first 10 years of its Jamestown settlement in 1607. In 1612 one of Capt. John Smith's principal assistants, John Rolfe, discovered that tobacco grew well in Virginia's warm and humid climate, and even though the initial shipments of the local leaf were found to be bitter and un-salable in England, he experimented with imported seeds from Trinidad and Venezuela which produced a sweet-scented leaf. The favorable reception to the new product created a veritable "gold rush" in Virginia where tobacco seeds were planted in every possible clearing including the interior of the local fort. In 1616, 11 commodities were sent to England, but by 1619, they were entirely replaced by tobacco and a small amount of sassafras. Ironically, the Virginia Company did not condone this one-product economy, and even King Charles I was outspoken in his criticism of the popular "deceivable weed" which provided no usefulness to the needs of his subjects.[1] The Virginia Company was unsuccessful in raising investment capital for the establishment of fishing, glass, iron, lumber, and shipbuilding industries, so they resorted to lotteries for funds which were so successful that in 1621, the Privy Council deprived the Company of its rights to hold lotteries on the grounds that they were undermining useful trade and industries. This was followed in 1622 by Indian massacres of 400 of the 1240 Jamestown settlers which finally led to the dissolution of the Virginia Company by the Crown in 1624. This, in turn, gave rise to the dramatic development of the Virginia tobacco trade which exported 60,000 pounds of tobacco in 1622, 500,000 pounds in 1628, and 1,500,000 pounds in 1639. By the end of the 1600's, Virginia and Maryland production reached 20,000,000 pounds annually, and by 1775 it exceeded 100,000,000 pounds which was equivalent to 75 percent of the total value of all commodities exported from the Chesapeake colonies. Tobacco proved to be easy to grow with minimum labor and production costs. Its use for pipe smoking and snuff created a fad among the British gentry, thereby demanding forced ever-higher market prices. Its growth was considered one of the easiest and quickest ways of realizing income and possible wealth especially if one could obtain land grants of sufficient size for producing large crops. It was during the early 1600's that George Washington's great-grandfather, John Washington, learned the workings of the tobacco trade while employed in a London counting house, and it was the lure of profitable trade that attracted him to enter the trans-Atlantic trade with America and particularly the export of tobacco to England and its re-export to the Continent.[1]

Growth and the Export Trade

With the rapid commercial success of tobacco, the English authorities soon gave their support because it brought significant income to the royal treasury through imposed duties. The vast quantities of imported tobacco also helped England's balance of trade and reduced her dependence on tobacco from Spain with whom it had an unfavorable balance of trade. In fact, the colonial imports were so great that the surplus allowed the re-export of tobacco from England to Europe and several other foreign markets, improving her export balances even more. However, the fascinating aspect to this entirely new colonial commercial endeavor was the impact it had on the political relationship between England and the colonies. During the early years of Virginia's settlement, there was no official British colonial policy regarding their administration. The success of tobacco prompted England to change that situation whereby Virginia was regarded as outside the fiscal limits of England and therefore subject to customs duties. Also, Virginia was required to export solely to England and was forbidden to trade directly with foreign countries. In return, the planting of tobacco in England was forbidden after 1619 and in 1624 foreign ships were denied trade with Virginia. Thereafter followed the Navigation Acts of 1650, 1660, 1663, and 1696—all of which were intended to secure revenue to the royal treasury. These measures were later extended to include most commodities from all the colonies which proved to be one of the principal contentious issues by 1775.

As the tobacco trade exploded it became a very significant source of revenue for the Crown growing from *L* 130,000 in 1689 to *L* 330,000 in 1775. Custom duties rose from two pence per pound in 1660 to over eight pence per pound by 1758. However, the policy of granting drawbacks on these duties from re-exportation saved the colonies considerable revenues. From 1660 to 1723, the re-export trade from England to other foreign markets was so great that the drawbacks resulted in net duty payments of only a half penny per pound. As colonial production continued to increase so did the re-export market, and after 1723 the entire duties were refunded. By 1700, two-thirds of the tobacco imported into England was re-exported to Germany, Holland, Spain, Portugal, Sweden, Russia, and the Baltic states, as well as the Turkish and African markets. The Dutch market took half of all English re-exports in the 1600's and over one-third in the 1700's. British merchants would send shiploads of tobacco to Amsterdam and Rotterdam to be sold on commission for British owners when prices were good. Frequently, the Dutch extended credit on more favorable terms than available in London while they waited for the market to improve. Both small and large British merchants could easily access this market. By 1750, total re-exports amounted to 75 percent, and by 1775 they reached 83 percent in England and 98 percent in Scotland. This meant that of the 100,000,000 pounds exported to England by 1775, only 10,000,000 pounds incurred a duty, and because of its popular use the merchants were able to pass the cost of duties on to the consumer with higher prices. The Crown granted further concessions to the colonies with delayed duty payments of 18 months, a 10 percent discount for payments in "ready money," and another 4 percent discount allowance for waste and decay. Also, a time limit for re-exportation was extended to 1 year, thereby allowing the importer to first try a sale in England and if unsuccessful then a re-export sale to foreign markets without losing the benefit of the drawback. The net effect of the British policy regarding the tobacco trade was to maintain high duties on English consumption and remove barriers to trade with foreign markets which generated further development of the re-export trade. The growth of the tobacco trade during the 17th and 18th centuries was so strong and secure that tobacco became a principal means of exchange. Almost everything could be paid for in tobacco including the purchase of wives in the 1620's for 120 pounds of the "finest leaf" to wages of soldiers to salaries of ministers. Even marriage services went for 200 pounds of tobacco while 100 pounds was the price for a funeral service. When the crops failed in 1758, the Virginia Assembly voted that ministers be paid in money instead of tobacco. The clergy was so upset with this they sent an agent to England where it was repealed.

Another important aspect of the tobacco market was the revenue it produced for the colonial governments of Virginia and Maryland. These amounted to *L* 3,000 for Virginia in 1680 and *L* 6,000 per annum in the 1758-62 period. Maryland received *L* 2,500 in 1700 to around *L* 3,000 annually by 1775. Another "Plantation Duty" of a penny per pound was granted for exports from Virginia and Maryland to other British colonies, but by 1693 it had produced so little income due to inefficiencies that the duty was granted to the College of William and Mary. The College tried to reduce the costs of collections, but by 1740 it received only *L* 200. While colonial production of tobacco increased dramatically from the early 1600's to the eve of the American Revolution, it was subject to wars, intermittent years of crop failures and abundance, price fluctuations, quality control, and regulation. Often these problems were interrelated such as low prices in 1660 which led to the shipping of "trash tobacco" which led to regulations on quality. Overproduction led to falling prices which led to regulations controlling the size of the plants, cultivation dates, prohibiting shipments of bulk tobacco, and fixing the size of hogsheads of tobacco. In 1663, 1666, and 1681 tobacco planting was actually banned, but this required approval of several colonies and was rejected by the Commissioners of Customs. In 1666, the bumper crop depressed prices in London, and this was exasperated by the recent plague which had so demoralized the country that no tobacco fleet had sailed to the colonies in 1665. The market rebounded in 1667 following a devastating storm that destroyed about 80 percent of the Virginia crop. In 1677, the record Virginia crop was equivalent to three normal years of production, and the glut caused tobacco to become nearly worthless. In 1680, Lord Culpeper of Virginia told the British authorities that continuing low prices would be fatal to the Colony. In 1682, plant-cutting riots occurred in several Virginia tidewater counties which reduced production that year by 10,000,000 pounds. The positive aspect to overproduction was the re-export trade and the opening of more foreign markets. The War of the Spanish Succession in 1702 and then the War of the Austrian Succession only temporarily disturbed the tobacco trade. In fact, the tobacco trade had become so important to England and France that during the Seven Years' War from 1756 to 1763, they had an informal agreement that British ships carrying tobacco to France were exempt from capture. Tobacco even played a role in financing the American Revolution when Benjamin Franklin and Silas Deane negotiated the sale of 5,000,000 pounds of tobacco to the French monopolists in return for the purchase of French armaments. It is even more startling to consider that between 1689 and 1815, France and Great Britain fought seven major wars, and yet during this period they continued to develop an expanding trade in tobacco. France became one of the largest purchasers of American tobacco for their own consumption and for the re-exports to western Europe and the East.[2]

The Traders and Planters

Although the Virginia Company initially controlled the tobacco trade in Virginia, their charters of 1606 and 1609 allowed private traders to participate upon appropriate fees paid to them. By 1620, the Company's attempt to monopolize the trade failed so they opened up trading to everyone which meant that private traders arrived at unspecified times going from plantation to plantation collecting cargoes. The planter was at a distinct disadvantage because he not only didn't know if or when the ships would arrive at his particular plantation, but he had to rely on the ship's captain for market information and the prices of the goods he offered thereby lessening his basis for negotiating the best terms. The captain was also at risk because he sailed without knowing what cargo he could get and incurred expenses going from place to place looking for it. He usually had to extend credit to unknown planters and then returned to England hoping to find a buyer at an acceptable price before the tobacco deteriorated. Competition and the Crown's practice of sending larger fleets improved the planter's position, but it made the private trader's role more precarious. As the market developed, merchants in London began to specialize in certain markets so we hear of "Virginia merchants" being separate from "Carolina merchants." These specialists developed a close working relationship between the British and foreign markets, and they became a significant force in shaping Parliament's policies on the tobacco trade.

The Revolutionary War

Virginia was perhaps the most critical colony in the cause for independence. When the British retaliated against the Boston Tea Party and unrest in Massachusetts, they passed the Boston Port Act in March of 1774. This effectively blocked all trade in an attempt to starve the Bostonians into submission. John Adams and other local leaders were not all sure if other colonies would support their opposition to Parliament. It was Virginia's House of Burgesses that responded by announcing a "Day of Fasting, Humiliation and Prayer" for their Massachusetts countrymen for June 1, 1774. They viewed the Port Act as an attack against all the colonies. Governor Dunmore immediately dissolved Burgesses which led to their proposing the First Continental Congress. This was followed by passage of the Fairfax Resolves which rejected Parliament's claim of authority over the American Colonies. George Mason authored the Resolves together with his neighbor and political protégé, George Washington. Mason then wrote Virginia's Bill of Rights which was one of the key documents used by Thomas Jefferson in writing the Declaration of Independence.

The British employed three different strategies in their attempt to defeat the Americans. The first was to isolate New England by controlling the Hudson River to Lake Champlain. That plan was abandoned when Generals Horatio Gates and Benedict Arnold defeated British Gen. Johnny Burgoyne at Saratoga in November of 1777. The second strategy was to capture key northeast port cities, particularly Philadelphia, which was the largest colonial city and in effect its capital. Although the British did occupy Philadelphia for six months, Gen. William Howe suddenly decided to retire, and he was replaced by Gen. Henry Clinton. In May of 1775, Clinton was becoming concerned about a possible Washington attack on New York City which was the British headquarters. He abandoned Philadelphia and left Philadelphia to the Americans. The third British strategy was to invade the South and take control of Georgia, the Carolina's, and Virginia. While Cornwallis did achieve some success in sweeping up from Georgia to Virginia, his victories came at a high cost in mortalities, wounded, and fighting ability. In this third phase, Virginia played a deciding role in the outcome of the conflict. Virginia's leaders moved the capital from Williamsburg to Richmond in 1780. Washington sent General Lafayette to defend Virginia, and Gen. Benedict Arnold invaded Richmond and came very close to capturing Thomas Jefferson. Nathanael Greene commanded the Continental Army in the South. When Cornwallis decided to march his 8,000 troops to Yorktown for evacuation to New York, Washington and Rochambeau saw an opportunity to trap the British. French Admiral de Grasse arrived early enough in the Chesapeake to block the entrance to the York River and to repel Admiral Graves from saving Cornwallis. Facing obvious defeat, Cornwallis surrendered on October 19, 1781 which marked the last major battle of the war. Actual peace didn't occur until November of 1783, but it was truly fitting that the war started in Massachusetts and ended in Virginia which were the two major colonies in the fight for American Independence.

Virginia's Ratifying Convention

When Virginia's 168 delegates met in Richmond in June of 1788 to debate passage of the proposed United States Constitution, everyone knew it was to be a hotly contested issue. This was due to the fact that several major leading figures were deeply divided between the benefits of a strong central government and those favoring greater individual rights. Anti-Federalists such as Patrick Henry, George Mason, James Monroe, and Benjamin Harrison believed there were serious flaws of too strong a central government—especially one that could tax individuals—as well as too powerful an executive office. The major opposition was the lack of a Bill of Rights guaranteeing fundamental individual freedoms. The delegates voted 89 to 79 for passage but included a strong recommendation for a Bill of Rights. Many of their ideas were later included in the United States Bill of Rights drafted by James Madison who was the leader in writing the United States Constitution.[3] Virginia was accepted as the 10th state on June 25, 1788.

Education

Even though the Jamestown settlement was founded in 1607 as a business venture with a charter to the Virginia Company of London, the Anglican

Church was headed by the Crown and therefore was influential in the religious education of the colony. When the Virginia Company was declared bankrupt in 1624, King James I assumed control and granted a Royal Charter to the colony. Leaders of the colony and the clergy were eager to bring their spiritual beliefs to the colonists and especially to the Native Americans. Because the Indians had different beliefs and practices and used odd writing and languages, the clergy assumed they lacked literacy and education. They wanted to correct this by introducing education in British "civic and religious practices." In 1618, the Virginia Company of London ordered that a school of higher education should be established in the Richmond area, and should include an Indian branch which they endowed with 10,000 acres of land. The school was specifically intended for Native American young men and the sons of colonists. In 1620, the Virginia Company appointed George Thorpe to be the first deputy of the project under the leadership of Sir Thomas Dale. In the Indian Massacre of 1622 Thorpe was killed, and the fledgling project was destroyed. In 1624, the college plans were abandoned when the company charter was revoked. However, the idea for a school was never lost, and in 1691 the House of Burgesses authorized the Reverend Dr. James Blair to go to London to obtain a new charter from King William III and Queen Mary II. It was still the intent of local Virginia leaders to educate the Native Americans, and this was a critical aspect for obtaining approval in London. Although this goal lay dormant for 70 years and proved elusive, it was revived through the will of the most famous English scientist of the time. Robert Boyle's will left *L* 4,000 for "pious and charitable uses," and his executors decided to construct a building on the campus and use rental income to annually fund the Indian schools at William and Mary and Harvard College. The Royal Charter was awarded in 1693 to "make, found and establish a certain Place of Universal Study, a perpetual College of Divinity, Philosophy, Languages and the good arts and sciences…to be supported and maintained, in all times coming…. that the Christian faith may be propagated amongst the Western Indians, to the glory of Almighty God."[4]

The colonists tried to enroll Indian boys for the Indian School at the College and were eager to find good candidates. Some came from North Carolina, the southern Appalachian Mountains, and the Delaware and the Ohio River Valley.

Enrollment reached a high of 24 in 1712 and declined to 8 in 1754 and stayed at that number until the school closed in 1779. The Indian students were sent there by parents who wanted them to serve as "envoys" to learn the English culture and to speak English or to trade their deerskins for weapons or goods they couldn't make themselves. Some students were even purchased from frontier traders to keep the peace with friendly tribes. The British deemed the school a failure as many of the students returned to their own culture and former behavior. Most of the students seem to have preferred their old ways more than the English ways. Despite sincere and well-meaning efforts by the British to build better relations, the Native American tribes preferred to align themselves with the French. This can be attributed to better integration with the French and their trading practices rather than the building of more permanent towns by the English. Also, Catholic priests lived among the natives. The French were adversaries to the English, and undoubtedly influenced the Indians to be anti-English. After the French and Indian War of 1752-1758 and the defeat of French Canada in 1763, the English made even greater efforts to win over the Indians. The Proclamation of 1763 forbid new English settlements west of the Allegheny Mountains, and in 1774, Parliament passed the Quebec Act in part to appease the natives by giving them living and hunting rights in the Ohio River Valley, Indiana, and Illinois.[5]

The College of William and Mary is the second oldest college in the United States. The charter named Blair as president, a post he held for 50 years until his death in 1743. It was financed from tobacco taxes and an export duty on furs and skins. Also, in 1693, a 330-acre parcel of land was purchased for *L* 170 near the Bruton Parish Church in "Middle Plantation" for the site of the college. In 1698, the statehouse at the capital of Jamestown was destroyed by fire, so the capital was temporarily moved to Middle Plantation which had its name changed to Williamsburg in 1699. The town was granted a Royal Charter in 1722, and during the American Revolution in 1780, it was moved to Richmond for better protection from advancing British forces. In 1788, George Washington was appointed as the first American Chancellor of the college, a position he held until his death in 1799. The college is known for educating a number of American presidents such as Thomas Jefferson, James Monroe, and John Tyler. George Wythe was regarded as the finest teacher of the law in all the colonies, and his students included Thomas Jefferson, John Marshall, Bushrod Washington (George's nephew), and Peyton Randolph.[5] While Thomas Jefferson was Governor of Virginia he brought several important changes to William and Mary. These include: establishing the first law school in America; the first honor system in the country was adopted; a chair of modern languages was introduced, and in 1776, the first intercollegiate fraternity, Phi Beta Kappa, was started. In 1781, the faculties of law, medicine, and the arts were united transforming the College into America's first authentic university.[6]

Chapter Two

New York

Founded as a colony by Peter Minuit in 1626
State on July 26, 1788

The Early Years—The Dutch

Long before the Dutch arrived, the Italian explorer, Giovanni da Verrazzano, discovered the New York area in 1524. He named it "New Angouleme" in honor of his patron King Francis I of France. In 1609, the Dutch hired an Englishman, Henry Hudson, to explore the northeastern portion of North America. When he returned on his ship *Half Moon*, he described the lands and rivers ranging from Delaware to Albany, Manhattan, and the coasts of Connecticut, Rhode Island and Massachusetts. In 1613 the Dutch hired Juan Rodriguez of Santo Domingo to study and trade in the beaver fur business to take advantage of the popularity of beaver fur which could be felted to make a waterproof hat. From these initial accounts, the Dutch West Indies Company was founded in 1621 to claim the lands as "New Netherlands," and they proceeded to set up trading posts from

Delaware north including New Jersey, Pennsylvania, Manhattan, and New York State, and along the shorelines of Connecticut, Rhode Island, and Massachusetts. In 1624, these posts were official settlements of the Dutch Republic and were established as private, profit-making enterprises for commercial purposes. The Dutch policy was to set these up as trading posts with some light defenses. Other than the town in the lower end of Manhattan which they named "New Amsterdam" and unlike the English, the Dutch did not build the larger and more permanent town structures. In 1620, the English Pilgrims who had lived in Holland for their religious freedom returned to England and set sail on the Mayflower to head for New Amsterdam. However, due to diminished supplies, they decided to settle in the Cape Cod area where they first sighted land.[1]

With its strategic location's access to the Hudson River and Atlantic Ocean, the Dutch settled at the end of New Amsterdam. This was an ideal location for the local American Indians to trade their large supply of beaver pelts for finished European goods. In 1624 Dutch families started to settle at present-day Governor's Island off the tip of Manhattan. The next year Fort Amsterdam was built on Manhattan at Bowling Green to protect them from attacks by other European countries, and this prompted many to move from Governor's Island to Manhattan which had been selected by Willem Verhurst as the permanent settlement location. Verhurst was then succeeded by the new director-general, Peter Minuit, in 1626. It was Minuit who negotiated the purchase of Manhattan from a Manahatta band of Lenape for 60 Dutch guilders ($1,100 U.S. in 2012). The Lenape chief, Seyseys, was eager to make the trade of useful merchandise in an exchange for an island that was controlled by the Weckquaesgeeks and which they did not own.[2]

The government of this new colony was led by Director-General Minuit together with four members appointed by the New Netherlands Company in Holland. By 1630, only 300 people had migrated to New Amsterdam primarily because Holland provided peace, religious freedom, and stability. Also, the colony did not offer self-rule or participation in the local government. The New Netherlands Company realized they had to offer attractive incentives to new settlers, and therefore introduced the "Patroon System." This granted members of the West India Company who would bring a minimum of 50 settlers a grant for an estate with 16 miles of river or bay frontage and as far inland as the occupant wanted. This New World feudal system established many new settlers in the Hudson Valley. The "System" provided a stocked farm, a schoolmaster, and a minister for each settlement. The tenants were required to stay for 10 years. The most successful patroons became some of the best-known families in New York such as Livingston, van Rensselaer, Schuyler, van Cortlandt, Bronck, van der Donck, and Pelham. As patroon privileges diminished with better government administrators, settlers from New England, Maryland, Virginia, and Europe migrated to the Hudson. By 1643, it was rumored that as many as 18 languages were spoken in New Amsterdam, and the city was acquiring a reputation as a budding cosmopolitan center.[3]

When William Kieft became Governor, New Netherlands fell into bitter disputes and warfare with most of its neighbors, including the Swedes on the Delaware River, the English in Connecticut, and Indian tribes on every side. The colony was nearly annihilated but was saved by John Underhill from Massachusetts. He commanded 150 Dutchmen, and one night slaughtered 700 Indians at their stronghold in Stamford, Connecticut thereby halting Indian power and bringing temporary peace to the colony. When hostilities resumed, the settlers appealed to the States-General for a new governor. Kieft was replaced by Peter Stuyvesant who was a man of great energy and an experienced soldier. He was obstinate and did not believe in democratic government. The colony was being governed by a despot, and this led to the settlers demanding a representative government similar to those in neighboring colonies. Although this was granted, it lasted less than a week, and for 10 years until 1663 there was no meeting of the representatives. By 1664, the population of New Netherlands reached 10,000 which was an enormous increase from the 2,000 in 1653.[4] Governor Stuyvesant did bring important changes with his autocratic rule. He achieved agreement with his New England neighbors on establishing the boundary between New York and Connecticut which brought peace to the Connecticut River Valley. With the Swedes settled on both banks of the Delaware River, Stuyvesant suddenly claimed their land belonged to the Dutch. He received authority from Holland to take it in 1665, and with 600 men bearing down on them, the Swedes were forced to yield thereby ending the New Sweden Colony. During this time, England and Holland were at war, and the Dutch lost their New Netherlands Colony.

The Early Years—The English

As English settlers flocked to New England and the northeast coast in the 1630's and 40's, Dutch influence gradually diminished until finally in 1664, England took over the Dutch settlements in a formal war between the two countries. At that time, the "Parliamentary Period," otherwise known as the "Interregnum," had ended in England and Charles II had been crowned in 1660. The name of the Dutch town was immediately changed by King Charles II to "New York" in honor of the king's brother, The Duke of York, who was later to become King James II. The years 1664-1667 witnessed several wars between England and the Dutch. These were fought on the continent and in the American colonies over the issue of commercial trade in the Atlantic World. While England dominated the East India trade and the West Africa slave trade, they also raided the Dutch colonies along the African coast and took the New Netherland colonies in New York and New Jersey prior to a declaration of war in March of 1665.[5] Albany was chosen as capital of New York State in 1797 and claims to be the oldest continuously chartered city in the United States. Its original Dutch name when it was a trading post was Fort Nassau. Explorer Henry Hudson founded the area when he was searching for a water route to the Orient. When the English took possession of the New Netherlands Company in 1664 they renamed it Albany again in honor of the Duke of York and Albany (England). The British crown granted the city a charter in 1686, and it was chosen as the capital of the state because it had the largest population in the colony at that time. In 1785, when John Jay returned from a diplomatic mission in Europe, he was offered the position of Foreign Secretary by the Continental Congress, but his acceptance was predicated on New York being named the capital of the United States which it was in 1789 and 1790. It was also the capital of New York State from 1784 to 1797

When the First Congress met in 1789 following George Washington's inauguration on April 30th, discussions were soon held on building a new Federal City in Virginia to be named to honor the first president. New York and

Philadelphia vied for the location, but a compromise was reached between the two principal advocates for the North and South—Hamilton and Jefferson. One of the very first pieces of legislation of the new Congress was the Assumption Bill which proposed to have all state debts incurred during the Revolution be assumed by the federal government. Virginia and other southern states had already repaid most of their debts and therefore were not in favor. New York and some northern states had sustained larger debts which had not been repaid and therefore were in favor of the measure. Concurrently, the north and south were opposed on locating the new nation's capital. A compromise was reached by each side support both Virginia as the location and passing the Assumption Bill. New York City was to remain the capital through 1790 whereupon it would move to Philadelphia for 10 years. The Executive Mansion in the District of Columbia would be completed by 1800 when John Adams was in his last year as President, and he was soon followed by the third president, Thomas Jefferson. Philadelphia was disappointed inasmuch as it had been an acting capital in colonial days with the First and Second Continental Congress, the signing of the Declaration of Independence, and the meeting of the Constitutional Convention. However, in recognition of its historic events, the new Executive Mansion was placed on Pennsylvania Avenue.

New York City quickly became a major trading port and prospered with its many agricultural products especially wheat which was ground to flour for export to England. It also was blessed with natural resources such as timber, iron ore, coal, and furs. It manufactured products like plows, tools, kettles, locks, nails, and exported blocks of iron to England where most of the finished goods were made for re-export back to the colony because American colonies were prohibited from manufacturing goods. New York also attracted settlers of most every faith as there was no dominant religion. It offered freedom to Catholics, Lutherans, Jews, and Quakers, as well as many other Protestant sects.

The Revolutionary War

At the start of the Revolutionary War, New York City had grown to 25,000 residents, most of whom lived at the southern end below Chambers Street. Because of its commercial activities and major port, it was difficult to distinguish

Loyalists from Patriots, but it is estimated that political preferences were evenly split into three groups, the last being those who were neutral and decided to wait for the outcome. After Washington had successfully ousted the British from Boston in March of 1776, he correctly assumed they would try to capture New York City and establish their headquarters there. He fully realized how difficult it would be to defend the City against the strongest navy in the world where the Atlantic Ocean and the Hudson and East Rivers provided deep water anchorage and therefore storage of armaments, horses, and men. On July 9, 1776, while Washington was having the Declaration of Independence read to his troops at City Hall, the British armada of 30,000 soldiers on 400 ships was barely visible on the horizon on their way to invade New York. The Americans had just torn down the gold-leafed lead statue of King George III and shipped the pieces to Connecticut where they were to be made into 40,000 musket balls, but their cheering soon stopped when the English forces advanced to Staten Island on the New York Harbor. Washington planned to repel the enemy on the western point of Long Island at Brooklyn Heights, but Cornwallis was able to find the only unguarded point at Jamaica Pass which threatened the Continental army encamped at the Heights. Washington realized the imminent disaster and managed to miraculously evacuate his entire army under cover of a sudden thick fog. Days later his army was unable to prevent the British from landing on Manhattan at Murray Hill (34th street), and Washington adopted a series of skirmishes and retreats from Upper Manhattan to Harlem Heights to White Plains to Fort Lee, New Jersey. The outcome was never in doubt, and even though he was leading inexperienced militia and was given poor support by his officers, he never cast blame but always claimed full responsibility. The losses on Long Island and New York haunted Washington for the 8-year duration of the war and played a part in his strategy for Yorktown, but his perseverance and leadership brought eventual vindication.

One of the saddest aspects of the war was the British use of many of its ships to house American prisoners. It is estimated that of the 25,000 American soldiers who died in the war, close to 11,500 died from wounds, sickness, and starvation while held as captives aboard these floating prisons stationed in New York Harbor. It is a vivid reminder of just how savage this war actually was. Keep in mind that the British had around 35,000 men in arms added to which were 29,000 mercenary Hessians, added to which were 20,000 American Loyalists fighting for England. Americans kept enemy prisoners in camps scattered across Virginia and Pennsylvania, and they were treated so humanely that many, including 25 percent of the Hessians, elected to stay in America after their release.[6]

Perhaps the most significant battle of the Revolutionary War took place in Saratoga, New York in the fall of 1777. The first British strategy was to isolate New England by controlling all of its surrounding waterways. They had already dominated the Atlantic Ocean, the Lower Hudson and East Rivers, and the Long Island Sound. The final piece was to be the Upper Hudson and Lake Champlain which would connect their New York City headquarters with their military control in Canada. America's northern army commanded by Gen. Horatio Gates was camped at Saratoga to resist the 7,000 men of British Gen. John Burgoyne. The first engagement opened on September 19th and was deemed a draw. The second battle launched on October 9th, but suddenly General Howe was unofficially joined by Gen. Benedict Arnold. Arnold had been instructed to stay away because of some prior disputes with his superiors, but he disobeyed orders and took the field. Considered by historians as the best field general in the army and known for his aggressive tactics, the Americans defeated Burgoyne and took his 7,000 men as prisoners in the first greatest battle of the war. The victory was a shock to England and the world, and it convinced a young, newly-arrived French officer named Lafayette to return to France and persuade King Louis XVI to support the Americans against their age-old enemy England. While the Treaty of Amity and Commerce providing men and materials to America was being negotiated, Washington and his army were encamped at Valley Forge being trained by Baron von Steuben. The major English army was occupying Philadelphia when their Commander-in-Chief, Gen. William Howe, suddenly decided to retire and returned to England. His replacement, Gen. Henry Clinton, evacuated Philadelphia in June of 1778 to reinforce New York in anticipation of French intervention. The tide of war had shifted and ended on October 19, 1781 at Yorktown where Cornwallis was forced to surrender his 8,000 troops to Washington. It took another two years for Treaty of Paris to be finalized, but it was only after the British sailed away in December that one could see the devastation that eight years of war had inflicted on New York City. Starting with the great fire that gutted the City in the fall of 1776 and then the destruction of buildings, furnishings, and framing used for firewood, there was devastation everywhere. The great conflict was over, but New York played its important role in attaining the victory.

The Constitutional Convention

The Constitution was adopted in Philadelphia on September 17, 1787, and New York's Ratifying Convention opened in mid-June 1788. By the end of May, a total of eight states had ratified the measure. Three states were scheduled to meet in June: Virginia, New York, and New Hampshire in that order. The remaining two states of North Carolina and Rhode Island did not ratify until the First Congress met and introduced amendments for the Bill of Rights. Before the June conventions met, the respective delegates were tied in Virginia at 52-52 and in New Hampshire at 84-84, but New York was heavily Anti-Federalist at 19-46.[7] There were a number of issues discussed such as determining the number of representatives in the House, terms of office, and checks and balances for the three branches of government. However, the most critical issue raised by several states was the lack of a Bill of Rights guaranteeing individual freedoms of speech, the press, and religious toleration. Rhode Island did not even attend the Constitutional Convention the prior year because of the absence of religious freedom. On June 24th, New Hampshire approved the Constitution, and on July 2nd, Virginia ratified it thereby bringing the total to ten states. However, one of the most essential states was New York which had not yet voted. The two political sides were the Federalists led by Alexander Hamilton and the Anti-Federalists led by Governor George Clinton, who outnumbered their opponents two-to-one. Strong upstate areas opposed the New York City area. Hamilton was well aware of the challenge, and being a prolific writer he joined with Madison and Jay to produce a series of 85 essays under the name "The Federalist Papers." The papers promoted the positive aspects of a central government, particularly in conducting foreign policy as well as the protections of the checks and balances of the three branches of government and the separation of powers. Madison argued that a large republic would prevent local interests from rising to create a tyranny and that a diverse economy of agriculture, manufacturing, merchants, and creditors would enable the nation to grow and would serve to offset controlling factions.[8] New York became focused on the issue of individual rights, and the delegates were very much aware that Rhode Island did not even attend the Constitutional Convention the prior year due to their strong convictions on religious toleration. On June 24th, New Hampshire approved the Constitution, making it the ninth state to ratify and thereby assuring adoption of the Constitution, and on July 2nd, Virginia became the tenth state to ratify the measure and thereby put extra pressure on New York to follow suit. However, New York continued their debates focusing on individual rights and the amendment process. This was finally resolved by proposing a list of 31 amendments to be attached to their vote for ratification. On July 26, 1788, New York voted in favor by 30-27 and became the 11th state to adopt the Constitution albeit with their conditions for a guarantee of individual rights.[9]

Most historians would agree that approval of the Constitution was due in large measure to the influence of George Washington who presided as president of the convention. While he did not participate in the debates or intervene in any way because he did not want to affect individual positions, he did express his thoughts privately outside the meetings. Also, in his letter of transmittal to the Confederation Congress he advised readers to not engage in partisan politics. He wrote: "the Constitution which we now present is the result of a spirit of amity" and he wished "that it may promote the lasting welfare of the country so dear to us all, and secure her freedom and happiness."[10] After the Constitution was completed, Madison wrote to the American minister to France, Thomas Jefferson, stating that passage was due to in large part to Washington's influence.

Education

In 1754, King George II granted a Royal Charter to establish King's College in New York City. It was located next to Trinity Church at the top of Wall Street and Lower Broadway and represents itself as the oldest college in the state and the fifth oldest in the United States. After considerable debate the school agreed to be affiliated with the Anglican Church, but its founders promised to adhere to the principles of religious liberty. The first president was Samuel Johnson who taught an initial student body of eight. It was a diverse school which included High Anglican Englishmen, members of some original Dutch families, and French Huguenots. Its principle studies were in law and the ministry, and in 1769 it was the first American college to grant an M.D. degree in medicine. The college was closely aligned with the Tories, but American revolutionary troops turned it into a barracks just before the British invasion. The English then converted it into a military hospital. After the war, it reopened in 1784 as Columbia College. Some of its famous graduates included Alexander Hamilton, John Jay, Robert Livingston, and Gouverneur Morris. George Washington's stepson, John Parke Custis, attended for one semester.[11]

The New York Stock Exchange

Because of its rising preeminence as a banking and mercantile center in the 1700's, it should not be surprising that New York City became the location for issuing and trading securities. It officially opened on May 17, 1792 with the signing of the Buttonwood Agreement at 68 Wall Street under a large Sycamore (Buttonwood) tree. The Agreement was signed by 24 brokers who had agreed to trade only amongst themselves at a 25 percent commission rate. They traded only five company stocks and mostly U.S. Treasury Bonds which were mostly Revolutionary War bonds. The first stock listed was the Bank of New York which had been founded by Alexander Hamilton. Prior to then, securities were exchanged through auctioneers who served as intermediaries between buyers and sellers, and they primarily dealt in commodities such as wheat and tobacco.[12]

Chapter Three

MASSACHUSETTS

Founded as a colony by the Pilgrim Fathers in 1630
State on February 6, 1788

Religious Issues

The name derives from one of the Native American tribes that lived in this region of New England. The Algonquian word "Massachusetts" translates to "at or about the Great Hill." The area referred to is the Blue Hills southwest of Boston. There seem to be several misconceptions about the founding of New England and Massachusetts in particular. The first of these is the landing in Plymouth by the pilgrims in 1620 whose intention was to escape persecution in England because of their religious convictions. While the pilgrims were "puritans" who tried for many years to purify the Anglican Church of its growing Roman Catholic tendencies in hierarchy and worship, they were viewed as "Separatists" and were regarded by King James I and his son, King Charles I, as enemies of the Anglican Church and the government. However, as this small group grew in size and secretly met primarily in the Essex area northeast of London, its practices and beliefs became a serious problem keeping in mind that the monarch was also the head of the Anglican Church. This left little distinction between following religious beliefs and adhering to civil laws and practices. During the first years of the 1600's, the group sought protection in Holland where religious tolerance was the norm. However, English puritans were still regarded as foreigners, and it was difficult for them to assimilate into Dutch society. They returned to England with the express purpose of gathering enough resources to emigrate to New England where they could establish their own religious settlement. That first group of 99 pilgrims arrived in Cape Cod in 1620 only to find an abandoned Native American settlement that lacked sufficient water or soil to sustain them. They proceeded to explore the surrounding land and choose to settle directly across Cape Cod Bay and called it Plymouth Plantation in remembrance of the town of Plymouth, England from where their ship had departed. It is important to note that this was not an official venture and was neither supported by the Crown, Parliament, nor the Church. It was motivated by religious fervor unlike the earlier settlers to Jamestown which was a commercial venture.

The idea for a Puritan New England settlement actually originated in Dorchester, England in the early 1600's. Its success prompted the formation in 1624 of the Dorchester Company which sent a group of settlers to Cape Ann on Massachusetts Bay for the purpose of duplicating Dorchester, England which had become a model religious and commercial town. It wasn't long before these settlers confronted Plymouth colonists over fishing rights and religious issues. In 1626, a prominent member of the Cape Ann group, Roger Conant, led around 30 people to an area called Naumkeag which was about 40 miles north of Plymouth. Although this was not approved by the English investors, who then sent a ship to retrieve them, Conant and a small number of followers elected to remain. In England, the man responsible for Dorchester's success, the Reverend John White, promised to send Conant more financial support and a charter. The Dorchester Company was disbanded and replaced with the Massachusetts Bay Company. Their priorities were changed from a purely commercial one to a puritan sanctuary. They sent planters, livestock, and supplies and appointed John Endicott as Governor. They then renamed the town "Salem" which translates to "peace" in Hebrew. This became the first official settlement of the Massachusetts Bay Company. It was a Corporate Charter with stockholders who agreed to transfer the government of the original plantation to those who would settle there. In effect, they transformed an investment company into a colony that provided self-rule and protection from the Crown and the Church of England. The charter would help build a legal and safe place and a religious community sometimes referred to as the "New Jerusalem." Governor Endicott emphasized that their government laws would be based on the rule of God's word. Massachusetts Bay Company was to remain loyal to the Church of England which was unlike that of the Plymouth settlers. Two of their leaders in England, Francis Higginson and Samuel Skelton, stated "We do not go to New England as separate from the Church of England, though we cannot but separate from the corruption in it, but we go to practice the positive past church reformation and propagate the gospel in America."[1]

The Real Beginning

The founding year of Massachusetts is recorded as 1630 because that is the year that supporters in England sent over 1,000 emigrants as well as animals, supplies, seeds, professional people, and armaments in an effort to establish a permanent colony. It was granted a Corporate Charter with stockholder proprietors. They also sent John Winthrop to replace John Endicott as Governor. Winthrop was a lawyer and devout Christian who spent months preparing for the governance of the colony. Massachusetts was to become a purpose-driven society, and that purpose was to advance God's interests upon earth. It was not a theocracy because ministers did not hold public office, but it was theocentric. Church and State were not officially united, but they were working together for the same objectives. Winthrop preached Christian charity and spoke of a society that held its wealth in common—hence the term "Commonwealth of Massachusetts." Winthrop recognized economic inequality and inequality in rank whereby some are rich and some are poor and this also applied to power and dignity. But there is total equality in man's value to God and man was made for the glory of his creator and the common good of the creature man. He spoke of the covenant between the emigrants and God and their need to obey his holy ordinances because they had replaced Israel as "God's Chosen People." Historians regard Winthrop's sermon as the greatest in 1000 years of western civilization.[2] When the 1000 emigrants arrived in 1630 they were shocked to see that only ten houses and huts had been built in Salem. Most of them had to move on to Charlestown, Roxbury, Dorchester, and Watertown. They emigrated across the Mystic River on to the peninsula where they built new houses and renamed the town "Boston" in honor of the Reverend John Cotton and many others who had come from Boston, England. As the towns with their local churches grew in number, they adopted the name "Congregationalists." The name dates back to 1582 when Robert Browne first published their principles which aligned closely with puritanism. The movement made significant progress during the English Parliamentary Period of 1640-1660 when it was protected from interference by the Crown and the Anglican Church. Government opposition had driven many puritans to exile in Holland which was well known for its policies of religious toleration. In Massachusetts where towns in and around Boston were growing rapidly, each local church (congregation) stood on its own but remained as part of a fellowship with all other local churches in a common family of believers in Jesus Christ. With the new charter of 1691, church membership was no longer required for one's right to vote. Also, with its modified and simpler worship service, bishops and presbyteries were eliminated.

When King Charles I appointed William Laud as Archbishop of Canterbury in 1633, pressure increased dramatically on those puritans living in England. This produced the "Great Migration" of the 1630's when 20,000 immigrants left for Massachusetts. Laud required all citizens to sign a Loyalty Oath to King and Church, and in 1634 he tried to have the Massachusetts Bay charter revoked, but they resisted the attempt. The colonists trained soldiers for a possible invasion and placed beacons on strategic hills to keep lookout for ships from England. This was the origin of "Beacon Hill."

Using some questionable legal maneuvering, the stockholders transferred the management and the original 1630 charter to "Massachusetts." This allowed for local management and their perceived right to regard the charter as a political constitution with some undefined dependence on the imperial one in England. After 50 years of growing friction with England, the renewed 1684 charter was revoked, and a Royal Charter was granted by monarchs King William and Queen Mary in 1691. It was the latter that merged the Plymouth Colony and the territory of Maine into the Massachusetts Bay Colony.[3]

The Road To Independence

Perhaps the Commonwealth of Massachusetts is best known for the key role it played in the American fight for independence. Although it was mainly the southern militias and particularly the Virginian one who fought as British-Americans against the French and Indians in the 1754-1759 period, it was the northern colonies that reacted most strongly to the taxing policies adopted by the British following that war. The justification for levying the many new taxes was the need to pay for past, present, and future costs of defending all the colonies from local and foreign intrusions. The most outspoken of the colonies was Massachusetts, which seems to have developed an organized opposition to British interference. This was personified in the Sons of Liberty, a Boston-based group of American Patriots who were led by Samuel Adams. It was Adams who reportedly orchestrated the Boston Tea Party in December of 1773, and it was Adams who the British were searching for in April of 1775. The Sons of Liberty was a secret society that was started in Boston to protect the rights of all the colonies from British interference and particularly increased taxation. It was composed of shopkeepers, tradesmen, and artisans who were initially called "The Loyal Nine." It contained members in every colony who were regarded as radicals and terrified royal governors and even held sway over local town governments. The Stamp Act of 1765 which taxed every piece of printed paper or document was the catalyst that set the stage for serious colonial protest and the formation of the Sons of Liberty. At the same time, the British withdrew the tariff on tea exported to the colonies in an effort to gain a competitive edge and also to save the East India Company from financial collapse. The Sons of Liberty committed their first consequential action on December 16, 1773 when they boarded three ships in Boston Harbor that had just arrived with 92,000 pounds of tea valued in today's terms at $1.7 million. The perpetrators were dressed to resemble Indians with blankets, painted faces, and hatchets. The tea was dumped into Boston Harbor, but no one was injured and there was no damage to the ships. However, the British East India Company sustained an enormous loss just as they were in poor financial condition and operating with government support. Simultaneously, in other towns along the coast like Baltimore and Wilmington, North Carolina, colonists prevented the unloading of tea as well and forced the ships to turn away. In retaliation, the British closed the Port of Boston, and under the Intolerable Acts passed the Administrative of Justice Act, the Quartering Act, and the Quebec Act, all of which led to suffocating acts of repression on the people of Massachusetts. The greatest significance of these reprisals was the sympathies it created in the other colonies. They convened the First Continental Congress in the Fall of 1774, which led to the events of April in 1775 in Lexington and Concord and then the Revolutionary War. There were two other events in Massachusetts during the early days of the war that are worth noting. Just before June of 1775 when Washington was appointed Commander-in-Chief of the Continental Army, the Massachusetts militia took control of Bunker and Breed's Hills to the north of Boston where 5,000 British troops were stationed. The hills had a commanding position over the Boston peninsula, and the British Gen. William Howe was slow to recognize its importance. After the Americans were in place, Howe decided to attack and used marines and war ships in a frontal assault which would expose his men. The Americans fought bravely, but the British won the day. However, Howe lost a staggering 40 percent of his troops to death and injuries, but it is baffling that he didn't simply capture the narrow neck of the Bunker Hill peninsula which would have forced the Americans to surrender and prevented their retreat back to the mainland. The most significant consequence of the battle was how it affected Howe over the following two years before his unexpected retirement to England. He apparently was reluctant to pursue the Americans at Chads Ford and Germantown and even from his stronghold in Philadelphia in 1777 while Washington was reorganizing his troops at Valley Forge.

The other significant event was the Siege of Boston in the winter of 1775-1776. Washington's headquarters and his army were encamped in Cambridge across the Charles River. His first objective of the war was to drive the British out of Boston, but he lacked trained soldiers, artillery, and ammunition. Again, Howe did not pursue the Americans in spite of superior forces and equipment.

In November of 1775, Henry Knox and a dozen men set out on a 300-mile journey to Fort Ticonderoga on Lake Champlain to remove the fort's cannons and drag them back to Cambridge on sleds. The fort had been captured in May of that year by Ethan Allen and Benedict Arnold without losing a single man. When Knox returned in January, the cannons were put in place on Dorchester Heights under cover of night. Dorchester overlooked Boston from the south, and again the British failed to appreciate its strategic position. When they woke on March 17, 1776 they were totally surprised to see the 59 cannons aimed directly at them. Bad weather intervened to discourage an assault on the dominating American advantage, so they soon packed their gear and left Boston. Washington had saved Boston and defeated the highly acclaimed British army without the loss of life. The statue of Washington astride his horse in the Public Gardens is in tribute to him.

Education

Massachusetts Bay Colony holds a great distinction for their introduction to the colonies of public education. The Puritans believed that their continued survival depended on the ability of future generations to govern and to maintain their spiritual beliefs by reading the Bible. They emphasized the importance of learning theology, philosophy, and government. By 1636, over 17,000 people had migrated to New England. In 1642, Massachusetts passed laws requiring all children to be taught reading and writing. The first public school was established in 1635 and named "Boston Latin School." It was started at a Boston Town Meeting where the voters agreed to collect rents from islands they owned in Boston Harbor to pay for a schoolmaster and school maintenance. Charlestown, Dorchester, and Salem soon followed. The "grammar" schools were intended primarily for boys who were expecting to enter the ministry. All children were required to learn reading and writing even though most of them were taught at home by their parents. Heads of households were required to teach all their dependents, including children, servants, and apprentices. If young children were found to be neglected, selectmen were authorized to have them removed from their parents who would then be fined. In 1647, the General Court required all towns to provide schools. The curriculum was reading, writing, and arithmetic. Students had to pay part of the cost in the form of tuition, lodging for the schoolmaster, and wood for the schoolhouse. Parents were not required to send their children to school, and not all towns allowed girls to enroll in publicly supported schools. If parents could afford fees, daughters could be sent to "Dame Schools" where a local woman taught reading, writing, and domestic arts. In 1636, the first American college was founded in Cambridge and named "New College," and it was formed to fill the need for training new clergy. It was established by vote of the Great and General Court of the Massachusetts Bay Colony. The name was changed in 1639 to "Harvard College" in honor of clergyman John Harvard, a Cambridge University, England alumnus who willed L780 and his library of 320 books to the College.[4]

Mercantilism and the Triangular Trade

Simply stated, mercantilism is the export of raw materials and the import of finished goods. This was the system in place in the American colonies from their first settlements until independence. It was restricted by the British whereby their Atlantic colonies could export only to English ports and were very limited in the types of products they were allowed to manufacture. Most of these were exported from England back to the colonies. Triangular trade describes the trade route patterns existing in the 1600's and 1700's. The colonies possessed an abundance of materials which were exported across the North Atlantic to England where finished products were shipped south to Africa and the West Indies from which slaves were sent to the American colonies particularly to the southern colonies. The economy of New England and especially Massachusetts with its well-developed port of Boston thrived with the export of timber, furs, whale oil, rum, whiskey, beer, and iron ore. Timber was a major material because of its many applications for ship building, house construction, barrel staves, and furniture. Whale oil was another valuable export with its many uses such as lighting oil for lamps, ingredient for soaps, candles, and ointments. Even the oil ambergris was essential for medicines and perfumes. Fishing was one of the most successful industries with a great variety including cod, mackerel, herring, halibut, bass, and sturgeon. Farming was another important industry that provided certain crops peculiar to North America. Corn, pumpkin, squash, beans, and fruits were popular in England. By 1774, three out of four families owned their own farms which ranged in size from 50 to 150 acres. New England was relatively limited in some of the exported foods because of their poorer soil and colder climate. However, their economy did well as they diversified their goods with timber and grist mills thereby producing jobs for carpenters, joiners, sail makers, barrel makers, painters, caulkers, and blacksmiths. By 1750, there were 125 shipyards in the colonies. In addition, many household industries were started making cloth, beer, rum, and whiskey.

Chapter Four

Maryland

Founded as a colony by George Calvert in 1633
State on April 28, 1788

Early Settlers

George Calvert, the first Lord Baltimore, was granted a charter in 1632 by King Charles I which gave him a proprietary interest in a large tract of land east of the Potomac River. The name Maryland derives from the king's queen consort, Henrietta Maria Calvert who died that same year. Their son, Cecil, inherited the state and the charter. Sir George was a convert to Roman Catholicism even though he had faithfully served the Protestant Kings James and Charles in many government functions including the Privy Council. He found the strong anti-Catholic policies too severe. He therefore took a keen interest in the North American colonies as a place for establishing a refuge for Catholics. He explored Virginia as a possible location for starting a settlement but found the Anglican Church there similar to that of England in their lack of religious tolerance.

The land granted to him was available because in 1624 the Virginia Company filed for bankruptcy, and the colony reverted to a Royal Charter. The enormous Virginia Colony stretched north to New York then to the Great Lakes and then due west, encompassing today's Wisconsin and Michigan and all of the mid-west thereby leaving large tracts available under royal rule for additional colonies. Calvert focused on land that was on both sides of the Chesapeake Bay. Cecil appointed his brother, Leonard, as governor of the province, who arrived in 1634 along with 200 planters. Cecil purchased the Bay area and the land at the mouth of the Potomac River from the Yaocomico Indians and formed a settlement they named St. Mary's. The colony grew rapidly because they enjoyed peaceful relations with the Native tribes who respected and appreciated their purchase of the land and opposition to acquisition by force. Other attractions were the mild climate and fertile soil. The most significant factors were the individual rights granted to the settlers. They enjoyed religious tolerance, civil freedoms, and were allowed to pass their own laws. In fact, no taxes could be imposed without their approval. In 1639, they formed an assembly with representatives elected by the people and others appointed by the proprietor, the governor, and the secretary. In 1650, they adopted a bicameral legislature with the upper house appointed by the proprietor and the lower house elected by the people.[1]

In 1635, the new colony did encounter civil war when an inhabitant living on Kent Island across from Annapolis refused to recognize Calvert's authority. William Clayborne and his followers took up arms against the local government but were defeated and Clayborne escaped. The government accused him of treason and took over his land. In 1645, Clayborne returned and overthrew the Calvert government for a year before being defeated again. In 1649, the Maryland Assembly reiterated their religious tolerance and support for those who believed in Jesus Christ. Those who abused others from practicing their faith were subject to fines that were payable to the victim. The strong support for religious freedom attracted Puritans from the south and others from the north to a colony that granted the greatest individual freedoms in all the colonies at that time. In 1651, during the Parliamentary Period of 1642 to 1660, Cromwell and his followers sent commissioners to Maryland to take control of the government. They chose William Clayborne for the job which gave rise to a civil war. Catholics sided with the proprietor and Protestants were allied with Parliament. In 1654, Protestants decreed that Catholics were no longer protected by the law. Civil War broke out in 1655, and many Catholics were killed. In 1660, the monarchy was restored with King Charles II. Lord Baltimore regained his rights and Philip Calvert was named governor. All former political enemies were pardoned, and Maryland returned to its liberal principles.[2]

In 1675, founding proprietor Cecil Calvert, Lord Baltimore, passed away. He had ruled the colony for 40 years and was greatly admired for his integrity and as a defendent of citizens' rights and welfare. He was revered for his wisdom and benevolence, and Maryland was fortunate that he was succeeded by his son, Charles, who possessed the same virtues as his father. In 1689, following England's Glorious Revolution when King James II was deposed, Parliament brought William of Orange to the throne. Soon thereafter, King William III married his cousin, Mary, and they reigned as king and queen equal in rank and authority which was the first and only time this occurred in England's history. Unfortunately for Maryland, a rumor was circulated that the Catholics were organizing to rid the colony of Protestants. However, it was the just the reverse, and the Protestants regained authority. In 1691, King William took control of Maryland and converted the proprietorship to a Royal Charter. Religious toleration was discontinued, and the Anglican Church became the established religion. In 1716, the infant heir to Lord Baltimore was reaffirmed, and the proprietary government was restored until the Revolution.[3]

American Revolution

As relations between the colonies and England steadily deteriorated with each new tax that was imposed, the merchants of Maryland became more alarmed. Even as Americans retaliated with non-importation of British goods and thoughts of independence, Marylanders were more concerned about the negative impacts to their trade and mercantile business. The delegates at the First Continental Congress championed moderation and compromise while decrying war and independence. However, the Boston Tea Party in December of 1773 followed by the British Port Act and then the complete blockage of Boston Harbor in October started to change attitudes. Radicals in Annapolis set fire to H.M.S.

"Peggy Stewart", destroying 2,000 pounds of tea, and by the end of the year Maryland formed its first militia, the Baltimore Independent Cadets. The outbreak of armed conflict in April of 1775 at Lexington ended any thoughts of conciliation with England. The Harford County Committee of Observation approved the Bush River Declaration calling for independence. In June of 1775, a Maryland Convention named themselves the "Association of Freemen of Maryland" and recommended that they prepare for war. Finally, in June of 1776, the eight delegates to the Maryland Convention voted for independence.

Like other colonies, Maryland's militia was composed of famers, merchants, lawyers, planters, and others with no real military training. Consequently, they were urged to read military manuals just as Washington, Knox, Greene, and Hamilton did. Because Chesapeake Bay was such a large part of the colony and an important maritime center, the British made every effort to disrupt American shipping there. In response, the colonists were constantly patrolling the Bay with privateers and state-owned ships. Maryland was a key part of the "Bread Basket" for the Continental Army, and it provided them with hay, flour, corn, and livestock. Maryland's soldiers quickly established themselves as one of the best trained and disciplined in the field. This was largely the work of Otho Holland Williams who was from Prince George County. When war erupted at Lexington, Williams left his mercantile business to join the Frederick City militia which soon marched to Boston. Williams became a student in the art of war, studying military tactics of commanders as far back as the Romans, and he directed his men to do the same. Upon arriving in Cambridge, Congress ordered the formation of riflemen regiments from Maryland, Virginia, and Pennsylvania. For most of the war, Maryland troops served under the command of Gen. William Smallwood who was a veteran of the French and Indian War. After the successful siege of Boston in March of 1776, the 900 Marylanders were sent to defend New York City where they participated in the battles of Long Island and Manhattan. At Fort Washington near present-day George Washington Bridge they fought under Marylander Moses Rawlings, but they were defeated by the larger and vastly superior British and Hessian forces after a turncoat revealed the fort's defenses. Over 3,000 Americans were captured including Williams who spent the next year in a New York City prison. He was released in a prisoner exchange and rejoined his Maryland troops in the spring of 1777. They fought with General Washington in New Jersey and Pennsylvania and were then stationed in Wilmington, Delaware to defend the Continental Army while encamped at Valley Forge for the next six months. For the first four years of the war, Marylanders fought in the north. When the British vacated Philadelphia in June of 1778, Washington attacked them at Monmouth Court House driving them back to New York City. He then moved his army to the Hudson River near Newburgh where Smallwood commanded four of his Maryland regiments.[4]

Another Maryland hero was Tench Tilghman who was a College of Philadelphia (later the University of Pennsylvania) graduate and merchant who early in his career opposed England's restrictive policies. His first mission in 1775 was to negotiate a peace for the neutrality of the Iroquois Indian Confederation. He then joined the Philadelphia militia and within the year was appointed captain of the Pennsylvania battalion attached to the Continental Army. In the summer of 1776, he was selected as an aide-de-camp to General Washington and remained with him for the entire war. While serving Washington at Valley Forge he was responsible for procuring supplies, horses, and weapons wherever he could find them, which was a demanding and almost impossible task. One of his finest moments was delivering the Articles of Capitulation of British General Cornwallis to Congress after his defeat at Yorktown in October of 1781. Tilghman was one of Washington's most trusted, competent, and admired aides and served him loyally without pay as a volunteer. After the war, he returned to his mercantile business and died in 1786 at 42 years old.[5]

At the end of 1779, the British launched their third major strategy for defeating the Americans. British Generals Clinton and Cornwallis took 8,500 men and began their campaign to capture and control the south. After losing Georgia and South Carolina, Washington sent 2,000 men of the Maryland Line to Camden, South Carolina where Gen. Horatio Gates was in command. The Americans were crushed and the Marylanders were decimated. When Washington learned of the 100-mile retreat by Gates, he immediately sacked him and sent Nathanael Greene to replace him and to reorganize the southern army. The Marylanders lost one of their most experienced generals, Johann de Kalb. The Maryland forces were reformed into five regiments under the command of

Generals Smallwood, Gist, and Williams. The "Maryland Line" was praised for its courage and gallantry in the southern theater where they fought for several years even after the victory at Yorktown. Gen. Henry Knox wrote, "The affair of Camden will not be more remarkable for its adverse circumstances than for the firm gallantry of the Maryland Line. The veterans of the army here admire their conduct and ardently wished to have been in such numbers, side by side with their old companions, as to have enabled them to have gained a victory which their bravery so richly merited." The state's nickname of the "Old Line State" derives from the bravery of their men in the Revolutionary War.[6]

Statesmen, Leaders, and Heroes

Ranked among the most influential early founders of Maryland would be the Carroll family. Daniel Carroll of Ireland married Eleanor Darnall of Prince George's County in 1727, and it was their son, John, and other Carroll relatives who assumed leadership roles in developing Maryland as well as the city of Baltimore. Daniel Carol II was born in 1730 and holds the distinction of being one of only five men to have signed the Articles of Confederation and the U.S. Constitution. Daniel's cousin, Charles, was an avid supporter of the Patriot cause and was the last surviving signer of the Declaration of Independence. He was the only Catholic who signed the Declaration and the first U.S. Senator from Maryland. But it was the son of Daniel and Eleanor, John, who was to leave a lasting legacy in America.

John was born on the ancestral Darnall estate in 1735 and was educated in French Flanders where the College of St. Omer had been established for English Catholics following the Protestant Reformation in 1536 initiated by King Henry VIII. John was joined at college by his cousin, Charles. In 1753, John commenced his studies of theology and 16 years later was ordained a priest. While in Europe, he taught at St. Omer and at Liege and was witness to the suppression of Jesuits which caused him to return to Maryland in 1774. In 1776, John was requested by the Continental Congress to travel to Quebec to explore whether the French Canadians were interested in joining the Americans in the fight for independence. While this was a distinct possibility because of their recent defeat by the British in 1763, they did decline the proposal. The positive aspect of the trip was his getting to know his companions, which included Benjamin Franklin, Samuel Chase, and his cousin, Charles Carroll. It was this trip that brought the Reverend Carroll directly into politics which, in turn, influenced the Bishop of Quebec to excommunicate him for his political activities.[7]

In 1783, Father Carroll assembled five other Jesuits for several meetings to discuss how the Roman Catholic Church should be organized in the new nation. The issue was sensitive and delicate because they fully realized the existence of a strong anti-British sentiment permeating the colonies. The Catholic leader in America had been the Vicar Apostolic of London, Bishop Richard Challoner. When he died in 1781, his successor, James Talbot, refused to assume jurisdiction. The Pope directed his official representative in France to discuss the matter with Benjamin Franklin in Paris who advised him that in the United States the church and state were separate and therefore the government was unable to interfere in the issue. In an effort to please Franklin, the papal nuncio asked him for suggestions whereupon Franklin recommended that John Carroll would be well qualified to determine the best course of action. Accordingly, on June 9, 1784, Pope Pius VI confirmed John Carroll to be the "Superior of the Missions in the thirteen United States of America." It wasn't long before the clergy realized a bishop would be needed. In 1783, American Protestants had readily accepted a Protestant Bishop, but Carroll had a more difficult assignment in not allowing the appearance that a foreign power (the Vatican) was appointing church hierarchy. Carroll first got assurances from the Continental Congress that a Catholic Bishop would be acceptable. Carroll then presented a report to the pope on the condition of the Catholic Church in America who was sufficiently pleased, so he requested that the American clergy send him a list of several possible candidates for the position of Bishop. The Maryland priests urged their support not only for John Carroll but also for the location of a cathedral. In April of 1789, Carroll was selected by a vote of all the clergy of 24-2 to become the Bishop of Baltimore thereby becoming the first Roman Catholic Bishop in the United States. Subsequently, he was consecrated in August of 1790 in Dorset, England where he did not have to take an oath to the English Church.[8]

Bishop Carroll took a leading role in the field of education. He wanted a higher education for all Catholics, including women, as well as proper training for priests. He founded and developed Georgetown University. He directed that it be administered by the Jesuits, and in 1791, the college accepted its first students making it the oldest Catholic school of higher learning in America.

Charles Carroll of Carrollton was born in 1737 to Charles Carroll of Annapolis and Elizabeth Brooke. He was a cousin of John Carroll and was educated at Bohemia Manor, a Jesuit school on the Eastern Shore. Like John, he studied at St. Omer College and in Paris and read the law in London. At age 28, he returned to Annapolis, but being a Roman Catholic he was not allowed to enter politics, practice law, or vote. He inherited an enormous tract of land and Carroll Manor from his father, and over the course of his life, he amassed a fortune that made him one of the wealthiest men in all of the colonies. Charles was not involved in politics until 1772 when he started to voice his opinions in the Maryland Gazette under the pseudonym "First Citizen." He was extremely critical of British taxing policies and was soon opposed by a Loyalist named Daniel Dulany who wrote under the name "Antillon." When the authors' identities were later revealed, Carroll's notoriety and reputation increased dramatically. He was soon appointed to several Committees of Correspondence and took a leading role in the Annapolis Tea Party where "HMS Peggy Stewart" was burned in October of 1774 destroying 2,000 pounds of East India Company tea. Carroll believed that American independence could only be achieved through armed conflict. In 1775, he was elected to the Committee of Safety and was appointed a delegate to the Annapolis Convention from 1774 to 1776 and was a member of the Continental Congress. In early 1776, he was sent on a mission to Canada to seek their assistance in the fight for independence. The committee included his cousin, the Reverend John Carroll, Benjamin Franklin, and Samuel Chase. They were not successful in persuading the French Canadians to join the fight because America had just failed in its attempt to invade Canada by Generals Montgomery and Benedict Arnold. Charles Carroll was elected a member of the Continental Congress on July 4, 1776. He was two days late to vote, but he did sign the Declaration of Independence, and after the deaths of Jefferson and Adams in 1826, he became the last living survivor of the original signers. Charles was elected to the Maryland Senate and served from 1781 to 1800. He opposed the confiscation of Tory property which did pass in 1780. He was elected to the U.S. Senate but preferred to remain in the Maryland Senate. As a major planter, he owned slaves, but he admitted slavery was evil. He did introduce a bill for the gradual abolition of slavery, but it did not pass, and he did not free his slaves. At age 91 he served as president of the State's Colonization Society, which was part of the national organization that promoted the founding of Liberia for the purpose of having a homeland for freed black slaves. In 1801, Carroll retired from public service but returned in 1827 to help create the Baltimore & Ohio Railroad. In 1832, he was invited to the first Democrat Party Convention but declined due to poor health. He died in November of that year at 95 years old.[9]

Daniel Carroll was born in 1730 into the wealthy Carroll family. His brother, John, became the first American Catholic Bishop, and his cousin, Charles of Carrollton, was a signer of the Declaration of Independence. Daniel studied at the Jesuit College of St. Omer in Flanders, and upon graduating he toured Europe before returning home to marry and begin his life as a planter and politician. In 1776, Maryland laws nullified the prohibition of Catholics to hold public office, so Daniel ran for and won a seat in the State Senate from 177 to 1781. He was then elected to the Continental Congress from 1781 to 1784. In 1781, he signed the Articles of Confederation, and he continued to befriend and advise George Washington and his policies for a strong central government. As a delegate to the U.S. Constitutional Convention, he voiced his objection of pay to the members of Congress by the states and was responsible for changing the proposed voting for the president by the legislature to voting by the public. He reportedly spoke 20 times, and one of his most important contributions was to change the final article stating that powers not delegated to the federal government were reserved to the states or to the people.[10] After the Convention, Daniel was elected a Maryland representative to the First Congress of 1789. He favored Alexander Hamilton's Assumption Bill allowing the federal government any remaining war debts of the states in return for supporting the new capital to be built in the south as proposed by Thomas Jefferson. Carroll served as a commissioner for the surveying land for the new capitol, some of which was owned by his relatives. He laid the cornerstone of the ten-square-mile District of Columbia near Alexandria. He then served in the Maryland Senate and worked with George Washington planning the Patowmack Company Canal. He passed away at his home near Rock Creek at 65 years old.[11]

Thomas Stone was born in 1743 in Charles County, Maryland and was descended from William Stone who was governor of Maryland in the 1650's. He was an extremely intelligent young boy who at age 15 chose to learn the English and Greek languages from a special school located ten miles from home. He travelled this distance every day on horseback, and when he graduated he went on to read the law in Annapolis and establish his own practice in Fredericktown and later in Charles County. In May of 1775, he was appointed a delegate to the Continental Congress. Like other delegates from Maryland, he was a loyal subject of the king and was even advised not to support any movement toward independence. One year later, that loyalty had dissipated when it became increasingly clear that resolution with England would not occur. Stone was a signer to the Declaration of Independence and was selected to write the Articles of Confederation which was debated 39 times before adoption in November of 1777. When completed, he returned to become a member of the Maryland legislature where he used his skills to mediate differences over the new confederation. In 1783, Stone was elected to return to Congress. The next year he resumed his law practice in Annapolis where his career flourished and his reputation blossomed. During this time, he was also a professor of religion and was noted for his piety. In 1787, his beloved wife died of smallpox, and Thomas was so bereaved that his health declined rapidly that he did not survive the year. He died at 45 years old.[12]

The Mason-Dixon Line

In 1632, King Charles I granted a charter to Sir George Calvert for land north of the Potomac River up to the 40th Parallel. In 1681, his son, King Charles II granted a charter to William Penn which defined the southern boundary of Pennsylvania as being the same boundary of the northern line of Maryland. Unfortunately, the Penn charter was inaccurate having been based on old, inaccurate maps. The resulting error showed that Maryland actually intruded into parts of Philadelphia which William Penn had planned for the capital. The problem was further complicated when Penn received an additional grant of the "Three Lower

Counties," which later became the Delaware Colony. At the time that territory was a satellite of Pennsylvania which Maryland claimed a part of their original grant.[13] The issue became even more contentious when the Maryland-Delaware line had to be determined. To resolve the issue, the Calverts and Penns hired the highly regarded services of two Englishmen; astronomer Charles Mason and surveyor Jeremiah Dixon of London's Greenwich Observatory. The entire project took four years from 1763 to 1767 and cost the Calverts and Penns *L* 3,512. The line is 244 miles long and encompasses four parts: the tangent line, the north line, the arc line (a 12-mile radius around New Castle) and the 39-degree and 43-minute North Parallel. The Mason-Dixon Line proved to be a cultural boundary between the North and the South as it marked the line where slavery was abolished or retained until the Civil War.[14]

Chapter Five

CONNECTICUT

Founded as a colony by Thomas Hooker in 1636
State on January 9, 1788

Founders and Settlers

The Province of Connecticut or the "River Colony" derives its name from the American Indian "Quinnehtukqut" which translates to "Beside the long tidal river." The first area to be explored was present-day Hartford by the Dutch in 1633. That same year, John Oldham of Massachusetts and Plymouth Colony explored the Connecticut River Valley, and his reports prompted the Reverend Thomas Hooker to begin a settlement in Hartford in 1636. Hooker migrated from Massachusetts because of his dissatisfaction with both the Puritan Church and the government there. He was joined by Governor John Haynes of Massachusetts Bay Colony who brought 100 followers with them to Hartford. The following year marked a major event in the Connecticut Colony when the English together with the Narragansett and Mohegan tribes fought a fierce and bloody battle against the Pequot Indians. Led by John Underhill and John Mason, the English defeated the Pequot and immediately established self-government with their refusal to surrender their authority to the Dominion of New England.

Their "Fundamental Orders of Connecticut" adopted in 1639 is regarded by some historians as the first governmental constitution in history that unequivocally separates church and state. It also declares the colonies in America as independent from the King of England. The Orders were reportedly inspired by a sermon from Thomas Hooker which espoused the tenets of God-given individual rights and freedoms. They were drawn by founder Roger Ludlow, approved by town magistrates in 1639, and established Connecticut as a self-ruled colony. The actual names of the framers were never officially recorded in order to discourage personal reprisals. It is also interesting that founders Hooker, Haynes, and Ludlow were granted approval by the Massachusetts General Court to settle the cities of Hartford, Wethersfield, and Windsor in Connecticut indicating that they had the authority to do this. The Fundamental Orders is composed of 11 paragraphs dealing with individual rights, the election of magistrates, terms of office, voter qualification, a justice system, and the mechanics of administrative government. Many of its principles were included in the U.S. Constitution and the Declaration of Independence. In 1662, Governor John Winthrop was instrumental in securing a Royal Charter, and he incorporated many of the Orders in a document he presented to King Charles II who then approved it. The colonists were guided by that charter and viewed it as preserving their Fundamental Orders. Years later with the reign of King James II in 1685, the colonists feared a more autocratic monarchy which wanted to annex Connecticut into the Dominion of New England. They took their charter and hid it in the hollow of a large white oak tree. Thereafter, it was referred to as the Charter Oak, and Connecticut became known as the "Constitution State."[1] Included below is the preamble to the Fundamental Orders of Connecticut which give a flavor to the document:

> *For as much as it hath pleased Almighty God by the wise disposition of his divine providence so to order and dispose of things that we the Inhabitants and Residents of Windsor, Hartford and Wethersfield are now cohabiting and*

dwelling in and upon the River of Connectecotte and the lands thereunto adjoining; and well knowing where a people are gathered together the word of God requires that to maintain the peace and union of such a people there should be an orderly and decent Government established according to God, to order and dispose of the affairs of the people at all seasons as occasion shall require; do therefore associate and conjoin ourselves to be as one Public State or Commonwealth; and do for ourselves and our successors and such as shall be adjoined to us at any time hereafter, enter into Combination and Confederation together, to maintain and preserve the liberty and purity of the Gospel of our Lord Jesus which we now profess, as also, the discipline of the Churches, which according to the truth of the said Gospel is now practiced amongst us; as also in our civil affairs to be guided and governed according to such Laws, Rules, Orders and Decrees as shall be made, ordered, and decreed as followeth.[2]

The second Connecticut Colony to be settled was New Haven in 1637 by John Davenport. As was the case with Hartford, it was not founded to be a state but instead was intended to be a place where God's work could be done without interference from other religions or governments. It was a Puritan stronghold that adhered to strict moral laws. They even did away with juries because those were never included in the Bible. Those accused of a crime were required to report it to the magistrate and await his decision and punishment. Laws were based on Scripture, and all residents were required to attend a Puritan church as no other religions were tolerated. They called themselves dissenters from the Anglican Church but were not "Separatists." Their life was strict and austere as they worked to purify and reform the Anglican Church. They had left England to escape persecution and arrest especially under the reigns of King James I and King Charles II.[3]

The Puritan church was called a "Meetinghouse" because it served as a place for town meetings, a courthouse, and even an armory. All citizens were required to attend church but only members could choose and ordain their own ministers and elect elders and deacons. Only they could elect new members and discipline those who disobeyed God's laws. Heretics and even those who were not Puritans could be fined, imprisoned, or physically punished. Hooker did relax some of these measures in 1639 with the passage of the Fundamental Orders that provided a full civil government, but still only adult male house and land owners were allowed to vote. Many of the changes in Connecticut occurred during the 1640's and 1650's. These were prompted by the Civil War in England when Oliver Cromwell led the Puritans in overthrowing the monarchy in 1642 and establishing England as a Puritan state. New England colonists supported Cromwell's movement and regarded them as aligned with their own cause in reforming the Anglican Church. Some Connecticut Puritans actually returned to England to fight in Cromwell's army and serve in his government. This "Parliamentary Period" in England from 1642 to the restoration of the monarchy in 1660 also energized the New England colonists to adopt more practices of self-government and greater personal freedoms.[4]

Two other English colonies were brought into Connecticut—the Saybrook Colony in 1644 and the New Haven Colony in 1662—and this was done largely through the efforts of John Winthrop the Younger who was the son of Governor John Winthrop of Massachusetts Bay Colony. Young John was born in England in 1606 and was educated at Trinity College in Dublin. In 1631, he joined his father in Massachusetts, and in 1633 he founded the town of Ipswich, Massachusetts. After a year of study in England, he returned to New England to be governor of land that had been granted to Lords Say, Sele, and Brook. He had a keen interest in minerals and in 1644 built iron works in Lynn and Braintree. The next year he gained title to lands in southeastern Connecticut and founded the town of New London where he constructed a grist mill that marked the first American monopoly on that trade for as long as he and his heirs maintained it. Winthrop went on to even greater accomplishments and served as Governor of Connecticut for consecutive terms from 1657 until his death in 1676. One of his greatest acts was gaining a charter that consolidated the New Haven and Saybrook Colonies into the Hartford Colony in Connecticut in 1662.[5]

When the first settlements started in the early 17th century, they were located along the Connecticut River Valley and its rich fertile soil. Subsistence farming developed into export products such as hemp, potash, whale oil, cattle, and timber primarily to the British colonies in the Caribbean. In the early 18th century, light manufacturing appeared with clocks and silverware. Mining produced iron ore and copper for export to England where finished goods were made for re-export back to the colonies. With its long shoreline on Long Island Sound, fishing and whaling were important trades. Much of Connecticut was forested with oak, birch, beech, maple, and hemlock trees which led to shipbuilding for domestic uses and export to England. When the American Revolutionary War began, trade with England declined dramatically, but this prompted the colonists to develop more manufacturing abilities. During the war, Connecticut became one of the principal sources of food for the Continental Army with a large supply of farm products, milk, and beef. Grist mills and textile manufacturing also started at that time and accounted for much of the colony's economy at the end of the century. Perhaps one of its greatest inventors was Eli Whitney, whose cotton gin proved a boon to textiles and cotton exports from the south.[6]

Fortunately for Connecticut there was little Revolutionary War damage because few campaigns were fought there. However, the colony did achieve much importance because of some of its local citizens and the role they played in the struggle for independence. Israel Putnam was born in 1718 in present-day Danvers, Massachusetts, but he is regarded as a son of Connecticut having spent most of life in Pomfret. He served in the French and Indian War in the 1750's and was captured by the Indians who were about to burn him at the stake when he was suddenly saved by a French officer. In 1762 when he was fighting against the Spanish in Havana, he survived a shipwreck, again showing his courage and daring. With the passage of the British Stamp Act, Putnam became a member of the Sons of Liberty and assumed an active role in opposing British oppression. His military heroics led to winning a seat in the Connecticut Assembly. Putnam became a successful farmer, but when he learned of the fighting at Lexington and Concord, he again joined the military to take a leading role in the Battle of Bunker Hill in June of 1775. The British military under Thomas Gage had been very much aware of the strategic position of the hills to the north overlooking their headquarters on the Boston peninsula, but they neglected to do anything about it. When they sent Gen. William Howe to strengthen their vulnerable position, the Americans were led by Israel Putnam to fortify Bunker, Breeds, and Moulton Hills which were on the peninsula jutting out from Charleston

Neck surrounded by the Mystic and Charles Rivers. On June 16th, Gen. William Prescott and his troops occupied the hills with most defenses centered at Breeds Hill. When General Howe saw the Americans continuing to fortify the area, he led 3,000 troops ashore while British ships pounded the hills with heavy canon fire. Howe was repulsed twice, but as American supplies dwindled, they retreated and were soon killed trying to escape the peninsula. Historians have never understood why the British didn't simply capture Charleston Neck and starve the Americans to surrender. The battle was relatively minor in terms of size, but it proved to be a very significant one. The British lost over 40 percent killed and wounded to the American loss of 450 men. However, the British losses affected Commander-in-Chief General Howe in his cautious approach to American resolve and fighting ability until his retirement to England in 1778. Before the hostilities commenced on June 16th, Israel Putnam's command to his troops "not to fire until you see the whites of their eyes" has been remembered to this day. Putnam survived Bunker Hill and served as one of Washington's generals. His first order was to take command of the American military in New York City and await the arrival of Washington.[7]

Certainly, one of the finest founding fathers was Roger Sherman who was born in 1721 in Newton, Massachusetts but spent most of his life in Connecticut after his father died in 1744. Sherman holds the distinction of being the only founder who signed four of America's most important documents: the Continental Association creating the First Continental Congress, the Declaration of Independence, the Articles of Confederation, and the United States Constitution. More importantly, he served on the committees which created all four of them. For the 30 years of his life, he worked as a public servant and occupied important political and judicial positions. Thomas Jefferson said he was "a man who never said a foolish thing in his life."

As a young boy, Sherman was taught his father's trade as a cordwainer in making shoes and leather products. At school he excelled in math, and he taught himself surveying which led him to an interest in land speculation. His first marriage produced seven children of which the three oldest sons served in the Continental Army. When he moved his family to New Milford, Connecticut in 1745, he opened a retail store that sold household goods such as tables, chairs, brooms, and an assortment of other goods. At the same time, he published an almanac which included weather, astronomy, religious festivals, and colonial currencies. In 1754, he took up the study of law, and the following year he was appointed Justice of the Peace for Litchfield County and was then elected to the Connecticut General Assembly. When his wife died in 1760, he moved the family to New Haven where he abandoned his law practice and surveying to open a general merchandising store next to Yale College. He soon met the 20-year-old niece of his brother's wife, Rebecca Prescott. They were married May 12, 1763 and went on to raise eight children. Sherman resumed his interest in politics and the law and was elected to the Connecticut General Assembly in 1764, was appointed as Justice of the Peace, and assumed the position of Treasurer of Yale for the next ten years.

The events of the 1760's and the growing hostilities between the colonies and Great Britain caught Sherman's attention. The various taxes imposed by Parliament without the consent of the colonists was troubling to him. The Tea Act of 1773 was vexing enough to prompt his greater involvement in government affairs. His noteworthy comment "no laws bind the people but such as they consent to be governed by" brought him broader notoriety, and subsequently he was elected to the First Continental Congress. Throughout the Revolutionary War, Sherman was regarded as a diligent and hard-working legislator who assumed growing responsibilities. He was well informed and attentive to the fast-moving events. His work schedule was similar to that of James Madison and other founders whose day started at 5:00 am and ended late at night. He served on the committees to draft the Declaration of Independence and the Articles of Confederation. He took on a variety of responsibilities including Native American issues and the post office system. He was appointed to the Board of War in 1776 and the Board of Treasury. He was a close friend of John Adams who said of him: "one of the most sensible men in the world."

In 1784, New Haven was a newly created incorporated city, and they elected Sherman to be their first mayor. He was also a judge of the Supreme Court and in 1787 was appointed to represent Connecticut at the Constitutional Convention in Philadelphia. He and Oliver Ellsworth are credited with writing the "Connecticut Compromise," breaking the deadlock on the issue of representation. The Articles of Confederation had been in effect since 1781, and it called for only one vote for each state, so the question of representation was an extremely sensitive one. The Connecticut Compromise proposed a bicameral or dual system whereby the number of representatives would be based on the population of each state while the Senate would have an equal number of two Senators. Upon his return to Connecticut, Sherman was elected to serve in the House of Representatives. In the First Congress, Sherman supported Hamilton's Assumption Bill allowing the federal government to assume the Revolutionary War debts incurred by all 13 states. Two years later in 1791, Sherman replaced Samuel Johnson in the Senate. He served only two years due to declining health, and he died in 1793 of typhoid fever. In summary, Roger Sherman was a man in many ways a combination of the discipline, integrity, and fortitude of a Washington and the intellect of a Madison and the creative mind of a Jefferson… a remarkable man who may be the greatest unsung hero of the infant United States.[8]

Connecticut was one of the first colonies to establish a school of higher learning. It claims to have had its roots in the 1640's, but the first charter and campus was granted in 1701 in Saybrook, Connecticut and was named the Collegiate School. It ranks as the third oldest college in the United States after Harvard (1636) and William & Mary (1693). The General Court of the Colony of Connecticut met in New Haven and passed "An Act for Liberty to Erect a Collegiate School." It was founded to be for the training of ministers and lay leaders for the church and the colony. Ten Congregational ministers agreed to donate their books to establish the school's first library. At this time, the Harvard president, Increase Mather, became embroiled with the Harvard clergy who he regarded as overly liberal and weak in ecclesiastical practices. Samuel Mather was one of ten Harvard alumni who supported the creation of the Collegiate School with its stated purpose of maintaining Puritan religious orthodoxy more successfully than Harvard had. Another important factor was over their concern over the growing frequency of Harvard students who were spending too much time across the Charles River visiting pubs and houses of ill repute. In 1718, the Reverend Cotton Mather was asked to contact a Welsh businessman, Eli Yale, whose father was one of the original founders of New Haven, to ask for financial help in constructing a new building for the college. Eli Yale donated nine bales of goods valued at *L* 560, and Mather proposed changing the name to Yale College in his honor. At the same time, a Harvard alumnus living in England persuaded 180 intellectuals to donate books. These 500 books were some of the best works in English literature, science, philosophy, and theology. In 1722, the rector and six of his colleagues abandoned Calvinism and became members of the Anglican Church thereby diluting the original Puritan objective. As Yale was fast developing as a significant intellectual center, it got caught up in the Great Awakening and Enlightenment movements of the 18th century. Under Presidents Clap and Stiles, a scientific curriculum was introduced just as the colonies were dealing with revolution, wars, and student unrest. It was President Stiles who introduced Hebrew to the curriculum and required all freshmen to study the language so they could read the Bible in its original language. When the British occupied New Haven in 1779, they threatened to burn it to the ground. As luck would have it, the Secretary to the British General in Command, Edmund Fanning, was a Yale alumnus and intervened to save the College.[9]

Chapter Six

Rhode Island

Founded as a colony by Roger Williams & Anne Hutchinson in 1636
State on May 29, 1790

Early Years

The earliest recorded use of the name was by the Italian explorer Giovanni da Verrazano in 1524 when he referred to an island near the mouth of Narragansett Bay which reminded him of Rhodes in the Mediterranean. Prior to the arrival in 1636 of its founder, Roger Williams, a Dutch explorer by the name of Adrian Block is credited with naming this land as "Roodt Eyelandt" which was later changed by the English to Rhode Island. The name derives from the red clay which abounds along its 400 miles of shoreline within its meager 47-mile width. Rhode Island was mainly inhabited by Native American Indian tribes until Roger Williams arrived in 1636 upon his banishment from Massachusetts Bay for his religious beliefs. Williams befriended the Narragansets and even learned their language. He was sympathetic to their culture and legal rights to their land and actually represented them in court successfully. Williams was born and educated in England where he studied law and religion at Cambridge University and became a Puritan. During his early years of ministry in England, Williams served under Sir Edward Coke, who was regarded as the greatest jurist in the country. It was Sir Coke who wrote the charter for the Virginia Company prior to their voyage to Jamestown in 1606. During this period, the key issue of the day was the divine right of kings and therefore the relationship between the church and state. King James I was a Protestant but was heavily influenced by his Catholic heritage and refused to reform or "purify" the Church. He introduced his version of the Bible, and those who didn't follow his policies were invited to leave the country. He called Puritans "enemies of monarchs." As the Puritans were increasingly persecuted by the Anglican Church, they sought religious freedom in the newly established colonies of Massachusetts Bay and Plymouth Plantation.

Flight From Massachusetts to Rhode Island

Williams and his wife, Mary Barnard, arrived in Boston in 1631, and soon Roger began preaching his doctrine of religious tolerance which was being threatened by the established theocratic Puritan government of Massachusetts. In spite of numerous warnings and pressures to mend his ways, he persisted with his strong convictions of religious freedom and separation of church and state until he was finally banished by Governor John Winthrop of Massachusetts in 1635 under threat of imprisonment. As he fled, leaving his wife and child behind, he wandered into the winter wilderness of New England until he was befriended by Native American Indians because of his many previous efforts to defend their rights as owners of the land. The Narragansets would sell some of their land only to Williams as sole proprietor. He named it "Providence" in thanks for "God's merciful providence unto me." He wished it to be a place for persons in distress of conscience. At first, it was a land without a charter or legal authority. However, with his extensive experience in law, religion, scripture, and politics, he established a government for himself and close to 50 followers. He had complete political control that he shared with a few heads of households, and decisions were made by majority rule. Although he owned all the land of

Providence, he kept only a parcel that was equal in size to what he made available to others. When he made back his original cost and no profit, he donated the remaining land to the Town of Providence. Most of the Rhode Island land was held by William Coddington under a land grant until 1652, when Williams travelled to England and had that land title annulled. Coddington founded Newport in 1639.

In 1638, another pioneer of religious tolerance, Anne Hutchinson, left Boston with her followers and settled in Providence Plantation where she founded the town of Portsmouth. As the colony gained in reputation for its policies of freedom of conscience, it attracted other minority groups such as Quakers and Jews. In fact, the first Jewish synagogue in America was established in Newport in 1763.

In 1640, Providence experienced internal pressure from those surrounding settlers who wanted more land to the point of causing civil unrest. Massachusetts and Plymouth wanted to exercise political and religious dominance which prompted Williams to sail to England to obtain a formal charter which would give him official recognition as a legal entity and thereby protect them from incursions and threats. While in England, Williams learned that the four Puritan colonies of Massachusetts Bay, Plymouth, New Haven, and Connecticut created their own military alliance in response to threats from Native American Indians, the Dutch in New York, and the French to the north. These united colonies stated: "whereas we all came into these parts of America with one and the same end and aim, namely, to advance the kingdom of our Lord Jesus Christ, and to enjoy the church liberties of the Gospel in purity with peace." Williams informed Parliament of how his neighbors were acting and of his banishment and of their pillaging of Providence. He told them how Massachusetts even expelled those who had tried to worship privately using the Book of Common Prayer. He charged that Massachusetts had combined the church and state, and he used a phrase that has resounded in American history to this day: "When they have opened a gap in the hedge or wall of Separation between the Garden of the Church and the Wilderness of the world, God hath ever broke down the wall itself, removed the Candlestick etc., and made his Garden a Wilderness as at this day." Williams was warning that mixing church and state corrupted the church.

He had found some sympathetic ears, and in 1644, some of the most powerful men in England signed the charter which gave the Providence Plantation their true legal standing and the freedom to form any type of government they chose as long as it conformed to the laws of England. The Committee on Foreign Plantations left all decisions about religion to the majority, knowing that it wanted to completely remove the state from the issue of worship. Williams had created the only such society in the civilized world.[1] The Royal Charter of Rhode Island was granted in 1663 by King Charles II who then appointed Benedict Arnold as the first governor. He was the great-grandfather of the notorious spy for the British in the Revolutionary War.

Roger Williams faced a challenging situation as he tried to stabilize his new-found colony. The area was inhabited by several Native tribes, some of whom were hostile to one another. In addition, neighboring Massachusetts Bay Colony and the Plymouth Plantation encroached on Rhode Island land. Williams played a critical role in his ability to pacify all warring factions until serious fighting erupted between the native Narragansett and the Pequots. The English settlers from Massachusetts, Connecticut, and Rhode Island finally subdued the Pequots, but this was followed by King Phillip's War in 1675 which marked an important turning point in Rhode Island's development.

Massasoit was the Native American chief who had befriended the Pilgrims in 1621. When he died in 1661, his son, Metacom (also known as King Phillip), became sachem of the Wampanoag Confederacy. As he grew more alarmed at the increasing number of English settlements, he developed more distrust of the colonists. In 1671, Metacom was required to sign a new peace agreement with the English whereby he was forced to surrender their guns. While he plotted revenge for this humiliation, he was betrayed by John Sassamon who was a Native American Christian convert who informed the Plymouth Colony officials of Metacom's intended attack. In 1675, three Wampanoag Indians were tried, convicted, and executed by the settlers for the murder of Sassamon. King Phillip was outraged at this affront to his tribal authority. He responded by raiding Swansea and other settlements in Plymouth Colony. Many other towns were destroyed, including Springfield and Providence in a massive Indian uprising. Colonists under Capt. William Turner of Massachusetts together with 150 men defeated and killed Narragansett Chief Canonchet. The next year Metacom was betrayed, captured, and executed thereby ending King Phillip's War. The consequences of the war were far-reaching, including: 1) greater distrust between settlers and native tribes and the conviction that the two cultures could not live peaceably 2) the important fur trade died 3) the local Indian culture and language all but disappeared 4) with thousands killed and major towns destroyed, economic and personal costs to the colonists was enormous 5) peace allowed for more settlers and faster future growth 6) a growing fear throughout all the colonies of potential Indian reprisals such as Bacon's Rebellion in Virginia in 1676.

The Revolutionary War

On May 4, 1776, Rhode Island was the first colony to declare independence from England. Its native son, Nathanael Greene, became one of General Washington's most trusted and talented field generals. In fact, Washington let it be known that upon his death or capture, Greene was to be his successor as Commander-in-Chief. Greene came from a Quaker family, but instead of assuming the family business, he chose the military and served in the local militia known as the Kentish Guards from Kent County. Greene became successful in business, but he also studied law and was elected to the Colonia Assembly from Coventry in 1771, 1772, and 1775. He took a special interest in military books, many of which he bought from his friend, Henry Knox, who was a Boston bookseller. Knox was to become General Washington's artillery general and then Secretary of War in the Washington Administration. Because Rhode Island was a self-governing colony, under its charter it was allowed to organize its own militia. Members were only admitted by application and approval and were required to supply their own uniforms and equipment. Green was not accepted as an officer, and historians believe the rejection was due to his slight limp which prevented him from a proper military bearing which this elite unit demanded. In spite of this huge disappointment, he joined as an enlisted man. He proved to be a resourceful member and was able to find a British army deserter to train and drill the Kentish Guards. He also arranged to hire an experienced fife and drum instructor. When hostilities with the British erupted in April and May of 1775, The Rhode Island Assembly ordered the formation of three regiments to support General Washington. The Kentish Guards were far more organized and trained than most of the other militias and eventually contributed 35 of their officers to the Continental Army. Greene went on to become one of Washington's closest advisors and distinguished himself at Valley Forge, the Battle of Camden, South Carolina, and as Commander of the southern army. He died in 1787 at age 44 and was regarded by South Carolina and Georgia as a great hero for his military gallantry and his successful administrative reorganization of their two states. He was survived by his wife, Catherine, and their three sons and two daughters. When President Washington toured the South in 1792, he visited his godson, George Washington Greene, and promised Kitty that he would provide for the boy's education. Nathanael Greene was truly one of the Revolutionary War's greatest unsung heroes.[2]

Another uniquely Rhode Island aspect to the Revolutionary War concerned the issue of blacks serving in the military. General Washington was opposed to this because he did not want to give the British a means of acquiring soldiers in the South by offering slaves their freedom in return for service in the British army. Such an event could give an enormous advantage while losing the support of the south in the fight for independence. The 1st Rhode Island Regiment was organized on May 8, 1775 under Col. James Varnum. It was immediately incorporated into the Continental Army and assigned to Gen. Nathanael Greene's Brigade in Washington's main army. In 1777, the Continental Army was reorganized, and the 9th Continental Regiment was re-designated the 1st Rhode Island Regiment. In 1778, Rhode Island was unable to fill its assigned quotas, so General Varnum suggested to Washington to consider the recruitment of slaves. Washington felt compelled to pass the suggestion on to the Assembly which approved the measure provided this was done on a voluntary basis only when the individual slaves chose to do so. In return for their service, they would receive their freedom, and the owners would be compensated for their loss. Even though less than half of the Regiment was black, the 1st Rhode Island became known as the "Black Regiment." In less than a month's time, no more black men were admitted to the unit mainly because of Washington's policy. His army was the first and only army in the country that was integrated until the Korean War in 1950.[3]

In 1784, it was the first state to legislate the abolition of slavery. However, Rhode Island did not participate in the Constitutional Convention at Philadelphia in 1787 because there was no provision for the freedom of religion. When President Washington went on his tour of New England in 1790, he bypassed Rhode Island because of their absence at the Constitutional Convention. Rhode Island was the last state to ratify the Constitution in 1791 after Congress adopted the Bill of Rights.

Rhode Island did play an important role in the Revolutionary War because of its strategic location on Long Island Sound. Also, its harbor was easy to access, and its deep water was ideal for large British navy vessels. With its vast naval superiority, the British could easily control the Sound and thereby protect its military headquarters in New York City. Attempts by the Americans and their French allies failed to oust the British from Newport Harbor in 1778 when French Vice Admiral d'Estaing abandoned his sea battle with the British due to stormy weather and left American Gen. John Sullivan alone to face the entrenched enemy forces. The following year, England left Newport to consolidate their headquarters in New York City, and the allies returned to recover the town in 1780. No other major battles were fought in Rhode Island, but their regiments participated in every major campaign of the war. Another famous son of Rhode Island was the artist Gilbert Stuart who painted the most prized portrait of George Washington as well as those of John Adams, Thomas Jefferson, James Madison, and James Monroe.

In the field of education, Rhode Island excelled by founding the third oldest school in New England: Brown University in 1764. It was first located in Warren and named the College of Rhode Island. It was moved to Providence in 1804 and renamed Brown University in recognition of a $5,000 gift from Nicholas Brown who was an alumnus and successful businessman from Providence.

In 1790, an English immigrant named Samuel Slater built the first textile mill in the United States. It was located in Pawtucket and marked the beginning of the New England textile business. Slater came to be known as the "Father of the American Industrial Revolution." By the mid-1800's, Rhode Island became a leading industrial state with many factories producing textiles, machine tools, silverware, and jewelry. This gave rise to the large-scale immigration of workers from Ireland following that country's potato famine from 1845-52.[4] During the Civil War, Rhode Island's strong industrial position enabled it to supply the Union with many necessary materials, including clothing, armaments, and 25,236 soldiers of which 1,685 died. In its Newport harbor, Fort Adams housed the United States Naval Academy which was moved from Annapolis, Maryland over concern about Maryland sympathizers for the Confederates. It also served as a recruit depot for U.S. Infantry regiments. Notable military men included Major Gen. Ambrose Burnside who commanded the army of the Potomac in 1862 and who later defeated at the Battle of Fredericksburg and the Siege of Petersburg. Maj. Gen. Silas Casey led a division of the army of the Potomac. Brig. Gen. Richard Arnold, the son of Rhode Island Governor Lemuel Arnold was Chief of Artillery who forced the surrender of two important Confederate towns: Mobile, Alabama and Port Hudson, Louisiana. Zenas Bliss led an infantry brigade at the Siege of Petersburg and later was awarded the Medal of Honor for gallantry at Fredericksburg. Others included Frank Wheaton of Providence, Fleet Captain William Rogers Taylor, and Gen. Thomas Sherman of Newport.[5]

Chapter Seven

New Hampshire

Founded as a colony by John Mason
State on June 21, 1788

The Early Years

The name "New Hampshire" was coined in 1629 by its founder, Capt. John Mason, who was Governor of Portsmouth in Hampshire, England. Mason and Sir Ferdinand Gorges received a grant of land in 1622 from the Council of Plymouth in Massachusetts which included part of present-day Maine and all the land between the Merrimac and Piscataqua Rivers in New Hampshire. In 1623, Mason sent David Thompson and a group of English fishermen to settle the area now called Rye which is on the Atlantic Ocean just south of Portsmouth. This was followed by another expedition led by Edward and William Hilton to settle the area of Dover farther up the Piscataqua River. In 1629, the new Company of Laconia was formed to settle in the Portsmouth area they named "Strawberry Banke," which was changed in 1653 to Portsmouth. Prior to this in the 1630's, Massachusetts claimed many of these territories, but in 1641 all parties agreed to have the Dover, Rye, and Portsmouth towns come under the jurisdiction of Massachusetts and were granted Home Rule. However, relations remained strained because of land claims by the heirs of John Mason. In 1679, the grants were separated from Massachusetts by King Charles II who then granted them a Royal Charter for the "Province of New Hampshire." In 1686, the Province was merged into the Dominion of New England, but this lasted only a short time until 1689 when King James II was deposed and replaced by King William III and his wife and cousin, Queen Mary. From 1699 to 1741, the governorships of New Hampshire and Massachusetts were shared, and confusion ensued when Massachusetts was granting some disputed New Hampshire lands, and Indian claims further complicated matters. In the 1730's, Lt. Governor John Wentworth brought these issues to local officials and to the Crown in England. In 1741, King George II ruled on the boundaries and separated the governments into their own provinces. However, Wentworth rekindled the issue when he granted lands west of the Connecticut River which were contested by New York. The lands remained outside the Colonial States until 1790 when they became the 14th American State of Vermont.[1]

The Beginning of Independence

In January of 1776, New Hampshire was the first colony to adopt a constitution although it stated that it was not their intention to terminate their dependence on Great Britain. A little-known event occurred in December of 1774 at Fort William and Mary on the small island of New Castle. The fort had been built by the earliest English settlers in the 1630's as a defensive measure to guard the entrance to Portsmouth Harbor and for the storage of munitions. With the Boston Tea Party having heated the tensions with England in December of 1773 and the closing of the Port of Boston as punishment, Great Britain became increasingly alarmed by American resistance. In October of 1774, King George III ordered the removal of all munitions from the fort and forbade the export of arms and munitions to America. Rumors spread in New England that Great Britain was sending troops to remove and protect the arms. On December 13, 1774, well before Lexington and Concord in April of 1775, Paul Revere rode to Portsmouth to warn local Patriots. On December 14, 1774, John Langdon gathered several hundred Patriots and sailed out the Piscataqua River to the fort where only one British officer and five soldiers protected it. When they refused to relinquish the arms, Langdon and his men rushed the fort and overtook the defenders. They took down the Union Jack and confiscated 100 barrels of gunpowder. No one was killed and the British soldiers were released. The next day John Sullivan and his rebels overtook the fort again and removed muskets, supplies, and 16 cannons.[2] The British declared the acts were high treason, and the cannons were sent to Boston for Washington's use in his siege that forced the British out of the city in March of 1776. After their departure, there were no British troops left in all the colonies.

One of New Hampshire's greatest colonial leaders was John Sullivan, who we first met at the siege of Fort William and Mary. He was born in 1740 in Somersworth, New Hampshire and lived a full and patriotic life as a major general in the Continental Army under George Washington, a congressman, a New Hampshire governor, and a judge. His life encompassed the Revolution and the political thinking of the times, and he made enormous contributions to establishing the states of New Hampshire and Vermont. Although there were no major battles in New Hampshire, it could be argued that the armed conflict at the Fort of William and Mary in 1774 marked the beginning of the Revolution, and Sullivan had the distinction of fighting for American independence four months prior to Lexington and Concord and six months before Washington was appointed Commander-in-Chief of the Continental Army.[3]

John Sullivan's parents emigrated from County Kerry in Ireland where his father was a schoolmaster. John was the third son, and his brother, James, became Governor of Massachusetts and another brother, Benjamin, served in the royal navy but died before the American Revolution. John married Lydia Worster of Kittery, Maine in 1760, and they had six children. He studied the law from 1758 to 1760 and established his own practice in 1763 in Berwick, Maine. He moved to Durham the next year where he was the only lawyer in town. As his law firm became established, he acquired significant financial interests in the milling trade where he earned substantial income. In 1767, John Wentworth was appointed by the Crown to be the new royal governor, and over the next few years he developed a friendship with Sullivan and appointed him a major in the New Hampshire militia. However, with Sullivan's legal background he began to shift his sympathies to the rebel cause, which ended his close relationship with Wentworth. In May of 1773, Virginia's House of Burgesses strongly suggested the New Hampshire Assembly form a Committee of Correspondence, and on the next day after they did so, Governor Wentworth adjourned the Assembly. Shortly after the Boston Tea Party and the closing of the Port of Boston the following March, Wentworth called for a new Assembly in April. He then closed the assembly in June when he couldn't prevent them from sending delegates to the Continental Congress in Philadelphia, which included Sullivan and royal governors, to secure all gunpowder and arms in local magazines. This move prompted the rebels to seize the weapons at Fort William and Mary. Wentworth elected not to arrest Sullivan because he mistakenly thought the militia would not take the action they did.[4]

The Revolutionary War

Sullivan and Langdon attended the Second Continental Congress in January of 1775 and tried to persuade Wentworth to call for a new Assembly. He responded by removing Sullivan from the militia, but he did not have the authority to arrest him. Sullivan was instrumental in convincing other delegates to prosecute the war for independence. He then went to Boston and served under Washington for the siege. After the British evacuated Boston in March, Washington sent Sullivan to assume command of the troops in Quebec. He succeeded in getting the sick and wounded to Crown Point at Lake Champlain, but his counter-attacks against a reinforced British army failed. Congress blamed Sullivan, but he was later exonerated and promoted to major general. Washington then summoned Sullivan to join him in the Battle of Long Island which ended badly due to misunderstood commands and poor communications. Sullivan exhibited great bravery in the field, but he was captured and used by the British to attempt a negotiated peace. Congress had no faith in the plan, but a meeting was held without any results. General Sullivan was eventually released in a prisoner exchange and joined Washington at the Battle of Trenton in December of 1776. His troops secured the north end of the bridge and prevented Hessians from escaping. A week later he fought successfully with Washington at the Battle of Princeton. This was followed by his unsuccessful assault of the British main garrison on Staten Island, but he was exonerated by a court of inquiry. He then fought at Brandywine and Germantown but was outflanked and forced to retreat albeit in an orderly fashion. Others were blamed for the defeat.

In 1778, Sullivan was sent to Rhode Island to work in concert with the approaching French fleet to oust the British from Newport. This was the first joint effort with France who had recently signed a Treaty of Amity and Commerce to provide both material and an army and navy to assist America. French Admiral d'Estaing encountered a severe storm just off Newport that caused him to cancel his attack. Also, the sudden arrival of the royal navy under Admiral Richard Howe influenced d'Estaing's decision to sail to Boston for repairs. Sullivan had no choice but to retreat, but his vociferous criticism of the failed attack did cause a serious breach in Franco-American relations and left in doubt the reliability of French assistance. In 1779, Sullivan led a major campaign against the Iroquois in western New York where the Indians had been harassing American troops and local settlers with assistance from the British army. He destroyed a large Indian settlement south of Ithaca which he reached by cutting a road through the Pocono Mountains. Known as Sullivan's Trail, it has been in service to this day. He reportedly exhausted his men and their horses which became useless, and this gave rise to the beginning of a town in New York named Horseheads. Although the campaign was successful, Sullivan received little appreciation from Congress and decided to retire from the army that year and return to New Hampshire. He was welcomed home and in 1780 was selected to be a delegate to the Continental Congress where he focused on the land disputes between New Hampshire and New York. The issue was further complicated when the British intervened and tried to persuade Vermont to become part of Canada. In 1781, Sullivan supported a committee to negotiate with Vermonters to become the 14th state, which was finally accomplished in 1791. That same year, Sullivan was asked to mend the Confederation's poor financial condition and weak international credit. As an ardent Francophile, he approached France for financial support. He then worked to have Benjamin Franklin as one of the American peace negotiators and for Robert Livingston to be appointed Secretary for Foreign Affairs. Sullivan retired from Congress on August 11, 1781.[5] When Sullivan returned to New Hampshire he was named the attorney general and served for four years. He was also elected to the State Assembly and was appointed Speaker of the House for New Hampshire. He led his state in the ratification of the United States Constitution in 1788. At the First Congress in 1789, Washington nominated Sullivan to be the first Federal judge for the District of New Hampshire, a position he held until his death in 1795 at 54 years old. His many accomplishments are memorialized in the large number of legacies honoring his service including: counties named for him in New York, New Hampshire, Pennsylvania, Tennessee, and Missouri; Sullivan Street in New York City; the General Sullivan Bridge near Durham, New Hampshire; towns named Sullivan in Illinois, New York, and New Hampshire, and Sullivan's Bridge at Valley Forge National Historical Park.[6]

The 18Th Century Founders

New Hampshire is another one of the original colonies that produced men who played an important part in the Revolutionary War, the Continental Congresses, the Constitutional Convention, and leadership roles in their respective states. Both John Langdon and Nicholas Gilman were sent by New Hampshire to Philadelphia in 1787, and while they lived long after the original settlers in the 17th century, they should be honored as founders of New Hampshire for their leading roles in achieving independence and statehood.

John Langdon was born in 1741 in Portsmouth. Like so many other leaders, his was a farming family that had emigrated from England in the 1600's. The family first settled at the mouth of the Piscataqua River which was developing as an important seaport in New England. Both he and his brother declined working at their father's successful agricultural business and became apprentices to naval merchants. At age 26, John acquired his first cargo ship and plied the waters between New England, London, and the Caribbean. By 1770, he was one of the wealthiest men in Portsmouth. Langdon was directly affected by the growing British control of the shipping industries and therefore became an ardent supporter of the revolutionary movement. He served on the Non-Importation Committee and the New Hampshire Committee of Correspondence. It was noted earlier of his leading role in confiscating the munitions stored at Fort William and Mary in New Castle. In 1775, Langdon was elected a member of the Continental Congress, but when war broke out the next year, he left to supervise the construction of several battleships including the "Ranger" which was captained by John Paul Jones. In 1787, he returned to the Continental Congress and was appointed as a delegate to the Constitutional Convention. He then served in the Senate from 1789 to 1801. This was followed by his two terms in the New Hampshire Legislature from 1801 to 1805 having been Speaker for his last two terms. Langdon was twice elected Governor of New Hampshire from 1805 to 1811, after which he retired to Portsmouth where he died in 1819. His legacy includes the town of Langdon, New Hampshire and Langdon Street in Madison, Wisconsin.[7]

Nicholas Gilman was born in Exeter, New Hampshire in 1755 where his homestead is the American Independence Museum. Having been born during the French and Indian War and having a father who was a leading local leader in the cause for liberty, young Nicholas learned very early in life about political events of the times. His education was limited to local public schools, and when he graduated, he worked as a clerk in his father's trading business. Because of that business, Gilman was engrossed in the plight of the merchants who were becoming incensed at the British imposition of the growing number of taxes. In 1775, at age 20, he became a member of the New Hampshire Provincial Congress. The next year he was appointed as an administrative officer of the 3rd New Hampshire Regiment under the command of Col. Alexander Scammel. Colonel Scammel was a combat officer who was trying to transform a group of raw recruits and aging veterans into a competent fighting force. He needed someone like Gilman for their administrative skills, and within a short period of time, the 3rd New Hampshire was highly regarded as one of the strengths of Washington's Continental Army. One of the most vulnerable areas of the colonies was in the north where British troops in Canada could attack. In early 1777, Washington assigned the 3rd New Hampshire to defend Fort Ticonderoga and the Lake Champlain area and resist advancing British and Hessian troops. The Americans were outflanked and forced to retreat. Their advance was slowed during the summer months which allowed the Americans to mobilize larger forces, including the 3rd New Hampshire Regiment led by Nicholas Gilman and his father. Their maneuvers also allowed Gen. Horatio Gates to better organize his defenses at Saratoga. Colonel Scammel with Gilman's assistance fought successfully at Freeman's Farm where British General Burgoyne was forced to surrender his army of 7,000 men. The victory was the first major American one and one of only three in the eight-year war where an entire army was surrendered. The others were the American surrender at Charlestown and the British surrender at Yorktown. The Saratoga victory convinced France that America could defeat England, and it resulted in the Treaty of Amity and Commerce the next spring whereby France committed to supply men and materials to the Americans.

A week after Saratoga, Washington sent the 3rd New Hampshire to assist him in the area just outside British-occupied Philadelphia. After American defeats at Chad's Ford and Germantown, Washington moved on to Valley Forge where Scammel and Gilman trained their regiment. They worked with Washington, von Steuben, Knox, and Greene. Gilman was promoted to captain and saw action at Monmouth in 1778 and Yorktown in 1781. Colonel Scammel was killed just before Yorktown, and Gilman's father died in 1783, at which time Gilman retired from the military and returned home to Exeter to manage the family business. In 1786, he was appointed to the Continental Congress where he supported changing the Articles of Confederation. He then was a delegate to the Constitutional Convention, and together with John Langdon they worked to debate and compromise on the issues. Gilman's brother, John, served as Governor of New Hampshire for 14 years and was helpful in the Ratifying Convention of 1788 which was adopted by a 57-47 vote. Nicholas was a member of the First Congress in the House of Representatives for four terms. In 1800, he served as a state senator. Although all his life he had been an ardent believer in a strong central government, he became concerned about possible abuses by too strong a government. In the election of 1800, he supported the Democratic-Republican Party of Thomas Jefferson. In 1804, he was elected to the United States Senate as a Jeffersonian. In 1812, he voted against the war with Great Britain which was approved by 19-13 by the Senate. As a signer of the United States Constitution, he later stated that it was "the best that could meet the unanimous concurrence of the States in Convention…it was done by bargain and compromise, yet, notwithstanding its imperfections, on the adoption of it depends (in my feeble judgment) whether we shall become a respectable nation or a people torn to pieces…and rendered contemptable for ages."[8]

Education

Like other colonies, New Hampshire ministers took the lead in bringing education to the settlers, including Native American Indians, to learn the basic skills of reading, writing, and learning about Christianity. After graduating from Yale in 1733 where he studied theology to become an ordained Congregational minister, the Reverend Eleazar Wheelock settled in the town of Lebanon, which is in the geographic center of Connecticut. To augment his modest salary, he taught school and invited several boys to live with his family where they paid a small sum for their room and board. In 1743, a Mohegan boy came to him by the name of Samson Occom. Wheelock became quite impressed with the boy's development and helped him later becoming a minister. The experience also inspired Wheelock to start a school for other Indians, and in 1755 he did so and called it "Moore's Charity School for Native American Indians." It was a charity school for Indians and poor English boys to prepare them for college and hopefully the ministry. He tried to raise sufficient funds to sustain the successful school, but he was forced to reach beyond his local area. It is surprising that the school even survived having started during the French and Indian War and its continuation in Canada as the Seven Years' War ending in 1763. Meanwhile, Wheelock's star pupil had become an ordained minister, and as a devoted follower of Wheelock, he agreed to travel to England with the Reverend Nathaniel Whittaker to raise money for a new and larger school. They preached from the pulpits of many English dissenting churches and were introduced to poor and wealthy people where contributions ranged from five schillings to 200 pounds from King George III. The greatest amount was from the Secretary to the Colonies, William Legge the Second Earl of Dartmouth. Occom and Whittaker raised 12,000 pounds which was placed in trust at a Scottish bank in Edinburgh where the account remains to this day.

Wheelock was concerned that the Connecticut school was not attracting sufficient numbers of Native American Indians, so he decided that it was too far away from larger native populations to the north. He considered many new locations in the western parts of Pennsylvania, New York, and Massachusetts. The best offers of land came from New Hampshire in the Connecticut River Valley which was on the direct route from the New England Coast to the Indian settlements in Canada. He approached the royal governor of New Hampshire, John Wentworth, who was also interested in education and the training of missionaries. In a request for a school charter, Wheelock outlined the kind he would need, and in a postscript added, "If you should use the word "college" instead of "academy"—it would please me." In 1869, acting on behalf of King George III, royal governor John Wentworth granted the charter. Wheelock offered to name the school after him, but Wentworth declined and suggested that it be named for his good friend, the Second Earl of Dartmouth who had been one of the school's largest donors. Little did either Wheelock or Wentworth imagine that the charter was to become one of the most important legal documents in the young nation. In the late 1790's, there arose a dispute over whether the state could assume control and ownership of the college. Many suits were filed as the case rose for decision before the Supreme Court in 1818 with John Marshall presiding as Chief Justice. Senator Daniel Webster spoke for the college pointing out that the key issue was the sanctity of a charter as a binding contract that would affect all schools, charitable organizations, churches, and private property. The college won its sovereignty, and since that decision, all law students read it as the "Dartmouth College Case." The charter is long and complex, but at the heart of it are two important sentences: "that there be a college erected in the Province of New Hampshire by the name of Dartmouth College for the education and instruction of youth of Indian tribes in this land in reading, writing, and all parts of learning which shall appear necessary and expedient for civilizing and Christianizing children of pagans, as well as in all liberal arts and sciences, and also of English youth and others." The Trustees were instructed not "to exclude any person of any religious denomination whatsoever from any of the liberties and privileges or immunities of the said College on account of his or their speculative sentiments on religion."

In searching for the location in New Hampshire to place the College, Wheelock received grants of 3,300 acres in Hanover (King George was of the

House of Hanover) and 1,400 acres just over the town line in Lebanon (NH). He began the move from Connecticut in 1770 to the Hanover Plain which was a forest of white pine trees where there were no settlers within two and half miles. Reportedly, the trees were 270 feet high with the first branches 100 feet from the ground. Workers started to construct a school building and a house for Wheelock's family. The snow was four feet deep, but the small band of 20 students and his family endured the first winter in log huts. The first class graduated in 1771 and consisted of four men who had been Wheelock students who were sent to Yale for their first three years because of the lack of food and shelter in Hanover. Just before the fifth commencement, the Revolutionary erupted and soon all the Indians left. Of the nine colleges existing at that time, eight suspended during the war, but Dartmouth remained operational.[9]

Eleazar Wheelock died in 1779 at the age of 69, having spent his final ten years establishing a college in the wilderness. The College seal depicts the sun shedding light on a Native American Indian holding a Bible. The Latin motto reads: "Vox Clamantis In Deserto," which is a verse from the Book of Isaiah proclaiming the coming of John the Baptist and translates: "A Voice Crying in the Wilderness."

Chapter Eight

Delaware

Founded as a colony by Peter Minuit & New Sweden Co. in 1638
State on December 7, 1787

Early Years

The name Delaware derives from Earl Thomas West, Lord De la Warr, who was the second governor of the Virginia Colony. The land Delaware now occupies was originally part of Virginia when that colony was started at Jamestown in 1607. Lord De La Warr arrived in Virginia in 1610 and remained governor for eight years even while he resided in England. Upon his return to Jamestown in 1618 he died at sea, supposedly in the Azores which was a new and quicker route from England to Virginia discovered by his contemporary, Samuel Argall. Argall was an English explorer who governed Jamestown in the absence of De La Warr and the one who originated the faster navigational route from the Azores directly west to the Chesapeake. While Jamestown was barely surviving its first year, it was Argall who brought food and supplies, enabling the settlers to survive. At the same time, Henry Hudson was in the employ of the Dutch West India Company exploring the northeastern coast of North America and was the first to sail into present-day Delaware Bay in 1609. His discoveries gave rise to Dutch claims to parts of Delaware, New Jersey, New York, Connecticut, Massachusetts, and Rhode Island. As these trading posts and towns were taking root and flourishing like Amsterdam (New York City), the Swedes made a foothold along the banks of the Delaware River in 1638. King Gustavus Adolphus of Sweden devised a plan for the settlement of a colony there. The first governor of New York was Peter Minuit who had a falling out with the Dutch and returned home. Adolphus appointed Minuit to take some settlers to the Delaware region for their new colony which he did on the western and eastern sides of the Delaware River. They first settled on Christiana Creek near Wilmington and built a fort there. The entire area of the settlement extended from Cape Henlopen to the Falls of Trenton and was named New Sweden. However, The Dutch claimed that the Delaware land belonged to them, so in 1623 they built Fort Nassau on the eastern part of the river about five miles south of Camden. To strengthen the Swedish position, their Governor John Printz built forts near Philadelphia and Lewistown. The Dutch and Swedes managed to co-exist from 1638 to 1655 when New Netherlands Governor Peter Stuyvesant received permission to subdue the Swedes and take control of their forts and land. The Swedes were allowed to stay if they took an oath of allegiance to Holland. Those who didn't left for Maryland, New York, or returned to Europe. The Dutch controlled the territory for close to ten years, but when the English won the Third Anglo-Dutch War in 1664, the New Netherlands was terminated and the land annexed to the renamed New York. In 1682, one of the principal proprietors, the Duke of York, sold New Castle and a 12-mile tract to William Penn which became known as the "Territories" and became today's Delaware. For twenty years it was governed by Pennsylvania, but in 1703 they were allowed to have their own assembly under the governorship of Pennsylvania until the Revolution. In 1776, the Delaware Assembly terminated their ties to both England and Pennsylvania to become the 13th separate independent colony.[1]

The Revolutionary War

Throughout the Colonial Period, Delaware was a territory governed by the Dutch, the Swedes, and the English. It was not until June 15, 1776 that it declared itself independent from England and its governance by Pennsylvania. The following July it voted as the 13th colony in favor of the Declaration of Independence. In anticipation of coming events it had organized the First Delaware Regiment which subsequently fought in every major battle in the middle colonies and in the south. In 1777, its militia fought against the British in the northern part of Delaware when they attacked Wilmington. This was the first battle in the British campaign to take the American capital of Philadelphia. General Howe and his 15,000 troops boarded 260 ships in Staten Island and headed for Elk Neck in the northernmost part of Chesapeake Bay. His strategy of sailing about 400 miles instead of marching 90 miles from New York to Philadelphia confounded everyone then as it still does today. One plausible reason could be Howe's fear of getting trapped by the Americans in the long baggage train such a march would entail. He seemed reluctant to venture too far away from his headquarters and preferred close proximity to his supply ships. Washington had established his headquarters in Wilmington and already had organized a corps of 800 marksmen under the command of Gen. William Maxwell to harass the enemy. Technically, the first actual battle fought on Delaware soil was a small skirmish near Newark at Cooch's Bridge on September 3, 1777. However, they were pursued by the British and returned to join Washington. After several skirmishes of hit and run tactics near Wilmington, Washington decided to take a stand at Chad's Ford on the Brandywine Creek. He had assured Congress that he could defend Philadelphia, but some historians think he never really believed that himself. He did want to buy more time for the arrival of needed arms and gunpowder expected from France, and he also wanted to prevent the British from moving inland where stockpiles of weaponry were stored at Reading. Chad's Ford was to be Washington's first head-to-head battle with European-style tactics, but he fell victim to the outflanking maneuver of Cornwallis by not extending his outposts far enough to the northwest along the Brandywine. It was another loss for him which was followed by a loss at Germantown, but he did manage to keep his troops intact to regroup in Reading while Howe proceeded to occupy Philadelphia.[2] The losses in Delaware and Pennsylvania convinced Washington that his troops needed more training. In December of 1777, Washington chose Valley Forge as the most strategic location for building a more unified Continental Army and to keep an eye on the British in Philadelphia only 20 miles away.

The First Delaware Regiment gained its greatest reputation for the battles it fought in the south. In 1779, the Regiment was placed under the command of a German-born volunteer, Maj. Gen. Johann De Kalb. In April of 1780, De Kalb was ordered to help the Americans in the Carolina's where they faced an advancing British force under Gen. Charles Cornwallis and Col. Banastre Tarleton.

After their failures to isolate New England at Saratoga, and thinking that the capture of Philadelphia and other key seaport cities would assure victory, the British employed their third strategy of conquering the southern colonies, especially Virginia which was at the heart of the initial rebellion and home to many leaders. The first city to fall was Savannah which was followed by Charleston in April of 1780. Congress directed Maj. Gen. Horatio Gates to lead the America's southern army, and he included troops from Delaware, Virginia, and North Carolina. In August of that year, the Americans were badly defeated at Camden, South Carolina where De Kalb was killed while leading his troops. When it was learned that General Gates had retreated 200 miles from the front line, Washington immediately relieved him of command and replaced him with Nathanael Greene. The Delaware were split into two companies under Captains Robert Kirkwood and Peter Jaquett, and they earned the highest praise from Greene and Washington for their bravery at Cowpens, Guilford Court House, Eutaw Springs, Ninety-Six, and Hobkirk's Hill forcing the British to surrender. In 1781, following the American victory at Yorktown in October, the Delaware marched south to join Greene. For their six straight years of service, several officers, including Kirkwood and Jaquett, were awarded furloughs. The other soldiers of the First Delaware Regiment stayed in the south until the fall of 1782, by which time peace negotiations were rumored as being arranged between England and America.[3]

Statesmen, Leaders, and Heroes

Richard Bassett was born in 1745 in Maryland where he was raised by his uncle, Peter Lawson. He began his successful law career in 1770 and eventually inherited his uncle's Bohemian Manor estate and purchased homes in Dover and Wilmington. During the Revolutionary War Bassett was appointed a captain in the Dover militia and also served at the Delaware Constitutional Convention. After the war, he sat in both houses of the Delaware legislature and was appointed as a delegate to the Annapolis Convention in 1786 and then the United States Constitutional Convention in 1787. At the Ratifying Convention, he joined in their 30-0 vote of approval. As a member of the U.S. Senate in the First Congress, Bassett voted against Hamilton's Assumption Bill of state debts being assumed by the federal government and supported the presidential power to remove government officials. For six years he served as chief justice for the Court of Common Pleas. Bassett was a strong supporter of Washington's Federalist policies, and in 1799 he was elected governor of Delaware. In 1801, President Adams appointed him a judgeship of the U.S. Circuit Court. However, Bassett became a part of the Adams "Midnight" appointments which were subsequently abolished by opposition from the Jefferson administration. He retired in 1801 and passed away in 1815 at 70 years old.[4]

Gunning Bedford, Jr. was born in 1747 in Philadelphia and was descended from one of the earliest families that originally settled in Jamestown, Virginia. He graduated from the College of New Jersey (Princeton) in 1771 where he was a friend and classmate of James Madison. He then read law with Joseph Reed, and with the outbreak of war he joined the Continental Army and reportedly was an aide to General Washington. After the war, Bedford began a distinguished career in local and national politics. He served in the Delaware legislature, on the state council, and in the Continental Congress from 1783 to 1785. He was the attorney general for Delaware from 1784 to 1789. As a delegate to the U.S. Constitutional Convention, he was an outspoken and strong advocate for the rights of small states and was a member of the committee that drafted the Great Compromise for a bi-cameral legislature. In 1789, Washington appointed him a federal district judge for Delaware which he retained for the rest of his life. He also served as an elector in the presidential elections of 1789 and 1793.

Bedford's other interests were Wilmington Academy, promoting abolitionism, and farming. He died in 1812 at 65 years old.[5]

Jacob Brown was born in Wilmington in 1752 and was educated at home. While he worked with his farming father he also learned surveying and worked in shipping and the import trade. His only involvement in the war was as a mapmaker for General Washington prior to the Battle of the Brandywine in 1777. At the age of 24, he became assistant burgess of Wilmington and served in that capacity six times and as chief burgess four times. He sat in the state legislature from 1784-86 and in 1788. He was a delegate to the U.S. Constitutional Convention and attended every meeting. After the Convention, he built a home on the Brandywine River. Brown held a number of local offices and was a director of the Delaware Bank in Wilmington and promoted development of Delaware's infrastructure. He died in 1810 at 58 years old.[6]

John Dickinson was born in Talbot County, Maryland in 1732. In 1740, the family moved to Dover where he was taught by private tutors. Dickinson studied the law in Philadelphia and in London's Middle Temple in 1753. In 1757, he started his successful law practice in Philadelphia. Three years later he entered politics and served in the Delaware assembly as a speaker. He then sat in the Pennsylvania assembly. His leadership as a conservative supporter of a proprietary governor was contrary to the policies of Benjamin Franklin, which hurt his popularity but gained respect for his integrity. Parliament's passage of the Stamp Act in 1765 set off a strong reaction in the colonies, and Dickinson took the lead in opposing the tax by having Americans pressure British merchants for its repeal. In 1767, Dickinson was regarded as the spokesman for a peaceful resolution between England and America. He used the "Pennsylvania Chronicle" as the media for his "Letters from a famer in Pennsylvania" wherein he opposed British taxation policy and promoted American resistance to unjust laws. He also took issue with the Townsend Duties in 1768 and called for strong rejection by recommending a halt to export and import of goods to and from England. In the early 1770's, Dickinson remained the principal spokesperson for peaceable policies, but the tide gathered in strength for a forceful response. In 1775, he composed petitions of redress for grievances directly to King George. While he continued to work for peace, he was reluctantly drawn into the confrontation.

Even when he was chair of the Philadelphia Committee of Safety and Defense, he was also a member of the first battalion to defend Philadelphia. In the Second Continental Congress of 1775-76, he was still seeking support for redress of grievances but insisted on maintaining ties to England. In 1776, Dickinson refused to sign the Declaration of Independence. He and Thomas McKean were the only two contemporary congressional members who joined the military, but when he was not reelected he resigned his brigadier general position and his Pennsylvania assembly membership. In 1779, Dickinson came out from retirement to join the Continental Congress to sign the Articles of Confederation which he had previously drafted. In 1781, he was elected president of the Delaware Supreme Executive Council and later moved back to Philadelphia where he became president of Pennsylvania from 1782 to 1785. The next year he chaired the Annapolis Convention. He was then chosen as a delegate to the U.S. Constitutional Convention. While opposed to the strong nationalist policies of Madison, he did actively support the Great Compromise. Illness forced him to leave the Convention, but he instructed George Read to sign it for him. Dickinson devoted the last 20 years of his life to writing about politics, and in 1801 he published two volumes of his work. He died in 1808 at 75 years old.[7]

George Read was born in 1733 in Maryland, and shortly thereafter his family moved to New Castle, Delaware. He was educated at a local grammar school and then at a private academy in New London, Pennsylvania. At the age of 15, he studied the law with an attorney in Philadelphia. At age 21 he began his successful law practice in New Castle. He married Gertrude Ross Till in 1763 who was the widowed sister of George Ross who later became a signer of the Declaration of Independence. From 1763 to 1774, Read served as attorney general for the "Three Lower Counties" of Delaware. He entered national politics with his strong opposition to the Stamp Act in 1765. In many ways, his political thinking was similar to his friend, John Dickinson. While he supported American independence, and fought unjust taxation and British laws, he believed in a peaceful solution to the conflict with England. He did not vote in favor of the Declaration of Independence probably because of the prevailing Tory sympathizers in Delaware and because of his strong belief in peaceful negotiation and reconciliation with England. He became the only opponent of the Declaration who actually signed the document. In 1776, Read focused his attention to state matters and chaired the Delaware Constitutional Convention. In 1777 and 1778 he assumed the presidency of the Delaware legislative council. In 1779, he directed the Delaware delegates to sign the Articles of Confederation. That same year poor health forced him to resign, but from 1782 to 1788, he was appointed judge of the Court of Appeals. In 1786, he attended the Annapolis Convention and the next year was selected as a delegate to the Constitutional Convention where he strongly advocated for the rights of small states. He supported a strong chief executive and led Delaware to ratify the Constitution making it the first state to do so. Read was elected to the First Congress as a U.S. Senator from Delaware from 1789 to 1793. He died in 1798 at 65 years old.[8]

Caesar Rodney was born in 1728 in Kent County, Delaware. His grandfather, William Rodney, came to America in 1681 together with William Penn who became Speaker of the Colonial Assembly of the Delaware Counties in 1704. The Rodneys built a 1,000-acre farm and became prosperous from the sale of wheat and barley to Philadelphia and the West Indies. Upon the death of Caesar's father in 1746, the Delaware Orphan's Court placed him under the guardianship of Nicholas Ridgely. Prior to that time, Caesar was educated at the Latin School in Philadelphia, and he was the only one of the eight brothers who received a formal education. He enjoyed an excellent reputation and possessed charm, wit, common sense, and wisdom. In spite of these attributes, he never married but did make several unsuccessful attempts. He later suffered facial cancer that eventually took his life, and it is speculated that this disease may have been a deterrent to marriage.

In 1755, Rodney was elected as the Sheriff of Kent County which was a financially beneficial position because it supervised elections and selected grand jurors. After finishing his three-year term, he was appointed Register of Wills, Recorder of Deeds, Clerk of the Orphan's Court, Justice of the Peace, and a lower court judge. He was commissioned a captain in the Delaware militia during the French and Indian War but never served active duty. From 1769 to 1777 he was Associate Justice of the Supreme Court of the Lower Counties.

In the 1700's, Delaware evolved into a politically divided colony dominated by the pro-Anglo Court Party which was centered in Kent and Sussex Counties.

The minority pro-independence Country Party was centered in New Castle County. The Rodneys aligned themselves with the latter and therefore advocated a break with England. At the Stamp Act Congress in 1765, Rodney was a leader of the Delaware Committee of Correspondence. He started his term in the Delaware Assembly in 1761, and he retained his position through 1776. One of the highlights of his career occurred on June 15, 1775 when, as chairman of the Assembly, it voted to declare its independence from England. From 1774 to 1776, Rodney served in the Continental Congress along with his friend and colleague, Thomas McKean. On July 1, 1776, while he was away in Sussex County, he learned that McKean and his Delaware political opponent, George Read, were deadlocked on the critical vote for American independence. Rodney immediately took off on his horse for Philadelphia to break the stalemate. He rode 70 miles in a severe thunderstorm entirely drenched and still in his soaked boots to arrive just as the voting began. He and McKean prevailed, and Delaware became the 11th state to vote for independence. Because Rodney was from pro-Anglo Kent County, he lost his bid for the Delaware Constitutional Convention and the next Delaware General Assembly.[9]

After the American defeat at the Battle of Brandywine and the British occupation of Wilmington and Philadelphia in 1777, Delaware held an election in October for a new General Assembly. Rodney and McKean were called back into the Continental Congress. Delaware's president, John McKinley, was held captive by the British, and George Read was physically unable to serve. Rodney was elected President of Delaware in 1778, and because of his popularity in the Assembly and in the militia, he was able to govern successfully. Declining health caused him to resign in 1781, three weeks after the decisive American victory at Yorktown. Rodney was then elected to the U.S. Congress by the Assembly in 1782 and 1783, but his poor health prevented him from attending. In the 1783-84 session, he served on the Legislative Council, but he died shortly thereafter at 55 years old. He is buried in an unmarked grave at the family's ancestral farm, "Byfield."[10]

Chapter Nine

North Carolina

Founded as a colony by Lords Proprietor & Carolina Charter in 1653
State on November 21, 1789

Early Years

The colonization of North America did not happen without early efforts that failed. The first recorded exploration of the Carolina coast was by Giovani da Verrazano in 1524 when he made a claim for his employer, King Francis I of France. He was closely followed in 1526 by Lucas Vasquez de Ayllon who started a settlement at Cape Fear which failed due to disease and starvation. The next Spanish explorer was Hernando de Soto in 1540 with his search for gold in western North Carolina. In 1629, King Charles I granted a charter to Sir Robert Heath who would honor the king by naming the area after him, but he did not establish a settlement (The name Carolina derives from the Latin "Carolus"). Finally, in 1563 some Virginians started a settlement in the Albemarle Sound area of northern Carolina. The most notable efforts were made by Sir Walter Raleigh who obtained a charter from Queen Elizabeth I in 1584 to establish a permanent English colony in America. Raleigh made five voyages, and the closest he came to success was the settlement at Roanoke Island which did not survive. It was not until 1663 that a new charter was granted by King Charles II to a group of eight proprietors for land south of Virginia at 39 degrees latitude. It was enlarged two years later to 36 degrees, 30 minutes to include present-day South Carolina and Georgia. For the other boundaries, the charter reads "from sea to sea" meaning the Atlantic to Pacific Oceans. The proprietors divided their land into three sections: the Albemarle District in the north that was already occupied by a small group of Virginians, the Clarendon District at Cape Fear which did not survive, and the Craven District which later became South Carolina. The leading proprietor was Lord Ashley Cooper, the Earl of Shaftesbury. Cooper introduced an unusual Government plan that historians believe was formed by John Locke, the English political philosopher. Called the "Grand Model" or the "Fundamental Constitutions," it called for a monarchy with aristocratic rule. The land was to be divided into counties each of which was to have an earl and two barons. After 20 years, the plan proved unpopular and unworkable and therefore was dropped. However, it did establish religious freedom, even though the Church of England was the established church.[1]

Initial authority was vested with Virginia Governor William Berkeley for the northern section of Albemarle who soon appointed William Drummond as governor. He was succeeded by Samuel Stephens in 1667 who called for an assembly to establish laws and enact policies that would attract settlers. These included the exemption of taxes for one year and the nullification of existing debts incurred outside the colony. Stephens was followed by Seth Sothel, but after five years as governor—and a corrupt administration—was sent into exile in 1688. The Albemarle settlement in the north continued to deteriorate, and over 15 years the population declined by 50 percent. The large colony proved too difficult to manage, so in 1710 the Lords Proprietors met in London to divide the colony into North and South Carolina with the same proprietors controlling both colonies. In 1729, the Crown bought out seven of the original eight investors and changed their status to Royal Charters. The first unofficial capital was its oldest town of Bath from 1705 to 1722. It was then moved to Edentown for 21 years and then to New Bern and finally to Raleigh in 1792.[2]

North Carolina grew from a 1752 population of 100,000 to 200,000 by 1765. Slaves totaled 25 percent of the total population. By 1776, North Carolina was the fastest-growing colony in America. They saw domestic immigration from Virginia and Pennsylvania. The Tidewaters area attracted settlers from rural England and the Scottish Highlands. The western part of the colony experienced immigrants of Scots-Irish, English, and German origin. Many of the settlers became increasingly upset with their proprietary leaders as well as savage attacks from local tribes. A series of uprisings occurred in the late 1600's and early 1700's including Culpeper's Rebellion, Carey's Rebellion, the Tuscarora War, and the Regulator Movement. In 1760, the western settlers fought a bitter war with the Cherokee Indians, and the colonist victory resulted in a treaty wherein the Native tribes surrendered significant tracts of land.[3]

The Revolutionary War

As various taxing measures were imposed on the colonies, political leaders and most citizens grew to resent the British government. In turn, the royal governor, Josiah Martin, was becoming more hostile as he learned of meetings to protest British policies. When colonial leaders in Massachusetts, Pennsylvania, and Virginia called for the formation of a Continental Congress in 1774, the leadership of North Carolina announced a convention for all 35 counties to elect delegates to the Congress scheduled for Philadelphia. Royal Governor Martin condemned such meetings, considered them illegal, and called out all civil and military officers to prevent them. In spite of such warnings, the First Provincial Congress of North Carolina took place on August 25, 1774 in New Bern and elected Richard Caswell, Joseph Hewes, and William Hooper to be representatives to the First Continental Congress on September 5th. They also stated their loyalty to the House of Hanover and King George III, recognized his sovereignty, and vowed to obey the established laws. This was immediately followed by flatly stating their intent to cease trade with Great Britain if their grievances were not addressed. Further, they would not import any East India Company goods or British manufactures, and they would not export any tobacco, tar, turpentine, or any articles whatsoever to Great Britain. Governor Martin was not invited to the meetings, but he learned of their resolves and met in New York with other royal governors who became alarmed at similar events throughout the colonies.

In February of 1775, a Second Provincial Congress was called for April. Once again, Governor Martin forbid such a meeting, but it took place on April 4th. On April 24th, leading Patriots seized all the artillery on the lawn of Governor Martin who soon fled New Bern for the safety of Fort Johnston off the Cape Fear River. After learning about the battles of Lexington and Concord in April, the Mecklenburg Committee of Safety adopted a resolution in May declaring their independence from Great Britain, which occurred 14 months before the Declaration of Independence. Meeting in February of 1776, the Third Provincial Congress agreed that it would pay their fair share for training the Continental Army, and it authorized the formation of two regiments of Provincial Troops. They also authorized each of the 35 counties to raise their own militia and "Minutemen" composed of all men between the ages of 16 and 60 to serve a minimum of three months. That same month, the first armed conflict occurred in North Carolina when a large force of militia clashed with the Loyalist troops of Highlander Gen. Donald McDonald at Moore's Creek Bridge in Pender County.[4] British Comm. Gen. William Howe ordered Gen. Henry Clinton to invade North Carolina thinking that large numbers of Loyalists in the south would come to their support. However, the initial battle of the war changed all that when the Highlanders sustained 39 killed, 20 wounded, and 850 captured. The Patriots lost only one. Clinton then decided to withdraw from North Carolina and move down to Charleston where he also expected support from local Loyalists. Again, the British were repulsed and did not reappear in the south until 1780 when they captured Savannah and Charleston and moved on to North Carolina. However, it was the first two encounters in early 1776 that led North Carolina to be the first colony to declare its independence in their Halifax Resolves adopted on April 12, 1776.[5]

In June of 1780, British General Cornwallis captured Charleston and marched north. The Continental Army was commanded by Gen. Horatio Gates who sustained a terrible loss at Camden, South Carolina and retreated more than 20 miles in what looked like a cowardly move, leaving the field to let his subordinate officers continue the fight. Washington was so outraged that he fired Gates on the spot and replaced him with Gen. Nathanael Greene who reorganized the southern army. The North Carolina line eventually peaked at 11 regiments and 7,000 soldiers. Some of their regiments had previously joined Washington's army in the failed attempt to defend Philadelphia before moving on to Valley Forge. In June of 1778, they had fought at Monmouth Court House when the British were leaving Philadelphia for New York. By then, they were reduced to three units which were sent to defend Charleston only to be captured by the British. At Cowpens, South Carolina, the British under Col. Banastre Tarleton were defeated by American Gen. David Morgan.[6] The loss prompted Cornwallis to move his men to the north where they faced General Greene at Guilford Court House, North Carolina. It what proved to be one of the fiercest and bloodiest battles of the war, the British were deemed the victors, but the price they paid was high. The Americans lost 79 killed and 185 wounded while Cornwallis lost 93 killed and 413 wounded, which represented 25 percent of his forces. When news of the victory reached London, a member of Parliament, Charles James, remarked, "another such victory would destroy the British Army." Cornwallis moved his army to rest and recuperate in Wilmington for a month before invading Virginia. Meanwhile, Greene returned to the south to liberate those areas of South Carolina and Georgia which had been lost.[7]

Willie Jones was born in 1741 in Virginia, and when he was 12 years old his family moved to the Halifax area in Northampton County, North Carolina. He was immediately sent to England to study at Eton for his four years of secondary schooling. Upon graduating he toured Europe before returning home. At the age of 35, he married Mary Montford who produced 13 children, and they lived a highly social and politically active life at "The Grove," which he had built prior to his marriage. Historians have never fully understood why Jones changed his pro-Anglo political beliefs and aristocratic lifestyle to favor the democratic society that was being pursued by American revolutionaries. He strongly supported colonial rights and feared a central government that could become too strong. In 1774, he served on the Halifax Committee of Safety and began his membership on the Five Provincial Congresses that brought North Carolina into the revolutionary war. At the same time, he served on the committee to draft the state constitution and bill of rights. From 1775 to 1787 Jones was the most powerful and influential politician in North Carolina. He was a member of the House of Commons and a state senator for three terms. In 1780, he was elected to the Continental Congress, but in 1787 he declined to attend the U.S. Constitutional Convention. When the document was completed for state ratification, Jones voiced his objection at the Hillsborough Convention knowing full well that the majority of the delegates would favor it. He did succeed in delaying North Carolina's approval until 1789 when the document was finally approved at the Fayetteville Convention by a vote of 195 to 77 thereby ending his political career. He died in 1801 at age 60, and his legacy is marked by a street in Raleigh, which he had selected for the state capital, a county in North Carolina, and the city of Jonesborough, Tennessee.[8]

John Penn was born in 1741 in Port Royal, Virginia. His paternal great-grandfather was James Taylor, who came to Virginia from Carlisle, England in 1635. Taylor married Frances Walker, and their descendants, James Madison and Zachary Taylor, became presidents of the United States. Penn received only two years of public education, and at age 18 his father died, suddenly leaving him to care for his mother and the extensive and successful farm his father had developed. Fortunately for John, his uncle, Edmund Pendleton, was a notable attorney who tutored him in the law. A friend of his, Thomas Jefferson, considered Pendleton "the greatest orator in the colonies," and another friend, George Washington, asked him to write his will just before going off to command the Continental Army in Cambridge. According to Adams and Jefferson, Pendleton possessed the finest library in all the colonies. Penn was exposed to many great legal minds, and by age 21 he received his license to practice law which he did for the next 12 years. In 1774, he moved his family to Williamsboro, North Carolina for several reasons: he was convicted in Virginia of the treasonous act of speaking ill of King George in a public place for which he was fined one penny but refused to pay, and secondly, he had outpaced his uncle in the cause for independence and found that North Carolinians harbored the same feelings of resentment as he did. Thirdly, he did not want to upset his highly regarded benefactor and uncle, Edmund Pendleton. In North Carolina, he found much deeper concern about British restrictive policies, and he was also upset with Virginia's unfair domination by wealthy planters and businessmen. He was very quickly accepted into North Carolina politics and in 1775 was elected to the First Provincial Congress and to the First Continental Congress. At the Provincial Congress, he was charged with several important issues: to gain more support for independence; to form a temporary government; to draft a constitution and statutes for an independent society. Penn returned home in the spring of 1776 to delineate specific grievances against England. The Provincial Congress authorized him to lead a committee to draft the first formal document in all the colonies declaring its independence from Great Britain. He led his fellow North Carolina delegates, William Hooper and Joseph Hewes, to affirm and sign the Declaration of Independence. In addition to his many duties and committee meetings, Penn participated in the financial affairs of the war with purchasing supplies and supervising their shipments. He did this for six years without pay. The trip home from Philadelphia to Granville County was 400 miles which was fraught with danger from highwaymen, Indians, and hardships of travelling on trails and poor roads.

In 1780, when the British adopted their third major strategy to win the war by capturing the south, John Penn played a key role in America's defense. General Cornwallis had taken Savannah, Charleston, and Camden and was about to invade North Carolina. Penn was appointed to a three-man Board of War to prepare for the attack. He quickly took charge of recruiting, funding, transporting, and finding supplies. He was surrounded by the pessimism of discouraged colleagues but rose to the occasion with confidence. Contemporaries described him as "indefatigable, cheerful, courteous…firm political principles… he went through the crisis with honor…and rendered services inestimable to the prosecution of the war." In 1781, after six years of devoted and constant work under stressful conditions, John Penn returned home to recover his health. He resumed his law practice until his death in 1788 at 47 years old.[9]

William Hooper was born in 1742 in Boston. His father, the Reverend William Hooper, was a Congregational minister who was educated at Edinburgh University and came to America in 1734 from Scotland. Years later he became an ordained Episcopalian and served in Trinity Church in Boston from 1747 to 1764. Young William attended the Boston Latin School and upon graduation entered Harvard as a sophomore and graduated at 18 years old. In 1761, he read the law under the outspoken colonial activist James Otis. He began his law practice in Wilmington, North Carolina and soon was appointed a Circuit Court judge. In 1767, he married Anne Clark of North Carolina whose brother became a brigadier general in the Continental Army. Her affluent and well-connected family was able to sustain the young couple throughout the privations of the revolutionary war. In 1773, Hooper sat in the Provincial Congress Assembly in New Bern representing Cambelltown (later Fayetteville). It was here that North Carolina's leaders came to know him. He was soon selected as a representative in the First Continental Congress in Philadelphia where he was joined by John Penn and Joseph Hewes. Their first assignment was to draw up a list of grievances against Great Britain. All the colonies were represented except Georgia whose governor blocked the election of delegates. The most significant work of the Congress was to protest the British closing of the Port of Boston. They created the Continental Association which banned the import and export of goods from and to Great Britain if colonial grievances were not resolved. Hooper was elected to the Wilmington Committee of Safety charged with the execution of the ban on trade. While in Philadelphia, Hooper served on the Committee of Secret Intelligence together with Joseph Hewes and Benjamin Franklin. It was an extremely important committee dealing with the hiring of secret agents, making agreements with other countries, and authorized to keep information from the Congress. Like his North Carolina colleague, John Penn, Hooper seemed to work around the clock, and by the end of 1776, he had attended three Continental Congresses, four Provincial Assemblies, and meetings of the Wilmington Committee of Safety. Hooper was absent from the July 4, 1776 vote for independence, but he did sign the amended document on the second of August. Later that year when General Washington was threatened from attack at the Delaware River, leaders feared for the safety of Congress in Philadelphia, so they moved the capital to Baltimore. Hooper took on more responsibilities with the post office, the treasury, intelligence networks, admiralty courts, and other critical areas of government. In December, he was charged with designing a Great Seal for the state of North Carolina. In April of 1777, he resigned his seat in the U.S. Congress declaring he was "weary of politics" and chose to return home never to reenter national politics. However, he did resume his law practice and once again rode the Circuit Court. He was also returned to the General Assembly from 1777 to 1781. When the British invaded Masonboro Sound they burned his Wilmington house to the ground, but he had fled with his family to his brother-in-law's house in Hillsborough. After the war, Hooper's law practice prospered with the myriad of legal actions involving confiscated estates, lands, and injustices claimed by Loyalists and Patriots. Hooper suffered from malaria for a number of years, and with declining health finally succumbed in 1790 at 48 years old. He is honored at the monument at Guilford Courthouse National Military Park in Greensboro and at his gravesite in Hillsborough. John Adams referred to William Hooper, Joseph Hewes, and Patrick Henry as the three outstanding "Orators of the Congress."[10]

Joseph Hewes was born in 1730 near Princeton, New Jersey. His ancestors emigrated from England to Pennsylvania around 1635. Joseph's parents settled in Connecticut where they became successful farmers and were free to practice their Quaker beliefs. However, within a few years, with frequent Indian massacres and persistent religious intolerance, the Hewes decided to move to New Jersey. Joseph received a secondary school public education and then went on to the College of New Jersey (later Princeton University). In 1760, he moved to Wilmington, North Carolina where he developed a successful shipping and mercantile business. In 1763, he moved the business to Edenton and formed a partnership with a local attorney, Robert Smith. Together they succeeded in buying ships and owning their own wharf. His fiancé, Isabella Johnston, passed away just before their planned wedding, and Joseph remained a bachelor for the rest of his life.

Joseph served in the local assembly from 1766 to 1775, and in 1774 he was elected to the Continental Congress where he represented North Carolina. He assisted in drafting the "Halifax Resolves" which were adopted on April 12, 1776 and represented an important turning point in colonial relations with England. The Resolves authorized its North Carolina delegates to approve a move in favor of independence from Great Britain. They document colonial grievances and justify a separation from the mother country. This was passed by the Fourth Provincial Congress of North Carolina when they had met in Halifax, North

Carolina. It was the first documented call for independence, and it was meant for all the colonial delegates meeting in Philadelphia. As a successful shipping merchant, Hewes was well aware of the British policies that were intended to restrain the colonies from their desire for independence. By 1776, he believed war was inevitable, so he left his Quaker membership which had been an important part of the Hewes family for many generations. At first, Hewes believed the move for independence was premature, but according to John Adams, he seemed to have an epiphany several months later when he approved the measure. Congress authorized the start of a small naval force known as the Naval Committee which included some of the most influential men in the colonies including: John Langdon of New Hampshire, John Adams of Massachusetts, Stephen Hopkins of Rhode Island, Silas Deane of Connecticut, Richard Henry Lee of Virginia, Christopher Gadsden of South Carolina, and Joseph Hewes. They armed eight vessels, including his own ships as part of the Continental Armed Forces, and Hewes had the responsibility for maintaining the fleet. In 1776, Hewes was the first unofficial secretary of the navy. He befriended John Paul Jones when he arrived from Scotland in 1773 at 21 years old. Hewes was later responsible for promoting Jones as the first Naval Captain for which Jones was eternally grateful. John Adams believed he and Hewes were the founders of the American navy. Hewes originated the navy plan of operation in coordination with General Washington. The next year he assisted in drafting the Articles of Confederation. In 1779, he resigned from the General Assembly and was planning his return home from Philadelphia to Edenton when he passed away at 49 years old. He has the distinction of being the only signer of the Declaration of Independence who died while serving in the Congress. Although his gravesite is unknown, he has been honored in Guilford Courthouse National Military Park in Greensboro, North Carolina. Also, near the Washington Monument in a park remembering the 56 signers of the Declaration, there is a granite boulder bearing the name of Joseph Hewes. In the Rotunda of the U.S. Capitol, he is shown in the famous painting by John Trumbull just to the left of John Adams.[11]

Chapter Ten

New Jersey

Founded as a colony by Lord Berkeley & George Carteret in 1664
State on December 18, 1787

Early Years

The Dutch East India Company was formed in 1602 and was considered the first major multi-national public corporation. The Dutch government extended many powers to the Company, including the right to found colonies, negotiate treaties, issue its own coins, and wage war. The Dutch East India Company's primary objective was to build trading relations with Asia, concentrating on the spice business. The Company operated from 1602 to 1796, and over that time, it conducted over 2.5 million tons of Asian goods. That is comparable to its closest European competitor of half a million tons. The Dutch East India Company established trading posts all over Asia and the South Pacific and bought up surrounding lands to protect the posts. Corruption eventually brought the Company to bankruptcy in 1800, and some of its territories became the Republic of Indonesia.[1]

In 1609, the English explorer Henry Hudson was employed by the Dutch to find a northwest passage to Asia. While searching along the northeast coast of North America, he discovered a major river that ran from Newark Bay, New Jersey to just below Lake Champlain. The river was initially called the North River but was later named the Hudson River. After reporting back to their government, the Dutch proceeded to establish trading posts from the north coast of New Jersey up to Albany and along the coasts of Connecticut, Rhode Island, and Massachusetts. In 1620, the first settlement was established in Bergen, which is several miles west of New York City. The next town to be settled was Fort Nassau in 1623, but it was soon deserted. More permanent colonization started when Philip Carteret was appointed governor at Elizabethtown in 1665. The government consisted of an executive branch with a governor and a council and a legislative assembly of representatives, who were chosen by each town. Immigrants from New York and New England were attracted to New Jersey because of its relatively milder climate and its fertile soil. The entire area of posts was named New Netherlands, but when the Dutch lost their third Anglo-Dutch War in 1674, they also lost their North American colony. The reigning King Charles II gave all the land between New England and Maryland to his brother James, the Duke of York. A few years later, James gave the land between the Hudson River and the Delaware River to two of his friends, Sir George Carteret and Lord Berkeley of Stratton. The land was named New Jersey after the Isle of Jersey in the English Channel where Carteret had been governor. The two men used several methods to encourage settlement, including the grant of religious freedom, which was not the usual custom of the Anglican Church. In return for the land, settlers paid an annual fee called "quitrents." Philip Carteret was appointed the first governor, and the first capital was Elizabethtown to honor his wife, Elizabeth.[2]

The two proprietors soon discovered that the quitrents were difficult to collect, and in 1674, Berkeley sold his share of the land to the Quakers.[3] Because of the sale, New Jersey was divided into East Jersey and West Jersey with the boundary line in dispute. George Carteret held East Jersey and Edward Billings took West Jersey, which was left to him by Lord Berkeley. In 1682, Carteret sold his East Jersey rights to William Penn and others who, in turn, sold half of it to the Earl of Perth. Robert Barclay was appointed governor. In 1688, the two New Jerseys and New York were annexed to New England. This change brought so much distress that the proprietors gave the government back to the crown in 1702. New Jersey was then annexed to New York under Lord Cornbury. After 26 years, an application was made by New Jersey to separate from New York. This was granted in 1738, and Lewis Morris was appointed royal governor by the crown.[4]

New Sweden

While the Dutch were concentrating on settling northern New Jersey, the Swedes gained a foothold along the banks of the Delaware River in 1638. The colony was named New Sweden and seems to have reached its pinnacle under Governor Johan Bjornson Printz, during his term of office from 1643 to 1653. Printz was responsible for building Fort Nya Elfsborg near Salem. Prior to the fort, the settlement was known as New Stockholm. The only other town established by the Swedes was Swedesboro, which was renamed from Raccoon in 1765. In 1655, the Dutch took control of the colony. After the English took over New Jersey in 1674, they embarked on a program to open the southern part of Gloucester County, so they constructed the King's Highway in 1691. The colony attracted farmers, fishermen, hunters, and lumbermen of Swedish and Finnish descent.[5]

Religion and Education

Because of the original settlement by the Dutch, New Jersey was predominantly a Dutch Reformed Church Colony. As many as 18 congregations were formed between 1660 and 1770. The area from the Hudson River to the Raritan River was known as the "Dutch Belt," and the Dutch Reformed Church played a major role in Dutch migration, which resulted in the establishment of towns and churches. Another important religious sect was the Society of Friends, also known as Quakers, which settled in the Monmouth County region. In 1665, they built their first Meeting House in present-day Little Silver. The English founder of the Quakers, George Fox, actually visited an early Meeting House which was built in 1672. Like the Dutch, the Quakers founded many towns in southwestern New Jersey. Other church groups, such as the Anglicans and the Baptists, also played a part in the settlement of the colony.

New Jersey's founders were especially eager to provide advanced education, and accordingly, they founded two major colleges and two secondary schools. The College of New Jersey was started in 1746 in Elizabethtown by a group of Presbyterians who were inspired by the Great Awakening taking place in Europe. The college was founded to train future ministers. Ten years later, it was moved to Princeton and was renamed Princeton University in 1896. Queens College was founded by a group of Dutch Reformed ministers in 1766 in New Brunswick, through a Royal Charter from King George III. The college was first named to honor the king's wife, Queen Charlotte, and it was renamed Rutgers University in 1825. The secondary schools included Rutgers Preparatory School (1766) and Newark Academy (1774).[6]

American Revolution

New Jersey was at the center of the conflict, and both sides crossed the colony on their way to engage the enemy in the North or in the South. Also, with the British headquartered in New York City and Staten Island and George Washington headquartered in Morristown, it is no wonder that most of the war's battles were fought in New Jersey. Of the ten large battles and hundreds of skirmishes there, three had great significance.

When Washington retreated from New York City, he was pursued by the British to Harlem Heights, White Plains and then across the Hudson to Fort Lee, New Jersey. Despite his losses, he kept his armies intact and appointed General Schyler to command the northern army while he led his 2,400 men to safety on the western side of the Delaware River. The retreat was swift and orderly, but British General Cornwallis was only a short distance away in Princeton, where he was preparing to crush the encamped Continental Army. Washington realized that he had to do something dramatic to survive, considering that half of his men were scheduled for discharge from their committed enlistment of 90 days on December 31, 1776. Although he was regarded as a risk-taker, Washington only acted when he believed the odds were in his favor. About 15 miles below his camp, the town of Trenton was being protected by 1,500 Hessian mercenaries under the command of Col. Johann Rall. During the battle in New York, Rall was one of the officers who slaughtered surrendering Americans at Fort Washington, and he had a reputation for pillage, rape, and brutality, which influenced many local Jersey farmers to side with the Americans. Of Washington's 2,400 men only 1,200 were fit to fight due to illness. The December 25th trip across the Delaware River—with supplies, cannons, and horses amid a bitter cold and snowy night—took 14 hours. When Washington attacked, it was swift and fierce, with 200 Hessian casualties and 950 prisoners. The Christmas night raid was a daring one that saw the Americans take the offensive for the first time. It was bold and risky, but Washington knew he had to take the initiative and could no longer fight defensively. His troops had gone for 48 hours without food and had marched for close to 30 miles, but their victory boosted American morale to a new level. Most historians would agree that if Washington had lost at Trenton, the war and the continent would have been lost.

After Trenton, Washington was faced with 1,200 of his men readying for discharge. He personally appealed to their sense of loyalty and service to their country and family, By the end of the day, all 1,200 volunteered to remain a while longer. It was enough time for Washington to plan a surprise attack on the British at Princeton. The news of the Trenton victory brought 1,600 new recruits, who joined their veteran comrades to drive the British into cover in Princeton's Nassau Hall. Washington took charge at the front of his troops, and his officers were horrified to see him so vulnerable to the firearms and cannons firing from both sides. He completely ignored the explosions and gun smoke while directing his troops, giving them the inspiration to face a superior force. When the battle was over, some called it a draw, others called it a significant American victory for the Continental Army in causing the British to retreat. When Benjamin Franklin learned of the two American victories, he informed King Louis XVI, who then sent four shiploads of guns and ammunition to the Americans. The British withdrew their forces from New Jersey to New York and abandoned their strategy of holding large pieces of land.

The third battle of significance was at Monmouth Court House in June of 1778, where Washington attacked the British as they withdrew from Philadelphia to consolidate their forces in New York. Their occupation of Philadelphia had lasted about one year when General Howe surprisingly announced his retirement. Meanwhile, in the spring of 1778, it was announced that France and America had signed the Treaty of Amity and Commerce, which increased French assistance in the form of material and fighting men, including their navy. There was little doubt that the British strategy had to change, so the newly appointed Commander-In-Chief, Gen. Henry Clinton, decided to abandon Philadelphia. Washington saw this as a great opportunity to inflict serious damage with an attack on the three-mile-long carriage and baggage line of British soldiers and material. While the battle at Monmouth did less damage than expected because of the retreating American Gen. Charles Lee–who was sacked on the spot by Washington—it did force the British to remain confined to New York City while Washington established new headquarters in Morristown, his troops nearby in Jockey Hollow. Monmouth was the first battle after the winter of 1777-78 in Valley Forge. The Continental Army had been transformed into a well-trained fighting force capable of matching the British veterans. This, together with the very significant aid coming from France, shifted the war's outcome in favor of America.[7]

Founding Fathers

The following five men were appointed as delegates from New Jersey to the Constitutional Convention held in Philadelphia in 1787. They are considered founders of the state and the country, and all but one signed the proposed Constitution of the United States. The reader will note the remarkable dedication, patriotism, courage, and work ethic of these men. Keep in mind that every colony had such men who were unsung heroes who put their lives, fortunes, and reputations at great risk. They are also a reminder that the American Revolution was led by men of learning, whether formal or self-taught. Most, if not all, revolutions started in the streets, where masses of underserved citizens rose against poverty and dictatorial administrators. This was not so in America where leaders emerged from the educated, who knew the importance of self-government through laws and a justice system.

David Brearley was born in 1745 in Spring Grove and was descended from a Yorkshire, England family. He attended the College of New Jersey (Princeton) but did not graduate. He chose the law for his career. During the Revolutionary War, he joined the New Jersey militia and rose from captain to colonel. In 1776, he served on the committee that drafted the state constitution. In 1779, he was elected chief justice of the New Jersey Supreme Court. At the Constitutional Convention, Brearley was a loyal follower of New Jersey colleague William Livingston. It was Livingston who introduced the rejected New Jersey Plan, which called for several changes to the existing Articles of Confederation but retained the one-vote system for each state. Brearley presided at the New Jersey Ratifying Convention in 1788 and was appointed by President Washington as a federal district judge for the last two years of his brief life.

Jonathan Dayton was born in Elizabethtown in 1760, and after graduating from the College of New Jersey (Princeton) in 1776, he joined the Continental Army. He attained the rank of captain by age 19 and served under his father, Gen. Elias Dayton, and Marquis de Lafayette. He participated in extensive action including the Battle of Yorktown in 1781, which was the last major battle of the war. Dayton's career encompassed a law practice and politics, and in 1787, he was appointed as a delegate to the Constitutional Convention. At the Continental Congress in 1788, he became a Federalist but chose not to serve in the 1789 First Congress. Instead, he became a member of the New Jersey Council and Speaker of the State Assembly. Dayton served in the United States House of Representatives from 1791 to 1799 and twice as Speaker of the House. He supported Hamilton's fiscal policies as well as most Federalist positions. He went on to the United States Senate for six years and supported the Louisiana Purchase in 1803. In 1806, his political career ended with his support of Aaron Burr's failed Southwest Expedition to conquer Spanish lands and create a separate empire. At home his popularity remained intact, and he served in the Assembly from 1814-15. In 1824, Dayton hosted Lafayette during his triumphant tour of the United States, but he died later that year at age 63. At the time of his passing, Dayton owned 250,000 acres of land in Ohio between the Big and Little Rivers, and the town of Dayton stands as a memorial of his service to the country. William Houston was born in 1746, and after graduating from the College of New Jersey (Princeton) in 1768, he worked as master and tutor at the college grammar school and later as professor of mathematics and philosophy. He changed careers and went into politics as deputy secretary of the Continental Congress from 1775-76. He then joined the militia and served as captain of the foot militia for Somerset County and saw armed conflict in Princeton. In 1777, Houston was again elected to the Continental Congress where he worked on supply and finance. He was admitted to the bar in 1781 and was immediately appointed clerk of the New Jersey Supreme Court. In 1784, he was elected to the House of Representatives. Houston was selected as a delegate to the Annapolis and Philadelphia Conventions but then passed away at the young age of 42.

William Livingston was born in Albany, New York in 1723 and graduated from Yale in 1741. Before completing his law studies in New York City in 1745, he married Susanna French, who bore them 13 children. During his early years practicing law, he took positions against conservative partisans in New York City. He strongly opposed attempts by the Anglican Church to take control of King's College (Columbia) and the pro-Anglican leaders in the city. From 1759 to 1769, Livingston fought Parliament's interference in the colony's business, and as a member of the New Jersey Assembly from 1759-61 he rose to be leader of his political faction. In 1770, he moved to Elizabethtown where he built his estate and planned to become a gentleman farmer. As the spirit of independence gathered momentum, Livingston was inspired to return to politics, and he soon became a member of the Essex County (New Jersey) Committee of Correspondence and then a representative in the First Continental Congress and then a delegate to the Second Continental Congress. In 1776, he joined the New Jersey militia as brigadier general and was then elected as the first governor of the state. He remained the elected governor for 14 straight years until his death in 1790 at 66 years old. In 1787, Livingston was appointed as a delegate to the Constitutional Convention, which he attended only when his governorship duties allowed. He supported the rejected New Jersey Plan but was a strong advocate at the state's Ratification Convention.

William Patterson was born in Ireland in 1745 and emigrated with his family two years later. By the time he was five years old, the Patterson family settled in Princeton. His father's prosperity as a merchant enabled William to attend private school and the College of New Jersey (Princeton), where he graduated in 1763. Patterson studied law under Richard Stockton, who was later to become a signer of the Declaration of Independence. When war erupted, Patterson served in many administrative positions, including the Provincial Congress (1775-76), the Constitutional Convention of New Jersey (1776), the Legislative Council (1776-77) and the Council of Safety (1777). He served as attorney general of New Jersey from 1776 to 1783. Four years later, he moved to New Brunswick where he concentrated on his private law practice. In 1787, he was chosen as a delegate to the Constitutional Convention. He co-authored the New Jersey Plan which primarily dealt with the contentious matter of one vote or representative voting according to population. The latter was a major change from the existing Articles of Confederation, which was to be supplanted by the Virginia Plan, allowing for a bicameral legislative system. Patterson signed the final document and advocated its adoption. In 1789, he was elected to the United States Senate (1789-90) and then as governor (1790-93). From 1793 to 1806, he served as Associate Justice of the United States Supreme Court and passed away at 61 years old.[8]

Chapter Eleven

South Carolina

Founded as a colony by Lords Proprietors & Carolina Charter in 1663
State on May 23, 1788

Early Years

Prior to the arrival of Spanish and French explorers in the early 1500's, this territory was inhabited by small tribes of Native Americans, the two largest being the Cherokee and the Catawba. History credits Hernando de Soto as the first European discoverer in 1540. However, there was no lasting colonization until 1663 when the English crown under King Charles II granted a charter to eight proprietors encompassing the present-day Carolinas, which was named the Province of Carolina in honor of King Charles I.[1] The Latin name of Charles is "Carolus." In 1629, King Charles I granted a patent to Sir Robert Heath for the lands south of 36 degrees and north of 31 degrees, "under the name, in honor of the king, of Carolina."[2] The grants were another instance of rewarding nobles who provided political and financial assistance to the future king while he was in exile during the English Civil War. King Charles wanted the new Province of Carolina to check the advance of Spain northward from their colony in Florida. Georgia was originally part of Carolina until 1732, and therefore in the 1600's, England was highly concerned with the possible threat of Spanish land claims and expansion. The English beneficiaries were wealthy planters who first settled in the Charleston area. They were attracted to the fertile soil and climate for the cultivation of rice, indigo, tobacco, and later cotton and sugar. The colony prospered with cheap slave labor and a great variety of commodities in demand domestically and abroad, and the Province of Carolina quickly became one of the wealthiest colonies in North America. It wasn't long before its administrators realized the difficulties in managing such a large area, so in 1710 the Province was divided into the colonies of South and North Carolina. With large numbers of slaves imported from nearby Barbados, the black population became the majority by 1720, and Charleston developed as the principal center for commerce and culture. As the coastal area grew, settlers moved ever westward, forcing the native tribes from their traditional homelands and hunting grounds. The conflict resulted in the Yamasee War of 1715-17, which was soon followed by the overthrow of the proprietors' rule in 1719 and the introduction of representative government. It also marked the end of proprietary ownership and the conversion to a crown colony.[3]

Colonial Period

The imposition of taxes on the American colonies by Great Britain was a major factor in fomenting unrest and ultimately war. The key event that led to open conflict was the Boston Tea Party in December of 1773, when the colonists refused to accept the delivery of tea that arrived in Boston Harbor. The protest led to the destruction of the tea, significant tax losses sustained by the British government, and losses by the financially weak East India Company. When the colonists refused to reimburse the British for the damage they had caused, Parliament responded by closing the Port of Boston, which led to colonial consolidation and their collective opposition to Great Britain's policies in America. It should be noted that similar "tea parties" were conducted in New York, Philadelphia, and Charleston, where the trading of commodities was the lifeblood of the local economy. Because the tax on tea is so little understood, a word of explanation should be helpful.

Towards the end of the 1600's continuing into the 1700's, the consumption of tea exploded in Europe, England, and North America. In 1698, the British government gave the East India Company the exclusive right to be the sole importer of tea.[4] In 1721, Parliament required the colonies to purchase their tea only from England thereby eliminating all competition.[5] Also, the East India Company could not sell tea directly to the colonies but were required to sell it at auction only to British firms, who then exported it to merchants in America. The East India Company paid a 25 percent tax on their sales in Great Britain, to which the government added another consumer sales tax. Meanwhile, the Dutch required no tax on their imported tea, thereby enabling them to sell their tea, which was smuggled into England and the colonies, at much cheaper prices.[6] By 1767, the East India Company was losing *L* 400,000 a year in revenue. In an effort to save the company, Parliament lowered the tax to British consumers and refunded the 26 percent duty on tea exports to America.[7] To compensate for the loss of revenue to the government, Parliament passed the Townsend Revenue Act of 1767, which included several new taxes in the colonies, including one on tea. After much protesting, all the new taxes were eventually eliminated, except for the one on tea. The Tea Act of 1773 was more than a question of imports, monopolies, and revenue, but it did raise the issue of whether Parliament had the legal right to impose taxes. The even larger issue was the fear that Parliament would impose taxes on any or all colonial commodities upon which cities such as Charleston were so dependent. An interesting consequence of the tea controversy was its impact on American drinking habits. The drinking of tea was now regarded as unpatriotic, which gave rise to the adoption of coffee as America's preferred hot drink.[8]

American Revolution

In March of 1776, South Carolina was one of the first colonies to establish its own independent government. Their President and Commander-in-Chief was John Rutledge, who immediately ordered the construction of Fort Sullivan on Sullivan's Island to protect the shipping channels into "Charles Town."

Col. William Moultrie was placed in charge of construction and named its commanding officer. In June, British Gen. Henry Clinton with his 2,000 troops tried to capture the city, but the fort withstood the attack, and the expected local Loyalist support did not materialize. The British withdrew, and the fort was renamed Fort Moultrie in honor of its commander. Colonel Moultrie designed the fort's "Liberty Flag," which was eventually adopted as the state flag. Charles Town was protected for the next four years until 1780 when General Clinton returned with 14,000 men and, with assistance from local Loyalists, forced American Gen. Benjamin Lincoln to surrender with his 5,400 troops.[9] This was the only major American defeat of the war and compares only to other British losses of 7,000 soldiers at Saratoga in 1777 and 8,000 men at Yorktown in 1781.

After the British abandoned their first and second strategies to defeat the Americans in New England and then in the mid-Atlantic coastal cities, they launched their assault to subdue the South. Gen. Henry Clinton assumed command of the British army when Gen. William Howe suddenly retired. Clinton's first move was to vacate Philadelphia in June of 1778 and consolidate his forces in New York City. The next move was to capture Savannah and Charles Town, leaving General Cornwallis in command. General Washington appointed Gen. Horatio Gates to stop the British advance through South Carolina, and the two armies then clashed at Camden. This important battle marked a significant defeat for the Americans, with 1,000 killed and 1,000 taken prisoner, compared to 345 British killed and wounded. It allowed the British to gain a strong foothold in South Carolina, but it also caused a change in American command. General Gates was relieved of his position when it was discovered that he had abandoned the field with the first British charge, leaving his inexperienced subordinates to do battle with the veteran enemy forces and retreating more than 20 miles from the front lines. General Washington immediately replaced him with his most trusted aide, Nathanael Greene, who became one of the war's greatest heroes and the greatest hero in the South. Greene commanded the southern army, could skirmish with the far more experienced British, and inflicted sufficient wounds on the enemy as they advanced through North Carolina and southern Virginia. Although Cornwallis was successful in his southern campaign, he lost 25 percent of his men and was forced to head for the Virginia coast where he planned to be retrieved by his navy and returned to New York City.[10]

The next important battle in South Carolina occurred in October of 1780, near the border with North Carolina nine miles south of King's Mountain in Cherokee County, South Carolina. British Major Patrick Ferguson was charged with recruiting Loyalist militiamen in advance of Cornwallis as he prepared to march into North Carolina. Ferguson was met by the Patriot militia led by Benjamin Cleveland, James Johnston, William Campbell, and Joseph McDowell. The British were pursued and surrounded and sustained heavy casualties including the death of Major Ferguson. It was a surprising victory when the American militia defeated the British, and provided a much-needed morale incentive for the Patriots. The victory is viewed as a pivotal battle that halted the constant British advance under Generals Cornwallis and Banastre Tarleton.[11]

The last of the five key battles fought in South Carolina was at Cowpens in January of 1781. Cornwallis was determined to defeat the southern army of Nathanael Greene, and he sent his most feared fighting unit commanded by Lt. Banastre Tarleton with his cavalry dragoons. Following the American loss at Camden in August of 1780, General Greene changed tactics and decided to split his southern army into two smaller groups to force Cornwallis to fight on separate fronts. He instructed Brig. Gen. Daniel Morgan to take 300 riflemen and 700 militiamen to attack the British at Fort Ninety-Six. Cornwallis responded by directing Tarleton and his 1,100 men to stop Morgan from organizing a backcountry uprising. Morgan instructed his front line to retreat after their first two rounds of fire. The British mistook the maneuver for a retreat, and as they pursued the Americans, they were suddenly met by heavy fire from the repositioned militia, long-range sharp shooting from far up in the woodlands, and a devastating cavalry charge that decimated the enemy. Tarleton escaped, but he lost 800 dead, wounded, or captured while the Americans suffered just under 100 casualties.[12] The route of the British at Cowpens was significant in several ways: it proved the American militia could defeat British regulars, the British loss of their light cavalrymen greatly impeded their campaign to capture the South, and the introduction of the new long-barrel rifle with its greater accuracy gave American soldiers an advantage. Lastly, the victory boosted the morale of the less-experienced American military.

Constitutional Convention

One of the most difficult issues to resolve at the Convention was the method of apportioning the state representatives, an issue which was at the heart of the republic the delegates were trying to establish. After the first month of deliberations, it was agreed by most that the existing Articles of Confederation needed more than just an overhaul. Every state had just one vote, and all legislation had to be unanimous, thereby giving veto power to each state, which gave equal power to both large and small population states. To satisfy every state with an equitable solution, a Grand Committee was formed with one member from each of the 11 states and included one of South Carolina's most influential delegate and legal scholar, John Rutledge. The Committee offered two major proposals: 1) revenue bills should originate in the lower house (House of Representatives) which could not be modified by the upper house (Senate); and 2) each senator could have one vote, thereby voting individually and not as a state's bloc, which had been their practice under the Articles. This allowed each senator to be a free agent, and each state would have an equal number of Senate seats. The Committee was chaired by John Rutledge, who was known as "Dictator John" for the strong power he practiced as South Carolina governor. Throughout the Convention, Rutledge firmly held to his beliefs that a stronger federal government was desirable but that power should not be limitless. Some even accused him of causing the Committee to go too far beyond the proposals presented at the Convention and claimed that he had hijacked the Constitution and altered critical agreements that had previously been made by the delegates. Another South Carolina delegate, Charles Cotesworthy Pinckney, expressed dire warnings to the Committee that they protect the practice of slavery in the southern states. He even reportedly advised Chairman Washington that South Carolina would return home if the subject of abolishing slavery was introduced. Pinckney also proposed that Congress prohibit the taxation of exports and that any legislation regulating foreign commerce through tariffs should require two-thirds majority votes in both houses of Congress.[13]

On May 27, 1788, South Carolina became the eighth state to ratify the Constitution. They offered only minor modifications to the proposed document, realizing they had won several important measures that greatly benefitted them. Although they opposed revisiting the slavery issue in 1808, they were appeased with favorable fugitive slave laws. They believed that proportional representation in Congress would prove helpful as South Carolina grew rapidly in population to become one of the larger states. They also wanted slaves to be counted in their population as that would allow for more representatives in the House. However, they did reluctantly accept the Three-Fifths Compromise towards including slaves in their numbers.

Slavery

It should be remembered that by 1787 South Carolina had become the most prosperous state in the Union, and their leaders were ready, willing, and able to make every effort to assure its continued financial success. The source of its wealth was its heavy dependence on the low cost of its manual slave labor. Their agrarian economy was dominated by the phenomenal expansion of rice production. However, the war devastated the rice fields and concurrently severely reduced the slave labor supply while a good number of slaves fought for the Patriot cause. The local economy was hard hit by rising costs for a limited number of slaves. This, in turn, sharply increased the slave trade in the 1780's, so that by 1790 there were as many black slaves as white citizens in South Carolina. More battles in the revolutionary war were fought in South Carolina than in any other state, and this resulted in the devastation of farms and plantations. The production of rice was especially labor-intensive because it required manual labor for both planting and harvesting. As the need for more slaves increased dramatically after the war to restore rice farms, the Constitutional Congress delegates from South Carolina and the other slave states did everything they could to protect their legal right to practice slavery. They succeeded in preserving the institution and in delaying the abolition of the slave trade for another twenty years until 1808, when the issue would be revisited.[14] Washington, as chairman of the Convention, warned that the practice would eventually divide the fledgling nation if left unresolved. He promised to support its abolition when such legislation was proposed in

Congress, but during his presidency from 1789 to 1797, the subject never came out of committee for a vote.

Statesmen, Leaders and Heroes

John Rutledge stands out from his peers as one of the most notable leaders of South Carolina. The son of an Irish immigrant and physician and the elder brother of Edward Rutledge, a signer of the Declaration of Independence, John was born in 1739 in Charleston. Without formal schooling, he was tutored by his father and an Anglican minister. He went on to study law at London's Middle Temple and at age 21 was licensed to practice in England. Rutledge then decided to return to Charleston, where he prospered as a lawyer and a very successful plantation owner. At age 24, he married Elizabeth Grimke, who produced their ten children. Upon his return to South Carolina, he began his long and impressive political career in Christ Church Parish where he was first elected to the Provincial Assembly and held his seat there for 15 years. While he maintained his strong position for colonial self-government, he was not prepared to sever ties with England. In 1765, he chaired a committee of the Stamp Act Congress, which petitioned the House of Lords for the act's repeal. Ten years later, he served in the First and Second Continental Congress and then returned home to reorganize the South Carolina government. When war broke out, he served on the Committee of Safety and participated in writing the state constitution. From 1776 to 1778, he served as President of the Lower House. After resigning in 1778, he was elected Governor of South Carolina, only to face his most challenging years when the British invaded the South and captured Charleston in May of 1780. They confiscated his property, and he never recovered from the financial losses he sustained during that time. Rutledge escaped to North Carolina, and when Gen. Nathanael Greene recovered South Carolina in 1781, he was able to reestablish the government. He resigned the governorship in 1782 and was elected to the Lower House. For two years he was a delegate to the Continental Congress, sat on the Chancery Court, and returned to the Lower House from 1784 to 1790. It was already noted above about his extensive service at the Constitutional Convention, where he strongly advocated for the interests of South Carolina and the southern states. In the election of

1789, Rutledge was appointed as an Elector, and President Washington made him an Associate Justice of the U.S. Supreme Court. In 1791, he became Chief Justice of the South Carolina Supreme Court. In 1795, President Washington appointed him as Chief Justice of the U.S. Supreme Court to replace John Jay. The Federalist-dominated Senate rejected his appointment mainly because of his opposition to the Jay Treaty, thereby ending his public career. He died in 1800 at age 60 and is buried at St. Michael's Episcopal Church in Charleston.[15]

Charles Cotesworthy Pinckney is another example of the better-educated 18th-century American who emerged as a leader for American independence. He was born in 1746 in Charleston to a prominent planter and an entrepreneurial mother who developed the indigo trade in South Carolina. His father was appointed a colonial agent, and he took his seven-year-old son with him to London where he received a European education. He went on to Christ Church College at Oxford, where he graduated in 1764 at 18 years old. Like his senior countryman John Rutledge, Charles received his legal training at London's Middle Temple and passed the English bar in 1769. The next year was spent touring Europe while studying chemistry, botany, and military sciences. He then returned to Charleston, where he was immediately elected to the Provincial Assembly while holding the position of a royal militia officer. In 1773, he served as an attorney general for several towns and, two years later, sat in the Provincial Assembly. He soon supported the Patriot cause and was elected to the Committee of Safety. As soon as South Carolina organized its forces in 1775, Pinckney joined the First Carolina Regiment as a captain. He fought in defense of Charleston and in the North at Brandywine and Germantown. He also fought in Florida and Savannah. When Charleston fell in 1780, Pinckney was imprisoned for two years, and after being released, he was discharged as a brevet brigadier general. His war years included terms in the Lower House and Senate. He attended all the sessions at the Constitutional Convention and advocated a strong national government. His proposal that senators should not receive pay was rejected, but he did move to have the Senate ratify treaties, and he supported the compromise to abolish the slave trade by 1808. During President Washington's first six years in office, Pinckney declined many important positions including commander of the U.S. army, justice of the Supreme Court, Secretary of War and Secretary of State. He did agree to help restore relations with France. In the notorious XYZ Affair, he vehemently opposed paying a bribe to the French as the price for entering negotiations, saying "Not a sixpence." When he returned to South Carolina in 1778, he was appointed major general in command of American forces in the South. For the last 25 years of his life, he practiced law and spent several terms in the legislature. He was a charter member of the Board of Trustees at South Carolina College (later S.C. University), first president of the Carolina Bible Society, chief executive of the Charleston Library Society, and an active member of the Society of the Cincinnati. He died in Charleston in 1825 at age 79 and is buried at St. Michael's Episcopal Church.[16]

Pierce Butler was born in 1744 in Ireland to an aristocratic family that practiced "primogeniture," whereby the first-born son inherited the family estate. Being the younger son, Pierce's lack of an inheritance prompted him to seek a military career. He first became a major, and in 1768, was sent to Boston with His Majesty's 29th Regiment to help calm the growing unrest there. In 1771, he married Mary Middleton, the daughter of a wealthy South Carolinian. He soon resigned his British military position and took a seat in the Provincial Assembly in 1778, a position which was followed by his appointment as adjutant general in the South Carolina militia. Throughout the 1780's, he served in the legislature, where he led the upcountry faction instead of his own plantation constituency. The revolutionary war took a heavy toll on his personal wealth, and he was forced to seek a personal loan in Holland. In 1787, Butler won his election to the Continental Congress and the Constitutional Convention, where he advocated a strong national government and supported southern slaveholders. He also defended the Constitution at the South Carolina Ratifying Convention. He then served in the U.S. Senate from 1789 to 1796. He supported Hamilton's fiscal policies but opposed the Jay Treaty. He returned to South Carolina in 1797 until 1803 when he was elected to the Senate for two years of an unexpired term. He continued to follow his past practice as an independent politician. His remaining 18 years were spent as a wealthy planter, before moving to Philadelphia to be near his daughter. He died there in 1822 at age 78 and is buried at Christ Church.[17]

Charles Pinckney was born in 1757 in Charleston to a wealthy planter and attorney, Col. Charles Pinckney. Young Charles was educated in Charleston where he opened his own law practice in 1779. He also enlisted in the South Carolina militia, where he became a lieutenant and fought in the siege of Savannah. He also saw action in Charleston in 1780 when he was captured and eventually released in 1781. He began his political career at age 20, serving in the Continental Congress from 1777-78 and again from 1784-87. He alternated between the Congress and the state legislature, where he served from 1777-80, 1786-89 and 1792-96. He focused on gaining American navigational rights on the Mississippi River. At the Constitutional Convention, Pinckney was outspoken and is widely credited for many contributions to the final draft. At the state Ratifying Convention, he strongly supported the proposed Constitution. In 1788 at age 31, Pinckney married Mary Eleanor Laurens, the daughter of a wealthy and influential South Carolina merchant. In 1789, he was elected Governor of South Carolina, and the next year, he chaired the South Carolina Constitutional Convention. His strong Federalist positions changed over time, and in 1795, he opposed the Federalist Jay Treaty. In 1796, he was again elected Governor, and he was then elected to the Senate in 1798. In 1800, he served as Thomas Jefferson's campaign manager in South Carolina. In 1801, Jefferson appointed him Minister to Spain, where he worked to assist in the transfer of Louisiana from France to the United States in 1803. He became a leader of the Democratic-Republican Party, sat in the legislature in 1805-06, and was reelected Governor from 1806-08. He returned to the legislature from 1810-14. In 1818, he was elected to the U.S. House of Representatives where he opposed the Missouri Compromise. Pinckney died in 1824, just shy of his 67 birthday. He is buried at St. Philip's Episcopal Church in Charleston.[18]

Chapter Twelve

Pennsylvania

Founded as a colony by William Penn in 1681
State on December 12, 1787

Early Settlers

The early history of Pennsylvania is more complex than most of the other original colonies because the Dutch, Swedes, and English all arrived there in the early 1600's. Also complicating the various claims made was the charter of the Virginia Company composed in London in 1606, which declared ownership of all the land from the North Carolina border north to New York City, then northwest along the eastern side of the Great Lakes and then due west, "from sea to shining sea." In such a vast area, many other colonies were discovered, explored and claimed by other countries, corporate investors, and monarchs. The first to do so in Pennsylvania was Capt. John Smith, who after he landed in Jamestown, Virginia in 1607, reportedly met with Native Indians in Pennsylvania in 1608. The following year, English explorer Henry Hudson worked for the Dutch in an attempt to find a new northwestern navigational route to Asia. When he sailed into Delaware Bay, he claimed the area for the Dutch. In 1610, English Capt. Samuel Argall not only sailed the Bay but named the area Delaware in honor of Virginia's first governor, Lord De La Warr, who served from 1610 to 1618. Another Dutch explorer Capt. Cornelius Hendrickson arrived in 1616 and navigated the Delaware River. Another Dutch navigator Capt. Cornelius Jacobsen May was granted a patent to Dutch West Indies Company. In 1638, the New Sweden Company was formed to establish the New Sweden Colony along both banks of the Delaware River. To protect the colony, Swedish Governor Johan Printz built Fort Elfsborg and Fort Gothenburg and thereby made New Sweden the first permanent European settlement in Pennsylvania, which included the Delaware Territory.

In 1655, Governor Peter Stuyvesant of New Amsterdam was ordered to occupy and control New Sweden. Ten years later, the British–under the new proprietor, James, the Duke of York–annexed the New Netherlands, and finally with the Third Anglo-Dutch War in 1674, England acquired all Dutch and Swedish possessions in North America. In 1660, the Parliamentary Period in England, known as the "interregnum," ended as Charles II assumed the throne, thereby restoring the House of Stuart to England. Prior to his return, his father, Charles I, was imprisoned in 1642 and beheaded in 1648. For 18 years, young Charles was protected in exile by English noblemen who were promised favors and repayment of debts for their loyalty and support. We are not sure if this was the cause of the debt of *L* 16,000 (adjusted to $3 million for today's value) owed by Charles to Sir William Penn. To satisfy the debt in 1681, the king granted Admiral Penn's son William 40,000 square miles of land, which he named New Wales. That name was rejected by the English Privy Council, so Penn named it "Sylvania." King Charles then modified it to "Pennsylvania" to honor Adm. William Penn.

William Penn sailed from England to America in August of 1682 and arrived in New Castle in October. He was joined by fellow Quakers of substantial means. Immediately, he and his friends went to Philadelphia to meet with Chief Taminend of the Leni Lenape tribe to purchase his grant of land, even though he was not legally required to do so. The Pennsylvania Assembly in 1682 and

1683 approved a constitution that provided an upper and lower house for the legislature. Penn attracted settlers by offering very attractive terms. For each 100 acres, he charged 40 shillings, and for a block of 5,000 acres, the cost was 100 pounds. Most immigrants came from England, Ireland, Wales, Holland, and Germany. Even African slaves were welcome to Pennsylvania. However, the colony was founded principally as a refuge for the much-maligned Quakers for their reform beliefs. Known for his religious tolerance and freedom of conscience, Penn attracted followers of other religions including Puritans, Huguenots, Catholics, Calvinists, Anglicans, and Jews. In 1684, Penn returned to England, but in his absence some serious conflicts arose in the colony. In 1696, after years of difficulties and imprisonment for disloyalty, Penn decided to return to Pennsylvania where he wrote the Charter of Privileges, which was formally adopted in 1701. It is a constitution that delineates in great detail the rights and privileges of Pennsylvania's citizens as well as the structure of government.[1]

William Penn died in 1718, and his sons succeeded him. As Philadelphia grew to be the unofficial capital of Colonial America for most of the 18th century, the colony expanded westward until the British Proclamation of 1763.[2] The act was passed at the conclusion of the Seven Years' War. It prohibited American settlers from occupying land west of the Appalachian Mountains and allowed Parliament to confiscate and void deeds of landowners there. These included a number of prominent Americans, such as George Washington. That same year the Treaty of Paris declared England the new owner of defeated French Canada, and in an effort to appease the Native American tribes, the Treaty set aside the present-day states of Ohio, Indiana, and Illinois–known as "New France"—for their use and possession. Both acts restricting American settlers served to alert them to the kind of British subjection that lie ahead.

American Revolution

Pennsylvania was at the center of the revolution in political and military activities. When the British followed the Proclamation of 1763 with the Stamp Act of 1765, considerable fuel was added to the fire of grievances. All 13 colonies sent delegates to Philadelphia to protest the measure, and this would mark the beginning of collective colonial concerns. After the Stamp Act was withdrawn, other taxes were introduced under the British policy of forcing the colonies to pay for recent war debts and continuing military protection. However, the tax measures were imposed without colonial discussions or assent, thereby infringing on their rights as British subjects. When such rights were denied, the colonies reacted by calling the First and Second Continental Congresses to Philadelphia in 1775. When attempts at peaceful solutions failed, Congress voted to declare their independence from England in July of 1776.

Pennsylvania witnessed a number of battles including the crossing of the Delaware River in December of 1776, the Battles of Brandywine and Germantown prior to the British occupation of Philadelphia, and the encampment of the Continental Army at Valley Forge from December of 1777 to June of 1778. At Valley Forge, one of the most significant events occurred which historians refer to as "the Crucible of Victory." In spite of losses at Brandywine and Germantown, Washington observed that his forces stood up well to the British, but they needed better training. Winter was just setting in by mid-December, and the British had just occupied Philadelphia. Not even his closest advisors were told by Washington of his destination. The small Pennsylvania rural town was 25 miles northwest of Philadelphia and 90 miles east of the relocated American capital in York. It was farm country with a small iron forge, but Washington believed it was a good strategic location. A common practice for combatants of that era was to refrain from conflict during the winter with its unreliable weather and poor roads. If General Howe had pursued the Americans the war would probably have been won by the British soon thereafter. Morale in the Continental Army was low, and popular support for the war was declining. Washington needed men, money and supplies, but the Congress did not have the authority to provide these essentials because those decisions were in the hands of the state governments, and they were not willing to raise new taxes or meet their required enlistments.

The six-month period at Valley Forge was filled with intrigue. It was a time when political and military forces influenced the future course of the war. Although no major battles were fought there, a new American army emerged, and its structural change left its imprint on America's unique interrelationships within the army that survive even to this day. When Baron von Steuben arrived from Prussia in February of 1778, and unofficially assumed the duties of inspector general, a new military era was born. Washington introduced a "Chain of Command" quite different from his British adversaries. Past defeats had shown glaring American weaknesses, but there was no infrastructure in place to deal with the problems. Unlike the British officers who did not participate in drills and exercises, von Steuben trained the troops and officers, and when a small contingent was ready, they in turn trained other men, one regiment at a time. The American officers were responsible for their own men, but when necessary, von Steuben stepped in to retrain those who needed it. Within three months, the Continental Army was transformed into an effective fighting force that would ultimately change the outcome of the war. Although still inferior to their British veteran counterparts, their skills at forming lines and moving in unison challenged the British enough to make a difference. The composition of the army also changed from the emotionally-charged farmers and merchants at Lexington who volunteered for several months, to younger more rugged men between 15 and 25 years of age who signed up for the long haul because they had few opportunities elsewhere. They included immigrants from Europe, indentured servants, and blacks. They respected Washington, and even though he was a tough disciplinarian and kept his distance, they all had an admiration for each other. Washington recognized their hardships and willingness to tough it out, and his devotion to them earned him their loyalty.[3]

As Americans grew more confident of winning their independence, their political leaders drew up the Articles of Confederation, which was adopted in Philadelphia in 1781. After the war, it became obvious to certain men like Washington, Madison, and Hamilton that the country needed a new form of government that could provide greater representation, a more comprehensive judicial system, and a chief executive officer. It should replace the restrictive Articles and enable the government to raise revenues to provide for national services. Delegates from all 13 colonies were invited to Philadelphia in June of 1787, and Rhode Island was the only one that chose not to attend, because religious tolerance was not on the agenda. After the U.S. Constitution was ratified in 1788 and Washington was inaugurated in 1789, the First Congress had to deal with the matter of strong fiscal credit and the location of the nation's capital. The Assumption Act proposed by Hamilton called for the federal government to acquire outstanding state debts from the war, but it was opposed in the South which had far fewer outstanding debts, and supported in the North which had the major portion of debt. Also under consideration was the placement of the new capital, which the South and North both wanted. At a dinner meeting at Madison's home in New York City, Hamilton and Jefferson arrived at a compromise whereby they would each support the Assumption Act and the location of a Federal City in Virginia named the District of Columbia. New York was to remain the capital for one year, and Philadelphia was to be the capital until 1800, when it would be transferred to the newly created District. Pennsylvania did receive somewhat of a concession when they were awarded the prominent address of Pennsylvania Avenue, for the location of the Executive Mansion, later called the White House.

Statesmen, Leaders and Heroes

When George Washington and James Madison corresponded about conditions in the new nation in the mid-1780's, they agreed that the existing Articles of Confederation were not sufficient. All 13 states were operating as quasi-independent entities with their own laws, currencies, customs, tariffs, and policies. There was no truly representative government at the national level, and each state had one vote for proposed legislation. There was no federal judicial system or Supreme Court. There were no means for financing national projects or defense, and there was no executive branch of government. Because of his experience in the war, where he had to seek approval from each of the 13 states and had to form an army from each state's militia, Washington was well-aware of the need for national unity. His initial intent was to correct the weaknesses by modifying the Articles. However, he soon changed his thinking, and with the concurrence of Madison and others it was decided to pursue an entirely new constitution. In 1787, 70 delegates from all states were invited to Philadelphia to discuss the situation and how to structure a new government. Not everyone could attend, but 55 came and 39 signed the document.[4] The following members represented Pennsylvania and are regarded as founders and heroes.

James Wilson was born in 1741 near St. Andrews, Scotland. After graduating from St. Andrews, Glasgow, and Edinburgh universities, he immigrated to America in 1765. He soon was hired as a Latin tutor at the College of Philadelphia (later University of Pennsylvania), but then he decided to read the law under John Dickinson. In 1771, he set up his own law firm specializing in real estate. He also lectured on English literature at the College of Philadelphia, where he later received an honorary Master of Arts degree in 1766. Wilson gravitated to politics with his chairmanship of the Carlisle, Pennsylvania Committee of Correspondence in 1774, and when he completed his paper entitled "Consideration on the Nature and Extent of the Legislative Authority of the British Parliament," he was regarded as a new political leader. In 1775, he was elected to the Continental Congress where he focused on Native American and military matters. On August 2, 1776, he signed the Declaration of Independence. The next year, he moved from Carlisle to Annapolis and then to Philadelphia, where he supported the policies of the conservative republicans. As a delegate to the U.S. Constitutional Convention, Wilson rose in influence, second only to James Madison. He attended all the sessions and sat on the Committee of Detail, which resolved legal problems, and he made the second greatest number of speeches. Wilson led the debate for ratification of the U.S. Constitution. At the Pennsylvania Constitutional Convention in 1789, he drafted the document that was adopted. That same year, President Washington appointed him as Associate Justice of the Supreme Court, and the College of Philadelphia chose him to be their first law professor. During his service on the Supreme Court, Wilson was severely criticized and almost impeached for trying to influence legislation favorable to land speculation. In the years 1792 to 1795, he invested large sums in real estate in western New York, Pennsylvania, and Georgia. The investments were heavily leveraged, and in order to escape arrest for unpaid debts he moved to New Jersey. A year later, while on court business in North Carolina, he suffered a mental breakdown and stayed at the home of fellow Supreme Court Justice, James Iredell, where he died a few months later at 57 years old.[5]

Benjamin Franklin and George Washington were two of the most celebrated Patriots in America. While Washington represented integrity, courage, and leadership, Franklin was the epitome of the American Dream. Born in Boston in 1706, Benjamin was the tenth son of a candlemaker who received little schooling and no college education. At the age of 12, he was working for his father, and at age 17 he left home for employment as a printer in Philadelphia. He quickly learned the publishing business and published "The Pennsylvania Gazette" from 1730 to 1748. At the same time, he annually produced his "Poor Richard's Almanac" starting in 1733 and continuing for the next 25 years. The Almanac proved wildly successful in the colonies and in London, where he acquired considerable popularity and notoriety. He became financially independent by age 42 and then devoted his resources to philanthropy, education, science, and politics. His first political job was serving as a clerk in the colonial legislation from 1736 to 1751 and then as a member from 1751 to 1764. He was Deputy Postmaster for Philadelphia from 1737 to 1753 and then Deputy Postmaster General for all the colonies from 1753 to 1774. A little-recognized idea of Franklin was the "Albany Plan" in 1754. Its purpose was to have all the colonies united with a single military force for protection during the French and Indian War. The Continental Congress approved of the Plan, but the individual colonies rejected the concept because they feared it would diminish their state independence. This was the first major effort to unite the colonies in America.

From 1757 to 1762, and then from 1764 to 1775, Franklin lived in London where he served as agent for Pennsylvania and then for Georgia, New Jersey, and Massachusetts. During those 16 years, he was content with British-American relations, but when Parliament passed increasingly harsh taxations and interfered with colonial governance, Franklin became alarmed. At first with the Stamp Act of 1765, he worked behind the scenes for its repeal, not realizing the depth of colonial opposition. As a result, his reputation suffered greatly because he was perceived as accepting the measure. He successfully recovered with his strong opposition to the bill in the House of Commons. When Franklin returned to Philadelphia in 1775, he was elected to the Continental Congress. The next year, he was on the five-man committee with John Adams and Thomas Jefferson to draft the Declaration of Independence. Despite his age, at 71 Franklin was to begin some of his most productive years. Throughout the war, he and Silas Deane were in Paris, where they procured experienced military officers from France and other European countries. In 1777-78, he led negotiations for the Treaty of Amity and Commerce with France, which provided the colonies with much needed munitions, men, and materials. This came at a time when American morale was low and the outcome of the war was very much in doubt. Franklin was greatly admired for his scientific knowledge and was regarded on the same level as Isaac Newton. He was the first American celebrity in Europe, and his reputation proved critically important in gaining easy access to King Louis XVI and his highest government officials. As commissioner to France from 1779 to 1785, Franklin joined John Adams in negotiating the Treaty of Paris, ending the war in 1783.

Returning to America in 1785, Franklin was elected to the Supreme Executive Council of Pennsylvania. He was a delegate to the U.S. Constitutional Convention at age 81 and is chiefly remembered for his common-sense compromises and his ability to diffuse emotional positions. In that same year, he was elected president of the Pennsylvania Society for Promoting the Abolition of Slavery. He died in 1790 in Philadelphia at 84 years old.[6]

Benjamin Franklin is considered the founding father of the present-day University of Pennsylvania, which dates its beginning to 1740. The date relates to the building that was constructed in Philadelphia to house a charity school that never came to fruition. In 1743, Franklin expressed his plans to establish a school of higher education. In 1749, he introduced his pamphlet *Proposals Relating to the Education of Youth in Pennsylvania*, which were to be incorporated in what he called a "Public Academy of Philadelphia." However, the school would not be for the education of clergy as were Harvard, William and Mary, Yale, and Princeton. Franklin's college was designed to teach both the classics as well as practical skills necessary to make a living and serve the public. The first Board of Trustees met in 1749 and the next year voted to take ownership of the uncompleted 1740 building and assume its outstanding debts. In 1751, the Academy of Philadelphia opened, and in 1755, the College of Philadelphia was incorporated into the school. Because of the Loyalist tendencies of its provost, the Reverend William Smith, the Pennsylvania legislature issued a new charter in 1791 naming the school the University of Pennsylvania.[7]

Thomas Mifflin was born in Philadelphia in 1744. After graduating from the College of Philadelphia (later the University of Pennsylvania) in 1760 at the age of 16, he worked for three years with William Biddle, then travelled abroad for two years and returned in 1765 to start his own commercial business with his brother George. His two terms in the Continental Congress (1774-75 and 1782-84) were interrupted by his tour of service in the Continental Army. As the son of a devout pacifist Quaker family, Thomas was expelled from the Society of Friends. He was first commissioned as a major general and then served as an aide to General Washington who appointed him as the army's first quartermaster general. Mifflin's military career suffered a setback at Valley Forge where he neglected to properly supply the troops with food and was accused of selling material for personal gain. Washington replaced him with Nathanael Greene, but Mifflin returned and later rebuilt his reputation in the field of battle, gaining promotions to colonel and then brigadier general. After the war, Mifflin returned to politics. During his last term in the Continental Congress, he served as its president in 1783 and accepted the commission of General Washington upon his retirement at Annapolis in December of that year. With the war ended, the states lost interest in the Congress, and it took until January 14, 1784 to gather enough delegates to ratify the Treaty of Paris of 1783. Mifflin was a Pennsylvania delegate to the U.S. Constitutional Convention and a signer of the document. He served in the Pennsylvania General Assembly and was a member of the Supreme Executive Council of Pennsylvania and then president on the Council in 1788, replacing Benjamin Franklin. In 1790, he became the last president of Pennsylvania and the first governor of the Commonwealth of Pennsylvania, with the adoption of the new state constitution. He was governor for nine years and was succeeded by Thomas McKean. Mifflin died in Lancaster on January 23, 1800 at 56 years old.[8]

Gouveneur Morris was born in Westchester, New York (later the Bronx) in 1752. He came from a wealthy family that had a long history of public service, and his older half-brother, Lewis, was a signer of the Declaration of Independence. Gouveneur was privately educated and graduated from King's College (later Columbia University) at 16 years old. He then studied law and was admitted to the bar at 19 years old. The Morris family was conservative with some Loyalist family members. For some unknown reason Gouveneur gravitated to the Whig position in 1775 and sat on the New York Revolutionary Provincial Congress for two years. He joined with John Jay and Robert Livingston in drafting New York's first constitution. In 1777, he served on New York's Council of Safety. From 1775 to 1779, he sat in the Continental Congress and later signed the Articles of Confederation. In 1783, he sent instructions to Benjamin Franklin in Paris for negotiating the Treaty of Paris. He supported President Washington's strong national policies and was considered a close advisor and friend. When Morris was defeated for reelection to Congress in 1779, he moved to Philadelphia to resume his law practice. In 1781, he returned to politics and for four years worked as an assistant to Robert Morris, who was Superintendent of Finance for the United States. At the U.S. Constitutional Convention, Morris served on many committees and delivered a record 173 speeches, primarily supporting nationalism. Some historians believe he was the one who drafted the Constitution. In 1788, he purchased the family's Morrisania Estate and returned to live there. The next year, he moved to France for ten years, during which time he travelled to London to resolve some of the problems that were straining American and British relations. Although he had little success, President Washington appointed him as Minister to France, replacing Thomas Jefferson who was the newly appointed Secretary of State. When Morris returned to the United States in 1799, he was elected to the U.S. Senate but was defeated for reelection in 1802. At age 57, he married Anne Carey Randolph of Virginia who bore one son. He frequently was critical of the emerging anti-federal Democrat-Republican Party, and he strongly opposed the War of 1812. He died in 1816 at 64 years old.[9]

Robert Morris was born in 1734 near Liverpool, England, and when he was 13 he left to join his father in Maryland. Having received very little schooling, he went to work for the shipping and banking firm of Willings. By age 20, he became a partner and for 40 years served as a director. When hostilities erupted in 1775 between England and America, the Continental Congress engaged the Willings Company to import munitions and arms, which marked the beginning of his involvement in politics. In that same year, Morris was elected to the Pennsylvania Council of Safety, the Committee of Correspondence, the Provincial Assembly, the Continental Congress, and a year later, the Pennsylvania legislature. However, he did not vote in favor of independence, thinking it was a premature move. During the war, he proved to be a critically important congressman who took the lead in financial matters and military supplies. He worked closely with General Washington, and he was largely responsible for keeping the Continental Army in the field with his financing skills and personal loans. While he served in the legislature from 1778-81, he was accused of profiteering, and although he was vindicated, his reputation suffered. After the war, he assumed the office of Superintendent of Finance from 1781-84. The country was in poor financial condition, so Morris drastically cut all government and military expenses, cajoled the states to fulfill their monetary obligations and used his own resources to guarantee government debts. In 1781, he obtained a loan from France to fund the Yorktown campaign. He also incorporated and funded the Bank of North America which was the first government-owned bank in America. In 1786, Morris attended the Annapolis Convention and then the Constitutional Convention the following year. President Washington selected Morris to be the first Secretary of the Treasury, but he declined and chose to serve in the U.S. Senate from 1789 to 1795. During this time, he engaged in excessive land speculation, and in 1789, he was arrested and thrown into Philadelphia's debtor prison. In 1801, he was released, but his homes and fortune were gone. For his last five years, he lived in poverty until his death in 1806 at 73 years old.[10]

George Clymer was born in 1739 in Philadelphia, and within the next year he was orphaned. He owes his life and success to a wealthy uncle who raised and educated him and upon his death bequeathed his successful mercantile business to him. Because of this and the restrictive British economic policies, Clymer witnessed firsthand their impact on business. He therefore became an early advocate for independence. He served on the Pennsylvania Council of Safety and the Continental Congress (1776-77 and 1780-82) and specialized in financial matters. He was reelected to the Pennsylvania legislature in 1784-88 and strongly supported a bicameral legislature. At the U.S. Constitutional Convention, he participated in composing the final document. He was elected to the House of Representatives for the First Congress (1789-91). In 1795, President Washington appointed his Secretary of War, Henry Knox, to negotiate a peace treaty with the Creek Indians in Georgia, and George Clymer was part of that mission. He was an active community leader during his retirement, supporting the Pennsylvania

Academy of Fine Arts and serving as the first president of the Philadelphia Bank. Clymer passed away near Philadelphia in 1813 at 73 years old.[11]

Jared Ingersoll was born in New Haven, Connecticut in 1749. After graduating from Yale in 1766, he read the law and assisted his Loyalist father with his financial affairs. On the advice of his father, Jared completed his law studies at Middle Temple Court in London and then toured Europe for two years before returning to Philadelphia, where he established his law practice. During his stay in England and the Continent, Ingersoll lost his Loyalist sympathies and gravitated to one of his family's friends Joseph Reed, who sat with the Supreme Executive Council of Pennsylvania. In 1780, he was elected to the Continental Congress. At the U.S. Constitutional Convention, he advocated for replacing the Articles of Confederation with a new constitution, but he seldom participated in the debates. Ingersoll was the attorney general of Pennsylvania from 1790 to 1799 and 1811 to 1817. His other public offices included Philadelphia City Solicitor, U.S. District Attorney for Pennsylvania, presiding judge for the Philadelphia District Court and the Federalist Vice-Presidential candidate in 1812 on the DeWitt Clinton ticket. Ingersoll gained an excellent reputation for managing the affairs of Stephen Girard who was one of the country's leading businessmen. In 1791, he practiced cases before the Supreme Court which concerned clarification of the Constitution. Ingersoll passed away in Philadelphia in 1822 at 73 years old.[12]

Chapter Thirteen

GEORGIA

Founded as a colony by James Oglethorpe in 1732
State on January 2, 1788

Early Years

Georgia was the last to join the preceding 12 colonies claimed and controlled by England on the mainland of North America. The first recorded claim was made by Giovanni de Verrazanno in 1524 when he was exploring the American coast under the sponsorship of France. However, the first actual attempt at colonization was made by Spanish settlers from Hispaniola under Lucas de Aylion in 1526. A band of 600 settlers was headed for western Florida, but they mistakenly landed in McIntosh County, Georgia where their settlement was named San Miguel de Guadalupe. The colony encountered native opposition, illness, starvation, and death and only 150 lived to return to Hispaniola. They were followed by Hernando de Soto, who was exploring Florida but crossed into Georgia in 1540. Again, de Soto's 600 explorers met a similar fate as Aylion's and close to half of them, including de Soto, died from starvation and illnesses like smallpox, measles. and chickenpox. The natives also contracted these diseases, and without any immunity, around one-third of the Southeastern American tribes perished. The next group of settlers arrived in 1559 from Mexico, led by Tristan de Luna. Their efforts in northwest Georgia failed within two years. In 1562, the French explorer Jean Ribault led a small band of French Protestants, who settled near present-day Savannah, which they named Port Royal. There they built Charles Fort, the first European fort built in North America. They also constructed Fort Caroline in present-day Jacksonville, Florida, but this was captured in 1565 by the Spaniards who executed the French and started the settlement of St. Augustine. One of the principal goals of the Spanish was to convert the Native Indians to Christianity, and they attempted this through the construction of 38 missions along the Georgia coast. Their missionary efforts were not successful, and they encountered a local Indian rebellion, which was finally subdued around 1600.[1]

England first appeared in the area in 1497 when their famous explorer John Cabot laid claim to the land that the French and Spanish tried to settle. Perennially at war with their two greatest enemies, the British constantly raided their settlements and burned their ships for the next 100 years. In 1586, Sir Francis Drake sacked St. Augustine, and England attempted settlements like Roanoke in North Carolina and then Jamestown in 1607, which took root to become the first permanent English colony in North America. The next most significant development occurred in 1663 when England established the colony of Carolina. They claimed the 31st parallel at its southern boundary, bordering Florida before the existence or colonization of Georgia. By 1645 all the Spanish missions in Georgia were abandoned due to British attacks, Indian raids, and little success in converting the natives. The three powers of England, France, and Spain claimed the Georgia territory, which became known as "the debatable lands."[2]

In 1712, England divided Carolina into North Carolina and South Carolina. In 1715, the Yamasee Indians revolted against English rule, and after they were suppressed, Sir Robert Montgomery proposed the creation of a buffer colony between South Carolina and Spanish Florida, but he never could gain enough financial support to have it established. However, in 1720, another

English explorer convinced the government to build forts along South Carolina's southern and western frontiers. They also spent the next six years constructing Fort King George, but Spanish threats and terrible working conditions forced its abandonment in 1727. Another explorer, Jean Pierre Purry of Switzerland made further attempts to colonize the area, and even though he failed, he is credited with naming the land "Georgia" in honor of the recently crowned King George I of England, who belonged to the House of Hanover in Germany. No one could have imagined that the House of Hanover was to survive for the next 290 years to the current descendant, Queen Elizabeth II.

Perhaps the most famous Englishman associated with Georgia was James Oglethorpe, who at the age of 33 took a humanitarian personal interest in England's prisons. His investigations and proposed reforms gained him national recognition. His brilliant idea was the potential transformation of poor incarcerated debtors into productive farmers, merchants, and artisans. He believed this could be accomplished with the transport of such unfortunates to Georgia where they could work the land and provide a viable living for themselves and the colony. In 1732, King George II was persuaded by Oglethorpe, who was granted a charter to create and govern the new colony along with 20 other trustees.[3] It should be remembered that England's overriding policy was the development of their colonies to enable them to produce raw materials to export for England's manufacturers and consumers, as well as to deter land claims from other countries. The transported felons were not to be treated as slaves or be bound by England's traditional class society. Their land grants were to be used to gain sufficient income to repay their debts and to provide incentives for a productive life. In fact, "transports" were given the opportunity to begin a new life that would have been impossible to attain in England. The trustees reviewed all potential candidates looking for skilled carpenters, tailors, bakers, farmers and merchants. By the time the first shipment was ready to sail in 1732, there was little thought given that Georgia was solely for debtors from England's prisons. Oglethorpe personally travelled with them to see that they were settled about 17 miles from the mouth of the Savannah River. The following year he returned to plan the town of Savannah with help from local militia, including African-Americans. He permitted all religious groups and opposed slavery in Georgia. Although he could not hold office in accordance with the trustee rules, he is regarded as Georgia's first governor.[4] It is interesting to note that Henry Williams was an English transport who became a grammar school teacher of George Washington.

Colonial Period

Oglethorpe and the settlers first landed in South Carolina before moving on to the site of present-day Savannah on February 12, 1733. That date is celebrated as "Georgia Day" (although February 1, 1632 is recorded under the old Julian calendar) and marks the beginning of Georgia as a new colony. One of Oglethorpe's initial steps was to befriend the local Yamacraw tribe and their chief, Tomochichi. He purposely invited them to Charleston, and with their friendly reception, he decided to bring the chief and his advisers to England the following year. In 1733, he concluded an agreement between the Lower Creek Indians and the Georgia colonists, entitled "Articles of Friendship and Commerce between the Trustees for establishing the Colony of Georgia in America and the chief men of the Natives of the Lower Creeks."[5]

In 1736, Fort Frederick was constructed on St. Simon's Island, and the next year, Oglethorpe returned to England to raise money and men for the new fort. Parliament assented to his request with sufficient funds and 600 soldiers and named him "Colonel of the Regiment of the Foot for the Defense of His Majesty's Plantations in America." In 1737, Fort Augusta was built north of Savannah. Oglethorpe continued to develop good relations with the native tribes, and when Chief Tomochichi died in 1739, he served as one of his pallbearers. That same year, he signed the Treaty of Coweta with the Creeks, which clarified the acres available to the British settlement. During the 1740's, Georgia was still struggling to find a viable cash crop and experienced a declining economy. Also, the war with Spain undermined economic development. All this time, the trustees were losing their control, and when they allowed the introduction of slavery, Oglethorpe attended his last trustees meeting. In 1752, the trustees surrendered their charter to the British government and thereby became a royal colony. The 12 years following the Treaty of Paris in 1763, which ended the Seven Years' War, witnessed events that led to the American Revolution. The

Proclamation of 1763, the Sugar Act of 1764, and the Stamp Act of 1765 all met with strong resistance, with royal Governor James Wright dissolving the General Assembly in 1768. In turn, this led to the Georgia merchants' boycotting of the import of British goods. Relations with the local royal government continued to deteriorate, and in 1772, the Georgia House of Assembly voted radical Patriot Noble Wimberly Jones as Speaker of the House, three times. Each time the ruling governor, James Habersham, rejected the elections, and when the Assembly refused to expunge the Jones elections, Habersham dissolved the Assembly.[6] This is noteworthy because it happened well before the Boston Tea Party in 1773, the closing of the Port of Boston in 1774, and passage of the Intolerable Acts.

As British-American relations frayed, the colonists called for the First Continental Congress to meet in Philadelphia. Georgia was the only colony to not send a delegate because they faced hostility from the Native Americans and needed the British soldiers for protection. However, they did vote to boycott all trade with Great Britain. The House of Assembly selected three Patriots as delegates to the Second Continental Congress: Noble Jones, Archibald Baldwin, and John Houston. When the Battles of Lexington and Concord broke out in April of 1775, celebrations erupted in Georgia which then sent money and food to the people of Boston. They voted to set up a Council of Safety in Savannah to enforce their boycott of British imports. They informed royal Governor James Wright that they were in solidarity with the other 12 colonies.[7] Early in 1776, Wright was placed under house arrest, but he soon escaped.

American Revolution

Georgia adopted its first constitution in May of 1777, and John Trentlen was elected its first governor. Later that year, Georgia was one of the earliest colonies to agree to the Articles of Confederation and ratified the document the following year. In 1778, the British captured Savannah, and former royal Governor Wright resumed his position. The next year, Augusta was lost, and the colony came close to being totally ruled by the British, who then controlled the two largest cities. By this time, the French had committed to supporting the American cause with men and materials and sent their navy to recapture Savannah. Commander Count D'Estaing brought 22 ships and 4,000 men to siege the city, but their military attempt failed. Georgia remained under British rule until 1781 when Washington replaced Gen. Horatio Gates, after his disastrous defeat at Camden, with Gen. Nathanael Greene. As Cornwallis advanced through South Carolina and North Carolina to Virginia, Greene began his campaign to recapture most of the South that had been lost. In 1782, Gen. Anthony Wayne's Continental Army took control of most of Georgia, except for Savannah. The British Commander-in-Chief, Henry Clinton, ordered the evacuation of all his forces from Savannah, and in July they surrendered the city to Col. James Jackson, thereby ending the revolution in Georgia approximately 17 months before the formal end of the war in all the colonies.[8]

Post Revolution Events

The Treaty of Paris of 1783 not only granted America its independence but also addressed a number of boundary issues extending to the Mississippi River. The treaty also established the southern border of Georgia, which at that time was the southernmost colony. The House of Assembly set aside 40,000 acres of land for the establishment of two new colonies and a school for higher learning. The Creek Indians ceded land that became the future site of the University of Georgia, and in 1785, the Assembly granted a charter making the school the first state-chartered school in the new nation. Additional treaties were signed with the Creeks and Cherokees, acknowledging and affirming earlier treaties. That same year, Georgia honored its war hero, Gen. Nathanael Greene, with a plantation, which he named Mulberry Grove. Greene died suddenly a short time afterwards, and when President Washington toured the South in 1791, he visited with Greene's widow, Kitty, and promised to pay for her son's education, to whom he had been named his godfather.

Constitutional Convention

The Convention was called for May of 1787 to be held in Philadelphia. Georgia sent six delegates: William Few, Abraham Baldwin, William Pierce, George Walton, William Houston, and Nathaniel Pendleton. The delegates arrived believing that they were to discuss amending the Articles of Confederation, but all of the delegates soon realized that an entirely new form of government would be necessary. One of the more difficult issues to resolve was representation in Congress, where larger states wanted the number to reflect their greater population and the smaller states wanted an equal say in legislative matters, as they were accustomed to under the one-state one-vote practice of the Articles. Georgia's Abraham Baldwin cast the deciding vote for a temporary adjournment to consider a solution to the stalemate. This produced the "Great Compromise," whereby the government would be composed of two bodies. The House of Representatives would be based on each state's population, while the Senate would have equal representation from each state. In 1788, Georgia was the fourth state to ratify the Constitution. When the United States Congress met for the first time following George Washington's inauguration in April of 1789, Georgia was represented in the House by James Jackson, Abraham Baldwin, and George Mathews and in the Senate by William Few and James Gunn.[9]

Statesmen, Leaders and Heroes

We have previously noted James Oglethorpe, who was a most remarkable man and humanitarian throughout his long life. He was born in 1686 in London into a wealthy family as the tenth and youngest child of Theophilus and Eleanor Oglethorpe. His father and two brothers had a seat in the House of Commons, so James was exposed to politics early in life. At the age of 20, he entered Corpus Christie College at Oxford University. He interrupted his studies to join a military school in Paris and went on to Austria to fight the invading Turks. He returned to Oxford but never graduated, choosing instead in 1712 to run for the seat his father and brothers had held in Parliament. When a friend of his, Robert Castell, was put in jail for failure to pay his debts, Oglethorpe was introduced to the dreadful conditions in London's prisons. Castell's cellmate was infected with the highly contagious smallpox, and he soon contracted the disease and died. The event prompted Oglethorpe to study England's prison system, and after exposing their widespread abuses, he was able to bring about many reforms. The experience brought about a life-changing time for him and shaped his humanitarian future work. He was also appalled at the number of English citizens who were incarcerated for nothing more than their indebtedness. When Oglethorpe and others began exploring the possibility of creating a new colony in North America around 1731, a brilliant idea emerged for its development. They proposed to transport able-bodied and skilled prisoners to Georgia to settle the new colony. He called them the "worthy poor" and arranged for hundreds and then thousands of them to come Georgia to become productive farmers and merchants. This would also alleviate the crowded prison population in England. Oglethorpe gained great notoriety, and in 1732, King George II granted him and 20 other trustees a charter to found and govern the colony of Georgia. Oglethorpe was unique in that he took a personal interest in assuring the fair and safe conditions of the settlers. He gave up the comforts of his life in London to travel with the "transports" and even designed the layout and streets of the new city to be called Savannah. Under his leadership, the trustees planned a classless society where slavery was prohibited. He was an enlightened leader who developed a close relationship with the Native Americans, particularly with the Creeks. Oglethorpe spent the rest of his life governing, promoting, and even militarily defending the fledgling colony. His legacy is Oglethorpe County, Oglethorpe University, and many schools, streets, parks, and businesses. He died in 1785, just shy of his 89th birthday and remains a most revered name in Georgia.[10]

The successful establishment of Georgia was due in large part to the work of two enlightened leaders, James Oglethorpe and Tomochichi, Chief of the Yamacraw Indians. It was their relationship that allowed for the peaceful settlement that started in the Savannah area where Tomochichi gave the land to the English for the building of Savannah. While the chief encouraged a closer working relationship with the colonists, Oglethorpe strictly observed native customs and adhered to their accepted formalities in transferring land and assuring fair and mutually-agreed terms. Tomochichi was born in 1644 into the Creek nation and had exposure to English settlers in South Carolina. At the age of 84, he encountered serious differences between the Creeks and Yamasees on how to deal with the English and Spanish settlers, so he formed his own Yamacraw tribe and settled on the banks of the Savannah River where his ancestors were buried. When Oglethorpe arrived in 1733, he soon met Mary Musgrove, the daughter of a Creek mother and English father. Mary served a vital role as an interpreter between Tomochichi and Oglethorpe. Despite some earlier hostile experiences with the English, the Native American chief decided to attempt a cordial relationship with the new settlers in an effort to promote trade. The two leaders developed a friendship from the beginning, and after only one year, Oglethorpe invited the chief and his family and advisers to England where they were introduced to many influential people. Tomochichi was successful in gaining their support and convinced them of his desire to educate his people and build a strong working relationship. When he returned to Georgia, he was able to convince other Native American leaders of the good intentions of the English. In 1736, Tomochichi met in Savannah with the famous Methodist leaders John and Charles Wesley and their friend Benjamin Ingham and implored them to educate his tribe. The Wesley brothers demurred, but Ingham responded by building a Native American school which confirmed the friendship of the 92-year-old chief. Even at that age, both Tomochichi and Oglethorpe travelled to southern Georgia where they negotiated with the Spanish to settle the boundaries of Georgia. The trip resulted in a treaty in 1739 which the chief could not attend due to an illness that took his life in October of that year. Oglethorpe served as a pallbearer for his good friend, and the chief was honored with an English military funeral.[11]

Button Gwinnett was born in Gloucestershire, England in 1735. At age 30, he immigrated to Savannah where he first attempted a merchant career. He then purchased St. Catherine's Island where he became a planter. He entered politics in 1769 by winning election to the Commons House of Assembly. Facing mounting financial problems, he sold most of his property and left politics. When Georgia's Provincial Congress met in early 1776, Gwinnett was elected commander of their Continental battalion. However, his election was challenged, so he was appointed to the Continental Congress, which met in Philadelphia. During his absence, his battalion was commanded by Lachlan McIntosh, who later became one of his greatest enemies. At the Congress, Gwinnett actively supported independence, and he was chosen as one of Georgia's three signers of the Declaration. When he returned home, he faced political problems, but nonetheless was elected Speaker of the Provincial Congress. He led the adoption of the Georgia Constitution of 1777, and he joined with supporters to oust those in the military who were deemed weak supporters of independence. In February of 1777, he was appointed by the Council of Safety to succeed the deceased Archibald Bulloch as president and commander-in-chief. Gwinnett then led a campaign against the British in East Florida, and when it failed, he was severely criticized but later exonerated. When his old enemy, McIntosh, publicly denounced him, he challenged him to a duel. Both men were shot, but Gwinnett died of his wounds. His legacy is Gwinnett County.[12]

Archibald Bulloch was born in 1730 in Charleston, South Carolina to James Bulloch, who had emigrated from Scotland, and to Jean Stobo, who was the daughter of a Puritan minister. He was educated locally and began his political career while practicing law. In 1758, his family moved to Georgia, and six years later, he married the daughter of a well-known and wealthy businessman, Judge James De Veaux. In Savannah, he resumed his political career and soon became the leader of the Liberty Party. In 1768, he was elected to the Commons House of Assembly, and in 1775, he was elected president of the Provincial Congress of Georgia. Bulloch then served in the Continental Congress where he was appointed to the Secret Committee responsible for the purchase of arms and ammunition. He served under Colonel Lachlan McIntosh in the Revolutionary War and saw combat in several local battles. In 1776, he was elected as Georgia's first president and commander-in-chief. He held that position for only eight months before dying in February of 1777, and the cause of his death remains a mystery.[13]

Abraham Baldwin was born in North Guilford, Connecticut in 1754. He was one of 12 children from his father's two wives, and his blacksmith father had to borrow money to send Abraham to Yale College. He studied theology to prepare himself for a career in the ministry. Graduating at age 18, he taught at Yale for the next seven years before becoming a chaplain in the Continental Army. After the war, Baldwin studied the law, and passing the Connecticut bar, he received a land grant in Wilkes County, Georgia. At age 30, he moved to Augusta, Georgia where he practiced law and began his political career. Baldwin declined a professorship of divinity at Yale and instead accepted a position proposed by Governor Lyman Hall to establish an educational system for secondary and college schooling. He strongly believed that education was essential for all states like Georgia. While serving in the state legislature, he developed a plan to fund a college in Athens, Georgia through land grants, and in 1785, the state granted him a charter to establish the University of Georgia. He became its first president from 1785 to 1801 when the first students were admitted. During that time, he held his seat in the Georgia Assembly and was elected to the Confederation Congress. He was one of the four Georgia delegates to the Constitutional Convention along with William Few, William Houston, and William Pierce. Only Baldwin and Few signed the Constitution. He is credited with adopting the "Great Compromise" that established representation in the House and Senate, and he considered this work his greatest achievement. Baldwin was an ally of James Madison and Thomas Jefferson and opposed Hamilton's policies. He died in 1807 at age 53 and is buried in Rock Creek Cemetery, in Washington, D.C.[14]

PART TWO

**From American Independence
In Chronological Order**

**DISCOVERY
To
TERRITORY
To
STATE**

Chapter Fourteen

Vermont

State on March 4, 1791

Early Years

The name "Vermont" is decidedly of French origin and was founded by French explorer and cartographer Samuel de Champlain in 1609. It is not certain whether the French word "vert" was referring to the color green or whether it was meant to denote the French translation of the word meaning "towards." The latter could have been used by Champlain as he was approaching the Green Mountains from the flat plains of Quebec across Lake Champlain.[1] The area included several Native American tribes until the early 1500's when the Iroquois Mohawks forced out most other tribes. Champlain brought the Abenaki to his side when he shot and killed the Iroquois chief in 1609. The incident made the Iroquois an enemy of the French and cost them dearly over the ensuing years. France had claimed that Vermont was a part of New France, an area they had been settling in the Ohio River Valley. They built Fort Sainte

Anne in 1666 as a defense for Lake Champlain, which they considered the first European settlement in Vermont. At the end of the 17th century, English and Dutch settlers from Albany established a trading post on Lake Champlain across from Crown Point, New York.[2]

In 1724, the British built Fort Dummer in southeastern Vermont. The fort protected the towns of Dummerston and Brattleboro. With the defeat of France in the French and Indian War in 1763, all French land claims were terminated. During much of the 18th century, many areas of Vermont were granted lands by New York and New Hampshire governors, but duplicate grants and claims were challenged, as was the authority of the governors who issued the grants. In 1761, Governor of New Hampshire, Benning Wentworth, even named the westernmost town in Vermont "Bennington" after himself. By then a total of 138 towns west of the Connecticut River were granted by New Hampshire. However, the holders of charters were required to clear the land within a stipulated time frame. The serious migration to Vermont started after the French and Indian War ended in 1763. Most settlers were from New Hampshire, New York, Massachusetts, and Connecticut, and they came by way of Lake Champlain and the Connecticut River. The early houses were built with log walls and floors and roofs of bark. It was a rugged and dangerous place to live, especially during the French and Indian War and the Revolutionary War when properties were plundered and burned to the ground.

In 1764, King George III settled the New York-New Hampshire-Vermont disputes by deciding to establish the boundary between New York and New Hampshire to be the Connecticut River. This prompted New York to claim the land west of the Connecticut River, and they refused to recognize New Hampshire grants in the Vermont territory. They went so far as to establish courthouses and took legal action against those who solely held New Hampshire grants. In 1767, the Privy Council reversed the New York position and forbid their selling of land in the Vermont area. However, the Connecticut River would soon become the boundary between New Hampshire and present-day Vermont. In 1770, in order to protect against further encroachments from New York and New Hampshire, a group of citizens formed a militia. It was founded by native son Ethan Allen and his two brothers, and they named it the "Green Mountain Boys."

On July 8, 1777 Vermont signed its own constitution, declaring itself the "Republic of Vermont."[3] Its constitution granted voting rights to non-property owners, it outlawed slavery and required public support of public schools. It issued its own currency, ran its own postal system, and named its governor, Thomas Chittenden, as president.[4] Although Vermont was not officially in the war because it was not an English colony, it did lend some support to the other colonies. Their most notable action occurred in May of 1775. Ethan Allen and Vermont's "Green Mountain Boys" together with Benedict Arnold's Connecticut militia attacked the British-held Fort Ticonderoga on Lake Champlain. They also took Crown Point and Fort George in New York. The Fort Ticonderoga capture was a most strategic one guarding Lake Champlain and proved to be very valuable when its cannons were later sent to Washington in his siege of Boston in March of 1776. Vermont's independent status led to a scandal that rocked its citizens and neighbors. In 1780, after the British burned Vermont settlements and took prisoners, Ethan Allen and Governor Chittenden entered into discussions with the British in Quebec to arrange a peace and the return of prisoners. Also, the talks included the possible return of Vermont to British control. The British Governor at Quebec was Frederick Haldimand, and when details of the meetings were leaked, the episode became known as the "Haldimand Affair." The Continental Congress was so enraged, they threatened to invade Vermont to bring her under control. Soon the Vermont militia was fighting the British in the western regions and in New York at Saratoga, and the "peace" talks ended. After the American victory at Yorktown, Vermont resumed its negotiations over land disputes with its neighbors. The ones with New York were settled upon payment of $30,000 by Vermont.[5]

England's first strategy to defeat the Americans was to isolate New England from the other colonies and starve it into submission. This was not only appropriate in British eyes because it was there that trouble began, but it was also the most logical and the easiest to execute. The Hudson River and Lake Champlain could block New England on the west and the Atlantic Ocean and Long Island Sound to the south could be controlled to surround New England. Commander-in-Chief Gen. William Howe assigned Gen. "Johnny" Burgoyne to lead the British from Canada down to Albany, where he would join up with

Lt. Col. Barry St. Leger coming from the Great Lakes and Adm. Richard Howe sailing north on the Hudson from New York City. They would form a formidable force to overcome Gen. Horatio Gates at Saratoga to complete the plan. As the plan unfolded, Burgoyne retook Fort Ticonderoga and drove the Continental Army south. When the retreating Americans reached Hubbardton, Vermont, which is south of Ticonderoga and east of Lake George, they were pursued by British Gen. Simon Fraser. The British won the day, but their losses held them back from further pursuit. The Battle of Hubbardton was the only battle of the Revolutionary War fought on Vermont soil. As the British advanced, burning everything in their way, New Hampshire feared an attack from the west and appointed Gen. John Stark to mobilize his troops. Burgoyne learned of the large number of supplies, munitions, and horses stored in nearby Bennington, Vermont and chose to take them on his way to Saratoga, New York. Meanwhile, Stark along with Lt. Col. Seth Warner attacked the British at Hoosick, New York, just across the border with Bennington, where they killed or captured 900 British soldiers. The victory weakened the British forces who then attacked Gates at Saratoga. The first engagement was a draw, but a few days later, the second battle ensued. Suddenly and unexpectedly, Benedict Arnold joined the second engagement in spite of being commanded by Gates to stand down. While Gates was awarded the victory, it very likely would not have happened without Arnold's help. The Americans took Burgoyne's army of 7,000 men as prisoners in what was the first major American victory of the war. The unexpected result shocked the British command and Parliament and caused them to devise a different strategy. It also encouraged a recently arrived 19-year-old French officer named Lafayette to return to France, where he persuaded King Louis XVI to support the Americans with arms and men. France and America signed the Treaty of Amity and Commerce, which took effect in the spring of 1778. This marked a major shift in the tides of war to the American cause.[6]

Vermont remained an independent republic during the war. Thomas Chittenden presided as chief magistrate from 1778-89 and again from 1791-92 and held office at Windsor in the eastern part of Vermont. The First General Assembly established Burlington County in the west and Unity County in the east. Its laws were adopted from the Common Law of England. The first tax in the republic was the confiscation and sale of Tory lands with proceeds used to finance their militia. Vermont became the 14th state (commonwealth) in early 1791. Its status as a non-slavery state contrasted with the 15th state of Kentucky, which was admitted as a slave-holding state later that same year.[7, 8]

The War of 1812

When the Americans gained independence from England with the Treaty of Paris in 1783, it soon became clear that the hostilities would not cease. Instead of fostering a friendly and peaceful relationship, the British nation assumed a domineering position over the colonies they had just lost. They did not respect the rights of Americans and adopted an attitude of superiority over the new nation. They blatantly violated many terms of the treaty and even refused to withdraw their troops from some towns which were south of the 45-degree latitude boundary with Canada. They incited the northern Native American tribes to commit acts of barbarism on the American settlers. They actually built and occupied Fort Miami on the western frontier from which they conducted constant raids. The British navy continued to impress American seamen by force for service in their navy under the excuse they were Englishmen and not true Americans. Even the British statesman Robert Castereagh admitted their records showed 1,600 cases of impressment by 1811. England acted with impunity against a weak America and her peaceful policy. Impressment was made mostly on the high seas but did reach inland to places like the Chesapeake Bay and Lake Champlain. Americans were outraged and insulted and wanted revenge. In 1807, President Jefferson issued a proclamation forbidding all British warships from entering harbor waters of the United States.[9]

In many cases, the British did not acknowledge their blatant disregard of the law, and this incurred greater animosity toward them. When word of the 1807 attack by *HMS Leopard* on the *USS Chesapeake* off the Virginia coast reached Vermont, the General Assembly passed the following:

> Resolved, that at this awful crisis, when our national honor and independence are insulted by a nation with whom we, forgetful of former injuries, have not only endeavored to act with harmony, by preserving

> a strict and perfect neutrality, but to conciliate their friendship by every act of benevolence, humanity and assistance compatible with the justice due to ourselves and others, it is the duty of every American to rally around the constituted authorities of his country and to support them with his life and fortune, in resisting any encroachments on our national and individual rights by any foreign power whatsoever.[10]

At that time, England was at war with France, and the United States was caught in the middle, much the same as it was in the 1790's during Washington's administration. England deemed it their right to treat all neutral powers as enemies if they were conducting trade with France, who was also impressing Americans. The United States was faced with the need to resolve this issue by going to war against either or both of them. In 1808, Napoleon ordered the seizure of all American commercial vessels in France. Between 1803 and 1810, 917 American ships were confiscated by England. In 1810, Napoleon sold 132 American ships and their contents for $8,000,000. Prior to the outbreak of war in 1812, the American State Department recorded 6,000 incidents of British impressment of Americans. The United States responded by issuing an embargo on all trade with France and England in 1807 and 1808. This was especially hurtful for Vermonters who could not export their timber and potash or sell their products to Canada. The embargo gave rise to an animosity toward the federal government and it divided many Vermonters over its fairness and effectiveness. The Jefferson and then the Madison administrations were deeply concerned whether the embargo would be supported by the affected states. Sensing the discord, the British government in Canada employed an agent, John Henry, to travel the state of Vermont to ascertain if there was sufficient non-support of the embargo and whether its government would break away from the Union to join Britain as part of Canada. When he later learned of this, President Madison confronted the British government in London which then denied any knowledge of the plot. However, Madison had incriminating documentation from material given to him by John Henry. Apparently, after having returned to Canada to report his opinion that support for seceding was not strong enough in Vermont, he was dismissed without political or financial reward for his efforts, and therefore supplied Madison with the information. The British had also conceived a plan to divide the American Union, and many believed this alone was sufficient cause to declare war against them. The question arose of whether the young nation was to support its government or oppose it with arms. By 1812, the nation was deeply divided. Its politicians were not trusted, and opponents of their policies were accused of being disloyal. Vermonters fully realized that if war did occur they would bear the brunt of it because of their proximity to invading British forces. In October of 1811, Vermont Governor Jonas Galusha addressed the Legislature:

> *At no period since the commencement of the differences has appeared to me so portentous as at present. Great Britain seems not inclined to relinquish her offensive orders in council, surrender up our impressed seamen, or permit us to enjoy the common and legal rights of a neutral nation – but assume the attitude of a threatening invader, although France has mitigated the rigor of her hostile measures and so modified her Berlin and Milan decrees that they have ceased to operate against the United States. Let us as far as possible, be prepared for any event which may occur. To be united is indispensably necessary to be prepared either for a state of war or for the full enjoyment of peace.*[11]

On June 12, 1812, Congress declared war on England. President Madison had previously mobilized 100,000 men from all the colonies. Vermont was led by Gen. Jonathan Orms and was headquartered in Burlington. The disputes with England had been growing for over 20 years, and most Americans were so used to them that they were unprepared for war. For over two years, fierce fighting took place on land and sea, especially along the coast. The English burned many seaport towns as well as the Executive Mansion and the city of Washington. Vermont played an important role in northern Vermont and on Lake Champlain. The Americans had made a good accounting of themselves, and hostilities ceased with the signing of the Peace Treaty of Ghent on December 24, 1814.[12]

Chapter Fifteen

Kentucky

State on June 1, 1792

Early Years

The significance of Kentucky is that it was the first "western" state because of its location west of the Appalachian Mountains. Established in 1792 as the 15th state, it is helpful to address the background of the American Southwest Frontier, where the major players were Spain, France, England, and the emerging independent country of the United States. In the beginning of European settlement, it was Spain that held the dominant position in discovery and exploration that started in the Caribbean and Central America and moved northward to the Gulf and southeastern North America. There is no consensus on the origin or meaning of the name "Kentucky." A large number of Native American tribes occupied the land and each spoke a different dialect including the Iroquois whose "kentake" meant "meadowland;" the Cherokee whose "kentathie" meant "land of tomorrow;" the Algonquian "kin-athiki" for "river bottom;" and for the Shawnee "head of a river." Also, the early pioneers used different spellings such as "Kaintuckee" and "Cantuckey." However, there is agreement on its nickname of the "Bluegrass State," which derives from the type of grass that grows in central Kentucky.

In 1539, Hernando de Soto began his exploration of southeastern North America, starting in western Florida, and two years later, entering the Kentucky area. Although some historians believe he never set foot in Kentucky, others record that he arrived at Fort Campbell before moving north to the Ohio River. On May 8, 1541, he and his band of 1000 men first entered the town of Quizquiz, which was located within Kentucky. After some minor skirmishes with the natives, de Soto marched another ten miles where he crossed the Ohio River and proceeded to build houses and start a settlement.[1]

The Spanish-American Frontier

While most students of history focus on England settling its North American colonies on the East Coast, we will now look to the Spanish-American frontier which included the land between the Mississippi River and the Appalachian Mountains and the Gulf of Mexico. Spain had made great inroads into Florida and northward into Georgia, Tennessee, and Kentucky, and they controlled much of the lower Mississippi River. However, their ability to control, protect, and advance their settlements was dealt a blow in 1588 when they attempted to invade England with their mighty naval power. With the defeat and destruction of their famous "Armada," Spain no longer ruled the seas, and England was empowered to explore and expand their North American colonies. At the same time, England took control of Spanish holdings in the Caribbean as well as parts of Georgia and Florida. The Bourbon dynasty under King Charles III staged a revival in the mid-1700's with stable finances and progressive reforms. Their more liberal commercial regulations also improved their colonization in North America as they acquired Louisiana in 1762, gained West Florida in 1779-81, and recovered East Florida in 1783. They controlled most of the Mississippi Valley from 1785 to 1795 and founded the far western settlements of San Diego, Los Angeles, Santa Barbara, and San Fernando Rey de España from 1760 to 1797. However, Spain's expansion was met head-on by England's territorial claims, and the two powers engaged in wars over many contested areas. By the end of the Seven Years' War in 1763, England had driven the Spanish out of the Savannah area and all the way back to the Mississippi River, and they then ousted them from their Pensacola region. Spain managed to hold onto East and West Florida and controlled the Mississippi River, which allowed them to dominate the Gulf of Mexico. Spain did not realize that an even greater threat to their North American colonies was the newly founded independent United States, which was growing rapidly and eager to expand westward. After eight years of war, Americans no longer had to deal with England's control of the frontier. Also, the western settlements had been extended during the war, and states such as Virginia had created new districts like Kentucky.[2]

The third factor that accounted for westward expansion was the economy following the revolution. Debt was high and hard currency was scarce. Taxation increased in established areas but was extremely low in the frontier. The states encouraged settlements with land grants and land sales but only some were in open unclaimed areas, while many were in established Native American hunting grounds. The conditions were ripe for land speculators who flocked there in droves. Land ownership rapidly passed from states to the private sector, and this caused greater conflict with many Indian tribes and caused the defeat of the Cherokees in North Carolina in 1785. From 1783 to 1793, more land ownership in North Carolina passed into private hands than in the preceding 100 years.[3] Georgia also had visions of their state extending to the Mississippi River. Their dreams were to become a nightmare to the Indians and Spanish who occupied these lands. With plentiful land and the American frontier expansionary nature and desire for more states, it was inevitable that the major losers would be Spain and many Indian tribes. The Mississippi River added to these pressures. Spain maintained sole rights to its use prior to the Seven Years' War. But the Treaty of 1763 ending that war gave England the right to navigate its entire length. That changed the fortunes of Spanish merchants and businessmen and ran counter to their policies of ridding the river of illicit trade and contraband. Spain wanted to protect its monopoly of the river and even opposed trade between the colonies and other nations. Spain recaptured control of the river during the last three years of the revolution and took back British West Florida, Natchez, Mobile, and Pensacola. They also controlled both banks of the lower Mississippi. Americans had traditionally used the river, thereby causing a conflict immediately after the war. Spain did permit the American Patriots to navigate the river from 1779 to 1783, and during this time the settlements of Kentucky, Holston, and Cumberland were established.[4] Such usage of the river came to be regarded as an "inalienable right" by Americans which set the stage for conflict and subsequent negotiations. In 1782, John Jay's efforts to negotiate a treaty with Spain failed. Spanish ambassador, Count Aranda, was instructed to regain exclusive rights to the river and to cede East Florida to England in order to create a buffer between West Florida and Georgia. The Treaty of Paris ending the Revolutionary War gave America and English subjects full navigational rights to the Mississippi and fixed the southern boundary of the United States at the 31st parallel. In their separate treaty with Spain, England made no mention of the Mississippi River. East Florida was ceded to Spain which was also allowed to retain West Florida. In both treaties—signed on the same day—Spain claimed that England ceded lands that were not hers.[5] Historians have debated whether England purposely put Spain into such a difficult position, but their government never formally protested the treaties. Americans held that, by her silence, Spain had acceded to the terms of the Treaty of Paris. The case can be made that the Revolutionary War and its resulting peace treaty gave rise to the Spanish-American conflict. However, the treaty did provide clear legal rights and thereby ultimately determined whose rights would prevail in settling the Mississippi Valley.

During the last decade of the 18th century, the stage was set to see whether Spain or the United States would win the territories of the American Southwest. Spain greatly feared armed aggression from the Americans in spite of their superior military and naval power. Also, they were not sure if France would enter such a conflict or which side they would support. President Washington, Jefferson, and Jay all agreed that peace would be the best course, as it would allow time for a greater number of settlers into the region, and they believed that European divisiveness could provide a better negotiating position. It should be noted that France controlled Louisiana, and Spain had treaties with both France and the United States. America was in no hurry to negotiate a settlement while it possessed a weak position and did not want to be forced to cede their rights to the Mississippi River. The eventual outcome was greatly determined by the type of government each country put into place. For Spain, their key holdings in West Florida and Louisiana served as protections for their other settlements. Each town was ruled by a military officer who reported to the governor who had authority in military and civilian matters. The governor was under the authority of the governor of Havana who answered to the king's ministers. It was a militarized centralized system that worked efficiently. However, its tight control over everything including land grants and overbearing post commanders were in stark contrast to the nearby free American settlements whose government allowed land speculation and lawlessness to prevail. Congress had little power over their frontiersmen and was afraid that too much control or the ceding of the Mississippi River could cause the secession of the West. The irony of the situation was that Spain had the major advantages of strong military and naval resources and a total population of ten million people. The fledgling United States had three million people, no navy and a fractious frontier. But it had a government responsive to the needs of its settlements.[6]

Another important aspect of the frontier was its economy and financial condition. The key products for Spain were furs, hides, rice, indigo, lumber, and tobacco. None of these had a market in Spain, nor could it supply the needs of its colonists. Expenses were greater than revenues. Louisiana alone cost the government $500,000 annually. Their trade imbalance was untenable, but to eliminate trade with other countries would end the colonies. Added to this were the constant rumors that Spain was considering the ceding of Florida to England and Louisiana to France. These rumors alone created insecurity, and thereby stemmed the flow of capital and labor to the colonies. On the American side were four key settlements: Georgia, Kentucky, Holston, and Cumberland. In 1785, their total population was 75,000 or three times the number in Spanish colonies. Close to 39,000 were in Kentucky and slightly more in Georgia, which was of little concern to Spain because of its distance from the Mississippi. Spain's chief settlements were Natchez in the North and New Orleans in the South. The Americans used the Mississippi River as a highway with their key settlements of Louisville and Nashville, and these were about 1,000 miles from New Orleans. There were no important American settlements on the Mississippi. America posed no real threat to Spain, and Congress had no intention of promoting a military attack. The only plausible problem for Spain was a possible alliance between the United States and England, but this was highly unlikely.[7]

The prosperity of the American frontier depended on its ability to transport its exports as cheaply as possible. It was not possible to reach the markets of Baltimore, Philadelphia, and New York over the Appalachian Mountains. Instead, they developed their own triangular trade with imports from the northeast and exports via New Orleans and the French West Indies. They depended entirely on use of the Mississippi, and therefore, maintained friendly relations with Spain and France. Even President Washington feared that keeping the Mississippi open to the United States could lead the Southwest settlements to becoming independent and closer to Spain. However, this was never a real threat, because the American frontiersmen would never have become docile to Spanish government laws, they didn't speak Spanish, and they were mostly Protestants who were unlikely to convert to Catholicism. The Americans aligned themselves more closely with the United States far more than subjects of Louisiana and Florida were to Spain. It is important to remember that most of the Americans were closely bound by language and culture of their government. The American system of local government, private land ownership, and freedom of trade and commerce were all derived from English laws and practices. Their desire to move westward was not based on discontent but rather to build a better place for themselves within the new country. They were state builders who used common institutions and wanted to be part of the new republic.[8]

Pioneers and Founders

Considered America's greatest frontiersman, Daniel Boone was born in Reading, Pennsylvania in 1734. He was one of 11 children born to Squire Boone and Sarah Morgan. At age 17, Daniel and his family moved to North Carolina where he worked as a wagon driver and blacksmith. In 1755, he joined the British army under Gen. Edward Braddock in his attempt to capture Fort Duquesne from the French. Braddock was killed, and Boone escaped the ambush, but before the attack, Boone had met John Finlay who had told him about the Kentucky territory. We should note that it was the Braddock campaign that brought much notoriety to a young aide by the name of George Washington, who took command of the disaster and was able to bring the regiment home to safety. Boone led his first expedition to Floyd County, Kentucky in 1767, and two years later, he and John Finlay cleared a trail through the Cumberland Gap that opened Kentucky to greater settlements. In 1775, Kentucky was formally designated a county of Virginia, and Boone was appointed a major in the militia. For 13 years, Boone held leadership roles including lieutenant colonel for Fayette county, legislative representative, and sheriff. In 1786, he and his family moved to Maysville, Kentucky where he was elected to the legislature. He acquired significant debts which plagued him for the rest of his life. In 1788, he moved to Point Pleasant which is now part of West Virginia. He was then appointed lieutenant colonel of Kanawha County in 1789, and two years later, was elected a legislative delegate. Nearing the age of 60, he moved his family to Spanish territory in Upper Louisiana (later Missouri), because he claimed Kentucky had become too crowded. Boone returned to Kentucky in 1810 to repay remaining debts, leaving himself with only $.55 to his name. His last years were spent with his son in St. Charles, Missouri where he died in 1820 at 86 years old.[9] His legacy is his reputation for bravery and leadership. He played a very significant role in opening the Mississippi Valley and paving the path for American settlement of the western frontier. His descendants continued the same tradition in their pioneering work all the way to California and Oregon. Many states from the current Midwest to the Far West owe a debt of gratitude to Daniel Boone, and many can give him credit for their formation.

One of the least known founding fathers of Kentucky was John Brown. Born in 1757, he was educated at the College of New Jersey (later Princeton) and then at the College of William and Mary, where he studied the law under George Wythe and was tutored by Thomas Jefferson and James Madison. At age 26, he established a law office in Danville, Kentucky, which was the seat of local government and a part of Virginia. He was immediately elected to the Virginia legislature from 1784 to 1788, during which time there was talk of statehood. Kentucky settlers were uneasy with the Richmond capital being so far away, but more importantly they were angry over the lack of support from Virginia in their conflicts with the Native American tribes and the little concern about keeping their right to navigate the Mississippi River. In 1787, Brown was also appointed to the Confederation Congress, and eventually he became the last surviving member of that Congress. The following year, he was a delegate to the Constitutional Convention in Philadelphia and was a strong supporter of its adoption, realizing it would pave the way for Kentucky becoming a state. He was then elected to the new House of Representatives where he worked for Kentucky's statehood. After several attempts over four years, his petition was accepted, and Kentucky became the 15th state in 1792. John Brown and John Edwards became Kentucky's first United States senators, serving from 1792 to 1805. When their capital was established in Frankfort, Brown moved his residency there. He retired from public life in 1805 and became an active member of the Frankfort community, including playing a leading role in the construction of the Old State Capitol building. He died in 1837 at 79 years old.[10]

James Harrod was born in Bedford County, Pennsylvania around 1742 to John and Sarah Moore Harrod. Like Daniel Boone, he had little formal schooling and grew up on the frontier, where he excelled in hunting, trapping, and fishing. When his father died in 1754, the family moved to Fort Littleton where James was employed as a ranger. He was exposed to all the hazards of frontier life, and his brother Sam and his father's first wife were killed by Indians. Both James and another brother William served under British Gen. John Forbes in the French and Indian War. Another notable officer in the Forbes campaign to capture Fort Duquesne from the French was George Washington. Harrod's military exploits took him to Illinois, where he lived among the French fur traders and learned to speak French. He also befriended local Indians with his hunting skills and learned their language as well. This was followed by his exploration of the Kentucky and Tennessee territories where he first met Daniel Boone.[11] In 1774, Virginia royal Governor Lord Dunmore appointed Harrod to survey the land in the Ohio River Valley that he promised to offer to all British-American officers who fought in the French and Indian War. With 37 men, he travelled down the Monongahela and Ohio Rivers and into today's Mercer County, Kentucky. On June 16, 1774, the explorers established Kentucky's first white permanent settlement which was named "Harrod's Town."[12] After building some structures, they were called back by Lord Dunmore to fight at the Battle of Point Pleasant but arrived just as it was ending. Harrod returned to his settlement where he and his men constructed more buildings and fortifications. They joined with the settlers in nearby Boonesborough to form the area's first governing regulations. In 1778, Harrod married Ann Coburn McDonald, whose first husband was killed by Native Americans, along with father's son by a first marriage. Harrod held important local government positions, and when Kentucky County was created in 1776, Harrodstown was selected as the County seat. He became a justice for the county and was elected to the Virginia House of Delegates. In the 1780's, he participated in many meetings in Danville that led to Kentucky's petition for statehood. He witnessed the rapid growth of Harrodstown and became a wealthy farmer acquiring over 20,000 acres throughout Kentucky. In 1792, Harrod and two other men went to hunt in the wilderness but never returned. Many theories have been proposed about his disappearance, from murder to abandonment, but no evidence has ever been found about how he died.[13]

Benjamin Logan was born in 1742 in Augusta County, Virginia to David and Jane McKinley Logan. Throughout his 60 years he served as a pioneer, soldier, and politician as a citizen of Virginia and Kentucky. Although the French and Indian War and its simultaneous Seven Years' War formally ended in 1763, wars and conflicts with many Native American tribes persisted for many years. In 1764, Logan joined the Virginia militia engaged in fighting the Shawnees. In 1774, he served as a lieutenant in Lord Dunmore's War against the same Indian nation. In 1776, he moved to Kentucky County, Virginia and established himself at Logan's Fort, which later developed into the town of St. Asaph's. During the Revolutionary War as the second ranking officer in the Virginia militia for Kentucky County, Logan served under George Rogers Clark against hostile Indians in the Ohio River Valley. After the war, he entered politics and served as Kentucky County's representative in the Virginia House of Delegates, where he devoted most of energy promoting statehood for Kentucky. He participated in the writing of the Kentucky Constitution in 1791-92, and after statehood, he was elected to the Kentucky House of Representatives from 1792-95. Logan passed away at 60 years old. His legacy is Logan County, Kentucky and Logan County, Ohio.[14]

George Rogers Clark was born in 1752 in Charlottesville, Virginia. He was the second son of John and Ann Rogers Clark. Five of their six sons became officers in the Revolutionary War, and their youngest son, William, achieved fame as a leader of the Lewis and Clark Expedition. George attended public school with James Madison and John Taylor, was tutored at home, and then learned surveying to help manage the family's 2,000-acre plantation. In 1772, Clark went on his first surveying trip down the Ohio River and into Kentucky. Ownership of the Kentucky Territory was in constant dispute, but it was Richard Henderson who purchased much of it from the Cherokees in what turned out to be an illegal treaty. His intention was to create a proprietary colony he named Transylvania. However, the settlers never recognized it as having legal authority. Instead, they engaged George Rogers Clark and John Gabriel Jones to petition the Virginia Assembly to incorporate Kentucky into Virginia. Governor Patrick Henry supported the creation of Kentucky County, Virginia, and Clark was appointed a major in the Kentucky militia. With the outbreak of war, the Native Americans were armed by the British, and thereby, hoped to regain the territories lost to the settlers. The Continental Army was in no position to help the distant frontier settlers who were left to fend for themselves. Clark convinced Virginia Governor Henry to attack the British forces north of the Ohio River in Illinois. In July of 1778, Clark captured Cahokia and Vincennes and several other British-held villages without firing a shot, because most of the local French and Indian settlers refused to fight for the British.[15] When the British retook Vincennes, Clark returned in a surprise winter attack, regained the town, and captured the commanding British officer, Henry Hamilton. The victory marked the peak of Clark's military career, and General Washington used it to further convince the French to become allies of America. Virginia used it to justify their claim to the old Northwest and named it Illinois County.[16]

In 1781, Clark defeated British and Indian forces that had invaded Kentucky and was rewarded with a promotion to brigadier general with command of all militia in Kentucky and Illinois counties. Between the end of the war and 1790, approximately 1,500 Kentucky settlers were killed by Indian raids. Clark tried to stop the bloodshed, but his campaign in the Northwest Indian War in 1780 ended in defeat, although he did gain a ceasefire. Clark was accused of drunkenness during the fighting, and when his plea for an official inquiry was denied by the Governor of Virginia, he never recovered from his lost reputation and left Kentucky for Indiana. Clark was also plagued by debts from personal expenses incurred while fighting on the frontier. He never received cash reimbursement, but Virginia did grant him 150,000 acres of land which later became Clark County, Indiana. He offered his services to France by proposing to oust the Spanish from the Mississippi Valley. The United States government was unresponsive to pleas from the western frontiers to remove Spain's control of the Mississippi River, which was being denied to Americans. The campaign was supported by Benjamin Logan and Kentucky Governor Isaac Shelby. When President Washington learned of this, he threatened to send the United States army to stop it and enforce his policy of neutrality. Clark's expedition failed, and he was never successful in his attempts to receive reimbursement for the $4,680 ($59,161 today) of his personal expenses. His personal finances continued to decline, and the former largest landholder in the Northwest Territory was left with only a small plot to construct a gristmill. In 1805, the Indiana Territory proposed the Indiana Canal Company and appointed Clark to the Board. Before construction could begin, two of the other Directors, including Vice President Aaron Burr, were arrested for treason. Furthermore, most of the $1.2 million seed money was unaccounted for and never discovered. Clark suffered a stroke in 1809 and became a dependent of his brother-in-law. In 1812, Virginia granted him a small pension. A second stroke in 1818 took his life, and he was buried in Locust Grove, Kentucky about eight miles from Louisville. A few years later Virginia granted his estate $30,000 for the debts they owed him. His legacy includes statues in Vincennes and seven other sites in Kentucky, Indiana, Illinois, Ohio, and Virginia. Nine high schools carry his name as a memorial for his many services in these same states.[17]

Chapter Sixteen

Tennessee

State on June 1, 1796

Explorers and Founders

Once again it was Spanish explorer, Hernando de Soto who was the first European to enter the Tennessee region from his Florida expedition in 1540. Other Spaniards soon followed into different parts of the area with Tristan de Luna in 1559 and Juan Pardo in 1567. All of the early explorers had to deal with a variety of Native American tribes, but no major conflicts were reported in their extensive chronicles. Nonetheless, they built a series of forts which were later destroyed by the local tribes, thereby leaving the land vulnerable to other European settlers. The name "Tennessee" is attributed to British Lieutenant Henry Timberlake, who created a map of the region when he was sent to visit the Cherokee who ruled much of the land. He named a part of the region "Tennessee," but historians believe the name really derives from the villages throughout the Cherokee nation called "te-na-si," located on the Little Tennessee River. This is validated by a state historical marker on the banks of Tellico Lake in Monroe County which cites the now underwater town from which the name "Tennessee" originated. However, credit is still given to Henry Timberlake, and the British Proclamation of 1763 still defines the current state boundary.[1]

One of the most famous explorers of Tennessee and the entire Mississippi Valley was Frenchman Rene Robert Cavelier, Sieur de la Salle who was born in Normandy, France in 1643. In 1666, he decided to sever ties to the Jesuits, after years of preparing for the priesthood, and leave France to settle in the Montreal area of New France in North America.[2] This region was first claimed for France by Jacques Cartier in 1534 when he explored the St. Lawrence River. New France included the colonies of Canada, Acadia, Newfoundland, and Louisiana. By the early 1700's, it reached from Newfoundland to the Rocky Mountains and Hudson Bay to the Gulf of Mexico and included all the Great Lakes. In 1763 with the Treaty of Paris ending the Seven Years' War, France was forced to cede Canada, Acadia, Newfoundland, and parts of French Louisiana east of the Mississippi River except for New Orleans, which, including the most western portion, went to Spain.[3] Upon his arrival in Montreal, La Salle was granted a large piece of land on the island and began to issue grants to other settlers. He also learned the language of the Native Mohawks who told him about the Ohio and Mississippi Rivers. His instincts and research convinced him that the Mississippi flowed all the way to the Gulf, so after selling all his Montreal land and convincing the French government to support him, he set out on his Mississippi expedition. In 1682, he claimed the Lower Mississippi area for France and named it Louisiana in honor of King Louis XIV. Prior to his Louisiana trip, La Salle focused on building the fur trade with the native Iroquois. The French had long dominated that trade, but by 1670, they were encountering competition from the Dutch and English in upper New York State. In an effort to control their position, La Salle built Fort Frontenac on Lake Ontario. Using the fort as his home base, he led expeditions to the west and southwest where he built a thriving fur trade. In 1679, he built a 45-ton barque named *Le Griffon*, which he sailed on Lake Erie, and then onto Lake Huron, and lastly onto Green Bay, Wisconsin. When the ship was lost on its way to Niagara, La Salle and his men canoed down Lake Michigan to the Miami River where they built Fort Miami near present-day St.

Joseph, Michigan. That was followed by an expedition to the Illinois River where they built Fort Crevecoeur, which later developed into Peoria, Illinois. It was from Peoria that he and his men, together with local Indians, canoed down the Mississippi. At present-day Memphis, they built Fort Prudhomme. This was the trip when he named the Mississippi Basin "La Louisiane," claiming it for France. The next year, La Salle returned to the same area and built Fort St. Louis of Illinois to replace the destroyed Fort Crevecoeur. On three more expeditions, La Salle searched for the mouth of the Mississippi River. In 1687, on his final trip, he was murdered by Pierre Duhart, who was then killed to avenge the slaying of La Salle. Historian Robert Weddle believes that La Salle was killed east of the Trinity River, about 20 miles northeast of present-day Huntsville, Texas. His legacy is enormous for the forts he constructed, the fur trading empire he developed, and the diplomatic and commercial policies he established with the Native Americans. His greatest achievement was putting New France on a firm footing in North America. His memory is revered from Ontario to the Gulf of Mexico with parishes, streets, towns, schools, and counties named for him in Canada and the United States.[4]

In the section on Kentucky, we learned about the exploits of Daniel Boone and how he cleared the passage through the Appalachian Mountains at a section called the Cumberland Gap in 1752. In 1769, William Bean brought his family through the Gap and settled by the Watauga River. He was soon followed by others, among whom was James Robertson who brought his family and friends to the same settlement despite many hardships and near-death experiences. Overcoming many difficulties, Robertson attracted a following and became one of the area's most respected leaders. Other families like Carter, Parker, Brown, Shelby, and Sevier came to settle in that same region on the Watauga River. Those first settlers named their homeland the "Watauga Association," which lay outside the boundary of North Carolina, and therefore prompted them to form their own independent government in what could be termed a "rogue colony."[5] The Association wrote its own Constitution and in so doing became the first non-European civil government in America. They wrote their "Articles of the Watauga Association" by using the laws of Virginia as a guide.[6] In 1772, the leaders of the Association leased lands belonging to the Cherokees at Sycamore Shoals near present-day Elizabethton, Tennessee. In 1775, at the same site, a North Carolina land speculator by the name of Richard Henderson purchased a large tract of land from the Cherokees through his Transylvania Company. The land included part of southwestern Virginia (later West Virginia) and Kentucky and part of Tennessee north of Nashville. More than 20 million acres were purchased for the price of *L* 10 million. After the land was purchased, Daniel Boone blazed the "Wilderness Road," connecting these lands with the Holston and Watauga settlements. The British Crown and the Cherokees believed the transaction with Henderson was illegal and dealings such as this propelled the Cherokee-American Wars of 1776 to 1794. At the same time, in 1775, the Watauga Association allied with the rebelling American colonies and reorganized as the "Washington District," which Virginia rejected but North Carolina accepted the next year as part of their state.

Statehood

As the population grew rapidly, the leaders sought the protection of North Carolina by asking to be annexed as a county. They also wanted to be associated with the colonies in their fight for independence from England and purposely chose the name "Washington" in honor of the new Commander-in-Chief of the Continental Army. They then voted to pay for their fair share of expenses for the war effort, which no doubt endeared them to North Carolina. However, England soon took steps to intervene by arming the Cherokees and Creeks, causing North Carolina to abandon their new Washington District. In 1779, the Wataugans approached their leaders, James Robertson and John Donelson, about moving westward, which they agreed to do. After leaving from the Kingsport area with more than 30 boatloads of settlers and supplies, they headed toward the Cumberland and decided to settle on the far side of the Tennessee River, which marked the beginning of the future city of Nashville. There they established a new government in 1780 by signing the "Cumberland Compact." The next three years, they were challenged by constant attacks from various Native American tribes, but under the strong leadership of Robertson and Donelson, they survived until the war's end and resumed building their settlement. However, the war debt proved overwhelming for North Carolina, so it abandoned its ownership of the Washington District, thereby angering its citizens enough for them to seek a new independent claim on their land. They created the State of Franklin, not only to honor the man but also to gain his support for future statehood. Although they adopted a new constitution and moved its capital to Greeneville, the State of Franklin lasted only four years before North Carolina declared it illegal and reclaimed the region. Meanwhile, other associations were formed outside Franklin, like "Government South of the Holston" and "French Broad Rivers." North Carolina didn't officially recognize them as they adopted their own constitutions and laws. Gen. John Sevier emerged as a leader of Franklin and the new associations and went on serving in the North Carolina Assembly as the representative for the Washington District.[7]

Although the State of Franklin did not survive, it did bring about several important changes. It awakened Congress to something it was not prepared for: namely, dealing with a rapidly expanding population and the pressures that would bring on creating new states. In 1789, North Carolina changed its mind again and ceded the Washington District to the federal government. This was prompted by the full payment of their war debts by paying veterans with land rather than cash. The federal government renamed the District "Territory South of the Ohio River," drew its new boundaries, and appointed William Blount as governor. Blount started the procedures for achieving statehood as soon as the population reached the required 5,000 male citizens. In 1796, President Washington signed the proclamation for statehood, and it was decided to use the name "Tennessee" instead of the other associations. The irony is that the name derived from the Henry Timberlake map of 1763, and the eastern boundary was formed from the British Proclamation of 1763 which had confined the American settlers to the eastern side of the Appalachian Mountains. Perhaps the most significant aspect of the new 16th state was that it was the first territory to become a state. All previous 15 states had been colonies or parts of colonies, but Tennessee was the first to be created from land owned by the United States government.[8]

The Revolutionary War

By their nature, the early settlers tended to be hardy independent pioneers who would not easily accept interference or domination by anyone. When England declared their Proclamation of 1763, restricting American settlement to east of the Appalachian Mountains, the issue was pretty much decided that the American frontier settlers would align themselves with the eastern colonies in their struggle for independence. This was further assured when the British armed the Native Americans to fight on their side. This, in turn, caused the Spanish to side with the Americans against their longtime adversary, England. Settlers in the Kentucky and Tennessee territories built a number of forts to defend themselves against Native American attacks, and the Continental Congress sent militia to help them. Despite peace treaties, the raids continued until 1779 when 900 militiamen destroyed most of the Cherokee and Chickamaugan villages, thereby confirming the animosity of most Native American tribes and their alignment with the British during the war. When the British failed in their first two strategies to defeat the rebels in the northeast and mid-Atlantic, they initiated an all-out attack on the South in 1780, hoping to enlist the support of local Loyalists and Native Americans. After sweeping up from Savannah and Charleston, they soon approached the North Carolina-Tennessee border where frontier leaders Isaac Shelby and John Sevier led 1,000 volunteers to assist the Americans at the western border of North and South Carolina. The Battle of King's Mountain was a decisive American victory and marked the turning point in the British southern campaign, which ended at Yorktown in 1781. The British had won victories along the way but sustained heavy-enough losses for Cornwallis to consider being evacuated from Yorktown. King's Mountain proved helpful to Tennessee's heroes John Sevier and Isaac Shelby, both of whom achieved political success. More importantly, the victory doomed the local Native Americans to relocate to another area in the west for having fought for the British.[9]

Statesmen, Leaders and Heroes

William Blount was born in Windsor, North Carolina in 1749 to descendants of Thomas Blount, who arrived from England in 1660. William served in the Revolutionary War as paymaster for the Third North Carolina Regiment and participated in the battles defending Philadelphia in 1777 and Charleston in 1780, where he was under the command of Gen. Horatio Gates. Blount sat in the North Carolina House of Representatives from 1780-84 and in the Upper House from 1788-90. He also served in the Continental Congress from 1782-83 and from 1786-87 when he was appointed a delegate to the Constitutional Convention. He signed the Constitution but only to make the support unanimous. When he failed to be elected to the United States Senate, he moved to the Tennessee Territory, where he had previously represented North Carolina in dealing with the local natives and where he had significant land holdings. He was also appointed to be Superintendent of Indian Affairs for the Southern Department and reportedly did a good job gaining the support of the frontiersmen. In 1796, he presided over the Tennessee Constitutional Convention and worked to attain their statehood. He was then elected as one of their first two United States Senators for 1796-97. Sadly, his land investments failed and caused him serious financial problems. For some unknown reason, he developed a plan to have American settlers join with England, France, and Native Americans to drive the Spanish from their colonies in Florida and Louisiana. When President Adams learned of the plan he turned it over to the Senate which promptly turned him out of office. His good reputation survived because in the following year he was re-elected to the Senate and became Speaker. He died in 1800 at age 51 and is buried in Knoxville, where his mansion is a museum and historic site.[10]

Gen. James Randolph Robertson is regarded as the "Father of Tennessee." He was born in Brunswick County, Virginia of Scots-Irish and English ancestry. He received little education, and at age 17, he joined Daniel Boone on his third expedition beyond the Appalachian Mountains. Boone moved on to Kentucky, but Robertson stayed for a while at an old abandoned Native American settlement on the Watauga River. He married then returned with a group of settlers to the old Watauga site in 1772. Their group established the Watauga Association but soon discovered they were on land belonging to the Cherokee tribe. While they were negotiating a lease with the tribe, one of Robertson's men killed a Native American warrior, which normally would have ended talks, but Robertson was able to placate the outraged Indians. He then built Fort Watauga and remained there in relative peace until 1776. Robertson together with John Carter and John Sevier successfully defended the fort from fierce Cherokee attacks, and afterwards, Robertson was appointed by the governor of North Carolina to be the local agent to deal with the Indians and report on British activities during the war. In 1779, Robertson and John Donelson built Fort Nashborough, which was named after Revolutionary War hero Francis Nash. The area grew rapidly into present-day Nashville, aided by its location on the Cumberland River which had access to the Ohio River and thereby the Mississippi, down to the Gulf of Mexico at New Orleans. While there, the Spanish offered Robertson's group free navigation on the Mississippi in exchange for abandoning the United States and consolidating Watauga and Kentucky into an independent political entity, but he declined. In 1790, President Washington appointed him as brigadier general of the territorial militia, and he held that position until 1796. He remained as Indian Commissioner until his death in 1814 at 72 years old.[11]

Donelson was born in 1718 somewhere in western Virginia, where his family had become established in commerce and planting. He is highly regarded as one of the more important founders of Tennessee. Donelson's interests and skills varied widely from being an explorer, frontiersman, ironmaster, politician, and city planner. Before moving to the Tennessee Territory, he served in the Virginia House of Burgesses. In the frontier, he joined with James Robertson in building Fort Watauga and Fort Nashborough, which developed into the city of Nashville. One of his greatest achievements was participating in the formation of the Cumberland Compact which bears the signatures of 256 colonists who settled on the Cumberland River. The document formed the future Constitution of Tennessee.[12] He married Rachel Stockley, and their daughter Rachel married Andrew Jackson who became the seventh president of the United States. Donelson died in 1785 at age 65, and his legacy is the town of Donelson which is six miles east of Nashville.[13]

John Sevier was born in Rockingham County, Virginia in 1745. In his early 20's he began exploring the Tennessee frontier and moved his family to the Holston River area in 1773. A few years later, he moved to the Watauga settlement in present-day Elizabethton. When it was discovered that Watauga sat on Native American lands, a condition prohibited by England's Proclamation of 1763, Sevier was instrumental in negotiating for a purchase of the land from the Cherokees, many of whom were not in agreement with the sale. When the Revolution started in 1775, Watauga changed its name to "Washington District" and appointed Sevier to their Committee of Safety. Wataugans first petitioned Virginia to be annexed, and when they declined, asked North Carolina, which accepted the proposal. Sevier was one of the first delegates to attend the North Carolina Constitutional Convention in 1776, which formalized the Washington District. He was then elected to one of North Carolina's two seats in the House of Representatives. In 1777, the District became Washington County, and Sevier was appointed a lieutenant colonel in the militia. In 1780, the British were making steady gains in their southern campaign when they reached the Appalachian frontier at the North Carolina–South Carolina border. British Major Patrick Ferguson threatened annihilation of the Tennessee settlements, but Sevier's and Isaac Shelby's 240 men joined with Virginia's 400 militiamen and organized an attack on Ferguson, but only after Sevier was able to obtain a personal loan to finance the battle. They proceeded to defeat the British and kill Ferguson in what is known as the Battle of King's Mountain, which changed the direction of the war. Two months later, Sevier fought off the Cherokees at the Battle of Boyd's Creek, and with Virginia's help, marched south to destroy settlements of a number of Native Americans who were supporting the British. In 1781, Sevier was appointed commander of the Washington County militia and fought against the Cherokees in North Carolina, destroying 15 villages before returning home. The next year, he defeated more hostile villagers in the northern Georgia and Alabama area.

When North Carolina ceded the expensive and unprofitable Washington District back to the federal government in 1784, the Tennessee frontiersmen organized their own independent State of Franklin and elected Sevier as their first and only governor. Rivalries from North Carolina for governing Franklin came to a head in 1788 with the "Battle of Franklin," a brief skirmish. For a period, Franklin had government officials from North Carolina and Tennessee. At the same time, attacks from Cherokees resulted in more deaths, forcing Sevier to destroy several Cherokee villages in the Tennessee Valley. After the Battle of Franklin, support for Sevier diminished, and the government of

North Carolina had him arrested. However, before the trial, he was released by a North Carolina judge who had been a veteran of King's Mountain. In 1789, Sevier took an oath of allegiance to North Carolina and was pardoned. He was then elected to the North Carolina Senate and supported ratification of the United States Constitution.

In 1790, Congress created "The Southwest Territory" to govern the former State of Franklin. Sevier was appointed brigadier general of the territorial militia, and William Blount was appointed governor. In 1796, the Southwest Territory was admitted to the Union as the State of Tennessee, and Sevier was elected as its first governor. He soon developed a political rivalry with United States Senator Andrew Jackson. However, he survived several elections for governor and an aborted duel with Jackson. He won three consecutive two-year terms as governor, and only term limits prevented him from seeking another. President James Madison offered him a command in the War of 1812, but he declined. Sevier died in 1815 at age 70 while surveying lands in the Alabama Territory. His legacies include Sevier County and its seat of Sevierville as well as highways and schools. His statue is in the United States Capitol Building, and a bust is in the Tennessee State Capitol.[14]

Isaac Shelby was born in Maryland in 1750 to Evan and Letitia Cox Shelby, who had left Wales in 1735. In his youth, Isaac worked on his father's plantation and engaged in several surveying projects. In 1768, he was appointed deputy sheriff of Frederick County, Maryland. In 1779, the family moved to Tennessee, where they built a fort and a trading post. In Lord Dunmore's War with the Shawnee and Mingo Native American tribes in 1774, Shelby served as a lieutenant in the Virginia militia, and afterwards, did surveying for the Transylvania Company that had purchased enormous tracts of land from the Cherokees, a purchase Virginia declared illegal. In 1777, Virginia Governor Patrick Henry appointed him a militiaman in the frontier, which was followed by his service in the Continental Army in 1778 and 1779. He was also elected to the Virginia House of Delegates and then commissioned as a major by Governor Thomas Jefferson to establish a boundary line between Virginia and North Carolina. When Shelby learned of the fall of Charleston, he rushed to join the Patriots. In July of 1780, he captured the British fort on the Pacelot River without firing a shot and took

94 prisoners. Later that year, he joined with John Sevier to defeat British Major Ferguson at King's Mountain. After the war, he resettled in Kentucky where he was instrumental in the change from Kentucky County, Virginia to the new state of Kentucky. He helped to organize the state and was elected its first governor. At the end of his term he retired from public life but was re-elected governor to guide Kentucky through the impending War of 1812. Gen. William Henry Harrison appointed Shelby to command Kentucky troops at the Battle of the Thames. At the end of that war, President James Monroe offered him the cabinet position of Secretary of War, but he declined. He died in 1826 at 76 years old. His legacies are numerous including nine different states with Shelby counties and 11 states with Shelby towns and cities.[15]

Chapter Seventeen

Ohio

State on March 1, 1803

Explorers and Settlers

When we think of present-day Ohio, we should keep in mind what the Ohio Country looked like in the 17th and early 18th centuries. At that time, it encompassed part of Pennsylvania, Indiana, and Illinois, and it was sparsely populated. It was the first American western frontier and a significant tract of real estate just to the west of the Appalachian Mountains and north of the Ohio River. The principal inhabitants were Native Americans who looked with increasing concern over the constantly growing number of European settlers on their hunting grounds. The name derives from the Iroquois word "ohi-yo" which translates to "Great River." The first European settlers to explore the area, creating trading posts and settlements, were the French, starting in the 1500's from the St. Lawrence River in northeastern Canada and then moving south to further develop their fur-trading empire. By 1663, Ohio officially became the centerpiece of New France. Their noted explorer Robert La Salle was the leader who expanded New France south of the Ohio River and down the Mississippi to a new territory he named "Louisiane" in honor of the reigning King Louis XIV. La Salle built many forts along the way, established settlements, and is credited with building French domination of the fur industry. With the eastern English colonies growing rapidly by the early 1700's, it was only natural for settlers to move westward into the near-empty frontier. But the French faced considerable obstacles from the Native Americans and the English settlers, who believed it belonged to them based on the charter given by King James I to the Virginia Company in 1606. With French immigration coming from the North and English immigration coming from the East, it was inevitable that a conflict would occur someday. This was further complicated by the large tracts of land held by wealthy and high-ranking English investors in the Ohio Company, which was the corporate entity that "owned" the land. Investors included some of the earliest Virginia families as well as the royal Governor Robert Dinwiddie. When the Governor learned that French forces were located in Fort Le Boeuf just south of Lake Erie, he called for volunteers to travel there and advise the French that they were on Virginia territory, and therefore should leave. The expedition was led by a young militia officer named George Washington who survived the 400-mile expedition and returned safely with his guides and surveyors. The trip was noteworthy, partly because Washington wrote a journal of the adventure, which he submitted to Governor Dinwiddie. Dinwiddie was so fascinated that he had it published in London, and thereby introduced the name Washington to the world. When the French did not leave but instead moved south to build Fort Duquesne at present-day Pittsburgh, Dinwiddie ordered Washington to form a regiment and forcibly remove them. It was on this second trip in 1754 that fighting erupted, and Washington succumbed to the larger French forces at Fort Necessity, deemed lucky to have survived. More significantly, the skirmish marked the beginning of the French and Indian War. Another note of interest is the question of why the natives allied with the French rather than the English. The most plausible answer could be that the native tribes traded with the French for over 100 years and seemed to integrate more easily with the Indians. While the French explorers established many settlements for trading purposes, they did not build towns with permanent buildings and institutions like the English. Also, the French Catholics brought over Jesuit missionaries to convert the natives, and many married and integrated. It is not certain exactly when the French and Indian War ended, because the American portion of the British-American forces seems to have ended with the capture of Fort Duquesne in 1758 while the British continued the fight to take possession of Canada. Sometime in the mid-1750's, the conflict evolved into the Seven Years' War, ending in 1763 with the Treaty of Paris. That war could have been deemed the First World War because it encompassed 11 countries in armed conflict on four continents. Its consequences were enormous as France lost Canada, Newfoundland, Acadia, Hudson Bay, and part of Louisiana to England and the remainder to Spain. New France from Ohio to the Mississippi River was also lost to England and eventually became the nucleus of the Northwest Territory that was ceded to the United States in 1783 in the Treaty of Paris, ending the Revolutionary War.

Another interesting part of Ohio's history is a piece of land in northeastern Ohio that was granted to the colony of Connecticut in 1662 by King Charles II. The land was named the "Western Reserve" and today still resembles features of New England's customs, town formations, structures, and architecture. The Ohio River Valley was considered prime agricultural land, and royal Governor Dinwiddie offered all officers who fought for England in the French and Indian War prizes in the form of pieces of a 200,000-acre tract. Washington almost always invested in good land and participated in the Dinwiddie offer. He reportedly accumulated around 20,000 acres including purchases from veterans who preferred cash. Several colonies had claims to land in Ohio, but activity in that frontier only took on significance after the Revolutionary War. In addition to Connecticut, New York claimed all of it, and Pennsylvania claimed everything west as an extension of its state. Connecticut and the other states gave up most of their claims to the federal government in exchange for the federal assumption of their war debts. Connecticut retained 3.3 million acres. The other portion they "gave" to the government became part of the Northwest Territory, which later was used in the 1787 Northwest Ordinance and from which the states of Ohio, Indiana, Illinois, Michigan, and Wisconsin were created. Connecticut's retained portion was sold to the Connecticut Land Company for $1.2 million in

1795-96. Some of it was used to compensate those who had lost their property in the war. In 1806, Moses Cleaveland (the "a" was dropped later) was hired to survey the land and lay out townships of 25 square miles. He founded the city of Cleveland which became the largest city in that area.[1]

Road to Revolution

One of the most historically-significant aspects of Ohio is that it played a major role in the evolution of the United States. Some historians claim that the American Revolution really started in Ohio because of the various pressures that came to a head there. While taxation and economic restrictions set the stage for open rebellion in the New England colonies in 1775, another event caused just as much friction between the American colonies and Great Britain in 1763. When the French and Indian War and the Seven Years' War ended in 1763, England realized it had to improve its relations with the Native American tribes, especially after they had allied themselves with the French. The British immediately announced their "Proclamation of 1763," which prohibited settlers in North America from moving to lands west of the Appalachian Mountains, and it forbid settlement on Native American lands as well as the purchase or lease of these lands by individuals. This was later followed in 1774 by the Quebec Act, which annexed parts of Ohio, Indiana, Illinois, Michigan, Wisconsin, and Minnesota into the Province of Quebec. It also reserved most of those lands for Native American hunting grounds and declared most of the existing land deeds null and void. They restored French civil law and guaranteed the practice of the Catholic faith. Both acts dealt a severe blow to all the colonists, especially to the English-speaking and Protestant settlers who saw these as punishment for the Boston Tea Party and evidence of British domination and loss of personal freedoms. Sandwiched between the two acts were a series of taxes, all adding ingredients for civil unrest and ultimate revolution. As settlers continued their westward migrations, ignoring the Proclamation, they encountered many bloody battles with the Shawnee and other tribes in the Ohio Territory, and it was primarily these violations that propelled the natives to align with the British in the Revolutionary War. It was Virginia that took the lead during the war to administer some of the Ohio Territory they named "Illinois County." Their legislature actually established the first American civil government there. In 1782, the Indians and the British defeated the Americans in Ohio, but with the Treaty of Paris in the next year, all those lands were ceded to the United States. Ohio then became a highly desirable place to settle especially for veterans of the Revolutionary War who preferred land in lieu of cash for their service.[2]

The Northwest Territory

The Northwest Territory consisted of present-day Ohio, Indiana, Illinois, Michigan, and Wisconsin. These lands were occupied for centuries by a great number of Indian tribes who waged constant war against themselves, as well as French and English settlers, for control over this vast area of fertile soil in the Ohio River Valley and the trapping of animals for their fur. No major Revolutionary War battles were fought here, but there was constant friction and savage attacks among the Native Americans and the French and English settlers. Hostilities became more pronounced from 1785 to 1795, which came to be known as the Northwest Indian War. The region included 45,000 Indians and far fewer European settlers. However, the English ceded this area to the United States in the 1783 Treaty of Paris without consultation with the Indians who were trying to retain control of the region. The Treaty required the British to vacate the area, but they ignored that provision and kept a series of armed forts along the southern border of the Great Lakes. The most heavily fortified was Fort Detroit from which the British would arm and assist the natives against American settlers. After the defeats of General Harmon in 1790 and General St. Clair in 1791, President Washington ordered Gen. Anthony Wayne to rid the region of the natives. In 1794, Wayne won a decisive victory at the Battle of Fallen Timbers, which forced the tribes to relinquish much of Ohio in the 1795 Treaty of Greenville. Emerging from the wars were several men who went on to achieve considerable fame including William Henry Harrison (President in 1841), William Clark and Merriweather Lewis. The Treaty also called for the Native Americans to recognize the United States as the sovereign power in the Northwest Territory rather than Great Britain and to surrender ten chiefs as hostages until all American prisoners were returned. In 1800, the region was divided into the Ohio Territory with the stipulated border of The Greenville

Treaty Line, and the remaining enormous area was temporarily named the Indiana Territory.[3]

The Northwest Ordinance of 1787

While the delegates from 12 of the 13 colonies (Rhode Island chose not to attend) debated the formation of the new government at the Constitutional Convention, each would occasionally excuse themselves to attend another meeting upstairs where the fate of the Northwest Territory was being discussed. It was Thomas Jefferson in 1784 who first proposed that the western lands which had just been ceded to the United States by the Treaty of Paris should be set aside for the creation of future states. Congress was well aware of the conflicting claims to that area by several states and realized the seriousness of the problems that could ensue. It was not until three years later that the issue was resolved by the Northwest Ordinance. Formally named "The Ordinance for the Government of the Territory of the United States North-West of the Ohio River," it included three major provisions: 1) there would be no less than three or more than five future states; 2) there would be a three-stage process for creating a new state whereby Congress would appoint a governor, a secretary, and three judges to rule in the first phase, an elected assembly and one non-voting delegate elected to Congress in the second phase when the population of the territory reached 5,000 male inhabitants, and a state constitution to be drafted and membership to the Union requested in the third phase when the population reached 60,000; and 3) a Bill of Rights would be written, protecting religious freedom, the right to a writ of habeas corpus, the benefit of trial by jury, and other individual rights. Also, the Ordinance encouraged education and forbid slavery.[4] In effect, the prohibition of slavery established the future boundary of the free and slave states at the Ohio River. The five free states that would emerge lay between the Appalachian Mountains and the Upper Mississippi River and the Ohio River to the border with Canada. The Ordinance is considered one of the most important acts of the Continental Congress, because it established precedent for the authority of the federal government to control westward expansion and the creation of future states. It provided for new states to be on an equal legal status as the existing ones. It also established the concept of private ownership in perpetuity with the right to own, sell, or give to a new owner. This was regarded as a "natural right" and included other rights such as religious tolerance and habeas corpus, which later were added to the United States Constitution as the Bill of Rights in 1791.[5]

Another revealing section of the Ordinance was the emphasis on education. Congress insisted on the creation of a public university as a condition for statehood and pronounced that "Religion, morality and knowledge being necessary to good government and the happiness of mankind, schools had the means of education and shall ever be encouraged." The year before Congress approved the Ordinance, a group of six public-spirited men met in a Boston tavern to discuss the future of the Ohio Territory and created the Ohio Company. One man in particular, Manasseh Cutler, took the lead and arranged for the current president of the Continental Congress, Gen. Arthur St. Clair, to serve as governor of the newly created Northwest Territory. The Ohio Company then negotiated with the Congress to purchase 1.5 million acres of Ohio land at the confluence of the Ohio and Muskingum Rivers for $1 million dollars of United States Treasury securities, which had a market value of $120,000. Townships were to be devoted to public schools, others for religious purposes, and two townships for a university. Unable to raise enough funds, the Company purchased 913,833 acres and negotiated a second contract for private purchase. In 1797, local settlers chose a section of Athens County near Marietta for the school they named American West University, but was changed in 1814 to Ohio University.[6]

Statesmen, Leaders and Heroes

Rufus Putnam was born in Sutton, Massachusetts in 1738. His father died when Rufus was seven, and in spite of very little schooling, he achieved successful careers in the military, as a surveyor and as a politician. At age 19, he fought for the British in the French and Indian War, and afterward, returned home to become a farmer and miller. Putnam joined the Continental Army at the start of the American Revolution and participated in the Siege of Boston and the defense of New York City and fought in the Battle of Saratoga. During the war, he rose from lieutenant colonel to brigadier general. Near the end of the war, Putnam became an advocate for the soldiers who had not been paid, and helped prepare the Newburgh Petition, which expressed their concerns and threatened to replace the government if compensation was not received as promised. Only when General Washington learned of the conspiracy was a serious crisis avoided. In 1786, Putnam was one of the six men who formed the Ohio Company, which was designed to purchase 1,500,000 acres of land in the Northwest Territory and establish uniform townships. They were to pay in cash and government securities, which were military warrants that were valued at 12 cents to the dollar. Their fundraising fell short, so they eventually purchased just under 1,000,000 acres, and Congress donated another 100,000 acres which was to be used as a buffer zone between the settlers and the Native Americans. Putnam is credited with the establishment of the first Ohio Company settlement, which was later known as the town of Marietta. He then became a significant political figure of the Northwest Territory. In 1790, President Washington appointed him to a judgeship while he was serving as a brigadier general in the United States army. In 1796, he was appointed as Surveyor General of the United States. Putnam also served in the Ohio Constitutional Convention in 1802, supported the Federalist Party, and took a strong stand in prohibiting slavery in the state. He died in Marietta in 1824 at 86 years old.[7]

Edward Tiffin was born in Carlisle, England in 1766, and from ages 12 to 17, he worked as a physician's apprentice. He moved with his family to Charles Town, Virginia (later West Virginia) in 1783, where he set up a medical practice. At age 32, Tiffin moved to the town of Chillicothe in the Northwest Territory with his brother-in-law, Thomas Worthington. Tiffin immediately entered politics when Governor St. Clair appointed him as clerk of the Court of Common Pleas. He then served in the legislature and was elected the Territory's first Speaker of the House. Statehood would require a constitution, and Tiffin presided as president on the Ohio Convention in 1802. As Democratic-Republicans, Tiffin and Worthington worked for Ohio's statehood, but they were opposed by Governor St. Clair and his Federalists, who wanted to shrink the proposed boundaries and delay admission to the Union in order to maintain their control. In 1803, Tiffin became the first governor of Ohio. However, he faced numerous problems, especially with the Indian tribes led by Shawnee Chief Tecumseh, who tried to form a Native American Confederacy to drive the Americans out of the Ohio and Indiana territories. His plan almost succeeded because he had weapons and military assistance from the British, who refused to abide by the terms of the 1783 Treaty of Paris requiring them to leave their American-based forts. Tiffin was reelected governor, and in 1807, was selected to replace Thomas Worthington in the United States Senate. Two years later, he was elected as Speaker of the House of Representatives. President James Madison appointed him Commissioner of the United States Land Office, after which he became Surveyor General of the Northwest Territory in 1814, which permitted him to return to Ohio, where he died in 1829 at 63 years old. His legacy is the town of Tiffin, Ohio.[8]

Thomas Worthington was born in 1773 in Charles Town, Virginia (later West Virginia), and following his father's early demise, he was raised by his brothers. As a teenager, he served two years in the merchant marines and then studied surveying. For his work with the Virginia Military District, he received compensation in the form of land near Chillicothe, Ohio. In 1798, he and his brother-in-law, Edward Tiffin, moved to that part of the Ohio Territory, where he built one of the earliest noteworthy houses in Ohio, having been designed by the nationally-known architect Benjamin Latrobe. The next year, Worthington served in the legislature until 1803. During that time, he worked diligently with Edward Tiffin towards Ohio statehood. He even travelled to Washington, D.C. to personally speak with President Jefferson about statehood and persuaded him to support the Enabling Act of 1802, which authorized Ohio to fulfill the requirements set out in the Northwest Ordinance. Worthington then became one of Ohio's first senators, serving for four years, then again from 1811-14, and again from 1814-18. He opposed the War of 1812, because he considered America to be much weaker than Great Britain. He resigned from the Senate in 1814 and went on to serve two terms as governor. He focused on many social reforms including prison conditions, welfare for the poor, and free public education. Even though several of his proposals were not immediately approved by the legislature, by the mid-1820's, Ohio did support public education and the construction of a canal system which Worthington had proposed. After his two terms as governor, he served two more terms in the Ohio legislature. He died in 1827 at 54 years old.[9]

Samuel Huntington was born in Coventry, Connecticut in 1765 and was educated at Dartmouth and Yale Colleges before studying law. In 1800, he visited the Connecticut Western Reserve, and the next year, moved his family to the small town of Cleveland. He stayed there for only six years before moving on to Painesville Township, where he founded the town of Fairport and established several businesses. When he first arrived in Ohio, he became involved in local politics and was active in pursuing statehood. He served as a member of the Ohio Constitutional Convention, and as a Democratic-Republican, worked closely with Edward Tiffin and Thomas Worthington. When statehood was granted in 1803, Huntington was appointed a judge on the Ohio Supreme Court, and the next year, was elevated its Chief Justice. In 1807, the Rutherford v. McFadden case presented the Court with its first major challenge. The Court held that it could rule on the constitutionality of laws passed by the General Assembly. Huntington followed the reasoning of the United States Supreme Court in its Marbury v. Madison ruling, where the Court could nullify legislative enactments as unconstitutional. The Ohio General Assembly was so upset by the Huntington Court that it tried to impeach two of his associates, but their convictions failed by one vote. Huntington escaped impeachment by being elected governor in 1808. After one term, he was elected to the Ohio House of Representatives. President James Madison appointed him a United States army district paymaster with the rank of colonel, which he held throughout the War of 1812. He died in 1817 at 52 years old.[10]

Ebenezer Sproat was born in Middleborough, Massachusetts in 1752. Little is known about his education, which was probably limited as he worked on the family farm at an early age. However, he did learn surveying before achieving prominence in the Revolutionary War, having served for the entire eight and a half years. He fought in the Battles of Trenton, Princeton, and Monmouth. He joined the Massachusetts Regiment in 1775 as a captain in April and by June was promoted to major. He wintered at Valley Forge under command of General Washington, with whom he enjoyed a friendly relationship. Near the end of the war, he was promoted to colonel. After the war, he moved to Rhode Island, where he married Catherine Whipple, the daughter of Commodore Abraham Whipple of the Continental navy. In 1786, he was appointed as surveyor for Rhode Island. He became a shareholder in the Ohio Company of Associates where he was employed as a surveyor. He joined Rufus Putnam in founding Marietta, Ohio, the first permanent American settlement in the Northwest Territory. Sproat was a very popular man, even among the Indians, who named him "Hetuck," which translates to "eye of the buck deer" or "Big Buckeye," because of his exceptional height. Some historians believe this is the origin of Ohio's nickname of "The Buckeye State." During the Northwest Indian Wars of 1785-95, Secretary of War Henry Knox appointed Sproat the superintendent of military affairs in Washington County. Having been at the Continental Army Headquarters at Newburgh, New York in 1783, he joined with Henry Knox in forming the Society of the Cincinnati, an organization designed to help Revolutionary War veterans after the war. He was the first sheriff for the Northwest Territories and served 14 years in Washington County, which encompassed half of the state from the Ohio River to Lake Erie. He died in 1805 at age 53 in Marietta and is buried at Mound Cemetery next to many Revolutionary War veterans.[11]

Tecumseh was one of the great Native American Indians who took a leadership role in trying to unify the native resistance to the white settlers. He was born in 1768 as the son of Puckshinwau, a Shawnee war chief, and a brother to Tenskwatawa, also known as "The Prophet." When his father was killed during Lord Dunmore's War in 1774, Tecumseh vowed to follow in his father's footsteps as a Shawnee war chief. In his youth, he joined the American Indian Confederacy, which was led by Mohawk Chief Joseph Brant. Tecumseh fought the intruding settlers under various warriors and participated in the annihilation of General St. Clair's 1,000-man army at the Battle of the Wabash, where 952 of the American soldiers were slain. At the Battle of Fallen Timbers in 1794, the Shawnees were badly defeated by Gen. Anthony Wayne and were forced to move on to Prophetstown (later Tippecanoe), where they formed a new Indian alliance. He was joined there by his brother, Tenskwatawa, and they began a large recruitment campaign from Alabama to Canada. Meanwhile, the governor of the Indiana Territory, William Henry Harrison, was busy subduing several Indian uprisings in that area. In 1809, Harrison signed the Treaty of Fort Wayne, which granted the Americans an enormous amount of Indian territory. When Tecumseh was away on a recruiting trip, Harrison attacked the tribe at the Battle of Tippecanoe, where the Indian encampment was destroyed. In the War of 1812, the Indian tribes sided with Great Britain, and Tecumseh was directed to attack the Americans at Detroit. After defeating Maj. Gen. Isaac Brock, Tecumseh failed at the Siege of Fort Meigs. In 1813, the British retreated from Detroit and moved on to Niagara. Their communications broke down and severe desertions left 500 Indians facing 3,000 Americans at the Thames River. Tecumseh was killed, and the battle marked the turning point to the Indian resistance in the upper Midwest.[12]

Chapter Eighteen

Louisiana

State on April 30, 1812

Explorers and Settlers

European discovery of the area later known as Louisiana began in 1528 by Spanish explorer Panfilo de Narvaez when he discovered the mouth of the Mississippi River. He was followed in 1542 by Hernando de Soto, who explored the land to the north and western part of the future state and sailed down the Mississippi River to the Gulf of Mexico. It is somewhat surprising that further exploration did not occur for the next 140 years until the French extended their Canadian expeditions from the Great Lakes region to the Mississippi River Valley. In 1682, their famous explorer Robert de La Salle claimed the region for France and named it "Louisiane" in honor of their King Louis XIV. France quickly claimed both sides of the river and most of the territory stretching all the way into their existing holdings in Canada. In 1722, they moved their controlling government of the Illinois Country from Canada to Louisiana and regarded the entire region between the Alleghenies and the Rocky Mountains as theirs. They officially called most of that area "New France," which is clearly stated on maps published in Paris in the early 1700's. Because of administrative disputes between the two governments in Canada and Louisiana, Governor Vaudreuil established the boundaries between the two regions with Louisiana reaching into southern Indiana and the Upper Mississippi being under Canada's rule. This arrangement allowed French-controlled lands to further develop their fur trading empire which was not only profitable but also served to align France with the Native Americans who were their principal trading partners. The oldest permanent settlement in Louisiana was established in 1714 in Natchitoches. Its purposes were to trade with the Spanish in Texas and to keep them from advancing into Louisiana. The town quickly became an important crossroads and river port, where other commodities like sugar cane and cotton were traded. Plantations developed along the Mississippi and were replicated in New Orleans and as far north as Indiana, Illinois, and Missouri. Louisiana soon became one of the wealthiest territories in North America. In the 1720's, a large number of German immigrants settled along the Mississippi which became known as the "German Coast."[1]

The French and Indian War and the Seven Years' War had a major impact on the future development of Louisiana. By the Treaty of Paris of 1763, France was forced to cede not only Canada to Great Britain but all its American settlements. While most of its possessions east of the Mississippi River went to Great Britain, their portion west of the river went to Spain, but they were allowed to keep New Orleans. Even though Spain controlled much of Louisiana, thousands of French from Acadia (later Nova Scotia) settled there, and their descendants were known as Cajuns. According to the census of 1800, Louisiana had 19,852 free people and 24,264 slaves, many of whom were brought there by white settlers to work on the expanding number of plantations. Also in that year, Napoleon reacquired Louisiana from Spain through the Treaty of San Ildefonso with the hope of reestablishing a North American French Empire. However, that ambition was never realized, because he lost two-thirds of his army trying to quell the revolution in Saint-Domingue (later Haiti) in 1803. Following his defeat, Napoleon sold Louisiana to the United States, which quickly divided the region into the Territory of Orleans and the District of Louisiana. The West Florida parishes of the Republic of West Florida were annexed to the United States by President James Madison.

The American Revolution

A much-overlooked theater of the Revolutionary War was the campaign fought in Louisiana by Spain and her allies against the British. Although Louisiana was under Spanish rule at that time, they sought revenge against England for the losses they sustained in the Seven Years' War. Towards the end of that war, Spain had offered to help France in exchange for the Louisiana Territory west of the Mississippi River, including the city of New Orleans. Upon England's victory, Spain was forced to give up their holdings in East and West Florida to Great Britain under the terms of the Treaty of Paris of 1763. When the American Revolution started, Spain quickly came to the aid of the American rebels by obstructing British military efforts in the Gulf and the Mississippi River Valley. The Spanish were principally led by three men: Oliver Pollack, Luis Unzaga, and Bernardo de Galvez y Madrid. Pollack was born in Ireland and emigrated to Philadelphia in 1760, where he became a successful businessman. He then moved on to New Orleans, where he married an Irish immigrant and continued to build his personal fortune as one of the most prominent merchants in the city. Through his close relationships with local politicians, Pollack aligned with Governor Unzaga and helped to finance the American fight against the British. His first major success was in defeating the English in the Illinois campaign led by George Rogers Clark, who captured British forts and thwarted their efforts in the region. Pollock then joined with the next Louisiana Governor de Galvez to finance strengthening the Spanish forts along the Mississippi River until 1779, when Spain officially declared war against Great Britain. Galvez provided Pollock with Spanish ships for the American rebels who then defeated the British on Lake Pontchartrain in the first battle of the Revolutionary War that took place in Louisiana.

Prior to becoming governor of Louisiana, Galvez fought in Europe and Africa, studied in France, and taught at a highly respected military academy in Spain. In 1779, when Galvez secretly learned of a planned attack by England on

New Orleans, he recruited a collection of Cajuns, Creoles, German immigrants, free people of color, and a variety of others to join his Spanish army. He attacked Fort Bute 100 miles north of New Orleans, which prevented British access to the Mississippi River. He then marched to Baton Rouge and took the new British Fort Richmond with its many canons and several hundred soldiers, including German mercenaries and Loyalists. When the British surrendered, they also gave up Natchez. Galvez then set his sights on Mobile and received reinforcements at Mobile Bay from Havana. His forces totaled 1,500 men while the British had only 300 troops to defend Fort Charlotte. The British surrendered after sustaining a week of bombardment.

The capital of West Florida was Pensacola, which was protected by Fort George, 3,000 British regulars, 500 Native Americans, hundreds of German mercenaries, and hundreds of Loyalists. Once again, Galvez requested reinforcements from Havana and received Spanish and French troops, 300 Irishmen, a contingent of Afro-Cuban soldiers, and supplies from New Orleans. His army totaled over 8,000 men. While preparing to invade Pensacola, Galvez encountered three consecutive hurricanes and was attacked by Choctaw Indians, but he was soon relieved by the Creeks, who persuaded him to leave the Spanish alone. The first major event was the capture of Fort Charlotte, which was followed by an attack on Fort George. After two more days of assault after the nine-week siege, ending on May 10, 1781, the British surrendered. The battle proved to be the longest siege of the Revolutionary War and a decisive factor in its outcome. The British lost their power in the Gulf and were prevented from attacking the Americans from that region. Spain regained much of its lost North American territory while France accumulated more debt.[2]

The Louisiana Purchase

When Spain ceded their Louisiana holdings to France, it also instructed their agent in New Orleans to terminate the American use of New Orleans and its port warehouses. The move angered the Americans to the point of calling for war. President Jefferson was forced to resolve the issue and attempted a diplomatic solution by sending his friend James Monroe to join Robert Livingston in Paris for negotiations. Monroe was authorized to spend up to $10 million for the purchase of New Orleans and part of Florida and to secure United States access to the Mississippi River and its ports in New Orleans. However, before Monroe reached Paris, the French had prepared an offer that was quite different and totally unexpected. France's Minister of Finance, Francois de Barbe-Marbois, had convinced Napoleon that their Louisiana Colony was of limited value without Saint-Domingue (later Haiti), which they had just lost. Also, he advised Napoleon that they were not in a financial position to send an army to defend their North American holdings in the event of war with England, which was looming on the horizon. In April of 1803, on the day before Monroe's arrival in Paris, Foreign Minister Talleyrand informed Livingston that France was willing to sell all of Louisiana to the United States for $15 million. The land totaled 827,000 square miles, which would double the size of the United States. Spain was opposed to the sale, but being unable to militarily block it, returned their western portion of Louisiana to France in November. After months of deliberations, surveys of boundaries, studies, and negotiations with England and Spain, the sale was completed on December 30, 1803. The Louisiana Purchase provided enough land for the eventual establishment of 13 states or parts of states. These include Arkansas, Missouri, Iowa, Oklahoma, Kansas, Nebraska, part of Minnesota, part of North Dakota, part of South Dakota, a section of New Mexico, and parts of Montana and Wyoming.[3]

The Lewis and Clark Expedition

Shortly after the Louisiana Purchase, President Jefferson directed that the newly-acquired land should be explored and evaluated, and he appointed Capt. Meriwether Lewis and William Clark to organize a team for that purpose. In May of 1894, Lewis and Clark left from St. Louis, Missouri with their Corps of Discovery and headed for the Pacific Ocean at present-day Portland, Oregon. They would not return until September of 1806. Both men were experienced army officers who were charged to study the area's geography, animals, and plants as well as the Native American tribes of the region. An important objective was to diplomatically transition the area from their French and Spanish cultures to those of the United States. Knowing that America would be expanding westward, Jefferson wanted to discover a possible waterway that would reach to the West

Coast, usually referred to as the "Northwest Passage." The Corps of Discovery initially included 40-plus people for the initial part of the journey up to St. Louis, and then for the major expedition westward it would be reduced to 35 people. The Corps developed a formal protocol for introducing themselves to the Native Americans, most of whom had never seen a white man. They eventually would meet 50 different tribes and would present each of their chiefs with a peace medal showing the face of their new "white father," President Jefferson, and an engraving of two hands clasped in peace. After offering other goods as gifts, the Corps would march in a short parade and fire their weapons to the air, undoubtedly to demonstrate their superior power. The Corps included a man named York, Clark's black slave; Sacagawea, a Shoshone Indian woman; her husband, Toussaint Charbonneau, who served as guide and interpreter; and their infant son "Pomp." The "Permanent Party" of the Corps included 34 men and one woman, who started the trip from Fort Mandan, North Dakota to Fort Clatsop, Oregon. All the members were carefully vetted and chosen for their skills in hunting, craftsmanship, and interpreting. Of the 35 total, only eight were non-military.

The first part of the expedition started in St. Louis, Missouri, and from there, travelled north on the Missouri River through present-day Kansas City and Omaha. In August of 1804, Sergeant Charles Floyd died of appendicitis, and thereby became the first American soldier to die west of the Mississippi River. When they reached the edge of the Great Plains, they met their first tribe, the Yankton Sioux, who were peaceful and unlike their next tribe, the Teton Sioux, who were hostile and threatened to end the journey through their lands. The first winter was spent with the Mandan tribe in Washburn, North Dakota for four months, until April of 1805. They sent their first report to President Jefferson, in which they recorded 108 plant species and 68 mineral types. They continued on the Missouri River to the Continental Divide, where they switched to horseback at the Montana-Idaho border. In northern Idaho past the Rocky Mountains, they took canoes onto the Clearwater River to the Snake River, and then, to the Columbia River to present-day Portland. The Corps reached the Pacific Ocean in December of 1805 and constructed Fort Clatsop, where they camped for the winter. They started their return home at the end of March and arrived back in St. Louis on September 23, 1806. The expedition produced over 140 maps, recorded 100 animal species and more than 170 plants, and documented a great deal of the area's geology. They had received important information and help from the many tribes they encountered and noted only the Teton Sioux as hostile.[4] After their famous expedition, Lewis and Clark became prominent in public service. Lewis was appointed governor of the Louisiana Territory, and Clark served under him as superintendent of Indian Affairs. Lewis died in 1809 from unknown suspicious causes, and Clark replaced him as governor of the renamed Missouri Territory from 1813 to 1820, when it became a state. In 1822, Clark was appointed superintendent of Indian Affairs for the United States government. He was approached to serve as a United States senator but declined from entering electoral politics. He died in St. Louis in 1838 at age 68, having served the country for most of his life. His greatest legacy is the prose he wrote in the journal of his Lewis and Clark Expedition.[5]

Diversity of Cultures and Laws

Owing to its many different explorers and governments, Louisiana may be the most diverse state in the Union. From the early Spanish under de Soto in the 1500's to the French rule under La Salle in the late 1600's and then the English in the late 1700's, Louisiana was settled by many cultures and races. During the French and Indian War and the Seven Years' War, the British demanded the Acadians in Nova Scotia to renounce Catholicism and swear allegiance to the crown or face exile. Thousands chose exile and migrated to Louisiana and the Caribbean, where they were welcomed by the French, who were predominately Catholic. They established farms along the Mississippi River and in the southern parts of the territory. The immigrants were named "Cajuns," which derives from the French pronunciation of Acadian or "A-can-Jan." Their region encompasses 22 parishes from the Gulf Coast up to Alexandria in the central part of Louisiana. The unofficial capital of Acadiana is the city of Lafayette. The Cajun language is part French and part English, their cooking is unique with unusual seasonings, and their music is both melancholy and lively.[6]

Another distinctive culture that is an important part of Louisiana is known as "Creole." The name comes from the Portuguese "crioulo," which translates to "slave born in the master's household." Creoles are considered descendants of European settlers from France, Spain, and Portugal. In Louisiana, their ancestors were upper class whites, many of whom were plantation owners. They were Catholic and adopted mostly French cultural traits and the French language. French explorers and settlers dominated Louisiana in the 17th century until 1768, when France ceded Louisiana to Spain following the Seven Years' War. In spite of Spanish rule, the French culture continued to thrive and actually increased in the 1790's when Saint-Dominique rebelled to become the independent country of Haiti. At that time, the island had 450,000 black slaves, 45,000 whites, and 32,000 free people of color called "mulatto." The rebels defeated a strong 20,000-man Napoleon force, causing whites to flee to Cuba and New Orleans. In 1801, former slave Toussaint L'Ouverture assumed control of Saint-Dominique, which caused even more migration to Louisiana, doubling the population in that ten-year period. With the mix of French, Spanish, white, black, and mulatto races, the term "Creole" represented people of racially mixed parents as well as children of French or Spanish descent with no racial mixing. The Louisiana Purchase in 1803 brought even more immigrants from the West Indies, and soon they were calling themselves Creoles to distinguish themselves from Anglo-Americans, immigrants, and Africans. Today, Creole can refer to people of mixed blood, a dialect of French, a way of cooking, or even a style of architecture.[7]

Because of its diverse cultural background, Louisiana's legal system is quite different from the other 49 states. Private law, which is primarily contracts and torts, is based on French and Spanish codes as well as Roman law. Administrative law is similar to the United States federal government and other state laws. Procedural law is similar to other states and is based on Federal Rules of Civil Procedure. The Louisiana Civil Code was written in French in 1808, and this has led to the mistaken belief that it was based on the Napoleonic Code. Recent historians have found the 1808 authors' notes stating they based their civil code on Spanish law, without any reference to the Napoleonic Code. Current Louisiana Civil Code incorporates 3,556 code articles, mostly from Spanish laws as well as old French law preceding the Napoleonic Code.[8]

Statesmen, Leaders and Heroes

Rene-Robert Cavelier, sieur de La Salle was born in Rouen, France in 1643. He was educated at a Jesuit college, but at the age of 23, he abandoned studies for the priesthood and moved to Canada to seek adventure and exploration. He first acquired a land grant in western Montreal and established a fur trading post. His frequent contact with Indian fur traders allowed him to learn a number of Native American dialects as well as new frontiers to the south. After three years in Montreal he sold his lands and left to explore the Ohio Territory. He befriended Count de Frontenac, the governor of New France, and together they extended French power on Lake Ontario and fur trading to the east with the Dutch and English. They built Fort Frontenac, and with the support of the governor and King Louis XIV, he was appointed a seigneur in 1675, thereby achieving a title of nobility. In 1677, he received the king's authority to explore the western part of New France, to build as many forts as possible, and to maintain French domination of the buffalo hide trade. The business required a great deal of cash, which La Salle borrowed in Paris and Montreal, but his debts continued to mount and came to plague him for the rest of his life. His business goal was to ship cargo to the Gulf of Mexico by using the Illinois, Ohio, and Mississippi Rivers. He built the sailing vessels with his new partner, Henri de Tonty, and drove his men exceedingly hard. After several failed attempts, they found the juncture of the Illinois and Mississippi Rivers and sailed down to the Gulf. In 1682, La Salle claimed the entire Mississippi Basin for France and named it "Louisiane" in honor of King Louis XIV. The next year, he built Fort Saint Louis on the Illinois River and developed a colony for several thousand Native Americans. He asked for help from Quebec, but the new governor was opposed to La Salle's work and ordered him to surrender the fort. La Salle appealed directly to the king, who directed the Quebec government to make full restitution to La Salle. In spite of his vision, courage, and tenacity, La Salle had a number of detractors who greatly disliked his arrogance and pride. Even the Jesuits were upset with him, because their missionary work with the natives in the North and the fur trading there were adversely affected by La Salle's activities in the East and South. His final expedition was to create a new French Empire in the Gulf with the invasion of a section of Mexico. The plan had the support of the king, but due to piracy, shipwrecks, miscalculations, quarrels, and lack of leadership, it failed. La Salle died in 1687 at age 44, at the hands of his own men. He is buried near Huntsville, Texas.[9]

Bernardo Vicente Apolmar de Galvez was born in Spain in 1746 into a military family. At the age of 16, he fought against Portugal in Europe in the Seven Years' War and in the French and Indian War in North America. He next saw action in New Spain, where he fought the Apaches, and then in North Africa, where he was badly wounded. In 1776, Galvez was appointed governor of Spanish Louisiana which encompassed an enormous region from the Gulf to Canada and the Mississippi River to the Rockies. We have already noted his military exploits in the American Revolution, having defeated the British in Baton Rouge, Natchez, Mobile, and Pensacola. He led soldiers from Spain, France, and Germany as well as Native Americans, Irish, and Italians. He commanded whites, blacks, and mulattos from Cuba, Mexico, and the Caribbean. He proved to be the right man, in the right place, at the right time. His timely assistance to the American rebels earned him the epithet "Hero of the Revolutionary War." George Washington acknowledged his great accomplishments and invited him to be alongside him in a July 4th parade. He died in 1786 at age 40 in Mexico City. His legacy includes Galveston, Texas and Galveston, Louisiana. He is honored in our nation's capital, where he sits astride his horse in a bronze statue at Virginia and 22nd streets.[10]

Chapter Nineteen

INDIANA

State on December 11, 1816

Settlers

The state of Indiana is appropriately named owing to the domination, size and number of Native American tribes who occupied the region for thousands of years. However, the area came to be significant when the French, led by their famous explorer Jacques Cartier, discovered the St. Lawrence River in the 1530's and established settlements throughout the Great Lakes. The French built forts for protection and developed a major fur trading empire throughout southeast Canada and the Ohio and Mississippi River Valleys. By 1600, there were two major native groups in the Indiana area—the Algonquians and the Iroquois. The Algonquians included the tribes of the Miami, Delaware, Potawatomi, Kickapoo, and Shawnee. The largest by far was the Miami tribe. In the mid-1600's, the Algonquians were challenged by the Iroquois for supremacy and control of the fur trade, a conflict that evolved into the

Beaver Wars and lasted for close to 50 years. For centuries, Europeans bought their furs from Russia and Scandinavia, but North American furs became an important new source in the 17th century. The Iroquois were supported and armed by their Dutch and English trading partners on the eastern side of the Great Lakes, while the Algonquians were backed by their French partners to the south and west of Lake Ontario. The Beaver Wars pitted tribes fighting for domination of the fur trade against each other, and they were savage and widespread and consisted of a series of wars over a 50-year period that displaced many tribes, groups, and clans who left the Midwest to avoid the violence and bloodshed. The Iroquois dominated the trade for a while, but when the English acquired the Dutch settlements in the 1760's, they lost their Dutch allies of the New Netherlands Colony and became close trading partners with the English. This proved to be a very significant event, as it formed the basis of the English claim to the area between the Appalachian Mountains and the Mississippi River, an area which, in 1783, was to become the Northwest Territory that England ceded to the United States in the Treaty of Paris ending the American Revolutionary War. It was an enormous piece of land that the Americans had not expected to receive, and it was to become very controversial over the next 25 years. This subject is discussed further below and in the Ohio chapter.[1]

The English attempted to align themselves with the Iroquois, not only for their fur trading but also to have them serve as a buffer against French expansion. When the English began colonizing western Pennsylvania, they encroached on Iroquois territory and caused the Indians to regard them as more of a threat than the French. At the same time, French policy began to change toward the Iroquois, who were regarded as indomitable. France befriended them to retain their control of the fur trade and to have them block increasing English expansion. The result was the "Great Peace of Montreal," which was signed in 1701 by 39 Indian chiefs and the French. The Treaty put a stop to the Iroquois savaging settlers and allowed thousands of tribe refugees to return to their homelands. The Shawnee resumed control of the Ohio Territory, and the Miami returned to control the Indiana Territory and the northwestern part of Ohio. The Pottawatomie went to Michigan and the Illinois tribe to Illinois. The Iroquois believed they achieved the balance of power between the French and English. The peace lasted 20 years and allowed the Iroquois to build a much stronger nation with better education and more advanced farming techniques.[2]

The Battle of Vincennes

At the end of January in 1779, British Lieutenant Governor Henry Harrison left his stronghold in Fort Detroit to retake Fort Vincennes in present-day Indiana. When American Lieutenant Col. George Rogers Clark was informed, he immediately organized about 170 men for a surprise attack in the middle of winter when fighting rarely occurred. About half of his men were French-Canadian volunteers who were sympathetic to the American cause. Clark felt a sense of urgency, because in the spring, he believed, the British would be pursuing further gains in the territory. Clark left on February 5, 1779 for a 180-mile march over land and icy water. They built canoes to cross swollen rivers choked with ice. Moving without food for days, Clark faced possible desertions, but his own confidence for success kept his men together throughout many hardships. They marched in water up to their shoulders, and just before reaching Fort Sackville (Vincennes), they crossed a flooded plain four miles wide. They captured a local sympathizer to send a message to the townspeople, instructing them to stay indoors to avoid being harmed. Clark's ploy worked as no one dared to go outside to warn British Commander Hamilton. Locals supplied Clark's army with dry gunpowder, arms, and food. When the town was secured, they commenced attacking the fort. Clark's men captured six of the enemy, and after releasing two of them, the other four were marched to the front of the fort in plain sight of the British. When Hamilton refused to surrender, the four prisoners were executed by tomahawk as an example to the British defenders. Hamilton then surrendered and signed the necessary papers. Clark and his 74men captured Vincennes and Fort Sackville without the loss of one man. Clark was recognized as a great hero, and his legacy abounds in the Midwest with statues and schools named in his honor. (See Kentucky for more about Clark). Virginia had made claim to the territory, but in 1781, they agreed to give it to the United States government, and the lands became part of the Northwest Territory.[3]

The Battle of Fallen Timbers

The Treaty of Paris of 1783 ending the Revolutionary War required Great Britain to withdraw its troops from American soil, which included the land between the Appalachian Mountains and the Mississippi River, which came to be known as the Northwest Territory. However, the British did not comply with those terms, and instead they manned their former forts and supplied Indian tribes with arms and supplies to attack and murder American settlers. These practices continued into the early 1790's, and in 1791, President Washington sent General Harmar and then General St. Clair to rid the territory of the native tribes. Both attempts failed with severe American losses. Finally, Washington resolved the problem in 1793 by ordering Gen. Anthony Wayne to organize a large new army named the "Legion of the United States." Wayne was a war hero, having fought in a number of battles and at Yorktown, which was the last major battle of the war. After the fighting, he went on to Georgia to negotiate treaties with the Creeks and the Cherokees. He had earned the epithet "Mad Anthony Wayne" for his brave and daring battles during the war. The problem in the Northwest Territory was the Native Americans who believed the British had no right to cede their lands, because the natives had no representation at the treaty negotiations, and any such treaty would require their consent. The United States government disagreed and believed they had won the land through their defeat of the British occupiers and combatants. Under Chief Tecumseh, the natives formed an alliance composed of several Indian nations that believed they had the ability to defend the region as they had done against Harmar and St. Clair. Some peace negotiations were attempted, but their delays and failures allowed both sides to prepare for war. Wayne amassed a professional army of 5,000 men, which he trained for two years. The Native American forces totaled 1,500 warriors composed of Shawnee, Delaware, Miami, Wyandot, Ojibwa, Ottawa, Potawatomi, Mingo, and a British Company of militiamen. Wayne swiftly and easily defeated the Indians, and the victory led to the Jay Treaty of 1795, with the British removing their troops from the frontier forts, and the Treaty of Greenville in 1795 with the Native Americans, who ceded lands in the Ohio and Indiana territories, thereby paving the way for future statehoods.[4]

The Battle of Tippecanoe

In 1808, two Shawnee brothers, Tecumseh and Tenskwatawa, left Ohio to start a new town at the juncture of the Wabash and Tippecanoe Rivers. It was named "Prophets Town" and was intended to become the capital of the Indian Confederacy. The goal was to unite many Indian tribes in order to defend against further incursions by white settlers into lands they had occupied for thousands of years. The town served as a center for combat training and cultural events and grew to about 1,000 warriors. Nearby settlers were alarmed at the growing strength of the Confederacy, so the governor of the territory, Gen. William Henry Harrison, formed an army of 1,000 men for the purpose of destroying Prophets Town. Harrison arrived there in November of 1811, and being wary of some treachery by the inhabitants, he camped about a mile away and arranged a meeting for possible peace discussions. While Tecumseh was away on a recruiting trip, his brother led an attack on the sleeping American soldiers in spite of explicit instructions from Tecumseh not to engage in any hostilities until the Confederacy became stronger. The soldiers fended off the surprise attack but not before losing 62 dead and 126 wounded. The defeated Indians were demoralized and left Prophets Town, which Harrison then burned to the ground. Tecumseh's Confederacy never recovered from the defeat, and Harrison claimed a great victory, which he later used to promote his successful presidential campaign in 1840 with the song "Tippecanoe and Tyler Too." The newspapers had carried very little about the battle, but when they picked up on it,Congress became enraged, accusing the British of interfering in American affairs. Also, Tecumseh was furious with his brother for starting the fight, and he was stripped of his authority. There were many conflicting accounts of the battle, but it did hasten the start of the War of 1812 with England. Tecumseh rebuilt his Confederacy and joined the British. Half of the British army that captured Detroit was composed of Tecumseh's warriors. Finally, upon Tecumseh's death at the Battle of the Thames in Ontario in 1813, the Tecumseh Confederacy no longer threatened the United States.[5]

European Control

In 1679, French explorer Robert Cavalier, Sieur de La Salle came to the area of the Kankakee River, where he claimed present-day Indiana for France. Two years later, he negotiated a treaty uniting the Illinois and Miami nations against the Iroquois, who were challenging all other tribes for control of the Indiana region. La Salle's goal was to establish a trading route between Canada and the Gulf of Mexico using a series of smaller rivers that connected with the Mississippi River, which continued all the way to New Orleans. In his quest, he claimed much of the lands he crossed for France, and thereby enlarged "New France" in the middle of the American Midwest. The French built trading posts and forts along the way including Fort Wayne, Lafayette, and Vincennes. They brought Jesuit missionaries to convert the natives to Christianity. The Jesuits brought the Marists, who also educated and preached to the Indians with whom they lived, hunted, and assimilated. Unlike the British, the French missionaries and settlers interacted with the natives but did not attempt to remove them from the land. In fact, the missionaries played a key role in developing close ties with the Indian tribes. By 1750, the French had expanded into the eastern Ohio and western Pennsylvania region as far as present-day Pittsburgh, until the English challenged them for occupying territory that belonged to them under the Royal Charter granted to the Virginia Company in 1606 by King James I. It was a young George Washington who, in 1752, volunteered to advise the French of their incursion, which then led to the French and Indian War which primarily was a British-American War against France and her Indian allies that expanded into the Seven Years' War. The Treaty of Paris of 1763 marked the beginning of British control of most former French colonies, including all of eastern Canada. The British expelled the Catholic missionaries, and many of the French settlers left the region even though the British allowed them to stay and continue with their fur and trading activities. In 1768, the British signed a treaty with the Iroquois and purchased their territorial land claims. The vehicle used to transfer the claims was the newly formed Indiana Land Company, which was the first recorded use of the name "Indiana." Virginia objected to the transfer of ownership because of their Royal Charter. The 13 colonies objected, because they fought with the British and therefore believed the land belonged to them.

However, that ownership lasted only 20 years until 1783 and the Treaty of Paris that ended the American Revolution and prompted the ceding of the Northwest Territory to the United States.

American Control

The ceded land between the Appalachian Mountains, the Mississippi River, the Great Lakes, and the Ohio River was formally established by the Confederation Congress in July of 1787 as the Northwest Territory. At that time, there were only two American settlements there–Vincennes and Clark's Grant, and the non-native "European" population was just under 5,000 people. In 1800, the Indiana Territory was officially formed, as was the Ohio Territory, which had begun the process toward statehood. The Supreme Court had dissolved the Indiana Land Company in 1798, but the name "Indiana" was retained to reflect the vast number of Indians who occupied the northern region. William Henry Harrison was appointed the first governor and served from 1800 to 1813. The first capital was in Vincennes and was moved in 1813 to Corydon. In 1809, the territory was permitted to vote its legislature for the first time. In accordance with Article 6 of the Northwest Ordinance, slavery was prohibited even though settlers from the South did bring some slaves with them. Blacks were free and entitled to vote. By 1816, the census showed a population of 63,897, which qualified for statehood. Their Constitutional Convention was held in June of that year, elections were held in August, and Congress approved statehood in November. Jonathan Jennings was elected president of the Convention, which included delegates Dennis Pennington, Davis Floyd, and William Hendricks. They all supported a ban on slavery which was incorporated in their constitution. Existing slaves remained in bondage, and free blacks were discouraged from immigration. Jennings was elected their first governor and then served in the state legislature for 18 years. As the population grew in the north, the capital was moved to Indianapolis in 1825.[6]

Statesmen, Leaders and Heroes

Jonathan Jennings was born in 1784 to Jacob and Mary Kennedy Jennings. Both parents were well-educated, Jacob being a medical doctor and a Presbyterian minister and Mary being a practicing physician with her husband. Around 1790, the family moved from New Jersey to Pennsylvania. Two years later, Mary died and left Jonathan to be raised and schooled by several of his five older siblings. He then studied law in Washington, Pennsylvania, and in 1806, moved to Steubenville, Ohio, where he assisted with his brother's law practice. In 1807, he moved to Vincennes, Indiana, where he opened his own law firm. With too few clients, Jennings changed his career to land speculation while serving as assistant to the clerk of the territorial legislature. In that same year, he was appointed clerk of the Vincennes University board of trustees while its president was William Henry Harrison, who was also Governor of the Indiana Territory. Harrison was a politically powerful man, and while serving on the University board, he and Jennings were opposed on several issues, causing Jennings to resign in 1808, realizing that Harrison's domination of western Indiana would be impossible to overcome. He then settled in Charlestown in Clark County, Indiana where his policies were more in line with the people there, particularly on the issue of slavery and his support of the abolitionists. That same year, a resignation in the legislature allowed Jennings to run for the opening. Harrison backed one of his favorites, Thomas Randolph, who was the attorney general for the territory. Jennings campaigned vigorously with his anti-slavery policy and won the seat. Randolph challenged the close election, and the House Committee called for a reelection, which Jennings won by a large margin. Jennings was an active delegate and frequently opposed Governor Harrison. He was reelected in 1811, 1812, and 1814. He strongly opposed Harrison's pro-slavery stand and accused him of improper personal gains while in office. He also cited suspicious land investments and inciting tensions with the Native Americans. He even wrote to President Madison, arguing against Harrison's reappointment as governor, but administration friends of Harrison secured his reappointment. In 1811, Jennings successfully won pensions for veterans, widows, and orphans of the Battle of Tippecanoe, even though his constituents blamed Harrison for the needless loss of life. Harrison was commissioned a general and went off to fight in the War of 1812. During his absence from government, Jennings assumed an active role in pursuing statehood for Indiana. Waiting for the war to end, he introduced a petition in 1815 for statehood. He was opposed by Harrison's successor,

Thomas Posey, on the grounds of insufficient tax revenues to financially support a government. President Madison ignored the plea and signed the petition. The Convention was held in June of 1816, and Jennings's friend and fellow delegate Dennis Pennington was able to gain the election of other anti-slavery delegates. The adopted constitution was modeled after those of Kentucky and Ohio. Slavery was banned, but indentured servants' contracts were preserved. After the Convention, Jennings ran for governor and was elected in 1816.[7]

William Hendricks was born in Pennsylvania in 1782 to Abraham and Ann Jamison Hendricks. His father was a prominent politician and a member of the state legislature. William attended public school in Ligonier Valley, Pennsylvania, where he was a classmate of his future good friends and advisors Jonathan Jennings and William Wick. Hendricks went on to Jefferson College (later Washington and Jefferson College). After graduation in 1810, he moved to Ohio and studied law in his brother's law office in Cincinnati and was admitted to the bar in 1812. The next year, he moved to Madison, Indiana, where he set up a printing press and started the *Western Edge* newspaper, which was the second paper in the Indiana Territory after the *Vincennes Sun*. Hendricks used his paper to promote his political beliefs, and he developed a large following in eastern Indiana while he opposed the views of the *Vincennes Sun*, which reflected those in western Indiana, especially on the issue of slavery. In 1813, Hendricks was elected clerk of the legislature in Vincennes, where he was chosen to publish the Assembly's records. The following year, he was elected as a representative for Jefferson County in his home town of Madison. Once there, he befriended Dennis Pennington and his anti-slavery followers. He soon succeeded Pennington and became Speaker of the Assembly. He then started his own law practice and was appointed prosecutor for several eastern counties. President Madison selected him to be the United States attorney general for the Indiana Territory. In 1816, he was an unofficial delegate to the Constitutional Convention and had become so well respected that he was asked to serve as the Convention secretary. Hendricks was elected to the 14th, 15th, and 16th Congresses, resigning in 1822 to run for governor. He succeeded Jennings and focused on restoring Indiana's poor financial condition. He also was responsible for building roads, canals, and the first state-funded school system in the country. He supported the construction of the State Seminary, which became Indiana University. He created the Indiana Code, which codified the state's laws for the first time. In 1824, he signed the bill which moved the capital from Corydon to sparsely-populated Indianapolis, in spite of strong opposition. In 1825, he resigned to become a United States senator. He promoted statehood for Illinois and Missouri and was regarded as the most popular politician in the state. He died in 1850 at age 68, having served the public for 29 years.[8]

Dennis Pennington was born in 1776 in Cumberland County, Virginia to Edward and Elizabeth English Pennington. The family moved to the Kentucky frontier, where they befriended Henry Clay and supported his efforts to make Kentucky a "Free State." In 1804, they moved to Clarksville, Indiana, where they purchased land from George Rogers Clark, four miles north of the capital city of Corydon. Prior to their moves, the Penningtons had met politicians and important leaders in Ohio who were responsible for adopting anti-slavery policies. In spite of Governor Harrison's pro-slavery positions, the Penningtons were more influenced by the anti-slavery arguments of Jennings, St. Clair, and Worthington. In 1807, Governor Harrison was close to having slavery legalized, but Dennis Pennington condemned the institution in open conflict with Harrison. In 1809, Indiana created a bicameral legislature, with the Lower House elected by popular vote and the Upper House appointed by the governor from candidates selected by the Lower House. The change reduced the governor's power. Pennington and many of his fellow anti-slavery representatives were elected by wide margins. That same year, Pennington wrote the resolution to move the capital from Vincennes to Corydon, citing the threat posed by Indian attacks and possible destruction of valuable records. In 1816, Delegate Pennington took a leading position at the Constitutional Convention in having slavery banned from the state. He became the first speaker of the state senate and served for four terms as well as serving in the Lower House for three terms. In the 1830's and 1840's, Pennington strongly opposed the Mammoth Internal Improvement Act, arguing that the costs would bankrupt the state. His predictions were accurate with the state losing $10 million, which was equivalent to 15 years of tax revenues. His last public service was his ten years on the Board of Trustees of Indiana University. He died in 1854 at 78 years old.[9]

As for Indiana's greatest hero, one must consider that person to be George Rogers Clark. In spite of all his sacrifices and personal expenses on behalf of the Indiana Territory and in the Revolutionary War, he was never compensated by the state or the United States government. His daring exploits were far-removed from the East, where his successes were unknown or appreciated. He was slandered by men who only sought personal gain and power. His last 15 years were spent on the frontier in a two-room cabin, after having fought for thousands of acres for the United States in the Northwest Territory. At his funeral in 1818, Judge John Rowan said, "The mighty oak of the forest has fallen, and now the scrub oaks may sprout all around...the Father of the Western Country is no more."[10]

Chapter Twenty

Mississippi

State on December 10, 1817

Explorers and Settlers

The name "Mississippi" derives from the Ojibwa Indian word "Misi-Sipi," which translates to "Great River." The name was first given to the river, and then to the territory, and then to the state. For thousands of years, the Mississippi River Valley was home to the "Five Civilized Nations" of the southeastern United States: The Cherokee, Chickasaw, Creek, Choctaw, and Seminole. These were considered civilized by the early European settlers, because they adopted many of the key European customs such as literacy, centralized government, written constitutions, market participation, and intermarriage with the white settlers. They were descendants of the Mississippian culture which flourished in the 800-1500 A.D. period. Other tribes who occupied the area included the Natchez, Yazoo, Pascagoula, and Biloxi. However, their culture vanished by the time of the first European explorers from Spain and France, who traded with them.[1]

Mississippi developed in much the same manner as Louisiana, on the western side of the Mississippi River, with a great diversity of races and cultures that emigrated from Europe, the Caribbean, and North America. The first to arrive was the Spaniard Hernando de Soto in 1540, with his discovery of the Mississippi River. However, he was an explorer and not a settler in the way the French and English were. While de Soto claimed territories for Spain, the settlements were relatively small and weak and could not be sustained by the mother country. This was partly due to the lack of exportable products or natural resources. Also, some historians believe Spain's loss of their Atlantic Ocean dominance in 1588, by the British victory over the Spanish Armada, may have had a direct and lasting impact on Spanish exploration and colonization. Close to 150 years passed before exploration was resumed in the Mississippi River Basin, and this time it was the French who were expanding their New France from lower Canada, down the Ohio River, and on to the Gulf via the Mississippi River. Their noted explorer Robert de la Salle claimed new territories for France along the way, culminating in the Louisiana and Mississippi region as belonging to France. In 1699, Pierre La Moyne d'Iberville established Fort Maurepas in Old Biloxi (presently Ocean Springs). In 1716, the French founded Fort Rosalie (presently Natchez) on the Mississippi River, which became a large trading post and the first capital of the future state. The French Catholic missionaries developed seven major parishes (districts/counties) in present-day Louisiana and two in present-day Alabama, all of which were incorporated into New France.

French domination of the American Midwest suddenly ended with the Treaty of Paris in 1763, when France succumbed to England in the French and Indian and Seven Years' Wars. All of their North American colonies were ceded to Great Britain from Canada to the Gulf of Mexico, with Spain receiving western portions of the lower Mississippi River Basin. This resulted in a population of mixed races and cultures that expanded beyond the French and Spanish to include black slaves, free blacks, and free people of color from the Caribbean, West Indies, Cuba, and Canada, thereby creating Creoles and Cajuns. Whites frequently mixed with black women and their descendants and intermarried, so a third culture called "mulatto" took root. British rule lasted only 20 years until American independence in 1783 ushered in a new wave of immigrants who quickly settled along the Mississippi River and Gulf Coast to take advantage of river trade and access to the Atlantic Ocean. However, the key attraction was the fertile land and a climate suitable for the growth of cotton. This was particularly appealing to tobacco planters in Virginia, Georgia, and the Carolinas whose land had been depleted of nutrients by the tobacco leaf. Cotton-growing land was cheap, and cotton prices were high. Migration to the Mississippi Territory was explosive, growing from 9,000 in 1798 to 220,000 in 1820, with the majority of the new inhabitants being African-American slaves.

Cotton

In 1793, Eli Whitney invented the first mechanical cotton gin (short for "engine"), and he had no idea of its far-reaching consequences. For cotton to be made into cloth, the seeds have to be removed from the lint fibers. This is a labor-intensive process that requires a full ten-hour day to produce a pound of useable fiber material. In contrast, two or three slaves using a cotton gin could produce 50 pounds of cotton a day. The effects of this vastly-increased productivity were enormous. Plantations sprang up throughout the Mississippi Territory, and fortunes were quickly realized, considering the very low cost of slave labor. The local and regional economies boomed as the ports of New Orleans, Mobile, Galveston, and Charleston became major trading centers. Cotton production in the United States grew from 750,000 bales in 1830 to 2.85 million bales in 1850. The population of the Mississippi Territory exploded from 7,000 in 1800 to 606,526 by 1850.[2] The dynamic growth occurred after Pinckney's Treaty of 1795 with Spain. During the prior 12 years, Spain had controlled use of the Mississippi River and used that power as a political tool in their dealings with the United States. They not only interfered with American shipping, but they also greatly restricted and sometimes prohibited American use of the great river. The Louisiana Purchase from France in 1803 enabled Americans to control more of the river, and finally in 1810, the settlers in the Spanish colony of West Florida (the "Panhandle") rebelled, declaring their freedom from Spain. President Madison announced that the land from the Mississippi River to the Perdido River, encompassing most of West Florida, was to be annexed to the United States under terms included in the Louisiana Purchase.[3]

The world-wide demand for cotton created a major increase in black slavery. Until 1793,

manumission had brought about a reduction in the percentage of slaves–to around 13 percent of the population, and therefore, a belief that the practice of slavery would continue to diminish. This dramatically changed with the introduction of the cotton gin. The need for manual labor to plant and harvest cotton increased the call for more slaves. In 1790, there were 700,000 slaves in America, and by 1850 they totaled 3.2 million. In 1790, there were six slave states, and in 1860 there were 15 slave states, and one in three Southerners was a slave. That growth is even more startling, considering that Congress forbid the importation of slaves in 1808 as agreed at the 1787 Constitutional Convention.[4]

Cotton production sparked the start of the American Industrial Revolution and soon replaced tobacco as the country's major export. Demand came from the textile mills in England and spurred the construction of American mills in New England. It came to be known as "King Cotton" because of its wealth creation, not only in Mississippi but in other southern states and New England. The cotton gin went through several developmental stages whereby its size was increased and wooden parts were replaced by metal parts for greater strength and longevity. The cultivation of cotton led to more land purchases and increased land values and speculation for more plantations. Financial organizations and investors shifted away from low return investors to those who were cotton-related, where prices were rising together with operating margins and returns were realized in a shorter period. All of this started before Whitney's cotton gin and continued throughout the 19th century. By 1860, the American South was producing two-thirds of the world's cotton supply. Due to its need for cheap labor, cotton was directly responsible for the increase in slavery. This, in turn, has been cited as a leading cause of the American Civil War. The threat of slavery prohibition weighed heavily on the South's economy and certainly influenced their decision to secede from the Union.

The growth of the cotton industry had a profound effect on the Native Americans who had been settled in the Southeast for hundreds and even thousands of years. During the Washington, Adams, and Jefferson administrations, the policy of acculturation was favored, because it was considered more humane for the natives to learn a second culture rather than to be forced to abandon their own customs. It was expected that, over time, this would lead to assimilation with the European-American cultures. Indians were encouraged to speak English and adopt new practices, such as private land ownership and other western practices. Settlers moving to the region were instructed to respect the rights of Native Americans, especially their homelands. The major five Indian tribes were to remain east of the Mississippi River and were expected to develop an agriculturally-based society. However, this changed in the early 1800's with the population explosion and the growing appetite for land. The problem came to a head in 1830 with the Indian Removal Act, which was proposed by President Andrew Jackson. He divided the land west of the Mississippi River into districts for Indian tribes as compensation for the lands they had to leave, and they could keep the new lands forever. Prior to the Act, in the Johnson v. M'Intosh case, the Supreme Court decided that Indians could only occupy land within the United States, but they could not hold title. Jackson opposed Washington's policy of treating Indian tribes as sovereign nations. He based this on Article 4, Section 3 of the Constitution, which stated that the creation of state jurisdictions violated state sovereignty. Jackson believed that he could allow Indian self-rule only on federal lands, which meant those which he had just created west of the Mississippi River. The Removal Act had an important impact on Georgia, which had claimed all the land from the Atlantic Ocean to the Mississippi River, including most of Mississippi. The Act was very controversial and was strongly opposed in the North. Jackson responded that they were being hypocritical because of how they had driven northern tribes to extinction and how tribal law had been replaced by state law. To him, the demise of the Indian nations was inevitable. He thought that transferring the natives was the only humane method of preserving their culture. If they had to remain in existing states, a fate similar to those in the North would follow. The Act started the removal of tens of thousands of Indians to the West. Although it was voluntary, the first to leave were the Choctaws of Mississippi, who ceded lands east of the Mississippi River in exchange for payment and new western lands. The next were the Cherokee from Georgia, who had ceded their claimed Mississippi land to the United States government in 1802. The Seminoles and several other tribes resisted the move and fought the United States in a Second Seminole War from 1835 to 1842. Most of the Indians eventually moved to the West, and those who elected to stay received citizenship.[5]

Road to Statehood

Before the Mississippi Territory became a state in 1817, it was preceded by close to 250 years of exploration with internal and external conflict. Although it was first discovered by the Spanish in 1540, the dominant force came from the French in Canada, whose ambitions were to develop their New France in the American Midwest. Starting in the late 1600's, New France grew from the Great Lakes to the Gulf of Mexico, but certain obstacles prevented them from achieving a permanent foothold in North America: 1) the Spanish who first arrived in 1540 and claimed much of it was theirs; 2) the English colonies who believed it belonged to them; 3) the French and Indian War, in which France was forced to cede their holdings to Great Britain; 4) the North American Indians who had occupied the region for over a thousand years; 5) the American Revolution, which won all the English lands south of Canada; 6) the Louisiana Purchase in 1803, which eliminated all remaining French interests in continental North America and 7) the War of 1812, which sorted out land boundaries and ownership in the Gulf region of the United States.

During the early years of the American Republic, it was the policy of Presidents Washington, Adams, and Jefferson to stay clear of frictions between France, England, and Spain in the Mississippi Territory. When the opportunity arose in 1795 to resolve Spanish claims along the Gulf Coast, President Washington sent Thomas Pinckney to Madrid to negotiate the Treaty of San Lorenzo, which defined the Spanish colony of West Florida (the "Panhandle") together with the ceding of their remaining lands east of the Mississippi River to the United States. The treaty also allowed the United States to freely navigate the Mississippi River. This was followed in 1798 by organizing the Mississippi Territory from lands in present-day Alabama and Mississippi. The territory was enlarged in 1804, after Georgia had abandoned its claim to most of Mississippi in 1802 to the United States government. The Mississippi Territory was enlarged again in 1812, when the United States annexed the western part of West Florida, thereby giving the territory a large section of land directly on the Gulf of Mexico. Spain complained about the move, but the United States justified the annexation under terms of the Louisiana Purchase and sent Gen. James Wilkinson with a military detachment to protect its interests there. The Spanish did not resist them. In 1817, the Mississippi Territory was split into two equal parts, with the future state of Mississippi on the west and the future Alabama to the east. Both sections experienced two waves of immigration—the first in 1798 and the second from 1815 to 1819. Most of the settlers came from Georgia, the Carolinas, and Virginia. Cheap land was only one of the attractions. Other incentives were the fast-diminishing number of Indian land titles as they moved west, improved roads and new access to the Gulf.[6]

The War of 1812

Sometimes referred to as part of the "Napoleonic Wars" and sometimes as the "Second American War of Independence," the War of 1812 between the United States and Great Britain lasted for three years. It was declared by President James Madison after many years of British hostility toward American trade restrictions, the impressment of approximately 10,000 American merchant seamen into the Royal navy, and the British attempt to establish a buffer Indian state in the Midwest by allying with Native Americans to impede American westward expansion. The three major theaters of conflict were the Atlantic seacoast, the Great Lakes, and the southern United States and Gulf region. Britain fought mostly a defensive war for two years, and when they defeated Napoleon in 1814, they were able to intensify their efforts in North America. After burning Washington, D.C. and many northeastern towns, they were repulsed in Baltimore and New York in 1814, which led to peace negotiations. Both countries wanted to end the conflict, but fighting continued in the Gulf where America defeated the British in the Battle of New Orleans. Although the war brought no boundary changes in the North, there were some significant changes in the South with regard to Native American tribes who had allied with the British. Indian Chief Tecumseh made valiant efforts to create an Indian Confederation, but even with British military support, he was defeated, thereby ending British and native interference with American settlers in that region. However, during the War of 1812 the Creek Nation in the Mississippi, present-day Alabama, and Georgia region erupted into a civil war that forced the United States into the conflict. The flash point was an attack on the Americans on Fort Mimms in West Florida, where an overwhelming force of Red Stick Creeks killed 400settlers. The warriors were mainly Upper Creeks whereas the Lower Creeks remained friendly with the United States. The attack caused The Mississippi and Georgia militias to join forces, accompanied by Lower Creeks and Cherokees. Soon North and South Carolina sent troops, and under Gen. John Floyd, a combined army of 5,000 men attacked the Creek homeland in a series of battles. Tennessee then came into the conflict under Maj. Gen. Andrew Jackson, who defeated the Creeks at Horseshoe Bend and then went on to defeat the English and Spanish at Pensacola in West Florida.[7]

In late 1814, Jackson with his army of 5,000 men moved to New Orleans. On January 8, 1815, British Gen. Edward Packenham with 8,000 men attacked New Orleans, but they failed to take it, thereby making Jackson a national hero, which started him on the road to the presidency. Although several battles were fought in early 1815, the Treaty of Ghent ending the war had been signed in December of 1814. Historians have disagreed about who won the war. The Treaty's main points were: 1) all occupied territory should be returned, 2) the pre-war boundary between Canada and the United States should be restored, and 3) the Americans should have fishing rights in the St. Lawrence Gulf. The treaty made no mention of American maritime rights or the ending of impressment. The Indian threat was ended, and Americans felt satisfied about their military victories. The British claimed to be the winner because they prevented the United States from capturing Canada, but the Americans responded by maintaining that they had no intention of seizing Canada. Americans believed they won, because they removed the British and Indian obstacles to their westward expansion into the Northwest Territories. The real losers in the war were the Native American Indians who lost their Creek War with the Treaty of Fort Jackson in 1814. They were forced to cede 23 million acres in present-day Alabama and southern Georgia without compensation. The land amounted to two-thirds of present-day Alabama and much of lower Georgia. The Alabama lands were merged into the Mississippi Territory, and in 1817, the entire block was split into two equal parts from north to south, from which the state of Mississippi was established on the western half. The eastern half of the remaining land was preserved for the future state of Alabama. Also, with the Treaty of Ghent, the Indians were left with no European allies, and in their weakened condition, their future was left to the mercy of the United States. Great Britain was finally forced to remove all their soldiers from every part of the United States, and England never came to their aid again.[8]

Statesmen, Leaders and Heroes

When the Mississippi Territory was first organized in 1798, President Adams appointed Winthrop Sargent as its first governor. Sargent was born in Gloucester, Massachusetts in 1753. Shortly after graduating from Harvard, he joined the local militia as a lieutenant on July 7, 1775 when General Washington first arrived in Cambridge, and in December, he was promoted to captain lieutenant in the Continental Army. He participated in the siege of Boston in Henry Knox's Artillery Regiment and fought in the battles of Long Island, White Plains, Trenton, Brandywine, Germantown, and Monmouth. In 1783, he was brevetted major. In 1786, he joined in the forming of the Ohio Company and served as its secretary. In 1788, the Confederation Congress appointed him as first secretary of the Northwest Territory, directly under Governor Arthur St. Clair. In 1798, President Adams selected him to be the first governor of the Mississippi Territory. Sargent was a member of the American Academy of Arts and Sciences and one of the first members of the Society of the Cincinnati, which was instituted in 1783 to assist those veterans who fought in the Revolutionary War. As a federalist, he was relieved of his Mississippi governorship in 1801 with the incoming Democratic-Republican President Jefferson. He then went on to develop the first major plantation in Natchez. He died in New Orleans in 1820 at 67 years old.[9]

David Holmes was born in 1769 in York County, Pennsylvania and moved to Virginia when he was a child. He enjoyed a distinguished political career which started in 1797 when he was elected to the United States House of Representatives, and he held that seat through six election cycles of two years each. In 1809, President Jefferson appointed him as the fourth governor of the Mississippi Territory, where he served until statehood in 1817. He dealt successfully with difficult issues of land policy and expansions, Indian claims, the

War of 1812, and the Mississippi Constitutional Convention, which he presided over as president. One of his major challenges was the conflict with Spain over their West Florida colony. However, he used his honesty, skillful diplomacy, and intelligence to manage the peaceful American occupation of that area.[10] When Mississippi gained its statehood in 1817, Holmes was elected unanimously as its first governor, but poor health forced him to resign after six months. He remains as Mississippi's longest-serving governor with 11 years of service. He returned to Virginia where he died in 1832 at 63 years old.[11]

Chapter Twenty-one

Illinois

State on December 3, 1818

Explorers and Settlers

The Illinois Confederation of Native Americans occupied a triangular area of Midwestern America from Iowa to Chicago to Arkansas. It included a dozen Algonquian tribes numbering around 10,000 natives. The area was also referred to as "Illiniwek." In a 1671 map drawn by French Canadian missionaries, the area southwest of Lake Michigan is called "Illinois." Other earlier French explorers in 1615 such as Etienne Brule and Joseph de La Roche did not leave any documentation of their explorations. French maps published in France in the early 1700's refer to the area as the "Pays des Illinois," which means "Lands of the Illinois." Its first European explorers were Father Jacques Marquette together with Louis Joliet in 1673, who travelled by canoe from Canada to the Lower Mississippi River Valley, claiming most of the territory for France. In 1717, King Louis XV claimed that such a vast area required more effective administration, so he annexed the Illinois Country to the Province of Louisiana, which was then referred to as "Upper Louisiana." Most of the French settlements were on the east side of the Mississippi River, and a few were in present-day Missouri and Indiana. However, the world changed in 1763 when the French were forced to cede most of their North American colonies to Great Britain with their loss of the French and Indian War. Their lands east of the river went to England, and west of the river went to Spain. The French who moved to the west founded the settlement of St. Louis. Another interesting change by the British was to incorporate eastern Illinois, Indiana, and Ohio into the Province of Quebec. This area was allocated for use by the various Indian tribes in an effort to gain their alliance and support. This was done at the same time as the Proclamation of 1763, which forbid white settlements west of the Appalachian Mountains and the voiding of existing land titles. Some historians view these moves as major causes of the American Revolution.[1]

Following the exploits of Marquette and Joliet in the Ohio River Valley and Mississippi River Valley, the French established settlements, missions, forts, and trading posts along the Arkansas, Illinois, and Mississippi Rivers. The first major fort was in St. Louis under Robert de La Salle in 1682, which was designed to defend against English incursions and to confine them to the East Coast. The American region of New France from the Canadian border to the Gulf of Mexico was intended to block the westward expansion of British-American settlers. The next major fort was built in 1720 to defend against Indian attacks. The Fort of Chartres was eventually taken over by the British with the Treaty of Paris of 1763. One of the earliest settlements was Kaskaskia, which was established in 1703 as a mission station. In 1778, American Gen. George Rogers Clark captured the village from the British, and the residents celebrated by ringing their "Liberty Bell" which was a gift from King Louis XV in 1741. The town prospered and became the capital of the Illinois Territory from 1809 to 1818 and then was the first capital of Illinois State from 1818 to 1820. For the help its citizens gave to General Clark, the Canadian and Indian residents were granted full citizenship. Clark had acted on behalf of Virginia Governor Patrick Henry, who declared them to be Virginia citizens because the town was in the County of Illinois in the state of Virginia. In 1787, Congress created the Northwest Territory, which included most of the Illinois Country, which was then changed to the Illinois Territory in 1809.[2] At that time, the Illinois Territory was a very large region that started at the confluence of the Ohio and Mississippi Rivers and northward included present-day Wisconsin and parts of Minnesota and Michigan up to the Canadian border. Upon the Louisiana Purchase in 1803, the Illinois Country area west of the Mississippi River became part of the United States. In 1818, the southern half of the territory near the bottom part of Lake Michigan was admitted to the Union as the 21st state. The northern half was designated part of the Michigan Territory. Virginia had ceded Illinois County back to the United States in 1784 to pacify complaints from the land-locked states and territories and make way for the creation of new states from the newly acquired Northwest Territory in the Treaty of Paris of 1783.

New France

In 1523, an Italian navigator from Florence, Giovanni da Verrazanno, persuaded King Francis I to commission an expedition to discover a westward route to China. He gathered 50 men and set sail in small boats called "caravels." These were highly maneuverable with shallow drafts, first invented in 1451 by the Portuguese, and were used by several major navigators, including Christopher Columbus and Bartholomew Diaz. Verrazanno first landed off the Carolina Coast and sailed north to be the first European to discover New York Harbor, which he named "Nova Galia" or "New France." Ten years later, Jacques Cartier claimed the Gaspe Peninsula for France, which became the first province of New France. However, the initial attempts to settle the area failed. French fishing boats continued to explore the St. Lawrence River, where they began to establish friendly relations with the native Indians. Recognizing the abundance of fur-bearing animals and the possibility of profitable trading, the French government decided to colonize the area. The lands were inhabited by the Algonquian and Iroquois tribes, and the French were able to deal with them peacefully to work together in the fur trading business. By 1680, trading posts were established to export furs back to Europe. Several other trading posts were attempted but failed. except for some very small ones farther inland called Acadia. Finally in 1608, Pierre Dugua and Samuel Champlain with 28 men founded the city of Quebec. Severe weather and disease took their toll, and the settlement's population by 1630 was only 106, but ten years later it had grown to 355.[3] Champlain continued his explorations down to present-day Burlington, Vermont (Lake Champlain), where he allied with the Algonquian and Huron tribes against their Iroquois enemy for control of the fur trade. His assistance not only won the battle, but it created excellent relations with the natives, which served French interests in the fur trade and further colonization. Champlain succeeded Cardinal Richelieu as the second governor of New France.

Cardinal Richelieu was the First Minister of King Louis XIII. The Cardinal viewed Canada as a great opportunity for New France to become a significant farming and mercantile center. He organized investors and offered land grants to settlers in an effort to match the English colonies to the south. He also forbid non-Catholics from settling there and made them renounce their Protestant faith if they chose to remain there. As a result, the Catholic Church established a firm foothold in Canada, which prepared the way for the Jesuit missionaries who converted thousands of natives, most of whom were Huron in the Great Lakes region. Conversion to Catholicism was not opposed by the Indians because of their reliance on French goods, trade, and weapons. Also, France denied trade with anyone who did not accept the missionaries.

It is important to remember that disease played a part in the development of French Canada. One of the most virulent diseases was measles, which brought certain death because the natives had no natural immunities to combat it. The Indians were far more receptive to conversion in order not to offend the priests, who were seen to be the cause of the illness. Another conflict arose when the missionaries tried to change the culture of the natives by diminishing the power of the women within the Indian family and community. The French wanted the native wives to be totally subservient to their husbands as they were in Europe. This caused much resistance, especially with the Iroquois, who almost annihilated the Jesuits and the Huron society in 1649.[4]

With increasing Iroquois attacks during the 1600's, King Louis XIV made New France a royal province in 1663. The French government provided transportation, land grants, and other incentives to settlers. In 1650, New France had 700 colonists, and by 1666 it had 3,215 colonists. The local government was reformed with a shift in power from the Bishop of Quebec to the secular system that existed in France. By 1720, the population reached 24,594, and the fishing, farming, and fur-trading industries were thriving. Also, the other French colonies from southern Illinois to the Mississippi River Valley were taking root. The economy of New France in the 1500's and 1600's depended on fishing, but in the 1700's, it shifted to the fur trade, which was centered in Montreal for the next 100 years. Located on the St. Lawrence River half way between Quebec to the northeast and Lake Ontario to the southwest, it was ideally suited for the fur trading capital. The agricultural economy was limited to local consumption and accordingly had limited expansion. On the other hand, the fur trade brought new foreign markets, tanneries, taverns, and shipping to an energized Montreal. This lasted until the end of the 1700's when market demand for pelts declined, Montreal was bypassed, and competition increased to the south from the British and Dutch.[5]

The French and Indian War

The French considered that the Ohio River Valley belonged to them because of their early explorations and settlements. Under the charter given to the Virginia Company by King James I of England in 1606, the boundaries of Virginia included not just the Ohio River Valley but most of the area between the Allegheny Mountains and the Mississippi River. In an effort to assure their ownership, the French built Fort Duquesne at present-day Pittsburgh, which marked an important strategic location. When Virginia's royal governor, Dinwiddie, learned of this and the presence of French troops just below Lake Erie, he ordered a series of expeditions to advise the French of their intrusions into British territory. The initial forays were led by the commanding officer of the Virginia militia who volunteered to deliver the message—George Washington. When he failed and was almost killed, England sent their veteran Gen. Edward Braddock in 1755. Braddock was killed, and his aide, George Washington, took command and brought the British troops safely home. Washington sustained bullet holes in his jacket and two horses shot from under him. These events started his illustrious career and international notoriety, even though he resigned from the military in 1758 after the capture of Fort Duquesne under British Brig. Gen. John Forbes.

The French and Indian War was subsiding, but it morphed into the Seven Years' War, which had started in 1756 and ended in 1763 with the Treaty of Paris. The French lost their North American colonies including Canada, Acadia, Nova Scotia, and all their lands east of the Mississippi River, as well as West Florida and East Florida.[6] By 1760, the European population in Canada was 70,000 compared to the 1.6 million who lived in the 13 British colonies and 450,000 who lived in New England. In spite of British control of the Ohio and Mississippi River Valleys, French culture, customs, and religion continued in New France. The next major changes came at the end of the American Revolution when Great Britain lost all their 13 colonies to the United States and unexpectedly gave all of their lands north of the Ohio River and east of the Mississippi River to the new republic which held it in reserve as the Northwest Territory. Four years later in 1787, the United States passed the Northwest Ordinance of 1787, which stipulated that this large tract of land was to be used for the creation of at least three and no more than five new states, and when each area achieved a population of 60,000, it would be considered for admission to the Union on an equal legal footing with the original 13 states. The states that were carved from this tract were Ohio, Indiana, Illinois, Michigan, and Wisconsin. A portion was used for the future state of Minnesota. Other American allies in the Revolutionary War did not gain meaningful lands. France got only small islands off the coast of Newfoundland but did incur enormous debt that contributed to the cause of the French Revolution.[7]

Statesmen, Leaders and Heroes

President James Madison appointed John Boyle as governor of the Illinois Territory in 1809, but he resigned after only serving for 21 days to take Ninian Edwards's job as Kentucky's chief justice. Madison then appointed Edwards as governor of the new territory. He was born in Montgomery County, Maryland in 1775 to parents from prominent political families. He was educated by private tutors including future United States Attorney General William Wirt. He left Dickinson College after two years to study law. At age 19, he moved to Kentucky and was soon elected to their House of Representatives, before he was eligible to vote. In 1892, he joined the Kentucky militia and then won several public offices including circuit court judge, presidential elector, judgeship, and chief justice of the Kentucky Court of Appeals. At age 34, he was the youngest governor to have ever held that position in Illinois's statehood or time as a territory. When he assumed the governorship, he received a land grant and brought along several slaves to work the new farm as other governors had done. This was in spite of the Northwest Ordinance which forbid slavery in the territory. At that time, Governor William Henry Harrison of the Indiana Territory stated that a person maintained the same legal status if brought into the territory if one was "under contract to serve another in trade or occupation." So, the law in Illinois allowed slavery if one was an "indentured servant." As Edwards appointed friends and distributed jobs, he could not avoid partisanship. The two-party system of Federalists and Republicans did not govern in early Illinois. Instead, political factions held sway depending on personal ties and friendships.[8] Edwards served three terms as governor and earned the reputation for his democratic governing style, whereby he solicited petitions from local residents and even asked for military leaders from the ranks. In 1812, he convinced Congress to change a voting provision in the Northwest Ordinance which restricted voting rights to freeholders of a minimum of 50 acres. Congress changed the law to allow for all white male suffrage in the Illinois Territory, making it the most democratic territory in the Union. He then moved for a referendum, which would allow the citizens of Illinois to directly elect a legislature and a non-voting delegate to Congress, and the measure passed. Edwards criticized the local judges because of their excessive absence away from the territory, and in 1814, he persuaded the legislature to reform the judicial system. The judges claimed that the legislature acted beyond their authority, but the next year, Congress passed a law supporting Edwards. In 1817, Edwards recommended that Illinois apply for statehood. Legislators who opposed slavery were anxious to proceed, because Missouri was moving for admittance and would be a slave state. Edwards vetoed the bill on constitutional grounds and was also an owner of several slaves. Illinois was granted statehood in December of 1818, and Shadrach Bond was inaugurated as the first governor of the state of Illinois. On the ballot for the Senate, Edwards was elected as the first United States senator from Illinois. During the nine years as governor of the territory, the Illinois population tripled from 12,283 in 1810 to 40,258 in 1818. By 1830, the population exploded to 157,445, making it the fastest growing area in the world. Edwards resigned from public life in 1830. For the last three years of his life, he performed charitable free medical care for those less fortunate. When a choleric epidemic came through Belleville, Illinois, he contracted the disease and died on July 20, 1833. Three of his sons continued in politics. Ninian Wirt Edwards was an Illinois Attorney General and its first Superintendent of Public Instruction. He married Elizabeth Porter Todd, the sister of Mary Todd Lincoln. Albert Gallatin Edwards was Assistant Treasurer of the United States Treasury under President Lincoln. In 1887, he founded the brokerage firm of A. G. Edwards in St. Louis, which survives to this day. Ninian Edwards is remembered by Edwards County, Illinois and Edwardsville, Illinois just east of St. Louis.[9]

Chapter Twenty-two

ALABAMA

State on December 4, 1819

Explorers and Settlers

The Native American Creeks were one of the oldest and largest Indian nations in the American South, going back for thousands of years. It was in the Creek language that the name "Alabama" originated, and it translates to "tribal town." Some historians disagree and believe the name derives from the Choctaw language, which translates to "a thick or mass vegetation." Colonization by Europeans included the Spanish, French, and English, but it was Hernando de Soto who is credited with discovering Alabama in 1539, with his documented report. At that time, it was part of a much larger area called "La Florida," which included all of today's Florida and parts of Georgia, Alabama, Mississippi, South Carolina, and southeastern Louisiana. The next to arrive were the English, who were granted charters in 1663 and 1665 by King Charles II that included Alabama to be part of the Royal Province of Carolina. Claims were further complicated in 1702 when the French built Fort Louis at the mouth of the Mobile River. That fort and settlement was replaced by Fort Conde, which became the town of Mobile and is now regarded as the first permanent European settlement in Alabama. The English and the French attempted to build trading relationships with the natives for the next 50 years until the French and Indian War broke out in 1753-54. Peaceful competition existed for most of that period, but the English seemed to succeed more than the French, mainly because London allowed their colonists far more freedom than Paris. During this same time, King Charles I granted James Oglethorpe and his partners a grant for colonizing Georgia in 1732, which included a portion of northern Alabama. Oglethorpe wisely befriended the Creeks and succeeded in gaining a treaty with them. After the victory over the French in 1763, the Treaty of Paris forced France to cede all of its colonies east of the Mississippi River, giving Great Britain control of the land between the Mississippi River and the Chattahoochee River. The part of Alabama below the 31st parallel went to British West Florida (the "Panhandle"), and north of it became part of the "Illinois Country" to be used by the Indians. This was done to placate the Indians in an attempt to build better relationships with them, especially after having fought them with their French ally.[1]

At the end of the Revolutionary War in 1783, England ceded West Florida back to Spain in the Treaty of Versailles. On exactly the same day in the Treaty of Paris, England also ceded the same land to the United States, thereby causing future problems. The issue was sorted out with Spain in 1795 in the Treaty of Madrid, whereby Spain ceded all of their lands east of the Mississippi River to the United States, except their colony of West Florida. South Carolina and Georgia also had claims to a large portion of the lands reaching as far west as the Mississippi River. Between 1787 and 1802, all of the lands in question were ceded to the United States government which then incorporated them into the Mississippi Territory. In 1812, the Mobile District in West Florida was annexed and added to the new Mississippi Territory in spite of Spain's strong objections. Congress justified the move by claiming it was included in the Louisiana Purchase in 1803. In 1817, the Mississippi Territory was divided into two equal parts, with each section having half of the newly annexed section directly on the Gulf of Mexico. Mississippi was granted statehood that year, and the eastern portion of the territory was preserved for the future state of Alabama. However, the Alabama Territory had been home for thousands of years to the Creek, Chickasaw, Choctaw, and Cherokee Nations. Civil War broke out with the Creeks in 1813 when the Upper Creeks attempted to control the region and rid it of European settlers. The Lower Creeks aligned themselves with the European-Americans and were joined by the other local Native American tribes to defeat the rebelling Upper Creeks in 1814, thereby ending threats to the frontier settlers. Gen. Andrew Jackson was the military leader for the Americans during the Creek War and the War of 1812. His victory over the British at the Battle of New Orleans in January of 1815 made him a national hero and paved the way for his future presidency. The War of 1812 was regarded as a draw, except for the Native American Indians who, under the Treaty of Fort Jackson, were forced to cede 23 million acres to the United States. The lands represented two-thirds of the Alabama Territory and a large portion of lower Georgia.[2]

Alabama became the country's 22nd state on December 14, 1819. Its evolution included the following territories: 1) Spanish-owned La Florida, 2) British-owned West Florida and 3) lands claimed by Mississippi, Georgia, and South Carolina ceded to the United States to form the Alabama Territory in 1817 and Alabama State in 1819.

Battle of Fort Bowyer

The town of Mobile, Alabama sits directly on Mobile Bay with direct access to the Gulf of Mexico. It was the first capital of French Louisiana in 1702 and was in the colony of West Florida, which was owned by the Spanish and then the French and then the British and then the Spanish again. In 1813, it was annexed by President Madison after the start of the War of 1812, under his belief that it was included in the Louisiana Purchase in 1803. Most of that three-year war was fought in the Great Lakes region along the Canadian border until the final major Battle of New Orleans in January of 1815. That American victory over England came only weeks after the Treaty of Ghent was signed in Belgium on Christmas Eve of 1814, but the news had not as yet reached commanding Gen.

Andrew Jackson in New Orleans. The Battle of New Orleans was decisive in that it truly ended a war that neither side wanted, but it gave the new American republic a sense of pride and confidence. However, the New Orleans victory would probably not have happened if the Battle of Fort Bowyer had not been first won by the Americans.

After the evacuation of Spanish forces from Mobile in 1813, American Col. John Bowyer built a small fort on Mobile Point that controlled the entrance into Mobile and was intended to impede a possible British invasion and capture of Mobile. The fort was briefly abandoned but was then re-armed with 160 men under Maj. William Lawrence in August of 1814. The British planned to take Mobile and then move on to Natchez and isolate New Orleans, cutting off American trade, food, and supplies. In September, British Capt. William Percy landed Lt. Col. Edward Nicolls and 60 marines to march on the fort. This was followed by a naval bombardment from two of the British warships. After two hours of heavy shelling and the loss of one ship, the British sailed away. The casualties showed the British with 34 dead and 35 wounded, compared to the four American casualties and five wounded. General Jackson was so elated that he recommended a promotion for all of the fort's defenders. The British then decided to attack New Orleans, and when they were repulsed by Jackson, they turned their attention back to Mobile. They landed a force of 1,000 men, realizing Fort Bowyer was vulnerable from the landward side. They took the fort after a five-day siege. Jackson quickly moved to reinforce Mobile only to learn that the war had ended. The War of 1812 resulted in no change of territorial ownership other than the annexation of Mobile from the Spanish. The Battle of Fort Bowyer was the last battle between the United States and Great Britain for the next 200 years.[3]

Economic and Social Conditions

The major aspect of Alabama's economy at that time was land, who would own it, and to what purpose would it be used. With rampant land speculation and government sales to the public, banks played a very significant role. The earliest white settlers were able to acquire land with their own saved capital or bank credit access, but those who recently emigrated from near and far were dependent on bank or state finance. Following the land auctions of the early 1800's, Alabama was awash with land debts, and private banks controlled by the wealthy were in a position to affect social conditions with how they distributed credit. The most desirable land sought was for agricultural purposes because of the rich, black, and fertile soil, especially in the Black-Belt region of southern Alabama. Like its neighbor Mississippi, its soil and climate was excellent for the growth of cotton. Farmers did have success in growing indigo, grapes, corn, and wheat, but cotton was a far more profitable product because of its domestic and international demand and because of its low cost of slave labor. As the cotton industry grew, so did the need for labor which meant the rapid rise in slavery. By 1820, Alabama's population soared to 125,000 people with over 30 percent being slaves. The impact of this was the growing distinction between the wealthier citizens of northern Alabama and the southern Black-Belt region. It is no wonder that the state's political system divided into the northern faction and the southern faction.[4]

Slavery had been a thorny issue for many years in emerging North America since it was first introduced in 1619 in Virginia. The initial purpose was to acquire cheap labor for the labor-intense growth and harvest of tobacco. The same criteria existed for the labor-intensive cotton industry throughout the Deep South states. When Eli Whitney introduced his cotton gin (short for ("engine") in 1793, it was believed by many that the need for more slaves would subside and slavery would end through manumission, but just the opposite happened. One pound of combed cotton by hand took an entire ten-hour day. The cotton gin enabled three men to produce 50 pounds of clean cotton in one day. The gin increased productivity so much that demands for it grew far faster than anticipated, and new markets developed from around the world. Cotton production brought about the construction of textile mills in New England, increased exports to England and Europe, and promoted ship building and traffic in major American ports from New Orleans to the Northeast. "King Cotton" far outpaced other crops and products to become America's largest export. It shaped the society of the South, and to some historians, it was responsible for the secession from the Union and thereby the Civil War.

Statesmen, Leaders and Heroes

The first appointed governor of the Alabama Territory was William Wyatt Bibb. He was born in Amelia City, Virginia in 1781 and attended the College of Willian and Mary, before moving with his family to Georgia upon the death of his father in 1796. He received his medical degree from the University of Pennsylvania Medical School in 1801 and began his medical practice upon returning to Petersburg, Georgia. In 1803, he was elected to the Georgia House of Representatives as a Democratic-Republican. Having been reelected four times, he was then elected a United States senator in 1813, where he served until 1816. President James Monroe appointed Bibb to be the first governor of the Alabama Territory, when it was formed in 1817. He immediately assumed his duties at the territorial capital of St. Stephens. His first legislative issues were focused on education, infrastructure, and transportation. Also, new counties were established and banks were chartered. In 1818, the legislature petitioned the United States Congress for statehood. The next step was a constitutional convention, held in Huntsville in July of 1819. Bibb appointed a committee of 15 to draft a constitution, and John Walker was elected president of the convention. Their model was the Mississippi Constitution, which provided for executive, legislative, and judicial branches of government. The Alabama Bill of Rights was modeled after the United States Constitution. Political factions began with the first gubernatorial election in November of 1819. Bibb's opponent was Marmaduke Williams, who had been a congressman in North Carolina. This immediately established the political parties known as the North Carolina faction and the Georgia faction and the conflicts between northern and southern Alabama. When Alabama became a state in 1819, Bibb was elected its first governor. The two major issues were the location of the first state capital and the method of representation in the legislature. The more-populace North wanted proportional representation, and the South wanted prescribed representation. A compromise called for proportional representation with the capital in the southern city of Cahaba. Bibb was particularly interested in developing roads and water transportation with the state's many rivers. This was just the beginning of the steamboat era with Robert Fulton's invention, which was first tried on the Hudson

River in New York and then brought to the Mississippi River and other Midwestern waters.

At this time, the great American hero of the Creek Wars and the Battle of New Orleans, Gen. Andrew Jackson, visited the temporary capital in Huntsville. Although the public idolized him, the planters and the well-to-do strongly opposed him. Bibb did not favor Jacksonian democracy and was more aligned with the better-educated and influential citizenry. In July of 1820, Bibb fell from his horse and sustained internal injuries that took his brief life at 38 years old. He was succeeded by his younger brother, Thomas, who as president of the Alabama Senate was automatically elevated to the governorship, where he served for the remaining 18 months of William's three-year term. Thomas was born in Virginia in 1784, grew up in Georgia and moved to Alabama in 1816. He was a delegate to the Alabama Constitutional Convention and then was elected to the state senate, where he was soon elected its presiding officer. As governor, he continued his deceased brother's policies, but he chose not to run for the next term.[5]

Thomas Bibb was succeeded by Israel Pickens in 1821. Pickens was born in North Carolina in 1780. He was educated at private schools and graduated from Jefferson College in Pennsylvania. He then studied law and was admitted to the North Carolina bar in 1802. He served in the North Carolina legislature and the United States House of Representatives. Pickens was a delegate to the Alabama Constitutional Convention. He became the leader of the North Carolina faction, which supported Jacksonian policies and opposed those of the Georgia faction. During his governorship, the University of Alabama was founded, and he served as the first ex-officio president of the board. Pickens was an active member of the American Colonization Society which was also supported by Presidents Madison and Monroe.[6] The ACS was founded to help resolve the slavery issue by freeing those slaves who wished to move to a new country in West Africa named "Liberia." Its capital was named "Monrovia" in honor of President James Monroe. Liberia modeled its constitution on that of the United States, and the concept of a free-black country is attributed to the Marquis de Lafayette, who suggested the plan to George Washington after the Revolutionary War. The idea lingered for over 25 years without success. The country was finally established, but the intended migration never fully succeeded. Pickens returned to the United States Senate after two years as governor. He then retired due to poor health and moved to Cuba to recuperate but died in 1827 at 47 years old.

One of the most prominent men who shaped the beginnings of Alabama was John Williams Walker. He was born in 1785 in Virginia, of Scots ancestry. His father, Jeremiah, was a Baptist preacher who founded 20 churches in Virginia and Georgia. Both of John's parents died when he was a young boy, but he was well cared for by his four brothers, who sent him to private school in South Carolina and then on to Princeton University, where he graduated in 1806. He soon joined his friend Thomas Percy in Natchez, Mississippi. In 1809, the United States government offered to sell land that had been previously owned by the Creek Indians. Walker and six other friends from the Broad River Group bought a large part of Madison County in the Mississippi Territory for $2.00 per acre. The Broad River Group was composed of relatives and friends who controlled the initial political power in the Alabama Territory. Walker was a licensed attorney who actively opposed making the Mississippi Territory into a single state, and when it was split into two sections, he was elected to the Alabama Territorial Legislature. He was politically opposed by Governor William Bibb of the Georgia faction, and when state borders were being decided, he was successful in getting his lands in the Huntsville area included. He was elected to the Alabama Constitutional Convention and was unanimously chosen as its president, and thereby he greatly influenced the choosing of the 15-member drafting committee. He strongly advocated proportional representation that would assure the continued domination by northern Alabama. He and his Broad River Group became known as the "Royal Party," which led to their defeat of the Georgia faction and pro-Jacksonian Israel Pickens in the 1821 gubernatorial election. At the Constitutional Convention prior to statehood, Walker introduced a bill to incorporate the colony of West Florida into Alabama, but the measure was narrowly defeated. In the legislature, Walker strongly supported the banking interests, opposed a bankruptcy bill that favored debtors, and opposed a tariff that would harm southern agricultural interests. Walker introduced the Land Law of 1821, which provided for the relinquishment of lands held by state debt, the resale of those lands, and the return to the original owners of proceeds over $1.25 per acre. The law reduced Alabama's debt by 50 percent and made Walker a local hero. As his health deteriorated, Walker resigned from office in November of 1822 and returned to Huntsville, where he died the following year at 40 years old.[7]

Chapter Twenty-three

Maine

State on March 15, 1820

Early Years

The name "Maine" derives its origin from two possible explanations; it could have been named after the French Province of "Maine," or it could have been a diminutive of the English word of "mainland," to distinguish it from its many islands. Maine is the largest of all six New England states. Maine was founded for commercial purposes, primarily for its timber and fur. Its two founders were Puritan members of the Anglican Church, but unlike most of the New England colonies, they were not fleeing religious persecution.

The earliest known European explorer to visit the area of Maine was Giovanni da Verrazano in 1524. However, the first recorded settler to actually set foot in Maine was Simon Ferdinando, who was a Portuguese explorer working for England in 1597. Seven years later, a Frenchman, Pierre du

Dugue, Sieur de Mons occupied a small six-acre island at the mouth of the St. Croix River that borders Canada and the United States, but it never took root. Another Frenchman explorer of note was cartographer Samuel Champlain who explored and mapped much of Maine and the entire New England coast. The French were followed by the English from the Plymouth Company, who attempted to establish a settlement at Phippsburg in 1607. They named it Popham Colony after their leader, George Popham. That settlement did not survive the first winter, and because no evidence remained of their presence, historians recognize Jamestown as the first permanent English settlement in 1607. The French established a trading post in Castine in 1613, which could be claimed as the first European settlement in New England. In 1622, a land grant was given to Ferdinand Gorges and John Mason for the territory between the Merrimac and Kennebec Rivers, which was named the Province of Maine. They split the land along the Piscataquis River in 1629 to form the Province of New Hampshire to the south and New Somersetshire to the north, in southwest Maine. The first attempt to settle the Maine Coast was in 1623 by the Englishman Christopher Levett. He obtained a royal charter for 6,000 acres at present-day Portland, where he built a stone house. He then returned to England to find financial support, but he died on his return to America, and his settlement failed. In 1629, Gorges received a second patent, which resulted in more Maine settlements along the Atlantic Coast. In 1641, Massachusetts purchased territorial claims from the Gorges heirs and took control of the Province of Maine with formal annexation in 1652, when the people of Maine requested to be placed under their jurisdiction.

From 1669 to 1763, Maine was engaged in constant land claims between the English, French, Dutch, and Native American Indians. Some of the most significant conflicts were King Phillip's War (1675); Queen Anne's War (1702-13); Father Rale's War (1723-24); King William's War (1745-47); the French and Indian War (1752-58), and finally the Seven Years' War (1756-63). With England defeating France and taking Canada from them, all French and Indian claims in Maine disappeared, and in 1675, King Charles II granted Maine a Royal Charter.

The Revolutionary War

Maine was somewhat in the middle of the war between England's Loyalist colony of Nova Scotia, which sometimes was called their 14th colony, and the erupting conflicts in Massachusetts. The British cut off all supplies to both the Americans and the Indians by controlling the coast. When the Port of Boston was closed in 1774, Maine could no longer ship their fish and timber or import much-needed food and goods. This affected the Native American tribes as well; so many of them travelled to the coast where they sided with the Americans. While most of Maine was protected from major fighting, it did engage in skirmishes along the coast. The Tea Act of 1773 gave rise to the Boston Tea Party in December, and that was followed by another Tea Party in York, Maine in 1774. Likewise, the Stamp Act of 1765 met with even more hostility in Maine because of its larger Patriot population relative to the number of Loyalists. In 1775, when the British cutter *Margaretta* entered the Portsmouth harbor, it was seized along with two other British ships by the rebel leader Jeremiah O'Brien. The action was called the first naval battle of the war. However, the Mainers were punished when British Admiral Graves burned Portsmouth, leaving 400 buildings destroyed along with the sinking of two American ships and the capture of 11 others.[1]

One of the earliest and most daring campaigns of the war was the American plan to invade Canada for the purpose of gaining French-Canadians to join in the fight for independence. France had just lost Canada to England in 1763, and American leaders, including Washington, believed they would find strong anti-British sentiment. American Brig. Gen. Richard Montgomery was sent from Fort Ticonderoga to join with Gen. Phillip Schuyler just south of Montreal. Montgomery and 1,100 men took control of Montreal in November of 1775, and he then moved on with 300 men to Quebec, where he was to join with Benedict Arnold's company. Arnold left Cambridge in September with 1,000 men, and they literally hacked their way through the forests and rivers of Maine, enduring snow, ice, hunger, and every sort of danger and deprivation. Their food was depleted, and they were forced to eat dogs and even their moccasins to survive. They arrived at the St. Lawrence River in November, where they constructed canoes from forest birches and quietly slipped past the anchored British warships. Once on shore, they scaled the cliffs outside Quebec. The city was defended by British Gen. Guy Carleton, who had been warned of the attack and had sent for reinforcements. He avoided being drawn out of the city and was able to repel the Americans. Montgomery was killed, and Arnold was forced to retreat after sustaining a bullet in his leg. The attack on Canada failed, mostly because the Americans did not accurately gauge the strength of British forces at Quebec and the little amount of anti-British sentiment by the Canadians, on which they had relied.[2]

New Ireland

In 1779, the British occupied Castine and burned Fort George on the eastern side of Penobscot Bay. The Americans tried to dislodge them during a 21-day assault but were repelled by British reinforcements. The British then blocked the sea escape, so the Americans went to Bangor, where they burned the British ships. Future attempts by the Americans failed. However, the easterly towns contained a large number of Loyalists who sought neutrality. This gave rise to a British plan to take control of northeastern Maine and create a new colony to be named "New Ireland." The intention was to have this become a permanent home for Loyalists and a military base during the war. Even though the plan never succeeded due to American resistance and Parliament's disinterest, it did reemerge after the war. In 1784, the British split off part of Nova Scotia and created the Province of New Brunswick, which reportedly came close to being named "New Ireland."[3]

The War Of 1812 and Maine Statehood

Tensions between Great Britain and the United States were building again in the late 1790's and finally boiled over in 1812. The two major factors that caused America to declare war were the impressment of American seamen and trade restrictions imposed by Great Britain on American trade with France, who was embroiled in the Napoleonic Wars. British ships raided and destroyed many American seaports from Maine to New Orleans, and they managed to capture and burn Washington, D.C. and the Executive Mansion. Some historians refer to the War of 1812 as the "Second War of Independence." In July of 1814, a British armada of warships and troop transports carrying 1,000 men captured

Fort Sullivan in Eastport. Mainers were deeply discouraged by the failure of the Massachusetts government to come to their defense for two years. There had been some talk for many years of seeking independence from Massachusetts since their annexation in 1652. Wealthier towns had always opposed it because such a move could disrupt the very profitable trade they enjoyed. British soldiers occupied Belfast, Castine, Blue Hill, and Machias. They looted Bangor and Biddeford, but there were no U.S. troops defending them. Maine citizens expected Massachusetts and the federal government to protect them, but nothing was done. The British occupied much of Maine and never bothered to invade the southern region primarily because of its proximity to Boston, which was the center for lucrative trade with the colony. Northeastern Maine thrived as the capital for smuggling and the black market for consumer goods that also benefitted England's factories. The war ended in 1815, and Massachusetts Governor Strong was severely criticized for his failure to support Maine. Even after the war, Massachusetts made no effort to administer Eastport, which the British regarded as part of New Brunswick. Massachusetts and Maine agreed to part ways, and a referendum was presented for statehood. It came at a time when slavery was dividing the country, thereby making Maine a pawn in the debate. This was resolved by the Missouri Compromise of 1820, which was the year of Maine's statehood. It was the 23rd state admitted to the Union.[4]

Education

Although Maine was not one of the original 13 colonies, as part of Massachusetts it was very much part of the early struggle for independence. It is another example of how important the founders regarded a literate and well-educated society. When the Constitutional Convention adjourned in 1787, Benjamin Franklin was asked by a friend what kind of government he gave us. He replied, "a republic, but only if you can keep it." Franklin and other founders knew that only a well-informed society could maintain self-government in contrast to the European leaders who claimed that a society could not govern itself. Nine colleges were established prior to the Revolution, and shortly thereafter, more sprang into existence. Bowdoin was one of them, having been chartered in 1794 by the Massachusetts State Legislature. Located in Brunswick, Maine, it was named for former governor James Bowdoin, whose son was a major donor. It quickly acquired a reputation for high academic standards, and it required knowledge of Latin and Greek as well as geography, algebra and, the works of Cicero, Virgil, and Homer. The college has a number of famous graduates including: U.S. President Franklin Pearce, Nathaniel Hawthorne, Henry Wadsworth Longfellow, and Brig. Gen. Joshua Chamberlain who led the "20th Maine" at Gettysburg and later became Governor of Maine. Bowdoin reports that it has the highest percent of alumni in all the northern colleges who fought in the Civil War.[5]

Chapter Twenty-four

Missouri

State on August 10, 1821

Explorers and Settlers

The name "Missouri" derives from the Sioux language and translates to "town of the large canoes" or "wooden canoe people." The Sioux Indians who lived in that region were referred to as the "Missouris." Native Americans lived there 12,000 years ago, but European settlements started in the late 1600's. Its initial period of exploration and colonization began in 1673 when French Canadian priest, Father Jacques Marquette, and fur trader, Louis Joliet, canoed down the Mississippi River in search for a water route to China. As they descended from the Great Lakes into the Ohio River Valley and the Mississippi River Valley, they met many tribal Indian chiefs, and due in large measure to Marquette's language skills, they were able to establish friendly relations with the local natives. Their principal goal was to discover a shorter trading route to the Orient, so they wanted to explore the Mississippi River as far south as possible and hopefully to its source at the Gulf. A secondary objective was to establish posts for the fur trading empire they were developing in Canada and the Midwestern part of North America. They were followed in 1682 by Robert La Salle, who also canoed down the Mississippi River in search of its entry on the Gulf. Along the way, he visited some of the natives who had met with Marquette and Joliet, and he also claimed much of the lands for France. Another Jesuit missionary, Father Pierre Gabriel Marest, established the first French mission on the west bank of the Mississippi River. In 1700, with a small number of French settlers and a much larger group of Kaskaskia Indians, they started a settlement called Kaskaskia that developed into a major trading and administrative center. Natives came from the eastern Illinois Country to escape from their Iroquois enemy, who were constantly trying to wrest control of the fur trade. At that time, Missouri was part of the Louisiana Territory, which the French in 1722 divided into a northern district controlled by Quebec and a southern Louisiana District, which reached as far as southern Illinois and Missouri. During this time, the French government in Paris made serious efforts to colonize the region. They built a string of forts north and west of Kaskaskia in Madison, St. Francis, Washington, and Carroll counties. The French continued to forge allegiances with many natives, but unlike English control of their American colonies, France paid little attention to Missouri.

The French and Indian War

The war broke out in 1754 over disputed land claims in the Ohio River Valley.[1] With their defeat by Great Britain, France lost Canada and all their North American colonies, as dictated by the Treaty of Paris of 1763. However, in 1762 with the Treaty of Fontainebleau, France gave its Louisiana holdings to Spain, including everything between the Appalachian Mountains to the Rockies. The treaty was held secret and was never disclosed when France was negotiating the Treaty of Paris in 1763. The later treaty gave the lands east of the Mississippi River to Great Britain, which Spain did not contest knowing they were to regain lands west of the river. In the same treaty, Spain ceded Florida to Great Britain, and in return, received western Louisiana. French settlers were granted 18 months to move to French colonies if they did not want to be under British rule. Many fled to Louisiana only to discover that it had been ceded to Spain in 1762. The French in western Louisiana rebelled against the Spanish government in 1768, but they were suppressed. In 1783, with the American victory over Great Britain, the United States returned Florida to Spain, which then controlled the entire ring around the Gulf of Mexico from Florida to the Pacific Ocean and north to Canada on the western side of the Missouri River.[2] When Spain regained control of western lands in 1762, there were only two established settlements in Missouri: Mine La Motte and Ste. Genevieve. Others soon followed: St. Louis in 1764, Carondelet in 1767, and St. Charles in 1769. Some of the Spanish-appointed administrators had to deal with the predominantly French settlers and therefore were forced to accept French culture and customs. Spain encouraged French settlers and even offered land grants and supplies to Catholic immigrants. In 1779, Spain declared war on England, and the next year, England attacked St. Louis, killing 21, wounding seven and taking 25 as prisoners. After the war, Spanish policy was remarkably forward-looking as it encouraged thousands of mostly Protestant American immigrants from the Ohio River Valley. Their intent was to develop the area as "New Madrid," but they were unsure of their loyalties to Spain, and it failed to take root.[3]

Spanish Control

In the 1790's, in an effort to better govern the region, Spain decided to divide the colony into five districts: St. Louis, St. Charles, Ste. Genevieve, Cape Girondeau, and New Madrid. The provincial capital was St. Louis, which—with a population of 2,500—was also the largest. By 1804, with more than 60 percent of the population being American, the Spanish authorities realized there was little loyalty to Spain, and there seemed to be no desire to convert to Catholicism from their Protestant heritage. In 1800, Spain and France had signed the Treaty of Ildefonso, whereby Spain returned their Louisiana colony, which included Missouri, to France. This came about because of their poor return on the time, money, and effort to colonize it, as well as pressure from Napoleon's growing threat at home. The colonial economy was subsistence agriculture, livestock, fur trading, lead mining, and salt production. The region was predominantly Catholic, and even though Protestant services were not allowed, the Protestant faith was tolerated. The social classes broke down into four or five segments: the wealthiest merchants at the top, followed by laborers, hunters, and soldiers, free blacks, servants and woodsmen traders, and black Indian slaves at the bottom. Black slaves accounted for 38 percent of the population in 1772, but by 1800, the number had declined to 20 percent.[4]

French Control

The period of 1800 to 1803 was a murky one for Missouri as the return to French control was kept a secret. The Spanish authorities in Missouri remained in their positions while Paris contemplated their next military moves in Europe, the Caribbean, and New France in North America. In 1802, they sent a force to quell unrest in St. Dominque, but it failed with continuing revolution in Haiti. When they suspended all foreign trade from New Orleans, the United States viewed this as an opportunity to purchase the city from France. The anticipated negotiations in Paris suddenly changed when Foreign Minister Talleyrand offered to sell all their French holdings on the North American continent to the United States for $15 million in an all-or-nothing package. Historians believe this was motivated by their need for cash to support Napoleon's intended exploitations in Europe. The resulting Louisiana Purchase included Missouri, as it was part of Upper Louisiana. In 1805, Congress divided the area into the Louisiana Territory for lands north of the 33rd parallel, and the Territory of Orleans for lands below that line. The latter became the state of Louisiana in 1812, and the Louisiana Territory to the north was renamed the Missouri Territory.[5]

During its territorial period of 1805 to 1821, Missouri had several appointed governors who were mediocre at best. The first was James Wilkinson, who was appointed by President Jefferson. He was not only an alcoholic and a thief, but he became a traitor to the United States when he participated in the Burr Conspiracy to create an independent country in the southwestern part of the country. Burr was acquitted, but the trial destroyed his political career.[6] Wilkinson was replaced with Meriwether Lewis in 1807, but he reportedly turned to alcohol and committed suicide in 1809. Lewis was followed by Benjamin Harrison until 1813 and finally by his former expeditionary partner, William Clark until statehood in 1821. Clark proved to be the most popular and successful of the territorial governors, and he managed the territory well during the War of 1812-15.

Missouri Compromise

In 1818, Missouri requested statehood as a "slave state," but the issue was complicated by the Congress, which wanted to keep an even balance between slave and free states. The slavery question became a critical issue, because in December of 1819, Alabama was admitted as a slave state, thereby maintaining the desired balance. Also, in January of 1820, there was a House bill in process for Maine to be admitted as a free state. A compromise was reached to admit Maine (March 1820) and Missouri (August 1821) but with the proviso that slavery would not be permitted north of the 36th degree line (the southern border of Missouri) in the future, with the exception of Missouri which could decide for itself. The Senate and the House were divided on the slavery issue, and while the Missouri Compromise was hailed as a great resolution, in fact it only delayed an inevitable conflict.[7]

Slavery

From 1810 to 1830, the black slave population in Missouri increased from 3,011 to 25,091. The proportion of slaves to the total population in 1830 was 18 percent, and by 1860 that number declined to 9.8 percent, due primarily to the population explosion of immigrants from Europe and neighboring southern states. The economy of the state was mainly agricultural, which was labor-intensive and required cheap labor to remain viable. Slavery was concentrated in the fertile soils next to the Missouri and Mississippi Rivers as well as in the center of the state, where large tracts of land were purchased by wealthy planters whose major crops were hemp and tobacco. The Missouri Constitution of 1820 required that slaves be protected from inhumane treatment. In 1825, a slave code was passed to protect against beatings, rape, and other abuses, but in fact, slaves did not have adequate protection of the law. Slavery was not widely practiced in the state, but it was an important aspect of the economy. More damaging was an 1847 law that prohibited slaves from learning to read and write or free blacks to move into Missouri. Slaves were not allowed to own real estate without permission from their owners. Also, they could not buy or sell liquor. To attend church services or assemblies of any kind required the owner's permission. The slave-owner relationship varied from state to state, usually depending on the size of the farm or plantation. In Missouri, there were far fewer overseers where abuses were more prevalent. Instead, many owners worked alongside slaves and even lived among them. A closer working relationship produced a greater family and personal bonding, that often led to their being freed in a greater sense of responsibility by the owner. In 1824, the Supreme Court of Missouri ruled that freed blacks could not be enslaved. In 1857, the famous Dred Scott v. Sanford case had a profound impact on the slavery issue. The United States Supreme Court ruled that because the Scotts had moved from a free state to a slave state, they lost their freedom. The decision also denied citizenship to blacks and ruled that Congress lacked the authority to prohibit slavery in the territories. The ruling overturned the Missouri Compromise of 1820 and prevented Congress from restricting the expansion of slavery into the western United States. This forced the abolitionist movement to adopt more clandestine operations. A small but determined portion of Missouri's citizens spoke out against slavery. They were led by ministers, journalists, college educators, and politicians, many of whom were forced to leave the state. During the 1840's and 1850's, the "Underground Railroad" was used extensively in Missouri to assist slaves in their escape to freedom.[8]

Religion

Admitted in 1821, Missouri was the first state to be established west of the Mississippi River. After the Louisiana Purchase in 1803, the presence and influence of the Catholic Church diminished for the next 15 years due to a lack of financing from its former Catholic owners Spain and France, a decline in missionaries, and an absence of leadership. However, this changed in 1818 when St. Louis Academy (later University) was the first founded west of the Mississippi River. That same year, Catholic Bishop Dubourg was installed, and he began a successful drive for church membership. Also, restrictions on Protestant services were ended, and a large number of Baptist, Presbyterian, and Methodist ministers arrived to build churches and preach throughout the state. Bishop Dubourg started a new cathedral in St. Louis, The Basilica of St. Louis, King of France, and he also built Catholic secondary schools and parishes throughout Missouri. Sizeable migrations from Ireland and Germany greatly expanded the Catholic communities. In 1818, the Baptist Church established churches throughout Missouri and started the first Sunday Schools in St. Louis, one for whites and another for blacks. In 1834, there were 150 established black churches in Missouri, and the number grew to 750 by 1860.[9]

Gateway to the West

When Missouri was admitted as the 24th state, its first capital was in St. Charles but was moved to Jefferson City in 1826. The population of the territory in 1820 was 66,586, and by 1850, it had grown to 682,044. The black slave population in the same period increased from 10,222 to 87,422. Its western boundary was a straight north-south line from Iowa to Arkansas, and a small portion in the northwest corner was deeded to the Iowa, Sac, and Fox Indian tribes. When white settlers intruded on those lands, Governor William Clark persuaded the Indians to accept $7,500 and new lands with the "Platte Purchase." The freed lands were attached to Missouri, thereby slightly enlarging the only slave state north of the 36th parallel. The population explosion can be attributed to the superb agricultural conditions that Missouri offered to Europeans and Midwestern Americans. The combination of the Missouri and Mississippi Rivers with their fertile lands, together with open grazing fields, served to attract small farming as well as large-scale farming. Livestock, hogs, corn, and tobacco became important products. Horses were the major work animal, but mule breeding was a unique Missouri activity. There was an abundance of waterway transportation systems with major rivers like the Mississippi, Missouri, Ohio, and Arkansas Rivers. Markets could be reached from New Orleans and through the Great Lakes, and with the completion of the Erie Canal in 1825, they reached New York City and the East Coast. The steamboat was introduced in 1811. By 1834, there were 230 steamboats on the Mississippi River. In addition, tributaries serviced barges, flatboats, and keel boats. Trips of 3-4 months were reduced to 6-7 days. From St. Louis, riverboat traffic could connect through the Ohio, Illinois, Cumberland, and Tennessee Rivers to the Missouri and Mississippi Rivers. By 1845, the telegraph connected St. Louis to the East Coast. Missouri attracted businessmen from the Atlantic Coast, farmers from the southern states, and immigrants primarily from Germany. The early 1800's saw major expeditions to the West from St. Louis and other cities across Missouri. The most noteworthy trip was in 1804 with the famous Lewis and Clark Expedition. which started in St. Louis. They were soon followed by Zebulon Pike in 1805 to the northern reaches of the Mississippi River and then to the mountains of Colorado, where he is memorialized at Pike's Peak. In 1810, another notable explorer Stephen Long went on the Yellowstone Expedition and then up the Platte River in 1820. The Gold Rush hordes on their way to California stopped in St. Louis, Independence, and St. Joseph to load supplies for the long trip. Missouri became the "Gateway to the West," long before the Gateway Arch was built in St. Louis in 1965.[10]

Chapter Twenty-five

Arkansas

State on June 15, 1836

Explorers and Settlers

The name "Arkansas" is interesting because it derives from native languages and is pronounced from the French language. The Quapaw tribe word of "akakase" means "land of downriver people," and the Sioux translates to "people of the south wind." However, the pronunciation is French, because it was French explorers and missionaries who were the first Europeans to settle there. The French silences the "s" in Arkansas, but the similar name of Kansas uses the "s" sound.

The Mississippi River marks most of the eastern boundary with Louisiana to the south, Texas to the southwest, Oklahoma to the west, and Missouri to the north. Like other states in the region, Arkansas was first occupied for thousands of years with Native Americans before the first Europeans settlers arrived. Again, it was the Spaniard Hernando de Soto who explored the area in 1541 and died there the following year. He and his expeditionary force were in search of gold, and like others who conquered the Mexican Aztecs, he was determined to let nothing stand in his way. While he was a daring and brave explorer, he was a brutal warrior who killed many natives as he cut his way through the forests and forged the rivers of Arkansas. The native Indians regarded him as a god, so he willed that he be buried in the Mississippi River to hide his mortality. As noted in the other Mississippi River Valley states, there was a lengthy pause in European settlement until the late 1600's, when French explorers moved down from Canada. Men like Jacques Marquette, Louis Joliet, Robert La Salle, and Henri de Tonti arrived from 1673 to 1681. In 1686, de Tonti established a trading post in a Quapaw village, making it the first permanent European settlement in the Arkansas Territory. It was from the Quapaw people who lived downriver from them and the European phonetic spelling that the name "Arkansas" was derived. The first settlement was used by French fur trappers, but nothing of significance developed until the French and Indian War, when France lost its colonies to the English. The major change in the region came in 1803 with the Louisiana Purchase, when France sold its 800,000 square miles of land, including the Arkansas Territory, to the United States.[1]

Robert La Salle came to the Arkansas region in 1681 to find the mouth of the Mississippi River. He was joined by his partner, Henri de Tonti, and the next year claimed the Mississippi River Valley for France. The first true settlers of the area were the Jesuit Father Jacques Marquette and the fur trader Louis Joliet. They left the Great Lakes to canoe down the Mississippi River to explore and document the wilderness of the region, arriving in Arkansas in 1673. This was 140 years after de Soto, which indicates the inability of Spain to follow through on their initial discoveries. This may be due in part to their loss of naval supremacy with the English defeat of their Spanish Armada in 1588. Marquette was born in France in 1637 to a family that had deep experience in military and civic responsibilities. He was educated at several Jesuit colleges, where he excelled at languages before leaving for Canada in 1666. Because of his skills, he was assigned to teach Indian tribes Christianity, which he did by first learning their different dialects. He chose to live among the Indians and therefore was well equipped for the job. In 1670, Canada's French governor Louis de Baude Frontenac proposed that Marquette go on an exploration of the Mississippi River

Valley. His travelling companion Louis Joliet was also a Catholic educated by the Jesuits, but his interest was in the fur trade. The two of them made maps of the area and were able to meet and converse with many Indian chiefs along the way, before landing in the Quapaw village of Kappa, which was 20 miles from the mouth of the Arkansas River. After staying there for three days, they concluded that the Quapaw were friendly, strong, and likeable enough to become allies in their anticipated settlement of the lower Mississippi River Valley. They were warned by their new found friends of the Spanish who were nearby in the south on the Gulf of Mexico, and not wanting to risk losing the work they had done, they decided to return to the Great Lakes to report their findings. They had learned that the Mississippi River emptied into the Gulf of Mexico and that a water route for trade from Canada was possible. Their discoveries paved the way for French colonization along the Mississippi River where they would build forts and ease the path for future explorers like Robert La Salle in 1682 and Henri de Tonti in 1686, when he established the first European settlement west of the Mississippi River. Father Marquette remained in Canada to work among the Kaskaskia Indians but suddenly died in 1675 at 39 years old.[2]

Louis Joliet was born in 1645 near Quebec. After studying religion and music, he decided to seek his fortune in the fur trade. His most famous trip was in 1673 with Father Jacques Marquette, which was described above. Their ultimate goal was to find a water passage to Asia via the large river named "Mesipi" by the local natives. The two men started their expedition in the Michilimackinac region. After a month of travel, they were greeted in the Illinois area by a local Indian tribe, whose chief befriended them with a peace pipe intended to help them with a safe journey. Their next encounter was in present-day St. Louis where some hostile Indians received them, only after seeing their peace pipe. After learning of the nearby Spanish, they decided to return home. The Indian guides showed them a shorter route to the Great Lakes via the Illinois River, and that is when they first discovered Lake Michigan and the surrounding rich prairie land. Father Marquette intended to return there to preach, but he died shortly afterwards from dysentery. On their return to Quebec, Joliet went on his own to travel the St. Lawrence River, where his canoe capsized, losing all his companions and the notes from his Arkansas trip. Fortunately, Marquette's records were available. In

1676, Joliet set up a trading post in the northern part of the St. Lawrence River, continued his explorations and surveyed the Hudson Bay area. He also surveyed the Labrador Coast and became a professor of hydrography at the University of Quebec. He died in 1700 at age 55, and his gravesite remains unknown.[3]

The discoveries by Marquette and Joliet led to an exploration in 1683 by Robert La Salle with 23 Frenchmen and 31 Indians. It was not meant to be an extension of New France but rather a discovery of where the Mississippi River ran into the Gulf of Mexico. It was also intended to further develop the French and Indian fur trading and military alliance.[4]

Rene-Robert Cavalier, Sieur de La Salle was born in France in 1643 and was educated there at a Jesuit college. He decided to abandon his studies for the priesthood and join his brother in Canada. He became a fur trader and explorer with his first major trip being down the Mississippi River to establish trading posts as far south as possible to the Gulf of Mexico. He and his aide, Henri de Tonti, reached the Arkansas region in 1682, and along the way, they initiated alliances with Indian tribes to assist them in their expanding North American empire of New France. In Arkansas, they stayed with the Quapaw tribe in Kappa where Marquette and Joliet had visited nine years earlier. The natives became closely allied with the French, who supplied them with firearms; formed trading, political, and military agreements; and even intermarried with them. While there, La Salle had the authority to give a land grant to de Tonti, who developed the land into the first permanent European settlement in Arkansas, which he named the Arkansas Post in 1686. La Salle went back to France to recruit more colonists for the new settlements. His next expedition was in 1684 to find the mouth of the Mississippi River, but he landed in Matagorda Bay, Texas. Poor judgement and bad decisions caused a great deal of frustration and anger among his settlers who then took his life in 1687. Although La Salle failed to establish the trading settlements he envisioned, he did pioneer excellent relationships with many Indian tribes that lasted another 100 years.[5]

Economy and Society

For most of its first 200 years, the economy of Arkansas was based on hunting and trading hides. Agriculture did play a role, especially along the Mississippi

River with its rich fertile soil. Cotton came to be a major product only after the Louisiana Purchase in 1803. In addition to animal furs, the new product of bear oil was introduced to the French by their Quapaw friends. They soon learned of the abundance of bears in the region, and their oil was used for cooking, protection from mosquitoes, and a cure for rheumatism. The French and the natives hunted together for bear oil, buffalo meat, tallow, and animal skins for trade, consumption, and export to New Orleans. Their trade was primarily with the French, which encouraged cultural exchange and mixing of the races. The French who traded with the natives also lived among them. By 1706, the French-Indian relationships stretched from the Great Lakes to the Ohio River and through the Mississippi River Valley. Considering the cold climate of Canada with its short growing season, the southern climate and fertile soil, the Indian alliances, a large animal population, and numerous rivers made Arkansas an attractive destination for Canadians. Another factor was the lack of female immigrants, which prompted the men to become attracted to native women. French hunters sought the meat of wild game, because there was little cattle due to limited cleared grazing land. They learned from the Indians about how to preserve bear meat with sun-drying and salting from the abundant salt springs in that area. In fact, salt was in such good supply that it became a trading product.

There were very few agricultural farmers in the 17th century. Farming was seriously affected by the annual flooding of the Arkansas River. Settlers were often forced to get their supplies from Illinois and local Indians. There was a limited supply of tillable riverfront land. This was alleviated by changing the land ownership system from plantations to the system along the St. Lawrence River. Land was formed into "longlots"—whereby strips were ten times longer than their width—which fronted on the river. This was done on the Arkansas River and its larger tributaries.

Even though the Treaty of Paris of 1763 ended the Seven Years' War, the French had ceded their Louisiana and Arkansas lands to their ally, Spain, in 1762. The area remained populated mostly by the French, and few Spaniards immigrated there. It was the American Revolutionary War that brought the first major change to Arkansas. In the Treaty of Paris of 1783, the British ceded their holdings east of the Mississippi River to the United States. This left the

Indians without an ally. The situation forced a peace between the Chickasaw, Quapaw, and Spain in the mid-1780's. The settlement of Arkansas Post became the center of activity and importance. The civil and military judges were the "commandants" who represented a small gentry class. Their terms of office were three to four years, and most of them were descended from French colonial soldiers. Their families were a small aristocracy loyal to the French king and governor. The Spanish also cultivated a military gentry that was well educated and refined. Officers often received a trading monopoly with specific tribes, which attracted them to such service. A non-military gentry was socially equal to the officers and were mostly composed of the local merchants. By the end of the colonial era in 1802, Arkansas had a population of 400,000 and a racially diverse community where French, Spanish, German, and several Indian languages were spoken. It included a small number of slaves, free mulattoes, and free blacks. The Spanish outlawed the enslavement of Indians. Records show that a great variety of Indian tribes moved to the Arkansas Post, including the Osage and Kansas from the prairies, Abenaki from New England, Cherokee from the Southeast, and Delaware from the Northeast. Most of the men who married Indian women were of French, English, and Spanish descent.[6]

Louisiana Purchase

With the sale of their 800,000 square miles in 1803 to the United States, French and Spanish dominance of Arkansas ended. For more than 100 years, the Spanish and French colonized and governed the Mississippi River Valley including Arkansas. After the defeat of France in the French and Indian War in 1763, Spain got control of Louisiana. However, as the United States grew stronger over the next 30 years, the Spanish felt threatened and returned the colony to France with the Treaty of San Ildefonso in 1800. This move prompted President Jefferson to seek protection from the French, so he sent his ambassadors, Robert Livingston and James Monroe to Paris in 1802 to purchase New Orleans and part of Florida. Unbeknown to them, the French Foreign Minister Talleyrand had just prepared an offering to the United States of all (or nothing) of the Louisiana colony for $15 million. The purchase was ratified in 1803, making the United States the largest republic in the world. Arkansas became part of the

District of Louisiana and the Territory of Orleans. The American legal system of English Common Law was immediately enforced, causing some to leave the area. The laws were denied to people of mixed races, and slavery was expanded in the farming sections. The United States army at Fort Smith was strengthened to protect against Indian attacks, and there was little resistance from the French or Spanish. The Louisiana Purchase ended European rule in the West and spurred immigration to the Mississippi Territory.[7]

Path to Statehood

The Arkansas Territory was formed from the Missouri Territory in 1819 and existed until statehood in 1836. The Missouri Territory had previously been named the Louisiana Territory, but the name was changed to avoid confusion with the state of Louisiana, which was established in 1812. The Arkansas Territory had Missouri to the north at the 36th degree mark, and then the boundaries went west to include present-day Oklahoma until 1907. The original lines were set through negotiations with the Choctaw Indians in 1820, but the lines were changed by President Jackson in 1824 and again in 1828, when he reduced the size of Arkansas to its present boundaries. The first capital was Arkansas Post, until it was moved to Little Rock in 1821 where it remained until statehood in 1836.[8]

It was Arkansas's first governor, James Miller, who was responsible for moving the capital to Little Rock. He was born in Peterborough, New Hampshire in 1776 and attended Williams College in Massachusetts. He first joined the New Hampshire militia and then the United States army in 1808. He fought in the famous Battle of Vincennes, Indiana where he was promoted to colonel. He then fought in the War of 1812 and was awarded the Congressional Gold Medal in 1814 and was promoted to brevet brigadier general. President James Monroe appointed Miller as the first governor of the Arkansas Territory and simultaneously the Superintendent of Indian Affairs for Arkansas. His was first challenged by the issue of land claims by the Quapaw, Cherokee, and Choctaw tribes. This was further complicated when warfare broke out in 1821 between the Cherokee and Osage tribes. Most of the credit for resolving the situation went to the territory's first secretary, Robert Crittenden, who served as acting governor in Miller's frequent absence. Even though Miller was governor from 1819 to 1824, his wife remained in New Hampshire, and he stayed there most summers for up to six months. In 1824, Miller was elected to the New Hampshire House of Representatives, but he never assumed office. He preferred to be Collector of Customs in Salem, Massachusetts, where he served until 1849. In 1851, he died at 75 years old in New Hampshire, but was buried in Salem.[9] The issue of statehood first surfaced in 1831 in the Little Rock Arkansas Advocate. It was opposed by the Democrats, who believed the required taxation den on such a small population. The Republicans and the Whigs were in favor, but when Michigan announced it was applying for statehood as a "free" state, Arkansas Territorial Delegate Ambrose Sevier realized that abolitionists would have the majority in the United States Senate unless Arkansas entered as a slave state. As a result, both Michigan and Arkansas applied for statehood. Arkansas got hung up on the issue of proportional representation, with southeast Arkansas wanting to include slaves in order to maximize their number of representatives in the House. Northwest Arkansas wanted to include only white males, which would give them a legislative advantage. A compromise was reached with eight representatives from the northwest, eight representatives from the southeast, and one from the central district. Their Constitution was approved, and President Jackson admitted them to the Union on June 15, 1836.[10]

As Arkansas was preparing for statehood, its economy was in such a weak condition that many in the legislature believed it was unable to support state functions. The planting of cotton was rampant as Arkansas began to compete with Alabama and Mississippi for the exploding domestic and international demand for the cotton. However, most planters were deeply in debt and fully-invested in slaves and land. Sufficient cotton was grown, but it was difficult to sell because Arkansas was unable to transport it to other markets. The federal government gave seed money to start a treasury for the planters, but the funds were wasted. As a result, tax and fee revenues were inadequate. To add to the problem, President Jackson introduced legislation requiring land to be purchased with gold or silver but not with paper money. This legislation reduced land sales, which were the major source of state revenues. In 1836, Governor James Sevier Conway became the first elected governor of the state of Arkansas. It was Conway who chartered the State Bank and the Real Estate Bank to help resolve the state debt and general economy. Private funding was not available, so the state funded both banks. These were contentious measures that caused physical confrontation in the legislature. Violence broke out, whereby Speaker of the House John Wilson, who was president of the Real Estate Bank, actually killed legislator Joseph Anthony, who had criticized Wilson's management of the bank. Wilson was acquitted but was banned from the legislature.[11] The inability of Arkansas to acquire sufficient credit in 1836 led to the Panic of 1837, which affected the entire economies of the United States and Great Britain. The preceding three years saw general economic expansion, but the bubble burst in domestic and foreign markets due to speculative lending in western states, a sharp decline in cotton prices and land values, and restrictive lending policies in Great Britain. Banks failed, prices declined, and unemployment soared up to 25 percent of the labor force. Deflation and recession lasted for seven years until 1844.[12]

Chapter Twenty-six

MICHIGAN

State on January 26, 1837

Explorers and Settlers

Like many parts of the United States, Native Americans occupied these lands for an estimated 10,000 to 15,000 years before they were discovered and settled by Europeans. The area that is now Michigan was home to eight Indian tribes, including the Ojibwa, Menominee, Miami, Ottawa, and Potawatomi, who were all Algonquians. Also, the Wyandot tribe of the Iroquois family lived there. By the 1500's, there were a total of 15,000 Native Americans and only a handful of Europeans who migrated from the Quebec region to explore the western Great Lakes. The name "Michigan" derives from the Chippewa word "meicigama," which translates to "great water," referring to the Great Lakes. One of Canada's earliest discoverers was Samuel de Champlain, who in 1620 ordered his countryman Etienne Brule to explore Michigan's Upper Peninsula, which later became part of Canada and one of its largest provinces in New France. One of the most notable French-Canadian explorers, Father Jacques Marquette, founded the first Michigan settlement of Sault Ste. Marie in 1668. He and his fellow explorer Louis Jolliet established several trading posts and forts in the Great Lakes and Mississippi River Valley. The next major settlement was Detroit, which was founded by French military officer Antoine de la Mothe Cadillac, in 1701. Their collective work was two-fold: conversion of the natives to Christianity and the development of the French-Canadian fur trade, which they dominated. Their pioneering efforts established close trading and cultural relationships with many of the tribes and fostered alliances which were later useful in their future conflicts with the British. The natives regarded the French as friends who integrated with them unlike the English, who kept their distance and pushed the Indians from their ancestral lands and hunting grounds. While the natives enjoyed an increasing amount of trade with the French, they also became more dependent on them for the arms the French supplied them. These were extremely important to the several tribes who were constantly fighting the Iroquois, who were always attempting to take control of the rapidly expanding fur business. In spite of the French-Canadian dominance of the Great Lakes region from 1600 to 1750, the growth of settlements was slow. By 1760, Michigan claimed only several hundred white colonists.[1] France devoted more energy to their colonies in the Ohio River Valley and the lands that bordered the Mississippi River and the Gulf of Mexico. They formally claimed this Midwestern region "New France," which encompassed practically all of the land between the Appalachian Mountains and the Mississippi River. In addition to acquiring rich fertile soil and navigable rivers, they strategically wanted to confine the English colonies to the eastern side of the Appalachians. It was only a matter of time before these two great adversaries would confront each other. As settlers arrived from England, Western Europe, and the East Coast, they migrated beyond the Appalachians, where they met resistance from both the French and the Indians. Land claims and jurisdictional disputes caused friction, which initially erupted in the Ohio River Valley where the French had established Fort Duquesne at present-day Pittsburgh. When Virginia's royal Governor Robert Dinwiddie was informed that French forces occupied Fort Le Boeuf just below Lake Erie, he was alarmed enough to send a small Virginia militia to the area, led by a volunteer named George Washington. The cause for Dinwiddie's concern was the long-standing charter granted to the Virginia Company in 1606 by King James I, which stated the boundaries of Virginia to be all of present-day Virginia, West Virginia, part of Pennsylvania, Ohio, Indiana, Illinois, Michigan, and Wisconsin. To further complicate matters, many prominent Virginians, including Dinwiddie, had invested in land in the Ohio River Valley and their deeds were now in jeopardy. Although Washington had a cordial meeting at Fort Le Boeuf, the French declined to abandon their position, but they confronted Washington again the following year at his Fort Necessity. Following his failure to oust the French, Governor Dinwiddie called on the regular British army under Gen. Edward Braddock in 1755. Braddock was killed and so nearly was Washington, when he successfully evacuated all of the British soldiers. The event marked the start of Washington's rise to notoriety and formalized the start of the French and Indian War, which morphed into the broader Seven Years' War with England's conquest of Canada and the Treaty of Paris in 1763. The treaty required the French to cede all of their continental North American colonies east of the Mississippi River to England. Part of that enormous tract of land included present-day Michigan. British control of the region incensed the Indians, who followed the lead of Chief Pontiac, who organized a revolt which is known as "Pontiac's War." Starting with Fort Detroit, the Indians captured a total of eight British forts, but they were unable to drive the British out of the Great Lakes or the Ohio River Valley. However, the war did bring about better British treatment of the Indians, who had been regarded as a conquered people. Just before the start of the Indian War in 1763, the British announced their bombshell document called the "Proclamation of 1763." This was intended to placate the many Indian tribes, but it did not prevent their uprising. However, it did contain certain provisions of the 1758 Treaty of Easton, which had promised that England would not expand west beyond the Appalachian Mountains. The Treaty and Proclamation were attempts by England to create better relations with the Indians. They took possession of the French forts but did not expand their settlements. One of the most important events to occur after the Proclamation of 1763 was its annexation of the Ohio River region in 1774 into the Provence of Quebec. It included the present-day states of Ohio, Indiana, Illinois, and part of Michigan and was seen as another gesture to the Native Americans to provide hunting grounds and a sanctuary from further European western expansion. However, the measure alarmed the British-Americans who regarded it as a further move to inhibit their western migration and settlements. British control of the former New France lasted for only 13 years until 1776. During the American Revolution, the British did get some help from various Indian tribes, particularly with their capture of Detroit. In return, the American rebels received assistance from the Spanish and French who marched from St. Louis in 1781 to liberate St. Joseph, Missouri from the British and immediately relinquished control to the Americans.[2]

The Northwest Territory

The Treaty of Paris of 1783 ending the Revolutionary War contained an unexpected provision whereby England ceded all of the former lands of New France to the United States, from the Canadian border to the Ohio River, between the Appalachian Mountains to the Mississippi River. Congress called the region the "Northwest Territory," and in 1787, passed the Northwest Ordinance, which stipulated the conditions for its future development. From 1787 to 1800, Michigan was part of the Northwest Territory. It should be noted that prior to the Northwest Ordinance, the states of New York, Massachusetts, Virginia, and Connecticut were required to relinquish their claims to any part of the Northwest Territory. However, once again the Native Americans in this vast area were so upset with this new arrangement that they formed the Western Indian Confederation, which was composed of a broad number of villages containing 15 different tribes. Their united forces resisted American ownership and settlements in the Northwest Indian War, which lasted from 1785 to 1795. The conflict ended in 1795 when Gen. Anthony Wayne with his 5,000 men defeated the Indians at the Battle of Fallen Timbers. Although hostilities with the natives ended, and treaties established the sovereignty of the United States over the Northwest Territory, the British continued to occupy several forts in the region, and boundaries remained unsettled until the War of 1812.[3]

The War of 1812

In 1800, Michigan was first annexed to the Indiana Territory, and in 1805, most of it was made into the new Michigan Territory, including the Lower Peninsula. The War of 1812 brought significant changes to the region. During the early part of the war, the British invaded from Canada to take control of Detroit and Fort Mackinac. They used their positions to incite the natives to fight the Americans. In 1813, Detroit was retaken by the United States, and even though the British and Native Americans were allied, the war ended in 1815 under agreement without a clear victor. The British were finally removed from their Midwestern forts, and the Indian tribes were compelled to sell their lands to the United States. The federal government took charge of the relocation process, which forced the natives to settle in lands to the west. In the decades of the 1820's and 1830's, the Michigan Territory experienced the rapid growth of immigrant arrival, mostly from the Northeast. The migrations started during the Revolutionary War when many New Englanders moved to upstate New York. This continued after the war until overcrowding prevented the next generation from obtaining their own acreage for viable farming. One of the most significant contributions to the westward expansion was the new Erie Canal which opened in 1825. It connected the Great Lakes to the Hudson River, with access to the markets in New York City and beyond the Atlantic Ocean. The Michigan Territory was considered by many to be the "Promised Land," because it also brought a more-cultured people from New York and New England, thereby becoming more politically prominent. Higher education was important, and in 1817, the University of Michigan was founded in Detroit and was later moved to Ann Arbor. As the population continued to expand in the Michigan Territory, it was deemed eligible for statehood by 1835. However, a dispute with the neighboring state of Ohio prevented the process from moving forward. Conflicting state and federal boundary claims between 1787 and 1805 caused both Ohio and Michigan to claim a 468-square mile strip of land around Toledo. The dispute was serious enough to prompt both states to field a militia in a face-off across the Maumee River. In 1836, Congress offered a compromise whereby Michigan would withdraw its claim in exchange for three-fourths of the Upper Peninsula. At first, Michigan rejected the offer, but under pressure from

President Andrew Jackson, they accepted the terms. The "Toledo War" ended without loss of life, and Michigan was redeemed when copper, iron, and timber were later discovered in the Upper Peninsula.[4]

Statesmen, Leaders and Heroes

Perhaps the first hero of Michigan was Etienne Brule, but he remains the most enigmatic figure in its history. It is estimated that he was born in 1592 near Paris. He left no records of his youth, but it is conjectured that he arrived in Quebec around 1608. Explorer Samuel de Champlain noted that he had spoken with a "youth" in 1610 who had spent two years in Quebec and had asked him for permission to live with the local Indians to learn their language. It is an educated guess that the youth was Etienne Brule, even though his name was first recorded by Champlain in 1618, confirming that he had lived among the native for eight years. Champlain was looking for volunteers to learn the local language and dialects, so he eagerly approved of the boy's request and sent him to Chief Iroquet of the Algonquians in exchange for a Huron boy by the name of Savignon, who he later took to France. In 1611, Champlain recorded the first anniversary meeting with Brule and his Indian mentors and noted with joy and pride the boy's accomplishments. He had lived among the Algonquians, dressed like them, and was accepted as one of them. Brule became an excellent liaison between the natives and the colonists and was to play an important role in the development of the fur trade for the French. During the next four years, he was the first European to explore the Huron Country. In 1615, he greatly expanded his exploits by joining the Huron in their battles with the Iroquois and the Susquehanna in upstate New York. He journeyed down to the Chesapeake Bay, but was captured and tortured by the Iroquois. After freeing himself, he was befriended by the Seneca and was instrumental in gaining a peaceful relationship between them and the French. He went on to discover Lake Superior and may have been the first white man to set foot on Pennsylvania soil. He is credited with having discovered four of the Great Lakes and the area west of Lake Michigan.

As daring, adventuresome, and intelligent as he was, Brule acquired a bad reputation because of his poor moral values. He adopted the Indian customs and beliefs, became a vicious person, and lived in a state of debauchery. He had little, if any, religious training. Champlain came to resent his work for the fur industry merchants and not for the colonization of the region. He did receive an annual salary to encourage Indians to trade with them. The final break came in 1629 when the English captured Quebec under the leadership of the Kirke brothers. Brule abandoned Champlain to work for the Kirke, and thereby was accused of treason. Champlain was forced to surrender, and Brule left to live again in the Huron Country. When Champlain returned to the region in 1633, Brule was dead. After having lived among them for 20 years as their brother, Brule was murdered and cannibalized by the Huron. To this day, his murder remains a mystery.[5]

Lewis Cass was born in Exeter, New Hampshire in 1782 to Molly Gilman Cass and Major Jonathan Cass, who was a Revolutionary War veteran. Lewis was educated at Phillips Exeter Academy, and then his family moved to Marietta, Ohio in 1800. Cass was active in the War of 1812, first taking command of the 3rd Ohio Regiment. He was quickly promoted to colonel in 1813 and then to brigadier general in the Regular Army. He participated in the defeat of the British-Canadians at the Battle of the Thames, and as a reward for his service, he was appointed governor of the Michigan Territory by President James Madison. During his term of office from 1813 to 1831, he negotiated several treaties with various Indian tribes who ceded significant tracts of land to the Michigan Territory. In 1820, he led an expedition to northwestern Michigan and into present-day Minnesota to find the source of the Mississippi River, which would mark the boundary of the United States and Canada. This was finally accomplished in 1832 when his geologist Henry Schoolcraft discovered the headwaters at Lake Itasca. In 1831, when Cass resigned as governor, he was appointed Secretary of War by President Andrew Jackson, who had just signed the Indian Removal Act. Cass was occupied with implementing the removal process which affected many tribes in Ohio and Illinois and their relocation to present-day Oklahoma and Kansas. In 1836, Cass was appointed Minister to France, where he served until 1842. He lost his nomination bid for Democratic nominee for the presidency to candidate James Polk. The Michigan legislature voted him to the United States Senate in the 30th Congress from 1845 to 1848. He then tried for the presidency in 1848 but lost to Zachary Taylor. He was returned to the Senate in 1849 until 1857 and then served as Secretary of State for President James Buchanan. He resigned in 1860, disagreeing with Buchanan's failure to protect American interests in the South and mobilize the federal army, which could have prevented the secession of southern states. Cass died in 1866 and is buried in Elmwood Cemetery in Detroit, Michigan.[6]

Stevens Mason was born near Leesburg, Virginia in 1811 into a prominent political family. His ancestry included a chief justice of the Virginia Supreme Court whose brother was George Mason—a neighbor, friend, and political mentor to George Washington; United States Senator for Virginia; United States Representative for Kentucky; Governor of the Louisiana Territory; Governor of the Missouri Territory; and United States Senator for Kentucky. His father, John Thomas Mason, was a lawyer whose business ventures failed but who went on to play an active part in the Texas Revolution of 1835. In 1830, John Mason was appointed by President Jackson as Secretary of the Michigan Territory and Superintendent of Indian Affairs. It was his son, Stevens, who protected him from political adversaries. When President Jackson sent John on a mission to Mexico in 1831, he replaced him with young Stevens as Secretary at 19 years old. When John Cass became Jackson's Secretary of War, he was replaced with Governor George Porter, who was often absent, leaving young Stevens as acting governor, which earned him the nickname of "Boy Governor." Young Mason first attempted a petition for statehood in 1832, which was rejected. He then ordered a census, which was completed in 1834 and showed a population of 86,000 people, which was well above the required minimum of 60,000. A dispute arose between Ohio and Michigan over a strip of land near Toledo, which delayed the statehood process. Mason would not agree to the arbitration, so Jackson replaced him with John Horner. Mason was elected in 1835 and agreed to cede the Toledo strip to Ohio in exchange for three-fourths of the Upper Peninsula. Mason also initiated the construction of three railroads and two canals. The financial panic of 1837 forced the abandonment of the projects and left the state with $2 million of debt. He decided to leave politics in 1839 and was replaced as governor by William Woodbridge, who blamed Mason for the financial mess. In 1841, Mason moved to New York City, where he tried unsuccessfully to establish a law practice. In January of 1843, he contracted pneumonia and died. Stevens Mason's legacy includes the City of Mason, Mason County, Mason Hall at Michigan State University, Mason Hall at the University of Michigan, the Stevens T. Mason Building at Lansing, two high schools, two elementary schools, and one middle school. One of his greatest achievements was the establishment of an educational and the relocation of the University of Michigan to Ann Arbor.[7]

Father Gabriel Richard was born in France in 1767, entered the seminary in 1784, and was ordained in 1790. Two years later, he arrived in Baltimore, where he taught mathematics at St. Mary's Seminary. He was then assigned by the first American-born Catholic Bishop, John Carroll, to engage in missionary work with the Indians in the Northwest Territory. He first went to Kaskaskia, Illinois and then to Detroit in 1798. In 1804, he opened a school in Detroit, but it was razed by a fire that demolished the city in 1805 and destroyed its grain and livestock. Father Richard organized a program to aid the victims with food from the countryside farms. He operated the first printing press in Detroit and published French language magazines. The Native Americans greatly admired Father Richard, and in spite of their hatred of white men, Chief Tecumseh would not fight for the British until Father Richard was released from his imprisonment. Father Richard was a co-founder of the University of Michigan, which had been authorized by the legislature in 1817. He served as its Vice President for four years. In 1821, the University board was reorganized, and Father Richard again served as Vice President and was appointed to the board of trustees. He was the first Catholic priest elected to the United States House of Representatives and served for one term from 1823 to 1825. In 1832, while assisting cholera patients, Father Richard contracted the disease and passed away at 65 years old. His legacy is Gabriel Richard High School in Ann Arbor, Gabriel Richard Elementary School in Detroit, and Pere Gabriel Richard Elementary School in Grosse Pointe Farms.[8]

Chapter Twenty-seven

Florida

State on March 3, 1845

Explorers and Settlers

Although it is likely that Florida was first explored by the Portuguese around 1500, credit is given to the Spaniard Juan Ponce de Leon, who organized an expedition in 1513 from Puerto Rico to Florida. Also, he may have had the opportunity to have studied the first map of the area, found in 1502 by the Italian Alberto Cantino, who reportedly smuggled it from Portugal. The "Cantino Planisphere" is the earliest existing nautical chart of many parts of the world and was composed using astronomically-observed latitudes. However, there is widespread belief that de Leon was the author of the name "Florida." He set foot in Florida on April 7, 1513 during Easter week and therefore named it "La Pascua de la Florida," meaning "Feast of Flowers." The land was soon referred to as "La Florida." The expedition of 200 men and women landed just south of St. Augustine and then sailed through the Florida Keys up the western coast to

Charlotte Harbor, where they were confronted by hostile Calusa Indians before returning home to Puerto Rico. Other Spanish explorers, including Hernando de Soto, explored the southeastern section of the continent without establishing lasting settlements. In 1564, Frenchman Rene de Laudonniere founded Fort Collins (present-day Jacksonville) for refugee Protestant Huguenots, but the next year, Spaniard Menendez de Aviles killed most of its defenders. In 1567, Frenchman Dominique de Gourgue recaptured the settlement and slaughtered the Spanish defenders. In 1565, de Aviles founded St. Augustine, which is regarded as the oldest continuously inhabited city in the United States. In 1586, Sir Francis Drake burned down the city, but it continued to be a major base for Catholic missionaries, from which they converted 26,000 natives over the following 100 years. In spite of frequent attacks and plunders from the British, French, and Spanish, St. Augustine became the most important settlement in Florida. From 1702 to 1704, The English under Col. James Moore attacked and burned St. Augustine but were unable to capture it. However, they did defeat the Spanish and their Indian allies, the Yamasee, Creek, and Appalachia. They went on to destroy the Spanish missions. In 1740, British forces under Georgia's founder, James Oglethorpe, attacked St. Augustine but were still unable to control it. Florida was becoming an attraction for African-American slaves who were fleeing from British slavery and who were offered their freedom by the Spanish if they converted to Catholicism. Many of them settled north of St. Augustine in a village called "Gracia Real de Santa Teresa," which became the first free black town in North America. The local Seminoles and Creeks welcomed the slaves and refused to assist the British Government when they made efforts to retrieve them for return to their former owners.[1]

European Rulers

The French and Indian War and the Seven Years' War occurred from 1752 to 1763 and ended with the Treaty of Paris. The impact of the wars was significant in many ways but especially for Florida. Spain and France were the major losers, and the British gained large colonies. Spain ceded all of Florida to Great Britain in exchange for control of Havana, Cuba, which the British had captured in the war that had just ended. The majority of the Spanish left Florida for Cuba, and the British were eager to replace them by giving veterans of the war land grants. Also, many people migrated there from South Carolina, Georgia, and Bermuda. Because it represented such a large area deemed too big to govern, the British divided it into two colonies: East Florida and West Florida. East Florida was the peninsula owned by Spain, and West Florida was the "Panhandle," which had been owned by France. Its western boundary was the Mississippi River, and the eastern boundary was the Chamahoochee River. The capitals were St. Augustine in the East and Pensacola in the West. During the Revolutionary War, both colonies remained loyal to Great Britain. Spain was indirectly involved because it was an ally of France and captured Pensacola from the British in 1781, two years before the end of that war. After the American War, Great Britain ceded East and West Florida to Spain.[2] Most of the English left, and Florida became a refuge for slaves and those fleeing Indian attacks from the Seminoles. Migrant British-Americans from Georgia and South Carolina moved into northern Florida, where they integrated with those British who had elected to stay. The Spanish authorities were not successful in keeping out the migrants, who became more resentful of Spanish rule or the lack of it. In 1810, the resistance by the British-Americans led to a rebellion which resulted in a three-month long Independent Republic of West Florida. The rebels went so far as to fly their own "Bonnie Blue Flag," which had a large white star on a solid blue field. This was later used as the initial flag of the Confederate States of America at the start of the Civil War. That same year, President James Madison annexed part of West Florida to the Territory of Orleans, claiming it was included in the Louisiana Purchase. In 1812, the United States annexed the Mobile District of West Florida to the Mississippi Territory. In 1817-18, the United States army led by Gen. Andrew Jackson entered East Florida in the First Seminole War. The American Government under Secretary of State John Quincy Adams viewed Florida as a derelict area void of effective government which served no purpose other than to harass the United States. Spain did not have the will or resources to maintain the colony, so they ceded it to the United States in 1821 with the "Adams-Onis Treaty."[3]

In 1822, Florida was organized into the Florida Territory by combining East and West Florida. The new capital of Tallahassee was established in the center between St. Augustine and Pensacola. Many free blacks and Indian slaves fled to Cuba to escape United States control. Black Seminoles and fugitive slaves moved to Andros Island in the Bahamas. Andrew Jackson was appointed by President Monroe to be the first military governor of the new territory. The major issue at the time was how to deal with the Seminole Indians. The United States government and the white settlers wanted them to move to the West. The issue was contentious and finally resolved in 1830 with passage of the Indian Removal Act, which required all Native Americans in the Southeast to move west of the Mississippi River. The act led to the Treaty of Paynes Landing, signed by the Seminoles in 1832. At that signing, their famous warrior chief Osceola declared his intention to fight. In 1835, he started a guerilla war against the United States. After many failed attempts by American generals, death and disease took their toll. Finally, Gen. Thomas Jesup captured most of the Seminole chiefs, including Osceola, who died in captivity. The fighting ended with the Seminoles forced to migrate.[4]

The Florida Territory

When Gen. Andrew Jackson was appointed military governor of the Florida Territory in March of 1821, he was not enthusiastic about the assignment. His fears were strained relations with the Spanish population that disliked him and of being isolated in an undeveloped area. However, Secretary of State John Quincy Adams believed Jackson was the best choice because of his extensive knowledge of the area. In July of that year, Spain relinquished control of Florida to the United States, and Jackson was faced with the enormous challenges of transferring Spanish property to the Americans, settling conflicting land claims, and mediating the many cultural differences that permeated the colony, knowing that the Spanish disliked and distrusted him. When the Spanish governor protested Jackson's policies, he was thrown in jail. Rather than selling their homes and properties at depressed prices, many Spaniards burned them to the ground. Florida was under-populated, lacked decent roads, and harbored hostile Seminole Indians. The government was poorly funded, and its legislature needed more diverse representation. A court of appeals was established in 1824, and new counties were chartered. The territory was in debt, and revenues were limited coming only from taxes on land sales, license fees, and poll taxes.

Half of the counties did not meet their tax return goals. The Whigs supported government spending for roads and public projects as well as charters for state banks. They were opposed by the rural small farmers of East Florida. Political differences began to take shape, especially when the new Peninsula Bank collapsed, harming many of the West Florida Democrat farmers who opposed the plantation aristocracy and called for lower taxes. Political power was the strongest among the plantation owners who were centered in the most fertile farmland between the Suwannee and Apalachicola Rivers. The early planters included family names such as Du Val, Call, Murat, White, and Milton. The middle-class consisted of merchants, shopkeepers, builders, and artisans. The small farmers were in the third class, and the black freedmen and slaves had the least status. Plantation life was very regimented for owners, workers, and slaves. Rising at dawn and stopping at sunset, everyone was assigned a specific task. Successful farming procedures were copied by other farmers, thereby producing uniform practices. Strict records were kept regarding all activities, especially the quantity and quality of crops and livestock as well as the health of workers. There were state statutes against cruelty to slaves. Cotton became the major crop after the introduction of the cotton gin (short for "engine") in 1793. Corn was grown for livestock and sugar cane for Consumption.[5]

Slavery

Slavery was a significant part of the Florida economy until it was abolished by the 13th Amendment of the United States Constitution in 1865. Slaves were the private property of individuals, and none were owned by the Florida Territory. There were very few slave rebellions in Florida, because it was a small closed society where escape was almost impossible. The free northern states were too far away, and the only practical possibility for escape was to the Caribbean by boat. Even free blacks preferred Florida over Mississippi and Alabama, where large plantations with overseers could make life even more unbearable. In Florida, slaves were generally trained in certain skills by their owners. Even free blacks were known to have returned to slavery when the right jobs and conditions were available. They lived in small cabins with fireplaces. Their daily routine was breakfast at sunrise, preparing lunch, and then going out to the fields. Work ended at 4:00 p.m. so they could tend to their own vegetable gardens. Some also work on construction or road projects. Skilled slaves could buy their freedom but were usually only freed when their owners retired or passed away. By law, slaves could not be fired, so there was a certain degree of security with a place to live and work. The key for them was to gain sufficient skills to increase their usefulness and value. This was evident during the Civil War, when many slaves were left to operate farms or work in towns.

The slavery system virtually ended African culture in America. They were not allowed to speak African words, practice African customs, or practice African faiths. They came from various tribes, and bondage was the force that brought them together. Children were raised by their mothers until they were old enough to help in the fields. Education was limited and dependent on the owner's attitude. The principal output for maintaining their identity was through the church where they could hold Sunday services, administer baptisms, sing, and listen to black preachers. With its small farms, Florida also offered the possibility of retaining slave family unity with some ties to their owner's family.[6]

Most of Florida consisted of small farms where owners were fearful of being overrun by northern planters, investors, and speculators. They were generally referred to as "Florida Crackers," which derives from the sound of their whips, driving teams of mules or oxen. They were Baptists or Methodists of Scots-Irish or non-Anglican English descent who migrated from Georgia and Alabama. They could not afford land in the rich soils of Middle Florida but instead worked in the peninsula with its poor sandy soils which were not suitable for plantation farming. They preferred the frontier life where their independent spirit drove them to work hard and pray often. They wanted to control their own destiny and promote strong family households. They did not participate in territorial politics, but they did believe in representative government. They were poor but proud and lived within their means. Their needs were satisfied with a monthly trip to town with a convoy of wagons to protect them from Indian attacks, help with wagon breakdowns, and provide companionship. They engaged in community house-raisings, corn shucking, and forest burning for pasture land. Religion was their foundation and could be practiced in their homes until sufficient community funds enabled them to collectively build a chapel or church. Florida Crackers were tough, stable, and reliable. When the plantation society disappeared following the Civil War, it was the Crackers who rebuilt the South.[7]

Statesmen, Leaders and Heroes

Three important figures stand out in the establishment of Florida as a state: Andrew Jackson, James Monroe, and John Quincy Adams. Probably the most outstanding was Jackson, who fought and governed valiantly over many years all over the South, and even at the age of 13, fought in Charleston against the British in 1780 in the Revolutionary War. Although he is usually regarded as a son of Tennessee, he was born in South Carolina in 1767 to parents who had emigrated from Ireland two years prior. His father died before Andrew was born. His mother was in Charleston, nursing the sick and wounded American soldiers in 1781, when she contracted cholera and died, leaving Andrew an orphan. At age 13, he volunteered to fight the British during their southern campaign, when he and his older brother Robert were captured. When the brash feisty Andrew refused to polish the British officer's boots, he was slashed with a sword to the arm and head, which nearly killed him, and he carried these scars for the rest of his life. Both of the brothers contracted smallpox while in prison and barely survived. Their mother was influential in gaining their release in a prisoner exchange; however, Robert soon died and Andrew lived after a long convalescence. After the war, Jackson finished school and briefly worked as a teacher. In 1784, he moved to North Carolina to study law and received his license three years later. He practiced in the back country of North Carolina and earned the reputation for being wild and ambitious. At age 21, his mentor John McNairy appointed Jackson as the North Carolina Western District prosecuting attorney. He then moved to Nashville, Tennessee. In 1802, Jackson was elected general of the Tennessee Militia to serve in the western and southern frontiers. He soon acquired the nickname "Old Hickory" from his soldiers, who regarded him as tough as a hickory tree. He gained his first public attention from his defeat of the Creeks and the Treaty of Fort Jackson, which forced the Creeks to cede 23 million acres of land to the United States. In the War of 1812, he acted on his own insights rather than government or military advice. He had no formal military training but still managed to defend New Orleans from a large military force of British veterans, forcing them to withdraw from Louisiana. The victory brought him national acclaim as the new American hero and marked the beginning of his path to the White House. At the end of the war in 1815, Major General Jackson was put in charge of the southern border of the United States. His two chief concerns were the Native Americans and Spanish Florida. The Seminole tribe had been steadily forced to southern Florida, where America had weak defenses. In 1818, he took the initiative to attack Spanish Florida and the Seminoles, declaring victory within three months. His action caused an international outcry, but he was supported by Secretary of State John Quincy Adams and President Monroe. In 1819, realizing that the United States was eager to control Florida, Spain agreed to cede their colony to the United States in the Adams-Onis Treaty, which took effect in 1821. Jackson was appointed military governor of the Florida Territory and immediately consolidated East Florida with those parts of West Florida that had not been previously annexed to Alabama, Mississippi, and Louisiana. He resigned in December of 1821 to serve two terms as the United States senator from Tennessee before becoming president in 1829.[8]

The acquisition of Florida at no cost to the United States would probably not have happened without the coordinated efforts of President James Monroe, Secretary of State John Quincy Adams, and Gen. Andrew Jackson. Presidents Madison and Monroe had been trying to purchase the colonies without success. When Napoleon invaded Spain in 1807, they needed to consolidate their resources and therefore paid less attention to their North American colonies. Florida's population exploded with Seminole, slave, and British-American migrants, and without adequate Spanish administration, conditions in Florida deteriorated into havens of lawlessness and the staging of attacks on nearby Georgia. Spain was well-aware of America's interests, but it did not act until Secretary Adams delivered a strong note of warning to Madrid. The conflict was initiated in January of 1818 when the Seminoles massacred a group of settlers and sought protection under the Spanish flag. When he learned of the attack, Secretary of War John Calhoun ordered General Jackson from Nashville to the Florida frontier to gather whatever troops he could from the neighboring territories. The governor could not be reached, so he acted on his own. Before starting, he wrote a letter to President Monroe suggesting that he take control of all of Florida and hold it as indemnity for all past outrages that were committed in the region. At the same time, Secretary Adams was negotiating with Spain for a peaceful acquisition of Florida and ordered that its boundaries should not be violated, but this was not sent to Jackson. President Monroe sent word to Jackson that he approved of his suggestions, thereby assuring Jackson of his authority to act. Jackson invaded Florida and captured St. Mark's fort in East Florida and the town of Pensacola in West Florida, killing Seminoles and executing two British military spies. The incident caused an international furor, but Jackson was exonerated when a trial revealed the guilt of the two soldiers and their role in the Indian atrocities. Madrid, London, and other European capitals were shocked, but American opinion favored Jackson. Congress wanted an investigation, but President Monroe and Secretary Adams supported Jackson. The next move was a letter from Adams to the Spanish minister that actually threatened Spain with American confiscation of Florida "if an officer of the United States should ever again be compelled to march into Florida." The letter reached London as well, which deterred England from interfering in the affair. By a large majority of congressional votes, Jackson was supported for his actions.[9] The incident led to negotiations for the Adams-Onis Treaty of 1819, which attempted to resolve the outstanding issues of borders and Spanish land claims: 1) both East and West Florida were ceded to the United States; 2) Spain abandoned its claim to the Oregon Territory; 3) a clear definition of the boundary of the Spanish Province of Mexico was established, making Spanish Texas a part of Mexico; 4) the United States agreed to pay up to $5 million for legal claims of Americans against Spain; 5) Spanish trade goods received most-favored-trade status in the ports of St. Augustine and Pensacola for the next 12 years; and 6) the United States relinquished claims to the part of Texas west of the Sabine River.[10]

Statehood

On March 3, 1845, Florida became the 27th state, on the last day of President John Tyler's term of office. Tyler was succeeded by the 11th president, James Polk, a Jacksonian Democrat from Tennessee. Florida's first governor was William

Moseley, and the leading advocate for statehood, David Levy Yulee, was elected to the United States Senate. The 1850 census showed the state's population at 87,445, which included 39,000 African-American slaves and 1,000 free blacks. Slavery very soon became the major issue in Florida and in the rest of the country. Abraham Lincoln won the next national election for president in 1860, but he received no votes in Florida. In January of 1861, Florida passed a new ordinance, allowing them to secede from the Union, which they did several weeks later to join the Confederate States of America.[11]

Chapter Twenty-eight

Texas

State on December 29, 1845

French Texas

Similar to many other American states, Texas had been occupied by several Native American tribes for thousands of years before the Spanish Conquistadors arrived, led by Hernando De Soto in 1519. However, Texas is somewhat unique in that it can specify just how long the natives lived here. In 1983, a full skeleton of a woman in her 30's was unearthed in Cedar Park, and carbon tests showed her to be 10,000 to 13,000 years old. She is a rare find and has been named "Neanderthal Lady" and "Leanne," referring to the nearby town of Leander. As we have seen in other Mississippi River Valley areas, the early Spanish explorers of the 1500's did little to establish permanent settlements other than a few missions over the next 150 years. With their explorations of the lower Mississippi River in the early 1600's, French explorers Marquette and Jolliet were the first Europeans to make significant inroads in eastern

Texas, as they searched for a navigable river connecting the Great Lakes to the Gulf of Mexico to market their fur products from the North. They were followed by Robert Cavalier de La Salle, who claimed the Mississippi River Valley in 1682 and named it "Louisiane" in honor of their King Louis XIV. In 1684, he convinced the king that a fort at the mouth of the Mississippi River was essential, not only for the protection of the southern borders of New France, but it also for attacking New Spain to the east and taking control of New Vizcoya and its extensive silver mines. He planned to do this by gaining alliances with the Native Americans who were at odds with the Spanish for enslaving them. King Louis wholeheartedly agreed with La Salle's plan and provided him with four warships, crews, supplies, and funds to hire skilled workers. In 1685, La Salle built Fort St. Louis near Arenas Creek and Matagorda Bay. He had planned to construct it at the mouth of the Mississippi River to protect his settlements and to access the Gulf, but poor maps and navigational errors caused him to land 400 miles west of there at the present-day town of Inez. The settlement lasted only three years because of illness and difficult conditions. La Salle expected to be supplied with necessary materials from the French colonies in the Caribbean, but these were abandoned, leaving him to depend on French colonies in the Illinois Country. During this brief period, he explored the Rio Grande and eastern Texas. In 1687, La Salle was murdered when a mutiny erupted against his leadership. The next year, the remaining colonists were murdered by a Kawakawa raid. However, Fort St. Louis enabled France to claim ownership of Texas. When the United States purchased the Louisiana Territory in 1803, it tried to include Fort St. Louis, but the claim was dismissed. Spain still considered Texas part of New Spain and sent several expeditions to expel the French and reestablish control. In 1689, they found the remains of Fort St. Louis, burned whatever was left, and buried any evidence of French settlement. Several years later, they built a fortified base called a "presidio" on the site in a further effort to destroy any evidence of the French occupation. In 1996, the Fort was rediscovered, and the French ship, *La Belle* was found at the bottom of Matagorda Bay. In 2000, more excavations unearthed several parts of the original Fort and the graves of Frenchmen.[1]

Spanish Texas

Spain resumed control of Spanish Texas in 1690 until 1821. Alonso de Leon, together with Catholic missionaries, established their first mission in east Texas in 1690. When the natives protested their presence, they left the area for almost 20 years before returning in 1716 to build several missions and a fort to protect them from the French district of Louisiana. In 1718, they built their first Texas civilian settlement, which was located in San Antonio to provide a shelter between missions. However, it was under constant attack from the Upper Apache for almost 30 years until peace was established with them in 1749. Other tribes which were enemies of the Apache resumed the attacks on the town, so it remained unsettled by immigrants until 1785 when the Spanish achieved peace with the Comanche. By the turn of the century, almost all tribes ceased hostilities. The French and Indian War changed the region when France was forced to cede Louisiana and part of Texas to Spain. In 1799, Spain returned Louisiana to France, and four years later, Napoleon sold its Louisiana Territory to the United States. President Jefferson believed the purchase included all the land east of the Rocky Mountains and north of the Rio Grande, even though a large portion of the southwestern part was located in New Spain. The disagreement was finally resolved in 1819 under the Adams-Onis Treaty in which Spain ceded West Florida to the United States in return for American recognition of the Sabine River as the eastern boundary of Spanish-Texas and the western boundary of the Missouri Territory. The Treaty took place during the Mexican War of Independence, which lasted from 1810 to 1821. Governor Manuel de Salcedo was overthrown in 1810, but he later organized a counter-coup. This was followed by the Republican army of the North, consisting of Indians and Americans who overthrew the government of Texas and executed Governor Salcedo. Spain was furious, but in 1821, it was forced to cede New Spain to the new nation of Mexico, which included Texas as a province.[2]

Mexican Texas

Mexican Texas has also been called "Tejas," because it was a province of Mexico when it won its independence from Spain in 1821. The name "Tejas" derives from the Caddo tribe of Native Americans and translates to "friends" or "allies."

For the next four years, Mexico was undecided about their political structure. They first wrote a provisional constitution which adopted many concepts of the Spanish Constitution of 1812, which granted equal citizen rights to all races. They then attempted a constitutional monarchy under Augustin I, but that ended in 1823 when he abdicated. Later that year, Mexico launched a federal republic with congressional representatives and named Luciano Garcia as the political head of Texas. In 1824, the country adopted a new constitution with 19 states and four territories. It was modeled on the United States Constitution, with the major exception that Catholicism was the official religion of the country.

In 1821, Texas was sparsely populated with an estimated population of 3,500 settlers, with most of them located in San Antonio and La Bahia. To promote more growth, the government passed the General Colonization Law in 1824, which permitted all heads of households to come to Mexico. The first land and settlement grant made under Spanish rule and later ratified by Mexico was to Stephen Austin, who brought settlers to the Brazos River area. Settlers were brought to the state from the United States, Europe, and Mexico by 23 other "entrepreneurs." In 1830, Mexican authorities became alarmed at the independent attitude of the Americans who were demanding more American democracies, so it outlawed further immigration. In 1833, colonists in Texas held a convention where they proposed that Texas become a separate Mexican state. The government tried to appease them, but Santa Anna's policies to transfer Mexico from a federalist to a centralist state caused the colonists to revolt. The first skirmish had occurred in 1832 at the Battle of Velasco. With the government of Santa Anna, the settlers in the border area of Texas and Mexico became even more upset with the loss of their individual rights under the dictatorial regime. Many of the American immigrants there became outspoken opponents of the government, and frictions escalated rapidly in October of 1835. In an effort to restore order, Santa Anna sent a large number of soldiers to the area, which marked the advent of the Texas Revolution. The Mexican army was defeated and it surrendered in December after the siege of Bexar (San Antonio). Santa Ana believed the Texans were "pirates" who were interfering in Mexican affairs, and he vowed to eliminate them. He even wrote to President Andrew Jackson to advise him of his intentions. After the Mexican defeat at Bexar, the Americans established a small garrison at the Alamo Mission which had previously converted to a fort by the Mexican army, built to defend against Indian attacks but not strong enough to withstand an army assault. Col. James Neill had requested more supplies and troops from Cmdr. Sam Houston, but he lacked spare troops and sent James Bowie to help defend the fort. On February 23rd, 1,500 Mexicans marched into San Antonio de Bexar, and for ten days the two armies exchanged fire. On March 6th, the Mexicans led two attacks which were repelled, but on the third attack, the walls were breached and the Texans were killed or executed while trying to surrender. Between 182 and 250 Texans died, and about 600 Mexicans were killed or wounded. The American loss was the motivation for many other Americans to join the Texan army, which achieved their revenge at the Battle of San Jacinto in April of 1836.[3] Gen. Sam Houston defeated Santa Anna, who was taken prisoner. The Mexican army was forced to leave the area. which paved the way for the eventual establishment of the Republic of Texas. The Mexican government did not recognize the new Republic, because they believed that any agreement or treaty signed by a prisoner was invalid. They were critical of General Filisola for retreating from Texas and replaced him with General Urrea, who promptly assembled 6,000 troops to recapture Texas. However, Urrea was soon ordered to defend other Mexican provinces which were rebelling. Colonists assumed that Mexico would again try to reconquer Texas, so thousands of volunteers from the United States arrived to join the Texan army. All "Tejanos" in the area between Guadalupe and the Nueces River were ordered to move to either Mexico or East Texas. Any remaining people were removed and replaced with new Anglo settlers who took over their land. Taxes in Mexico were raised to build a larger army to retake Texas, but it was primarily used to quell other rebellious provinces which threatened to ally with Texas.[4]

The Republic of Texas

The Republic of Texas was created on March 2, 1836 and existed until statehood on December 29, 1845. It was bordered on the southwest and west by Mexico, on the southeast by the Gulf of Mexico, to the east by Louisiana and Arkansas, and to the north by territories that included future Oklahoma, Kansas, Colorado, and Wyoming. The boundaries were based on the Treaty of Velasco, signed in

1836 by Texas and Mexican President Santa Anna, and the treaty following the Battle of San Jacinto, signed by the Republic's President David Burnet and President Santa Anna. Neither treaty was recognized by the Mexican government, because they claimed they were signed under duress. Mexican authorities regarded Texas as a breakaway province, and they did not sanction the word "treaties" to indicate an end to hostilities between the two parties. Throughout the Republic's ten-year history, their southern border remained in dispute. Texas claimed it was marked by the Rio Grande River, but Mexico claimed it was the Nueces River farther to the north along the Gulf. In 1844, President James Polk offered to purchase the land between the two rivers for the United States. Upon its rejection by Mexico, Maj. Gen. Zachary Taylor and his troops were moved to this area known as Coahuila, and while there, the Mexican soldiers killed 12 and imprisoned 52 Americans. They also destroyed an American fort on the Rio Grande. The actions led to the Mexican-American War of 1846-1848.[5] As a result of the several conflicts, the United States forces occupied Santa Fe de Nuevo Mexico (New Mexico), the Alta, California Territory, and parts of northeastern and northwestern Mexico. The United States army imposed a blockade in Baja, California and took control of several garrisons to the south of Baja. Maj. Gen. Winfield Scott captured Mexico City. It was well-known that President Polk wanted to expand the United States to the Pacific Coast, but the war with Mexico was controversial and widely unpopular. It ended in 1848 with the Treaty of Guadalupe-Hidalgo, which had Mexico ceding Santa Fe de Mexico (New Mexico) and the Alta, California Territory to the United States. America agreed to pay for the physical losses sustained in these areas, totaling $15 million, and it assumed the $3.25 million debt owed by Mexico to American citizens. In the United States, the war with Mexico was a partisan issue and divided the country into sectional rivalries. Whigs in the North opposed it while southern Democrats supported it with the hope it would expand slavery-owning territory. The Treaty had far-reaching consequences for the future expansion of the United States. Mexico relinquished claims to lands that would someday become nine states including New Mexico, Nevada, Utah, Arizona, California, most of Colorado, and parts of Wyoming, Kansas, and Oklahoma. Before the war, Mexico claimed to own a total of 1.7 million square miles. After the war in 1849, that amount shrank to 800,000 square miles. The land annexed by the United States contained 14,000 non-indigenous people in Alta, California and 60,000 in New Mexico. In addition, there were many large Indian nations which migrated to Mexico, but the majority remained in the United States. The Treaty did offer all Mexicans living in the ceded territories the opportunity to become United States citizens, but it withheld citizenship from the southeastern Indians until the 1930's, even though they were legal citizens of Mexico.[6]

The war had devastating effects on the Mexican government and its people. They blamed it on the aggressiveness of the United States and their own weakness in defending their lands. Following their independence from Spain in 1821, Mexico had left its northern territories vulnerable to attacks from the Comanche, Apache, and Navajo Indians. The natives constantly invaded far into Mexico for several hundred miles where they acquired cattle for themselves and to sell in Texas and beyond. To help stabilize the area, Mexico encouraged United States citizens to settle in the western provinces, but they chose to live in East Texas where the soil was fertile and the American markets were much closer. For Americans, the newly acquired lands created a stampede of settlers and a wave of patriotism. The extension of the country was seen as an obvious development that promoted the American concept of "Manifest Destiny," which was simply a belief in what was meant to be. Opposition to the Mexican War included notable leaders such as Congressman Abraham Lincoln and poet Ralph Waldo Emerson, who were very outspoken against it. President Polk was for the war, and in the election of 1848, the country praised Gen. Zachary Taylor, their new president, for his military conquests. Future president Ulysses S. Grant was a young army lieutenant under General Taylor, and he recorded in his "Memoirs" that he was strongly opposed to the war with Mexico, believing it was extremely unjust for a stronger nation to wage war against a weaker nation for the purpose of acquiring territory.[7] Another junior officer, Capt. Robert E. Lee, began his fighting experience in the Mexican War. Under Generals Wool and Scott, he took seven major cities and was cited for his extraordinary physical and moral courage. Just before the American Civil War erupted, it was commanding Gen. Winfield Scott who recommended Lee to President Lincoln to be appointed as the commander of the Union army. Lee declined the offer because he strongly objected to invading his southern homeland. The actual fighting of the Mexican War lasted only 17 months, but it took a heavy toll on the 115,000 mostly volunteer soldiers. Death, injuries, and disease accounted for 35-40 percent of casualties, which made it the deadliest war in American history. Politically, it caused great dissension among those who wanted and those who opposed the complete annexation of Mexico. It raised the question of slavery and whether the ceded territories would become slave or free states. Disputes lingered into the 1880's when Congress declared the war to be "one of the darkest scenes in our history."[8]

Statesmen, Leaders and Heroes

Both Sam Houston and Stephen Austin are regarded as the "Fathers" of Texas. Houston was born near Lexington, Virginia in 1793, the son of a Revolutionary veteran. When his father died in 1807, the family moved to eastern Tennessee. Five years later, he joined the military and fought in the War of 1812 under Andrew Jackson, who accorded him praise for his valor. Houston enjoyed a good relationship with Jackson, who convinced him to move to Texas and enter politics. He then earned his law degree and was elected the district attorney general. In 1823, he was elected to Congress, where he served for two terms. In 1827, Houston was elected governor of Tennessee. When his first marriage dissolved in 1829, he resigned his governorship and moved to Arkansas, where he married Tiana Rodgers, a native Cherokee. Houston had earlier in life become close to the Cherokees, even learning their language and being adopted as one of their citizens. He then began to represent the Cherokee Nation in Washington, D.C. In 1832, he became involved in a legal fight with United States Congressman William Stanberry of Ohio. He was found guilty of assault and let go on bail but suddenly left for "Tejas," which was still a Mexican province. He soon became involved in the Texas Revolution, which simmered for several years and finally broke into war in 1836. Houston's fame was assured that year when he defeated Mexican Gen. Santa Anna at the decisive Battle of San Jacinto. The victory was completed with the Treaty of Velasco, which Santa Anna was forced to sign and which granted Texas its independence. Sam Houston was elected president of the Republic of Texas in 1836 for two years and again in 1841 for three years. He supported annexation of Texas by the United States in 1845 and then became a United States senator for one year, which established him as the only person to become governor of two different states—Texas and Tennessee. He was re-elected governor in 1859, and two years later, he refused to accept secession into the Confederacy, which caused his removal from office in 1861. At the start of the Civil War he declined an offer to fight for the Union army and instead chose to retire to Huntsville, where he died on July 26, 1863 at 70 years old. His legacies are many, including the City of Houston and being remembered as one of the fathers of Texas.[9]

Stephen Austin was also born in 1793 in Virginia but was raised in southeastern Missouri. His great-great-grandfather Anthony and his wife migrated from Hampshire, England in the 1600's to Suffield, Massachusetts, which became part of Connecticut in 1749. At the age of 11, Stephen was sent to Connecticut and then to the University of Kentucky for his education. After beginning his law studies, he served in the legislature of the Missouri Territory. The financial panic of 1819 forced him to move south to the Arkansas Territory. He lost his first run for Congress but was soon appointed a judge for the First Circuit Court. While in Arkansas, his father received a grant to bring 300 families to Texas, which became known as the "Old Three Hundred." Upon the death of his father, his mother persuaded Stephen to continue Anthony's work of colonizing Texas. In 1817, on his way to San Antonio, he met Jose Antonio Navarro, who befriended him and helped him secure his father's impresario grant. The contracts allowed him to explore the Gulf Coast between the San Antonio and Brazos Rivers for a future colony. Austin travelled to New Orleans, where he advertised the opportunities to obtain inexpensive land in Texas. Farmers could purchase 177 acres, and ranchers could buy 4,428 acres for 12.5 cents per acre. In December of 1821, the first American colonists went to settle in present-day Brazoria County. However, in that same year, the Mexican government claimed its independence from Spain, and the new laws voided all land grants. Austin travelled to Mexico City to appeal his case, which was approved but was later denied in 1823 when Emperor Augustin de Iturbide abdicated. In 1825, the former laws were reinstated, allowing impresarios to open and administer public lands. The law also allowed married men 4,428 acres for a $30 fee to the state, payable within six years. By the end of that year, Austin had brought 300 families to his settlement of Austin County, which history refers to as the "Old Three Hundred." Over the next four years, Austin went on to bring 900 more families. Having virtual control over his settlement, he introduced civil laws as well as armed groups to protect them, which evolved into the Texas Rangers. Austin made almost nothing for his work, as most settlers did not compensate him. During the 1830's, Austin worked closely with the Mexican authorities in helping to develop the Texas economy. He even sided with them in suppressing the Fredonian Rebellion by organizing local troops to join the Mexican army in fighting the Texas rebels. The Americans who had settled there totaled around 11,000 by 1832, and there was a rapidly increasing desire for independence. Mexican authorities were becoming increasingly concerned, so they restricted their immigration policies but allowed Austin to continue accepting immigrants. The introduction of tariffs caused further complaints from the colonists. Austin used his political connections to keep the colonists under control, and he even supported the emerging power of Santa Anna. He was able to gain some reforms, including lifting the ban on immigration. In 1834, the Mexican government arrested him for supporting Texas independence and inciting insurrection. After being moved from prison to prison in Mexico City, he was finally freed by general amnesty in 1835, at which point he returned to Texas. He took command of the Texas military, and with confrontations in several towns, Santa Anna prepared to rid the province of the Anglo population. In March of 1836, the Republic of Texas created its constitution and won its independence the next month at the Battle of San Jacinto under Gen. Sam Houston, who captured and imprisoned Santa Anna. Both Austin and Houston ran for president of the new Republic, but Houston easily won with 5,119 votes to Austin's 587 votes. Houston appointed Austin Secretary of State, but he served only two months before dying at 43 years old. His legacies are numerous including the capital city of Austin, many public buildings, schools, and roads as well as being regarded as one of the two great founders of Texas.[10]

Chapter Twenty-nine

Iowa

State on December 28, 1846

Early Years of The French and Indians

The state name of "Iowa" derives from the name of the North American tribe that lived there for thousands of years. There were many other tribes who also occupied the region including the Sauk, Mesquakie, Oto, Omaha, and the Sioux. The natives were attracted to the area's rich soil and proximity to the Mississippi River, which forms the eastern boundary, and the Missouri River, which defines the western border. Iowa is the only state that has two parallel rivers that mark two of its boundaries. Two notable French explorers are credited with being the first European white men to set foot in present-day Iowa. Father Jacques Marquette and his fellow explorer Louis Joliet came from France to Quebec in the mid-1600's to convert the natives to Christianity and to assist in the further development of the French-Canadian fur industry. While the English were expanding their colonies on the Atlantic Coast and the Spanish were gaining footholds along the Gulf Coast and the lower Mississippi River Valley, the French saw their best opportunity to establish colonies from the St. Lawrence River to the Great Lakes and then southward to the Gulf. Marquette and Joliet intended to find the best possible water route to the far East in 1673, so they started down the Mississippi to set up trading posts on both sides of the river. Father Marquette had learned a native tongue and used the journey to pave the way for future French explorers, which included Robert de La Salle and Julien Dubuque in the late 1700's. Although Marquette made much progress and claimed enormous amounts of land for France and King Louis XIV, he never found the mouth of the great river. He did found "Louisiane," thereby honoring the king. Important aspects of his explorations were the many friendships he acquired among the Indian tribes. These proved to be valuable in the future conflicts with the British, who claimed to own certain lands in the Ohio River Valley. The first serious confrontation between the two great European powers occurred in 1754 when England tried to oust the French just below Lake Erie and above present-day Pittsburgh. The ensuing French and Indian War had an enormous impact on the evolution of the North American continent and the development of the American states. France lost most of its holding to England and some to Spain. Their largest losses were Canada, the Ohio River region, and the Louisiana region, which stretched from New Orleans to present-day Missouri and Iowa. All of these areas played an important part in the shaping of the emerging United States.[1]

With the Treaty of Paris of 1763 ending the French and Indian War, England acquired the former French colony of New France, which included present-day Ohio, Indiana, Illinois, Michigan, and Wisconsin. When the United States won its independence from Great Britain 20 years later, the Treaty of Paris of 1783 ceded that entire area to the United States, which became known as the Northwest Territory. Because the Americans did not expect it to be part of the treaty, there were no specific plans for its development. However, in 1787, while delegates were debating the new constitution, they were also attending another important meeting, in that same building in Philadelphia, which was determining the future of the Northwest Territory. Those deliberations produced the Northwest

Ordinance, which proposed that the ceded lands should be preserved for no less than three or no more than five future states which would have the same rights as the existing states. Each new state was to have a minimum population of 60,000 people, a constitution, and the financial ability to administer their government. The Ordinance established conditions that were intended to be a model for all future states. The lands were opened to settlers, with Ohio gaining its statehood in 1803 as the 17th state, followed by Indiana in 1816, Illinois in 1818, Michigan in 1837, and Wisconsin in 1848.

By the late 1600's and early 1700's, the largest tribes in the Upper Mississippi Valley had moved to western Illinois along the banks of the Mississippi River. In the War of 1812, the British in alliance with the Sauk Indians attacked and burned Fort Madison in 1813. The alliance was due to the prior signing in 1804 of the Treaty of St. Louis, that ceded Sauk land to the United States. Sauk Chief Quashquame rejected the treaty, which was not authorized by their council and thereby led to Chief Black Hawk's decision to fight with the British against the United States. In 1829, the Indians were ordered to leave Illinois and move across the Mississippi into Iowa. They were deeply opposed to the move, and three years later, Black Hawk returned to take part of Illinois. He was defeated and ordered to surrender a 50-mile-wide strip of land on the eastern side of Iowa, extending from the Missouri border to northeastern Iowa. Known as the "Black Hawk Purchase," it consisted of six million acres and was purchased for $640,000 or $.11 per acre. Its boundary was the Mississippi River on the east and included the present-day cities of Dubuque, Fort Madison, and Davenport on the west. Part of the tract was awarded to Chief Keokuk and his Sauk tribe in thanks for their neutrality. Another section west of the Missouri River was given to Antoine Le Claire, who was the founder of Davenport, Iowa. The entire tract had been governed by the legislature of the Michigan Territory, the Wisconsin Territory, the Iowa Territory, and lastly the state of Iowa. With the signing of the Black Hawk Purchase, the land was opened to settlers on June 1, 1833. At that time, there was an estimated number of 40-50 settlers. Most of the earliest settlers were French looking to trade fur, search for lead mines, and convert natives. The very first settler was Julien Dubuque, who had arrived from French-Canada in 1787. He received a grant from the Mesquakie tribe to work the lead mines. There was very little population growth prior to 1833, but that year saw a surge of settlers from Ohio, Indiana, Illinois, Missouri, Kentucky, and Tennessee. Most of them came in family units and had already lived in one or two other states. Also, a good many of them moved on to the Dakotas and the Great Plains. By 1836, the first census of Iowa showed 10,531 people, but that was only the beginning.[2] By 1845, nearly all the Indians had left Iowa resulting from their treaties with the United States. The Sioux were the last tribe to leave in 1852. During the next five years, the Mesquakie appealed to Governor James Grimes to allow them to purchase some of their former land. They were able to acquire 3,200 acres, and the governor was able to get them additional compensation in the form of annual payments from the federal government.

As more settlers arrived, they had recognized the need for proper transportation. This initially was provided by transporting goods down the Mississippi River to New Orleans and the Gulf. By the 1850's, steamboats became popular, and by the 1860's, Iowans caught the railroad fever. Chicago had become the railroad hub of the Midwest, with a dozen lines serving the surrounding area. City officials could see that railroads would soon reach the Mississippi River across from the Iowa cities of Dubuque, Clinton, Davenport, and Burlington. They organized railroad companies which eventually resulted in five lines crossing Iowa. From those beginnings, major railroads developed including Union Pacific, Central Pacific and Chicago, Milwaukee, St. Paul and Pacific, Illinois Central, and the Chicago and North Western Railway. In later years, railroads paved the way for enormous economic changes, including the establishment of food processing, farm machinery, the export of corn, wheat, beef, and pork. Also, coal mines were started to produce the fuel for rail power. Whether by rail or the Mississippi River, or the Great Lakes, or the Erie Canal to the Hudson River, Iowans could reach the major markets of the United States as well as abroad.[3]

Road to Statehood

Iowa followed the stipulated plan for statehood as directed in the Northwest Ordinance of 1787. Before a region reached a population of 5,000 it was deemed to be a district. Only free white males could vote, and it was ruled by a governor and three judges appointed by the president of the United States. When its population reached 5,000, the district could become a territory, and settlers could elect their own legislature, but the governor was still appointed by the president. The territory could send a non-voting representative to Congress, who was allowed to speak out on the issues under discussion. When the territory reached 60,000 people, it could apply for statehood. In 1834, Iowa was still a part of the Michigan Territory. In 1836, Iowa was directed to be a part of the Wisconsin Territory, because Michigan had applied for statehood. In 1838, Iowa formed its own territory. Robert Lucas was appointed the first Iowa Territory governor by President Martin Van Buren, with Burlington as the first capital. Two years later, the newly-elected President William Henry Harrison appointed John Chambers as the second governor of the Territory, and the capital was moved to Iowa City. The appointments were political, and therefore, the governors were selected from the president's party. The settlers were not too anxious to become a state, because the costs of government would then switch from the federal government to the state's tax-paying residents. In 1844, the new President James K. Polk was a Democrat, who appointed the third governor, James Clarke. The Iowa population had grown to 75,000, and the tax concerns abated because the size of the population lessened the burden. The next issue that affected statehood was that of controlling slavery, which continued to divide the country. The United States Senate had worked out a plan to keep the number of slave states and free states equal. Iowa was established as a free state, so its admission to statehood depended on finding another slave state. In 1845, Florida as a slave state was ready for statehood, thereby clearing the way for Iowa. Another issue was the question of borders. At that time, Iowa was larger in size, reaching farther north into future Minnesota. Most northern states wanted Iowa to be smaller in order to leave sufficient room for additional free states west of the Mississippi River. The Senate arrived at a plan to make the Iowa border 60 miles further east of the Missouri River. After negotiating agreeable borders on the western side and the southern side with Missouri, President Polk approved Iowa's admission to the Union as the 29th state on December 28, 1846.[4]

Statesmen, Leaders and Heroes

The man who is honored as the first European to have settled in Iowa is Julien Dubuque. He migrated from Champlain, Quebec in 1785 to the area that came to be named Dubuque. It is assumed that he chose to settle there because of the lead mines he discovered. In 1788, he sought permission from the Mesquakie tribe to operate the mine. He befriended their chief, Peosta, and remained in that area his entire life and reportedly married the chief's daughter, Potasa. The nearby town of Petosa was named in her honor, but her marriage to Julien has never been confirmed. When Julien died in 1810 at the age of 48, the settlement was named Dubuque in his memory. The town became the first city in Iowa and grew to become one of its largest. The Mesquakie constructed a wooden crypt overlooking the Mississippi River as his memorial, and it was replaced in the 1890's with a large stone tower honoring him as the founder of Dubuque, Iowa. When Chief Peosta died, his tribe buried him next to his close friend's monument. The city of Peosta is a suburb of Dubuque and was named in honor of the Indian Chief.[5]

Robert Lucas was born in 1781 in western Virginia to William and Susannah Barnes Lucas. His schooling focused on math and surveying, and at the age of 19, he moved with his family to southern Ohio, where he became a licensed surveyor. In 1803, he joined the local militia and rose to become major general and then a lieutenant colonel in the United States army. In the War of 1812, he served under Generals William Hull and William Henry Harrison. Starting in 1808, he was twice elected to the Ohio House of Representatives and seven times to the Ohio Senate. In 1832 and 1834, he was elected governor of Ohio. His vision was to organize a new state, and in 1838, he became instrumental in the Iowa Territory, where President Van Buren appointed him as their first territorial governor and Superintendent of Indian Affairs. His major objectives were to establish an educational system of free public schools, construct roads, organize a militia, develop a good library, and establish strict criminal codes. In 1839, he initiated the building of the capital site in present-day Iowa City. His ultimate goal of statehood was rejected by a vote of its citizens. The issue of statehood introduced the subject of state boundaries with neighboring Missouri, when they tried to collect taxes in the southern part of Iowa. Surveyors disputed the matter, causing Lucas to send representatives to Washington to appeal the conflict, and he even brought out the militia to protect their claims. In 1850, the issue was resolved by the Supreme Court who ruled in favor of Iowa. When the new Whig president, William Henry Harrison, was elected in 1840, Lucas was replaced with John Chambers as the second territorial governor. In 1844, Democrat James Polk was elected president, and much to his disappointment, Lucas was not reappointed governor, just as it was getting close to becoming a state. However, he remained extremely active in the development of Iowa. He was a delegate to the first state constitutional convention and served on the committees to define the state's executive powers and revenue policies. He continued to fight for the state's larger boundaries and was successful in his appeals. In 1846, he tried to become the state's Democratic candidate to run for the state's first governorship but failed. Although he was a Democrat his entire life, he suddenly switched to supporting the Whigs in the 1852 elections, mainly because of his disapproval of the Democratic Party's pro-slavery policy. Lucas backed Whig candidate Gen. Winfield Scott, who lost to Democrat Franklin Pierce. After the election, he retired to his home near Iowa City, where he died in 1853 at 72 years old.[6]

James Clarke was born in Greensburg, Pennsylvania in 1812, and started his business career as a printer. At age 24, he moved to Belmont in the Wisconsin Territory and married Christiana Dodge, who was the daughter of the territorial governor Henry Dodge. James then entered politics and moved to Burlington (later Iowa) in 1837, where he founded the *Wisconsin Territorial Gazette* and the *Burlington Advertiser*. In 1839, President Van Buren appointed Clarke as secretary of the new Iowa Territory. When the capital was moved from Burlington to Iowa City in 1842, Clarke became an assistant to Governor Robert Lucas. He joined with Governor Lucas in proposing statehood, and President Polk appointed Clarke as governor of the Iowa Territory in 1845. He immediately inherited the boundary dispute with Missouri and in setting up the first constitutional convention. In office for only one year, Iowa became a state in December of 1846 and elected Ansel Briggs as its first governor. Clarke returned to his newspaper work in Burlington and became the first president of the Burlington School Board. In 1850, his wife and infant son were stricken with cholera, and both died soon thereafter. Only two weeks later, Clarke was taken ill with the cholera that was sweeping the Mississippi River area and died at 38 years old. His legacy is Clarke County, Iowa.[7]

Ansel Briggs was born in Vermont in 1806 and was educated at the Norwich Academy in Connecticut. He worked as a mail carrier and a stagecoach driver in Ohio and then Iowa. In 1842, he served in the Iowa Territory House of Representatives for a four-year term, while also holding the position of Sheriff of Jackson City. In 1846, he was elected the first governor of the new state of Iowa. While in office, he assisted with developing the school system and resolving the boundary dispute with Missouri. He retired from politics in 1850 and worked on various business interests. He was deeply involved in the founding of Florence, Nebraska and died in Omaha in 1881 at 75 years old.[8]

Chapter Thirty

Wisconsin

State on May 29, 1848

French Wisconsin

Like many of the Midwestern states, Wisconsin became a part of New France in the 1600's, and it was settled by French-Canadians in their quest to expand their fur industry. With Lake Michigan to the east and Lake Superior to the north, the region was home to many Native American tribes such as the Algonquian, Chippewa, Ojibwa, Anishinabek, Ho-Chuck, and Sane Dakota. Although the origin of the name has never been definitely identified, it has been attributed to the Indian word "ouisconsin," which translates to "long river" or "gathering of the waters," which could refer to the Great Lakes. The natives had lived there for thousands of years and had developed extensive trading posts along the Mississippi River. Artifacts such as shells from the Gulf of Mexico and copper from Lake Superior have been found in Wisconsin.

The first European to discover the area was Jean Nicolet in 1634. He was ordered there by Samuel de Champlain, who was the unofficial governor of New France. His charge to Nicolet was to find a water route to Asia and to establish friendly relations with the natives to foster French ambitions to dominate the fur trade. Nicolet made some progress, but the Canadian efforts were interrupted by the Beaver Wars (or Iroquois Wars), which pitted the Iroquois trying to take control of the trade from the Huron and Algonquians. The Iroquois were armed by their Dutch and English trading partners, while the Algonquians were supported by the French. The wars were brutal and affected the entire trading relationships in European countries in more than just the fur industry. Prior to this time, the Scandinavians had been the major supplier of furs to Europe, but this changed when pelts arrived from North America. The superior forces of the Iroquois destroyed the Huron, Erie, Susquehannock, and Shawnee when they took control of the Ohio River Valley and the Lower Peninsula of Michigan. Many natives fled to escape the Iroquois and settled to the west of the Mississippi River. When England defeated the Dutch in the 1670's and took their New Netherlands Colonies, the Iroquois lost one of their key supporters and became allied with the French to check the English expansion westward. In 1673, Father Jacques Marquette and his partner Louis Joliet set out to explore the Mississippi River Valley. They entered the Fox River at Green Bay and reached the Mississippi River at Prairie du Chien, Wisconsin. The French commander of their western settlements, Nicolas Perrot, built a series of forts in Wisconsin from 1685 to 1718. The forts were used more as trading posts and storage. They housed no permanent settlers but served as meeting and business places for fur traders and missionaries.[1]

British Wisconsin

As noted in most of the French holdings in North America, their world changed dramatically as a result of their loss to England in the French and Indian War. Although the conflict started in the Ohio River Valley in 1752-54, it exploded into a much larger war that eventually shaped the future United States. The British-Americans terminated their participation after they stopped the French expansion in western Pennsylvania at Fort Duquense and southward from Lake Erie. The British finished the war in 1763 by taking Canada and all of New France east of the Mississippi River, from the Great Lakes to the Gulf of Mexico, including Wisconsin. British control of this vast area lasted only 20 years until the Americans won their independence in 1783. England retained Canada, which became part of their British Commonwealth. France regained its Louisiana Territory, and the new American Republic acquired the Northwest Territory, which would eventually be converted into Ohio, Indiana, Illinois, Michigan, and Wisconsin. During the 20 years of British control, little colonization occurred. Instead, the focus was on building the fur trade and closer relations with the various Indian tribes. In 1766, royal Governor Robert Rogers employed Jonathan Carver to explore and map the area and to search for the elusive Northwest Passage to the Orient. The existing French settlers as well as the newly-arrived English settled peaceably under British rule, because they needed each other in developing the fur business and granting trapping licenses. Towns like Green Bay and Prairie du Chien prospered and built self-sustaining communities.[2]

The Wisconsin Territory

The United States acquired the Wisconsin region in the Treaty of Paris of 1783 and included it in the Northwest Territory in 1787. Under the Northwest Ordinance, this enormous tract of land was destined to be converted to no less than three or no more than five states, which eventually included Wisconsin. In 1800, it became part of the Indiana Territory, but the United States did not take much control of it and allowed the British to dominate the fur industry and continue their alliances with the native tribes. This changed with the advent of the War of 1812, when the British aligned with the Native Americans to capture Fort Shelby at Prairie du Chien. The war ended in a stand-off, and the Treaty of Ghent in 1815 allowed the United States to regain Wisconsin, which had become part of the Illinois Territory. To protect the area from future attacks, the United States built Fort Crawford and Fort Howard in 1816. Two years later, Wisconsin became part of the Michigan Territory, because a smaller Illinois became a separate new state. Settlements in the area slowed considerably due to the turmoil of two Indian wars. The Winnebago War of 1826 involved the killing of settlers and natives but was short-lived, when the Winnebago surrendered to the United States army at Portage, Wisconsin. The Black Hawk War of 1832 was more significant and resulted from natives being dispossessed of their homelands in Illinois, Iowa, and Wisconsin. Chief Black Hawk led native warriors of the Fox, Sac, and Kickapoo tribes, but the war ended with the Bad Axe Massacre, where over 150 Indians were killed and 75 were taken prisoner.[3]

With the end of the internal Indian conflicts and the resolution of the Midwest region when the British military finally left American territory, the Wisconsin settlements grew rapidly. One of its primary attractions was the lead mining opportunities. Prior to their removal to western territories, the Indians had operated the mines. These jobs were then taken over by the white settlers who arrived in droves from the mid-Atlantic and the coal mines of Cornwall, England. Many new towns arose from the mining areas such as Mineral Point, Platteville, Shullsburg, Belmont, and New Diggings. The federal government opened land offices in Green Bay and Mineral Point in 1834. By the end of the next decade, half of the nation's lead was mined in Wisconsin. After it achieved statehood, it was named the "Badger State," because the miners protected themselves from the harsh winter weather by digging tunnels and living like badgers underground. The next surge of settlers came to the Milwaukee area at the old trading posts like Sheboygan, Manitowac, and Kewaunee. An important developer emerged in the 1820's by the name of Solomon Juneau, who purchased one of the trading posts at the mouth of the Milwaukee River. Sensing the decline of the fur trade, he concentrated on building that area, and with two partners, bought 160 acres between Lake Michigan and the Milwaukee River, which he named Juneautown. Another businessman named Byron Kilbourne purchased land west of the Milwaukee River and named his settlement Kilbournetown. In 1840, the Wisconsin legislature built a bridge over the river and several towns competed to become the largest town in the territory. In 1846, the three settlements of Juneautown, Kilbournetown, and Walker's Point were incorporated into the town of Milwaukee, bringing the population to 10,000 and making it the largest city in Wisconsin from that time to today.[4]

The Wisconsin Territory was formally created by the United States Congress in 1836. It included present-day Wisconsin, Minnesota, Iowa, and parts of

North and South Dakota. Henry Dodge was appointed the first territorial governor by President Andrew Jackson. His first task was to build a capital, and he suggested Belmont in the lead mining area of southeastern Wisconsin. Other lawmakers disagreed, so he left the decision to them. Led by James Doty, they decided to build a new city for the capital and named it Madison. Burlington served as a temporary capital for two years, and when Madison was completed, Burlington was made part of the Iowa Territory, as were all the Wisconsin Territory lands west of the Mississippi River. By 1845, the population of the Wisconsin Territory totaled 150,000 people with a large and diverse economic and cultural background. Three centuries of settlers included Native Americans, French-Canadians, Englishmen, fur traders, frontiersmen, miners, loggers, and Catholic missionaries. By 1848, it had become a laboratory of democracy. It had applied for statehood in 1846 and came very close to adopting a progressive constitution that banned commercial banking, allowed married women to own property, and left slavery to a popular vote. It failed, and a more moderate constitution was passed in 1848. Wisconsin was admitted to the Union as the 30th state on May 29, 1848.[5]

Statesmen, Leaders and Heroes

Jean Nicolet was born in Cherbourg, France in 1598, and while a young man, he was befriended by Samuel de Champlain the noted explorer, navigator, and cartographer. When Champlain first developed his plan to train young explorers and traders to work in the fur business in Canada, Nicolet became intrigued with the idea of living among the natives to learn their language and culture. In 1618 at age 20, he moved to Quebec, where he worked as an interpreter for the Compagnie des Marchands, which was a trading company owned by members of the French aristocracy. In 1820, he was sent to live among the Algonquian and Odawa tribes. He fathered a Nipissing daughter and had her educated by the French upon his return to Quebec. When the Kirke brothers took control of Quebec for England in 1629, Nicolet and his daughter fled to live among the Huron until the French regained control. In 1634, he was the first European to cross Lake Michigan and explore present-day Wisconsin in search of the Northwest Passage to the Orient. He firmly believed it existed because of the native tribe called Ho-Chuck, which translates to "people of the sea." He assumed the "sea" was the Pacific Ocean which would provide the route to Asia. When he canoed down the Wisconsin River, he was so convinced he had found the Passage that he returned to Quebec to announce his discovery. He never realized how close he came to discovering the upper Mississippi River. In 1642, while travelling on the St. Lawrence River, his boat capsized, and he drowned. His accomplishments are memorialized with the city of Nicolet in Quebec, Nicolet Area Technical College, Nicolet High School in Milwaukee, the Jean Nicolet Chapter of the Daughters of the American Revolution, and a statue of him near his first landing in Green Bay, Wisconsin.[6]

Another notable French explorer of the western Great Lakes region was Nicolas Perrot, who was one of the first Europeans to set foot in present-day Wisconsin and Minnesota. Perrot was born in France in 1644 and immigrated to New France as a teenager in the 1660's. New France was discovered by Jacques Cartier in 1534, when he sailed up the St. Lawrence River and claimed the land for France. Cartier is considered the Father of French Canada and set up trading posts along the St. Lawrence River. He was followed by Samuel de Champlain, who explored and mapped the eastern region of the Great Lakes in the early 1600's. Champlain founded the city of Quebec in 1608 and the large lake in northern Vermont named in his honor. It was not until 1663 that Nicolas began his expeditions to Lake Michigan and Lake Superior. As a young man under the supervision of the Jesuits, he worked in the fur trade and learned the native language and customs. New France Governor Frontenac directed Perrot to claim the upper Mississippi area for France in 1670. When he returned to New France the next year, he settled into farming and the fur trade until 1683, when Governor La Barre sent him to establish good relations with the natives in Wisconsin and enlist their support against the hostile Iroquois who were fighting the Algonquians and Huron to wrest control of the fur trade. In 1684, Perrot established peace treaties with several tribes. In 1685, he was made the military commandant of the region and built Fort St. Nicolas at the junction of the Wisconsin and Mississippi Rivers.[7] He then constructed Fort Saint Antoine near the headwaters of the Mississippi River, and five years later, he built Fort Saint-Pierre at the mouth of the Wisconsin River. In 1690, he broke through a blockade by the Iroquois of the Ottawa River and thereby resupplied the tribes loyal to France, saving New France from the hostile Five Nations. Perrot is credited with keeping the peace among the Miami, Sauk, Menominee, Potawatomi, and Fox tribes in their effort to defeat the Iroquois. In 1701, Perrot was instrumental at the Great Peace of Montreal, where 1,300 representatives among 40 Native American tribes signed a peace treaty with New France. He died in 1717, at age 74, and his legacy is a state park in Wisconsin.[8]

Solomon Juneau was born in Quebec, Canada in 1793. At the age of 23, he moved to Fort Michlimackinac at the northern tip of Michigan's Lower Peninsula. He worked as an administrator in the fur trade before becoming an agent for the American Fur Company of Milwaukee. In 1818, he purchased 160 acres near the mouth of the Milwaukee River, which he named Juneautown, and concentrated on building a settlement there. After he sold a good number of lots to settlers, he joined with two other developers, George Walker of Walker's Point and Byron Kilbourne of Kilbournetown, to incorporate their settlements into the city of Milwaukee. In 1820, he married Josette who was a native Menominee with French ancestry. Because of her family relations, Solomon prospered in the fur business and was popular among the Menominee tribe. After consolidating his business in Milwaukee, he built its first store and first hotel. In 1837, he founded the *Milwaukee Sentinel*, and in 1846, became the city's first mayor and then its first postmaster. In 1854, he moved to Dodge County, where he founded the village of Therese, named in memory of his French-Canadian mother. In 1855, his wife died, and the following year he passed away at age 63 in Keshena, Wisconsin. At his funeral, six Menominee Indian chiefs were his pallbearers, and his legacy is an enormous statue memorializing him as the founder of Milwaukee, which remains as Wisconsin's largest city. His cousin Joseph Juneau was the founder of Juneau, Alaska. His grandson Paul Husting became a United States senator in 1914.[9]

Henry Dodge was born in 1782 in Vincennes, Indiana to Israel and Nancy Hunter Dodge. Israel Dodge was a Revolutionary War veteran who fought in the Battle of Brandywine and later served under the command of George Rogers Clark. At age 14, Henry moved to live with his divorced father in Missouri. At age 18, he married Christiana McDonald. In 1806, he became involved with Aaron

Burr and his failed attempt to create a separate nation in the Southwest. When he learned that the Burr Conspiracy was deemed a treasonous act, he returned home to be indicted, but the charges were dropped. In the War of 1812, Dodge joined the Missouri State Volunteers as a captain, and by the end of the war, he had been promoted to major general. During the Red Bird Uprising in 1827, he served as militia commander. His notoriety rose dramatically in the Black Hawk War of 1832 when he organized a formidable fighting force in the western Michigan Territory militia. Known as the "Michigan Mounted Volunteers," they saw action at the battles of Horseshoe Bend, Wisconsin Heights, and Bad Axe. In 1833, he was commissioned a colonel in the United States Regiment of Dragoons, where one of his captains was Nathan Boone, the youngest son of Daniel Boone. The regiment was the first mounted Regular Army unit in the United States army. One of Dodge's greatest achievements was as a successful negotiator in the 1835 peace commission initiated by President Andrew Jackson. The reward for his many accomplishments and bravery was his appointment as the first Territorial Governor of Wisconsin in 1836 and again in 1848. The territory was large enough to include the future states of Wisconsin, Iowa, and Minnesota. In the election of 1844, Dodge declined the nomination for the presidency. Both he and President Van Buren were opposed to the annexation of Texas, but James Polk favored it and was elected president. When Wisconsin was admitted as the 30th state in May of 1848, he was elected as one of its first United States senators where he served two terms. In 1857, President Franklin Pierce offered Dodge the territorial governorship of Washington, but he declined. He died in 1867 in Burlington, Iowa at 85 years old. His legacies include Fort Dodge, Iowa, Dodge County, Wisconsin, Dodge County, Minnesota, Henry County, Iowa, and the 5,270-acre Governor Dodge State Park.[10]

Chapter Thirty-one

California

State on September 9, 1850

Explorers and Settlers

It is estimated that close to one-third of the total United States population of one million Native Americans lived in present-day California. They were composed of approximately 100 tribes dating back for 15,000 years. The name "California" derives from the fictional writings of Spaniard Garcia Rodriguez de Montalvo, who used Greek mythology in describing an island named "California." His fantasies were published around 1500 A.D. when Spanish explorers first believed that southern California (Baja California) was an island and not a peninsula. The island myth persisted for many years, and the name was applied to northern (Alta) California as well. The earliest known map using the name "California" was published in 1562. Stories evolved from the earliest days about cities of gold located along the coast of California, inhabited by fierce warriors. The initial Spanish explorers were also motivated by the possibility of finding the rumored Northwest Passage to the far East. In 1542, the first European to explore California was a Portuguese working for Spain by the name of Juan Rodriguez Cabrillo. He discovered that there was no wealth or cities of gold and its natives barely survived on limited foods. The area was arid, requiring irrigation, and there were no herds of cattle. Even corn and potatoes couldn't grow without extensive care. The natives ate deer, elk, fish, grass seed, berries, and edible plants. Their only staple was a mush of ground acorn flour, which many Indians consumed, as much as one ton of acorns annually. Cabrillo found no redeeming qualities in the region, so serious exploration ceased for over 230 years. However, the Spanish did develop a trading route off the coast of California. It was used to transport gold and silver that was mined in South America in exchange for spices and goods from Asia. Spanish galleons sailed from Mexico to their central base in the Philippines and then returned to the northern coast of California about 300 miles north of San Francisco, where they turned south for 1,500 miles back to their home port in Mexico. The Bay of San Francisco was not discovered until 1769.[1]

Although the English never colonized California, they did claim part of it when Sir Francis Drake landed about 30 miles northwest of San Francisco in 1579. His exact landing has never been proven, but the name "Drake's Bay" is widely regarded as the port where he repaired and resupplied his ship *Golden Hind* during his second circumnavigation of the globe in 1579-1580. Drake claimed all the land south of 42 degrees latitude, north of existing Spanish claims, and then eastward from "coast to coast" for England. His records show this as "Nova Albion," which translates to New England and is an ancient name for Great Britain. The name "albion" means "white" and refers to the white cliffs of Dover. It is interesting to note that many maps made during these early days of discovery were never published, because the government regarded them as state secrets. This led to many occurrences of conflicting claims by other countries as well as by the natives, who were often not consulted.[2]

When the Spanish realized Baja California was a peninsula, they still regarded the region as two distinct territories. Baja ended in the north at San Diego, and Alta (the upper part) started at San Diego and had no definitive reliable boundaries to the east or to the north. In 1697, a Jesuit named Juan

Maria Salvatierra founded the first mission of Loreto in Baja California. Similar to the French missionaries in Canada, the Jesuits founded most of the missions in California. In the 1760's, the Spanish monarchy under King Charles III had a political falling-out with the Jesuits, who were seen as too powerful and autonomous, especially in colonial territories. Charles closed all the Jesuit colleges in Mexico and all of South America. The missions were then assigned to the Franciscan and Dominican friars, but many were abandoned. After 1769, the Spanish government administered Baja and Alta California as a single entity of New Spain with its capital at Monterey. When the French were defeated in the French and Indian War (also called the Seven Years' War) in 1763, they lost all their North American colonies, and only England and Spain remained as the Europeans in present-day United States. Before the Treaty of Paris of 1763, Spain had been secretly given the Louisiana Territory by the French but feared they could lose their California holdings to England. King Charles III took defensive measures to prevent this by building more missions and forts in northern California. However, Spain lacked the military and financial resources to defend such a vast and remote area that was constantly harassed by Indian raids and reprisals by Spanish soldiers who treated them badly. The native tribes were not well-organized, and their meager food supply was not sustainable or attractive enough to foster further colonization.

Several valiant attempts were made to establish footholds in Alta California. In 1769, Gaspar de Portolo commanded a major expedition with three units by sea and two by land. They left Baja California to rendezvous in San Diego 50 days later. One ship disappeared and the other two took 90 days to reach San Diego. The soldiers, missionaries, and settlers suffered from scurvy and many died. The expedition started with 219 men but was reduced to 100 men before they set foot on their journey north on July 14, 1769. They arrived at San Francisco Bay on November 2nd and returned to San Diego in January of 1770.

Another expedition under Juan Bautista de Anza left Tucson, Arizona in January of 1774 to find a land route into California and arrived in the Mission San Gabriel Arcangel 74 days later. That settlement became the future Los Angeles. In 1775, Anza led 240 colonists, soldiers, and friars from Tubac, Arizona on October 22nd and arrived at San Francisco Bay on March 28, 1776. There they established the Presidio of San Francisco and the Mission San Francisco de Asis, which became the city of San Francisco. The Spanish succeeded in building 21 missions between San Diego and San Francisco, all of which were located around 30 miles from the coast. No attempts were made to settle in the central valley of California or in the Sierra Nevada region. The settled parts accounted for 15,000 square miles of California's future size of 156,000 square miles or 10 percent of the total land. The missions represented a major factor in the development of California. Each one contained about one million acres and in total claimed one-sixth of available land. Each was manned by two or three friars and from three to ten soldiers. Construction was done by the local natives under the supervision of the friars. The non-missionary land was owned by the Spanish monarchy. Large land grants were given free to friends and relatives of government officials and to foreign colonists if they accepted Spanish citizenship and became members of the Catholic Church. Protestants were not allowed to live in Mexican-held territory. The mission settlements were protected by four royal forts called "presidios," which were defended by ten to 100 men and located in San Diego, San Francisco, Santa Barbara, and San Jose.[3]

Nationhood For Mexico

In 1821, Mexico became independent of Spain but remained unstable with 40 changes of government over the next 27 years. During this period, the population declined, and Alta California produced no net revenue to the Mexican government. The Indian population decreased, and the missions deteriorated. With the new Mexican government, California was ruled by the First Mexico Empire. It feared control by the Roman Catholic Church, so it closed all the missions and nationalized the Church's property. Many of these missions became small towns called "pueblos," and some eventually grew into large cities like Los Angeles and San Jose. In 1834, Governor Figueroa ordered the missions to surrender their property and begin the secularization of the Franciscan-run missions with his "Decree of Confiscation." However, the new Mexican government abolished the old Spanish rule of non-trading with foreigners. Emigration from Mexico stopped, but new settlers from the United States and Europe began to emerge and become "rancheros" and traders. Prior to 1825, Alta

California saw two or three trading ships a year, but that increased to about 25 ships annually from 1825 to 1848. Tariffs were high at 25 percent where ships unloaded in the principal port of Monterey.[4]

The Mexican-American War

Hostilities between the United States and Mexico resulted from territorial disputes across the Southwest, but the most contentious were those in Texas. In 1846, the American government annexed Mexican Texas to the United States. Prior to that time, Mexico had welcomed Americans to settle in the area, but they changed their policy when they observed a growing sense of American independence and loyalty to Washington, D.C. In 1846, a small group of Americans in Sonoma seized control of the area and declared it as the new California Republic. It lasted only 26 days before it accepted United States government control. The Californians who revolted were joined by John Sutter with his men and supplies at Fort Sutter. They hoisted their "Bear Flag," but the revolt lasted only one week. However, it should be noted that today's California State flag incorporates the original Bear Flag and the words "California Republic." On May 13, 1846, the United States declared war on Mexico. The United States navy and marines were ordered to capture every town and port along the California coast. They encountered token resistance and ended the war in January of 1847 with the Treaty of Cahuenga. California was annexed and paid for by the Treaty of Guadalupe Hidalgo in 1848. The treaty dictated that Mexico had to abandon any claim to California. It also called for the United States to pay Mexico $15 million and assume the debt owed by Mexico to the United States. The boundaries of California, New Mexico, Texas, and the large unsettled southwest territory were all resolved by the treaty.

California Statehhood

With the discovery of gold in 1848, California suddenly became an important and influential region. It bypassed the usual procedure of being first declared a territory and was allowed to choose its own boundaries and immediately write its state constitution, admitted as the 31st state in 1850. Statehood could have come even sooner, but the slavery issue slowed the process. California determined its own status, rather than Congress, and declared to be a free state. Once again, slavery was an issue in the establishment of new states. With the emergence of Texas in 1845 and then California in 1850, Congress could anticipate many more additional states from existing territories as well as the large unorganized areas in the West. By September of 1850, there were the four official territories of Oregon, Utah, New Mexico, and Minnesota. Additionally, there was an enormous unorganized section that eventually would include states like North Dakota, South Dakota, Nebraska, Colorado, Wyoming, and Idaho. When California achieved statehood in 1850 as a free state, the slavery issue was resolved with the "Compromise of 1850." It was a hard-fought contest drafted by Henry Clay of Kentucky and brokered by Stephen Douglas of Illinois. Neither side received everything they wanted, but it did calm the sectional rivalries for another ten years. Its major provisions were:

1. Texas relinquished its claims to New Mexico and lands north of the Missouri Compromise. It retained the Panhandle section, and the federal government assumed its public debt;
2. California was admitted as a free state;
3. The Wilmot Proviso which would have prohibited slavery in all the new states was defeated by the South, and the new territories of Utah and New Mexico could vote for their choice;
4. The slave trade, but not slavery, was abolished in the District of Columbia;
5. A tougher Fugitive Slave Law was adopted.[5]

California Gold Rush

The discovery of gold in California in 1848 had a profound impact on the area that was to become the 31st state. By the end of that year, 6,000 people from many countries had arrived in their search for gold. They came by sea and by land and were referred to as "Argonauts," which derives from Greek mythology. Around 1300 B.C., a group of Greek heroes sailed on the ship *Argo* in search of the "Golden Fleece" of the winged ram. The fleece was its golden hair and symbolized authority and kingship.[6] The Argonauts migrating to California were composed of all classes and races, and most of them were men. By the end of 1849, it is estimated that 80,000 had arrived in the Sierra Nevada and northern California areas. Half came by land over the California Trail, and half came by sea to the official port of entry in San Francisco. Prior to 1848, 25 was the average number of visiting ships. In 1849, the total number jumped to 793 ships, and in 1850, they totaled 803 ships. Tariffs of 25 percent were collected by Customs on food, clothing, lumber, building materials, tools, hardware, and livestock. The San Francisco population grew from 200 in 1846 to 36,000 in 1852. While the search for gold created an economic bonanza, it also did some environmental damage and forced many natives to leave their homeland. Streams and rivers were diverted, allowing miners to dig deep into the gravel beds where gold had been freed from the ore. In the first five years of the Gold Rush, about 12 million ounces were removed. Techniques were improved, and hydraulic systems brought another 20 million ounces out with a current value of $12 billion. The new found wealth enabled the settlers to create roads, bridges, towns, businesses, steamships, churches, schools, and an entire culture in northern California and later in southern California.

The Founder of California

Perhaps the most notable of the early leaders of California was Junipero Serra, who was a Franciscan friar who started a series of mission settlements in 1767 when he was appointed to the task. He is considered the founder of California and spent all of his adult life establishing missions along the coast of the region more than 80 years before it became a state. Serra was born in 1713 on the island of Majorca. After his religious training, he was designated a monk in 1729 and was ordained a priest in 1737 after earning his doctorate of philosophy degree. His calling was to become a missionary in the New World, so in 1749, he and some fellow Franciscans sailed to Mexico and spent most of the next ten years teaching Christianity to the native Indians. In 1767, he was assigned to take charge of establishing missions in Alta (upper) California. His first project was in Sierra Gordo, Mexico, where he was joined by his friend, biographer, and successor as President of the Missions, Father Francisco Palou.[7] They found the village in disarray and devoted the next eight years to rebuilding it and converting the native Pames tribe to Christianity. When the Jesuits were banned from Mexico for political reasons in 1767, Serra was appointed President of the Missions for Baja California, and he soon acquired spiritual and secular administrative control of the region with his Franciscan friars. In 1768, he was chosen to lead his missionaries to San Diego and arrived there the next year after a 900-mile, tortuous journey. In July of that year, he founded the Mission of San Diego de Acala. In 1770, Serra moved to Monterey and founded the second of his nine missions which included:

1. 1769 – Mission Basilica San Diego;
2. 1770 – Mission San Carlos Borromeo in Carmel-By-The-Sea;
3. 1771 – Mission San Antonio de Padua;
4. 1771 – Mission San Gabriel Arcangel;
5. 1772 – Mission San Luis Obispo de Tolosa;
6. 1776 – Mission San Juan Capistrano;
7. 1776 – Mission San Francisco de Asis;
8. 1777 – Mission Santa Clara de Asis;
9. 1782 – Mission San Buena Ventura.[8]

The missions were founded to convert the natives to Catholicism. Other purposes were to assimilate them into the Spanish culture and to organize them into a productive workforce and train them for future ownership and management. Father Serra died in 1784 at the age of 70 and is buried at the Mission San Carlos Borromeo. In 1988, Pope John Paul II beatified Junipero Serra. He was canonized by Pope Francis in 2015, which marked the first canonization of a saint on American soil. Pope Francis said that "Friar Junipero was one of the founding fathers of the United States, a saintly example of the Church's universality and special patron of the Hispanic people of the country."[9]

Chapter Thirty-two

MINNESOTA

State on May 11, 1858

Explorers and Settlers

There is clear evidence of Native American tribes having lived in present-day Minnesota around 9000 B.C. In 1931, a body known as "Minnesota Woman" was found in Otter Tail County, and carbon tests aged the bones to be 8,000 years old. Stone tools from this period are on display at the Olmsted County Historical Society Museum in Rochester, Minnesota. Around 5000 B.C., natives in the Lake Superior area are credited with making the first metal tools on the continent. They were made from copper ore that was heated and beaten into shape and could be sharpened into knives and tips for spears. The most prominent tribes to live in this area were the Dakota, Ojibwe, and Winnebago who still occupied the land when the first Europeans arrived in the mid-1600's. The name "minnesota" is a Dakota-Sioux word meaning "sky-tinted water." which refers to the Minnesota River and the numerous lakes in the region. The Indian word "minni" translates to "water," and "sotah" means "cloudy" or "sky-tinted."[1] Two French explorers are honored to have been the first Europeans to set foot into the region: Pierre Esprit Radisson and his brother-in-law Medard des Grosseilliers. Their expeditions to the north and west of Lake Superior led to the establishment of the Hudson Bay Company in 1670, even though most of their explorations focused on the south shore of the lake. The lands north of the lake were explored by a French Jesuit named Claude Allouez, who mapped the area in 1671. During that same year, France signed a trading agreement with several tribes. However, tensions mounted between the Ojibwa and Dakota for control of the fur trade. Another notable French explorer was Daniel Greysolon, Sieur du Lhut, who is regarded as the first European to explore the western side of Lake Superior at the headwaters of the Mississippi River, where the fur-trading city of Duluth was named in his honor.[2] In 1679, du Lhut negotiated a peace treaty between the Ojibwa and Dakota tribes which enabled the fur industry to continue to operate without further disruptions. du Lhut performed another rescue the next year, when he learned that the Dakota had captured the well-known explorers Father Louis Hennepin, Michel Aco, and Antoine Auguelle, who were being led by Robert de La Salle. While travelling as a captive of the Dakota, Father Hennepin is credited with discovering the Falls of Saint Anthony, which is located northeast of downtown of present-day Minneapolis. He named the Falls after his patron saint, St. Anthony of Padua, and he also brought the world's attention to Niagara Falls. Saint Anthony Falls became a very significant source of power for Minneapolis and the development of saw mills, textile mills, and flour mills.[3]

Many French explorers were attracted to the area in search of the fabled Northwest Passage to the Orient and the headwaters of the Mississippi River. The early "voyageurs" included the ones named above and others like Pierre-Charles Le Sueur, Pierre La Verendrye, Jonathan Carver, Henry Schoolcroft, Major Stephen Long, Zebulon Pike, and George William Featherstonhaugh. In the 1830's, Joseph Nicollet explored the upper Mississippi River, the St. Croix River, and the region between the Mississippi and Missouri Rivers, most of which he mapped and paved the way for future settlers.

The state of Minnesota started to take shape in 1783 with the Treaty of Paris ending the American Revolutionary War. Great Britain ceded the enormous triangle of land between the Ohio and Mississippi Rivers. It included present-day St. Paul but only a part of Minneapolis, but the northern boundary with Canada was uncertain due to landmarks reported by fur traders. That area was determined by the Anglo-American Convention of 1818 and the Webster-Ashburton Treaty of 1842. The boundary was set at the 49th parallel west of the Lake of Woods. Minnesota went through several territorial stages, beginning with the Northwest Territory, the Illinois Territory, the Michigan Territory, and the Wisconsin Territory.[4] After the Treaty of Paris of 1783 by which Great Britain ceded the lands noted above, the next major event affecting the future of Minnesota was the Louisiana Purchase. That story is covered in the creation of Louisiana and the Mississippi River Valley. The purchase executed in 1803 was for 828,000 square miles, which immediately doubled the size of the United States. The land included all of present-day Arkansas, Iowa, Missouri, Kansas, Oklahoma, Nebraska and parts of Louisiana west of the Mississippi River, parts of New Mexico, South Dakota, northern Texas, and parts of Wyoming, Montana, and Colorado. One of the biggest impacts was in Minnesota, whose size was more than doubled.

Disputes between the Dakota and Ojibwa tribes noted above continued into the early 1800's. The friction was due to control of the fur trade, so it was decided to build a fort at the confluence of the Minnesota and Mississippi Rivers on land that was owned by Zebulon Pike. The fort was started in 1819 and took six years to construct. It was first administered by Col. Josiah Snelling and was named Fort Snelling in his honor. In addition to monitoring Indian disputes and serving as a training center for army inductees, it played a role in the Underground Railroad, protecting runaway slaves. The most notable event in the slavery issue of that time was the Dred Scott Case, which was heard by the United States Supreme Court. The Court's decision had a major impact on American labor and constitutional laws. Dred Scott and his wife were taken by their owner, United States army surgeon Dr. John Emerson, to live in the free state of Illinois at Fort Snelling, which was also in a free territory which prohibited slavery. Scott pleaded that he therefore was entitled to become a free man. However, the Court ruled against him on the grounds that "a negro, whose ancestors were imported into the United States and sold as slaves, whether enslaved or free, could not be an American citizen and therefore had no standing to sue in federal court… and that the federal government had no power to regulate slavery in the federal territories acquired after the creation of the United States." This decision was only the second in the Supreme Court's history to rule on the constitutionality of a congressional law. The Dred Scott Case has been cited as one of the major causes of the American Civil War, because it so enraged the anti-slavery citizenry, who were mostly in the North.[5]

Fort Snelling marked the site for the future cities of Minneapolis and St. Paul. In its earliest days, the soldiers stationed there constructed roads and buildings in the attempt to make the fort a self-sufficient town. A grist mill was built, and in nearby St. Anthony Falls, they erected a sawmill. Entrepreneurs John Stevens and Franklin Steele built stores and bought more land on the eastern and western sides of the Mississippi River, and in 1850, the first residential house was built in Minneapolis. Eventually, in 1872, St. Anthony was absorbed by Minneapolis. Likewise, St. Paul started with squatters outside Fort Snelling, who were later forced to move a few miles from the fort and proceeded to build a settlement named Lambert's Landing, which was later renamed St. Paul. The two cities became known as the "Twin Cities" after 1872, after talk of them merging into one. Citizens wanted the two of them to keep their own identity, so they introduced the Twin Cities name. Both of them still remain as the two largest cities in Minnesota.[6]

Road to Statehood

Thanks to the efforts of Senator Stephen Douglas of Illinois, Minnesota survived to become a separate state. When Iowa was formed in 1846, he prevented it from absorbing Fort Snelling and St. Anthony Falls. In 1848, when Wisconsin gained statehood, Douglas fought to keep it from including St. Paul and St. Anthony Falls. In 1849, the Minnesota Territory was formed from Iowa lands and Wisconsin lands. The Minnesota Territory also included parts of North and South Dakota. In 1853, Henry Rice replaced Henry Sibley as the territorial representative to the United States Congress. Rice was responsible for bringing a railroad to connect St. Paul and Lake Superior to the Illinois Central. In 1856, he introduced bills to allow Minnesota to write a state constitution and acquire a railroad grant. He defined the Minnesota boundaries with Iowa to the south, Wisconsin to the east, Canada on the north, and the Red River to the west. The question of slavery again came to the fore when Senator Douglas introduced the enabling bill for Minnesota statehood. Senator Thompson of Kentucky and 21 other senators opposed it on the grounds of too small a population and too great an expense to the government for roads, canals, and forts. However, the real reason was the losing of political power to the northern free-state majority if Minnesota was admitted. In spite of Democratic opposition, the enabling act was passed in February of 1857, but the Republicans and Democrats were so at odds, that they formed two separate constitutional conventions. They finally came together to write an agreed constitution, but the two parties remained divided and actually had each party sign the constitution on two separate papers—one was white for Republicans, and the other was blue for the Democrats. In October of 1857, the constitution was approved by 30,055 votes and rejected by 571 votes. While the southern states debated the slavery status of the Kansas application for statehood, they had delayed the Minnesota application until May 11, 1858 when it was admitted as the 32nd state.[7]

Dakota War of 1862

On April 12, 1861, the Confederate army fired on Fort Sumter in Charleston Harbor, South Carolina, thereby opening the first shots of the American Civil War. Minnesota Governor Alexander Ramsey happened to be in Washington, D.C. at that time, so he went to the War Office, making Minnesota the first state to offer its assistance to suppress the rebellion. Matters grew worse for Minnesota in 1862 when the Dakota Indians realized they would starve with the lack of United States government aid, the loss of their hunting grounds, and the crop failures that year. Their frustrations exploded, and while searching for food, four Dakota Indians killed a white family. The incident sparked a wider conflict, which resulted in the death of 400 more white settlers throughout the Minnesota River Valley, that came to be known as the Dakota War of 1812. The six-week war ended with the trial of 425 Native Americans and the conviction and death sentence for 303 of them. Bishop Whipple intervened to ask President Lincoln for clemency, which he granted to all but 39 men who were hanged in a mass execution at Mankato, Minnesota on December 26, 1862. Non-combatants were imprisoned at Pike Island, where 300 perished from disease that winter. Survivors went into exile in Nebraska, except for the Sioux, who did not fight in the Dakota War but actually helped the French missionaries escape the Indian warriors. Some Dakota moved back to Minnesota 20 years later, but after then the Dakota were prohibited from living there.[8]

Statesmen, Leaders and Heroes

Famous early founders of New France who explored the Minnesota wilderness included Frenchmen Father Jacques Marquette, Louis Joliet, and Robert de La Salle, all of whom are discussed in states to the south and southwest of the Great Lakes. However, the one explorer of Minnesota who was comparable to these more famous explorers was Daniel Greysolon, Sieur du Lhut. His name was anglicized to Duluth, and the city in northern Minnesota was named in his honor. Daniel was born in France in 1639, and at age 35, he first visited New France at Montreal. After four years, he journeyed to western Lake Superior to arrange a peace treaty between the Dakota and Ojibwa tribes, who had been fighting each other for control of the fur trade. The next year, while living among the Sioux people, he learned of the capture of a Franciscan Catholic priest named Louis Hennepin by another Sioux tribe. After successfully bargaining for his release, he had inadvertently violated French rules about banning trade with the natives without government approval. While still in the wilderness, he explored the region and reached the upper Mississippi River by way of the Saint Croix River in 1680. He then returned to Montreal and Quebec, where his activities with the natives were severely criticized and forced him to return to France to defend himself. In 1682, he went back to Lake Superior and established trading posts at Thunder Bay, Ontario, and Port Huron between Lakes Erie and Huron. He died in Montreal at 71 years old. His legacy is the city of Duluth in Minnesota and Duluth Avenue in Montreal.[9]

Father Louis Hennepin was a Franciscan missionary who was born in Belgium in 1640, according to his recorded baptism on April 7th of that year. He joined the Recollect Friars in France, where he was ordained a priest in 1666. The Recollects were a branch of the Franciscan Order who played a major role in the colonization of New France. In 1675 at his request, Father Hennepin left for Quebec and spent the next three years in the eastern St. Lawrence River area, serving the colonists and Native American communities. In 1678, he was selected to join Robert de La Salle on an expedition to explore the Mississippi River. On the trip, he and two other men were sent by La Salle to explore the upper part of the great river. They left in March of 1680 and were captured by Sioux warriors in April and went to live with them at Lake Mille Lacs until July. That summer, they were allowed to canoe down the Mississippi to the Wisconsin River to retrieve supplies that La Salle had left for them. It was during that trip that Hennepin discovered the largest waterfall on the Mississippi River, which he named St. Anthony Falls in honor of his patron saint, Saint Anthony of Padua. That settlement went on to become the city of St. Paul. That summer, Daniel Greysolon du Lhut heard about the captured Frenchmen and negotiated their release. Father Hennepin returned to Canada, and in 1681, left for France, where he began a literary career. His works describing North America brought him notoriety as well as criticism because of his exaggerated and fictional accounts of his life among the Dakota and the nature of his surroundings. He was also accused of plagiarism using the reports of Robert de La Salle. In 1700, he travelled to Rome seeking funds from the Franciscans. Some historians believe he died there the following year. In spite of his poor literary reputation, Father Hennepin has been remembered by the many schools, streets, and parks in his name in Minnesota, Canada, and his home town in Belgium.[10]

Henry Mower Rice was born in 1816 in Waitsfield, Vermont. His ancestors were from England and arrived in the Massachusetts Bay Colony in the early 1600's. At the age of 18, he moved to Detroit, Michigan, where he surveyed the canal along the Sault Saint Marie rapids between Lake Huron and Lake Superior. In 1839, he got a job at Fort Snelling and became a fur trader with the Ho-Chunk and Chippewa Indians. He acquired an excellent reputation for trust and integrity among the natives, and in 1847, he negotiated a treaty with the Ojibwa tribe, which resulted in large tracts of land being ceded to the United States by them. In 1849, Rice lobbied in the Congress for establishing the Minnesota

Territory, and he then served as a delegate to the United States Congress from 1853 to 1857. It was his work on the Enabling Act that allowed Minnesota to gain statehood in 1858. That same year, Rice and James Shields were elected as Democrats to the United States Senate, and Rice served in the 35th, 36th, and 37th Congresses. During this time, he was a board member of the University of Minnesota and president of the Minnesota Historical Society. His best work seems to have been negotiating treaties with the Indians which included: 1) the 1847 treaties with the Ojibwa at Fond du Lac and Leech Lake; 2) the 1854 Treaty with the Ojibwa at La Pointe, Wisconsin; 3) as United States Commissioner in 1887-88 with the Ojibwa tribe; and 4) negotiator with the Dakota at St. Paul after the Senate revised the 1851 Dakota Treaties of Mendota. He also was instrumental with the removal of the Ho-Chunk from Iowa in 1848. Henry Rice died in 1894 at age 78 while on a visit to San Antonio, Texas. His legacy is a life-size marble statue of Rice, which was given by the state of Minnesota to the National Statuary Hall Collection at the United States Capitol in 1916. He was also honored with the name of Rice County, Minnesota.[11]

Chapter Thirty-three

OREGON

State on February 14, 1859

Explorers and Settlers

In 1938, archeologist Luther Cressman discovered bark sandals near Fort Rock Cave that have been dated to around 11,200 B.C. Other discoveries along the lower Columbia River include artifacts dated to 8,000 B.C. By the 1500's, natives across the state of Oregon consisted of many tribes including the Umpque, Takelina, Nez Perce, Molalla, Bannock, Chasta, Chinook, Kalapuya, and Klamath. Early European arrivals were generally welcomed by the natives, because they provided more trading possibilities. However, as the immigrants steadily increased, they brought diseases that decimated the tribes and caused friction in competing for the local natural resources.

The origin of the name "Oregon" has been the subject of much debate, owing to the influence of original native inhabitants as well as Spanish and French explorers. The Columbia River is at the root of most interpretations of the name.

The Sioux Indians called the river "The River of the West," which derives from the Shoshone words "ogwa" for "river" and "pe-on" for "west." Also, the French word "ouragon" means "hurricane," and they called the river "Hurricane River," due to the strong winds of the Columbia Gorge.

Oregon is another state that was discovered by the Spanish but settled by the French. In 1543, the man credited with first recording the area was Juan Rodriguez Cabrillo. Juan de Fuca studied and mapped the area 50 years later and has been honored with the naming of the straits to the north flowing into British Columbia. The area remained dormant for over 100 years, until Juan Jose Perez Hernandez sailed his frigate *Santiago* to the Oregon coast in 1774. Although Vasco de Balboa was the first European to see the Pacific Ocean and West Coast, claiming it all for Spain in the early 1500's, it was Perez who started settling Oregon. Balboa was searching for gold, but Perez and other explorer-navigators were using the Oregon coast as an important trading post in their triangular trade from Mexico to the Philippines to Oregon and their return to Mexico. A major objective for the Spanish and then the British was to discover a sea route to the Orient.[1] In 1778, English Capt. James Cook explored the Oregon coast in search of what the English called the "Northwest Passage." He was one of the many Europeans and Americans in search of the elusive path that connected the Atlantic and Pacific oceans. When such a path was deemed non-existent on the North American continent, explorers continued their search farther to the north in the Arctic. Cook did confirm that ocean water did in fact freeze and thereby produced icebergs of fresh water.[2] However, it was the fur trade that attracted so much interest in the Pacific Northwest. The American merchant Capt. Robert Gray had circumnavigated the world from 1787 to 1790. His primary business was sailing to China, where he traded fur pelts for tea. When he returned to Boston in 1790, he immediately set sail for the Northwest Coast and became the first explorer to enter the Columbia River. It was this trip that provided the basis for America's future claim to the region. His ship *Columbia Rediviva* was the inspiration for naming the river. Gray was heading for Nootka Sound when he experienced strong currents at latitude 46'16", emanating from a river he couldn't enter after nine days of trying. He returned to the area in October and built Fort Defiance. He and his crew wintered on Vancouver Island and returned in April to that area where muddy waters were flowing into the Pacific. On April 29th, he exchanged greetings with British Capt. George Vancouver on the *HMS Discovery*, who doubted Gray's theory of finding the water route of the Northwest Passage. Gray proceeded to find a channel through the treacherous breakers, and on May 11, 1792, he entered the Columbia River for five miles. He disembarked, planted an American flag, and claimed the area for the United States. After nine days of trading with the natives, he collected about 450 pelts to trade in China. Before leaving on May 12th, he named the river "Columbia," the entrance "Cape Hancock," and the south point "Adams." When he returned to Boston in 1793, the British and Americans disagreed on their respective claims to the territory. It took another 50 years to resolve the issue with the 1846 Oregon Treaty, which divided the Oregon Country equally between the United States and Great Britain.[3] That treaty was preceded by the Treaty of 1818 among Great Britain, Ireland, and the United States, which attempted to resolve the boundary disputes. It permitted all three parties to occupy the Oregon Country known by Canadians as the Columbia District of the Hudson's Bay Company. The British and Americans agreed to set the boundary at the 49th parallel. Both countries gave up some territory from both sides of the line. The concessions were the last ones by Great Britain in the continental United States and the only ones in the history of the American Republic to a foreign country. Great Britain ceded land south of the 49th parallel and west to the Rocky Mountains. The United States ceded the northern tip of the Louisiana Territory above that parallel.[4]

Another significant settlement occurred in the 1810-1812 period, initiated by American John Jacob Astor. He founded the city of Astoria, named in his honor, where he brought large numbers of fur traders. Fort Astoria became the first permanent white settlement in that area and was to become an important supporting factor in the future American claim to Oregon. Near the start of the War of 1812, in an effort to avoid capture by the British, the fur trading assets of the Pacific Fur Company at Fort Astoria were sold in 1813 to the North West Company based in Montreal. Pacific was the dominant factor in the fur industry until it was bought by the Hudson's Bay Company in 1821. Hudson's Bay copied the Astoria model of sending supplies by sea to their Columbia River base for direct export to China. Known as "The Bay" and "HBC," it was not only the dominant fur trading company, it was once the largest land-holding company in North America, owning 15 percent of all existing land. HBC's original charter by King Charles II in 1670 granted trapping rights in the vast area surrounding Hudson Bay, including all the rivers and tributaries that flowed into the bay. Being the first such entity to explore and settle the lands that reached to the Rocky Mountains, HBC assumed the role of the government. It controlled and administered the area for 200 years while its explorers and trappers established trading posts all over northern and western Canada. In the late 1800's, with the "Deed of Surrender," it formed the basis for the creation of the Dominion of Canada. HBC went on to become the largest retailer in Canada and one of the largest in the world. A competing group, the North West Company was founded in 1779, and by 1821, the British government ended the often-violent competition by merging it with the Hudson's Bay Company. The government issued a new charter, allowing them to expand their control to the Arctic Ocean and the creation of the Columbia District in the Pacific Northwest. Pacific headquarters were moved from Fort Astoria, Oregon to Fort Vancouver. The newly combined company had 25 chief factors, 25 chief traders, and its trading covered three million square miles with 1,500 employees. Although commercial operations were shared to some degree in the Columbia River area by the Treaty of 1818, HBC controlled the fur industry and discouraged Americans from settling there. In 1834, they established another base at Fort Boise (not yet in Idaho) to compete with the American Fort Hall operation about 300 miles to the east, which they bought three years later. However, the Oregon Trail in the 1840's would bring significant changes to that region.[5]

Oregon Trail

The trail was started by traders around 1811, and for many years it was passable only by foot or horse. By 1846, wagon trains were organized at Independence, Missouri to travel through present-day Kansas and then to Fort Hall in Idaho. When completed, the trail was 2,170 miles long and stretched from the Missouri River to the Willamette Valley in Oregon and could handle large-wheel wagons. When it breached the Rocky Mountains at South Pass and entered Oregon in 1841, it was named the Oregon Trail. At that time, major migrations occurred, and in the 1846-1869 period, an estimated 400,000 settlers travelled across it including farmers, ranchers, miners, and businessmen. Other offshoots developed from it such as the California Trail, Mormon Trail, and the Bozeman Trail. In 1869, the first transcontinental railroad was completed, which provided faster and cheaper transportation, causing the usage of the Oregon Trail to decline.[6]

Road to Statehood

As the Treaty of Oregon in 1846 avoided a potential war with Great Britain over major land disputes and the Oregon Trail brought thousands of immigrants into the Pacific Northwest, the Oregon Country was ready to begin the process for statehood. When it was organized in 1848, it consisted of present-day Washington, Oregon, Idaho, and parts of Montana, Wyoming, and British Columbia. The northern boundary was the 49th parallel, and the southern boundary was the 42nd parallel. The capital moved several times from Oregon City to Salem to Corvallis and then back to Salem, where it stayed following statehood in 1859. The impetus for organizing the region into a territory was the massacre of the missionary doctor Marcus Whitman and 15 of his followers in 1847 near Walla Walla, Washington. Several tribes in the area became incensed with the belief that Whitman was intentionally infecting 200 Cayuse Indians with the measles while they were under his care. Some historians believe the real cause was the native conflict with Whitman when he came to settle in the Columbia River area as the leader of the first wagon train to arrive by the Oregon Trail. The cause has never been determined, but the massacre did prompt Congress to move the area to territorial status, which became effective on August 14, 1848. The new territory was governed by a governor, a marshal, a secretary, an attorney, and a three-judge supreme court, all of whom were appointed by President James Polk. In 1853, the northern part of Oregon was organized into the Washington Territory. When Oregon entered the Union in 1859, its boundaries were reduced to its present size. Idaho and parts of Montana and Wyoming made up part of the Washington Territory.[7]

Statesmen, Leaders and Heroes

Certainly, Robert Gray is one of the leading heroes of Oregon. He was born in 1755 in the town of Tiverton, Rhode Island. Very little is known of his youth other than he may have served in the Continental navy in the Revolutionary War. As a merchant sea captain, he circumnavigated the world in 1790 and again in 1793. His sea voyages to the Orient brought him into the Pacific Northwest, where he explored the coasts of Oregon, Washington, and Alaska and became the first significant American seaman to enter the fur trade. In 1788, Gray made his first attempt to enter the Columbia River but was thwarted by strong tides and dangerous shoals. He then went on to China to trade his furs for tea. Leaving China, he sailed through the Indian Ocean and around the Cape of Good Hope and then across the Atlantic to Boston. The trip was so profitable that Gray set out again within six weeks for the Pacific Coast. His successful sea trading trip to the Orient also motivated other American merchant ships to enter the trade, which led to more American territorial claims in the Oregon Country. Other countries like Great Britain, Spain, and Russia followed suit, which eventually led to conflicting claims. In 1790, Gray sailed to the Pacific Northwest under papers signed by President George Washington, which meant Gray was acting on behalf of the United States government. He landed in Nootka Sound, and while he wintered there, he and his crew built Fort Defiance. In April of 1792, Gray left Nootka to sail south on his ship *Columbia Rediviva*. In May, he searched for the mouth of what he believed was a great river. After finding a safe channel, he sailed into the river he would name "Columbia." He was met by many natives with whom he traded, and then he continued up the river for 15 miles over a nine-day period. He made a chart and map of the bay and mouth of the river, copies of which were soon acquired by British Captain Vancouver. It was because of Gray's explorations and discoveries that the United States could support claims to the Oregon region when the disputes among several countries came to a head in the early 1800's. Gray continued his trading in South America, England, and southeastern United States until 1806, when he died at sea, reportedly from the yellow fever. Gray's legacy is extensive with Gray's Bay and Gray's River near the Columbia River. His name adorns three elementary schools in Washington and Oregon; two middle schools; Gray Avenue in Tiverton, Rhode Island; and Gray Harbor in Washington.[8]

Doctor John McLoughlin was born in Quebec in 1784. He studied medicine and in 1803, was licensed to practice in Lower Canada. He was hired as a doctor for the North West Company on Lake Superior, and it was there that he learned the fur business as well as several Indian languages. He was made a partner in 1814 and was a leading negotiator in the 1821 merger of North West with the Hudson's Bay Company. In 1825, McLoughlin built Fort Vancouver to replace Fort George (formerly Fort Astoria, Oregon) on the north side of the Columbia River. From there he managed the growing empire of the Hudson's Bay Company. He broadened the fur company by introducing trade in salmon and timber and expanding into the markets of California, which was owned by Mexico and also into Hawaii. The company had two major headquarters—one in York on Hudson Bay and the other at Fort Vancouver, which oversaw their Columbia Department and the Pacific. Under McLoughlin there were 600 employees, 34 outposts, 24 ports, and 6 ships. The operations were very successful, especially with the fur trade in Europe where beaver hats were in great demand. When the British government decided in 1821 to apply the laws in Upper Canada to British subjects in the Columbia District, it gave the Hudson's Bay Company the legal authority to enforce the law. Because McLoughlin was Superintendent of the Fort Vancouver office, he became the unofficial governor of the region, charged with maintaining law and order and keeping the peace with the natives and the Americans living there.

With the opening of the Oregon Trail reaching the Pacific in the 1840's and the arrival of many Americans, who the HBC discouraged from settling there and competing with their dominating position in the fur trade. However, McLoughlin violated company policy and gave considerable aid to them. Frictions developed rapidly to the point of possible war between Great Britain and the United States over differing land claims. In 1843, Hudson's Bay Governor George Simpson ordered McLoughlin to move the headquarters farther north to Vancouver Island and build Fort Camosun, which later became Victoria, British Columbia. McLoughlin never moved there, mainly because of his strong attachment to the Willamette Valley and partly due to his growing dissatisfaction working for the HBC. He promoted debates on his proposal to convert the region into an independent sovereign nation. Initial support for such a move gradually died as Great Britain and the United States began negotiations for establishing agreeable borders. Americans had set up a provisional government of Oregon in 1843. After the Oregon Treaty of 1846 settling the border dispute, the provisional government remained in control until 1859, when it became the Oregon Territory and then part of the United States when it was admitted as the 33rd state.

McLoughlin resigned from the Hudson's Bay Company in 1846 and moved back to Oregon City in the Willamette Valley. In 1847, Pope Gregory XVI awarded McLoughlin the Knighthood of St. Gregory. In 1848, he became a United States citizen, and in 1851, he served as mayor of Oregon City. McLoughlin died in 1857 at 73 years old. His legacies are many, with schools, streets, and bridges bearing his name. But the two greatest honors are the bronze statue of him in the National Statuary Hall in the nation's Capital and being officially entitled "The Father of Oregon" by the Oregon legislature in 1957.[9]

Chapter Thirty-Four

Kansas

State on January 29, 1861

Explorers and Settlers

Although a broad range of Native Americans traversed present-day Kansas as far back as 8,000 B.C., it was the Pawnee, Kansa, and Osage natives that came to dominate the area in the 17th century. The Spaniards under Francisco Vazquez de Coronado were the first Europeans to explore the region in 1541. The Indians saw horses for the first time when Coronado arrived, and from that time onward, their life style changed as they purchased greater numbers of them from the Spanish. The Kansa claimed to have settled there in 1673 on the Kansas River in the north, and the Osage occupied land on the Arkansas River in the south. The Pawnee dominated the western portion. The key attraction for all of them was the large herd of bison that roamed the area. In 1720, Spanish Lt. Gen. Pedro de Villasur led an expedition into the Nebraska section of the territory to thwart French intrusions there, but they were annihilated by the Pawnee and Otoe, which effectively ended further Spanish exploration in that region. In 1724, the French built a trading post at the mouth of the Kansas River, but there was little settlement by the French or Spanish during the 200 years from the discovery by Coronado. As the French expanded their fur trading from the Great Lakes to the Ohio River Valley and down the Mississippi River under the leadership of Marquette, Joliet, La Salle, and others, they claimed the lands they entered for France. These included territories on both sides of the Mississippi, which together with Canada constituted New France. Conflicts arose with existing claims by Spain and Great Britain, and these frictions led to the French and Indian War and the Seven Years' War. The two simultaneous wars morphed into one major conflict, which resulted in France losing Canada and all of its colonies east of the Mississippi River to Great Britain. Their colonies to the west of the river, including Kansas, went to Spain. Terms were dictated by the Treaty of Paris of 1763, but conditions changed again with the American Revolutionary War, when the Treaty of Paris of 1783 required England to cede most of their colonies south of Canada and from the Atlantic Ocean to the Mississippi River to the new American Republic.[1]

The Kansas region was owned by Spain for only 20 years until 1803, when they returned it to France. That same year with the Louisiana Purchase, France sold its entire holdings of 828,000 square miles to the United States, thereby doubling the size of the American Republic. Kansas was included and then became part of the Missouri Territory. Spain was allowed to keep 7,500 square miles in the Texas portion on the Gulf of Mexico until it became part of the newly-independent Mexico. After the Mexican-American War in 1846, it became part of the United States in 1848. The Lewis and Clark Expedition in 1804 was charged with mapping the newly acquired Louisiana Territory, and one of their earliest tasks was in 1806, when they met with French fur traders in Kansas at the confluence of the Kansas and Missouri Rivers to map that area. For the next 40 years, it was used by the United States government as a resettlement area for the displaced American Indians. In 1821, Kansas shifted from being a part of the Missouri Territory to being an "unorganized territory," where there was little daily government administration. This was a temporary status before Congress would recognize it as a formal territory with an appointed governor and various state officials. The Santa Fe Trail ran through Kansas and was used by settlers headed to the Southwest and by those going to the Northwest onto the Oregon Trail. The United States army built posts along the trails to protect the settlers and the rapidly expanding trade that was developing. Kansas became a strategic stopping area with other lesser trails crisscrossing the region.[2]

During the 1820's to the 1840's, the United States government entered into several treaties with many tribes, whereby certain natives were directed to specific sections of Kansas in exchange for large tracts of Indian land. In 1825, the Kansa Nation ceded 20 million acres to the United States. That same year, the Shawnee and Delaware from Ohio and Missouri were moved to Kansas. In 1831, the Ottawa were moved to Kansas. All of the designated lands assigned to the Indians were not to be settled by white Americans or Europeans. However, by 1850, squatters were pressuring the government to settle there. The United States army even built Fort Riley deep in the Indian territory to protect the immigrants who were streaming west.

In 1852, Congress began to consider the creation of the Kansas Territory. The next year the House of Representatives passed a bill calling for the establishment of territorial status for a large tract of land from the western boundaries of Iowa and Missouri to the Rocky Mountains. However, the Senate delayed the motion with exhaustive deliberations on the status of slavery in the new territories.[3]

The Kansas-Nebraska Act

The purpose of the act was to open millions of acres of fertile land to farmers without violating the Missouri Compromise regarding slavery. Adding additional pressure to the issue were the railroad interests who wanted to construct a transcontinental rail line which would run through the Territory of Kansas. Senator Stephen Douglas of Illinois was a strong supporter of the railroads, and he was also a strong believer of popular sovereignty, which would allow the residents to decide on whether to permit slavery. The Senate Committee on Territories was headed by Douglas, and the first step in resolving the issue was a bill to organize the Nebraska Territory. Opposing Douglas was Senator David Atchinson of Missouri, who would only support the Nebraska bill if it allowed slavery, which was prohibited under the Missouri Compromise. The Nebraska bill was tabled by a vote of 23 to 17, with all the senators from the states south of Missouri voting with the majority. After months of antagonistic debates between pro-slavery and anti-slavery members of Congress, the Kansas-Nebraska Bill was passed on May 30, 1854. The Act established the two new territories of Kansas and Nebraska. The Kansas boundaries were Missouri to the east to the summit of the Rocky Mountains on the west. Its southern boundary was the 37th parallel, and the northern boundary was the 40th parallel. The key provision originally introduced by Senator Douglas was to remove the slavery issue from Congress and allow the residents of Kansas to decide the matter themselves. This effectively repealed the Missouri Compromise of 1820, which prohibited slavery in any new state north of the 36"30' line. The immediate reaction was a large-scale migration into Kansas from some northern states but mostly from the southern states, especially Missouri, in an attempt to win their respective positions on the slavery issue. Organized militias on both sides were formed and reached a fever-pitch by the time of the legislative elections in March of 1855. The large numbers of migrants from the South gave victory to the pro-slavery candidates in every polling district except one. This led to open hostilities for the next three years, which came to be called the "Border War" or the "Bleeding Kansas" period. The battles also took place in the legislature, which eventually elected sufficient anti-slavery members to propose free-state constitutions. Among these were the Topeka Constitution, the Lecompton Constitution, the Leavenworth Constitution, and the Wyandotte Constitution. The latter was adopted on October 4, 1859. It prohibited slavery and was approved by Congress, which was essential for admission to statehood on January 29, 1861. The Border Wars of the 1850's were regarded as the preview to the American Civil War.[4]

The Civil War

Civil strife ended in Kansas with the Wyandotte Constitution in 1859, and the local militias rapidly declined from little use. When the Civil War erupted in April of 1861, the Kansas government had no effective military forces, armaments, or meaningful supplies. They supported the North and formed their first regiments in June of 1861, which was in response to an assigned quota of 16,654 men. They eventually raised a total of 20,097 soldiers, which indicates their strong support of the Union. The number killed in battle and by war-related disease per thousand was the highest of all the states. There were no major strategic battles fought on Kansas soil, but there were 29 Confederate raids into the new state during the war.[5]

Railroads

Kansas played a key role in the development of the United States as it expanded westward. As noted earlier, the major impetus for organizing the Kansas Territory from the Missouri Territory was the construction of a transcontinental rail line that would connect the East Coast to the Pacific. Planning began in the 1850's with the first step being the Leavenworth, Pawnee, and Western Railroad in 1855, which was reorganized in 1863 as the Union Pacific Eastern Division. The original objective was to build a line from Kansas City across Kansas to Fort Riley and travel north to join the Union Pacific at Fort Kearny, Nebraska. Construction started in 1863. In 1869, the name was changed to the Kansas Pacific Railway by Congress, which extended land grants to homesteaders who would settle towns near the rail line. Residents in the Colorado Territory were anxious to join a national rail system, so in 1868, President Andrew Johnson signed into law a congressional bill that extended the line to the Rocky Mountains. It was to first reach Denver and then travel through the Rockies to the Pacific. The extension started in 1869, and by August of 1870, the first trains arrived in Denver. The Kansas Pacific and the Denver Pacific lines intersected three miles north of Denver. The Denver-Pacific Railway linked with the Union Pacific in Cheyenne, in the Nebraska Territory. The joining of the two rail lines marked the completion of a coast-to-coast network. The previous year the Golden Spike in Utah witnessed the linking of the Union Pacific with the Central Pacific Railroad, but passengers had to detrain at Council Bluffs, Iowa and at Omaha, Nebraska in order to cross the Missouri River.[6]

Statesmen, Leaders and Heroes

Cyrus Holliday was born in Carlisle, Pennsylvania in 1826. After graduating from Allegheny College, he pursued various business ventures and made a sizeable profit ($20,000) from the construction and sale of a small railroad in

Pennsylvania. In 1854, he moved to the Kansas Territory and settled in the town of Lawrence, where he soon acquired a reputation for integrity and leadership. Holliday firmly believed in the future of Kansas and was convinced that it would become a successful and important state. Less than two months after arriving, he searched for a future permanent capital along the Kansas River and proceeded to purchase large tracts of land. He and seven other investors formed the Topeka Town Company, and Holliday was elected president. The company profitably sold most of the building lots it owned, and when it closed for business, Holliday remained as the trustee who settled all outstanding debts and title claims. He became the largest individual tax payer in Topeka, and he still owned a good amount of land there when he died in 1900. Five years after settling in Kansas, Holliday began to fulfill his dream of building a railroad by chartering the Atchinson and Topeka Railroad, which was to be built along the Santa Fe Trail connecting the two cities. It was approved in 1860 by territorial governor Andrew Reeder, with Holliday as its first president. In 1863, the railway became the Atchinson, Topeka, and Santa Fe Railroad. Holliday continued to acquire land through government grants reaching far into the western parts of the state. He was a fervent free-stater and founder of the Republican Party of Kansas. Holliday was a member of the Free State Conventions in Topeka in 1857 and 1858. In 1861, he was chosen as the state senator for the Sixth District. In the Civil War, he was appointed adjutant-general of Kansas and was responsible for the business affairs of all the state regiments. It was his successful work there that earned him the honorary title of colonel, which he used for the rest of his life. In 1866, he was elected to the state legislature as representative for the Topeka District. He served on the boards of Atchinson, Topeka, and Santa Fe Railroad, the Excelsior Coke and Gas Company and as president of the Merchant's National Bank and the State Historical Society. Cyrus Holliday died in 1900 at 74 years old.[7]

The Reverend Thomas Johnson was born in Virginia in 1802 and later moved to Missouri, where he married Sarah Davis in 1830. It was during this time that the United States government was moving many Indian tribes from the Midwest to designated lands west of Missouri. In 1830, Congress passed the Indian Removal Act, which accounted for the resettlement of 10,000 American Indians. The natives had little choice but to sell their lands to the government and move to an area of the Kansas Territory known as the Great American Desert. The Shawnee received a 1.6 million-acre tract, and when they arrived, they requested a missionary to teach them English and other useful skills. The man chosen was a Methodist minister named Thomas Johnson, who immediately moved with his bride to Wyandotte County, Kansas. Johnson proposed to build a school that would serve many tribes, and he chose a place on the Santa Fe Trail that ran through Shawnee lands. The school opened in 1839 and taught academics, manual arts, and agriculture to more than 15 tribes. Named the Shawnee Mission School, it grew to 16 buildings on 2,000 acres with an enrollment of 200 boys and girls ranging from five to 23 years old. Classes were held from Monday to Saturday. Boys worked in the shop or on the farm while the girls did sewing, washing, and cooking. When the Kansas Territory was formed in 1854, its first governor, Andrew Reeder, had his office at the school, and the first legislature met there as well. Being from the South, Johnson was a slaveholder and brought his slaves with him when he moved to Kansas. During this time, there were bitter and fierce disputes over slavery and whether it should be allowed in Kansas. To complicate matters, the Kansas-Nebraska Act of 1854 displaced the Indians again. Johnson was a firm advocate of slavery, and records show he had purchased more of them up to 1856. Oddly, the previous year, Johnson County was named in his honor. According to historian John Bowes, Johnson joined with those who wanted Kansas to become a slave state. Just before the Civil War broke out in 1861, John publicly claimed to support the Union. During the war, his mission school closed and served as barracks for the United States army. In 1865, Johnson was murdered in his home, and to this day his death is an unsolved crime. Some believe it was committed by southern sympathizers who were angered by Johnson's reversal in supporting the Union abolitionists. He is buried at the Shawnee Methodist Mission. After his death and several legal battles, the mission property was given to the Johnson family. In 1927, it was sold to the State of Kansas and is administered by Kansa Historical Society and operates as the Shawnee Indian Mission State Historic Site.[8]

James Butler Hickok was born in 1837 in Homer, Illinois where he grew up in a farm house that was part of the Underground Railway, assisting runaway slaves seeking freedom from their southern masters. At a very young age, Hickok was known as an excellent marksman. His father died in 1852, and three years later, James left Illinois to settle in Leavenworth in the Kansas Territory. There he joined Gen. Jim Lane's Free State army, which was a vigilante group also known as the "Jayhawkers." It was there that he first met William Cody (Buffalo Bill), who was serving as a scout for the United States army. In 1857, Hickok made claim to a 160-acre tract in Johnson County, Kansas, and in 1858, he was made a constable of Monticello Township. The following year, he worked for the Russell, Waddell & Majors Freight Company, which was the parent company of the Pony Express, and he then became a teamster for the Union army in Missouri. In 1861, Hickok began using the name "Wild Bill," which reflected his many episodes of shootouts and dealing with lawless gunmen. He was discharged from the army in 1862 and joined Gen. James Henry Lane's Kansas Brigade, where he reportedly worked as a Union spy. After the war, Hickok lived in Springfield, where he acquired his reputation as a gambler, ruffian, and gun slinger. In an interview with *Harpers New Monthly Magazine,* he used the name "Wild Bill Hickok," claiming to have killed hundreds of men. He left Springfield in 1865 and served as a scout for Gen. George Custer. After he claimed to have killed a number of Indians who attacked him, he left for Nebraska, where he engaged some brawling cowboys and ended up taking on four of them at once and killing three of them. He moved on to Hays, Kansas to work as a scout there and then to Lincoln County, Kansas. In 1869, he was elected city marshal of Hays, and in his first month, killed two disorderly men who tried to attack him. In 1871, Hickok was hired as marshal of Abilene, Kansas. He then became involved in more shootings of alleged outlaws, but when he accidentally killed his deputy, Mike Williams, while he was coming to Hickok's aid, he was relieved of his duties as marshal. In 1873, he joined Buffalo Bill Cody and Texas Jack Omohundro in their new show "Scouts of the Plains." Three years later, he was diagnosed with glaucoma which ended his days of marksmanship. In 1876, while playing poker in Deadwood in the Dakota Territory, Hickok befriended another player named Jack McCall, who had lost all his money. When Hickok offered to help him, McCall was offended and left the saloon. The next day, McCall snuck up behind Hickok and shot him in the head. After two trials, McCall was found guilty and was hanged. Wild Bill Hickok remains a hero of the Old West. Historians are still trying to separate fact from fiction because of his tendency to exaggerate his exploits as a soldier, scout, and marshal. We are still not certain about the number of men he killed in defense, brawls, or otherwise. His birthplace is listed as a historic site and is administered by the Illinois Historic Preservation Agency. He is the hero in the first dime novel of the West, and his life captures the rough and dangerous world of the Kansas frontier.[9]

Chapter Thirty-five

West Virginia

State on June 20, 1863

Settlers and Founders

The state of West Virginia is unique in that it is the only state in the country to have been formed by seceding from the Confederacy, and it was one of the only two states (other was Nevada) to have originated by seceding from another state. The secession of West Virginia from Virginia came about because of the Civil War in 1861, but the causes were far more fundamental and encompassed political, economic, social, and geographic factors over a 150-year period.

West Virginia's "parent" state of Virginia was the country's first colony (1607), and its charter from King James I designated its boundaries over the largest tract of land in all the colonies that were to follow. The Virginia Company Charter showed land that ranged from the North Carolina line on the south to northerner New Jersey and then northwest to Canada east of the Great Lakes, with both northern and southern boundaries reaching from "sea to shining sea"—

meaning the Atlantic and Pacific Oceans. Its size and shape were to change with the establishments of new states, but for many years, it included the present-day states of West Virginia, Ohio, Indiana, Illinois, Michigan, Wisconsin, and part of Minnesota. As the western portions of Virginia were explored by English, Spanish, French, German, and other settlers, disputes over claims arose, especially with the Native American tribes who had lived in this region for thousands of years. Land claims in western Virginia were primarily from the Iroquois, Shawnee, and Cherokee natives who used the lands west of the Blue Ridge Mountains for hunting. There were very few European settlements there until the 1700's, when the region's natural resources were discovered.

Virginia's royal Governor William Berkeley, who served from 1660 to 1677, is credited with sending two Englishmen, Thomas Batts and Robert Fallum, into western Virginia in 1671. They were followed in 1716 by the efforts of royal Governor Alexander Spotswood, who explored the rich veins of iron ore in the upper Rappahannock River region and present-day Pendleton County in the Shenandoah Valley. As more Europeans moved to the western part of Virginia, the Iroquois voiced their strong objections, which resulted in the Treaty of Albany of 1722, which set the Blue Ridge Mountains as the western boundary for white settlers. In spite of the treaty, settlers continued to move into the northern part of present-day West Virginia where the Shenandoah River flows into the upper reaches of the Potomac River. That area had very few settlements, but it did attract Indian traders and German settlers from Pennsylvania, who founded the towns of New Mecklenburg and Shepherdstown in the late 1720's. In 1734, Orange County was organized, which included all of West Virginia west of the Blue Ridge Mountains. That measure infuriated the Iroquois, which led to an outbreak of hostilities in 1743. A major conflict was avoided by Virginia royal Governor William Gooch, who negotiated the Treaty of Lancaster whereby he purchased the Indian claims for 400 pounds sterling.[1]

In the years of 1749 to 1751, a young 17-year-old surveyor named George Washington began his new career mapping the area. His youngest brother, Charles, later moved to the region and built his home "Happy Retreat." He gave 80 acres to the local government for the establishment of Charles Town in 1786, which was named in his honor. Another of George's brothers, Samuel, built his estate there named "Harewood," and George himself owned land there in Berkeley County. Another notable surveyor named Christopher Gist explored and mapped the area for the Ohio Company, which was formed in 1748 by Thomas Lee, who was president of the Virginia Council of State. Other partners included royal Governor Robert Dinwiddie, John Hanbury, Col. Thomas Cresap, George Mercer, and a number of wealthy Virginians. In 1751, the company attempted to charter another colony there with the name of "Vandalia," but it was not approved. Their land was partly in Ohio and mostly in present-day West Virginia, encompassing the rich soil of the Ohio River Valley. As more settlers moved into the region, disputes with the Iroquois resumed, and it became apparent that the Treaty of Albany of 1722 was not explicit in describing precisely which lands they had sold to Virginia. In 1752, with the Treaty of Logstown, the Iroquois recognized the rights of Virginians to settle south of the Ohio River. At the end of the French and Indian War, the English made another effort to placate the Indians with the Proclamation of 1763. The Parliament's edict prohibited further white settlements west of the Allegheny Mountains and dedicated lands to the west of the mountains strictly for use by the Native Americans. It took another five years for the Iroquois to surrender their claims south of the Ohio River with the Treaty of Fort Stanwix. However, the Shawnee and Cherokee who occupied the southern areas of western Virginia still had unresolved claims. The Cherokee soon settled their issues by selling their land to Virginia in 1770 under the Treaty of Lochaber. Sadly, some Cherokee under Chief Dragging Canoe continued to oppose white settlers from 1776 to 1794 in what came to be known as the Cherokee-American Wars. The Shawnee decided to physically oppose the English in armed battle. Royal Governor John Murray, Lord Dunmore with Col. Andrew Lewis led British troops to the confluence of the Kanawha and Ohio Rivers, where they decisively defeated the natives. The conflict, called Dunmore's War of 1774, ended with the Shawnee ceding their lands south of the Ohio River to West Virginia and Kentucky.[2]

Early Economy

Because of its many rivers and waterways, West Virginia provided excellent places for trading posts and mills. One of its earliest ventures was a flour mill built by Thomas Shepherd in 1739. It was powered by the upper Potomac River at the Falling Springs Branch, and the town prospered to become present-day Shepherdstown whose name honors its founder. Two of West Virginia's first commercial ferry operations were authorized in 1748 by Virginia's General Assembly, with one in Berkeley County and the other at Harper's Ferry. During the first half of the 1700's, the demand for beaver skins increased sharply as beaver hats were widely purchased in Europe and America. Other natural resources were exported such as salt, coal, and timber, which were transported up the Ohio River through the Great Lakes to the St. Lawrence River and also southward via the Mississippi River to the Gulf of Mexico. Keel boats, barges, and steamboats were built in towns like Wheeling, Parkersburg, Point Pleasant, Morgantown, and Mason City, with an abundant supply of lumber railroad ties made for the rapidly expanding rail lines to the west. West Virginia's early economy did not depend on trade with eastern Virginia or the Atlantic Coast markets, and this became an important point in deliberations 100 years later, when West Virginia decided to secede from Virginia.

Post Revolution Period

During the American Revolution, settlers in western Virginia supported the war and fought in the Continental Army. After the war, the two sections of the state resumed their separate development. Plantations in the east operated with slaves, while farmers and miners in the western areas had few slaves and performed most of the manual labor themselves. The populations of the two sections were quite different, with many Germans and Ulster-Scots coming from Europe and states to the north, especially Pennsylvania. In 1776, settlers in western Virginia attempted to form a new state by the name of "Westsylvania," but the war intervened, putting an end to the effort. In 1829, Virginia held a convention to create a new constitution which would grant suffrage only to white male property owners. It also would allow counties with slaves to count three-fifths of them to be included in their official populations for determining the number of elected officials to the House of Representatives. Both measures were overwhelmingly opposed by all but one of the counties west of the Allegheny Mountains. The new rules gave the eastern Virginians tremendous control over the entire state, as was illustrated shortly afterwards when the Virginia Board of Public Works embarked on a costly internal infrastructure program, to be paid by all state residents with only a small proportion of improvements for the western counties. Another issue that isolated western Virginians was the distance to the capital in Richmond and the difficulty of getting there. As noted above, the economies of eastern and western Virginia were very different. The east was dominated by tobacco and cotton farms, agricultural crops, fishing, and shipping. In the western section, the major focus was on mining, timber, and salt. Their raw materials and products were shipped north, west and south. The westerners believed their interests were not supported in Richmond. Conditions were ripe for a significant event to rupture the two sections, and that event occurred in April of 1861.

The Civil War

When the war erupted in Charleston, South Carolina, one of the first states to secede from the Union was Virginia. The process began in Richmond on April 17, 1861 with the Ordinance of Secession. The 49 delegates from western Virginia voted 30 to 17 against the measure, which was an early indication of the divisiveness that lie ahead. At the next meeting in May, secession was ratified by a wide margin, but the western vote was 34,677 against and only 19,121 in favor. A leading member of the proceedings, state senator John Carlile made an interesting point that the Secession Convention was illegal, because it was called without the consent of the people. More importantly, he stated that the government in Richmond had been terminated by those voting for the Ordinance of Secession, thereby requiring the reorganization of the government. The Restored Government of Virginia was established, and Francis Pierpont was chosen as governor. The new additional government elected two United States senators, who were immediately accepted by Congress. There were now two governments representing Virginia—one which owed its allegiance to the Confederacy and the other its allegiance to the United States. However, the change violated the United States Constitution, which forbade new states from being created from existing states without the latter's permission. The Restored Government maintained its authority and formed the new state of Kanawha, which included most of West Virginia's present-day counties. The name was changed one month later to West Virginia, and in October, a popular vote resulted in 18,408 in favor and only 781 against the new state. On December 31, 1862, President Lincoln approved the new state on the one condition that the gradual abolition of slavery be included in their constitution. On March 26, 1863, their new constitution met Lincoln's requirement, and West Virginia was admitted to the Union on June 20, 1863. When the Unionist Restored Government approved the separation, its constitutionality was confirmed.[3]

Statesmen, Leaders and Heroes

Regarded as the "Father of West Virginia," Francis Harrison Pierpont was born in Morgantown, Virginia in 1814. His great grandfather Col. Zackquill Morgan was the founder of Morgantown. Young Pierpont moved with his family to Fairmont in 1827, where his father built a successful tannery, enabling Francis to enter Madison College (later Allegheny College) and afterwards to study the law. Among his youthful friends were men who were to shape the future of West Virginia, gaining its status as a state. These included Waitman Willey, John Carlile, and James Otis Watson. Early in his legal career, Pierpont worked as an attorney for the Baltimore & Ohio Railroad. In 1854, he became a partner with James Watson in his family-owned Consolidation Coal Company. Two years later, he began to work on founding the Male and Female Seminary, which eventually became Fairmont State University. At the start of the Civil War, Pierpont spoke out forcibly against Virginia's secession and cautioned not to act too soon for the establishment of a new state. He strongly believed that such a move would be unconstitutional. When the western counties met in Wheeling in 1861 to debate their future following Virginia's secession from the Union and joining the Confederacy, Pierpont first served as a representative and then was unanimously elected governor of the new Restored Government of Virginia. He raised funds for their militia and actively supported the Union. He moved the capital to Alexandria, Virginia during the war to keep it safe on federal lands and under their control. At the end of the war, President Andrew Johnson directed Pierpont to head the new state from Richmond, where he served until 1868 to be replaced by Gen. John Schofield under the Military Reconstruction Act of

1867. When he returned to West Virginia, he served one term in their House of Delegates. In his retirement, he devoted time to community affairs such as the West Virginia Historical Society and the Methodist Protestant Church. He died in 1899 at age 85, in his daughter's home in Pittsburgh. His legacy is the epithet "Father of West Virginia" and his statue in Wheeling's Independence Hall and in the Statuary Hall in the nation's Capital building.[4]

Waitman Willey was born in a log cabin near present-day Farmington, Virginia in 1811. After graduating from Madison College (later Allegheny College), he studied the law and settled down in Morgantown, Virginia, where he practiced law. After losing a bid for the Virginia General Assembly in 1840, he became involved in several local political groups. At the Virginia Constitutional Convention in 1850-51, he spoke about the inequities of the state's political structure, which heavily favored the eastern counties. He also advocated universal white male suffrage without property requirements. In 1861, Willey was elected to Virginia's convention in Richmond to discuss the issue of secession. He warned that such a move would dissolve the state, but when President Lincoln called on federal troops to subdue the rebellion in Charleston, the Assembly voted to leave the Union and join the Confederacy. When Willey returned home and attended the First Wheeling Convention in 1861, he urged his peers to claim that the government in Richmond was illegitimate and that they should form a new government. His recommendation was accepted, and he was appointed as one of the two United States senators from the Restored Government of Virginia. He was then appointed to the West Virginia Constitutional Convention. In Congress, the bill to consider West Virginia for statehood became embroiled over the slavery issue. Willey supported emancipation but only if there was compensation to the former slaveholders. He then offered a compromise that provided all slaves under age 21 on July 4, 1863 would attain their freedom, and the offer assumed statehood for West Virginia. In 1863, when West Virginia was accepted into the Union, Willey was elected to the United States Senate and was reelected in 1865 to serve another six years. Waitman Willey died in 1900 at 89 years old.[5]

Chapter Thirty-six

NEVADA

State on October 31, 1864

Founders and Settlers

After the Spanish conquered the Aztecs in 1521, they established their first of four viceroyalties in their kingdom known as New Spain. It consisted of Mexico, Central America, Central America, Southwestern North America, Florida, the Philippines, Guam, Mariana, and the Caroline Islands. To the east of the continent, it included Cuba, Hispaniola (Haiti and Dominican Republic), Puerto Rico, Jamaica, the Cayman Islands, Trinidad, and the Bay Islands. On the continent, it claimed most of present-day United States south of Canada and west of the Mississippi River. It is important to note that most of the western and southwestern parts of the United States were known as borderlands, which were of no value to Spain and therefore were scarcely populated. Spain did not entirely ignore these areas and sent explorers and missionaries to the Pacific Coast of California, British Columbia, and Alaska. The heart of the Spanish Empire was central Mexico, and the discovery of silver in the 1500's became the foundation of their economy in their development of New Spain. In 1821, Mexico won its war for independence from Spain and was first formed as the Mexican Empire and then as simply Mexico. In an effort to populate and develop its borderlands, the Mexican government invited immigrants from the United States to settle there. As settlements grew in Alta (upper) California, which was present-day Arizona, and Santa Fe, which was present-day New Mexico, the residents there demanded more individual freedoms to the point where Mexican-American relations deteriorated into open hostilities. The ensuing war lasted from 1846 to 1848 and ended with the Treaty of Guadalupe Hidalgo whereby Mexico lost California, half of New Mexico, most of Arizona, Nevada, Utah, and parts of Wyoming and Colorado. The Mexicans who lived in those areas had the choice of relocating to Mexico or remaining as American citizens. The treaty also established the Rio Grande River as the boundary between Texas and Mexico. The United States paid the Mexican Government $15 million and $3.2 million for American citizen claims against Mexico.[1]

Spain and Mexico had never developed or effectively administered Nevada, but it was inhabited by Americans since the 1820's. The region was known as Washoe, after the name of the local Indian tribe. After being a part of the Mexican territory, it became a part of the American Utah Territory and then the Nevada Territory in 1861. Three significant events impacted Nevada after its annexation to the United States in 1848: gold and silver were discovered in the 1850's; the Mormons established the first permanent white settlement in Nevada in 1851; and Congress passed the Homestead Act of 1862. Miners and speculators poured into Nevada, especially in 1859 with the Comstock Lode discovery in Carson County. This was an enormous event that yielded $300 million in gold and silver by the year 1882. However, land claim disputes put a serious strain on the local government and judicial system. Bribery was rampant and record-keeping of titles was almost impossible. Mining laws were complicated and difficult to uphold. Matters came to a head in 1864 when the territorial supreme court all resigned, thereby temporarily stopping further litigation. In 1860, there was a major discovery of gold in Aurora, which was on the border with California. Earlier it was a California county, but when the border dispute was resolved,

Aurora was deemed to be part of Nevada. The eastern boundary of the Nevada Territory was first fixed at the 116th meridian, but when gold was discovered to the east of that line, Nevada gained approval from Congress to move their boundary farther east to the 115th meridian in 1862. After statehood in 1864, more gold was discovered still farther to the east, and again Congress approved their request to move the boundary to the 114th meridian in 1866. In 1867, with another discovery of gold beyond its southern boundary, Congress approved the state's request to expand to the Colorado River to include the northwest tip of Arizona. Arizona protested, but Congress had little regard for them because of their past membership in the Confederacy. Also, with very little water available in Nevada, its access to the lower Colorado River would be an important asset for their future development.

When gold was first discovered in California in 1848, it sparked a massive gold rush from across the United States. Most speculators came by land through Nevada, and before attempting to travel through the Sierra-Nevada Mountains, they rested and resupplied their wagons in the Carson Valley. In 1850, a small group of Mormons established a trading post on the west side of Carson, and their favorable reports to their leaders in Salt Lake City prompted them to send more of their sect to the Carson area to establish a permanent settlement there. In 1851, they organized a government, and the Utah Territorial Legislation established Carson County. The Mormons renamed their settlement from Mormon Station to Genoa. Utah Territorial Governor Brigham Young sent Orson Hyde to be their spiritual head and local judge. Mormons flocked to Carson until 1857, when Young ordered all able-bodied men to return to Salt Lake City to defend against an expected attack from the United States army. In 1861, the Territory of Nevada was approved by Congress, and James Nye was appointed governor by President Lincoln. The capital was established in Carson City.[2]

The Homestead Act of 1862

The purpose of the Homestead Act was to entice farmers with families to settle the western territories and states. The first such bill was attempted in 1858 but was defeated in the Senate by one vote. The following year, another bill was passed by both the House and Senate but was vetoed by President James

Buchanan. Opposition was led by southern Democrats who feared many of the new western states would be free and thereby hold a political advantage against their interests. When Democrat Buchanan completed his four-year term, he fulfilled his promise to serve only one term. In 1860, the new president Abraham Lincoln and the Republican Congress soon approved the Homestead Act, that granted any adult citizen with a family could qualify for free public land of up to 160 acres by paying a small registration fee plus $1.25 per acre and living on it continuously for five years. Passage of the measure was assured with the secession of the southern states in 1861. Any American citizen, including freed slaves, was allowed to submit a claim. In three years, by the end of the war, 15,000 claims had been filed. The last claim was in 1988 for 80 acres in Alaska. Under the Act, a total of 420,000 square miles of land was granted to 1.6 million people.[3]

The Civil War

Nevada raised 1,200 men for their 1st Battalion Nevada Volunteers Cavalry, but they never fought against any southern state. Instead, they were used to scout and protect overland routes and settlements from possible Indian attacks. Nevada's major contribution to the war was $400 million of silver from the Comstock Lode. They did experience some isolated strong support for the Confederacy, but any open hostilities were immediately subdued. During the war, Nevada was put under martial law with support from Fort Churchill, ready to use military force.[4]

Statehood

The Nevada Territory was established on March 2, 1861, only one month before the outbreak of the Civil War. Prior to that time, the area was known as Washoe, in recognition of the local Washoe tribe. It was also part of the Utah Territory, and the separation was welcomed by both territories due to a history of friction and open hostilities between the Mormons of Utah and the non-Mormons of Nevada. The three-year period from a territory in 1861 to a state in 1864 was not an unusually brief time, but when the process was speeded up in 1864 it gave rise to rumors and misconceptions. One of these was the notion that Congress needed Nevada's extensive silver treasure to finance the war. This has been disputed, because as a territory under United States control, the silver could have been taken by an act of Congress. Because Nevada's population in 1864 was around 35,000, it did not comply with the 60,000-resident requirement of the Northwest Ordinance of 1787, to which all previous new states had conformed. This exception was viewed with skepticism and caused more speculation for the apparent fast-track to statehood. Upon closer examination of the Northwest Ordinance, this theory is incorrect, because the actual wording reads that a state could be admitted, "provided, the constitution and government so to be formed, shall be republican, and in conformity with the principles contained in these articles, and so far as it can be consistent with the general interests of the confederacy, such admissions shall be allowed at an earlier period, and when there may be a less number of free inhabitants in the state than sixty thousand." The third theory of supporting hastiness of admitting Nevada was that President Lincoln needed Nevada's two electoral votes for the November presidential election. This theory was given credence when Nevada's new constitution was telegraphed to Washington, D.C. in late October and signed by the president on October 31, 1864, which was just eight days before the election. It was the first constitution to be telegraphed and its thousands of pages cost $3,416.77 or close to $57,000 in today's currency value. It was the longest and most expensive telegraph in American history. The theory proved false when the Electoral College voted 212 to 21 in favor of Lincoln over George McClellan. The more plausible reason for Nevada's prompt and favorable acceptance had to do with becoming a free state and supporting the Lincoln agenda of reconstruction and reconciliation during and after the Civil War, which outcome had become apparent by 1864. In that election, Nevada voted Republican in the presidential, congressional, and legislative elections.[5]

Founders and Statesmen

Francisco Garces is credited with being the first European to have set foot in present-day Nevada. He was born in north-central Spain in 1738, entered the Franciscan Order in 1758, and was ordained a priest in 1763. Shortly thereafter, he travelled to the Spanish province of Mexico in New Spain to serve in the Franciscan College of Santa Cruz in Queretaro. For close to 200 years, the earliest Spanish explorers of Mexico and southwestern United States were accompanied by Jesuit missionaries, who proceeded to build missions from Mexico to the California Coast. As the power and influence of the Jesuits increased, the Spanish government became alarmed, and in 1768, the king of Spain, Charles III expelled them all from their missions in northeast Mexico and southwestern United States. He replaced them with the Franciscans, with whom he had more trust and confidence. Garces was one of the first Franciscans to arrive at his new post of Mission San Xavier in the Sonoran Desert near present-day Tucson, Arizona. Other Franciscans took over missions in Mexico City, Baja California, and upper (Alta) California. They worked with the Viceroy of New Spain in building road connections between upper California and central New Spain. Francisco Garces was at the center of these projects, as he personally explored the Sonoran, Colorado, and Mojave Desert regions, including the Gila River and the lower Colorado River to the northern California Coast. Along his journey, he established good relations with the Quechan, Mojave, Hopi, and Havasupai tribes. He joined another explorer, Juan Bautista de Anza, in his expedition to reach upper California from the east and his 1775 journey to the San Francisco Bay. In 1776, he explored the San Joaquin Valley, just after crossing the Mojave Desert. Garces and Juan Diaz built two mission churches at Yuma Crossing on the lower Colorado River in 1779 to 1781. When Spanish settlers violated a treaty with the local natives in 1781, the Yuma tribe revolted, killing a number of Franciscans including Garces. The Catholic Church declared those Franciscans to be martyrs and started the process for their sainthood.[6]

Abraham Van Santvoord Curry was born in New York in 1815. After marrying Mary Ann Cowen in 1835, the family moved to Ohio in 1848, where Abraham worked as an agent for the Michigan Southern Railroad. In 1854, Curry and his son Charles travelled by steamship to San Francisco, and by 1856, they were living in the California mining town of Red Dog, where they met their future business partners: Benjamin Green, John Musser, and Frank Proctor. In 1858, the partners moved east to Genoa, Nevada, which had been abandoned by the Mormons, who were called back to Salt Lake City to defend against the United States army in what was known as the Utah War or the Mormon War. The conflict lasted 15 months in 1857-58, and though there were no major battles, there were a total of 150 victims who died in isolated skirmishes. Frictions between the Mormons and the United States government were running high for a number of years, due primarily to religious persecution and fears of permanent Mormon control of Utah. After the "war," the two sides negotiated a peaceful resolution with a transfer of political power from Mormon President Brigham Young to the non-Mormon Alfred Cumming. In Genoa, Curry found real estate too expensive, so he moved on to Eagle Valley, where the partners bought a ranch and 865 acres. He and his attorney partners tried to develop a separate territory from Utah, but when it was blocked, they founded Carson City. They then donated ten acres of their land for the future site of the state capital for Nevada. In 1859, Musser was appointed President and Proctor was named Vice President for the Nevada Constitutional Convention to establish the Territory of Nevada. Curry became the delegate for Eagle Valley. That same year, the Comstock Lode was discovered just east of Carson City, bringing thousands of miners to the area. In 1861, Curry built a large hotel east of the city, and the next year, the Nevada Territorial Legislature leased it for meetings and for holding prisoners. In 1864, the legislature purchased the hotel for $80,000 (close to $1.5 million in today's currency value), and it became the Nevada State Prison. The Carson City Mint opened in 1870, and Curry was appointed its first superintendent. He then supervised the construction of engine houses and machine shops servicing several railroads. Curry died unexpectedly in 1873 at age 58 from a stroke. His funeral was the largest one ever held in Carson City.[7]

James Nye was born in New York in 1814. He was educated at home, and after working four years as a stagecoach driver, he studied the law with an eye toward politics. He won his first election as Madison County District Attorney in 1839 and then as County Judge from 1840 to 1848. He lost his bid for Congress in 1848, running as a Democrat who opposed slavery in the territories. After losing, he moved to Syracuse, New York, where he became President of the Metropolitan Police Commission in 1857. In 1860, he switched to the Republican Party and campaigned for Abraham Lincoln. When the Nevada Territory was created in 1861, President Lincoln appointed Nye as its governor. His policies were to bring law and order to the new territory and to move it toward statehood. He organized judicial districts and created a legislative body. As Superintendent of Indian Affairs, he met with leaders of the Northern Paiutes to craft a peace treaty. He also signed a Peace and Friendship Treaty with the Shoshone Indians. Natives and relatives of their chiefs stated that Nye was the only governor who helped them. He supported civil rights and strongly opposed gambling. Upon statehood in 1864, Nye was elected governor but served only two months before resigning to run for the United States Senate. He was reelected in 1867 and served until 1873. Nye was regarded as a Radical Republican and became a political opponent of Secretary of State Seward. He was far ahead of his contemporaries in that he advocated universal suffrage and women's right to vote. Nye lost his bid for the Senate in 1873 and returned to New York City, where he died in 1876 at 62 years old.[8]

Chapter Thirty-seven

NEBRASKA

State on March 1, 1867

Explorers and Founders

Nebraska is an Indian name that translates to "flat water," which is in reference to the Platte River that runs through the state. The Oto Indian word for the Platte River was "Nebrathka." In 1844, United States Secretary of War William Wilkins suggested that the name "Platte" or "Nebraska" could be an appropriate name for the new territory. It was the Platte that attracted the Pawnee and the Arikara about 500 years ago. In the 18th century, other tribes migrated to the area, including the Ponca, Oto, Lakota, Arapaho, Omaha, and Cheyenne. By the year 1800, an estimated 40,000 Native Americans lived in Nebraska. The natives subsisted on bison for food and clothing and on crops such as beans, corn, and squash. When the Spanish arrived in 1541, led by Francisco Vasquez de Coronado, the local Indians welcomed them for their trading as well as their horses and guns. Both of these items allowed the tribes to hunt for bison over a larger territory, and they quickly adapted their culture around the use of horses. Coronado travelled through Nebraska, Kansas, and much of the Southwest beyond the Mississippi River, and he claimed much of the region for Spain, even though they did not build settlements there. It was close to 100 years before the French appeared with their explorers Marquette, Joliet, and La Salle, who also claimed most of the Mississippi River Valley for France and named it "Louisiane" in honor of King Louis XIV. Spain was alarmed by the French incursions, and in 1720, Pedro de Villasur with 45 of his men attempted to remove the French from Nebraska. At the Platte River, the Pawnee attacked and killed the Spaniards. Other French explorers continued to expand their dominant position in the fur industry and established trading posts and trading relationships with the natives throughout the Mississippi River region, extending west to Kansas and Nebraska. It was two French explorers, Pierre and Paul Mallet, who gave the Platte River its name as they travelled the length of Nebraska. Control of the region shifted to England and Spain after the French and Indian War. France ceded its colonies to England east of the Mississippi River and to Spain west of the river. The new ownerships lasted for only 20 years for England, who lost their American colonies with the Treaty of Paris in 1783. In 1800, Napoleon pressured Spain to return its former Louisiana Territory. As Napoleon continued to overrun Europe, he required more resources, so in 1803, he initiated the sale of the entire Louisiana Territory to the United States for $15 million.[1]

The first United States explorers to visit the region were Lewis and Clark, who travelled up the Missouri River in 1805-06. That same year, Zebulon Pike explored south-central Nebraska under another government program. In 1812, a party travelled from the Astoria Trading Post in Oregon through Nebraska to New York City. Headed by a fur agent, Robert Stuart, they followed the North Platte River to its connection to the South Platte and then to the Missouri River. The route marked the beginning of the Oregon Trail, which opened the Northwest to future settlers from the Midwest. In 1819, Fort Atkinson became the first United States army military post in Nebraska. It was located near the present-day town of Fort Calhoun in Washington County. In 1820, an expedition led by Major Stephen Long travelled from the Missouri River to the Platte River to the South Platte close to Denver. Long observed the region to be a desert and not suited for settlement because the land was barren and could not be cultivated. The first permanent white settlement in Nebraska was founded in 1823 at the town of Bellevue on the Missouri River.[2]

Both Kansas and Nebraska became the first crossroads for the massive American migration that started in the 1840's and grew rapidly with the discovery of gold in California and silver and gold in Nevada. The river valleys of the Platte and Little Blue gave rise to the Mormon, California, and Oregon trails, which were used by settlers, speculators, homesteaders, miners, and the Pony Express to deliver mail to the Pacific Coast. In the 1830's, steamboats made their appearance, and up to 50 of them conducted river trade. With the construction of railroads in the 1860's, trails gave way to a faster and safer way of crossing the plains and through the Rocky Mountains. White settlers were prohibited from staying in much of the area, because it was designated strictly for the Indians until the establishment of the Nebraska Territory in 1854. Plans for a Nebraska Territory started in 1844 with a bill introduced by Senator Stephen Douglas of Illinois. The bill was defeated primarily over the slavery issue, and it took another ten years of debate and compromise for it to be approved by Congress. Resolution was reached when Congress agreed to withhold the slavery question from the federal government and allow the local residents of Nebraska and Kansas to vote on the issue themselves. Being above the latitude of 36'30", the Kansas-Nebraska Act clearly violated the Missouri Compromise of 1820 and brought about conflicts between pro-slavery and anti-slavery advocates pouring into the Kansas and Nebraska territories in an effort to turn the vote in their favor. The conflict gave birth to the new anti-slavery party called "Republican" and served as a catalyst for the coming Civil War. Nebraska's initial boundaries were from the 40th parallel in the South to the Canadian border in the North. On the east was the Missouri River, and the western line was at the Continental Divide. It was much larger than today's Nebraska, including present-day Montana, North and South Dakota, Wyoming, and Colorado. Over the next ten years, new territories were carved out, which reduced Nebraska to its current size. President Franklin Pierce appointed Francis Burt of South Carolina as the first governor, but after his sudden death two days after taking office, Thomas Cuming became acting governor. Omaha was chosen as the capital, but this changed with statehood in 1867 to Lancaster, the name of which was changed to Lincoln in memory of Abraham Lincoln.[3] It took 13 more years for Nebraska to attain statehood, primarily due to the slavery issue and the Civil War. The territory grew rapidly with passage of the Homestead Act of 1862 and the construction of the Union Pacific Railway from 1865 to 1867, which ran across the entire state. The population grew from 28,841 in 1860 to 122,993 by 1870. The railroads received land grants from state and local governments, and an extensive advertising program attracted settlers from the eastern United States and Europe. Another boost came from discharged Civil War veterans who sought free farming land. Statehood was briefly delayed in early 1867, due to a clause in its newly proposed constitution which limited voting to free white males. President Johnson vetoed the bill, but the clause was later corrected and Nebraska was admitted as the 37th state.[4]

The Homestead Act of 1862

One of the most significant acts of Congress to affect western migration and Nebraska in particular was the Homestead Act, which was intended to settle the western territories. It reads: "any person who is head of a family, or who has arrived at the age of 21, and is a citizen of the United States, or who has filed his declaration of his intention to become such…and who has never borne arms against the United States or given aid and comfort to its enemies" was authorized to acquire a quarter section (160 acres) of public land with a small registration fee. Residents for five years who cultivated the land could get title immediately from the United States government. After the Civil War, veterans could count their years in service towards the five-year requirement for themselves, widows, and orphans. Many thousands of Union soldiers took advantage of the offer and headed west.[5]

The Civil War

The census of 1860 shows only 15 slaves in the Nebraska Territory. In spite of this exceedingly small number, Nebraska contributed 3,300 men to the Union army. Slavery was not an issue in Nebraska, especially in comparison to neighboring Kansas, where serious hostilities erupted. The entire population was only 30,000, and yet they formed separate companies of Germans, Pawnee, and Omaha. Many Nebraskans also joined regiments in Iowa and Kansas. However, the Nebraskans strongly objected when the United States government redeployed troops from Fort Kearny and Fort Randall thereby leaving homes and settlements vulnerable to Indian attacks. The issue was resolved when the War Department proposed to replace the men from the newly recruited troops of the First Nebraska Volunteer Infantry. Within four months, the Nebraska regiment was fighting in Missouri, Arkansas, and Tennessee. Their commanding officer, John Thayer, commended them for their "courage and proficiency," and in the summer of 1864, they were given a three-month furlough. During that time, the Cheyenne Sioux attacked wagon trains and ranches along a 250 mile range. The Nebraska Volunteers then introduced horses and changed their name to the "First Nebraska Veteran Volunteer Cavalry." In 1863, the Sioux were thoroughly defeated. Casualty reports for Nebraskans in the Civil War are recorded: 35 were killed in battle, 159 died from disease, 23 died from accidents, and 22 died from other causes, bringing the casualty total to 239 or 7 percent of its men in the war. One of the beneficial aspects of the war was the diminishing of sectional disputes within Nebraska, especially with the question of locating the rail lines. With the secession of the southern states, President Lincoln's legislature placed the line through central Nebraska from Omaha. In 1868, the Union Pacific was completed and made major contributions to the development of Nebraska.[6]

Politics in Nebraska

In the territorial years of Nebraska, sectional disputes evolved between the North Platte and South Platte regions. The south Platte had a much larger population and thereby held a majority in both houses of the legislature. They voted to move the capital from Omaha to a "paper town" named Douglas, but Governor Izard's veto retained it in Omaha. Bitterness rose to such a level that fist-fights erupted in the legislature, and on January 8, 1858, a majority of the House adjourned to the town of Florence, six miles from Omaha. There they passed laws that were dismissed by Governor William Richardson, who was a Democrat from Illinois. At the end of 40 days, both the Omaha and Florence sessions disbanded with nothing accomplished. In 1858, most settlers in Nebraska were Democrats, because they immigrated from states where that political party was dominant. The Kansas-Nebraska bill of 1854 gave rise to the new Republican Party, which further exasperated the issue of slavery. The South Platte Democrats believed that slavery should be permitted in any place in the territory. The North Platte Democrats believed that each state should decide for itself, and the Republicans said slavery should be prohibited everywhere. Most Nebraskans opposed slavery, and on June 18, 1855, the first meeting was called to form the new Republican Party. Meeting in Omaha, they were called "Black Republicans" and were held in low regard. In the fifth legislative session, Republicans were responsible for the repeal of prohibition and authorized the issuance of state liquor licenses. In 1860, with the new Republican Party together with its nominee for president, Abraham Lincoln, Nebraska's politics shifted from Democratic to Republican. The change lasted for 30 years and persisted due to Democratic President Buchanan's veto of the Homestead Bill and the veto of the anti-slavery bill by Democratic Governor Black.

Nebraska's Early Economy

The year 1859 marked the turning point in the history of Nebraska when its first corn was shipped to market. Steamboats on the Missouri River were collecting corn from towns along the way, and from that year onward, there was no doubt that Nebraska was to become a viable farming state. The settlers had endured the earlier harsh weather and overcame the arid soil which had been called the "Great American Desert." However, the early settlers introduced irrigation, tree orchards, wheat, corn, and maize and transformed the state into a major agricultural region. Its largest industry was the production of corn, which had to be "husked," and the importance of this crop for consumption and feed for its cattle is the reason why Nebraska adopted the nickname, "The Cornhusker State."[7]

Adding to their early success that year was the discovery of gold at the foot of the Rocky Mountains. Miners and speculators came by the thousands in covered wagons with signs painted "Pike's Peak or Bust," the mountain top of which was visible in the distance in Colorado.[8]

Statesmen, Leaders and Heroes

Thomas B. Cuming was born in 1828 in Genesee County, New York. After graduating from the University of Michigan at the age of 16, he worked as a geologist in the Lake Superior region before joining the Michigan Volunteers as a lieutenant to fight in the American-Mexican War in 1848. When the war ended, he moved to Keokuk, Iowa to operate the telegraph for the Democratic weekly the *Dispatch*. When the Nebraska Territory was formed in 1854, Cuming was appointed as its first secretary to serve under its first governor, Francis Burt. The new governor was not well and died ten days after taking office. Cuming immediately assumed his duties as the acting governor and faced the current crisis over the location of Nebraska's first capital. The issue exasperated the existing riff between the North Platte Republicans and the South Platte Democrats, with the latter preferring Bellevue, and the former wanting Omaha. However, politicians in Iowa exerted their influence for selecting Omaha because of its proximity to western Iowa and the positive impact it would have on nearby Council Bluffs. Also, it was the Iowans who had helped Nebraska attain territorial status and were responsible for Cuming getting his position. Cuming selected Omaha and went to work organizing the territory. He ordered a census, created districts, and apportioned legislators. Sectional rivalries grew worse when he gave more legislators to the North even though the population of the South was greater. In 1855, he ordered the first legislature to meet in Omaha. The move infuriated the southern faction to such an extent that they proposed to secede and become annexed to Kansas. Fortunately, Kansas was not ready for even more internal strife, so the matter was dropped. In 1867 upon its statehood, the capital was moved to Lincoln. Cuming proved to be a strong leader, but he was not popular because of his Iowa leanings and had always retained his Council Bluffs residence. In 1855, Mark Izard was appointed the second governor to succeed Burt. Izard resigned in 1857, and again Cuming was chosen to be the acting governor. He died in 1858 at 30 years old.[9]

John Milton Thayer was born in 1820 in Bellingham, Massachusetts. After graduating from Brown University, he established a law practice in Worcester, Massachusetts. In 1842, he married Mary Torrey Allen, with whom he had six children. In 1854, the family moved to Nebraska, where Thayer entered politics in the Republican Party. He joined the Nebraska Territorial Militia and was soon elevated to major general. In 1860, he served as a delegate at the Nebraska Constitutional Convention, and that same year, was elected to the Nebraska Territorial Legislature. With the outbreak of war in 1861, Thayer asked for permission to form the First Nebraska Infantry Regiment. Starting as colonel, he spent the entire war fighting in the Western Theater. His bravery is legendary, having fought in many battles including Fort Donelson, Shiloh, Chickasaw Bayou, Arkansas Post, Vicksburg, Prairie D'Ane, Jenkin's Ferry, and Fort Smith. He commanded the District of the Frontier with headquarters at Fort Smith. He was relieved of command in 1865 and was brevetted major general of volunteers. In 1866, he was a member of the Nebraska Constitutional Convention. Upon statehood the next year, he served as a United States senator from 1867 to 1871. In 1875, President Grant appointed Thayer as governor of the Wyoming Territory, and in 1878, he returned to Nebraska to practice law. In 1886, he was elected governor of Nebraska by popular vote and served two terms until 1888. John Thayer died in Lincoln, Nebraska in 1906 at 86 years old. His legacy is Thayer County, Nebraska and his bust is on the grounds of the Vicksburg National Military Park in Mississippi.[10]

Chapter Thirty-eight

COLORADO

State on August 1, 1876

Founders and Settlers

Many powerful and well-known North American tribes lived in this region for thousands of years, and yet it was not until the Spanish arrived in the mid-1500's that it was named. The name "Colorado" is clearly Spanish and translates to "color red," which is the dominant color of its soil. This is most evident as one drives to southern Colorado with its mesas and carved monuments that many thousands of years of erosion have sculpted. The major Indian Nations who lived here include the Pueblo who lived in the valleys and mesas of the Colorado Plateau; Apache who lived in the Great Plains in the 1700's and migrated to Texas, New Mexico, and Arizona, leaving this region to be occupied by the Arapaho and Cheyenne; Comanche who lived on the High Plains of southeastern Colorado; Shoshone who occupied the intermountain valleys in the northern part of the state; and the Ute who have lived in the southern and western Rocky Mountains for centuries. The Ute controlled almost all of Colorado west of the Continental Divide and frequently were clashing with the Arapaho and Cheyenne when they entered their territory. The Ute Nation was led by Chief Ouray and his wife, Chipeta, who we will discuss later.

The first European who is credited with discovering the area was Juan De Onate, who founded the Province of Santa Fe de Nuevo Mexico in 1598, which was incorporated into the Viceroy of New Spain from that year until 1821. At this time, became the territory of the First Mexican Empire for two years, until it became the territory of the First Mexican Republic. After Onate, the next Spaniard to explore much of Colorado was Juan de Ulibarr, who in 1706 claimed most of the region for Spain. He was followed by Juan Bautista de Anza in 1787, who attempted to establish a settlement named San Carlos near present-day Pueblo, but that failed and marked the last attempt by Spain to start a settlement north of the Arizona River. Colorado had become part of the Province of Santa Fe de Nuevo Mexico (today's New Mexico) and therefore, part of the Viceroyalty of New Spain.[1]

In 1803, with the purchase of the Louisiana Territory, the United States believed it had included land on the eastern side of the Rocky Mountains. However, Spain contested the claim. American explorer Zebulon Pike led an army unit into the area, but it was arrested by the Spanish cavalry and expelled by Mexico. In 1810, Mexico declared its independence from Spain. In 1814, the United States and Spain signed the Adams-Onis Treaty, whereby the United States purchased Florida and settled the border dispute in the western lands—particularly in the Spanish–Texas area. The treaty set the boundaries of the United States and its claims through the Rocky Mountains and west to the Pacific Ocean. The United States agreed to cede its claims to those lands to the south and west of the Arkansas River to Spain. In 1821, with the Treaty of Cordoba, Mexico won its independence from Spain and assumed its territorial claims. For the next 25 years, the area remained sparsely settled due to the lingering uncertainties of land ownership. Trading posts were established for traders and trappers, but only small settlements were set up along the Arkansas and Platte Rivers. When the United States went to war with Mexico in 1846 and overpowered them within two years, the region began to reorganize into more definitive boundaries. By the Treaty of

Guadalupe Hidalgo in 1848, Mexico ceded its northern territories to the United States and thereby opened up southern Colorado to American settlement. The land was divided into the Territory of New Mexico and the Territory of Utah, which were organized in 1850. That same year the United States signed a peace treaty with the Ute Nation. Four years later, two more American territories were established: the Territory of Kansas and the Territory of Nebraska.[2] Colorado's first permanent European settlement is the small town of San Luis, which was founded by Spanish settlers from Taos, New Mexico in 1851. Today, the town is still small with a recent census population of 739 people. However, when the Colorado Territory was established in 1861, San Luis was located in Colorado, and it remains the oldest continuously inhabited town in the state.[3]

The Colorado Gold Rush

Some of the most significant events to shape the formation of the American Southwest were the Mexican-American War and the discovery of gold in California and Colorado. The initial discovery at Sutter's Mill, California in 1848 caused a stampede of miners, speculators, and settlers across the Great Plains and through the Rocky Mountains. The timing of these events was fortuitous, having started in 1848 with gold and the end of the Mexican War together with the establishments of new territories in New Mexico, Utah, Kansas, Nebraska, Oregon, Nevada, and Colorado. Silver was discovered in Nevada in the 1850's, and gold was discovered in the eastern edge of the Colorado Rocky Mountains in 1859. Returning war veterans were lured to the West, and the Homestead Act of 1862 allowed homesteaders to choose 160 free acres of public lands to cultivate farms and raise a family. For several centuries, most of these territories were occupied by natives and Spanish settlers. Now, these same areas were being invaded by European-Americans for the first time. Small mining camps sprang up in Denver and Boulder, which grew into prosperous cities. There were others like Central City, Black Hawk, Georgetown, and Idaho Springs that survived to become viable cities.

William Greeneberry Russell of Georgia and Sam Bates are the speculators who are credited with the start of the Colorado "Gold Rush." After years of working the gold fields of California in the 1850's, they organized a party of

107 miners along the south Platte and Arizona Rivers. They followed the Santa Fe Trail and turned north to the suburbs of Denver in 1858 and extracted a small deposit yielding 20 ounces of gold. Their discovery marked the beginning of the Colorado "Gold Rush." For the first few years, the miners concentrated along the South Platte River at the base of the eastern side of the Rockies. They occupied towns such as Golden City, Breckenridge, Coma, Fairplay, and Alma. The population explosion speeded the formation of the Colorado Territory in 1861. The migration quickly was identified as "Pikes Peak or Bust," which was only a short distance from Colorado Springs. In 1861, total gold production reached 150,000 ounces, and in 1862, production was 225,000 ounces. By 1865, the cumulative production of gold was 1.25 million ounces of which 60 percent was placer gold. With the discovery of gold and the many thousands of people it attracted, Congress was quick to establish the Territory of Colorado in 1861. The move enabled Congress to maintain control of the mineral wealth of the area and actually led to the construction of the Denver Mint, which has remained operational since. Statehood was expected in the near future, but the process was stopped by a veto from President Andrew Johnson in 1865. For the next 11 years, the subject was debated and became mired in politics.[4]

Statehood

In spite of its expanding population and gold and mineral wealth, the road to statehood was not smooth. Statehood was finally approved on August 1, 1876 after 16 years, four Colorado votes, three proposed constitutions, and many discussions in Congress covering two administrations. The events were a classic illustration of politics and personal egos that have plagued the American political system since its founding. Colorado could have become a state far sooner if it had considered the options more clearly from the beginning of its territorial status. In 1860, Coloradoans voted to become a territory rather than a state by a vote of 2,007 to 1,649. The simple reason was that the federal government paid for the administration of a territory, but states assumed such expenses. This same attitude prevailed in the 1864 presidential election year when Lincoln's administration would have welcomed more Republican support and its three electoral votes. Instead, at the state Constitutional Convention, Coloradoans again rejected statehood, because they enjoyed having a territorial government paid by the federal government. President Johnson succeeded the assassinated Lincoln on April 15, 1865, and his highest priority was to reinstall the southern states and pay little attention to other new state applications. Although Johnson had been on the Republican ticket and did support the Union, he was more Democrat than Republican. He was not a Radical Republican Reconstructionist. In 1865, Coloradoans approved a constitution, but in 1866, Johnson vetoed a bill admitting Colorado to statehood and pocketed a like bill for Nebraska. He claimed that Colorado did not have the required population of 60,000 and did not even have enough population to qualify for a single congressman.[5]

In 1866, Congress passed the Civil Rights Act which declared every male citizen was free and no state could deprive them of their fundamental rights. That same year, President Johnson vetoed the Act on the grounds that it violated states' rights and that it favored colored against the white race. Congress overrode the veto and introduced the 14th Amendment to the Constitution which stated that all persons born or naturalized in the United States cannot be deprived of their life, liberty, or property without due process of law, nor could any person be denied equal protection of the law. If any male inhabitant was denied the vote by a state, that state's representatives would be reduced. President Johnson used his influence to defeat the measure and opposed it in the 1866 and 1868 elections. In spite of this, ratification was achieved in 1868. In 1867, Republican Senator Ben Wade of Ohio introduced admission bills for Colorado and Nebraska, except this time he included some new wording that was not previously used in their constitution, namely suffrage for African-American males. Johnson attacked the bills and again cited Colorado's inadequate population, which as of 1860 was 34,277 inhabitants. The Senate overrode his Nebraska veto, and it became the 37th state on March 1, 1867. The Colorado vote was 29 in favor and 19 against and 4 absent. Once again, Colorado could not obtain a two-thirds vote to override a veto. Another attempt at statehood was made that year, but this time a Republican, Henry Teller, opposed the measure based on inadequate population. In fact, the real issue was Teller's desire to become a senator, and the two potential seats were reserved for John Evans and Jerome Chaffee.

In 1868, the Senate impeached President Johnson, but he was acquitted by votes of 35 guilty and 19 not guilty, but if only one of the latter had voted guilty, Johnson could have been removed from the presidency. When Johnson was succeeded by Ulysses Grant in 1869, there was little effort to secure Colorado's statehood, because Grant as a Republican secured their political positions. In 1875, Jerome Chaffee, with only one week left in office as territorial representative, was able to get through an enabling act for statehood. To succeed, he had to convince Congress that Colorado had a population of 150,000. He did that, and on August 1, 1876, Colorado was admitted as the 38th state. Chaffee was vindicated with the 1880 census showing Colorado with 194,000 residents.[6]

Statesmen, Leaders and Heroes

Chief Ouray was born in 1833 in present-day Taos, New Mexico. His father, Guera Murah, was an Apache who was adopted into the Ute tribe, and his mother was an Uncompahgre Ute. The boy learned to speak the English, Spanish, Apache, and Ute languages which proved to be an important asset in negotiating future treaties. When he was 18, he travelled into Colorado and joined the Tabeguache Ute. In 1859, after the death of his first wife, he married 16-year-old Chipeta, who was a Kiowa Apache adopted by the Ute when she was a child. His father had become a leader of the Tabeguache, and when he died in 1860, Ouray became Chief of the Ute. He was greatly admired and known for his patience and diplomacy. Although he opposed the white man's settlements, he tried to work with them. In an 1863 treaty, the Ute were assigned reservation but found that most of their land east of the Continental Divide ended up with the United States government. In 1868, Chief Ouray and his wife, Chipeta, travelled to Washington, D.C., where he was appointed Chief of the Utes. He gained more reservation lands in Colorado for the Tabeguache, Moache, Capote, Wiminuache, Yampa, Grand River, and Uinta, but the Utes ended up with a net loss of land. He always tried to do the best for his people, but each treaty brought less total land. He was known as "The White Man's Friend," but resentments brought hostilities with attempts made on his life. When discoveries of gold were made in Colorado in the 1850's to 1870's, white settlers and miners occupied Indian land, causing relations to severely deteriorate. In 1878, the American

Indian Agent at the White River Agency, Nathan Meeker, was determined to convert the natives from primitive savages to God-fearing farmers. He forced the natives to adopt western ways and abandon their culture. The Indians watched in horror as he plowed under their horse racing tracks and killed some "excess" horses. Hostilities erupted, and Meeker wired for help, which arrived in the form of 200 troops. The Utes rebelled and attacked the agency buildings, killing Meeker and nine of his employees. Relief troops from Forts Steele and Russell put down the revolt at the Battle of Mill Creek. Orders to desist from Chief Ouray were not followed, and what became known as the "Meeker Massacre" ended badly, with the Utes forced to resettle in Colorado near Gunnison and to the Uinta Reservation in Utah. In 1880, Chief Ouray and Chipeta travelled to the southern Ute Agency for more negotiations, but shortly after arriving, he passed away on August 24, 1880 at 47 years old.[7] His obituary in the Denver Tribune reads:

> In the death of Ouray, one of the historical characters passes away. He has figured for many years as the greatest Indian of his tribe, and during his life has figured quite prominently. Ouray is in many respects…a remarkable Indian…pure instincts and keen perception…a friend to the white man and protector to the Indians alike." His legacy includes: Ouray County, Town of Ouray, Mount Ouray, Ouray Peak, and Camp Chief Ouray.[8]

William Palmer was born in 1836 in Delaware into a Quaker family. At age five, his family moved to Germantown, Pennsylvania, where William attended the Friends School and Boys' High School. After finishing school at age 15, he went to work as a clerk in the engineering department of Hempfield Railroad in western Pennsylvania. For the next four years, he worked for Hempfield as an assistant to the chief engineer, a rodman, and a transit man. His uncle Frank Jackson was president of Westmoreland Coal Company, and it was Jackson who encouraged his nephew to go to England to study the coal and railroad industries. While there for six months, Palmer immersed himself in both fields and had the opportunity to meet with such famous engineers as

Isambard Brunel and Robert Stephenson. Two of the most important things he learned were that coal was a better source of power and that the narrow-gauge rail lines he observed in England could be useful in the Rocky Mountains. He returned in 1856 to work as secretary and treasurer for Westmoreland Coal. The next year, he worked as private secretary to Pennsylvania Railroad President Jon Thomson. He wrote reports on coal and railroad operations and was credited with the conversion from wood to coal for American locomotives. At Pennsylvania Railroad, he was befriended by Thomas Scott, who was soon to become Assistant Secretary of War in the Lincoln Administration, in charge of military transportation in the Civil War.

Palmer joined the Union army because of his strong abolitionist beliefs. He organized a small independent group that was intended to guard Brig. Gen. Robert Anderson of Pennsylvania, but he was so successful that it developed into the 1st Anderson Cavalry. The unit grew to become the 15th Pennsylvania Cavalry and was immediately sent to assist the army of the Potomac in defending against the Confederate invasion of Maryland. Palmer personally spent a week gathering information on Lee's movements in the Antietam area, sending the information by telegraph to Gen. George McClellan. Palmer was in civilian clothes when he was captured and was then imprisoned in Castle Thunder in Richmond. After four months of interrogation, he was set free in a prisoner exchange, and his true identity was never discovered. He rejoined his regiment, which then went on to distinguish themselves at the Battle of Chickamauga. They then covered the Union army retreat to Chattanooga, where Union Maj. Gen. George Thomas rewarded a brigadier star to Palmer for his leadership. He went on to achieve several battlefield victories, followed Jefferson Davis' escape through the South, and came within 20 miles of capturing him. Years later, in 1894, Palmer was awarded the Medal of Honor.[9]

After retiring from the army, Palmer left Philadelphia in 1867 to join the Kansas Pacific Railway to serve as secretary, treasurer, and then managing director. His charge was to extend service into Colorado. He had his chief engineer, Col. William Greenwood, recommend a route from Kansas to Pueblo and then to Santa Fe, New Mexico. The board rejected the plan in favor of a direct line from Kansas to Denver, which was finished in 1870. Palmer was still determined to build a North-South line in Colorado. His vision was to connect Denver to New Mexico and on to Mexico City. He gathered prominent Coloradoans including Governor Alexander Hunt, formed the Denver and Rio Grande Railway, and was elected its president. The line went to Colorado Springs by 1871, to Pueblo in 1872, and to the coal fields of Trinidad by 1873. In addition to another number of coal fields, it also went to the mining towns of Leadville and Saguash County. He resigned in 1883 to build the Rio Grande Western Railway with lines from Denver to Ogden and Salt Lake City, Utah which used a narrow-gauge railway to navigate the sharp turns and steep topography. During 1880, Palmer organized the Mexican National Railway. Sadly, his life-long friend and chief engineer, Col. William Greenwood, was robbed and murdered near Mexico City, but within three years, the line was completed to the capital of Mexico.[10]

After moving to Colorado in 1867 to work in the railroad business, it was only four years later that Palmer founded Colorado Springs. Soon thereafter, he founded Manitau Springs at the base of Pike's Peak. It is estimated that he spent around $1 million in parks and roads, which would be equivalent to $27 million in today's currency. He funded Colorado College and established parks in other towns. He donated 1,638 acres for parks, churches, libraries, hospitals, and schools, and he founded the *Colorado Springs Gazette*. In 1880, he built the Colorado Coal and Iron Company's steel mill, and it became one of the most successful iron and steel plants in the United States. His wife, Mary Lincoln (Queen) Mellen, suffered from poor health attributed to having lived in high altitudes for so long. She died in 1894 at 44 years old. Palmer retired in the late 1890's, and during his remaining ten years, he was immersed in philanthropic activities to the extent of $4 million, or over $106 million by today's values. In 1906, his fall from a horse left him partially paralyzed and confined to a wheelchair. He died in 1909 at age 72, and on that day all local schools, businesses, and trains stopped to mourn his loss. The mayor of Colorado Springs commented that he was "the soldier, the builder of an empire, the philanthropist, the friend of the people, whose life was a blessing." His legacy is monumental including land grants for the Union Printers Home, the Colorado School for the Deaf and Blind, several churches, Cragmore Sanitarium, the

University of Colorado in Colorado Springs, the creation of Colorado College, the Lewis and Palmer High School, Palmer Drive, and the General Palmer Hotel (originally the Palace) in Durango. William Palmer is considered as "The Father of Colorado."[11]

Chapter Thirty-nine

North Dakota

State on November 2, 1889

Explorers and Settlers

A great variety of Native American tribes lived in this area for hundreds of years, even though there is archeological evidence of other cultures being there as far back as 10,000 years. The tribes included the Dakota, Assiniboine, Cheyenne, Mandan, Hidatsa, and Arikara. Some tribes were nomadic, and they roamed the plains in search of bison herds from which they derived the basic necessities of life, especially food and clothing. When the first European settlers arrived in the 1700's, they introduced the horse, which changed the lifestyle of tribes such as the Dakota, Assiniboine, and Cheyenne, who could then hunt at greater distances and enjoy better living conditions. Other tribes like the Mandan, Hidatsu, and Arikara lived a more sedentary farming life and settled along the Missouri River. Their villages became trading centers primarily for the fur trade with the French Canadians, who were continuously expanding their fur trading empire. Explorers like Marquette, Joliet, and La Salle explored the Mississippi River Valley, but the first recorded French explorer in the Dakotas was La Verendrye, who travelled the Missouri River from Canada in 1738. He and his sons were searching for a water route to the Pacific Ocean. Their objective was to discover a faster sea route to trade in the Orient, but most explorations were used to establish trading posts and relationships with the natives. The French from Canada and France were the first Europeans to develop the fur trade through the Great Lakes and the St. Lawrence River directly to the expanding demand from Europe for beaver and other furs. The French were overtaking the Scandinavian countries as the leading supplier of furs. The Americans came later in 1804, after the Louisiana Purchase and the opening of the West with the Lewis and Clark expedition up the Missouri River.[1]

Sovereign Ownership

Control and ownership of the Dakota lands changed several times over a 50-year period. The first of these occurred in 1763 with the Treaty of Paris. British America first became involved when France was expanding its colony of New France, which basically was the Midwestern section of America from Canada to the Gulf of Mexico. When the French pushed eastward from the Ohio River Valley and the Great Lakes into lands claimed by England, it was Virginia royal Governor Dinwiddie who asked his militia to advise them of their intrusion. The request was answered by a volunteer named George Washington, who took a small party of guides, cartographers, and Indians to Fort La Boeuf, just below Lake Erie, to deliver Governor Dinwiddie's message. After two failed attempts to oust the French, British veterans were called in to do the job, which they did in 1758 by taking Fort Duquesne at present-day Pittsburgh. The French and Indian War was principally held in the western British-American colonies. However, it morphed into the existing Seven Years' War, when England defeated France and acquired all French lands drained by Hudson's Bay, including the tributary of the Red River in the North. France also ceded its lands drained by the Missouri and Mississippi Rivers to Spain, but in 1800, they were returned to France and became part of the Louisiana Territory. The Dakotas were part of that territory, and when it was sold in 1803 by Emperor Napoleon Bonaparte to the United

States to raise money for his European exploits, the Dakota Territory was then owned by the United States. As Americans migrated west, they became a factor in the fur trade and built major trading posts at Fort Union and Fort Clark. The Americans offered Indians guns, tools, cloth, and beads in exchange for furs and meat. Relations between the Americans and Indians remained peaceful during the first half of the 1800's. The major catastrophe was the smallpox epidemic, that decimated the Mandan tribe at Fort Clark in 1837. An interesting outgrowth of the fur trade was the birth of a new Indian Nation called the Metis. It was the result of European-American traders mixing with the Chippewa women and blending the two cultures. The Metis would send their buffalo robes and foodstuffs from the Red River to St. Paul for trade. However, with the decline in buffalo herds east of the Missouri River, the Metis eventually disappeared.[2]

The Dakota Territory

John Blair Smith Todd, a delegate from the Dakota Territory to the House of Representatives, was a first cousin of Mary Todd Lincoln, the wife of Abraham Lincoln. In 1861, he lobbied the Congress for the territorial status of Dakota, and it was granted on March 2nd of that year. It originally included part of the Nebraska Territory and part of the Idaho Territory to the west, but in 1863 more than half of its lands were delegated to the Idaho Territory, and a much smaller section to the southwest was given to the Wyoming Territory in 1868. The Dakota Territory was the northern most section of the original Louisiana Territory and was included in Napoleon's sale to the United States in 1803. The name "Dakota" is a Sioux Indian word meaning "friends." Immigration to Dakota began in earnest in 1872-73, with the completion of the Northern Pacific Railway to the Missouri River. Settlers came in droves from other western territories as well as northern and western Europe, particularly Norway, Germany, Sweden, and Canada.[3] The growth of Dakota was uneven partly due to the extremes in weather and partly due to periodic Indian uprisings. The Great Dakota Boom occurred around 1873 and lasted until 1889. The greatest growth was in the 1878 to 1887 period, and the peak year is designated as 1883. There were few settlements prior to that time, and some did not survive. Even successful cities like Sioux Falls faltered and were abandoned due to locusts, drought, and

Indian attacks. The Homestead Act of 1862 did not have an immediate impact on the Dakotas, because it was passed during the first turbulent year of the Civil War. The westward migration suddenly shifted to an eastward flow as men from the West were shipped East to fight in the war. This had the added negative of leaving western forts undermanned and vulnerable to Indian raids. This, in turn, slowed the expansion of the railroads. By 1878, there were only two rail lines connecting northern Dakota to southern Dakota. Survival on the isolated plains with inadequate transportation, harsh weather, drought, and the constant fear of Indian uprisings was daunting to even the hardiest settlers.[4] During the seven years of 1879 to 1886, over 100,000 immigrants settled in the territory.

The Long Depression

The eight-year period following the end of the Civil War marked an international economic boom that abruptly ended with the Panic of 1873. Economists have referred to the ensuing depression as "the first truly international crisis," and it is called the "Depression of 1873-1879" in the United States and even longer for Europe, according to the National Bureau of Economic Research. It lasted for 65 months, which was far longer than the official 43 months of economic contraction of the Great Depression.[5] From 1873 to 1879 over 18,000 businesses in the United States went bankrupt including 89 railroads, states, and hundreds of banks. Unemployment ranged between 8 and 14 percent. The Long Depression started in Vienna in April of 1873 with the collapse of the Vienna Stock Exchange that then hit the United States in September of that year, with the closing of the Jay Cooke bank when it failed to underwrite $100 million for the Northern Pacific Railway. The New York Stock Exchange closed for ten days. At the same time, Germany stopped production of the "thaler" coin (origin of "dollar"), and the United States passed the Coinage Act of 1873, which took the country off the silver and gold standard on to a purely gold standard. The price of silver collapsed, and the Denver Mint closed. This, in turn, deeply affected the financing of the railroads and brought production of silver to a halt in Nevada, Colorado, and Idaho. Western miners and farmers strongly objected to the gold standard, which was finally relieved by the Sherman Silver Purchase Act of 1890. Another theory on the cause for the Depression was that the supply of gold was inadequate to support the economy and that the gold rushes in California, South Africa, and the Klondike were only alleviating the shortage and hiding its negative impact on the booming world-wide economies. The protracted depression destroyed prices for commodities, with prices falling by 50 percent from 1872 to 1877. The price of grain and cotton fell by 66 percent, which devastated farmers. These events promoted protectionism in France, Germany, and the United States, and this prompted mass emigration from Italy, Spain, Austro-Hungary, and Russia.[6]

In spite of deflationary prices, noted economists like Friedman and Schwartz have pointed out that, from 1869 to 1879, money national product grew by 3 percent annually, gross national product grew by 6.8 percent annually, and real product per capita grew by 4.5 percent. They argue that monetary contraction never occurred, and the money supply grew by 2.7 percent per annum.[7]

Real per capita income stayed constant throughout 1873-1880 and 1883-1885. Income rose from 1881-1882 and 1886-1896. By the end of the 23-year period, the average consumer was better off than beforehand.[8]

Statesmen, Leaders and Heroes

In 1889, North Dakota was admitted to the Union as the 39th state. Its first governor was John Miller, who aligned with the Republican Party and the "McKenzie Gang." Politics was controlled by the conservatives, who initiated liberal banking and regulatory and taxation policies. Aided by government policies, they developed mines, brickworks, and flour mills. The Great Northern Railway was completed in 1887, and the Soo Line was finished in 1893. Both railroads built branch lines, and together with land grants for the railroads and the settlers, communities were established and took root assuring North Dakota of future prosperity.[9]

George Crook was born near Dayton, Ohio in 1828 and graduated from West Point in 1852. The first part of his military career was spent fighting Indians in Oregon, Washington, and California. Historians consider him to be the greatest Indian fighter in the army's history. Ironically, he sympathized with the plight of the Native Americans, and his skills developed because of his study and respect for their culture. He was known to prefer negotiating rather than engaging in battle. In 1861, he was sent to the East and fought in the battles of Second Bull Run and Chickamauga. In 1864, as major general, he was appointed to command the army of West Virginia. At the end of the Civil War, Crook was sent to the Northwest to defeat the Paiute. Two years later, President Grant put him in charge of the Arizona Territory and ended the hostilities there by placing the Apaches on reservations, which he felt was the only way to protect them. By 1872, he had brought peace to Arizona by drawing up a treaty with Apache Chief Cochise. In 1875, Crook was appointed Commander of the Department of the Platte, just when the Sioux were preparing to retake the Black Hills, where gold had recently been discovered. The Black Hills became overrun by white settlers and speculators. The Indian Bureau, including Crook, made several attempts to get the tribes back onto their reservations in the Dakota Territory and Nebraska. Segments of Cheyenne, Arapaho, and Lakota instead went to join the great Sioux Chief Sitting Bull, who was lying low while building a formidable force of warriors from several tribes. In 1876, the War Department ordered that those who disobeyed should be brought in. Crook was forced to retreat from Cheyenne and Lakota warriors led by Crazy Horse at the Battle of Rosebud Creek, thereby preventing Crook from bringing relief to Major General Custer at the Battle of the Little Bighorn.[10]

In the winter of 1876-77, Crook enlisted the Arapaho, Ute, Bannock, Shoshone, Crow, and Winnebago to defeat the Sioux. On May 6, 1877, Crazy Horse surrendered 1,100 of his warriors in the last Battle of the Plains. In 1882, Crook was sent back to Arizona to face the Apache under Geronimo. For four years, Crook routed the Apache, only to see Geronimo escape each time. In 1886, Crook was replaced by Gen. Nelson Miles, who captured the Apache and their elusive leader and exiled them to Florida along with the Apache scouts who had helped Crook and Miles for so long. Crook never forgave Miles for his actions. In 1888, President Cleveland promoted Crook to major general and put him in charge of the Department of the West. For the last two years of his life, George Crook spoke out against the unfair treatment of his former enemies as well as the broken treaties and failed federal policies. He died in 1890 while serving as Commander of the Department of the West. He and his wife are buried in Arlington National Cemetery.[11]

Chapter Forty

South Dakota

State on November 2, 1889

Explorers and Settlers

The first Europeans to set foot in the Dakotas were the French in the late 1600's. The Verendrye brothers were exploring the area in 1743, in search of a water route to the Pacific. Their ultimate goal was to expand the French-Canadian fur trade as far as the Orient. They were preceded by other French explorers such as Marquette, Joliet, and La Salle. As France was building its empire in North America, it was also firmly establishing its domination of the fur industry. This was accomplished by building trading posts along the Ohio, Mississippi, and Missouri Rivers and developing trading relationships with many Indian tribes. New France stretched from the St. Lawrence River to the Great Lakes and down the Mississippi and Ohio Rivers to the Gulf of Mexico. However, that changed with their defeat by England in the two simultaneous wars known as the French and Indian War and the Seven Years' War. The Treaty of Paris of 1763 required

France to cede all of its North American colonies east of the Mississippi River, including Canada, to Great Britain, with one exception. In the prior year, with the Treaty of Fontainebleau, France gave its lands west of the Mississippi to Spain, and in so-doing hoped to persuade Spain to accept defeat to Great Britain in the Seven Years' War. The treaty was done in secret, with most settlers unaware of the change except in later years when controversies arose on titles and land ownership. Spain wanted to defend its interests in the South and West of North America, but never made a serious effort to find a water route to the Pacific or to solidify its colonies in New Spain. France regained its lands 20 years later with the defeat of Great Britain by the United States.[1]

In 1803, Napoleon sold the Louisiana Territory to the United States, which doubled its size and included the Dakota Territory. The next year, Lewis and Clark, under direct orders by President Thomas Jefferson, started on their "Corps of Discovery." They started in May in St. Louis on the Missouri River with 45 men and 15 tons of supplies in three boats. It reached South Dakota in August, near present-day Vermillion. They left Missouri in October and spent the winter with the Mandan tribe in North Dakota. They returned by the same route and arrived back in St. Louis two years later.

American settlement of South Dakota began in earnest in 1817 with its first fur trading post at Fort Pierre. During the first half of the 1800's, more than 100 trading posts were built with fur trading as the major economic activity in southern Dakota. Fort Pierre became the center for the United States fur industry, until around 1840 when demand declined. In 1856, the center of activity switched when the United States army abandoned Pierre in favor of Fort Randall. In 1858, the Yankton Sioux ceded most of the eastern portion of southern Dakota to the United States. The cities of Sioux Falls and Yankton grew rapidly through rampant land speculation and became the two largest cities in southern Dakota. In 1859, Bon Homme, Elk Point, and Vermillion were established along the Missouri River. The Dakota Territory was organized in 1861, and settlers arrived from Scandinavia, Germany, Ireland, Russia, and the eastern United States. Motivating the flood of immigrants was completion of rail lines to the territorial capital of Yankton in 1872 and the discovery of gold in the Black Hills. Congress passed the Enabling Act of 1889 allowing both North and South Dakota to be admitted to the Union on November 2nd, Montana on November 8th, and Washington on November 11th. When gold was discovered in the Black Hills, the United States government attempted to purchase that region from the Sioux. The land had been clearly granted to the Sioux in the Treaty of Fort Laramie in 1868, and the Sioux had refused to grant mining rights to speculators. In spite of the treaty, white speculators encroached on the Great Sioux Reservation, causing armed conflict between the Lakota Sioux and the Northern Cheyenne against the United States government in 1876 and 1877. The best-known battle of the war was the Battle of the Little Bighorn, which military historians call "Custer's Last Stand." Fierce fighting took the lives of 280 natives and 300 Americans, including that of George Custer. The war took place under President Grant's administration and marked the last major war between Native Americans and the United States government. The Agreements of 1877 resulted in the annexation of the Sioux Reservation to the United States Territory of Dakota.[2]

Statehood

South Dakota became the 40th state on November 2, 1889, after being the southern half of the Dakota Territory for 28 years. Also, on that same day, North Dakota became the 39th state, and to this day, no one is certain which state was approved before the other, because no time stamp was put on the papers. The papers signed by President Benjamin Harrison were shuffled at his request, so he would not know which was executed first.[3] The Dakota Territory was enormous and included parts of Montana and Wyoming. For years since its meeting in Philadelphia in 1787, Congress abided by the guidelines of the Northwest Ordinance and tried to keep all future states to a reasonable and manageable size. This as well as the fact that its two largest populations were so far apart prompted Congress to sever the western half of the territory for the future states of Montana and Wyoming. South Dakota selected Pierre as its capital in spite of the fact that Sioux Falls is centrally located and their largest city, and Rapid Falls is their second largest city. The state has a diverse cultural population that includes Native American, rural Western, and European backgrounds. The Missouri River, which is the largest and longest river in the state, divides the state into two distinctly different sections known as "East River" and "West River." East is predominantly agricultural due to its rich fertile soil. West is dominated by ranches and was "home" to Native Americans on reservations. In the Southwest are the Black Hills with their low forested mountains and land that is sacred to the Sioux Indians. The Great Plains cover two-thirds of western South Dakota. Also, in the southeast of the Black Hills are the "Badlands." Specifically, it is known as the White River Badlands, that has yielded numerous fossils since first inhabited by the Lakota Indians. A number of distinguished archeologists from around the world have explored the Badlands. In 1854, Dr. Joseph Leidy published a book in which he records that of the 84 significant fossils found in North America, 77 of them were found in the White River Badlands. The area has become world-famous for its fossil research, and mammals have been dated back to 33 million years ago. The native Indians had also researched fossils including sea shells and turtle shells. They also correctly stated that the entire area had at one time been completely under water.[4]

Statesmen, Leaders and Heroes

Sitting Bull was born in 1831, along Yellowstone River just below Miles City, Montana in a place that was later in the Dakota Territory. By the age of 14, he was joining raiding parties with his father. After stealing horses of the Crow tribe, his father celebrated his bravery by giving him his own name of "Tatanka Iyoyanka," which is in the Lakota language and translates to "Buffalo Bull Who Sits Down," and which later got abbreviated to "Sitting Bull." His father also gave him an eagle feather, a warrior's horse, and a shield to mark his passage into manhood. During the period of 1863 onward, Sitting Bull led many attacks against white settlers and the United States army. He attacked Fort Berthold, Fort Stevenson, and Fort Buford as well as attacks against smaller forts in the upper Missouri area. In 1868, the United States government signed a peace treaty with some Lakota leaders, but Sitting Bull openly declared he would not honor the Treaty of Laramie nor would he agree to sell any part of his country. He continued to fight the white settlers well into the 1870's. When the Northern Pacific Railway began surveying Lakota lands in the early 1870's, they were stopped by Sitting Bull's forces. With the discovery of gold in the Black Hills in 1874, tensions rose with the Lakota. That same year Lt. Col. George Custer was sent to find a good location for a fort in the Black Hills. In 1875, President Grant ordered all Sioux tribes to live within their reservations, and in 1876, the government declared that those who did not comply would be deemed hostile, knowing that this would justify the search and capture of Sitting Bull. During the period of 1868 to 1876, Sitting Bull had emerged as the most important political Native American leader. Unlike other Sioux leaders, Sitting Bull refused to live on the reservation or become dependent on the United States government. Whenever relations between the government and the Lakota became inflamed, more and more natives chose to live under Sitting Bull's protection. The first six months of 1876 saw an enormous expansion of Sitting Bull's camp, estimated at 10,000 natives from various tribes. On June 25, 1876, Custer and his 7th Cavalry attacked Cheyenne and Lakota tribes on the Little Bighorn River. They did not realize that more than 2,000 Indian warriors had joined Sitting Bull's forces, and when they counterattacked Custer's men, the Americans were overwhelmed and annihilated. The public was shocked by the defeat, which led to more soldiers joining the war. The revitalized American army forced many Native Americans to surrender on July 19, 1881. They were held as prisoners and sent to Fort Randall. Sitting Bull and 172 of his people spent 20 months there, before being allowed to return north to the Standing Rock Agency. In 1890, the local Indian Agent James McLoughlin feared that Sitting Bull would escape from the reservation, so he had the police arrest him. During the arrest, a skirmish erupted and one of the policemen shot Sitting Bull in the chest, and another policeman shot and killed him. His body was taken to Fort Yates, and in 1953, his family had him reinterred at Mobridge, South Dakota, which was his birthplace. Sitting Bull's legacy includes a postage stamp in 1989 and the renaming of Standing Rock College to Sitting Bull College in 1996.[5]

George Armstrong Custer was born in 1839 in New Rumley, Ohio into a farming family. He went to the local public schools in Monroe, Michigan and then attended Hopedale Normal College before going to the United States Military Academy at West Point in 1857. He graduated in 1861 at the bottom of his class of 34 cadets. He appears not to have taken his classes seriously while accumulating 726 demerits and the worst record in the academy's history.

Historians have conjectured that Custer would have been expelled from West Point, if the Civil War had not intervened. He was commissioned a Second Lieutenant in the 2nd Cavalry Regiment and fought at the First Battle of Bull Run. In April of 1862, he served in the 5th Cavalry Regiment and was an aide to Maj. Gen. George McClellan. His pursuit of notoriety started at Chickahominy River in Virginia, where he captured 50 Confederate soldiers and the first Confederate battle flag of the Civil War. Major General McClellan personally thanked Custer for his bravery and promoted him to captain. In 1863, Custer became an aide to Brevet Lt. Col. Alfred Pleasanton, who was commander of the Cavalry Corps. Two days prior to the Battle of Gettysburg, Custer was promoted to Brigadier General of Volunteers, thereby becoming one of the youngest generals in the Union army at 23 years old. He again served as aide to Pleasanton and acquired a reputation for aggressiveness in leading charges at Gettysburg and Hunterstown, where he was knocked from his horse amidst the enemy and saved at the last minute by jumping onto a comrade's horse. At Gettysburg, Custer volunteered to intercept Stuart's cavalry just behind the Union army, and for his bravery, was cited "For Gallant and Meritorious Services at the Battle of Gettysburg, Pennsylvania." In 1864, Custer, fighting under Maj. Gen. Philip Sheridan, defeated Confederate Gen. Jubal Early in the Valley Campaigns and then advanced to Petersburg for the winter. When the Confederate lines broke in April of 1865, Robert E. Lee began his retreat to Appomattox Court House, when Custer blocked his army. General Sheridan praised Custer for his gallantry and later presented the surrender table to his wife, Elizabeth.[6]

In the early 1870's, the United States government increased its pressure on the Sioux for selling their Black Hills land. In 1873, Custer led an expedition to that area and announced the discovery of gold. For years, Sitting Bull as the leader of the Lakota Sioux openly professed no interest in selling any portion of their land, and the discovery of gold only strengthened his resolve. The Grant Administration set a final date of January 31, 1876 for all Lakota Sioux, Cheyenne, and Arapaho to vacate the Black Hills and move to their designated reservation. Custer was sent to that area in the summer of 1876 to round up all the natives who had remained in the Black Hills. At the same time, Chief Sitting Bull held meetings with various tribe leaders to discuss their position.

On June 25th, Custer's scouts discovered a large Sioux encampment on the Little Bighorn River. Being discovered by the Sioux, Custer decided to form three battalions for an attack. One of his units, under Scout Reno, dismounted 500 yards from the village but was quickly overrun and lost one-quarter of his men. Custer fought his way to a nearby ridge, and most of the other units tried to join him, but many were cut down by the Sioux. Custer started the campaign with close to 600 soldiers, but the Indians numbered an average of an estimated 3,500 warriors. Every man in Custer's command was killed in what is known as "Custer's Last Stand." At his death until this day, Custer remains a controversial figure. General Grant was highly critical, calling it a "sacrifice of troops brought on by Custer himself." President Theodore Roosevelt praised Custer. His legacy includes Custer Counties in six states, townships in Michigan and Minnesota, villages named Custer in Michigan, Ohio, South Dakota, and Wisconsin, Custer National Cemetery, Fort Custer National Military Reservation, Custer Hill in Fort Riley, Kansas, the Black Hills of South Dakota with counties, towns, and parks in his name, and the Custer Monument at the United States Military Academy that stands next to his grave.[7]

Chapter Forty-one

MONTANA

State on November 8, 1889

Explorers and Settlers

Like many of the other western states, there is archeological evidence of people who lived in the Montana area as long ago as 12,000 years. However, Montana is unique in that it claims the oldest human burial site in North America, near Wilsall. The remains of an infant male have been analyzed to show genome of what is called the "Anzick Boy." Its DNA proves it dates from people of the Clovis Period, who are regarded as the ancestors of all North Americans. It also confirms that the indigenous peoples of North America originated in Asia and migrated east, probably through the Bering Sea area and across Alaska. The first native nation to settle here were the Crow, who migrated from Alberta, Canada around 1700 A.D. In the 1800's, the Crow were allied with the United States army, and their reservation was the largest in Montana, located in the southwestern part of the state. Just east and adjacent to the Crow are the

Cheyenne, who were first recorded by early explorers. In total, there were 11 different tribes who roamed the area in a nomadic way, following the herds of buffalo for food and clothing. Although no one person is deemed to be the founder of Montana, the French explorer Pierre de la Verendrye is credited with discovering the Rocky Mountains in 1743. "Montana" is a Latin word meaning "mountainous regions." The natives referred to it as the "land of the shining mountains."

In 1803, France sold its Louisiana Territory to the United States for $15 million, which was equivalent to $.03 per acre. The land doubled the size of the United States and included the mid-section of America from the Mississippi River on the east and the Continental Divide on the west. It was bounded on the north at the 44'30" parallel, and it funneled down to the Gulf of Mexico at New Orleans. Most of Montana was included except for a small portion to the west that was part of future Idaho. Very little was known about the area, so President Jefferson asked his personal secretary Meriwether Lewis to lead an expedition to study this vast region and learn as many facts as he could find about its geography, natural resources, and indigenous people. Lewis brought in William Clark as co-leader of the expedition. Clark was a soldier and frontiersman, and both of them assembled a group of scouts and guides including a Shoshone Indian woman named Sacagawea, who we will discuss later. They called themselves the "Corps of Discovery," and in 1804, they started north from St. Louis on the Missouri River and wintered with the Mandan natives between Montana and North Dakota. In the spring, they reached the headwaters of the Missouri River where they purchased horses from the Shoshone to traverse the Continental Divide and eventually discovered the Columbia River, which is the largest river in the Pacific Northwest. They used it to sail southward and then westward between Washington and Oregon to the Pacific Ocean. Although the Columbia River originates in British Columbia, Canada, it is 1,243 miles long and is the fourth longest river in the United States, and it runs through seven American states including its drainage basin. Lewis and Clark returned to St. Louis in 1806 through Montana, which was the area where they spent most of their time on their two-year exploration.[1]

The first European settlement in Montana was St. Mary's Mission, and its origin can be attributed to the Louis and Clark Expedition. In middle and southeastern Montana, there is a small Indian tribe known as the Salish. We don't know if Lewis and Clark ever met them, but they did interact with other tribes such as the Iroquois. In the 1812 to 1820 period, the Salish learned of the Jesuits who had come to the area to teach medicine, farming, and religion to the Iroquois. This was a similar pattern as the French Catholic missionaries from the Great Lakes to the Ohio, Mississippi, and Missouri River valleys where they became known as the "blackrobes." When the Salish learned of them, they were sent to the home of Gen. William Clark in St. Louis in 1831. From there, they met with Bishop Joseph Rosati, who promised to send the Jesuits they requested. Nothing was done until 1839 when the Iroquois joined the Salish to meet Father Pierre DeSmet in Council Bluffs, Iowa. Again, nothing happened until 1841 when Father DeSmet arrived in Stevensville, Montana. He immediately built a chapel, log cabins for classrooms, and a drug store for medicines, and he called the settlement St. Mary's Mission.[2] In 1847, Montana started a series of forts that also served as trading posts. The first of these was Fort Benton, named after Senator Thomas Benton who was a strong supporter of western expansion. It was located on the upper Missouri River, and its water access enabled it to develop into a major trading center which locals today promote as the "Birthplace of Montana." In 1850, Major John Owen established another fort and trading post just above St. Mary's Mission to protect the settlers, missionaries, and Indians in the region. In 1867, Fort Ellis was built at the mouth of the Gallatin Valley and was home to the 2nd Cavalry, who fought in the Great Sioux War of 1876-77. Fort Ellis served many explorers and surveyors of the territory, and it eventually became the nation's first national park, Yellowstone. One of the most important forts that was built by the infantry in 1867 was Fort Shaw, which was in the Sun River Valley to the west of Great Falls. It had a hospital, trading post, and barracks that could house 450 soldiers. The fort was used to protect the major supply line from Fort Benton to the southwestern gold mines of Montana. After decommissioning in 1891, it was converted to the local Indian Industrial School. It taught natives the English language and new technologies for as many as 300 students, some of whom boarded there.[3]

The Montana Territory

After gold was discovered by James and Granville Stuart in 1858 near present-day Drummond, Montana, the United States government reorganized the Idaho Territory and carved out Montana under President Lincoln in 1864. The new territory came from land that had been part of the Dakota and Nebraska territories to the east of the Continental Divide. Land to the west of the Divide was the Oregon Territory, and the part that had been split off for the future Washington Territory was delegated to be the western part of Montana. What is unusual is that the boundaries of the Montana Territory remained the same when it became a state in 1889.[4] The Organic Act of 1864, which created Montana, was part of President Lincoln's plan to establish a greater number of free states, considering this was at a critical point in the Civil War. The Act described the type of government to be installed which included executive, judicial, and legislative branches. The federal government reserved the right to nullify any laws passed by the territorial legislature. The president appointed the governor, secretary, and three members of the territorial Supreme Court. The local citizens elected the legislature, which consisted of a Council and House of Representatives. The citizens also elected a single delegate to Congress who was not permitted to vote, but only served as an advisor to the House. Montana's territorial status lasted 25 years, which was comparatively lengthy, but this period of time was intended to allow its fledgling government to mature and its population to grow. For Montana, as well as other territories, Congress was willing to pay for their government administrations until they were satisfied that they could be economically viable and able to stand on their own as a state.[5]

Montana's remoteness accounts for its sparseness during its territorial period. In 1870, the census shows only 20,595 residents, and by 1880, it had doubled to 39,159. However, as the railroads were introduced, the population soared to 142,924 people by 1890.[6] The key railroad was the Northern Pacific, which obtained grants from the federal government and was able to reach Billings by 1882. The railroad sold most of its "surplus" land to speculators who, in turn, sold it on credit to individual farmers and ranchers who wanted to be situated on or near the rail line. The Great Northern Railroad bought its land from the federal government and sold it directly to promote settlements in the northern part of the state. It opened offices in Germany and Scandinavia and brought families to Montana at a very low cost. In 1882, the Northern Pacific developed Livingston, Montana for a major maintenance center, and years later, it also served as the major gateway to Yellowstone National Park. Other rails included the Utah and Northern Railway which was part of the Union Pacific, which completed a narrow-gauge line from Utah to Butte in 1881. Smaller lines included the Oregon Short Line and Montana Railroad.[7]

The other important factor in Montana's development was the Homestead Act of 1862, but it was six years before the first claim was made, because the allocated 160 acres of free land under the act was not sufficient to sustain a family in the area's marginal soil. This changed in 1877, with passage of the Desert Land Act, which offered settlers up to 640 acres at $.25 per acre and their promise to irrigate the land. The settlers could buy the land after three years and pay another fee of $1.00 per acre. These terms attracted cattle and sheep ranchers, who used the central and western valleys of Montana for grazing.

Early Business Leaders

Marcus Daly was born in 1841 in Ulster, Ireland and immigrated to America from there as a young boy. He worked his way from New York City to California and got caught up in the Nevada gold rush and the silver mines of the Comstock Lode in 1860. While working in Virginia City, Nevada, Daly met George Hearst (father of William Randolph Hearst) and Lloyd Tevis. In 1872, Daly convinced Hearst to buy the Ontario Mine near Park City, Utah, and over the next ten years, it produced over $17 million in silver and $6.25 million in dividends. In 1876, Daly arrived in Butte, Montana to look at a mine named "Alice" while working as an agent for the Walker Brothers of Salt Lake City. After purchasing Alice, the Walkers made Daly its superintendent and offered him a fractional share in it. Daly continued to inspect other nearby mines and recommended purchases to the Walkers. They declined one of Daly's most interesting mines named "Anaconda." Daly sold his share of Alice for $30,000, and with other partners, purchased the Anaconda. Although it contained a good amount of silver, Daly was focused on its copper deposits. Together with his friends Hearst, Higgin, and Tevis, he poured millions of dollars into developing what was to become the "richest hill on earth." After exhausting the silver, Daly closed the mine and watched silver prices decline. He then purchased other bankrupt mines and reopened the Anaconda around the time that Thomas Edison invented the light bulb, which used copper as a conductor. Daly then built a smelter to process the ore. With that operation alone, Daly was worth millions of dollars. He not only owned the Anaconda Mining and Reduction Company but also the Butte, Anaconda, and Pacific Railroad, lumber interests in the Bitterroot Valley, prized horse stables, and an enormous mansion. He founded the city of Anaconda for his employees, and in 1894, unsuccessfully tried to move the state capital from Helena to Anaconda. In 1899, he sold the Anaconda Mining Company to William Rockefeller and Henry Rogers for $39 million. Daly was made president and died in 1900 at 59 years old. His legacy includes a statue by world-famous sculptor Augustus Saint-Gaudens at the University of Montana, a drawing of Daly acquired by the American National Portrait Gallery in Washington, D.C., and the Marcus Daly Memorial Hospital in Hamilton, Montana.[8]

William Clark was born in Connellsville, Pennsylvania in 1839. At age 17, his family moved to Iowa, where William taught school and studied the law. In 1862, he travelled to Colorado to work in the quartz mines, and the following year, he moved to Montana to work in the newly discovered gold fields. After some small success in gold prospecting, he went into banking in Deer Lodge, Montana. With his savings, he purchased repossessed mining properties. He proceeded to make a fortune in copper mining, railroads, newspapers, electric power companies, and trolleys in Los Angeles and Salt Lake City. Clark, Daly, and Heinze were known as the three "Copper Kings" who controlled business in Butte. Clark served as president of Montana's state constitutional conventions of 1884 and 1889, and he used his newspaper *The Butte Miner* to promote his own political career. He strongly campaigned to keep the capital in Helena when his business rival Marcus Daly was trying to get it moved to Anaconda. With its local gold deposits, Helena became one of the richest cities in the country. By 1888, 50 millionaires lived in Helena, and on a per capita basis, it was the wealthiest city in the world. Clark was eager to gain political influence, but in 1899, he was accused of bribing existing senators for their votes when he ran for the Senate. At that time, senators were elected by the Senate, and it was Clark's activities that gave rise to the adoption of the 17th Amendment in 1913, whereby senators were elected by popular vote. Clark did gain a senate seat in 1901 and served until 1907. He died in 1925 at 86 years old. His extensive art collection was left to the Corcoran Gallery in Washington, D.C. as well as funds to construct the Clark Wing. When he died, he was one of the 50 richest Americans in history. His reputation was mixed between his business success, his philanthropy, and being regarded by his detractors such as Mark Twain for his corruption.[9]

James J. Hill was born in 1838 in Ontario, Canada. He received some early education at Rockwood Academy, but when his father died when James was 14 and working as a grocer, he studied under Reverend William Wetheraid, who taught him English and math, where he excelled in algebra and geometry. At 17, he moved to Kentucky to work as a bookkeeper and then to St. Paul, where he worked for a steamboat company. He moved on to work for the St. Paul and Pacific Railroad, where he learned selling, shipping, and trading. Exempt from service in the Civil War due to blindness in one eye. He helped to form a volunteer corps in Minnesota. While he was acquiring a variety of skills, he looked to the Northwest as the most likely area for economic expansion. In 1879, at age 41, he and some partners started a company that purchased the bankrupt St. Paul and Pacific Railway Company and transformed it to the successful St. Paul, Minnesota & Manitoba Railway Company. Several years later, he was appointed president of the company, and he earned an excellent reputation as a railroad executive. Hill was eager to have his railroad reach the Pacific, and in spite of negative opinions, he surveyed the Rockies to find the lowest crossing point at the Marias Pass, thereby avoiding the need for expensive tunneling. He repeated this feat later when he was expanding the Great Northern Railway in Washington. When the Union Pacific Railway started to compete with him, he teamed with banker J.P. Morgan and added the Northern Pacific and then the Chicago, Burlington, and Quincy railroads to his holdings. Hill was greatly responsible for developing the Pacific Northwest by bringing settlers from Europe, especially Scandinavia. His fee for transporting the immigrants was only $10.00. The governor of Minnesota called him "the greatest construction genius of the Northwest." Hill earned a reputation for high standards and hard work, and even after he sold the business to his son in 1907, he went to work every day until a week before his death in 1916, at 77 years old.[10]

Chapter Forty-two

WASHINGTON

State on November 11, 1889

Explorers and Settlers

In 1996, one of the most complete Paleoamerican skeletons was discovered on the banks of the Columbia River in Kennewick, Washington. Recent DNA testing has found the 9,000-year-old "Kennewick Man" to be very similar to the living Native Americans of today. Scientists from many countries have performed exhaustive studies of its bones for 25 years, and some have concluded that the Kennewick Man was related to Japanese ancestors or to white Europeans. Local Indian tribes have filed legal claims to the skeleton, and it was only in 2016 that the United States Senate and House agreed to return the ancient bones to a coalition of tribes for proper burial. We can conclude that aboriginal Americans lived in the Washington region for thousands of years before the Europeans arrived.[1]

The first recorded European to land in Washington was Spanish Capt. Don Bruno de Heceta in 1775 on the ship *Santiago*. Under the Treaty of Tordesillas of 1494, Portugal and the Crown of Castile had agreed on the division of lands outside of Europe, and based on this, Heceta claimed the Washington coast up to Prince William Sound for Spain. In effect, that treaty gave Spain the right to claim almost all the Pacific. That would change when British explorer Capt. James Cook discovered Cape Flattery off the San Juan de Fuca Straits in 1778, and Charles William Barkley travelled into the Straits in 1787. In fact, it was Barkley who named the Straits after Juan de Fuca, who was a Greek maritime pilot from Iona in the late 1500's in the service of King Philip of Spain. The Spanish-British Nootka Conventions of 1790-94 ended Spain's exclusive rights and opened the area to others like Great Britain, Canada, Russia, and the United States. In 1792, British Capt. George Vancouver claimed the Puget Sound for England and named the waters around Tacoma Narrows in honor of Peter Puget, who was a lieutenant on his expedition. Also in 1792, American Capt. Robert Gray discovered the entrance to the Columbia River from the Pacific Ocean, and he named it the Columbia River after his ship *Columbia*. Lewis and Clark arrived at the Columbia River from the east side in 1805. David Thompson, a Canadian explorer, started his Pacific Northwest expedition in 1807. In 1811, he became the first mariner to navigate the entire length of the river to the Pacific Ocean. On that trip, he posted notices that the North West Company planned to build a fort there, and when it was finished, they named it Fort Nez Perce.[2] During this time, the Americans had established a settlement in Astoria on the coast and were looking to build an inland trading post for the Pacific Fur Company. The PFC was owned by millionaire financier John Jacob Astor from 1810 to 1913 and operated in Fort Astoria at the mouth of the Columbia River. It faced strong competition from the Canadian North West Company, the British, and the Russians. When the War of 1812 erupted, the PFC lacked military protection and was forced to sell its depleted assets to the North West Company in 1813. Workers and settlers returned to St. Louis, and on their way, they made an important discovery, finding the South Pass through the Rocky Mountains. This came to be a major trail for thousands of settlers who used the Oregon, California and Mormon routes in the great migration west.[3]

Territorial Issues

The issue of sovereign boundaries became complex because of the competing claims by the United States, Great Britain, Canada, and Russia. The Treaty of 1818 following the War of 1812, established the 49th parallel as the border between British Columbia and the United States. The two countries also agreed to joint control and occupancy of the Oregon Country, which was an area west of the Continental Divide, north of the 42nd parallel, and south of the 49th parallel. This was followed by Russia in 1824 and 1825, who signed separate treaties with the United States and Great Britain that they had no claims to lands south of 50'40" latitude. In the 1819 Adams-Onis Treaty, Spain ceded their rights to the United States to lands north of the 42nd parallel. As traders and settlers flocked to the Oregon Country over the next 25 years, tensions developed with the joint ownership arrangement with Great Britain. In 1846, both countries agreed to fix the boundary between British Columbia and the United States at the 49th parallel. Two years later, the Oregon Territory was established, which included present-day Washington, Oregon, Idaho, and parts of Montana and Wyoming. In 1853, the Washington Territory was created and included Washington and parts of Idaho and Montana, which were taken from the Oregon Territory. The name "Washington" was selected to honor George Washington, and it is the only state named for one of America's founding fathers. The "Pig War" of 1859 was a bloodless conflict that arose over the boundaries in the San Juan Islands and between Vancouver and the mainland. The dispute was settled by arbitration in 1872, which established the present-day United States-Canada border.[4]

Statehood

Only after the boundary agreement of 1846 at the 49th parallel could American settlers in the northern Oregon Territory pursue an independent government. In 1853, a small group of settlers petitioned Congress to divide the Oregon Territory above the Columbia River. In 1855, gold was discovered in the upper valley of the Colorado River on the eastern side of the Rockies, which brought the usual rush of prospectors and settlers. Additional mineral deposits were discovered in the Idaho portion, so it was removed from the Washington Territory in 1862. From 1860 to 1864, there were several attempts to move the territorial capital from Walla Walla to Vancouver, but they all failed. Some business leaders even proposed a new territory for eastern Washington but to no avail. When the Northern Pacific Railroad permit was approved by Congress, it allowed Portland, Oregon to be its terminal point with only a branch line up to the Puget Sound. Washington renewed its appeal several times for statehood, but voter apathy doomed the effort. The financial panic of 1873 and the seven-year depression that followed prevented any near-future approval for statehood. Businessmen in Walla Walla became so despairing of Washington statehood that they came very close to becoming a part of Oregon. In fact, the prospect of losing Walla Walla and northern Idaho to Oregon awakened the residents of Washington to move more aggressively for statehood. The county votes for calling a constitutional convention were overwhelmingly positive. Only the counties below the Snake River and close to the Colorado River wanted to be with Oregon. Another obstacle to statehood was when Republican Colorado was admitted to statehood in 1876. When the electoral commission gave every disputed vote to the Republicans, giving them an unexpected victory for Rutherford Hayes, the Democrats in Congress were so upset that they promised not to admit another Republican state for the foreseeable future. In spite of such dire opposition, the Washington delegates met in Walla Walla in 1878 for their constitutional convention. The territory voted 2:1 in favor, but Congress stayed firm in their opposition and refused to vote the measure out of the Committee on Territories. Again, in 1880, the Washington Territory Legislature passed a motion to draft a bill for convening a constitutional convention. However, Congress buried it for six years. Many admission bills were passed by Dakota, Montana, Wyoming, Utah, Idaho, and Washington during the 1880's. At the same time railroads were expanding into these same territories, bringing a rapid increase in population that would soon force Congress to take action. Other territories were not likely candidates for statehood for other than political reasons. New Mexico had a heavy Hispanic population. Oklahoma had a large number of Indians, and Congress was not amenable to Indian citizenship. Utah was inhabited by a large Mormon population, and Congress remained hostile to their religious practices, especially polygamy. There was an effort to annex northern Idaho to eastern Washington which was supported by southern Idaho, but Congress rejected it.

Another problem arose when miners in the Washington and Wyoming coal mines went on strike, protesting the hiring of cheaper Chinese and black laborers. The unrest gave statehood opponents more reasons to withhold approval, citing the instability of the area.

By 1888, statehood became an important issue in that presidential election. Benjamin Harrison won the electoral votes while Grover Cleveland won the popular vote. Before leaving office, Cleveland signed a bill in February of 1889 that started the process of statehood for Dakota, Montana, and Washington. In July of 1889, 75 delegates met in Olympia to draft a constitution. The vote on October 1st was 40,152 in favor and 11,789 opposed. With a new Republican-controlled Congress, President Harrison admitted Washington to the Union on November 11, 1889.[5] The Washington Territory waited 36 years for statehood, and Olympia remained its capital.

Statesmen, Leaders and Heroes

Isaac Stevens was born in Andover, Massachusetts in 1818, and graduated from the United States Military Academy at West Point in 1839, ranked first in his class. He fought in six major battles of the Mexican-American War, including the Battle of Mexico City where he was seriously wounded. He was recognized for his bravery and steadily rose in rank until after his death in 1862, when he was awarded major general posthumously. In the presidential campaign of 1852, Stevens strongly supported Franklin Pierce, who rewarded him in March of the next year with the governorship of the Washington Territory and the position of Superintendent of Indian Affairs. On his journey to the Northwest to assume his new position, he was also selected by the United States government to survey the best possible route for a railroad across the northern United States.

As Washington's first governor, Stevens acquired the reputation of being a strong-willed disciplinarian who would use military force to achieve his goals. He intimidated the natives and forced them to sign treaties that ceded their lands to the United States. Those included the Treaty of Medicine Creek, Treaty of Hellgate, Treaty of Neah Bay, Treaty of Point Elliot, Point No Point Treaty, and Quinault Treaty. He used martial law against Indians and whites who opposed him. Several highly placed citizens appealed to President Pierce for his removal, but the president merely expressed his concern and refused to dismiss him. Somehow, Stevens retained enough popularity to be elected as the territorial delegate to Congress in 1857 and 1858. In 1861, Stevens was commissioned in the Union army and was appointed as colonel of the 79th New York Volunteers. Later that year, he was elevated to brigadier general and fought at Port Royal, the Sea Islands of South Carolina, and the Battle of Secessionville near Charleston. He was then sent to Virginia, where he fought in the Second Battle of Bull Run and in the Battle of Chantilly, where he was struck in the temple, and died on September 1, 1862. He is buried in Newport, Rhode Island, and his legacy includes Stevens County in Washington and Minnesota; Fort Stevens in Washington and Oregon; Isaac Stevens Camp at Washington State Camp; Stevens Hall at Washington State University; City of Lake Stevens, Washington; Stevensville, Montana; Isaac Stevens Middle School in Washington; Isaac Stevens Elementary School in Seattle; Stevens Peak in Idaho; and Upper and Lower Stevens Lake in Idaho.[6]

Elisha Ferry was born near Detroit, Michigan in 1825. His family soon moved to Waukegan, Illinois, where Elisha's father served as a judge. Elisha was educated there through high school and then studied law at Fort Wayne Law School in Indiana. He practiced law there for 23 years, and in 1859, he was elected its first mayor. In 1862, he was selected as a delegate to the Illinois State Constitutional Convention. During the Civil War, Ferry organized the Illinois regiments, which enabled him to make friends with Gen. Ulysses Grant and President Lincoln. After the war in 1869, President Grant appointed Ferry to be Surveyor General of the Washington Territory, causing his move to Olympia. Three years later and then again four years after that, President Grant appointed him to be the territorial governor. During that eight-year period, Ferry became instrumental in the building of the Northern Pacific Railway, and with his surveying experience, he planned the extension line from Tacoma to the capital at Olympia. As territorial governor, he was a financial conservative, and by the time he left office in 1880, Washington was nearly debt-free. He then returned to law and banking, but in 1889 when Washington was declared a state, his Republican supporters urged him to run for governor, and he won handily with 58 percent of the vote. During his first year in office, the cities of Seattle, Ellensburg, and Spokane Falls were destroyed by fire, and Ferry saw that they were rebuilt properly with brick and stone, thereby giving them a sense of permanence. After retiring from office in 1893, Ferry was plagued by failing health. He died from a cold in 1895 at 70 years old. Elisha Ferry is remembered as one of the most respected leaders in Washington's history. His legacy is Ferry County, Washington.[7]

Chapter Forty-three

Idaho

State on July 3, 1890

Explorers and Settlers

Like its Pacific Northwest neighbors, Idaho was home to ancient humans for 12 to 15 thousand years. Some of North America's oldest artifacts have been found here, including those of the Native American tribes of Shoshone and Nez Perce, who occupied Idaho for hundreds of years before the Europeans discovered the area. Americans Lewis and Clark entered Idaho on their Voyage of Discovery in 1805, but it was American Andrew Henry of the Missouri Fur Company in 1810 who built the first settlement, Fort Henry, on the Snake River. The next pioneer was Wilson Price Hunt, an employee of John Jacob Astor, who attempted to find a water route from St. Louis to Astoria, Oregon. He navigated the Snake River from the east and arrived at the mouth of the Columbia River, completing the journey in 340 days. By the 1820's, the Hudson's Bay Company explored Idaho and soon controlled the fur trade along the Snake River. In June of 1816, the North West Company was created, and it employed Donald Mackenzie to head the operation. Mackenzie was an experienced fur trader who had worked for Hudson's Bay and Astor's Pacific Bay Company. He soon made North West a major force in the Snake River area. He used Fort Nez Perce as his strategic staging point. He then attempted to find a navigable route from there to Boise, and while he found it wasn't possible, he did reach the Boise River in 1819.[1] The American efforts at building a competitive fur industry in that region were extremely challenging due to the difficulty of maintaining adequate supply lines from the Missouri River to the west of the Rockies. Other Americans like William Ashley and Jedidiah Smith were able to expand their St. Louis fur trade into Idaho by 1824. Meanwhile, the area attracted missionaries to educate the natives and assist the settlers. The Kullyspell House was constructed in 1831 and was the first trading post in Idaho. The first mission-school was started by the Reverend Henry Spalding. His wife, Eliza, and missionary wife Narcissa Whitman were the first non-native women to enter Idaho. In 1842, Fathers Pierre De Smet and Nicholas Point and Brother Charles Duet built another mission on the St. Joe River. The oldest standing building in Idaho today is the Cataldo Mission, which was built in 1848 by the native Coeur d'Alene and Catholic missionaries. It quickly became a key resting place for traders, settlers, and miners. They could also purchase supplies for wagon travelers or those going up the Coeur d'Alene River. During the early years of the 19th century, Idaho was part of the much larger Oregon Country. It was still unorganized and jointly claimed by the United States and Great Britain. With the Oregon Treaty of 1846, the United States acquired the sole jurisdiction of the Oregon Country. The original size of the territory was enormous and included Washington, Oregon, Idaho, and parts of Montana and Wyoming. Its boundary on the west was the Pacific Ocean, and to the east, it was the Continental Divide in the Rockies. In 1853, the region north of the 48th parallel became the Washington Territory, which split Idaho in two. In 1859, Oregon became a state, and the part of Idaho that had been taken by Washington was reunited with Idaho.[2]

When the Mormons moved west to escape persecution from those who objected to their customs and beliefs, they settled in Utah, Idaho, and the surrounding area. Idaho's first organized town of Franklin was settled by

Mormons in 1860. Another large group of immigrants came from England. They found more personal freedoms in America as well as opportunities to rise above the confining social classes that existed in Great Britain. Today, the English make up 20 percent of Idaho's population. Another major number of immigrants were the Germans, who now account for 18 percent of the state's population. The first Germans to settle in Idaho were farmers, and the German language was the most prominent in Idaho until World War II. The period of 1845 to 1852 marked the peak of the Great Potato Famine in Ireland, which forced many Irish families to leave their country. Some settled in the Midwest, Montana, and southern Idaho around Boise. Though not as numerous as the English or Germans, close to 10 percent of Idaho's population have Irish origins. The first African-American in Idaho was an aide to Lewis and Clark by the name of York. Many blacks from the South migrated to the West after the abolition of slavery in 1862 by President Lincoln. They were mostly ranchers and farmers trying to escape discrimination. By the year 2000, African-Americans became the fourth largest ethnic group in Idaho. Another large ethnic group is the Chinese, who arrived in the mid-19th century to work on the railroads. They came through San Francisco and migrated to the mountains to work with gold and mineral speculators from California to Idaho.[3]

The Idaho Territory

The name "Idaho" is credited to a political lobbyist named George Willing. He reportedly suggested it because of its Shoshone origin meaning, "the sun comes from the mountains." Another interpretation is "gem of the mountains." The latter translation is more appropriate in that Idaho was about to yield billions of dollars in gold, silver, and precious gems over the next 40 years.[4] On March 3, 1863, President Abraham Lincoln signed the Act of Congress that officially made Idaho a Territory. It covered all of present-day Idaho and Montana and almost all of Wyoming, except for a very small part of its southwest corner. It was spanned by the Oregon Trail and a portion of the California and Mormon trails. The first capital was Lewiston, but three years later, it was moved to Boise. The move caused much controversy and ill will between the northern counties near Lewiston and the southern counties near Boise. Some historians believe

Lewiston was named after Meriwether Lewis. It was founded just one year after gold was discovered in nearby Pierce. Moving the capital to Boise in 1866 was extremely unpopular in the North, and that was also based in part on how it was done. Caleb Lyon was the territorial governor, and together with the territorial secretary Clinton De Witt Smith, stole the government seal, archives, and treasury and fled to Portland, Oregon. Before arriving in Lewiston to assume his new position, Lyon had stopped in Boise, where he was allegedly approached by lawmakers with a bill designating Boise as the new capital. Lyon signed it before leaving for Lewiston. When Lyon was away in 1865, Secretary Smith became acting governor and favored the move to Boise. Smith and his accomplices reportedly stole the government documents. When Lyon returned in late 1865, he pursued statehood because of his ambition to become a United States senator. The Republican legislature blocked his attempts, and when he resigned in 1866, he absconded with the entire Idaho Indian Fund of $46,418.[5]

In 1864, the Montana Territory was removed from Idaho, as was the Dakota Territory. In 1868, the Wyoming Territory was removed, leaving Idaho with its current boundaries. The 1860's saw Idaho blossom with gold, silver, and mineral discoveries and the completion of the Transcontinental Railway. By the 1870's, Idaho had established a public-school system and regular stage coach service. Newspapers appeared in Lewiston, Boise, and Silver City, and in 1874, Lewiston was the first Idaho town to be linked into the telegraph. Mormons represented a significant portion of the population, but in 1882, they were disenfranchised in the entire territory because of their polygamy practices. Ever since the territorial capital of Lewiston was moved to Boise in 1866, there seems to have been friction between the northern and southern counties of Idaho. When Edward Stevenson was appointed governor of the territory by President Grover Cleveland in 1885, he was immediately faced with several challenges. The first was his desire to have more control of territorial appointments, and the second was to have residents vote for president and vice president, but he was unsuccessful in both goals. The next issue was far more serious and occurred in 1889 when the northern counties requested to be joined to western Montana or to the eastern Washington Territory, which was about to acquire statehood. At the same time, Nevada wanted to annex Idaho's southern counties. Congress was in favor of the moves, but Stevenson was able to prevent the changes with help from his friend, President Cleveland. The two sections of Idaho were at odds partly due to the large influx of Mormons in the north. When the Mormons became disenfranchised and consolidated more into Utah, the issue of statehood became dominant. On July 3, 1890, with President Benjamin Harrison's signature, Idaho was admitted to the Union as the 43rd state.

Statesmen, Leaders and Heroes

William H. Wallace was born in 1811 in Troy, Ohio into a family that was deeply political. His father, Andrew, was a close friend of William Henry Harrison, and his mother was a relative of Revolutionary War hero John Paul Jones. William's brother, David, was governor of Indiana, and his son was a Civil War general and a New Mexico territorial governor. William served in the Iowa legislature, and in the 1850's, he was befriended by Abraham Lincoln, and the two men remained lifelong friends. Wallace moved to the Washington Territory in 1853 when Idaho was still a part of Washington. While on a business trip to Washington, D.C. in 1861, President Lincoln appointed him governor of the Washington Territory, but before he could assume that position, the Washington Republicans chose him to be their territorial delegate to Congress. While in the nation's capital, he succeeded in getting Congress to approve of Idaho as a new territory. President Lincoln immediately appointed him as the first territorial governor of Idaho in 1863. In the fall of that year, he was elected as the territorial delegate to Congress and left for the capital in December, thereby leaving Idaho without a governor. His secretary, W.B. Daniels then became acting governor. Wallace served two terms as delegate. While there, President Lincoln invited Mr. and Mrs. Wallace to join him at Ford's Theater, but he declined due to his wife's illness. Wallace served as one of Lincoln's pall bearers, and after retiring the next year, he returned to the Washington Territory to practice law until he died in 1879 at 68 years old.[6]

Edward Stevenson was born in 1831 in Lowville, New York but spent most of his early years in Ann Arbor, Michigan. One of his brothers was governor of Nevada, and another brother was the first Speaker of the Legislative Assembly of Ontario. Edward's cousin Adlai was vice president under Grover Cleveland. Adlai

Stevenson, Jr. was nominated by the Democratic Party to run for president against Dwight Eisenhower in 1956. At the age of 18, Edward joined the California gold rush in 1849. At age 22, he was elected to the state legislature, where he served four terms. His other civic jobs were Justice of the Peace, deputy sheriff, and mayor of Coloma, California. While still in California, Colonel Stevenson actively fought against the Modoc Indians, and he also negotiated peace treaties with them as well as with other tribes. In 1855, he married Harriet Marcy, and they settled on a farm in Tehama County. While away on business in 1859, Indians allegedly set fire to his house, and his wife and three children were burned to death. In 1860, he remarried, joined the Idaho gold rush, and resettled in Boise. In 1863, when President Lincoln created the new territory, Stevenson was drawn back into politics, serving three two-year terms in the territorial legislature. In 1874, he was elected Speaker of the House, and in 1876 at the age of 45, he began to study the law. In 1882, he moved to Payette Valley, where he engaged in farming and stock raising. In 1885, President Cleveland selected him to serve as the first and only Democratic territorial governor of Idaho. Such positions were usually filled from outside the territory, but Stevenson may have been selected because of his cousin's influence as vice president under President Cleveland. However, both Democrats and Republicans thought highly of Stevenson, and he went on to become Idaho's most successful governor. He promoted policies of non-partisanship, moderation, fiscal frugality, local authority, and less federal control. He pushed for statehood, the bill for which Republican Benjamin Harrison signed on July 3, 1890. Governor Stevenson died in 1895 at 64 years old.[7]

George Shoup was born in 1836 in Kittanning, Pennsylvania, northeast of Pittsburgh. At age 16, he graduated from the local public school and then farmed with his father. The Panic of 1857 financially ruined him, so he moved to the Colorado Territory in 1859 to work in mining and merchandising in Colorado Springs and Denver. He spent four years in the Union army and fought in the Battle of Apache Canyon in New Mexico and the Sand Creek Massacre in Colorado. He was honorably discharged in 1864 as a colonel, moved to Montana and then to Idaho, where he assisted in the founding of the town of Salmon. In 1874, Shoup was elected to the Idaho Territorial Legislature. In 1889, President Benjamin Harrison appointed him governor of the Idaho Territory. After it was admitted as the 43rd state in 1890, Shoup was elected Idaho's first governor, where he served for only a few weeks before being elected to the United States Senate. As a senator for ten years, his priorities were education and military issues. As Chairman of the Committee on Territories, he promoted justice for Native Americans. He retired to Boise in 1901 and passed away in 1904 at 64 years old. His legacy includes the community of Shoup on the Salmon River, a World War II liberty ship, a men's dormitory at the University of Idaho, and a marble statue of him presented by the state of Idaho to the National Statuary Hall Collection at the United States Capitol.[8]

President Grover Cleveland is honored as the savior of Idaho. When the Idaho Territory was formed in 1863 and approved by President Lincoln, its capital was first established in Lewiston. Located in the northwestern part of the territory, lawmakers considered it too distant and difficult to reach. Unscrupulous politicians collaborated with Governor Caleb Lyon and Secretary Clinton Smith and pushed through a bill that moved the capital to Boise in 1866, which many in the northern counties believed was done illegally. That move set the stage for poor internal relations for over 25 years. In 1878, the northern citizens voted to support a proposed move to join neighboring Washington. Nine years later, both houses of Congress voted in favor of the measure. However, President Cleveland prevented it from happening by using a "pocket veto," just before retiring from office in 1890. To appease the northerners, the University of Idaho was placed in northerly Moscow, and Congress created the first and only county in its history and called it Latah County in northern Idaho.[9]

Chapter Forty-four

Wyoming

State on July 10, 1890

Explorers and Settlers

The name "Wyoming" was first introduced to the United States in reference to a section of Pennsylvania called the Wyoming Valley. It became well-known from a popular Scottish poet whose work "Gertrude of Wyoming" was published in 1809. The poem depicts a massacre which occurred in 1778, when 300 American Patriots were killed by English Loyalists and their Indian allies. The name derives from the Algonquian-Lenape language of the tribe that lived in the New York City, New Jersey, Pennsylvania, and Delaware area. A United States Representative, J. M. Ashley of Ohio, used it in Congress when he introduced the bill for "the temporary government for the territory of Wyoming," just before its passage in 1868.

The Wyoming region contains ancient human artifacts dating back 13,000 years. Evidence strongly suggests that the ancient cultures of Clovis, Folsom, and

Plano lived here. Certain medicine wheels and rock formations have been found in Yellowstone National Park, which occupies an enormous part of Wyoming. The ancient cultures gave way to the Native American tribes which included the Arapaho, Bannock, Blackfeet, Cheuenne, Crow, Gros Ventre, Kiowa, Nez Perce, Sioux, Shoshone. and Ute. These nomadic tribes were called the Plains Indians. Two of the most famous Indians are buried in Wyoming. Sacagawea was the female Shoshone guide for Lewis and Clark's Expedition. Shoshone Chief Washakie is buried at Fort Washakie. He died in 1900 at the age of 102 and was the first Indian chief to be buried with full military honors.[1]

Like many other states along the northern frontier, the earliest settlers of Wyoming were fur trappers who thrived on trading fur skins, especially those of the beaver whose fur was in great demand due to the growing popularity of beaver hats in Europe. The French dominated the fur industry in the 1700's, but with their independence, Americans migrated west to compete with the English and the French. It was the Louisiana Purchase in 1803 that gave the migration its greatest impetus and the Lewis and Clark reports following their two-year "Voyage of Discovery" that attracted traders and businessmen to the Pacific Northwest. John Colter was a member of the Lewis and Clark Expedition, and in 1807, he was probably the first white American to explore Wyoming. In 1812, Robert Stuart and his party returning from Astoria, Oregon discovered South Pass through the Rockies and also explored Wyoming. Stuart and Colter focused on the Yellowstone area. Their accounts spurred the arrival of the "Mountain Men," who were male trappers who lived in the wilderness, particularly in the mountains of western Wyoming. Another explorer of note was Jim Bridger who found the Bridger Pass which enabled the Union Pacific Railroad to traverse the Rockies in 1868. The Mountain Men prospered in the 30-year period from 1810 to 1840 and were instrumental in clearing paths and widening wagon trails and opening the Emigrant Trails, namely the Oregon, California, and Mormon trails. As demand for beaver declined in the 1840's, it was replaced by the silk trade with the Orient, so the Mountain Men disbursed into other work like becoming army scouts, guiding wagon teams, and operating trading posts to service the settlers heading west.[2]

The Oregon Trail was built over a 30-year period from 1810 to 1840, and it served as a major thoroughfare for the 400,000 settlers, miners, farmers, ranchers, and businessmen who migrated to the Pacific. The trail spanned almost all of Wyoming, and was used by those going on to the California Trail and those going on the Mormon Trail to Utah. When the transcontinental railway was completed in 1869, use of the trail declined because the trains provided a faster, cheaper, and safer means of transportation.[3] The most instrumental railroad to develop Wyoming was the Union Pacific. It used its land grants from the government to support bank loans to finance the construction of bridges, rail beds, tunnels, and rail cars. The land was ideal for ranches, but rails were necessary to bring the cattle to market and manufactured goods for the ranchers. The Union Pacific built towns with the kinds of facilities that were needed, such as housing for the crews, eating halls, and repair shops. It eventually covered the entire state and created some of its largest cities like Laramie, Rock Springs, and Evanston, and it reached Cheyenne, which became the state capital in 1867.[4]

As the railways brought a greater number of settlers to the region, it was necessary to protect them, so the United States began to build a series of strategic forts along the key east-west trails and rail lines. In 1851, the first of these was Fort Laramie which, together with the Treaty of Fort Laramie, was intended to establish peace with the local tribes. The larger white population brought tensions with the Indians in the 1860's, when settlers encroached on land that was dedicated for the natives' hunting grounds in the Powder River Country. Maj. Gen. Grenville Dodge was ordered to settle the conflict, which ended with the Battle of the Tongue River against the Arapaho. In 1866, the first major battle between the United States and the Wyoming tribes of Arapaho, Cheyenne, and Sioux was Red Cloud's War. The Americans at Fort Kearny sent out 81 soldiers, who were drawn into an ambush by Chief Crazy Horse, and none of them survived. Another Treaty of Fort Laramie in 1868 closed the Powder River Country to the white settlers. Again, in 1876, miners violated the treaty in the Black Hills area, which led to another war.[5]

The Road to Statehood

In 1867, gold was discovered in Wyoming, which led to the founding of South Pass City and the likely approval of territorial status. The act was passed by Congress on July 25, 1868. Anticipating that event in the prior year, lawmakers had already divided the region into four counties: Laramie, Carter (later Sweetwater) and Albany. Their boundaries extended from north to south at the existing lines of the territory. When it was officially declared a new territory, Congress added portions of Utah and Idaho to Wyoming. John Campbell was named the first territorial governor by President Grant. Wyoming is unique in that it was the first government in the world to extend the right to vote, serve on juries, and hold public office to women. The act was signed by Governor Campbell in 1869. In 1870, Esther Hobart Morris became the first woman to be appointed a Justice of the Peace, and for that she is honored as the "Mother of Women Suffrage."[6] Although no statehood enabling act was passed or presented to Congress, Wyoming did something not done before. They proceeded to call for a Constitutional Convention in 1889 which was approved by a vote of 6,272 in favor and 1,923 opposed. In December of 1889, both Houses of Congress introduced bills for Wyoming's statehood. On July 10, 1890, President Benjamin Harrison signed the bill admitting Wyoming to the Union as the 44th state.

Statesmen, Leaders and Heroes

One of the best-known names in American history is "Sacagawea," and this Shoshone woman's story is placed in this chapter because her gravesite is located in Fort Washakie, Wyoming. She was born in Salmon, Idaho in 1788. At the age of 12, she was captured by a band of Hidatsa Indians, who had just killed several Shoshone men, women, and children. She was then taken to Washburn, North Dakota. The next year, a nearby fur trapper from Quebec, Toussaint Charbonneau, allegedly purchased Sacagawea and another squaw from the Hidatsa to have as wives. In 1804, Meriwether Lewis and William Clark left on their famous "Voyage of Discovery" from St. Louis and planned to spend the winter in a Hidatsa village on the Missouri River. After building Fort Mandan, they realized they would need local guides and interpreters, so they interviewed trappers who knew the territory. The logical choice was the Frenchman Charbonneau, because his Shoshone wife, Sacagawea, spoke that language and they would be travelling in Shoshone territory. She did not speak English, but her husband spoke French and Hidatsa. Another member of the team, Francois Labiche, spoke French and English, thereby making it possible for all 33 members to understand the dialogue with the natives.[7] At that time, Sacagawea was pregnant and soon gave birth to a son she named Jean Baptiste Charbonneau. When the expedition reached the headwaters of the Missouri River, they met the Shoshone and discovered that their chief was Sacagawea's brother. The Indians traded their horses and provided several guides for the hazardous trip through the Rockies. Sacagawea proved to be extremely valuable and was included in all the council meetings with the Indians. On their journey, they met many tribes who had never seen a white man, but their initial fears and doubts subsided at the sight of an Indian woman with her infant son. When they reached the Pacific Ocean, a meeting was held to decide on the location for a winter fort. It is interesting to note that both Sacagawea and Clark's black manservant York were included in the decision which was to be Astoria, Oregon. On their return trip as they approached the Rockies in July of 1806, Sacagawea informed Lewis and Clark that she was familiar with the area and could find a good place to pass. It was called "Gibbons Pass" on the Continental Divide in Montana. A week later, she directed them to cross into the Yellowstone River Basin at a place later named "Bozeman Pass." This was the place where the Northern Pacific Railway chose to cross the Continental Divide, 50 years later.[8]

Sacagawea's contributions to the Lewis and Clark Expedition have been described differently. She has been depicted as a guide, but that was a limited role. Her assistance as an interpreter was greater, but her greatest help could simply have been her presence. When potentially hostile natives saw a mother and child, they quickly viewed the strangers as peaceful people who would not endanger themselves with warring intentions.[9]

When the great expedition ended in 1806, Sacagawea and her husband lived with the Hidatsa for three years before moving to St. Louis to be near Clark. During the two years together, Clark had treated Jean Baptiste as a son and called him "Pomp." When the Charbonneau family settled in St. Louis, Clark sent the boy to St. Louis Academy and offered to adopt him. Although there have been conflicting stories about Sacagawea's remarrying and dying in 1884, historical evidence shows that she died in 1812 at 25 years old. To quote historian Bonnie Butterfield:

> An 1811 journal entry made by Henry Brackenridge, a fur dealer at Fort Manuel Lisa Trading Post on the Missouri River stated that both Sacagawea and Charbonneau were living at the fort... *'Sacagawea had become sickly and longed to revisit her native country.' John Luttig, a clerk at Fort Manuel Lisa recorded in his journal of December 20, 1812 that... 'the wife of Charbonneau, a Snake(Shoshone) squaw died of putrid fever.' Documents held by Clark show that her son, Baptiste, already had been entrusted by Charbonneau into Clark's care for a boarding school education at Clark's insistence.... An adoption document made in the Orphan's Court Records in St. Louis, Missouri states... 'On August 11, 1813 William Clark became the guardian of Tousant Charbonneau, a boy about ten years, and Lizette Charbonneau a girl about one year old.' For a Missouri Court at that time to designate a child as orphaned and to allow an adoption both parents had to be confirmed dead in court papers."*[10]

John Colter was born in Virginia sometime between 1770 and 1775. Around 1780, the Colter family moved to Kentucky. Growing up, he acquired extensive outdoor skills that impressed Meriwether Lewis when they met in October of 1803. Lewis hired him for the planned "Corps of Discovery" at $5.00 per month at the rank of private. Colter was a tough and independent mountain man who could blaze trails, hunt, and survive in the most severe weather possible. The records show he never had a sick day, and he had an unusual ability to barter and trade with various local tribes. He could find passes in the mountains and retrieve trails to find lost horses and supplies. He earned the respect of Lewis and Clark, who honorably discharged him two months early to allow him to return to join Forrest Hancock and Joseph Dixon to further explore the upper Missouri River. His work prompted Lewis and Clark to pay him a bonus of double pay and 320 acres of land. Colter was the first white man to enter the Sunlight Basin of Wyoming, and on his return home near the mouth of the Platte River, he met

Manuel Lisa, who owned the Missouri Fur Trading Company. Colter was only a week from St. Louis, but he decided to join the Lisa party of former Lewis and Clark veterans to explore the Yellowstone region, when he helped build Fort Raymond. When he left Fort Raymond in 1807, he trekked over 500 miles to establish trade with the Crow nation. On that trip, he spent the winter exploring the area that later became Yellowstone and Grand Teton National Parks.

In 1808, Colter teamed with John Potts and other veterans of the Lewis and Clark Expedition to establish more trading relations with Indian tribes. The part was attacked by 1,500 Blackfeet, but Colter managed to escape. The next year he was in trouble again with the Blackfeet, who shot and killed Potts from the shoreline. Colter was stripped naked and ordered to run for his life. After several miles, he was accosted by a Crow who tried to kill him with a spear, but miraculously it missed, and Colter managed to retrieve the broken spear and killed the warrior. He took the Indian's blanket and ran for five miles, followed by avenging Indians. He spent a day in a beaver lodge, and at night, he climbed and walked for 11 days to a trader's fort. In 1810, he learned that two of his partners were murdered by Blackfeet, which prompted him to leave the wilderness forever and return to St. Louis. He had lived in the wild for six years. That same year, Colter met with William Clark and provided him with reports and maps of his exploits, from which Clark created the most comprehensive map for the next 75 years. Colter's death is still undetermined but is believed to have been on May 7, 1812. He is buried near his home in Miller's Landing, Missouri. His legacy is Colter Bay on Jackson Lake in Grand Teton National Park, Colter's Peak in Yellowstone National Park, and a Kentucky Historical Marker commemorating Colter as a member of the Lewis and Clark Expedition.[11]

Esther Hobart Morris was born in 1814, in Tioga County, New York, and she was orphaned at a young age. After an apprenticeship, she opened a successful millinery business in her grandparents' house. When her husband died in 1844, she moved to Illinois, where her husband had left some property. At that time, women were not allowed to own or inherit property, so she had great legal obstacles in settling his estate. She then moved to Peru, Illinois, where she married John Morris in 1850. In 1868, her husband and two sons moved to South Pass City, Wyoming to open a saloon during the last years of the local gold rush. Esther and her two sons followed the next year. As the gold rush subsided in 1870, the town of 4,000 residents dwindled to 460, and by 1875, it shrank to 100. In 1870, Esther Morris was appointed to be the first woman Justice of the Peace. Her predecessor, Justice R. S. Barr had resigned in 1869, following the legislature's passage of the women's suffrage amendment. Esther appointed her son Archibald as district clerk and her son Robert as deputy clerk. She got no support from her husband, and when he made a scene in her court, she had him jailed. During her eight months in office completing Justice Barr's term, she ruled on 27 cases, and all were upheld. She failed to get nominated by both parties for the next election, in spite of her excellent record and reputation. In the years that followed, Esther's life was unsettled. She left South Pass City and moved to Albany, New York and then to Springfield, Illinois. In the 1880's, she returned to Cheyenne to live with her son Robert.

Although the Wyoming legislation granting women's suffrage was written by a local citizen named William Bright a year before the Morris appointment, critics claimed that she was the author of the measure. Even her newspaper son was accused of promoting her political interests. However, she did receive much acclaim for her pioneering work on behalf of women's rights. Years later in 1919, influential people like H. G. Nickerson wrote a letter to the *Wyoming State Journal* in which he praised Esther Morris "for advocating and originating women's suffrage in the United States." Another highly regarded Wyoming historian, Grace Hebard, promoted Morris as a founder and co-author of the state's suffrage legislation. The great significance of Morris and the Wyoming legislation of 1869 is that, from that day forward, human rights became a critical issue in the United States. Esther Morris died in 1902 at 87 years old. The state of Wyoming donated a life-size statue of her to the National Statuary Hall Collection in Washington, D.C. The statue is inscribed "Mother of Women Suffrage."[12]

William "Buffalo Bill" Cody was born in 1846, near Le Claire, Iowa. The family lived in Canada for several years, and in 1853, they sold their Iowa land and moved to the Kansas Territory near Fort Leavenworth. At that time, slavery was an explosive topic, and with the Cody family being firmly antislavery, they encountered deadly hostilities from which Bill's father never recovered, dying in

1857. Fatherless at age 11, Bill got his first job delivering messages by horseback up and down wagon trains. He then worked as a scout for the United States army in Utah, helping to put down a rebellion by the Mormons. At age 14, he signed on with the Pony Express. At age 17, he joined the 7th Kansas Cavalry for the Union army, until being discharged in 1865. In 1868, he rejoined the army as the Chief of Scouts for the Third Cavalry during the Plains Wars. He fought in 16 battles over four years, and he was also employed to kill bison for the army and the Kansas Pacific Railroad. During an 18-month period at this time, he reportedly killed 4,282 buffalo. He then competed with Bill Comstock to claim the epithet "Buffalo Bill." In 1872, Cody was awarded the Congressional Medal of Honor for his gallantry in the Indian Wars from 1868 to 1872. He then went to Chicago to start his famous "Wild West" shows, and for the next 20 years, he took his shows throughout the United States and Europe. The shows were a combination of a circus and a parade interspersed with shooting and riding skills. They included the military, cowboys, American Indians, Turks, gauchos, Arabs, and Mongols on their magnificent horses and dressed in their native costumes. He was able to get famous people like Sitting Bull, Wild Bill Hickock, Annie Oakley, and Frank Butler to perform. The show played in England to Queen Victoria, King Edward VII, Kaiser Wilhelm, and King George V. Cody became an international celebrity.

In 1895, Buffalo Bill was back in Wyoming, where he founded a town that was named "Cody" in his honor. His vision was for thousands of tourists flocking to see glimpses of the Old West and to include side trips to nearby Yellowstone National Park. About 35 miles from Cody, he built a dude ranch, stocked with a thousand head of cattle. He acquired over 8,000 acres of land for grazing. He organized camping trips and big-game hunting and entertained distinguished guests from Europe and America. Buffalo Bill Cody died in 1917, at his home in Denver. His fortune had dwindled to $100,000 (equivalent to $1,869,000 today). In life, Cody respected and supported Native Americans and their civil rights, and he claimed that every hostility resulted from broken treaties by the government. He was outspoken about women's rights and equal pay. His legacy is extensive and includes the Congressional Medal of Honor, two United States postage stamps, the town of Cody, the Buffalo Bill Historic Center, Buffalo Bill's

Wild West, and the Progressive Image of American Indians at the University of Nebraska in Lincoln, and the National Museum of America's History's Photographic History Collection at the Smithsonian Institute.[13]

Chapter Forty-five

UTAH

State on January 4, 1896

Explorers and Settlers

The person who is credited with being the first European to enter the Utah region was the Spanish explorer Francisco de Coronado in 1540. He led an expedition of 1,000 men to find the "Seven Cities of Gold," also called "Seven Cities of Cibola." Instead of finding the wealth he expected, he found the tribes of Apache, Navajo, Hopi, Zuni, and Rio Grande Pueblo scattered across Arizona and New Mexico. After exploring the Texas Panhandle, Oklahoma, and Kansas, he returned to Mexico. Other Spanish expeditions followed in 1594 by Francisco Bonilla and Antonio Humana, and in 1601, the governor of New Mexico, Don Juan de Onate, travelled as far as central Kansas in search of the Quivera region that Coronado had described in his reports. The next significant exploration was much later in 1776, when a group of Spanish priests left from Santa Fe to find a route to the California coast. They travelled north to Utah Lake, which is a tributary of the Great Salt Lake. They were soon followed by French-Canadian fur trappers in the late 1700's and early 1800's, including Etienne Provost in 1825, for whom the city of Provo was named. Also, a leading Hudson's Bay Company trapper was Peter Skene Ogden, for whom the city of Ogden was named. However, the development of Utah really started with the arrival of the Mormons in 1847.[1]

The Mormons and the Utah Territory

As the Mormons were entering the Utah region in the late 1840's, other important events were about to take place that would greatly impact the area. The Mexican-American War that started in 1846 was to end in 1848 with the Treaty of Guadalupe Hidalgo, which transferred Utah from Mexico to the United States. In finding no permanent Indian settlements, the Mormons regarded the land as the public domain of the United States. Years later, the Shoshone petitioned for compensation, but no titles or treaties existed to support their claims. The Compromise of 1850, regarding the boundaries of slavery, allowed the future territories of Utah and New Mexico to decide the issue themselves through a popular vote. Because slavery was such an explosive issue, Congress was very sensitive to maintain a balanced number of free and slave states. There was little concern about Utah and New Mexico, because there was no real demand for slaves owing to the arid and poor soil for farming or agricultural production. Other events, such as the discovery of gold in California in 1848 and in neighboring territories, impacted the future boundaries of Utah. Under the leadership of Brigham Young, the Mormons petitioned Congress in 1849 to form the new state of "Deseret." With the pressure of timing as California and New Mexico were applying for statehood, Young decided to skip a territorial status and aim directly for statehood. It was a brash move, considering the size of the proposed Deseret, which included all of present-day Utah and Nevada, large sections of California and Arizona, and parts of Colorado, New Mexico, Wyoming, Idaho, and Oregon. While the size was enormous, the populations at that time were sparse, and much of the land was unsuited for agriculture. Congress did not like the size and the difficulty of governing such a large area, but they did not dismiss it entirely. President Taylor even proposed combining

California and Deseret, which would have decreased the number of free states, thereby preserving the balance with the slave states. The Mormon practice of polygamy was also a controversial aspect of the Territory, which was specifically mentioned in its terms. Utah was declared a new territory in September of 1850, and in February of 1851, Brigham Young was inaugurated as its first governor. Congress drastically reduced the size of the Utah Territory over the next 18 years by transferring most of its border regions to neighboring territories. The eastern portion went to the new Territory of Colorado. Its western portion went to the new Territory of Nevada. Its northern portion went to the Territory of Nebraska. Another 106 miles of its eastern lands were given to the Nevada Territory. The Northeast corner of Utah went to the new Territory of Wyoming.[2]

However, for a brief period prior to becoming a territory, there was a provisional government of Deseret that had a General Assembly under a bicameral legislature. Judges were appointed, a criminal code was adopted, and the Church of Jesus Christ of Latter-day Saints was incorporated. Even though the official name was Utah, the Mormons did not abandon the Deseret concept, and from 1862 to 1870, the elders met as a shadow government to ratify new legislative laws under the state of Deseret, which was a name taken from the Book of Mormon, written by their founder, Joseph Smith. As Utah grew with new railroads, more non-Mormon settlers gradually influenced the citizens to forgo the concept of a religious state.[3]

Utah had to wait 46 years before being admitted to the Union as the 45th state. The unusually long delay for statehood can be attributed to several factors. Starting with the gold discovery in California in 1848, other neighboring regions were also discovering gold, silver, precious stones, and minerals. The Comstock Lode of silver discovered in 1859 was actually in the western part of the Utah Territory, so in 1861, it was transferred to the new Territory of Nevada. Likewise, Wyoming's and Colorado's discoveries prompted Congress to create more new territories using part of Utah's original lands. Some historians maintain that the Mormon practice of polygamy and its past hostilities with the United States government were partly to blame for the delay. Also, there is little doubt that the United States government was eager to secure the wealth that was being unearthed, and their control of territories assured it stayed in federal hands. For example, Nevada had to wait only three years for statehood, in spite of a small population. Colorado waited 15 years before statehood in 1876. It should be noted that the polygamy matter was only revealed to the public in 1852, only two years after receiving territorial status. Many settlers and politicians viewed the practice as un-American, and in 1857, President Buchanan sent troops to prevent open rebellion. He also replaced Brigham Young with Alfred Cumming as governor. At the same time, the Mormons became fearful of an attack and decided to go on the offensive. With the help of some Paiute warriors, they staged an attack on 120 immigrants from Arkansas based on fear-mongering that led to the Mountain Meadows Massacre. Scholars agree that Brigham Young was not involved, and the one man who was convicted was executed. Meanwhile, the United States army with 2,500 soldiers marched to Salt Lake City, and Young ordered his people to evacuate the city and instructed close to 10,000 able-bodied men to slow the army's advance. No blood was shed, and negotiations enabled a peaceful settlement and transfer of government. The army camped 40 miles away, and Governor Cummings entered a deserted city. The event is known as the Utah War.[4]

Women's Rights

Mormon leaders in Utah were well aware of the animosity from non-Mormons near home and in the rest of the country. The practice of polygamy had ostracized them as immoral. Even Protestant ministers were calling their religion non-Christian. Federal laws were passed in the 1870's and 1880's prohibiting polygamy, and with the 1890 Manifesto, the Church of Latter-day saints reversed its policy and declared an end to plural marriage. However, the issue did bring national attention to women's rights. The Mormons were accused of mistreating women, and in an effort to counter that reputation, they promoted the right of women to vote as early as 1869. It is interesting that it came from the Mormon leadership without any organized effort from women themselves. Non-Mormons thought the women of Utah would vote to end polygamy. Mormons like Young realized plural marriage would not be ended, and they supported their suffrage just to show the country that Utah women were not oppressed. The act was passed in February of 1869 with no dissenting votes. At that time, there were no states which permitted women to vote, and Utah was the only territory to offer suffrage. Wyoming followed Utah's lead later in that same year. The Utah non-Mormons were concerned that suffrage could strengthen the political power of the Church of Latter-day Saints. In 1887, the Edmunds-Tucker Act, also called the Anti-Polygamy Act, was passed by Congress, which also took away women's suffrage. With that setback, women's suffrage groups began to mobilize and managed to get their rights into both Democratic and Republican party platforms in 1874. In Utah's Constitutional Convention of 1895, despite strong opposition and the fear that Congress would not accept it, women's suffrage was voted into the Utah constitution by a significant majority. On January 4, 1896, Utah was admitted as the 45th state in the Union.[5]

Statesmen, Leaders and Heroes

There can be no question as to which state is so closely related to a particular individual, and that is Utah. Brigham Young is synonymous with Utah, for having led the members of the Mormon Church away from hostilities in the East to settle in a remote unorganized area of the United States that had been part of Mexico until the Mexican-American War of 1846-1848. Brigham Young was born in Vermont in 1801, and grew up in various upstate New York towns. He was one of 11 children, and his family was a highly moralistic one that exposed him to religion. He had very little formal education and joined the Methodist Church at 23 years old. He supported himself by working in carpentry and painting. In 1830, while living in Mendon, New York, he was introduced to the teachings of the Mormon Church. Their beliefs and practices appealed to him because of their primitivism and Puritanism. He cautiously agreed to be baptized in 1832, but only after other family members agreed to join him. Young soon met the founder of the Mormon Church, Joseph Smith, whom he believed was a man of God. By 1835, Young had completed the preliminary steps before being appointed to the Council of the Twelve Apostles. In 1838, he was charged with leading the Mormons to Illinois after being expelled from Missouri.[6]

As he acquired more leadership responsibilities, he was sent to England in 1840, where he supervised the extensive missionary work in that country. When he returned in 1841, he confirmed his loyalty to Joseph Smith by accepting polygamy. His initial hesitation was short-lived, having eventually married 55 wives and produced 57 children by 16 of the women. In 1844, Smith was assassinated in Illinois, and Young successfully competed to succeed him as the new leader of the Mormon Church. With growing anti-Mormon violence in Illinois, Young organized one of the most successful migrations in American history in 1846-1847. He personally led his flock to the Great Salt Lake Valley and continued to ring many thousands of followers to that area over the next 30 years. He also organized many Mormon communities throughout Utah, Nevada, Idaho, Wyoming, Arizona, and California.[7]

When Utah was declared a territory in 1850, Brigham Young was appointed its first governor. Relations with the federal government steadily deteriorated over the next seven years, especially when the Mormon Church informed the public in 1852 of its practice of polygamy. That issue fueled the friction that burst into flame in 1857, causing President Buchanan to send federal troops to quell the unrest and to replace Young as governor with Alfred Cummings. Negotiations prevented a potentially serious "Utah War," but in 1862 the army was called again to intervene. Congress passed anti-bigamy laws in 1862 and 1874, and Young was held in house arrest for several weeks in 1872 and was jailed in 1875. As a religious leader, Young was not a theologian like Joseph Smith. Young was a serious, no-nonsense organizer and businessman, whose skills were focused on building a Kingdom of God throughout a harsh frontier environment. He later was referred to as the "Mormon Moses," who led his people away from persecution into the desert. In addition to building religious-based communities, he developed several businesses including a wagon express company, a ferryboat company, a railroad, and the manufacture of lumber, wool, iron, and whisky. His greatest wealth came from real estate, and at his death, his estate had an estimated wealth valued at $600,000, which is close to $10 million in today's currency. As successful as he was, events were overtaking Utah's economy. With more mineral discoveries and new railroads bringing more non-Mormon settlers, the once-dominant Mormon influence declined.[8] Brigham Young died in 1877, from a ruptured appendix. His legacy is impressive, and he is credited with settling an enormous part of the American West during the last 30 years of his life. He founded 350 towns in the Southwest and colonized the immense region between the Rocky Mountains and the Sierra Nevada. He also founded the University of Utah. The state of Utah donated a life-size statue of Young to the National Statutory Hall Collection in the national Capitol building. Several large monuments can be seen in Salt Lake City honoring his memory. A newspaper article in 1974 noted that Brigham Young was "one of the outstanding organizers of the 19th century…If the circumstances of his life had worked out differently he might have become a captain of industry…an Andrew Carnegie or John D. Rockefeller or a railroad builder. Instead, this able, energetic, earthy man became the absolute ruler and the revered and genuinely loved father figure of all Mormons everywhere."[9]

Chapter Forty-six

Oklahoma

State on November 16, 1897

Explorers and Settlers

Like most of the southwestern section of North America encompassing the region between the Mississippi River and the Pacific Ocean, the first Europeans to enter there were Spanish explorers in the mid-1500's. The first recorded documentation of Oklahoma was made by Spaniard Hernando de Soto. However, instead of finding the legendary cities of gold, he found the indigenous natives known as Plains Caddoan. Their Caddoan-Mississippi culture had occupied the greater Mississippi Basin for over 600 years prior to his arrival. Other Native Americans who lived there included the Wichita Plains and the Kiowa-Apache cultures. While Spanish explorers like de Soto and Coronado claimed lands they entered for Spain, they did not follow up with strong roots other than missions along the California Coast and in isolated parts of the Southwest, as well as in their key city of New Orleans. When the French-Canadian fur trappers and Jesuit missionaries began their explorations down the Mississippi River in the mid-1600's, they also claimed much of the Mississippi River Valley for France. They were able to build close relationships with the natives, especially through trading agreements but also through social and religious integration, education, and even marriage. Father Marquette and Louis Joliet concentrated on the north-central regions of Ohio, Illinois, and Missouri, while Robert de la Salle claimed all of the Mississippi River and its tributaries for France. It was his work that created the enormous region of the Louisiana Territory, that included Oklahoma which France controlled from 1682 to 1763. However, Oklahoma was so distant that it was not affected by French colonization. The name "Oklahoma" is a Choctaw Indian word meaning "red people."

When France lost the simultaneous Seven Years' War in Europe and the French and Indian War in America to Great Britain, the Treaty of Paris of 1763 required them to cede all their New France colonies and Canada to the British.[1] Unknown to everyone was the Treaty of Fontainebleau in 1762, by which France had given all of its Mississippi River colonies, including New Orleans, to Spain. In 1763, land east of the Mississippi was given to Great Britain, and lands west of the river were controlled by Spain. Spain ceded Florida to Great Britain, and western Louisiana was their compensation. Spain did not really care much about British control of the eastern part of Louisiana, because they wanted the western part, which would serve to consolidate their colonies of New Spain. When the French colonists in western Louisiana learned they were under Spanish authority, they were outraged but were given the opportunity to move to French colonies. After America achieved its independence in 1783, it returned Florida to Spain, thereby giving her control of the Gulf of Mexico from Florida to the Pacific Ocean. The Spanish wanted to control New Orleans, so it did not attempt to colonize Oklahoma. In effect, whether the French or Spanish controlled Oklahoma, it was free from European colonization. This would change in 1803, when Napoleon offered to sell Louisiana's 828,000 square miles to the United States.[2]

The Oklahoma Territory

With the Louisiana Purchase, the size of the United States immediately doubled. All of Oklahoma was included, and it was obvious that the enormous area acquired would result in the formation of future territories, which would eventually become states. In 1890, Congress had passed the Oklahoma Organic Act, which was the first step in the preparation for an Oklahoma Territory. It also was intended to assimilate the Indian tribes in Oklahoma and the Indian territories and to eliminate tribal reservations and communal ownership of property by the tribes. To better understand Oklahoma's evolution, one can start with the Indian Intercourse Act of 1834. That measure gave Native Americans their own lands, partly in exchange for their lands in the Midwest they were forced to vacate. The lands west of the Mississippi River were considered "unorganized territory" but could not be located in Missouri, Louisiana, or Arkansas. The Indian Territory eventually became Oklahoma, except for the Panhandle and Old Greer County. Changes were made after the Civil War, when the United States government proceeded to execute new treaties with those tribes who supported the Confederacy. The Five Civilized Tribes of the Cherokee, Choctaw, Creek, Chickasaw, and Seminole were ordered to free their slaves and offer them citizenship in their tribes if they elected to stay. They then forced the tribes to cede 2,000,000 acres of Indian Territory to so-called "Unassigned Lands," where white settlers were prohibited from entering. Pressure grew to open those lands, but President Hayes issued proclamations in 1879 and 1880 denying entry. Capt. David Payne was a strong advocate for settling in the Unassigned Lands, and he gathered 10,000 followers to settle in the prohibited area east of Oklahoma City, which they named "Ewing." They were immediately arrested by the United States Fourth Cavalry, who took them back to Kansas. Being a civil matter, the military were not allowed to intervene, so the federal government was forced to free them. A few months later, Payne tried to occupy the lands again, but he was arrested and fined for trespassing. In 1884, Payne tried a fourth time and was arrested for bringing whiskey into Indian Territory. The judge ruled it was not a crime to settle on unassigned lands. Payne planned another entry, but he died suddenly and was replaced by Capt. William Couch as the new leader of the "Boomers." They were also known as the "Boomer-Sooners" because of their efforts to enter the run for land sooner than the starting date of April 2, 1889. In December of 1884, Couch and his followers entered the Indian Territory and founded Camp Stillwater. President Arthur sent a small detachment of federal troops to oust them, but when they resisted, the army cut off their food line, which forced them to abandon the area. In 1885, Congress passed the Indian Appropriations Act, allowing negotiations for the cession of unoccupied lands belonging to the Creek, Seminole, and Cherokee. Couch spent the next four years trying to persuade Congress to open the Oklahoma lands. The Creeks were the first to capitulate and offered to sell 3,000,000 acres of their land to the United States. In 1889, Congress provided for the creation of homeland settlements in the Unassigned Lands, which they named the Oklahoma Territory. That same year on March 23rd, President Benjamin Harrison opened an Oklahoma Land Run to start on April 22nd. On the first day, over 50,000 people participated, as well as 14,000 of the Boomers. During the melee of horses, wagons, carts, and vehicles, William Couch was shot and died from his wounds one year later. Many lawsuits were filed due to duplicate claims, and tent cities appeared in Oklahoma City, Kingfisher, El Reno, Norman, Guthrie, and Stillwater, which all became some of Oklahoma's largest cities.[3]

In 1860, Oklahoma's Indian Territory had a population of 55,000 Indians, 8,400 black slaves which were owned by Indians, and 3,000 whites. Confederates signed alliances with all the major tribes, and the United States government withdrew all its forces from the territory. Not all Oklahomans supported the Confederacy thereby creating internal hostilities. In 1863, Union soldiers and their Indian allies defeated the Confederates at Honey Springs and then took control of Fort Smith in nearby Arkansas, ending any chance for them to take over the Oklahoma Territory.[4]

Statehood

In 1890, Congress passed the act to create the Oklahoma Territory for the western half of the Indian Territory while the eastern half stayed under the control of the Five Civilized Nations. The Panhandle, known as "No Man's Land," was included in the Oklahoma Territory. Later that year, the Sac and Fox, Iowa, and Pottawatomie reservations were opened for settlement. The next year, the Arapaho and Cheyenne lands were opened. In 1893, the Cherokee section was opened, and in 1895, the Kickapoo area was available. In 1896, by a decision of the Supreme Court, a portion of Texas was given to the Oklahoma Territory.

Its total size consisted of 24,000,000 acres, of which 1,725,646 acres remained as Indian reservations. The territory existed from 1890 to 1907, and during that time, it started the University of Oklahoma, the University of Central Oklahoma, and Oklahoma State University, but little else happened, as the local government was considered to be in a transitional period in anticipation of statehood. From 1902 to 1905, representatives from the Five Civilized Nations met to compose a constitution. They drew up their Sequoyah Constitution with maps showing the counties that would be created and petitioned Congress for statehood. The referendum in Indian Territory was approved by a wide margin but was not well received by Congress. President Theodore Roosevelt decided that there should be only one Oklahoma and rejected a separate Indian state. However, the Sequoyah Constitution was used at the Oklahoma Constitutional Convention in 1906, and it served as the basis for the constitution of the state of Oklahoma when the two territories were joined in 1907. In their election on September 17, 1907, the state adopted the United States Constitution, and the citizens elected Democrat Charles Haskell as its first governor. Oklahoma was accepted into the Union as the 46th state on November 16, 1907 by President Roosevelt.[5]

Statesmen, Leaders and Heroes

David Payne is considered to be the "Father of Oklahoma." He was born in 1836, in Indiana, was educated at the local public schools, and in his youth worked on the family farm. At age 22, he and his brother left home, and David ended up in Kansas as a scout for the federal government for their expeditions in the West. At the start of the Civil War, Payne joined the 4th Kansas Volunteer infantry and saw action over the next three years in Kansas, Arkansas, Missouri, and in the Cherokee Nation. Upon his return to Kansas, he was elected to the Kansas House of Representatives and served for three different sessions. In 1868, Payne joined the 19th Kansas Cavalry and served as a scout for Gen. Philip Sheridan, against the Indians in the western Great Plains.

As noted earlier in this chapter, when certain tribes sided with the Confederacy in the Civil War, they were punished by Congress and forced to cede over 2,000,000 acres of land in the middle of their Indian Territory, which was prohibited to whites even entering. Newspaper editor Dr. Morrison

Munford of the *Kansas City Times* referred to it as "Unassigned Lands," and the people who wanted it open to the public were named "Boomers." In 1880, Payne and his men entered the prohibited lands and tried to establish the town of Ewing, which was in present-day Oklahoma City. The United States 44th Cavalry arrested them and returned them to Kansas. They protested and were freed on the grounds that the military was not allowed to interfere in a civil manner. Payne tried several more times to return to Ewing, but was arrested and fined. Payne wanted a public trial, and when he tried to reenter the Indian Territory, he was arrested again. He and his followers were marched and dragged for several hundred miles through Cherokee Country to Fort Smith. The army seized his printing equipment and burned his buildings. The action caused a public outcry and forced the government to hold a trial. The United States District Court in Kansas overturned the indictments, stating that entering Unassigned Lands is not a criminal offense. Payne and his Boomers celebrated, but in November of 1884, Payne suddenly died of heart failure at 48 years old. His legacy is being honored as the "Father of Oklahoma." The Unassigned Lands were opened to the public four years after his death.[6]

George Washington Steele was born in 1839, in Fayette County, Indiana. He was educated at the local public schools and earned his law degree at Ohio Wesleyan University. Steele was practicing law when the Civil War erupted in 1861, and he immediately joined the 12th Indiana Regiment. He was later transferred to the 101st Indiana, in which he served until the end of the war. He fought under Maj. Gen. William Sherman in his "March to the Sea," and after the war, he joined the regular army with the rank of major and served until 1876. Upon retiring from the army, he started an agricultural business and became active in local politics. In 1880, he won a Congressional seat from Indiana and was reelected four times. In 1890, the western part of the unorganized territory became the Oklahoma Territory. President Harrison had learned of the chaos there, so he looked for a military man to serve as its first governor and selected George Steele. His first act was to declare a state of emergency. He then vetoed bills to move the capital from Guthrie to Oklahoma City, and then to Kingfisher. His next move was to organize a public-school system and lay the groundwork for two universities. The legislature approved one for Norman and the other for

Stillwater. The first became the University of Oklahoma, and the latter became Oklahoma State University. Steele served only 17 months and was followed by Abraham Jefferson Seay. Steele returned to Indiana and again was elected to the House of Representatives in 1895, where he served for eight years until 1903. In Congress, Steele introduced a bill to establish a Home for Disabled Volunteer Soldiers, which President Grover Cleveland signed in 1888. In 1890, he became the first president of the First National Bank in Marion, Indiana. He also served on the Board of Managers of the National Military Home from 1890 to 1904. He died in 1922 at 83 years old. Although Steele was born and died in Indiana, his legacy is located in Oklahoma, where he founded the public-school system and was instrumental in establishing two of its universities.[7]

William Couch was born in North Carolina in 1850, and in 1865, his family moved to Kansas, where he stayed and married Cynthia Gordon in 1871. He first tried farming, but when the railroad was completed from Emporia to Wichita, he became involved with several businesses, including selling grain, operating a grain elevator, horse trading, and managing a grocery and hardware store. He then experienced several financial setbacks, but continued to receive a steady income from his livestock business. In 1879, he learned about the homestead land in Oklahoma from David Payne, and he soon became a close friend and follower of Payne and the "Boomers." He even contributed funds to the fledgling colony, which earned him a leadership position. In 1883, he led an expedition to the Oklahoma Country after earlier Payne expeditions failed. Couch too was arrested and released. He tried again in 1884 and actually staked a land claim at the future site of the University of Oklahoma. When David Payne unexpectedly died in 1884, Couch became the sole leader of the Boomers, a position he did not desire. In December of that year, Couch entered the Indian Territory and established Camp Stillwater. President Chester Arthur sent a 600-man detachment to remove the Boomers, but they refused to leave. After their food and supply lines were cut, they surrendered and were taken back to Kansas. Congress then passed the Indian Appropriations Act of 1885, which authorized the negotiations for ceding the unoccupied lands of the Creek, Seminole, and Cherokee. Couch spent four years in Washington, D.C., lobbying to open the Oklahoma lands. Within a few weeks, the Indians sold close to 3,000,000 acres to the United States. In 1889, Congress passed another Appropriations Act, opening millions of acres to homesteaders by means of a land run. Over 50,000 people entered the race for free land scheduled for April 22, 1889. Those who attempted entry before that date were called "Sooners," which has become the nickname for Oklahomans to this day. William Couch entered the race, and during the chaos, he staked his claim in present-day Oklahoma City, but he was shot and never lived to receive the title for himself or his wife and children. He died from his wounds one year later in April of 1890. Five thousand mourners attended the funeral of their hero. His close friend, the Honorable Sidney Clarke eulogized Couch with an eloquent and heart-rending message, the last lines of which are: "…Brave, generous, heroic friend! Noble in life, true to duty and humanity, what a sublime lesson you have left to us, and to those who live after us in the presence of death! We enroll your name with the heroes of this age and of all the ages who have dared to suffer and to die for principle, for friends, for country, for the good of their fellow man."[8]

Chapter Forty-seven

New Mexico

State on January 6, 1912

Explorers and Settlers

The first Europeans to enter New Mexico were Spanish Conquistadors in the early 16th century. At that time, Spain ruled New Mexico, and from that base, they explored north beyond the Rio Grande River in search of gold. Their first major expedition was led by Panfilo de Narvaez in 1527, but only four men survived to tell of the rumored fortunes that lie ahead somewhere in the New Mexico region that was identified as the "Seven Cities of Cibola (gold)." In 1540, Francisco de Coronado organized a large expedition to find the legendary cities, and he travelled through New Mexico to central Kansas without success. He did encounter the Pueblo who lived on that region since the 13th century, but the Spaniards badly mistreated them, thereby preventing colonization there for hundreds of years. Juan de Onate led 500 Spanish soldiers and settlers to found the first Spanish settlement in New Mexico in 1598, 50 years after Coronado.

He named it San Juan de Los Caballeros. He then built a 700-mile trail from New Spain to his colony. Onate was appointed the first governor of the new Province of Santa Fe de Nuevo Mexico. After constant attacks on San Juan, he moved the capital to Santa Fe in 1610, thereby making it the oldest capital city in the United States.[1]

Like the Catholic French-Canadians in the Midwest, the Spanish also brought missionaries to their New Spain colonies. However, the Franciscan missionaries had little success in converting the Pueblo in New Mexico. This could be contributed to the internal conflicts between the Spanish governors, civil authorities, and the missionaries. The former acquired a reputation for exploiting the natives for their own personal wealth. They used the Pueblo for labor, slavery, and the sale of Indian products made with slave labor. The Franciscans also used Pueblo labor and competed with the local government to control them, but they did not have the same desire for personal gain. The friction came to a head in 1650, when Governor Bernardo de Mendizabel and his assistant Nicolas Aguilar prohibited the missionaries from punishing the Indians or employing them without pay. When they also allowed the natives to engage in their religious practices, the missionaries protested and had them arrested and sent to the Inquisition in Mexico City. Afterwards, the Franciscans ruled the natives, which led to their revolt in 1680. Some historians attribute the Indian conflicts to the missionaries. There seems to have been little or no integration between the Spanish and the natives, and unlike the French and Indian fur traders, there was little economic basis for mutual gain or trust. The Spanish were unable to rule the Pueblo, who were the first tribe to challenge them. Other factors were the European diseases that decimated the natives, as well as the severe drought that hit the region in the 1670's. The Pueblo lost what little faith they harbored in the Spanish government and the Catholic Church to protect them. Further conversion efforts by the missionaries only created more resentment from not being able to practice their traditional ceremonies. In 1680, under their charismatic leader Pope (pronounced "po-pay"), the Pueblo drove the Spanish out of most of New Mexico. They destroyed all crosses and vestiges of the Catholic Church. Even Catholic marriages were voided and Spanish crops were destroyed and discontinued. However, internal power struggles among the scattered and distant Pueblo tribes eventually weakened them. In 1692, Diego de Vargas led Spanish forces to confront the Indian rulers in Santa Fe. He made them swear allegiance to the king of Spain and granted them clemency in exchange for peace. Santa Fe remained as a trading center, but in 1706, settlers founded Albuquerque along the lower Rio Grande. The Spanish then ruled more successfully and gave land grants to each Pueblo and passed laws to protect their rights.[2]

Following the Pueblo were the Comanche, who terrorized the Spanish colonies and became the dominant tribe in the Southwest. Historian Hamalainen refers to it as "Comacherin," or the "Comanche Empire." They built a military force by obtaining arms from the Americans, Mexicans, and other Indian tribes, through trade and a sophisticated commercial network. They spread their culture throughout the Southwest and developed their own political system. Their economy was based on raiding the Spanish colonies and other tribes as well. The Comanche were nomads who were nimble, elusive, and violent. Much of their dominance was due to their raiding the colony for horses and breeding them. In 1778, they killed 127 Spanish settlers and Pueblo, which prompted the Spanish to send 500 soldiers to Pueblo, Colorado to kill the Comanche war leader. The battle brought peace to New Mexico, until the United States won the territory in the Mexican-American War in 1846-1848. It was the smallpox and cholera that finally destroyed the Comanche. Their population declined from 20,000 in the mid-18th century to 1,500 by 1875. They were no longer strong enough to face the United States army and the growing number of white settlers.[3]

Mexican Independence

In 1810, a Catholic priest named Miguel Hidalgo started the movement for Mexico's independence in Central Mexico. He and his countrymen wanted independence, redistribution of land, and racial equality. The next year, Captain Los Casas in the Spanish military attempted a coup in support of the revolutionaries, but he was arrested and executed. The central authorities in Mexico could not achieve effective control, but it was Napoleon's occupation of Spain that prompted revolts in Spanish America. Hidalgo, Jose Morelos, Mariano Matamoros, and Vicente Guerrero all fought the Spanish and the

Royalists but were unsuccessful. Surprisingly, it was the Royalists in 1821 who achieved Mexican independence under Agustin de Iturbide. He established an independent constitutional monarchy, maintained the position of the Catholic Church and achieved equality of Mexicans of Spanish descent with the Spaniards. In 1821, Mexico achieved independence with the Treaty of Cordoba, and Iturbide was proclaimed emperor. In 1823, republican leaders deposed Iturbide and established a republic with Guadalupe Victoria as the first president.[4]

By the mid-1830's, the republican system failed, and a new more centralist constitution was drafted. Mexico drifted away from their national concepts and embraced despotism. In 1835, Texas declared its own independence, and in 1837, a revolt in New Mexico executed its appointed governor and demanded its own authority. As central Mexico fell into chaos, New Mexico moved economically closer to the United States. By 1845, most New Mexicans had grown to distrust the central government. Rumors spread that Mexico was planning to sell the New Mexico Territory to the United States. Although false, New Mexico's leaders drafted a secession document from their central government. In August of 1846, the United States invaded New Mexico.[5]

At the beginning of the Mexican-American War, Gen. Stephen Kearny marched his 2,400 men into Santa Fe to establish law and order with a joint civil and military government. He then appointed Col. Sterling Price as military governor to maintain order in Santa Fe. Other officers were sent to California to control the area from Sacramento to San Diego and also to the Arizona area that was still a part of New Mexico. Kearny encountered no resistance in New Mexico, and the Mexican authorities peaceably returned to Mexico. The Provincial governor Charles Bent pleaded with the American officers to respect the rights of local citizens, and while General Kearny ruled fairly with his highly regarded "Kearny Code," abuses appeared and resentments festered. In January of 1847, local New Mexicans and some Pueblo allies initiated their "Taos Revolt." They killed Governor Bent and ten other local officials. Colonel Price soon arrived and attacked the rebels, killing 150 men and capturing 400 others. He fought in four separate battles before bringing the area under control. Courts were assembled, and six rebels were convicted of treason and hanged.[6]

Treaty of Guadalupe Hidalgo

The treaty ending the Mexican-American War in 1848 did much to shape present-day United States. Most of California and the American Southwest were ceded by Mexico in exchange for removal of American forces in Mexico City, the recognition that Texas was part of the United States, and the American assumption of $15 million of debt owed by Mexico. Residents of the affected lands could choose to remain as citizens of the United States or return to Mexico and seek citizenship. Only 1,000 people decided to leave, and those who remained became American citizens with full voting rights. Also, Texas gave up eastern New Mexico to the United States, thereby settling a long-standing border dispute.

Territorial New Mexico

The Compromise of 1850 was a comprehensive measure that dealt with new territories and slavery. In September of 1850, the New Mexico Territory was established by Congress. The new territory included all of Arizona, New Mexico, and parts of southern Colorado, and its capital remained in Santa Fe. At that time, its total population was 61,547. The citizens were allowed to decide for themselves whether to choose slavery or not, but this only applied to their status as a territory. Statehood would be another matter. Congress was deeply divided on the issue, with such notables as Stephen Douglas arguing for slavery under the Missouri Compromise and Abraham Lincoln arguing against slavery under the old Mexican traditions of prohibiting slavery. The Gadsden Purchase of 1853 involved a 29,670-square-mile tract of land at the southern border of Arizona and New Mexico. It cost $10 million ($270 million today) and was the last piece of land acquired in the contiguous United States. The purpose was to construct a transcontinental railroad below the Gila River and west of the Rio Grande and to settle border disputes between the United States and Mexico. The United States was eager to build trade to the Pacific and with the newly acquired regions of California, Nevada, Utah, Arizona, New Mexico, and Colorado. A more northerly route would be too mountainous and costly. The Southern Pacific Railway Company completed the line in 1883.[7]

The next event affecting New Mexico's territory was the removal of lands to create the Colorado Territory in 1861. In 1863, all land west of the 109th meridian was taken from New Mexico to create the Arizona Territory, and it included all of present-day Arizona plus land that would be added to the southern part of Nevada in 1864. That left New Mexico with its present-day boundaries. When the Civil War broke out in 1861, New Mexico was in a disputed area, where southern sections joined with the Confederacy and created the Confederate Territory of Arizona and sent a representative to the Confederate capital in Richmond, Virginia. With the Battle of Glorietta Pass in 1862, the Union army took control of Santa Fe, but the government of the Confederate Arizona Territory remained until the end of the war in 1865.[8]

Road to Statehood

The road to statehood for New Mexico was a long, arduous, and frustrating adventure that met with many obstacles. Some of the roadblocks were internal like cultural differences, poor education, and having a predominantly Catholic population and Spanish as the major language. Outside barriers were the slave issue, land boundaries, remoteness, the Civil War, Indian hostilities, and a poorly disguised prejudice toward another culture that was distinctly different from the rest of America. When the Treaty of Guadalupe Hidalgo was signed in 1848, it promised statehood "at the proper time," but generations passed for 64 years before that time would arrive. The difficulties began from the very beginning, with the Mexican-American War and the annexation of land resulting from the war. The Hispanic and Indian people resented the American army presence and the abuses that inevitably erupted under martial law. Raids by the surrounding Apache, Navajo, and Pueblo were eventually brought under control by Col. Sterling Price, but the tensions remained. Politically, Washington, D.C. had a distrust of New Mexico's culture. In 1850, the citizens drafted a constitution which was approved by a vote of 8,371 to 39, but the New Mexican acceptance of slavery prevented Congress from pursuing the subject of statehood. Religion was an essential part of life for Spanish Catholic New Mexico. However, this was not easily accepted by a Protestant Congress and the Midwestern and Eastern population. The citizens of New Mexico were divided on whether to become a state or to remain a territory. Taxes and administrative costs were debated over a long period of time. Congress considered the matter on six separate occasions and came very close on two of them. New Mexicans themselves weakened their cause in 1866, when a quorum couldn't be reached in a call for a constitutional convention. Again, in 1890, voters declined a proposed constitution by 2:1. The real problem seemed to have been a lack of unity among the politicians and their constituents.

By the year 1900, New Mexico's population reached 200,000, and a good number of railroads were serving most of the area. Other neighboring states came into or were about to enter the Union like Oklahoma, Utah, and Arizona. In 1905, Congress considered a bill to combine New Mexico with Arizona that would be named "Montezuma." It was pointed out that the two territories contained different cultures and were separated by a mountain range. In 1906, the two territories would be called Arizona. Voters in New Mexico approved the referendum, but Arizona rejected it. By 1910, the population of New Mexico reached 327,301, and it contained a dozen railroads. Pressure was building for statehood, and even President William Howard Taft toured the territory. Both New Mexico and Arizona adopted new constitutions, and in 1911, President Taft signed a bill promoting statehood for each of them. On January 6, 1912, New Mexico became the 47th state, and Arizona joined the next month.[9]

Statesmen, Leaders and Heroes

San Juan Pope (pronounced "po-pay") was a Pueblo religious leader who was born in New Mexico in 1630. At the time of his birth, his people numbered between 40,000 and 80,000, from many towns and speaking many different languages and dialects. The Pueblo were subjected to many abuses by Spanish rulers, soldiers, priests, and Mexican Indian allies. They suffered from violence, forced labor, suppression of their religious practices, illness, and death from European diseases that decimated their population to 15,000 by the late 1600's. In 1675, Pope was arrested for witchcraft and was sentenced to be sold into slavery. Local Pueblo begged for his release, which was granted only because the governor did not want to risk the Pueblo from joining the Apache and Navajo who were attacking the Spanish settlements at Santa Fe. Upon his release, he moved to Taos, where he planned a major revolt to destroy the Spanish. He met with the leaders of the many different Pueblo tribes, who all agreed to rise up on August 13, 1680. When the Spanish authorities in Santa Fe learned of the revolt, they took refuge in the governor's palace, before Pope arrived with his warriors that totaled between 1,000 and 2,500. On August 21st, the Spanish broke out and marched south until they reached El Paso, Texas. The rebels did not harm the 2,000 survivors on their retreat, but the Spanish sustained 400 dead. Pope succeeded in removing the Spanish from New Mexico, and as the new leader, he went about destroying all vestiges of Spanish culture and religion. In 1681 and again in 1687, Spanish forces tried to reenter New Mexico but were repelled. However, Apache and Navajo resumed their raids, and old internal Pueblo rivalries returned. Pope lost his popularity and was regarded as a tyrant. The Pueblo once again could not remain united. Pope died in 1688, and in 1692, the Spanish Governor Diego de Vargas led an army of 150 men to retake New Mexico. He granted the citizens a pardon, and the Spanish again ruled, even though animosities continued. Conditions for the Pueblo improved, and forced labor was abolished. Franciscan priests no longer interfered with Pueblo ceremonies, and their warriors united with the Spanish soldiers to fight their common enemies, which were the Apache, Navajo, and Comanche.

Pope was finally recognized in 2005 by New Mexico for his bravery and leadership, when his statue was included in the National Statuary Hall Collection in the nation's capital. The local Pueblo consider him a great hero who saved their cultural identity.[10]

Christopher "Kit" Carson was born in 1809, in Kentucky. His father was a farmer who had fought in the American Revolutionary War and the War of 1812. The family moved to Missouri when Kit was one year old and settled on land owned by Daniel Boone's sons. The Carsons and Boones became life-long friends through socializing and intermarriage. At that time, Missouri was on the western frontier, where Indian attacks were so frequent that most cabins had stockade fences and armed sentries stationed around the fields. His father died when Kit was eight, and his mother remarried. Kit and his stepfather were not compatible, so he was apprenticed to a saddler in Franklin, Missouri when he was a teenager. Located at the beginning of the recently opened Santa Fe Trail, young Kit learned from the trappers and traders many tales of the West, which lured him to run away with them in 1826 when he settled in Taos. Living with explorers and trappers, he learned frontier skills and became fluent in Spanish and several Indian languages. Carson became a "Mountain Man" for 12 years and met notable men like Jim Bridger, Bill Williams, and Ewing Young. At the age of 21, he went on an expedition with Young into Apache country by the Gila River in southwest New Mexico, where he experienced an Apache attack. He survived and went on to explore and trap in California, from Sacramento to Los Angeles. He spent the next ten years building a reputation as a good fighter and reliable explorer and trapper. In 1841, as the beaver trade was in decline, Carson was hired to hunt buffalo, deer, and antelope to feed people at Bent's Fort in Colorado, in return for pay of $1.00 per day. In his memoirs, he wrote of many encounters with hostile Indians like the Crow and Blackfeet. During this period, he had little regard for Indian warriors who threatened his life and his livelihood. As he matured and spent more time with them, he grew more mature and made sure that those under his care were treated honestly and fairly, clothed and fed. Some attribute his changed attitude followed his first marriage to an Arapaho woman. In 1842, Carson met John Fremont, who was on his way to do some engineering work in the West for the United States army. He hired Carson as a guide for $100 per month, which was the best pay he ever received in his life. Carson guided Fremont over the Oregon Trail to Wyoming. The purpose of the work was to produce a guidebook with maps and descriptions for future settlers going to the South Pass through the Rockies. The printed reports became widespread and gave Carson national exposure and notoriety. In 1843, Carson guided Fremont to the Columbia River in Oregon. Along the way, they entered the Great Salt Lake and California, which was then owned by Mexico. Those reports made them both even more popular, and Freemont was promoted to captain in the United States army and earned the nickname of "The Pathfinder."[11]

Carson's third and final trip with Fremont was completely different from the others. They went to California in 1845 to visit the American settlers under the guise of doing scientific work. Fremont could have been sent by President Polk to gain support for his ambitions to take California from Mexico. The men were ordered to leave by the Mexican government, so they moved on to Klamath Lake in southern Oregon. On March 16, 1846, they were attacked by 20 Indians, and three of Carson's men were killed. He was so outraged by this, that he mutilated a dead Indian. He and Fremont then retaliated by attacking a Klamath Indian camp, where they massacred men, women, and children. In 1846, Fremont and Carson joined local settlers in an uprising against Mexico to be free of Mexican rule. Mexico ordered all Americans to leave, but they chose to stay and fight in what came to be known as the "Bear Flag Revolt." Fremont became the military governor, and Carson undertook three dangerous trips to Washington, D.C. with messages and reports. One of Carson's most daring feats was in 1846, when he was ordered to guide General Kearny and his men from Socorro, New Mexico to San Diego, California. Kearny was ambushed 25 miles from San Diego and was surrounded with no chance for survival. Carson slipped away, and losing his shoes, he walked across the desert's prickly pear and rocks with bare feet to get reinforcements from San Diego. They arrived the next morning to save Kearny and his troops.[12]

During the Civil War Carson joined the Union army as a lieutenant. He initially trained men, and then in 1863, his commanding officer, Gen. James Carleton, ordered Carson to round up the Apache and Navajo for transport to their reservations. By this time, Carson was tired and not eager to carry out the assignment. In 1864, he did manage to gather close to 8,000 Navajo, and when he witnessed them suffering from cold and hunger, he got them food and clothing for their famous "Long Walk of the Navajo" to Bosque Redondo. In 1868, they signed a treaty with the Navajo, who were allowed to return to their homeland. As the Civil War was ending, Carson was promoted to brevet brigadier general and was sent to command Fort Garland in Colorado. He retired from the army and settled into ranching and helping the Ute tribe by representing them in Washington, D.C. When he returned home, his wife died, and then he died a month later on May 23, 1868, from an abdominal aneurysm. His legacies include his Taos home as a museum; a monument in the Santa Fe Plaza; a statue in Denver and another in Trinidad, Colorado; a national forest in New Mexico; a county in Colorado; a river in Nevada; and Carson City, which is the capital of Nevada. Carson's reputation changed over the years from being a genuine hero to one of being a racist, thoughtless Indian killer. While he did kill many Apache and Navajo, he has been remembered as a champion of the Ute. His biographer Harvey Carter maintained that Carson was not overrated and that he deserves the admiration of later generations. He believed that he had more good qualities and fewer of the bad qualities of the men in his generation.[13]

Chapter Forty-eight

Arizona

State on February 14, 1912

Explorers and Settlers

The first Europeans to settle the American Southwest were Spanish Conquistadors, who occupied the region during the 15th, 16th, and 17th centuries. Their purpose was to seek personal fortune with little regard for the natives who had lived there for thousands of years. They frequently brought missionaries with them, whose goal was to preach Christianity and to convert as many natives as possible to the Catholic Church. Their motivation was for the glory of God, but both groups managed to destroy ancient cultures and to displace and decimate many Indian tribes. Thousands of natives died by the sword or gun, and many thousands more perished from diseases for which they had no natural immunization. One of the driving forces for the explorers was to find the legendary Seven Cities of Cibola, which were rumored to be made of gold. Arizona was thought to be a possible location of Cibola, but in spite of expeditions throughout the region including New Mexico, Texas, Oklahoma, and Kansas, the city was never found. Other Spanish explorers who are given credit for being among the first to enter Arizona were Marcos de Niza in 1539 and Coronado in 1540 in his quest to find Cibola.[1]

The first recorded account of the search for gold in America was made in 1527 by Panfilo de Narvaez and his assistant Alvar Nunez Cabeza de Vaca. Their destination from Spain was Florida, and when they returned home, de Vaca recorded their adventures. Their first stop was in Cuba, where the governor was a cousin to Narvaez, who authorized the explorers to conquer the lands between the Cape of Florida and the Rio Grande. The party consisted of 600 men, and they split into two groups, with one proceeding by land and the other by water. After shipwrecks, Indian attacks, starvation, and desertions, the expedition was doomed. The last 40 survivors were shipwrecked at Galveston, Texas, where they became laborers for the local tribes. Many tried to escape but died from starvation. Within the year, only four of the original 600 men survived including de Vaca. He reached the Brazos and Colorado Rivers and was befriended by some natives, who regarded him as a religious healer. His reports mentioned gifts he received of copper and metal riches. He mentioned "signs of gold" in the mountainous areas. He appears to have reached southern Arizona and New Mexico and wrote about the Pueblo dwelling made of earth. He also received beads of coral and arrow points of emerald. When de Vaca reached the Pacific, he was introduced to the Spanish viceroy and reported his findings, which prompted expeditions to the north of Mexico into a region which today we call Arizona. It is not certain when the name "Arizona" was first adopted, and historians disagree on its origins. Most do agree that it derives from the O'odham language, which refers to an area of Arizona called "Ali-Shonak" or "Aleh-zon," which translates to "small spring." Another theory is that the name comes from a Basque word that means "the good oak tree." The area referred to is at the border of southern Arizona and northern Mexico. It was called "Arissona," "Arisona," or "Arizona," which was occupied by Basque settlers. The name of Arizona has been referred to in Basque settlements well beyond the O'odham tribe, which lends credibility to this theory.[2]

Territorial Arizona

When Mexico acquired its independence from Spain in 1821, it took ownership of the New Spain State of Sonora, which was later to become part of the New Mexico Territory. With the Treaty of Guadalupe Hidalgo in 1848 ending the Mexican-American War, Mexico ceded their New Mexico Territory to the United States. For two years, that area was not organized, and it was the Compromise of 1850 concerning slavery that also assured the future territorial status of the Territory of New Mexico. At that time, it consisted of present-day New Mexico, Arizona, and part of Colorado. The next major change occurred in 1853 with the Gadsden Purchase. It was President Franklin Pierce who sent the American Minister to Mexico, James Gadsden, to Mexico to purchase land along the northern border of Mexico for the purpose of constructing a transcontinental railroad across the southern New Mexico (including Arizona) border. It consisted of 30,000 square miles for $10 million and avoided a costly mountainous route north of the Gila River. Another purpose was to settle a boundary dispute with Mexico and the United States, between the Rio Grande and the Colorado Rivers. The additional land was the future site of Tucson, and the area just north of the Gila River became the metropolitan area of Phoenix, Scottsdale, Mesa, Glendale, and Tempe, Arizona.[3]

At the start of the American Civil War in March of 1861, the citizens of southern New Mexico sided with the Confederacy. One year later, Union troops from California captured the Confederate Territory of Arizona, which was the southern region of New Mexico including Arizona, and returned it to the northern section of the American Territory of New Mexico, including Arizona. In 1863, Congress divided the New Mexico Territory in half on a north-south axis and created the Arizona Territory from New Mexico's western lands. Starting in 1851, the United States army built forts to protect the settlers from Indian attacks, with Fort Defiance as the first. In 1860, one thousand Apache warriors attacked the fort and were defeated. The fort was closed during the Civil War and was reopened in 1864 by Col. Kit Carson, who forced the Navajo on their famous "Long Walk" to their reservation. In 1870, the next significant fort was Fort Apache, built on the Indian reservation. It functioned for 54 years until 1924, when the Native Americans became full United States citizens. Fort

Huachuca was built in 1877, east of Tucson, and it has remained in operation since then and now serves as the United States Army Intelligence Center.[4]

After the Gadsden Purchase enlarged the New Mexico Territory, discussions began in earnest for reducing its size to a more manageable level. The initial efforts to create another territory in the southern part of New Mexico were held in Tucson in 1856 and 1857. The proposed bills were defeated by Congress, which did not want to see another slave territory like New Mexico. They also feared that a southern territory with an east-west boundary across the middle of New Mexico and Arizona would dominate both the northern and southern territories. This fear was proven accurate in 1861, when the southern parts supported the Confederacy and created the Confederate State of Arizona. In 1858, the New Mexico Territory Legislature approved the move to authorize the Arizona Territory by dividing New Mexico with a north-south line from the center, thereby creating two territories of equal size at the 107th meridian. President Lincoln signed the bill creating the Arizona Territory on February 24, 1863. In 1864, the first capital was Prescott in central Arizona because of a nearby gold discovery. Three years later, a small section of northwestern Arizona was transferred to Nevada to incorporate Las Vegas into Nevada. In 1867, the capital was moved to Tucson, and in 1869, it was moved to Phoenix because of concerns about the large Spanish population in Tucson.

Road to Statehood

Arizona waited 49 years to be admitted to the Union. In 1891, they wrote the prerequisite constitution and took it with them to present to Congress, only to be shocked when it was rejected. In 1910, President Taft signed the Enabling Act, which allowed Arizona to write a new constitution and begin the process to statehood. In Phoenix, 52 delegates met with 41 Democrats who supported progressive legislation favoring labor unions but rejecting women suffrage and segregated schools. They supported the right to petition the government, the right for a referendum, and the right of voters to recall judges who were deemed unfit. The last issue was toxic, and they were warned that President Taft was not in favor of judicial recall. The convention approved the progressive constitution by a vote of 12,534 in favor and 3,720 against. However, President Taft held firm and vetoed the Arizona constitution. The local leaders realized they had to withdraw the recall provision, so they sent the amended constitution to the voters in December of 1911, who approved the document by an even larger margin than the previous version. President Taft signed the bill on February 14, 1912, admitting Arizona as the 48th state and the last state to be formed in the contiguous United States. In their first elections after statehood, Arizona amended their constitution to allow the recall of judges and granted women the right to vote.[5]

Statesmen, Leaders and Heroes

Charles Poston is considered the "Father of Arizona." He was born in Elizabethtown, Kentucky, in 1825, and was educated at the local public schools. When he was orphaned at the age of 12, he was apprenticed to the local county clerk, and moving to Tennessee, he clerked for the Tennessee Supreme Court while studying the law. In 1851, he was lured by the California gold rush and took a job at the San Francisco Custom House. While there, he met some French bankers who wanted to purchase land that Mexico was planning to sell to the United States under the Gadsden Purchase. Poston joined mining engineer Herman Ehrenberg on an expedition to the Gila River and met the commander of Fort Yuma. He soon bought land a mile below the fort in Colorado City for an undisclosed sum and sold it for $20,000 a short time later when he went back to San Francisco. He returned to the East Coast in search of capital to start a mining company. In 1856, Poston and his friend, the Fort Yuma Comm. Maj. Samuel Heintzelman, secured $2 million and founded the Sonora Exploring and Mining Company with headquarters in Tubac, Arizona. For five years, that operation produced $3,000 per day in silver until the Civil War began in 1861. When Union troops were withdrawn, the Apache intensified their attacks, forcing the closing of the mines and settlement.

Poston then moved to Washington, D.C. to work as a civilian aide to General Heintzelman. It was at this time that Poston lobbied Congress and President Lincoln to create an Arizona Territory, emphasizing its mineral wealth. In 1863, President Lincoln signed the Arizona Organic Act, and Poston was appointed the Superintendent of Indian Affairs. The next year, he was elected as the delegate to the United States House of Representatives. His major job was to settle land claims and establish Indian reservations along the Colorado River. After losing his Congressional seat in 1866, Poston travelled in Europe, China, and India, studying their cultures and writing books and serving as editor for the New York Tribune. He returned to America in 1876 and worked as a presidential campaign manager for Samuel Tilden. For the last 26 years of his life, he supported himself as a writer, speaker, and promoter of mining and railroads and as an employee of the United States Geological Survey. When his poor financial condition became known, the Arizona Territorial Legislature awarded him $25.00 per month. He died of heart failure in 1902 and was buried in a pauper's grave. In 1925, his remains were moved to his beloved Primrose Hill in Florence, Arizona, which was his last wish. The monument is a white pyramid, and the area was renamed "Poston's Butte."[6]

George W. P. Hunt was born in 1859, in the town of Huntsville, Missouri, which was named in honor of his grandfather. At the age of 19, he ran away from home and supported himself as a waiter, a mine mucker, a rancher, and a clerk in a general store. When that store was bought by a much larger company, Hunt stayed on and eventually was appointed president of the company. In 1890, he entered politics but lost his bid for Recorder of Gila County. In 1892 and 1899, he won a seat for the Territorial House of Representatives. He then was elected to the upper house called the Council in 1896. The next year, he sponsored a bill requiring children aged eight to 14 to attend a minimum of 12 weeks a year in school. He was reelected to the Council in 1898, briefly retired, and then was reelected in 1894, 1906, and 1908. He successfully sponsored other bills that introduced primary elections and outlawing gambling in the territory. At Arizona's Constitutional Convention, Hunt presided as president, and he supported initiative, recall, and referendum, which were progressive planks of the Democratic Party. In 1911, he was elected to become the first governor of the new state of Arizona when it was admitted in February of 1912. Governor Hunt immediately went to work promoting workers' compensation and old age pensions. In 1914, Hunt was reelected governor and was faced with border conflicts resulting from the Mexican Revolution. Mexico actually attacked Naco, Arizona, and Secretary of War Linley Garrison had to restrain

Hunt from sending his national guard to allow the United States army to settle the matter. In 1916, Hunt lost his bid for reelection to the governorship by 30 votes to Thomas Campbell, but he contested the outcome, claiming there was fraudulent voting. The Arizona Supreme Court confirmed Campbell's victory, but in December of 1917, the Court reversed its decision and declared Hunt the winner by 43 votes. Hunt retired from the governorship in 1919 and was soon appointed United States Minister to Siam in May of 1920. When he returned, he ran for governor and was reelected in 1923 for six consecutive years.[7] The major issue he faced was the water rights affecting seven states in the Southwest, including Colorado, Utah, Wyoming, New Mexico, Arizona, and California. The "Colorado River Compact" provided for an even distribution of water from the Colorado River to all seven states, as well as provisions for future water projects such as Hoover Dam and Lake Powell. Governor Hunt opposed the Compact, believing it gave California an "unfair share of Arizona's birthright." Hunt became the target of jokes. During his fifth term as governor, he was called "George V." Comedian Will Rogers said he wanted to be adopted by Hunt so he could inherit the governorship. Pundits claimed that while Jesus walked on water, Hunt ran on the Colorado River.[8] Hunt was reelected in 1930 for his seventh term. He died of a heart attack in 1934 and was buried in a white pyramid in Papago Park in Phoenix.

Chapter Forty-nine

ALASKA

State on January 3, 1959

Explorers and Settlers

Although Alaska is sparsely populated and has been part of the United States for a relatively brief period, it is most likely the place where North America was first settled thousands of years ago. Many historians believe Paleolithic people migrated from Asia across a Bering Land Bridge around 15,000 B.C. and settled in the southeastern coastal region. Sometime between 500 and 1,000 A.D., the Indian tribal groups made their appearance and included the Tlingit, Haida, Tsimshian, Athabascans, and Aleut. Other groups of natives who settled into central Alaska were the Eskimo tribes of Inupiat and Yup'ik. The name "Alaska" is an Aleut Indian name which translates to "object toward which the action of the sea is directed" or more simply "mainland." Spanish explorers in the 1770's and 1780's made claims for Spain, but they never colonized Alaska with forts and settlements. In fact, they visited some Aleutian Islands, where they met Russian fur traders in the first permanent white settlement at Three

Saints Bay on Kodiak Island. The man credited with establishing the first non-native settlements there and at Cook Inlet was Grigory Ivanovich Shelikhov in the 1780's. He was the founder and co-owner of the first major fur company in Alaska, the Shelikhov-Golikov Company. British explorer James Shields was employed by that company and carried out important surveillance for them in the 1790's. However, it was Alexander Baranov in the 1790's who managed the operation and also sailed into Sitka Sound, claiming the area for Russia. Known as the "Lord of Alaska," Baranov also founded the settlement of New Archangel, which became the colonial capital of Russian America. After the purchase of Alaska by the United States in 1867, it was renamed Sitka and remained as the territorial capital.[1]

The British were not far behind the Spanish when Capt. James Cook sailed three expeditions starting in the 1770's along the west coast of North America from California up to Bering Strait. It was during his final trip that he discovered the passageway that later was named Cook Inlet in his honor by George Vancouver in 1794. The Cook and Vancouver explorations prompted the British to establish a greater presence in the Pacific Northwest. In 1799, Shelikhov's son-in-law Nikolay Rezanov formed the Russian-American Company to compete with the British Hudson's Bay Company and hired Alexander Baranov to manage the operation in 1804. In 1818, management was turned over to the Russian navy. In 1825, the Anglo-Russian Convention permitted the British to trade in Alaska, thereby putting further pressure on the Russian-American Company. In 1833, the Hudson's Bay Company built another operation on the edge of Russian America, which competed strongly with the Russians and contributed to their willingness to sell their colony 30 years later. Actually, it was a combination of several issues that brought about the sale: 1) Russia was experiencing financial problems; 2) Russia did not want Britain to control Alaska; 3) trade was declining and profitability of the trading posts was low; 4) there was continuing hostility and harassment from the Indians; and 5) Russia feared that the region eventually would be overrun by American settlers and lost without any compensation.[2]

From the American perspective, Secretary of State William Seward long held the belief that Alaska someday would be part of the United States. When he learned at the end of the Civil War that Russian America might be for sale, he urged President Johnson to pursue the matter. Seward was given the authority to negotiate the purchase, and when the Russian minister Baron Eduard de Stoeckl returned from home leave in 1867, he strongly suggested that his government sell the colony. Seward made the first offer of $5 million, and following some negotiations, the two men settled at $7 million on March 15, 1867. Some Russians still had some concerns, so Seward sweetened the offer to $7.2 million, and it was signed on March 30, 1867.[3] The purchase was not popular and was soon referred to as "Seward's Folly." However, when gold and oil were discovered there in the late 1800's, Seward was vindicated, and his acquisition was considered brilliant and Seward's greatest achievement.

Road to Statehood

Alaska at that time was unique in that it went through different stages of organization before the granting of territorial status. At the time of purchase, very little was known about the vast wilderness the country had just bought. Congress created the Department of Alaska and placed it in the hands of the United States army from 1867 to 1877, when it was transferred to the Department of the Treasury for two years and then switched to the United States navy from 1879 to 1884. All three supervisory groups conducted surveys, drew maps, and collected data. In 1884, Congress changed the name from Department to District of Alaska. Little happened until 1896, when gold was discovered in the Yukon Territory of Canada. The most direct path to the goldfields was through Alaska, which brought speculators, miners, and settlers who started new towns. In 1899, gold was found in Nome, Alaska, which resulted in more new towns like Fairbanks and Ruby. In 1902, they began to build the Alaska Railroad, which was to run from Fairbanks to Seward by 1914. Highways were built to connect to the Pacific Northwest, which contributed to the start of several industries like copper mining, fishing, and canning. The latter were instrumental in the canning of cod, herring, and salmon from the Aleutian Islands. Finally, in 1912, Congress passed the Second Organic Act of Alaska, thereby reorganizing it into the Territory of Alaska. With a population of 58,000 in 1916, a statehood bill was introduced but failed primarily because of little interest by the Alaskans. The Great Depression of the 1930's severely impacted Alaska's economy. Their key exports of fish and copper declined with falling prices and rising unemployment. President Roosevelt supported measures to entice settlers in the northern states like Michigan, Wisconsin, and Minnesota to move to Alaska to develop an agricultural industry, but he had little success. It was the aircraft industry that brought an influx of workers and some economic stability. In the early 1900's, many in Congress were concerned that Alaska was too distant and economically fragile to ever become a viable state. That attitude changed dramatically with the bombing of Alaska by the Japanese in World War II and the discovery of oil at the Swanson River in 1957. In June of 1942, the Japanese invaded and occupied the Aleutian Islands of Attu and Kiska. They captured the villagers and imprisoned them in Japan until the end of the war. Many died and starved there due to poor health care, food, and shelter. The United States army retook the two islands in 1943 and sustained casualties of 3,929 soldiers killed, wounded, diseased, or injured. The invasion and occupation of America's homeland did affect how Washington viewed the strategic importance of Alaska. President Eisenhower signed the Alaska Statehood Act in 1958, and Alaska was admitted to the Union on January 3, 1959 as the 49th state.[4]

Statesmen, Leaders and Heroes

Alexander Baranov was born in 1757 in St. Petersburg, Russia into a modest lower-class merchant family. He was an adventuresome young man, who took his family to Siberia to explore business opportunities and first settled into trading and tax collecting. When he was on the verge of bankruptcy at the age of 43, he was offered a job to manage the fur trading companies in the Kodiak Islands of Russian America owned by Grigory Shelikhov. In 1792, Baranov moved the firm to Three Saints Bay to a more suitable business area on Kodiak. The next year, he founded the Port of Voskresensk in Chugach Bay. In 1795, he started a new settlement in Yakutat Bay for farming families from Russia. Meanwhile, the Russian-American Company took over the Shelikhov Company and appointed Nikolay Rezanov as chairman. That position was a powerful one, because the Tsar used the Russian-American Company to rule all of its Alaska Colony. In 1799, Baranov was promoted to manage all of the company's operations in Alaska. Considering the isolation and distance to St. Petersburg, Baranov virtually controlled Russian America as an independent governor. One of his first steps was to build a fort on Sitka Island to protect the settlement there but also to prevent the British from annexing southeastern Alaska to Canada. In 1802, Baranov was faced with a revolt from the Tlingit tribe which massacred the entire Russian Sitka settlement. As he organized a 700-man army to rid the island of the Tlingit, he was promoted to the position of collegiate counselor, which was in the mid-nobility rank and equivalent to a Russian navy ship captaincy. Baranov defeated the natives on Sitka but lost to them on Yakutat, where they had also massacred the Russian settlement. In 1805, Chairman Rezanov visited Alaska to inspect the rumored mismanagement by Baranov. He found the rumors to be false and praised Baranov in his report to the Tsar. When Baranov asked to return to Russia to see his family, Rezanov declined, because he considered Baranov as indispensable to Russian America. In 1807, Baranov was awarded the Order of St. Anna, 2nd Class for his leadership. In spite of his success, some dissatisfied soldiers tried to assassinate him, and Tlingit natives shot him with arrows, which failed to penetrate the iron mail he wore under his shirt. In 1812, Baranov built Fort Ross in Spanish northern California to develop a food supply for the Alaska settlements. In 1815, he sent Dr. Georg Schaffer to Hawaii to arrange accommodations for Russian ships transporting furs to the China market. Dr. Schaffer became involved with local politics, and the Russians were told to leave. The episode was an expensive failure which ultimately led to Baranov's removal from office. An audit exonerated Baranov. In 1818, he left Alaska to return home, but he fell ill in the Dutch East Indies and died on April 16, 1819 at 62 years old. His legacy is Baranof Island in Alaska and a United States Coast Guard Cutter and Liberty ship named in his honor.[5]

William Seward was born in 1801 in Florida, New York about 60 miles north of New York City into a wealthy land-owning family. He was a bright student, and at age 15, he was sent to Union College into the sophomore class. At Union, he was elected into Phi Beta Kappa. After graduating at age 17, he and a friend Alvah Wilson left home to sail for Georgia, where William unexpectedly landed a job as principal of a new academy. He returned home in 1820 to study the law and then moved to Auburn, New York, where he practiced law and became involved in politics. In the 1828 presidential campaign, Seward supported the reelection of John Quincy Adams. In 1831, he was elected to the New York State Senate, where he sided with dissident Democrats and focused on penal reforms. President Jackson was reelected in 1832, thereby causing the creation of the opposition Whig Party. The Whigs were in favor of legislative measures to manage the country and not the autocratic rule favored by Jackson. Seward emerged in 1834 as the Whig candidate for governor of New York, but he was soundly defeated by 11,000 votes. At that time, the term of office was two years, so Seward ran again in 1838 and won by 10,000 votes. He was reelected in 1840, and Gen. William Henry Harrison was elected president. In 1843, Seward left politics and returned to Auburn to resume a profitable law practice in order to repay his large personal debts that he accrued during his costly political life. In 1844, Seward declined the Whig presidential nomination and supported Henry Clay, who was defeated by Democrat James Polk. Seward did not approve of the Mexican-American War, because he believed the additional territory was pursued by southerners who wanted to expand slavery. In 1849, Seward reentered politics by running for the United States Senate. He won by an enormous majority voted by the legislature that still voted for senators until that practice was discontinued in 1913 under the 17th amendment. As Governor Seward worked to advance the agenda of President Taylor, he acquired great notoriety for his anti-slavery speeches and writings. The Compromise of 1850 did not settle the slavery issue, and with Taylor's death that year, many in the federal government were replaced with President Fillmore's appointees. At home, the Sewards opened their house to fugitive slaves as part of the Underground Railroad. His wife, Frances, was a fervent abolitionist and frequently wrote to her husband about helping certain people. When Senator Stephen Douglas introduced the Kansas-Nebraska Bill in 1854 allowing new territories to decide on slavery themselves, Seward vigorously opposed it in the Senate. More significantly, the Kansas-Nebraska Bill spurred the founding of the Republican Party. In 1857, President Buchanan supported the admission of Kansas as a slave state, but the move split the Democratic Party. To further complicate the issue, the United States Supreme Court had just ruled in the Dred Scott Case that neither Congress nor a local government could ban slavery in their territories. For the upcoming election in 1860, Seward was seen as the likely Republican candidate, and with his outspoken comments condemning slavery, he was hated by southerners. At the Republican Convention, party leaders feared he could not win in Illinois, Indiana, Pennsylvania, or New Jersey. On the first ballot, Seward received 173 votes to Lincoln's 102. On the third ballot, Lincoln got 231 votes and Seward had 180 votes. The winner would need 233 votes. After the roll call, Ohio changed 4 votes to Lincoln, giving him the victory. Seward calmly received the news and commented that Lincoln had the qualities to be elected president. Although Seward was devastated, he agreed to campaign for Lincoln. He travelled throughout the Midwest, Minnesota, Missouri, and Kansas. He appeared with Lincoln in Springfield, Illinois and spoke about a future Union that could include Canada, Latin America, and Russian America. After winning the presidency, Lincoln offered Seward the Secretary of State position, which he accepted seven weeks later on December 28, 1860.[6]

While he was a senator, Seward was opposed to the acquisition of Mexican land under the Gadsden Purchase in 1853 as well as President Buchanan's desire to buy Cuba from Spain. His reasoning was based on fears that the new territories would bring more slavery which he adamantly opposed. After he served as Secretary of State, he completely changed positions and even spoke of expanding the Union to include Canada, Latin America, Greenland, Iceland, and Russian America. He learned from the Civil War that the Union could have benefitted from overseas bases and the country could have expanded trade through distant territories. In 1865-66, he toured the Caribbean and made attempts to purchase the Danish West Indies (later Virgin Islands), St. Thomas, and Samara Bay Port in the Dominican Republic. None of the attempts came to fruition. In 1860, he had predicted that Russian America would become part of the United States, and in 1864, when he learned that it might be for sale, he pursued the matter. In 1867, he received permission to negotiate with Russian minister Baron Eduard de Stoeckl. After some negotiation on price, it was agreed at $7.2 million and signed on March 30, 1867. In the election of 1868, the Republicans chose Gen. U. S. Grant, who had no interest in retaining Seward as Secretary of State. After advising the new president on a few issues, Seward returned home to Auburn. He then took a tour of the Pacific Northwest for nine months, visiting Alaska, Oregon, Utah, California, Mexico, and Cuba. In 1870, he travelled to Japan, China, India, the Middle East, and Europe. In 1872, while working on his memoirs, William Seward passed away at 71 years old. His reputation during his lifetime, and to this day, remains controversial. He has been praised as an outstanding Secretary of State, especially for his work in the Civil War. Others, like navy Secretary Gideon Welles, thought he had no principles. However, Seward and Lincoln were the two most important leaders of that time. Seward led Lincoln in popularity before 1860, and then he was overshadowed by him afterward. His legacy is Alaska.[7]

James Wickersham was born in 1857 near Patoka, Illinois. After attending the local public schools and then studying the law, he married and moved to Tacoma, Washington in 1883. He was appointed a district court judge by President McKinley in 1900. Wickersham was one of the three federal judges who practically ruled all of Alaska, and he was quick to have his authority known and understood. He soon gained notoriety with the Nome Gold Conspiracy, which involved some important National Republican Committee members. He was able to clean up the mess left by the ousted Judge Noyes. Wickersham acquired the reputation of being a man of swift and fair action. He played a key role in developing the small settlement of Fairbanks into one of Alaska's important cities. He worked closely with local Capt. E.T. Barnette, and together they incorporated Fairbanks and arranged important federal appointees. When his term ended, he ran for the congressional delegate position in 1908 and began a lifetime of dedication to the interests of Alaska from his new and influential position in Washington, D.C. His first priority was to gain territorial status. Many Alaskans were upset with the lack of home rule since being acquired by the United States in 1867. All the government positions from governor to clerks and marshals were appointed by the president and confirmed by the Senate for terms of four years. None were elected by Alaskans. Next, Wickersham wanted to break the "Alaska Syndicate," which was a group of private business interests who controlled the copper industry, transportation, and steamship lines. In 1909, he introduced a bill for territorial status, but it was rejected by President Taft. It was also opposed by the Alaska Syndicate, who feared local government rule and government taxes. However, in 1912, Wickersham's tenacity won passage of the Alaska Organic Act. He then proposed a federal railroad for the territory, and his record-breaking five-hour speech in Congress won its approval and started competition with the Syndicate's stranglehold on transportation. Wickersham served several terms as congressional delegate with the last one from 1931 to 1933. He was able to bring Alaska's many resources under state control while still depending on the federal government for economic assistance. Even today, it is the Department of Defense that heavily supports Alaska, but Wickersham believed that the federal government was better than having private outside business people gain from the wealth of Alaska's vast resources.

James Wickersham died in Juneau, Alaska in 1939 at 82 years old. His legacy includes founder of the University of Alaska and a residence building on the Fairbanks campus named in his honor. Some historians regard him as the unofficial "Father of Fairbanks."[8]

Chapter Fifty

Hawaii

State on August 21, 1959

Explorers and Settlers

Archeologists disagree on the early settlement of Hawaii, with some placing the arrival of Polynesians in the 100-300 A.D. period while others put their arrival around 1000-1200 A.D. when Tahitians established settlements and created the Hawaiian civilization. For the next 500 years, Hawaii remained isolated and undeveloped until 1778, when English explorer James Cook landed there on his third expedition to the Pacific. It was the British military that enabled King Kamehameha I to conquer and unify the islands from 1782 to 1819 and establish the Kingdom of Hawaii in 1795. The Americans came to Hawaii soon after Cook's arrival, but it was not until 1835 that they started building a sugar industry under the leadership of William Northey Hooper from Manchester, Massachusetts. The first major sugar producer in Hawaii was Ladd & Company, which was started by Hooper, who also served as consul to the Kingdom of

Hawaii. Hooper's job was to start and operate sugar plantations. His first move was to lease 980 acres of land owned by King Kamehameha III for the planting of sugarcane. Within 30 years, sugarcane transformed the economy of Hawaii and was grown on Hawaii's four main islands. In 1846, President Tyler sent Secretary of State John Calhoun to formally recognize Hawaii's independence under King Kamehameha III. With its newly-formed independence, Hawaii established 90 legations and consulates all over the world. With the preponderance of American plantation owners, they began to play a role in Hawaii's politics in the 1850's, in spite of the British takeover in 1843. The major American issue was land tenure.[1]

King Kamehameha relented under the pressure and decided to invoke the "Great Mahele" or division of land distribution in 1848. The result was that one-third of the land went to the Crown. The next one-third went to the 245 chiefs, and the last one-third went to the public. Most of the public land was bought by foreigners, and the local Hawaiians ended up with less than one percent. Other land acts soon followed. The Alien Land Ownership Act of 1850 allowed foreigners to hold title to the land under the pretext that this would bring much needed capital and labor. The Kuleana Act of 1850 was similar to the American Homestead Act that allowed that people who cultivated the land were entitled to petition for ownership.[2]

Another difficult issue resulting from the expanding sugarcane production was tariffs. The United States kept tariffs very high on Hawaiian imports while Hawaiians kept tariffs low on American imports. King Kamehameha tried to gain reciprocity, but the United States Senate denied it. Around 1870, the United States began to consider the military importance of Hawaii in order to protect the American West Coast. An American, Charles Reed Bishop, married into the royal family and became Hawaii's Minister of Foreign Affairs. He pursued the American purchase of several Hawaiian ports, but the reigning monarch William Lunalilo sensed local opposition and cancelled negotiations in 1873, just three months before his death. He was succeeded by David Kalakaua, who was pressured by the United States government to cede Pearl Harbor to the Americans for a defensive base. The lease was for seven years, but at the end, the Americans showed no interest for its renewal. Shortly after the start of the lease in 1887, a group of non-Hawaiians started a rebellion. They called themselves the

Hawaiian Patriotic League, and they wrote a new constitution. They enlisted the Hawaiian Militia to threaten King Kalakaua into adopting the new constitution, even though it required him to fire his cabinet and it weakened his authority. The voters and candidates had to have certain property and asset values that would immediately disenfranchise two-thirds of the native population. Americans could retain their United States citizenship and still vote and hold office in Hawaii. Asians could no longer vote or gain citizenship. The new constitution was soon called the "Bayonet Constitution" because of its passage by use of force.[3]

When King Kalakaua died in January of 1891, he was replaced by his sister Queen Lili'uokalani, who arrived in the middle of a financial crisis. The McKinley Tariff Act of 1890 eliminated the tariff on sugar imported into the United States from other countries, thereby hurting Hawaii's exports to the United States. The negative impact on business and government revenues was severe and required the queen and her government to seek new sources of revenue. Against all of her advisors' pleas, she introduced opium licensing for more revenue but later paid a political price. Her next priority was to regain power to the monarchy by replacing the Bayonet Constitution. She personally campaigned throughout the islands and received widespread support among the native Hawaiians. However, when she introduced the plan to her cabinet they withheld their support, because they knew what the reaction would be from the Americans and Europeans. Nonetheless, the queen decided to pursue her plan, but a small group of five Americans, one Englishman, and one German plotted to overthrow the monarchy, depose the queen, and attempt to be annexed to the United States.

Territorial Hawaii

Lorrin Thurston, the grandson of American missionaries, was a leading member of the Committee of Safety, which was the group that deposed the queen. The Committee consisted of American and European business people who were also citizens of Hawaii. They included legislators, government officials, and even a Supreme Court justice of Hawaii. The marshal of the kingdom, Charles Wilson, declared martial law and tried to negotiate with Thurston. Meanwhile, the Committee of Safety gathered 1,500 armed non-native men who were becoming concerned for the safety of Americans and their property. The United States government supported the coup, placed the queen under house arrest, and transformed the kingdom to the Republic of Hawaii. The United States Minister John Stevens called in 162 marines and sailors to maintain order, which they accomplished without firing a shot or taking over any buildings. Sanford Dole was elected the Republic's first and only president. He had served as the Supreme Court justice and was a close friend of Queen Lili'uokalani. He later was appointed as the first territorial governor.[4] The Republic lasted close to five years. In 1897, the Republican William McKinley succeeded Democrat President Grover Cleveland. McKinley's bill to annex Hawaii never got the two-thirds approval in the Democrat-controlled Senate. President Cleveland was opposed to annexation and wanted the queen to be restored. An investigation of the marines' behavior in the coup resulted in the Morgan Report, which showed that the American troops were neutral and therefore exonerated of any complicity. In Congress, a new joint resolution needed only majority support to pass and was approved in the House and Senate. Its passage was spurred by the outbreak of the Spanish-American War in 1898 and the move by Japan to send warships to Hawaii to oppose annexation by the United States. President McKinley signed the annexation bill on July 7, 1898, thereby creating the Territory of Hawaii. Withstanding opponents who believed the queen was the legitimate ruler of Hawaii, President McKinley appointed Sanford Dole as the territorial governor, and the new legislature elected Robert Wilcox as their congressional delegate.[5]

As a territory, there was no longer a tariff on sugarcane shipped to the United States. This freed capital, thereby giving planters more resources for equipment, land, and labor. Annexation was a boon to the "Big Five" old-line companies like Castle & Cooke, Alexander & Baldwin, C. Brewer & Company, American Factors, and Theo H. Davies & Company. Another beneficiary was the Dole Company built by James Dole, when he came to Hawaii in 1898 and built the first pineapple plantation in Hawaii. In 1901, he built his first cannery, and the business exploded. He built his second cannery in 1907 near Honolulu Harbor where it remained in operation until 1991. In 1922, he purchased the island of Lanai and developed it into the largest pineapple plantation in the world. For many years, Dole produced 75 percent of the world's pineapple and earned the epithet "Pineapple King." The fruit became Hawaii's second largest industry behind sugarcane.[6] Another industry started in 1882 when William Matson founded Matson Navigation Company, which transported goods between San Francisco and Hawaii. He was then encouraged to purchase steamships that would carry passengers who wanted to vacation in Hawaii. His fleet rivaled the best sailing ships in the world and included the *SS Wilhelmina*, *SS Mariposa*, *SS Monterey*, and *SS Lurline*. Matson then opened two resort hotels in Honolulu and the Moana Hotel in Waikiki in 1901. One of finest hotels was the Royal Hawaiian, which opened in 1927 and served as the residence for President Franklin Roosevelt when he visited the islands during World War II.[7]

When the Japanese attacked Pearl Harbor on December 7, 1941, Hawaii was placed under martial law. Only pro-Japanese leaders were arrested, but the enormous Japanese-American population was left to live their normal lives. The local government formed the 442nd Regimental Combat Team of the United States army. It was composed of American soldiers with Japanese ancestry. They fought in Italy, France, and Germany and became the most decorated for its size and time of service in United States history. Close to 14,000 men served and earned 9,486 Purple Hearts and were awarded 21 Medals of Honor.[8] With Hawaii under martial law from 1941 to 1944, all civil authority was terminated, including the governor. The constitution was suspended, and all residents were subject to military law. A military government was formed and governed from Iolani Palace, which had been the home of the past monarchy. All residents over age six were fingerprinted, blackouts and curfews were imposed, food and gas were rationed, and mail was censored.[9]

Statehood

The issue of Hawaii's statehood had not received congressional approval in 1935 or in 1937. The matter was tested again in 1940 when it was placed on the ballot. Two-thirds of the electorate supported the measure. The war intervened, but when it was over, an even greater number voted in favor of Hawaii joining the Union as a state. There was no doubt that Hawaiians were ready for statehood based on a number of factors: 1) they wanted to elect their own governor, 2) they wanted to vote for a president of the country, 3) they wanted to end taxation without representation, 4) they had sustained the first deaths and destruction in World War II, 5) their non-white and mostly Japanese residents fought in the war and proved their loyalty, and 6) Hawaii was composed of 90 percent United States citizens, most of whom were born in the United States.[10]

In 1956, John Burns was elected as Hawaii's congressional delegate, mostly from non-white local Japanese and Philippino support. In Washington, D.C., he worked tirelessly, convincing congressmen and governors that Hawaii was ready for statehood. In March of 1959, Congress passed the Hawaii Admissions Act, and on June 27, 1959, President Dwight Eisenhower signed the bill admitting Hawaii as the 50th state.[11]

Statesmen, Leaders and Heroes

Lorrin Thurston was born in Honolulu in 1858. His grandparents on his father's and mother's side were part of the first American missionaries to come to Hawaii in 1820. His father, Asa Goodale Thurston, was speaker of the house of representatives for the Kingdom of Hawaii, but he died when Lorrin was only one and a half years old. Lorrin received an excellent education at the Punahou School and Columbia University Law School in New York City. At the age of 28, Thurston entered the Kingdom of Hawaii legislature aligned with the conservative Missionary Party, which was opposed to the policies and seeming corruption of the Hawaiian royalty. The Missionary Party soon changed its original name to the Reform Party. His first notable political work was writing the so-called "Bayonet Constitution," which was passed under the threat of using local militia. The document limited the power of King Kalakaua and based voting rights on property ownership and wealth. He acquired a great deal of power as the Interior Minister, and with Englishman William Green as Minister of Finance, they both ruled the country. When the king died in 1891, his sister Queen Lili'uokalani inherited the monarchy. She tried to regain the monarchy's former power by introducing a new constitution, but she failed against Thurston and his Annexation Club (later Committee of Safety), which planned to make Hawaii a territory of the United States. In 1893, the monarchy was overthrown by the Committee of Safety with the United States government's approval, and Thurston led the Commission to Washington, D.C. to negotiate for territorial status. Queen Lili'uokalani also went to Washington to argue that the new government did not have the support of the Hawaiian people. Rumors of American military force in the overthrow caused the territorial negotiations to end. In 1894, Thurston helped to draft a new constitution which was approved and created the Republic of Hawaii. He declined the opportunity to become its first president, realizing his reputation was too controversial. Instead, he appointed Sanford Dole as president. In 1897, when William McKinley became president, Thurston again lobbied for annexation. With the Spanish-American War in 1898 and fighting in the Philippines, Congress had greater appreciation of Hawaii's strategic location. Annexation was approved in July of that year, and Thurston retired from politics.

In 1898, Thurston purchased the *Pacific Commercial Advertiser* newspaper, where he promoted the sugarcane and pineapple industries. With Hawaii as a territory, all tariffs on exports to the United States were removed, resulting in greater profits and wealth for businessmen like Thurston. He went on to help build the railroads and brought the first electric street cars to Hawaii. He also fought to keep billboards out of the country. He took a keen interest in the study of volcanoes and raised money to build the Hawaii Volcano Observatory in 1912. He also promoted national parks with support from President Theodore Roosevelt, conservationist John Muir, and Senator Henry Cabot Lodge. He died in 1931 in Honolulu with a legacy that includes markers throughout Hawaii, a street named in his honor, a chapel at the Punahou School, and the Hawaii Volcanoes National Park.[12]

Sanford Dole was born in 1844 in Honolulu, into a family of Protestant missionaries from Maine. He attended Punahou School for one year where his father was principal, and then went on to Williams College for one year. He did not attend law school but did receive an honorary LLD from Williams in 1897. In 1884 and again in 1886, he was elected to the legislature of the Kingdom of Hawaii. In 1887, with the Honolulu Rifles militia at their side, a group of businessmen, planters, and politicians deposed the cabinet and governor and adopted a new constitution for the Kingdom of Hawaii. Dole, Thurston, and lawyers of American descent drafted the new document, which reduced the authority of the monarchy and imposed property and wealth franchise requirements limited to literate males of Hawaiian, American, and European descent. King Kalakaua appointed Dole a justice of the Supreme Court, and after the king died, his sister, Queen Lili'uokalani, appointed Dole to her Privy Council. The monarchy was overthrown in 1893 by most of the same men who were responsible for the coup in 1887. Dole also helped to write the Committee of Safety Declaration in 1893. After the coup, he was named president of the Provisional Government of Hawaii and was immediately recognized by the major countries of the world. President Cleveland was opposed to the coup and tried to reinstate the monarchy. The Blount Report to the president accused the Committee of Safety of calling in the Marines to remove the Queen. President Cleveland offered her reinstatement in return for clemency for members of the Committee of Safety. The Queen refused and demanded their execution, but she later denied this in a book she wrote about the coup. The Morgan Report in 1894 found that the Marines only protected American lives and property, and therefore were exonerated. Dole served as president of the Republic from 1894 to 1898. During that period, he withstood several attempts to restore the monarchy. The rebels led by Robert Wilcox were captured and sentenced to death, but Dole commuted the sentence. The Queen abdicated and swore allegiance to the Republic. In 1900, Dole was appointed the first territorial governor and served for three years before accepting an appointment by President Theodore Roosevelt to be a United States District Court Judge, a position he held until 1915. He died in 1926 at 82 years old. He was the cousin of James Dole who founded the Hawaiian Pineapple Company in 1899.[13]

John Burns was born in 1909 in Fort Assinniboine, Montana into a military family that was sent to Hawaii in 1913. When his father abandoned the family, John was sent to live with various friends and relatives. He was educated at several Catholic high schools, dropped out to join the army, and finally graduated in 1930. His first work as a police officer was with Japanese and native Hawaiians. He moved into politics around 1950 and was elected as a party delegate to the 1956 Democratic Party Convention. He lobbied for statehood, which he achieved in 1959 when President Eisenhower signed the bill. He then ran for the governorship but lost to Territorial Governor William Quinn. In 1962, he won the gubernatorial election and focused on the state economy, tourism, and capital investment. Some of his achievements include making Hawaii a center for oceanography, building a new state capitol building, expanding the University of Hawaii, and making Hawaii a leader in environmental management. He was reelected in 1966 and 1970. He died of cancer in 1975 in Honolulu. His legacy includes the John Burns School of Medicine at the University of Hawaii, the Interstate H-3 named in his honor, and the road to the summit of Mauna Kea, named in his memory.[14]

EPILOGUE

As I have noted earlier, the story of the United States of America started as an experiment in individual freedom and evolved into a republic whereby its citizens determined its laws and regulations. With its Constitution, it established a world-wide reputation as a nation of laws which also provided a framework for other nations of the world. The country began in 1607 in Jamestown, Virginia and fought a revolution to retain its freedoms and independence. Its Declaration of Independence proclaimed the nation's moral beliefs. It survived a civil war, sectional differences, and economic depressions. It adopted an international policy of protecting individual freedoms all over the world and voluntarily acted to defend against foreign oppression of individual human rights. It devoted its treasure and sacrificed its blood for others in two world wars without financial repayment or land. Contrary to the advice of some of its founders, it became entangled in the affairs of other nations only because there were few, and at times none, other countries who were willing or able to intervene on behalf of victims who suffered under inhuman conditions. What other country in history has rebuilt its former enemies? One must ask what the world would be like without the aid and leadership of America.

Today, we see an America that faces many challenges. While leading in technology and rebuilding other parts of the world, we have neglected our own infrastructure. Our younger generations do not possess the skills to assume the millions of job opportunities currently available. Many of our laws are ignored with impunity. Our government has not been managed, properly evidenced by a national debt of $20 trillion most of which was accumulated over recent years. We have a failing healthcare system that is on the verge of bankruptcy. For every dollar we spend as a nation, our government borrows 44 cents. The very rock of our foundation has been through immigration, but our laws are no longer followed and our system is broken. This book has told the story of brave men and women who dared to face the challenges of building a family, a home, a town, and even a nation from a harsh wilderness. People who are now long forgotten were driven by a pursuit of happiness and the desire of a better life for their children and their children's children. Hopefully, their story will inspire present and future generations to learn from our forefathers and gain the necessary skills to correct our flaws. Respect for our parents, teachers, and leaders has declined dramatically. Accordingly, our nation is losing the patriotism and loyalty of the younger generations. May this book serve to awaken an interest in the greatest experiment in history—the United States of America.

Acknowledgements

I would like to thank the team at Morgan James Publishing for publishing my second book. Founder and CEO, David Hancock, together with Vice President of Operations, Cindy Sauer, have been a great help in getting my historical writing career started. Also, Aubrey Kosa performed an excellent job of editing and proof-reading my material and Margo Toulouse put it in good order. The maps were digitized with great assistance from Beverly Smith of the Omohundro Institute of Early American History and Culture and Michael Harris of the Swem Library at the College of William and Mary. Lastly, when one engages in the writing of a book it often impacts others who share our lives, and yet they are the ones who provide encouragement and balance, and for that I want to thank my wife Martha.

About the Author

A. Ward Burian first developed his love of history as a student at Dartmouth College. His 41 years of business experience started in 1959 at the Federal Reserve Bank of New York and several New York City banks, before he partnered the creation of a money market and bond trading firm in Wall Street and London. In 1986, he co-partnered a residential real estate brokerage in Connecticut that was the first affiliate of Sotheby's International Realty. Upon retirement, he was attracted to Williamsburg where he became an associate member of the Omohundro Institute of Early American History and Culture, a volunteer for the Colonial Williamsburg Foundation, a volunteer researcher for the Jamestown-Yorktown Foundation, and an instructor at the Christopher Wren Association which is operated under the aegis of the College of William & Mary. His initial book, *George Washington's Legacy of Leadership*, published in 2007, tells us about Washington's ancestors and the possible source of his natural leadership skills with military and political responsibilities. We see how he developed as the commanding officer of the Virginia militia during the French and Indian

War and how he was transformed from a loyal British-American into a fiercely independent American who first recognized the potential of the United States. This latest book, *The Creation of the American States*, provides the reader with a sweeping view of how the country came together. It is chock-full of details about the major events and people who created the country. Although the story of each state had to be condensed, the author believes a comprehension of its contents will enable the reader to understand and appreciate the remarkable experiment which came to be named the United States of America.

Table A

Origin of Original 13 States by Chronological Order

Date	State	Type of Charter	Changes	Official Religion	Founders & Leaders
1607	Virginia	Corporate	Revoked by Crown to Royal in 1624 when Virginia Co. filed for bankruptcy	Anglican	John Smith /John Rolfe Lord De la Warr
1626	New York	Proprietary	Holland lost war with England Changed to Royal Charter in 1664	Anglican	Henry Hudson Peter Minuit Dutch West India Company
1630	Massachusetts	Corporate	Changed to Royal Charter in 1684 and back to Corporate in 1691	Congregational	John Winthrop
1633	Maryland	Proprietary	Changed to Royal in 1691	Anglican	Sir George Calvert Cecil Calvert
1636	Connecticut	Corporate	Self-ruled in 1639 and changed to Royal Charter in 1662	Congregational	Thomas Hooker Joseph Wadsworth MA Bay Gov. John Haynew
1636	Rhode Island	Corporate	Changed to Royal in 1663 by petition of Roger Williams	None	Roger Williams Ann Hutchinson
1638	New Hampshire	Corporate	Changed to Royal in 1674	Congregational	John Mason

1638	Delaware	Proprietary	Ruled by the Dutch and then England 1664 after Third Dutch-Anglo War	None	Lord De la Warr Samuel Argall
1653	North Carolina	Proprietary	Changed to Royal in 1729	Anglican	Lord Ashley Cooper
1660	New Jersey	Proprietary	Insecure land titles & multiple proprietors let to request for Royal Charter in 1702	None	John Lord Berkeley Sir George Carteret
1670	South Carolina	Proprietary	Converted to a Royal Charter in 1719	Anglican	Sir Robert Heath
1682	Pennsylvania	Proprietary		None	William Penn James Wilson
1732	Georgia	Proprietary Trusteeship	Changed to Royal Colony in 1752	None	John Cabot JamesOglethorpe

Table B

The American States by Date of Statehood

STATE	DATE JOINED	NAME or STATUS PRIOR TO STATEHOOD	
1	Delaware	December 7, 1787	Lower Counties on Delaware/Sovereign State in Confederation
2	Pennsylvania	December 12, 1787	Province of Pennsylvania / Sovereign State in Confederation
3	New Jersey	December 18, 1787	Province of New Jersey/Sovereign State in Confederation
4	Georgia	January 2, 1788	Province of Georgia/Sovereign State in Confederation
5	Connecticut	January 9, 1788	Connecticut Colony/Sovereign State in Confederation
6	Massachusetts	February 6, 1788	Province f Massachusetts Bay/Sovereign State in Confederation
7	Maryland	April 28, 1788	Province of Maryland/Sovereign State in Confederation
8	South Carolina	May 23, 1788	Province of South Carolina/Sovereign State in Confederation
9	New Hampshire	June 21, 1788	Province of New Hampshire/Sovereign State in Confederation
10	Virginia	June 25, 1788	Virginia Colony/Sovereign State in Confederation
11	New York	July 26,1788	Province of New York/Sovereign State in Confederation
12	North Carolina	November 21,1789	Province of North Carolina/Sovereign State in Confederation
13	Rhode Island	May 29, 1790	Colony of Rhode Island & Providence Plantations/Sovereign State in Confederation

14	Vermont	March 4, 1791	Province of New York & New Hampshire Grants/Vermont Republic
15	Kentucky	June 1, 1792	Virginia
16	Tennessee	June 1, 1796	Province of North Carolina/State of Franklin/Southwest Territory
17	Ohio	March 1, 1803	Northwest Territory
18	Louisiana	April 30, 1812	Orleans Territory
19	Indiana	December 11, 1816	Indiana Territory
20	Mississippi	December 10, 1817	Mississippi Territory
21	Illinois	December 3, 1818	Illinois Territory
22	Alabama	December 14, 1819	Alabama Territory
23	Maine	March 15, 1820	Massachusetts
24	Missouri	August 10, 1821	Missouri Territory
25	Arkansas	June 15, 1836	Arkansas Territory
26	Michigan	January 26, 1837	Michigan Territory
27	Florida	March 3, 1845	Florida Territory
28	Texas	December 29, 1845	Republic of Texas
29	Iowa	December 28, 1846	Iowa Territory
30	Wisconsin	May 28, 1848	Wisconsin Territory
31	California	September 9, 1850	California Republic/ Mexican Cession/Alta California
32	Minnesota	May 11, 1858	Minnesota Territory
33	Oregon	February 14, 1859	Oregon Territory

34	Kansas	January 29, 1861	Kansas Territory
35	West Virginia	June 20, 1863	Virginia
36	Nevada	October 31, 1864	Nevada Territory
37	Nebraska	March 1, 1867	Nebraska Territory
38	Colorado	August 1, 1876	Colorado Territory
39	North Dakota	November 2, 1889	Dakota Territory
40	South Dakota	November 2, 1889	Dakota Territory
41	Montana	November 8, 1889	Montana Territory
42	Washington	November 11, 1889	Washington Territory
43	Idaho	July 3, 1890	Idaho Territory
44	Wyoming	July 10, 1890	Wyoming Territory
45	Utah	January 4, 1896	Utah Territory
46	Oklahoma	November 16,1907	Oklahoma Territory & Indian Territory
47	New Mexico	January 6,1912	New Mexico Territory
48	Arizona	February 14,1912	Arizona Territory
49	Alaska	January 3,1959	Alaska Territory
50	Hawaii	August 21,1959	Kingdom of Hawaii/Territory of Hawaii

SOURCE: www.simple.wikipedia.org/wiki/list_of_U.S._states_by_date_of_statehood

Maps

Territorial and State Maps

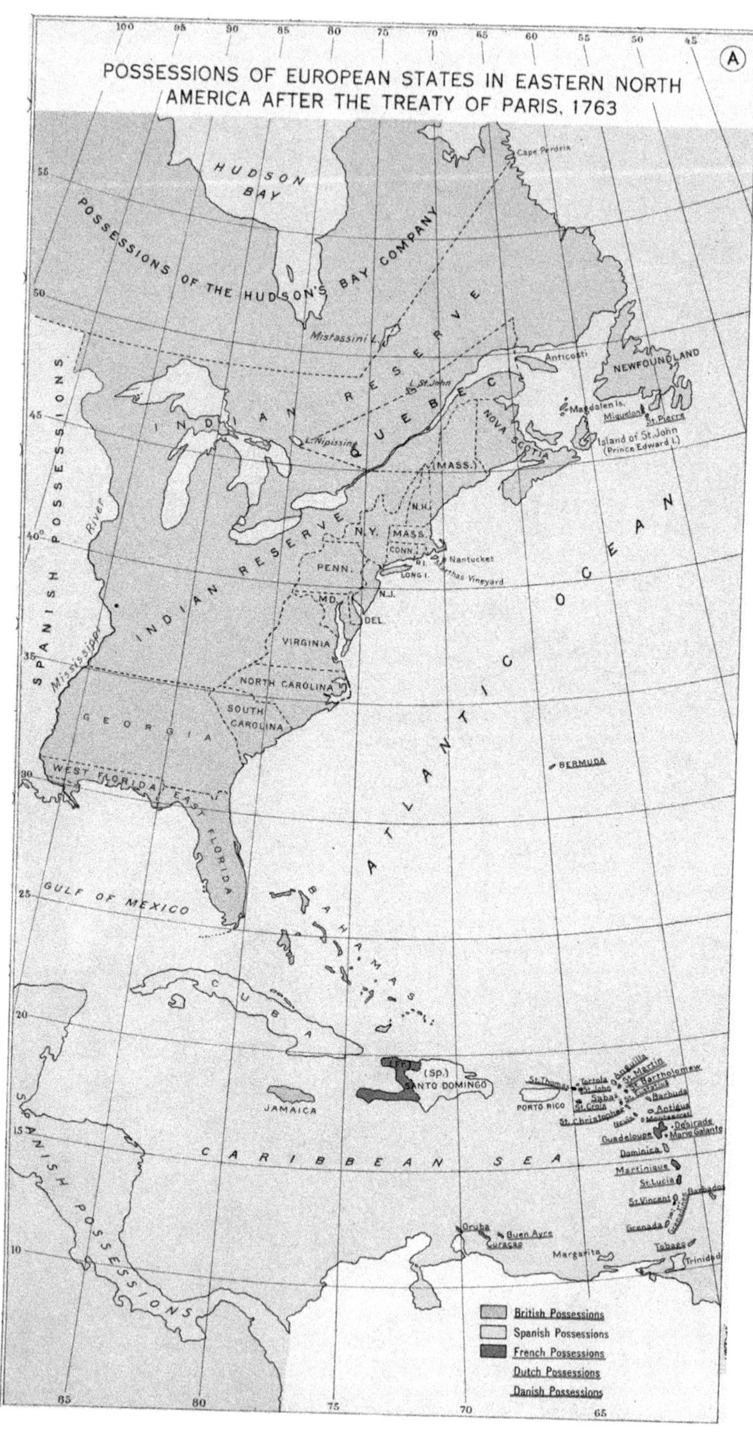
A
POSSESSIONS OF EUROPEAN STATES IN EASTERN NORTH AMERICA AFTER THE TREATY OF PARIS, 1763
HUDSON BAY
POSSESSIONS OF THE HUDSON'S BAY COMPANY
Mistassini L.
INDIAN RESERVE
QUEBEC
Anticosti
NEWFOUNDLAND
Magdalen Is.
Miquelon
St. Pierre
Island of St. John (Prince Edward I.)
NOVA SCOTIA
MASS.
N.H.
N.Y.
CONN.
R.I.
LONG I.
Nantucket
Marthas Vineyard
PENN.
N.J.
MD.
DEL.
VIRGINIA
NORTH CAROLINA
SOUTH CAROLINA
GEORGIA
WEST FLORIDA
EAST FLORIDA
SPANISH POSSESSIONS
Mississippi River
ATLANTIC OCEAN
BERMUDA
GULF OF MEXICO
BAHAMAS
CUBA
JAMAICA
(Fr.)
(Sp.)
SANTO DOMINGO
PORTO RICO
St. Thomas
St. John
Saba
St. Croix
St. Christopher
Nevis
Anguilla
St. Martin
St. Bartholomew
Barbuda
Antigua
Montserrat
Guadeloupe
Desirade
Marie Galante
Dominica
Martinique
St. Lucia
St. Vincent
Barbados
Grenada
Tobago
Trinidad
Oruba
Buen Ayre
Curaçao
Margarita
CARIBBEAN SEA
SPANISH POSSESSIONS
British Possessions
Spanish Possessions
French Possessions
Dutch Possessions
Danish Possessions

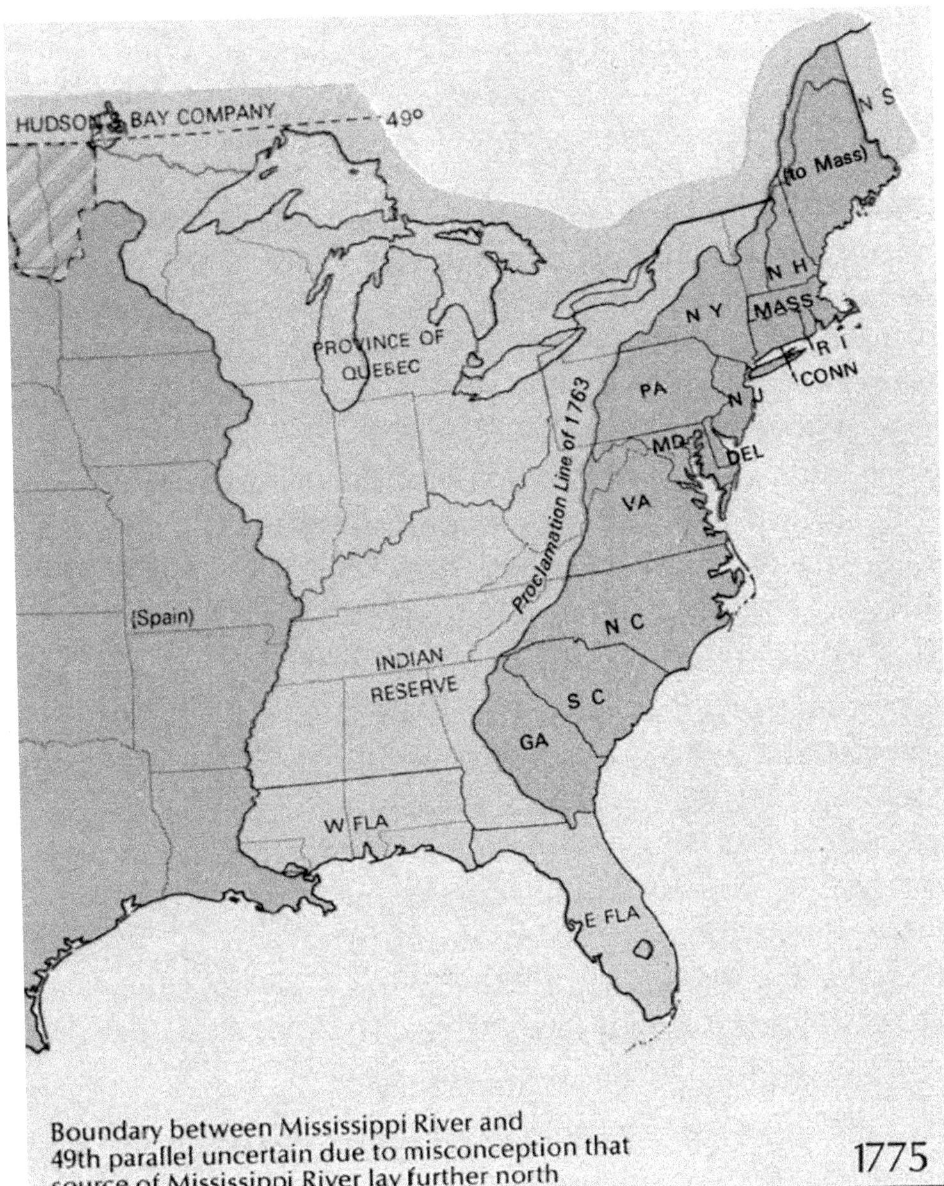

Boundary between Mississippi River and 49th parallel uncertain due to misconception that source of Mississippi River lay further north

1775

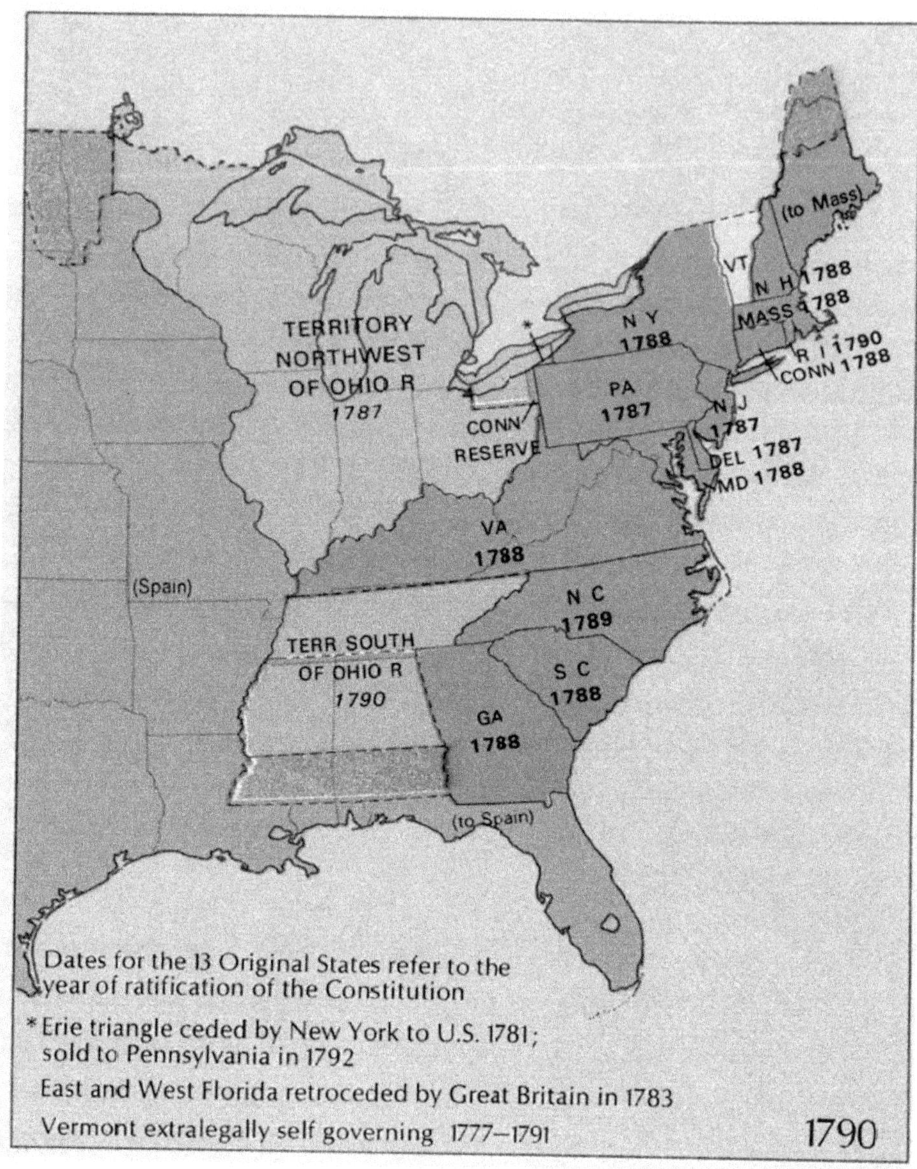

(to Mass)
VT
N H 1788
MASS 1788
R I 1790
CONN 1788
N Y
1788
PA
1787
N J
1787
DEL 1787
MD 1788
TERRITORY
NORTHWEST
OF OHIO R
1787
CONN
RESERVE
VA
1788
(Spain)
N C
1789
TERR SOUTH
OF OHIO R
1790
S C
1788
GA
1788
(to Spain)
Dates for the 13 Original States refer to the year of ratification of the Constitution
*Erie triangle ceded by New York to U.S. 1781; sold to Pennsylvania in 1792
East and West Florida retroceded by Great Britain in 1783
Vermont extralegally self governing 1777–1791
1790

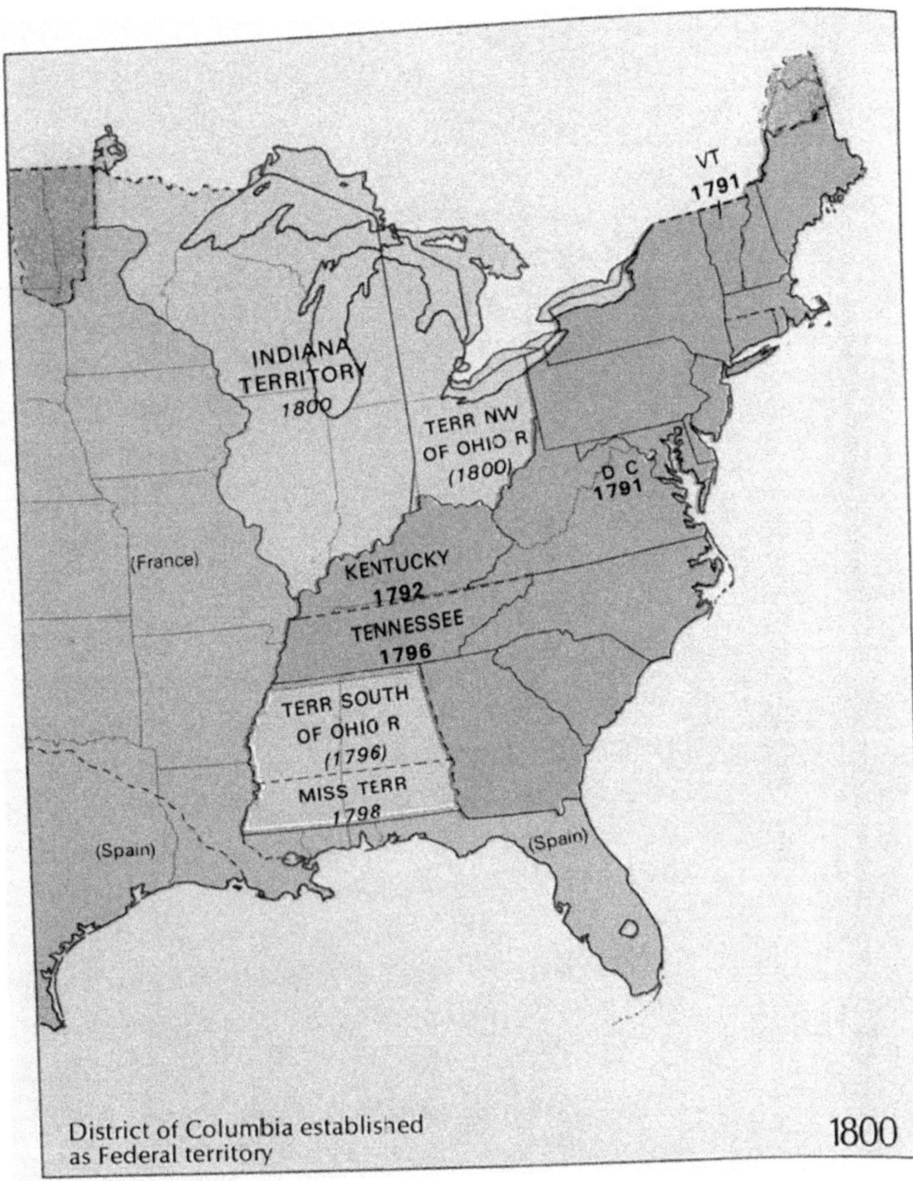
VT
1791
INDIANA
TERRITORY
1800
TERR NW
OF OHIO R
(1800)
D C
1791
(France)
KENTUCKY
1792
TENNESSEE
1796
TERR SOUTH
OF OHIO R
(1796)
MISS TERR
1798
(Spain)
(Spain)
District of Columbia established
as Federal territory
1800

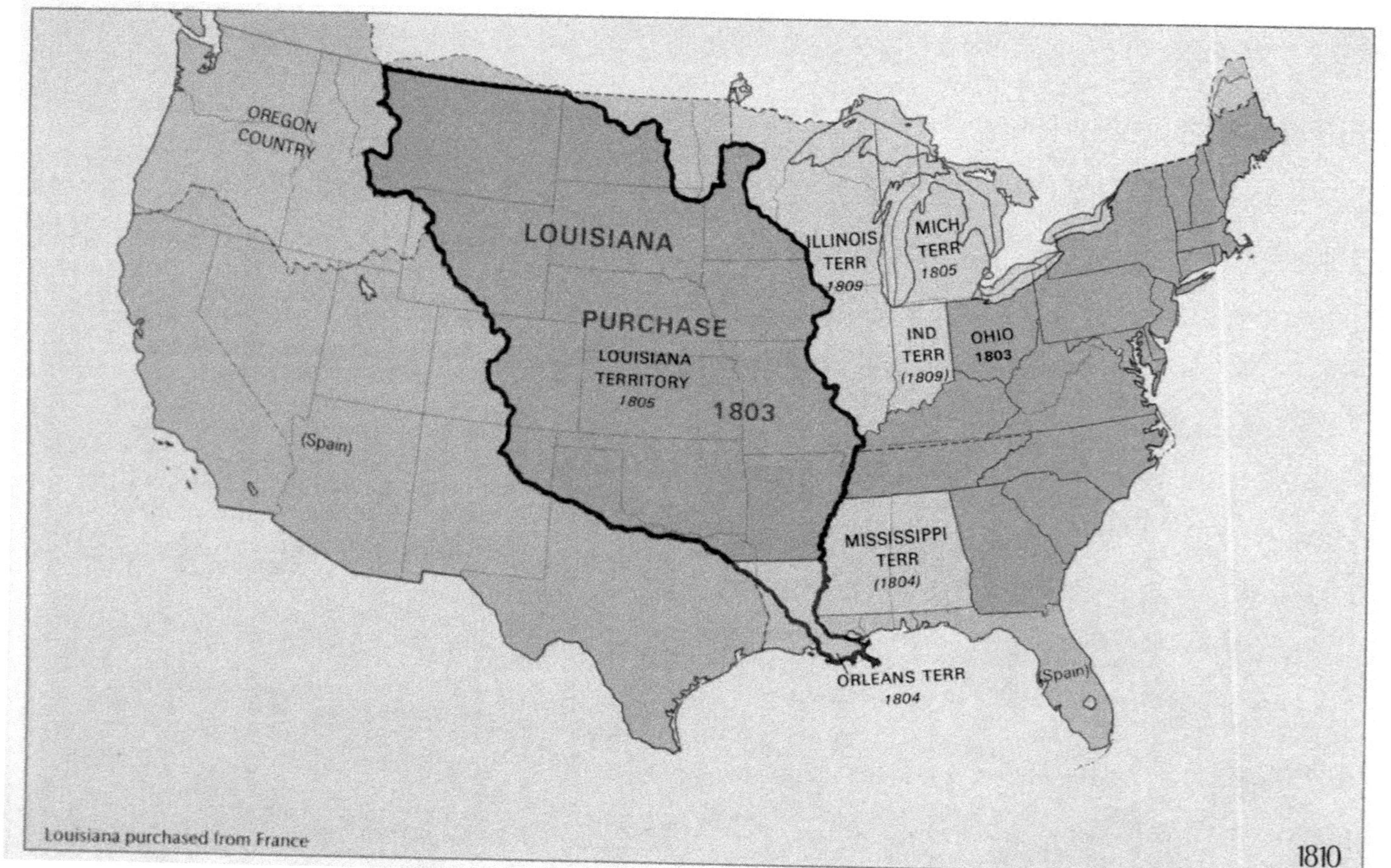

Louisiana purchased from France

1810

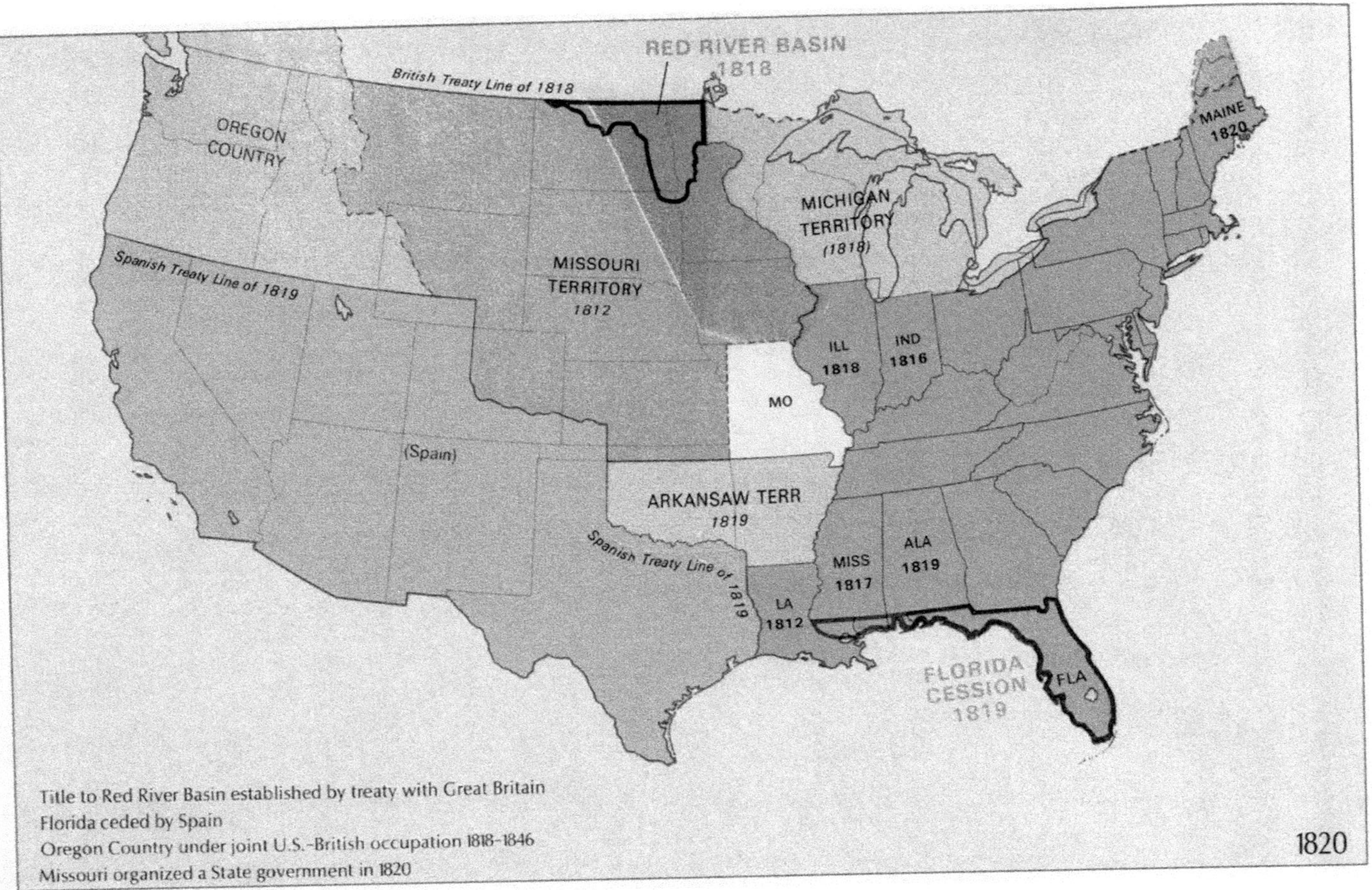
RED RIVER BASIN
1818
British Treaty Line of 1818
OREGON
COUNTRY
MAINE
1820
MICHIGAN
TERRITORY
(1818)
MISSOURI
TERRITORY
1812
Spanish Treaty Line of 1819
ILL
1818
IND
1816
MO
(Spain)
ARKANSAW TERR
1819
Spanish Treaty Line of 1819
MISS
1817
ALA
1819
LA
1812
FLORIDA
CESSION
1819
FLA
Title to Red River Basin established by treaty with Great Britain
Florida ceded by Spain
Oregon Country under joint U.S.-British occupation 1818-1846
Missouri organized a State government in 1820
1820

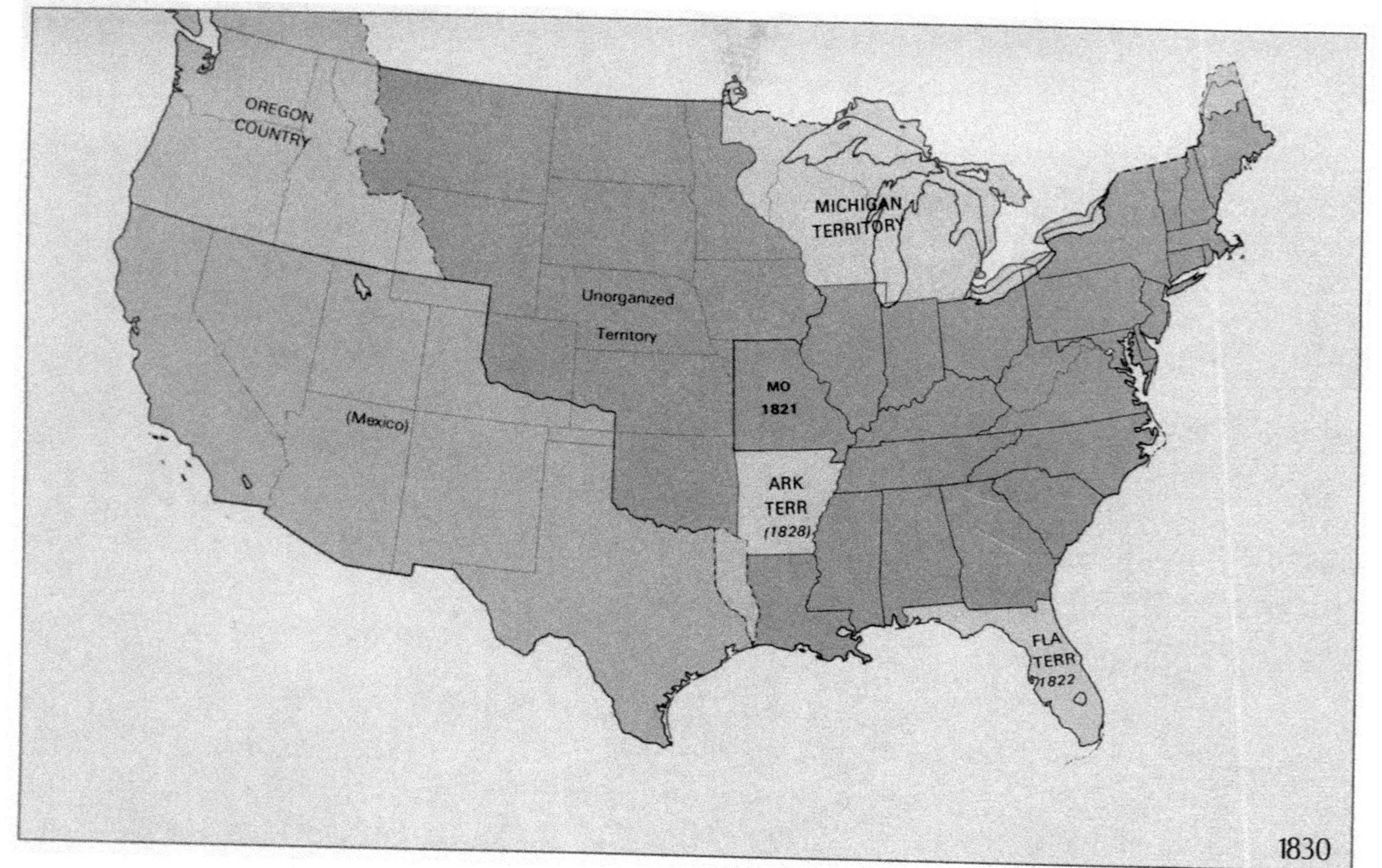
OREGON
COUNTRY
MICHIGAN
TERRITORY
Unorganized
Territory
MO
1821
(Mexico)
ARK
TERR
(1828)
FLA
TERR
1822
1830

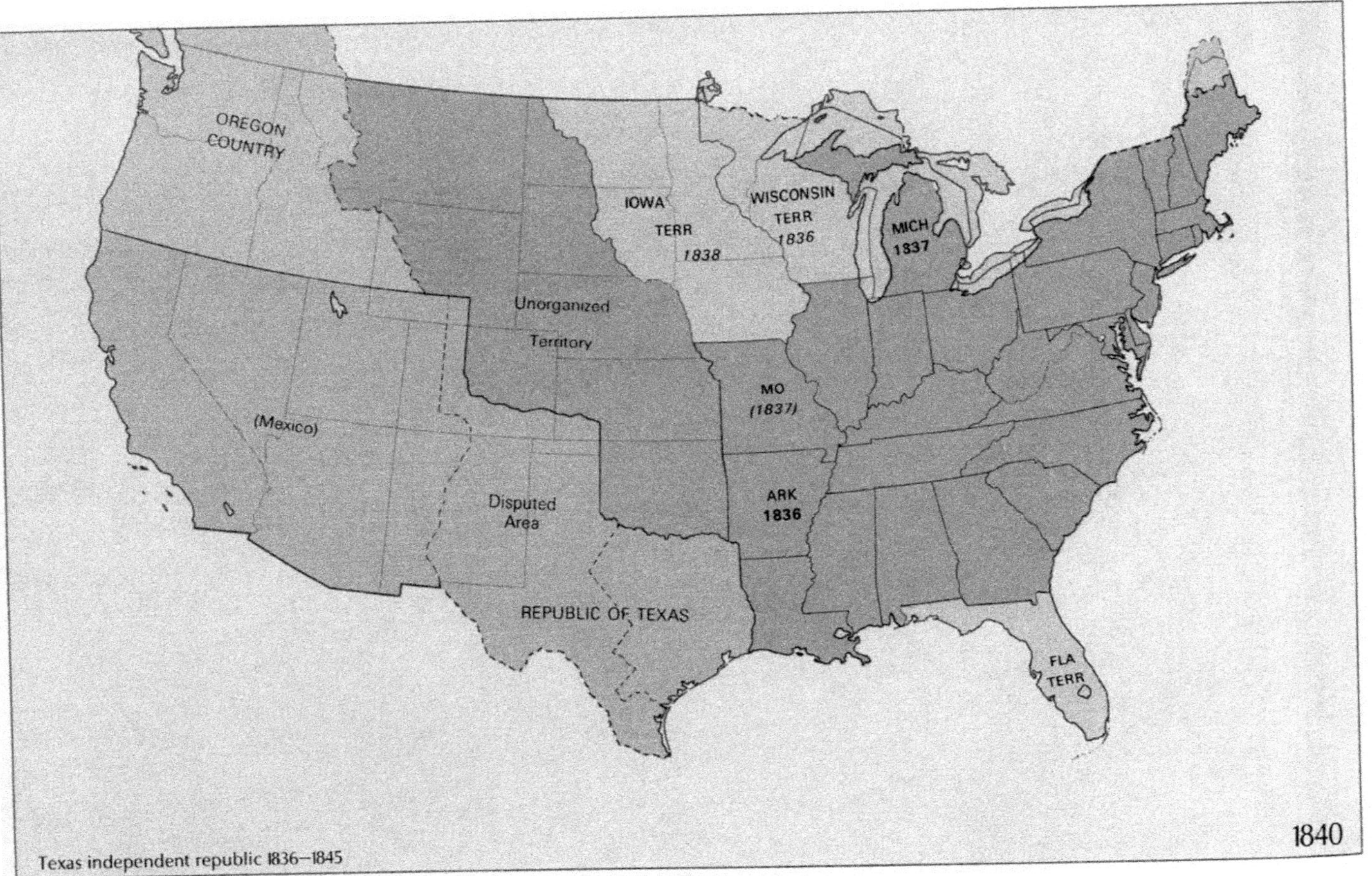

1840

Texas independent republic 1836–1845

Treaty Line of 1846
OREGON TERR
1848
OREGON COUNTRY
1846
Treaty Line
of 1842
MINNESOTA TERR
1849
WISCONSIN
1848
Treaty Line of 1842
MAINE
(1842)
UTAH TERR
1850
Unorganized
Territory
IOWA
1846
CALIF
1850
MEXICAN
CESSION 1848
NEW MEXICO TERR
1850
GREER
COUNTY
TEXAS
ANNEXATION
1845
(Mexico)
TEXAS
1845
(1850)
FLA
1845
Title to Oregon Country established by treaty with Great Britain
*Disputed area: Treaty of Guadalupe-Hidalgo 1848
Western area of Texas purchased in 1850

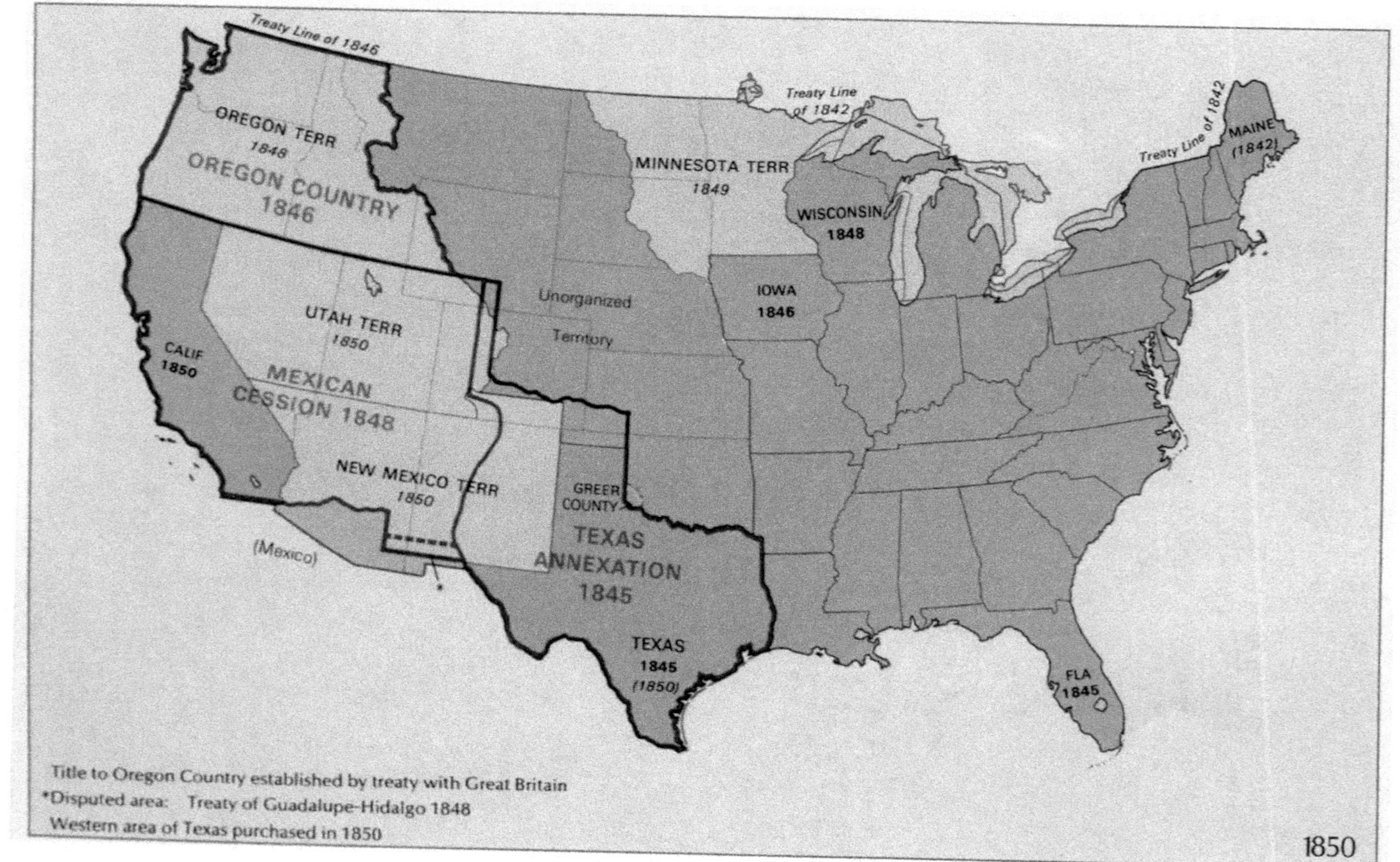

1850

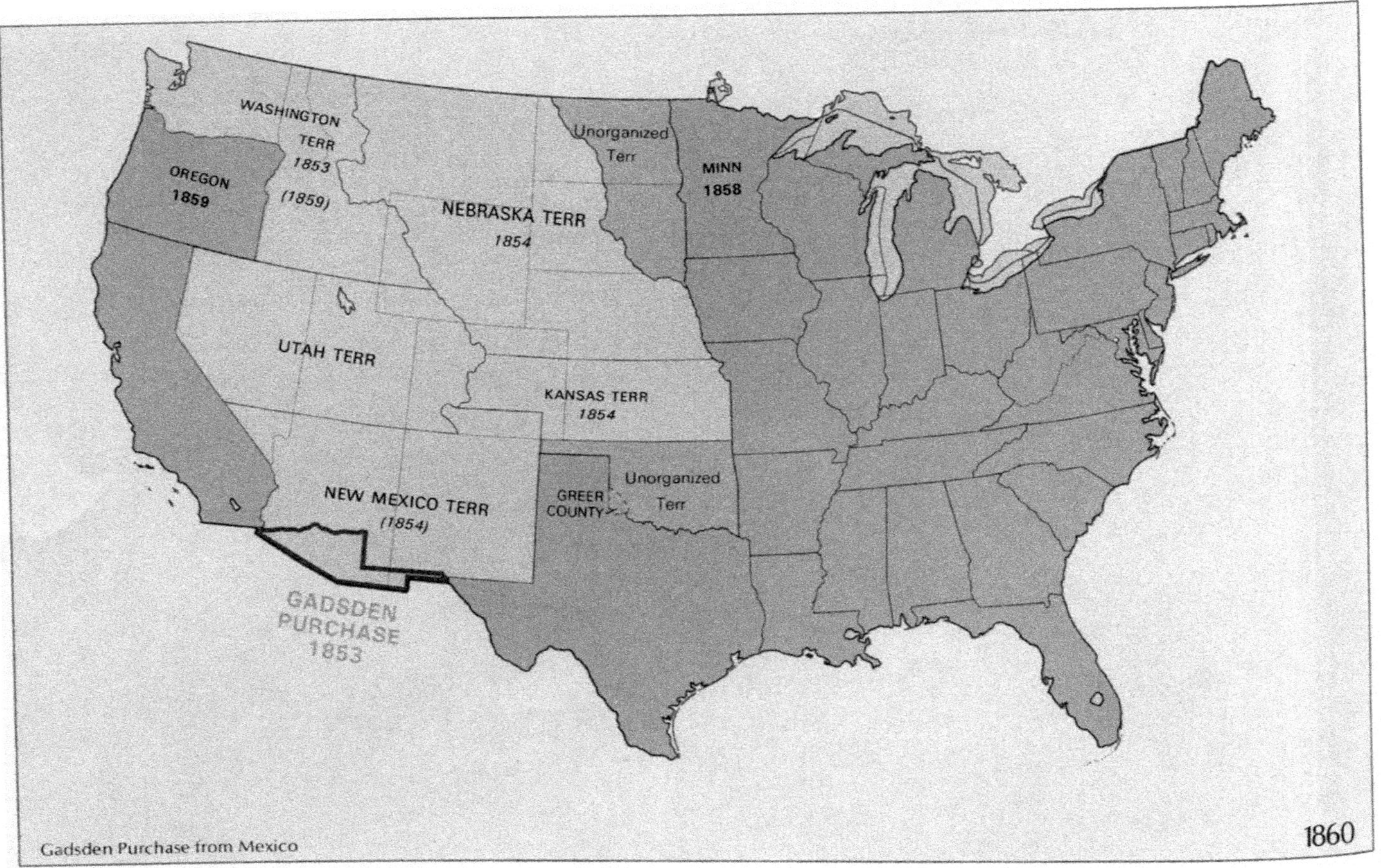

Gadsden Purchase from Mexico

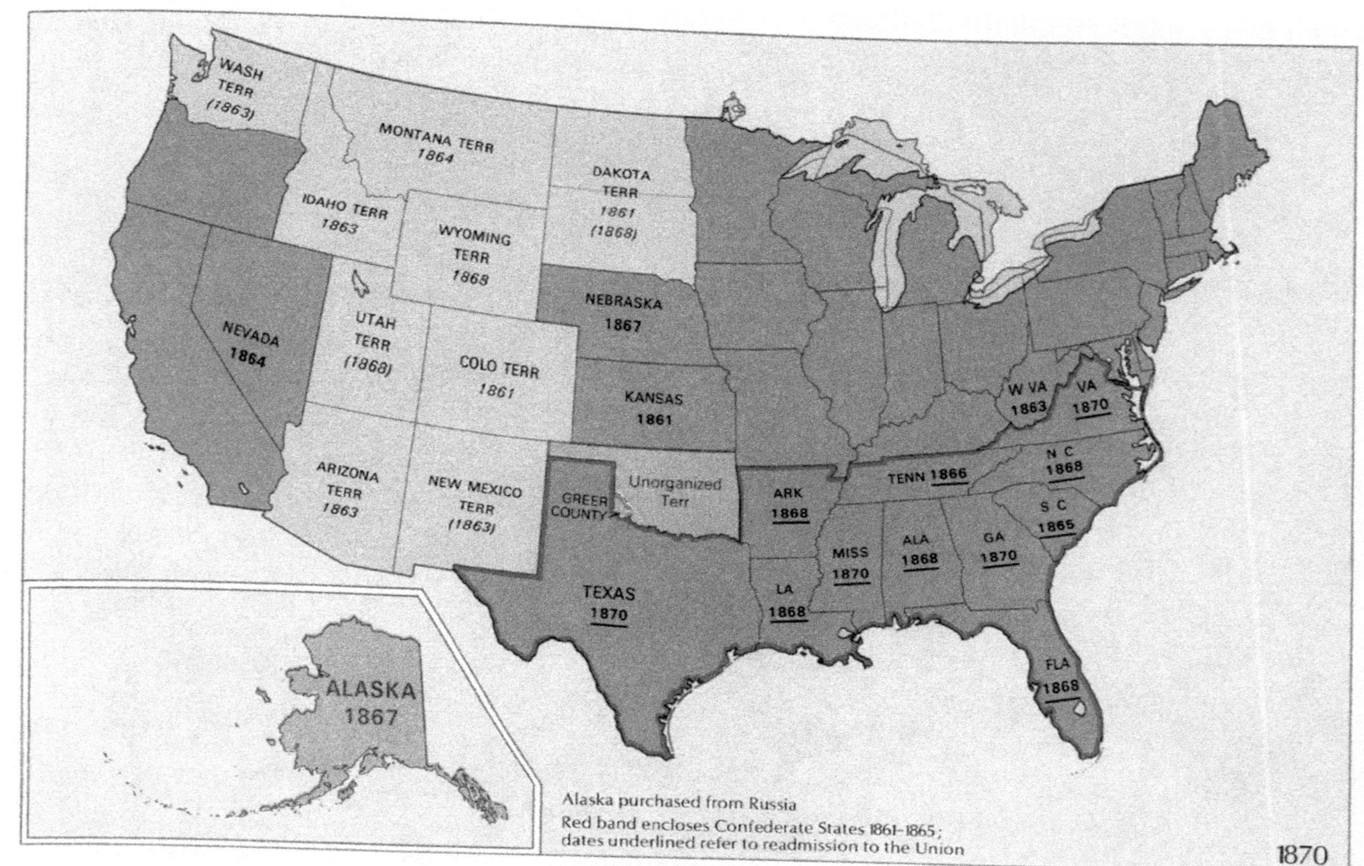
WASH TERR (1863)
MONTANA TERR 1864
IDAHO TERR 1863
DAKOTA TERR 1861 (1868)
WYOMING TERR 1868
NEBRASKA 1867
NEVADA 1864
UTAH TERR (1868)
COLO TERR 1861
KANSAS 1861
W VA 1863
VA 1870
N C 1868
TENN 1866
ARIZONA TERR 1863
NEW MEXICO TERR (1863)
GREER COUNTY
Unorganized Terr
ARK 1868
S C 1865
MISS 1870
ALA 1868
GA 1870
TEXAS 1870
LA 1868
FLA 1868
ALASKA 1867
Alaska purchased from Russia
Red band encloses Confederate States 1861–1865;
dates underlined refer to readmission to the Union
1870

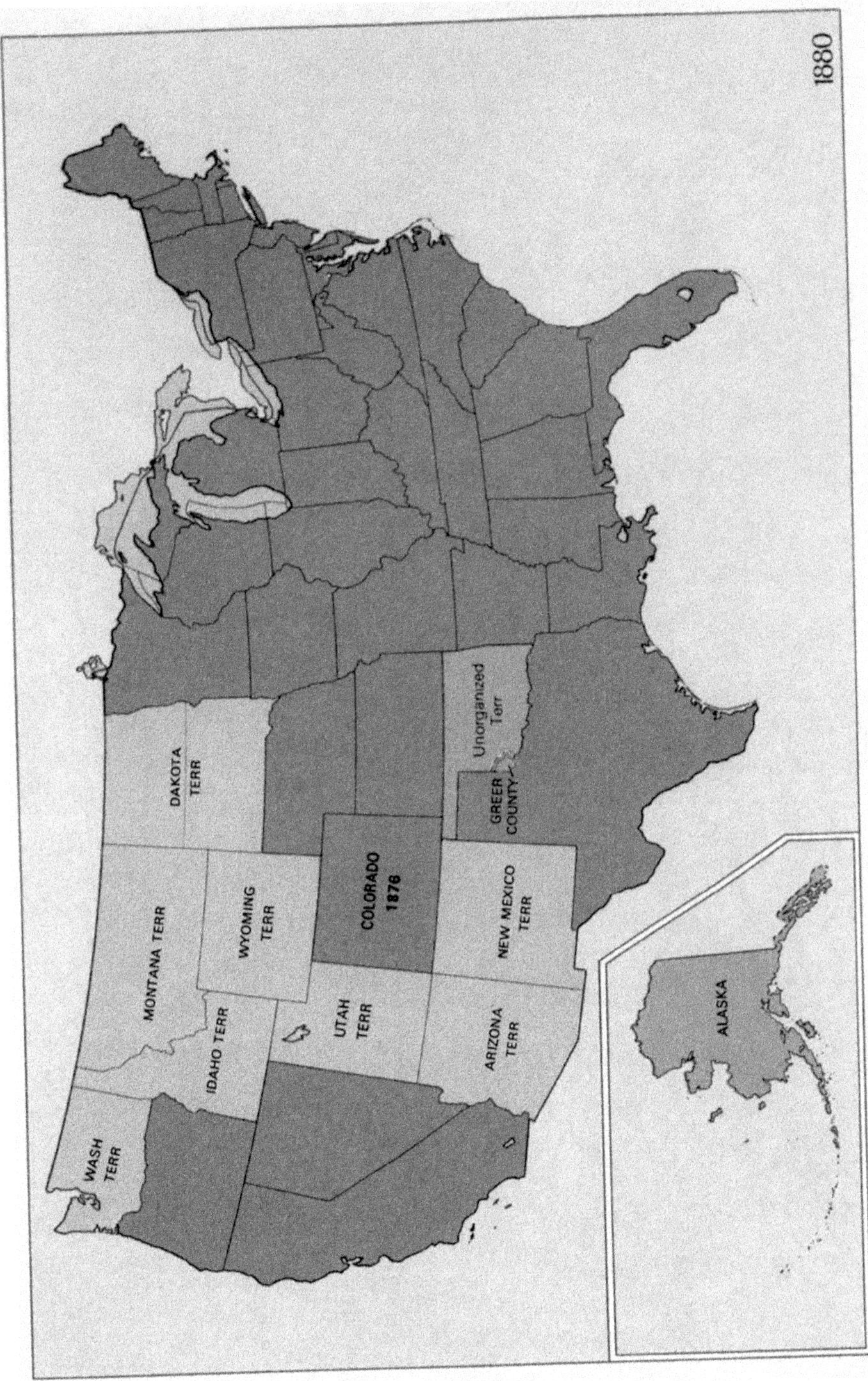
1880
WASH TERR
MONTANA TERR
IDAHO TERR
DAKOTA TERR
WYOMING TERR
UTAH TERR
COLORADO 1876
ARIZONA TERR
NEW MEXICO TERR
Unorganized Terr
GREER COUNTY
ALASKA

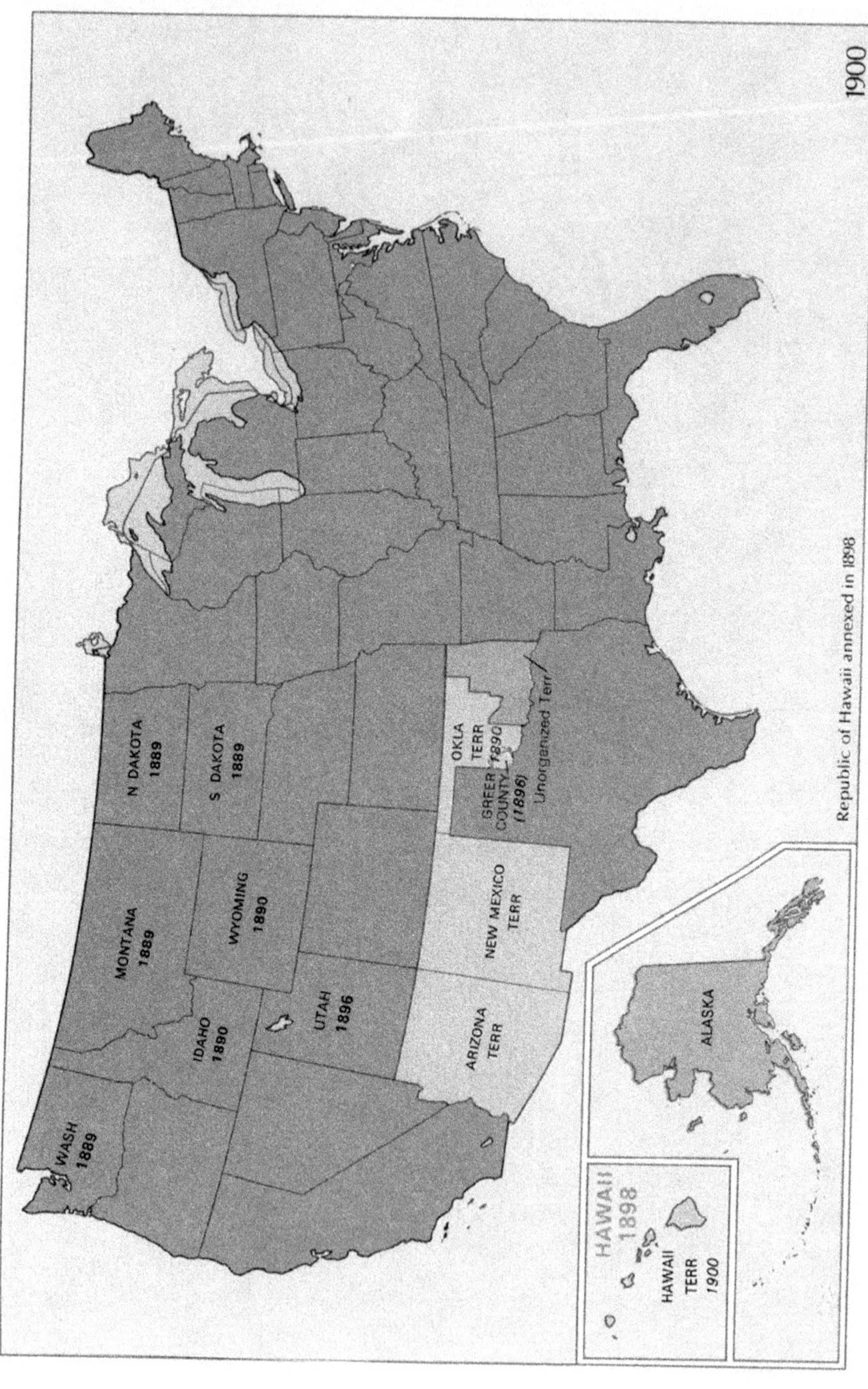
WASH
1889
MONTANA
1889
N DAKOTA
1889
S DAKOTA
1889
WYOMING
1890
IDAHO
1890
UTAH
1896
ARIZONA
TERR
NEW MEXICO
TERR
OKLA
TERR 1890
GREER
COUNTY
(1896)
Unorganized Terr
ALASKA
HAWAII
1898
HAWAII
TERR
1900
Republic of Hawaii annexed in 1898
1900

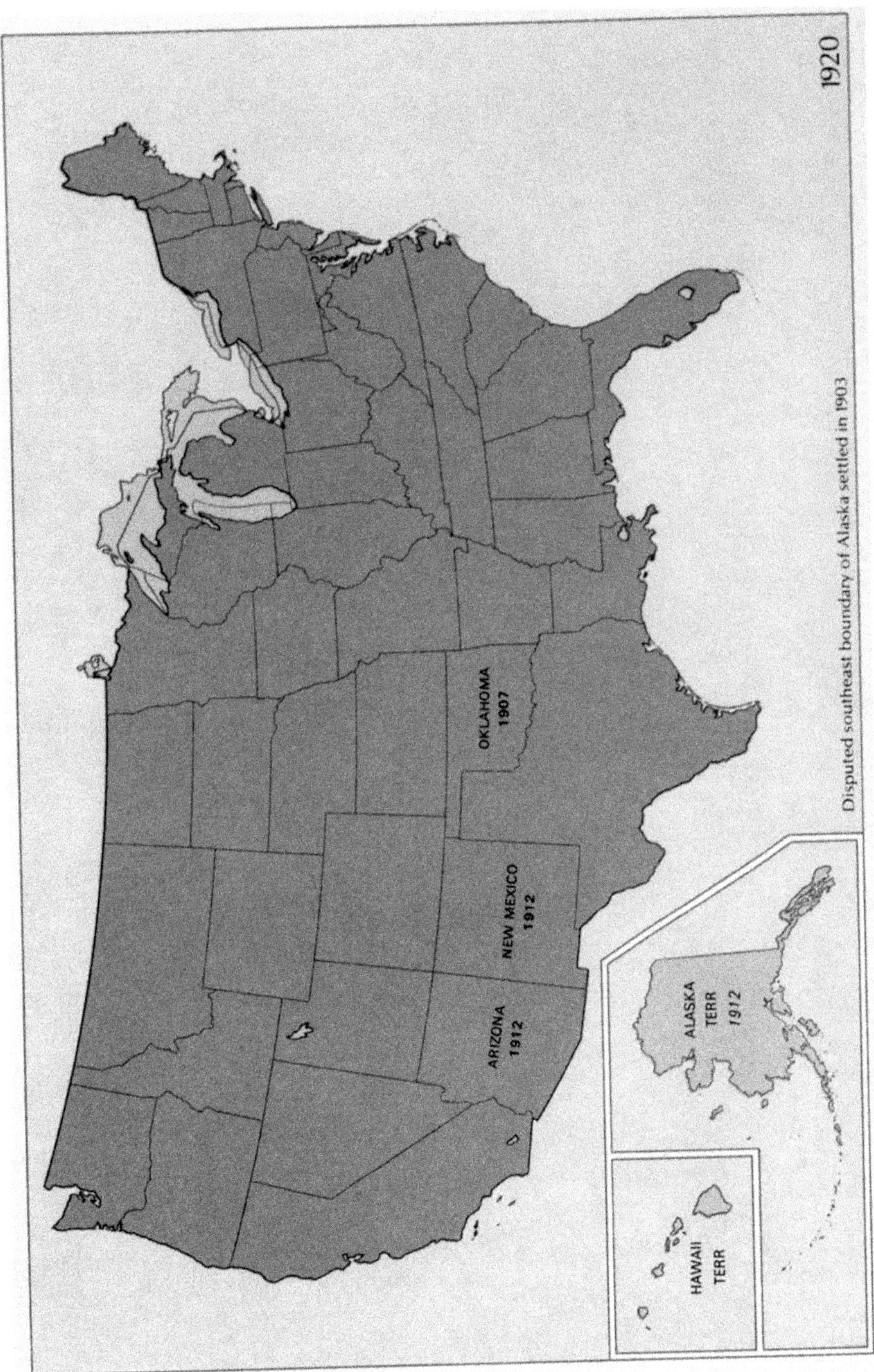
1920
OKLAHOMA
1907
NEW MEXICO
1912
ARIZONA
1912
ALASKA
TERR
1912
HAWAII
TERR
Disputed southeast boundary of Alaska settled in 1903

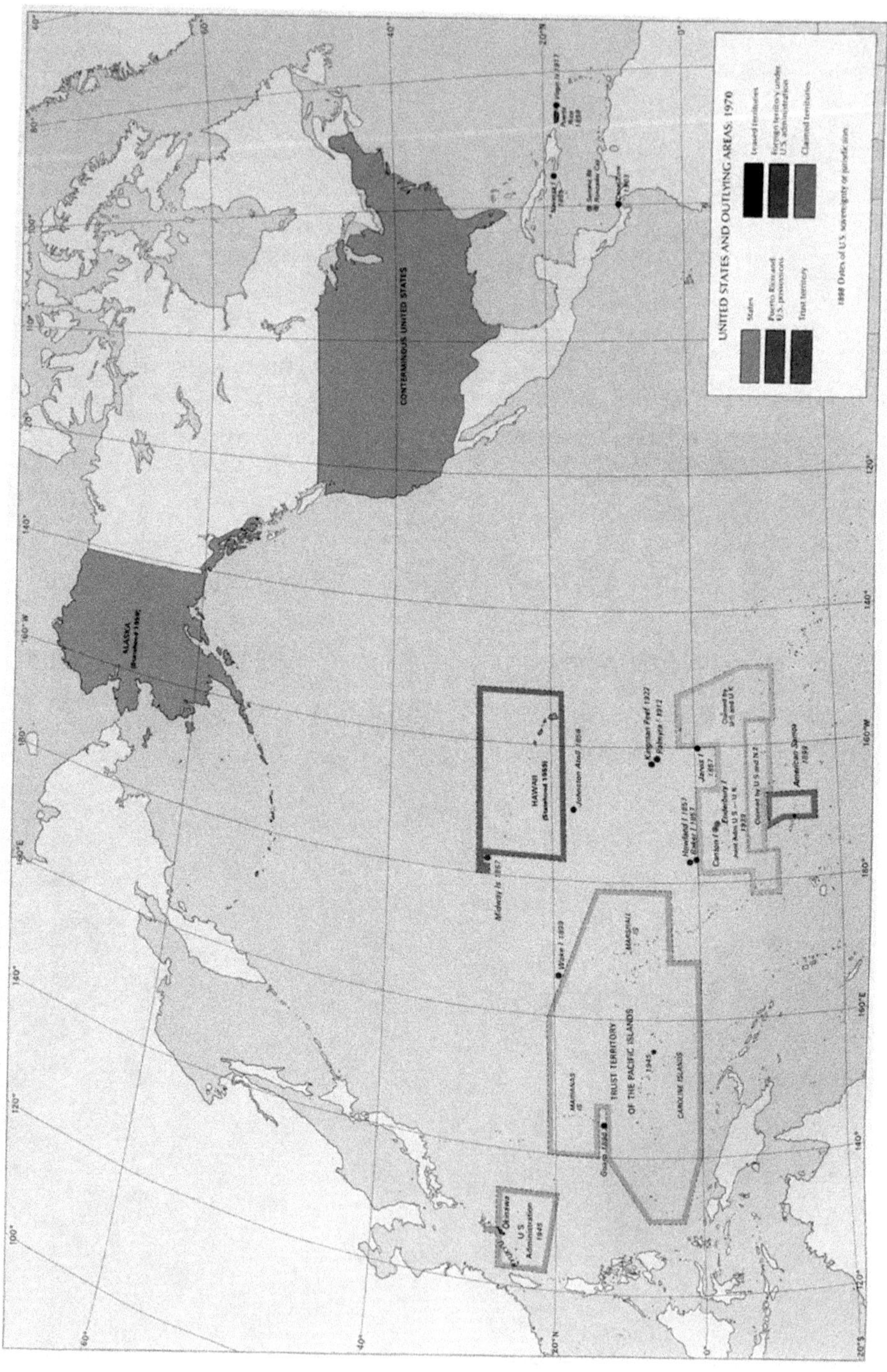
UNITED STATES AND OUTLYING AREAS: 1970
States
Puerto Rico and U.S. possessions
Trust territory
Leased territories
Foreign territory under U.S. administration
Claimed territories
1898 Dates of U.S. sovereignty or jurisdiction
ALASKA
CONTERMINOUS UNITED STATES
HAWAII
(Statehood 1959)
Midway Is 1867
Wake I 1899
Johnston Atoll 1858
Kingman Reef 1922
Palmyra I 1912
Howland I 1857
Baker I 1857
Jarvis I 1857
Canton I
Enderbury I
Joint Adm U.S.—U.K. 1939
Claimed by U.S. and N.Z.
Claimed by U.S. and U.K.
American Samoa 1899
TRUST TERRITORY
OF THE PACIFIC ISLANDS
1945
MARIANAS IS
MARSHALL IS
CAROLINE ISLANDS
Guam 1898
Okinawa
U.S. Administration 1945
Virgin Is 1917
Puerto Rico 1898
Canal Zone 1903

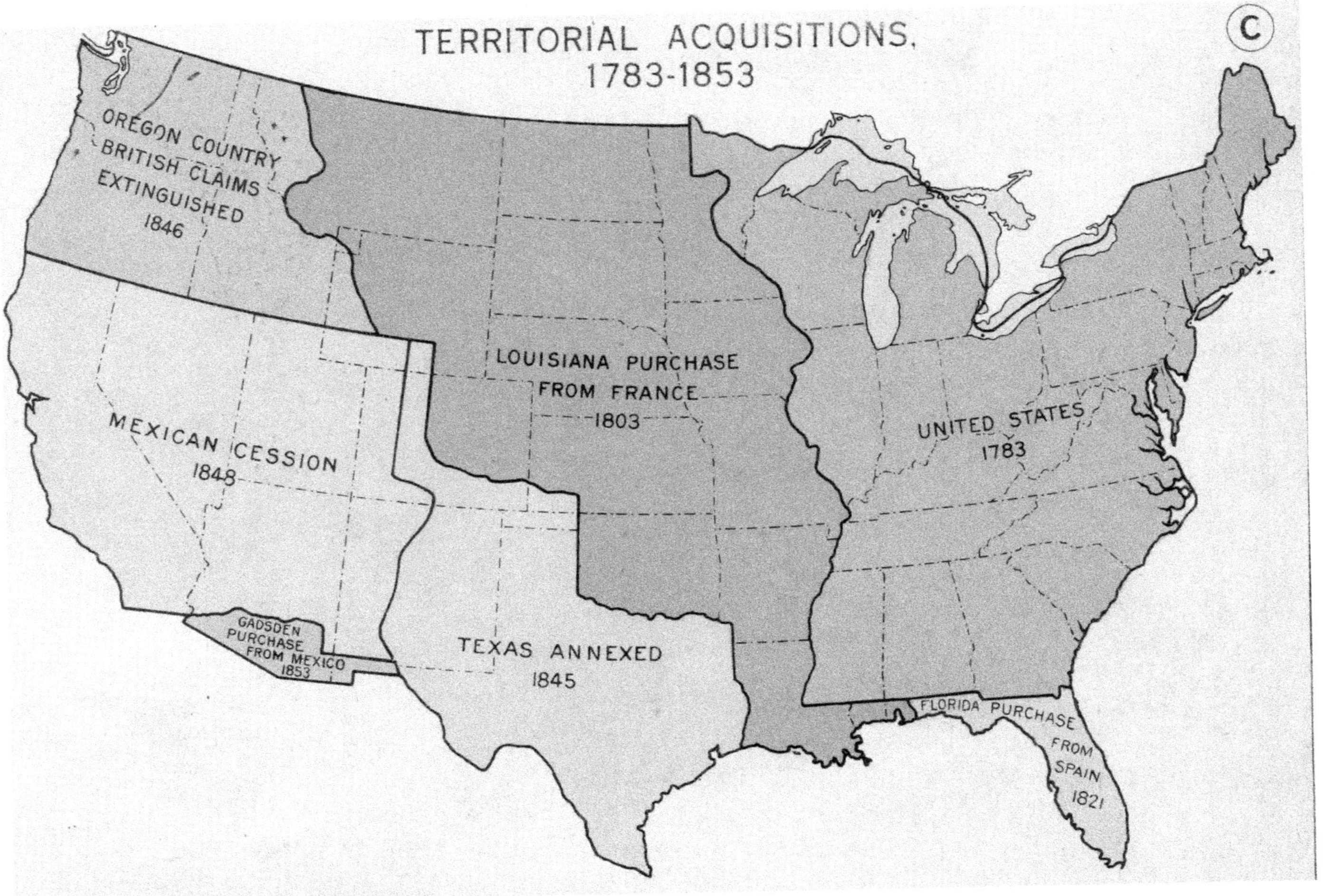
TERRITORIAL ACQUISITIONS, 1783-1853
C
OREGON COUNTRY BRITISH CLAIMS EXTINGUISHED 1846
MEXICAN CESSION 1848
GADSDEN PURCHASE FROM MEXICO 1853
LOUISIANA PURCHASE FROM FRANCE 1803
TEXAS ANNEXED 1845
UNITED STATES 1783
FLORIDA PURCHASE FROM SPAIN 1821

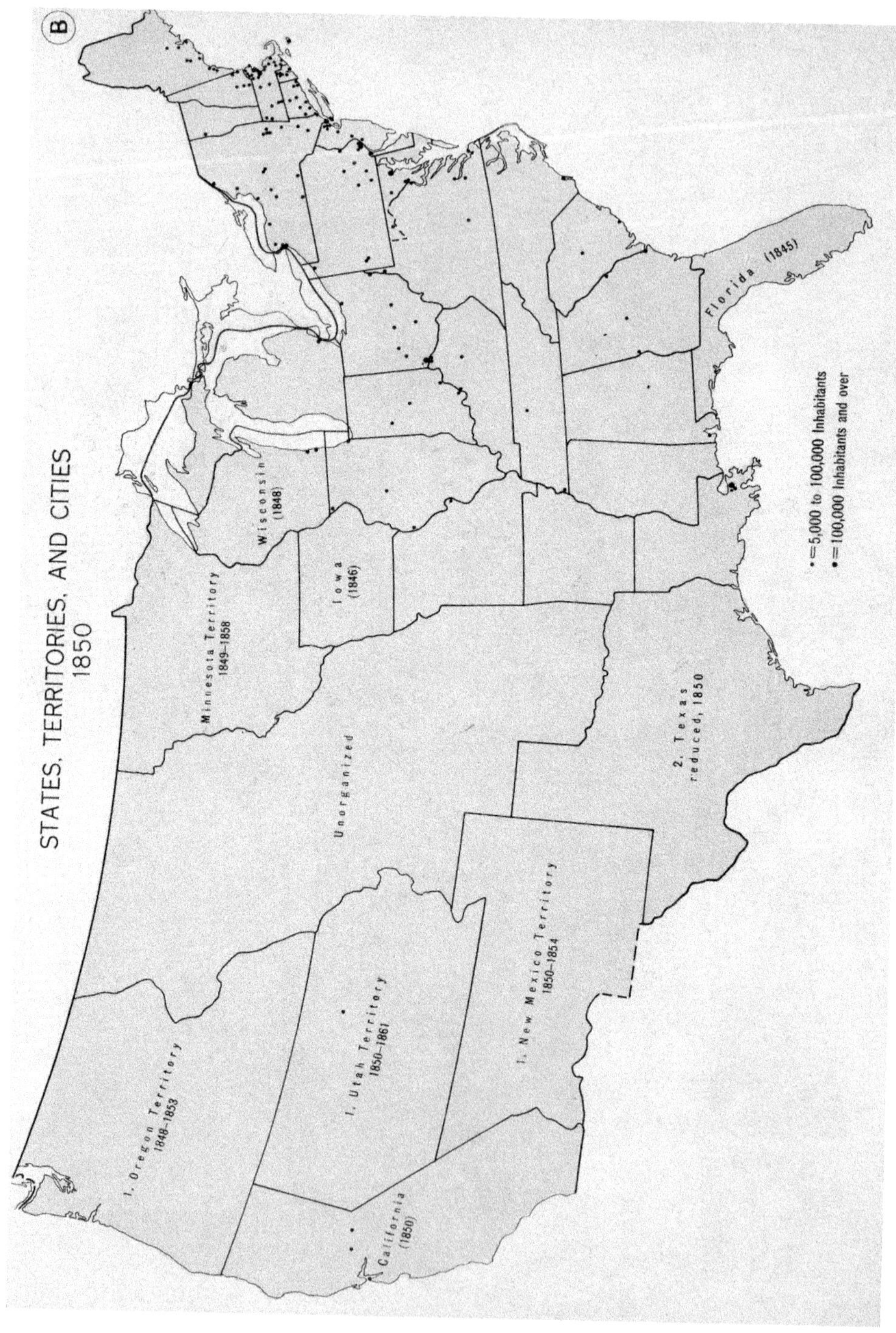
B
STATES, TERRITORIES, AND CITIES
1850
1. Oregon Territory
1848–1853
1. Utah Territory
1850–1861
1. New Mexico Territory
1850–1854
California
(1850)
Unorganized
Minnesota Territory
1849–1858
Wisconsin
(1848)
Iowa
(1846)
2. Texas
reduced, 1850
Florida (1845)
• = 5,000 to 100,000 Inhabitants
● = 100,000 Inhabitants and over

Sources For The Creation Of The American States

PART ONE: The Original Thirteen Colonies

Introduction

SOURCES FOR THE INTRODUCTION

1. Games, Alison. "Migration and the Origins of the English Atlantic World"; Harvard University Press, Cambridge, MA; 1999 (pp. 17-77).
2. Games (pp. 90-91).
3. Barry, John. "Roger Williams and the Creation of the American Soul: Church, State and the Birth of Liberty"; Viking (Penguin Group), N.Y., N.Y. 2012
4. Games (pp. 152-153).
5. Games (p. 164).
6. Games (p. 174).
7. Horsman, Reginald, "The Northwest Ordinance and the Shaping of an Expanding Republic", Wisconsin Magazine of History, 1989 (pp. 21-32).
8. Wikipedia'org/wiki/Northwest Ordinance
9. Games (p. 216).

Chapter One

SOURCES FOR VIRGINIA

1. "The Seed From Which Virginia Grew" by George Arents, William and Mary Quarterly, Vol. 19, 2nd series, No. 2, 1939
2. "Tobacco in Atlantic Trade" by Jacob M. Price, Ashgate Publishing Limited, Aldershot, Great Britain, 1995
3. www.wikipedia.org/wiki/Virginia_Ratifying_ Convention
4. www.en.wikipedia.org/wiki/History_of_the_College_of_William_Mary

5. www,wm.edu/offices/deanofstudents/services/studentconduct/studenthandbook/history_of_the_ college/index.php
6. Ibid.

Chapter Two

SOURCES FOR NEW YORK

1. www.Wikipedia.org/wiki/New_Amsterdam
2. Benchley, Nathaniel, "The $24 Swindle: The Indians Who Stole Manhattan were Bilked Alright, but they didn't mind—the Land Wasn't Theirs Anyway." American Heritage, Vol.11, No. 1 (Dec.1959)
3. www.usahistory.info/colonies/New-Amsterdam
4. "History of the United States of America," The MacMillan Company, New York, 1904 (transcribed by Kathy Leigh)
5. Columbia Electronic Encyclopedia, 6th ed. Columbia University Press. 2012
6. www.amny.com/nyc-has-a-lot-more-revoltionary-history-than-you-might-think
7. www.teachingamerican history.org/ratification/newyork
8. www.ushistory.org/us/16d.asp
9. www.myway.com/search/GGmain
10. www.gilderlehrman.org/history-by-era/creating-new-government/resoures/ratification-us-constitution-new-york-1788.
11. www.wikicu/king's_College
12. www.loc.gov/rr/business/hottopic/stock_market

Chapter Three

SOURCES FOR MASSACHUSETTS

1. Barry, John / "Roger Williams and the Creation of the American Soul: Church, State and the Birth of Liberty"; Viking (Penguin Group), N.Y., N.Y. 2012
2. Ibid
3. www.britannica.com/place/Massachusetts Bay Colony. Retrieved 12/14/15
4. www.wikipedia.org/wiki/History of Harvard University: "John Harvard Facts, Information" The Columbia Encyclopedia, Sixth Edition 2008, retrieved 200hn Harvard Facts, Information etc)

Chapter Four

SOURCES FOR MARYLAND

1. Goodrich, Charles A., "A History of the United States." 1857
2. Ibid.
3. Ibid.
4. www.societyoftheCincinnati.org/pdf/downloads/exhibition_maryland.pdf
5. Ibid.
6. Ibid
7. "Cardinal Foley entertains Knights dinner, asks for lifting of excommunication." Catholic News Agency, August 5, 2008. www.en.wikipedia.org/wiki/John_Carroll_(bishop).
8. www.en.wikipedia.org/wiki/John_Carroll_(bishop)
9. www.en.wikipedia.org/wiki/Charles_of_Carrollton, United States National Archives and Records Administration. 1943
10. www.en.wikipedia.org/wiki/Daniel_Carroll
11. Ibid.

12. Goodrich, Charles A., "Lives of the Signers to the Declaration of Independence". William Reed & Co., New York. 1856. www.colonialhall.com/stone/stone.php.
13. Hubbard, Bill, Jr. "American Boundaries, the nation, the states, the Rectangular Survey:" The University of Chicago Press. 2009. www.en.wikipedia.org/wiki/Mason_Dixon_Line.
14. Ibid.

Chapter Five

SOURCES FOR CONNECTICUT

1. Barry, John / "Roger Williams and the Creation of the American Soul: Church, State and the Birth of Liberty"; Viking (Penguin Group), N.Y., N.Y. 2012
2. www.kentishguards.org/nathael-greene.htm/www.kentishguards.org/nathael-reene.htm
3. www.wikipedia.org/wiki/1st R.I. Regiment. Lanning, Michael Lee. "African Americans in the Revolutionary War" (pp. 75-79).
4. www.wikipedia; History of Rhode Island:; George M. Dennison, "The Dorr War: Republicanism on Trial, 1831-76"; 1976
5. www.wikipedia.org/ "List of Rhode Island Civil War Units"; retrieved 12/8/15

Chapter Six

SOURCES FOR RHODE ISLAND

1. www.en.wikipedia.org/wiki/Fundamental_Orders-of_Connecticut
2. Waters, T.F., "Sketch of the Life of John Winthrop the Younger"; Ipswich, Massachusetts, 1899
3. www.ushistory.org/us/3f.asp
4. www.connecticuthistory.org./the_importance_of_being_purian: church_and_state_in_colonial_connecticut
5. www.en.wikipedia.org/wiki/Fundamental_Orders_of_Connecticut
6. www.britannica.com/place/connecticut
7. www.us-history.com/pages/h1294.html
8. www.connecticuthistory.org/people/roger-sherman/gregg mangan
9. www.en.wikipedia.org/wiki/Yale_University#Origins

Chapter Seven

SOURCES FOR NEW HAMPSHIRE

1. www.en.wikipedia.org/wiki/History_of_New_Hampshire
2. www.en.wikipedia.org/wiki/Fort_William_and_Mary
3. www.en.wikipedia.org/wiki/John_Sullivan_(general)
4. Whittemore, Charles P., "A General of the Revolution: John Sullivan of New Hampshire". Columbia University Press. New York. 1961 Whittemore (p. 166).
5. www.en.wikipedia.org/wiki/John_Sullivan_(general)
6. www.constitutionday.com/langdon-john-nh.html
7. www.Wikipedia.org/wiki/Nicholas_Gilman
8. www.dartmouth.edu/library/rauner/dartmouth/dartmouth_history.
9. Francic Lane Childs, Dartmouth Alumni Magazine. 1957

Chapter Eight

SOURCES FOR DELAWARE

1. Goodrich, Charles A., "A History of the United States" 1857
2. Clark, Ellen McCallister and Sxhulz, Emily L.; "Delaware in the American Revolution,"
3. The Society of the Cincinnati, Washington, D.C. 2002

4. Ibid.
5. www.archives.gov/exhibits/charters/constitution_founding_fathers_delaware
6. Ibid.
7. Ibid.
8. Ibid
9. Ibid
10. Ryden, George Herbert. "Letters to and from Caesar Rodney." Historical Society of Delaware. 1933

Chapter Nine

SOURCES FOR NORTH CAROLINA

1. www.en.wikipedia.org/wiki/History_of_North_Carolina
2. www.u-s-history.com/pages/h624
3. Ibid.
4. www.en.wikipedia.org/wiki/Battle_of_Moore's9627s_Creek_Bridge
5. www.en.wikipedia.org/wiki/Halifax_Resolves
6. www.societyofthecincinnati.org/pdf/downloads/exhibition_NorthCarolina.pdf
7. www.militaryhistory.about.com/od/americanrevolution/p/guilfordch.htm
8. Lefler, Hugh. "Willie Jones: The Patriots: The American Revolution Generation of Genius." Ed.VirginiusDabney, NewYork: Atheneum, 1975. www.en.wikipedia.org/wiki/Willie_Jones_(statesman)
9. McCullough, David. 2008. www.dsdi1776.com/signers_by_state/john-penn/
10. Lowry, Harold D. 2006. www.dsdi1776.com/signers_by_state/william-hooper/
11. www.dsdi1776.com/signers-by-state/joseph-hewes/

Chapter Ten

SOURCES FOR NEW JERSEY

1. www.en.wikipedia.org/wiki/Dutch_East_India_Company
2. Ibid.
3. Streissguth, Thomas. "New Jersey", San Diego Lucent Books, Inc. 2002.
4. Goodrich, Charles. " A History of the United States. 1857
5. Shorto, Russell. "The Island at the Center of the World: The Epic Story of Dutch Manhattan and the Colony that Shaped America." Random House, New York, 2004
6. www.en.wikipedia.org/wiki/Colonial_History_of_New_Jersey
7. Burian, A. Ward. "George Washington's Legacy of Leadership." Morgan James Publishing, LLC. Garden City, New York. 2007
8. www.archives.gov/exhibits/charters/constitution_founding_fathers_new_jersey

Chapter Eleven

SOURCES FOR SOUTH CAROLINE

1. Charles Hudson (September 1998). "Knights of Spain, Warriors of the Sun: Hernando de Soto and the South's Ancient Chieftans. University of Georgia Press. Retrieved February 16, 2012.
2. N.C. Board of Agriculture (1902), "A Sketch of North Carolina", Charleston. Lucas-Richardson Co. p. 4. Retrieved May 26, 2014
3. www.en.wikipedia.org/wiki/History_of_South_Carolina
4. Larabee, Benjamin Woods. "The Boston Tea Party". Boston originally published 1964. Northeastern University Press, 1979.
5. Ibid

6. Ibid
7. Ibid
8. www.en.wkipedia.org/wiki/Stamp_Act-1765.
9. www.halseymap.com/flash/window.asp?HMID=47
10. www.britishbattles.com/battle-camden.htm
11. www.en.wikipedia.org/wiki/Battle_of_Kings-Mountain
12. www.history.com/topics/american-revolution/battle_of_cowpens
13. www.en.wikipedia.org/wiki/Constitutional_Convention_(United_States)
14. www.social.rollins.edu/wpsites/list120/2012/12/06/slavery-in-south-carolina
15. www.let.rug.nl/usa/biographies/john-rutledge/
16. www.let.rug.nl/usa/biographies/charles-cotesworthy-pinckney/
17. www.let.rug.nl/usa/biographies/pierce-butler/
18. ww.let.rug.nl/usa/biographies/charles-pinckney/

Chapter Twelve

SOURCES FOR PENNSYLVANIA

1. www.ushistory.org/pennsylvania/pennsylvania
2. www.enwikipedia.org/wiki/History-of-Pennsylvania
3. Burian, A. Ward. "George Washington's Legacy of Leadership"; Morgan James Publishing. Garden City, New York. 2007
4. www.archives.gov/exhibits/charters/constitution-founding-fathers
5. Ibid.
6. Ibid.
7. www.en.wikipedia.org/wiki/University_of_Pennsylvania
8. www.En.wikipedia.org/wiki/Thomas_Mifflin
9. www.archives.gov/exhibits/charters/constitution-founding-fathers gouv
10. www.Teachingamerican history.org/static/convention/delegates/morris
11. www.archives.gov/eshibits/charters/constitution founding fathers pennsylvania
12. Ibid.

Chapter Thirteen

SOURCES FOR GEORGIA

1. www.georgiainfo.galileo.usg.edu/topics/history/article/timeline-prehistoric-era-and-early-history.
2. Ibid.
3. Ibid.
4. www.georgiaencyclopedia.org/acrchives/history-archeology/james-oglethorpe-1696-1785.
5. www.georgiainfo.Galileo.usg.edu/topics/history/articles/Georgia-as-an-english-colony-1732-1775/timeline-georgia.
6. Ibid.
7. Ibid.
8. Ibid.
9. Ibid.
10. www.georgiaencyclopedia.org/articles/history-archeology/james-oglethorpe-1696-1785
11. Sweet, Julie A. "Tomochichi (1644-1739)." New Georgia Encyclopedia. 06 January 2016. Web. 16 May 2016.
12. Denton, Stan. "Button Gwinnett (1735-1777)." New Georgia Encyclopedia. 10 March 2016. Web. 16 May 2016.

13. Schmidt, Jim. "Archibald Bulloch (1730-1777)." New Georgia Encyclopedia. 30 September 2014. Web. 17 May 2016.
14. Smith, Gerald J. "Abraham Baldwin (1754-1807)." New Georgia Encyclopedia. 06 January 2016. Web. 17 May 2016.

PART TWO: From the Constitutional Convention in 1787 to the Present

Chapter Fourteen

SOURCES FOR VERMONT

1. www:en.wikipedia.org/wiki/History_of_Vermont
2. Ibid.
3. www.Historicsites.vermont.gov/Vermont_history/early_settlement
4. www.Militaryhistorynow.com/2013/05/07/the-14th-colony-vermont-curious-role-in-the-American-Revolution.
5. Ibid.
6. Ibid.
7. Ibid.
8. www.newworldencyclopedia.org/entry/vermont
9. LaFayette, Wilbur. "Early History of Vermont", Roscoe Printing House. Jericho, Vermont. 1902
10. Ibid.
11. Ibid.
12. Ibid.

Chapter Fifteen

SOURCES FOR KENTUCKY

1. Sheppard, Donald E. "de Soto's Kentucky Trails", Florida History, October 27, 2015. www.en.wikipedia.org/wiki/History_of_Kentucky
2. Whitaker, Arthur Preston. "The Spanish-American Frontier", Peter Smith Publisher, Gloucester, Massachusetts. 1962. 1783-1795. "The Western Movement and the Spanish Retreat in the Mississippi Valley."
3. Ibid.
4. Ibid.
5. Ibd
6. Ibid.
7. Ibid.
8. Ibid.
9. www.notablebiographies.com/Be-Br/Boone-Daniel.html
10. www.libertyhall.org/john-brown/founding-faher-of-Kentucky#page
11. www.wow.com/wiki/James_Harrod
12. Ibid.
13. Ibid.
14. www.wow.com/wiki/Benjamin_Logan
15. www.wow.com/wiki/George_Rogers_Clark
16. Ibid.
17. Ibid.

Chapter Sixteen

SOURCES FOR KENTUCKY

1. www.en.wikipedia.org/wiki/History_of_Tennessee#Early_Spanish_and_French_Exploration
2. www.en.wikipedia.org/wiki/Rene_Robert_Cavelier,_Sieur_de_la_Salle
3. www.en.wikipedia.org/wiki/New_France
4. www.en.wikipedia.org/wiki/Rene_Robert_Cavelier_Sieur_de_la_Salle
5. www.Tennesseehistry.com/class/FoundingTN.htm
6. Ibid.
7. Ibid.
8. Ibid.
9. www.tn4.org/articles.cfn/a_id/264/minor_id/82/major_id/26/era_id/3
10. www.archives.gov/exhibits/chaters/constitution_founding_fathers_north_carolina.html
11. www.en.wikipedia.org/wiki/James_Robertson_(explorer)
12. www.en.wikipedia.org/wiki/Cumberland_Compact
13. www.en.wikipedia.org/wiki/Donelson_Tennessee
14. www.en.wikipedia.org/wiki/John_Sevier
15. www.en.wikipedia.org/wiki/Isaac_Shelby

Chapter Seventeen

SOURCES FOR OHIO

1. www.en.wikipedia.org/wiki/Connecticut_Western_Reserve
2. www.en.wikipedia.org/wiki/Ohio_Country
3. www.en.wikipedia.org/wiki/Northwest_Indian_War
4. www.ourdocuments.gov/doc.php?flash=true&doc=8
5. www.en.wikipedia.org/wiki/Northwest_Ordinance
6. Ibid.
7. www.ohiohistorycentral.org/w/Rufus_Putnam
8. www.ohiohistorycentral.org/w/Edward_Tiffin
9. www.ohiohistorycentral.org/w/Thomas_Worthington
10. www.ohiohistorycentral.org/w/Samuel_Huntington
11. www.en.wikipedia.org/wiki/Ebenezer_Sproat
12. www.ohiohistorycentral.org/w/Tecumseh?rec=373

Chapter Eighteen

SOURCES FOR LOUISIANA

1. www.en.wikipedia.org/wiki/History_of_Louisiana
2. www.yatlagniappe.com/2015/01/15/louisiana's-fight-in-the-revolutionary-war/ TO 2
3. www.en.wikipedia.org/site/Jefferson/louisiana_purchase. Wilson, Gaye-2003. "Jefferson's Big Deal: The Louisiana Purchase," Monticello Newsletter, 14 (Spring 2003).
4. www.geography.about.com/ed/historyofgeography/a/lewisclark
5. www.history1800s.about.com/od/lewisandclark/fl/William-Clark-b
6. www.everyculture.com/multi/Bu-Dr./Creoles. Caver, Helen Bush and Williams, Mary T.
7. www.louisiana.gov/explore/About_Louisiana
8. www.en.wikipedia.org/wiki/Law_of_Louisiana.
9. www.britannica.com/biography/Rene-Robert-Cavelier-sieur-de-La-Salle.
10. www.nps.gov/foma/learn/historyculture/galvez

Chapter Nineteen

SOURCES FOR INDIANA

1. www.en.wikipedia.org/wiki/History_of_Indiana
2. www.en.wikipedia.org/wiki/Beaver_Wars
3. www.en.wikipedia.org/wiki/Siege of Fort_Vincennes
4. www.en.wikipedia.org/wiki/Battle_of_Fallen_Timbers
5. www.en.wikipedia.org/wiki/Battle_of_Tippecanoe
6. www.en.wikipedia.org/wiki/History_of_Indiana
7. www.en.wikipedia.org/wiki/Jonathan_Jennings
8. www.en.wikipedia.org/wiki/William_Hendricks
9. www.en.wikipedia.org/wiki/Dennis_Pennington
10. www.in.gov/history/2958

Chapter Twenty

SOURCES FOR MISSISSIPPI

1. www.en.wikipedia.org/wiki/Five_Civilized_Tribes
2. www.en.wikipedia.org/wiki/cotton_gin
3. www.en.wikipedia.org/wiki/History_of_Mississippi
4. www.en.wikipedia.org/wiki/cotton_gin
5. www.en.wikipedia.org/wiki/Indian_Removal_Act
6. www.en.wikipedia.org/wiki/Mississippi_Territory
7. www.en,Wikipedia.org/wiki/War_of_1812#Creek_War
8. Ibid.
9. www.en.wikipedia.org/wiki/Winthrop_Sargent
10. www.en.wikipedia.org/wiki/David_Holmes. McCain, William D., "The Administration of David Holmes, Governor of the Mississippi Territory; 1809-1817", Journal of Mississippi History, Vol 29, No. 3 (1967) (pp. 328-347).
11. www.en.wikipedia.org/wiki/David_Holmes

Chapter Twenty-one

SOURCES for ILLINOIS

1. www.en.wikipedia.org/wiki/Illinois_Country
2. Ibid.
3. www.en.wikipedia.or./wiki/New_France
4. Ibid.
5. Ibid.
6. Ibid.
7. Ibid.
8. www.en.wikipedia.org/wiki/Ninian_Edwards
9. Ibid

Chapter Twenty-two

SOURCES FOR ALABAMA

1. www.en.wikipedia.org/wiki/History_of_Alabama
2. Ibid.
3. www.en.wikipedia.org/wiki/Fort_Bowyers
4. www.encyclopediaofalabama.org/article/h-1548. Hagood, Thomas Chase, University of Georgia.

5. Stewart, John Craig. "The Governors of Alabama," Pelican Publishing Company, Gretna, Louisiana, 1998 (pp. 51-59).
6. Ibid.
7. www.encyclopediaofalabama.org/article/h-1181. Balley, Hugh. Valdosta State University

Chapter Twenty-three
SOURCES FOR MAINE

1. www.penobscotmarinemuseum.org/pbho-1/our-maine-ancestry/revolutionary-war
2. www.us-history.com/paes/h557
3. www.en.wikipedia.org/wiki/History_of_Maine
4. www.pressherold.com/2012/06/24/200-years-ago_2012-06-24/
5. www.em.wikipedia.org/wiki/Bowdoin_College

Chapter Twenty-four
SOURCES FOR MISSOURI

1. www.en.wikipedia.org/wiki/History_of_Missouri
2. www.en.wikipedia.org/wiki/Treaty_of_Fontainebleau_(1762)
3. www.en.wikipedia.org/wiki/History_of_Missouri
4. Ibid.
5. Ibid.
6. www.en.wikipedia.org/wiki/Burr_Conspiracy
7. www.en.wikipedia.org/wiki/Missouri_Compromise
8. www.en.wikipedia.org/wiki/History_of_Missouri
9. Ibid.
10. Ibid.

Chapter Twenty-five
SOURCES FOR ARKANSAS

1. www.en.wikipedia.org/wiki/History_of_Arkansas
2. www.encyclopediaofarkansas.net/encyclopedia/entry-detail.aspx?entryID =2208
3. www.biography.com/people/louis_joliet-20973103#north-american-travels.
4. www.encyclopediaofarkansas.net/encyclopedia/entry-detail.aspx?entryID=2916&media=print.
5. www.encyclopediaofarkansas.net/encyclopedia/entry-detail. Aspx?entry/ID2207&type=Time+Period&Item=European+Exploration+Settlement+(1541+-+1802)&p.
6. www.encyclopediaofarkansas.net/encyclopedia/entry=detail.aspx?entryID=2916
7. www.encyclopediaofarkansas.net/encyclopedia/entry=detail.aspx?en
8. www.en.wikipedia.org/wiki/Arkansas_Territory
9. www.en.wikipedia.org/wiki/James_Miller_(general)
10. www.Wikipedia.org/wiki/History_of_Arkansas#statehood_and_antebellum_Arkansas
11. Ibid.
12. www.en.wikipedia.org/wiki/Panic_of_1837

Chapter Twenty-six
SOURCES FOR MICHIGAN

1. www.en.wikipedia.org/wiki/History_of_Michigan
2. Ibid.
3. www.en.wikipedia.org/wiki/Western_Confederacy
4. www.en.wikipedia.org/wiki/Toledo_War

5. www.Jurgins,Olga.UniversityofToronto/UniversiteLaval/1966-2016. www.biographi.ca/en/bio/brule_etienne_1E.html
6. www.en.wikipedia.org/wiki/Lewis_Cass
7. www.en.wikipedia.org/wiki/Stevens_T._Mason
8. www.en.wikipedia.org/wiki/Gabriel_Richard

Chapter Twenty-seven

SOURCES FOR FLORIDA

1. www.en.wikipedia.org/wiki/History_of_Florida
2. www.en.wikipedia.org/wiki/East_Florida
3. www.en.wikipedia.org/wiki/History_of_Florida
4. www.en.wikipedia.org/wiki/Florida_Territory
5. www.floridahistory.org/territorial.htm
6. Ibid.
7. Ibid.
8. www.The hermitage.com/learn/andrew-jackson/general
9. Dyer, Oliver. "General Andrew Jackson." Robert Bonner's Sons, New York, 1891.
10. www.en.wikipedia.org/wiki/Adams-Onis Treaty
11. www.dos.myflorida.com/florida-facts/florida-history/a-brief-history/statehood/

Chapter Twenty-eight

SOURCES FOR TEXAS

1. www.en.wikipedia.org/wiki/French_colonization_of_Texas
2. www.en.wikipedia.org/wiki/Spanish_Texas
3. www.en.wikipedia.org/wiki/Mexican_Texas
4. www.en.wikipedia.org/wiki/Battle_of_the_Alamo
5. www.en.wikipedia.org/wiki/Republic_of_Texas
6. www.en.wikipedia.org/wiki/Mexican-American War
7. Ibid.
8. Ibid.
9. www.en.wikipedia.org/wiki/Sam_Houston
10. www.en.wikipedia.org/wiki/Stephen_F._Austin

Chapter Twenty-nine

SOURCES FOR IOWA

1. www.en.wikipedia.org/wiki/History_of_Iowa
2. Ibid.
3. Ibid.
4. www.iptv.org/iowapathways/mypath.cfm?ounid=ob_000124.Sage,Leland."A History of Iowa," Iowa State Press, 1974; Wall, Joseph. "Iowa: A Bicentennial History," New York; Norton, 1978; Schwieder, Dorothy. "Iowa: The Middle Land." Ames: Iowa State Press, 1996.
5. www.en.wikipedia.org/wiki/Julien_Dubuque
6. Randak, Leigh Ann. "Lucas, Robert. The Biographical History of Iowa." University of Iowa Press, 2009. Web. 10 November 2016.
7. www.en.wikipedia.org/wiki/James_Clarke_(Iowa_politician)
8. www.en.wikipedia.org/wiki/Ansel_Briggs

Chapter Thirty

SOURCES FOR WISCONSIN

1. www.en.wikipedia.org/wiki/History_of_Wisconsin
2. Ibid.
3. Ibid.
4. Ibid.
5. Ibid.
6. www.en.wikipedia.org/wiki/Jean_Nicolet
7. www.en.wikipedia.org/wiki/Nicolas_Perrot
8. www.en.wikipedia.org/wiki/Great_Peace_of_Montreal
9. www.en.wikipedia.org/wiki/Solomon_Juneau
10. www.en.wikipedia.org/wiki/Henry_Dodge

Chapter Thirty-one

SOURCES FOR CALIFORNIA

1. www.en.wikipedia.org/wiki/History_of_California
2. Ibid.
3. Ibid.
4. Ibid.
5. www.en.wikipedia.org/wiki/Compromise_of_1850
6. www.en.wikipedia.org/wiki/Golden_Fleece
7. www.sfmuseum.net/bio/jserra.html
8. www.en.wikipedia.org/wiki/Junipero_Serra
9. Ibid.

Chapter Thirty-two

SOURCES FOR MINNESOTA

1. www.statesymbolsusa.org/symbol-official-item/Minnesota/state-name-origin/origin-minnesota
2. www.en.wikipedia.org/wiki/History_of_Minnesota
3. www.en.wikipedia.org/wiki/Saint_Anthony_Falls
4. Ibid.
5. www.en.wikipedia.org/wiki/Dred_Scott_v._Sandford
6. www.en.wikipedia.org/wiki/History_of_Minnesota
7. Ibid.
8. Ibid.
9. www.en.wikipedia.org/wiki/Daniel_Greysolon,_Sieur_du_Lhut
10. www.mnopedia.org/person/hennepin_louis_c1640-c1701
11. www.en.wikipedia.org/wiki/Henry_Mower_Rice

Chapter Thirty-three

SOURCES FOR OREGON

1. www.en.wikipedia.org/wiki/History_of_Oregon
2. www.en.wikipedia.org/wiki/Northwest_Passage
3. www.en.wikipedia.org/wiki/Robert_Gray9627s_Columbia_River_expedition
4. www.en.wikipedia.org/wiki/Treaty_of_1818
5. www.en.wikipedia.org/wiki/Hudson%27s_Bay_Company
6. www.en.wikipedia.org/wiki/Oregon_Trail
7. www.en.wikipedia.org/wiki/Oregon_Territory

8. www.en.wikipedia.org/wiki/Robert_Gray_(sea captain)
9. www.en.wikipedia.org/wiki/John_McLoughlin

Chapter Thirty-four

SOURCES FOR KANSAS

1. www.en.wikipedia.org/wiki/History_of_Kansas
2. Ibid.
3. Ibid.
4. Ibid.
5. Ibid.
6. www.en.wikipedia.org/wiki/Kansas_Pacific_Railway
7. www.robinsonlibrary.com/america/uslocal/west/kansas/history/holliday/htw
8. www.kshs.org/kansapedia/shawnee-indian-mission/11913
9. www.en.wikipedia.org/wiki/"Wild_Bill_Hickok

Chapter Thirty-five

SOURCES FOR WEST VIRGINIA

1. www.wikipedia.org/wiki/History_of_West_Virginia
2. Ibid.
3. Ibid.
4. Sturm, Philip. "Francis Harrison Pierpont." E-wv: The West Virginia Encyclopedia 07 March 2016. January 2017. www.wvencyclopedia.org/articles/1853.
5. Fredette, Allison. "Waitman T. Willey (1811-1900)." (2014, June 20). In Encyclopedia Virginia. Retrieved from www.EncyclopediaVirginia.org/Willey_Waitman_T_1811-1900.

Chapter Thirty-six

SOURCES FOR NEVADA

1. www.en.wikipedia.org/wiki/Treaty_of_Guadalupe_Hidalgo
2. www.parks.nv.gov/parks/mormon-station-state-historic-park/
3. www.history.com/topics/homestead-act
4. www.en.wikipedia.org/wiki/Nevada_in_the_American_Civil_War
5. www.onlinenevada.org/articles/nevada-statehood
6. www.en.wikipedia.org/wiki/Francisco_Garces
7. www.en.wikipedia.org/wiki/Abraham_Curry
8. Southerland, Cindy. 8 November 2010. www.onlinenevada.org/articles/james-warren-nye

Chapter Thirty-seven

SOURCES FOR NEBRASKA

1. www.ereferencedesk.com/resources/state-history/nebraska.html
2. Ibid.
3. www.ereferencedesk.com/resources/state-history/nebraska.html
4. Ibid.
5. Berry, Myrtle D. "Nebraska in the Civil War." Nebraska State Historical Society. www.usgennet.org/usa/ne/topic/military/CW/neincs.htmlhttp://www.usgennet.org/usa/ne/topic/military/CW/neincw.html
6. Ibid.
7. www.wisegeek.com/why-is-nebraska-called-the-cornhusker-state.htm
8. Sheldon, Addison Erwin. "History and Stories of Nebraska." www.odlden-times.com/oldtimenebraska/n-csnyder/nbstory/nbstory5.html

9. www.nebraskahistory.org/lib-arch/research/manuscripts/politics/thomas-cuming.pdf
10. www.en.wikipedia.org/wiki/John_Milton_Thayer

Chapter 38

SOURCES FOR COLORADO

1. www.en.wikipedia.org/wiki/History_of_Colorado
2. Ibid.
3. www.en.wikipedia.org/wiki/San_Louis_Colorado
4. www.en.wikipedia.org/wiki/History_of_Colorado
5. Kopel, Jerry. www.Jerrykopel.com/b/Colorado-statehood-struggle
6. Ibid.
7. www.en.wikipedia.org/wiki/Ouray_(Ute_leader)
8. www.en.wikipedia.org/wiki/William_Jackson_Palmer
9. Ibid.
10. Ibid.
11. Ibid.

Chapter Thirty-nine

SOURCES FOR NORTH DAKOTA

1. www.history.nd.gov/ndhistory/firstpeople.html
2. www.history.nd.gov/ndhistory/furtrade.html
3. www.en.wikipedia.org/wiki/Dakota_Territory
4. Lee, Shebby. "The Great Dakota Boom." www.exploretheoldwest.com/the_great_dakota_boom.htm
5. www.en.wikipedia.org/wiki/Long_Depression
6. Ibid.
7. Friedman, Milton and Schwartz, Anna Jacobson. "A Monetary History of the United States, 1867. 1960." Princeton University Press. 1971. www.en.wikipedia.org/wiki/Long_Depression.
8. Rothbard, Murray N. "A History of Money and Banking in the United States." www.en.wikipedia.org/wiki/Long_Depression.
9. www.history.nd.gov/ndhistory/statehood-html
10. www.Blackhillsvisitor.com/all-articles-directory.html?pid=878&sid=907:George-Crook-A-Short-Biograohy-Parts 1 & 2
11. Ibid. Parts 3 & 4

Chapter Forty

SOURCES FOR SOUTH DAKOTA

1. www.en.wikipedia.org/wiki/History_of_South_Dakota
2. www.en.wikipedia.org/wiki/Great_Sioux_War_of_1876
3. www.history,com/topics/us-states/south-dakota
4. www.en.wikipedia.org/wiki/Badlands_National_Park
5. www.en.wikipedia.org/wiki/Sitting_Bull
6. www.en.wikipedia.org/wiki/George_Armstrong_Custer
7. Ibid.

Chapter Forty-one

SOURCES FOR MONTANA

1. www.en.wikipedia.org/wiki/History_of_Montana

2. Ibid.
3. Ibid.
4. Ibid.
5. www.en.wikipedia.org/wiki/Montana_Territory
6. www.en.wikipedia.org/wiki/Montana
7. www.en.wikipedia.org/wiki/History_of_Montana
8. www.en.wikipedia.org/wiki/Marcus_Daly
9. www.en.wikipedia.org/wiki/William_A._Clark
10. www.biography.com/people/james_j._hill-38025#synopsis

Chapter Forty-two

SOURCES FOR WASHINGTON

1. www.en.wkipedia.org/wiki/Kennewick_Man
2. www.en.wikipedia.org/wiki/History_of_Washington (state)
3. www.en.wikipedia.org/wiki/Pacific_Fur_Company
4. www.en.wikipedia.org/wiki/History_of_Washington (state)
5. Murray, Keith A. "Statehood for Washington." Columbia Magazine. 2.3 (winter 1988-1989): 30-35. Accessed 2/19/17. www.columbia-washingtonhistory.org/anthology/fromtriballands/statehood.aspx.
6. www.en.wikipedia.org/wiki/Isaac_Stevens
7. www.en.wikipwdia.org/wiki/Elisha_P._Ferry

Chapter Forty-three

SOURCES FOR IDAHO

1. www.en.wikipedia.org/wiki/History_of_Idaho
2. Ibid.
3. Ibid.
4. www.Wikipedia.org/wiki/Idaho
5. Preston, Seth. "Those Dirty Scoundrels Stole the Capital," The Lewiston Tribune, July 3, 1990. www.Lmtribune.com/feature/those-dirty-scoundrels-stole-the capital_bdb95913-fcbe-5170-8819-841FOaa34886.html
6. www.history.idaho.gov/sites/default/files/uploads/ES5_Wallace.pdf
7. www.idahofallmagazine.com/2016/03/forgotten-idaho-heroes.
8. www.en.wikipedia.org/wiki/George_L._Shoup
9. Burnett, David. "Grover Cleveland Saves Idaho." www.580KIDO.com/grover-cleveland-saves-Idaho/

Chapter Forty-four

SOURCES FOR WYOMING

1. www.wyo.gov/wyoming-history
2. www.en.wikipedia.org/wiki/History_of_Wyoming
3. www.en.wikipedia.org/wiki/Oregon_Trail
4. www.en.wikipedia.org/wiki/History_of_Wyoming
5. Ibid.
6. www.enzi.senate.gov/public/index.cfm/aboutwyoming?p=wyoming-facts
7. Butterfield, Bonnie. "Spirit Wind-Walker Sacagawea: Captive, Indian Interpreter, Great American Legend: Her Life and Death." www.pbs.org/lewisandclark/inside/saca.html
8. Ibid.
9. Ibid.

10. Ibid.
11. www.en.wikipedia.org/wiki/John_Colte
12. Hebard, Grace Raymond. "The Independent Feminine Life, 1861-1936" by Virginia Scharff. From "Lone Voyagers: Academic Women in Co-Educational Universities 1870-1937." Edited by Geraldine Joncich Clifford. The Feminist Press of the City University of New York (1989). www.en.wikipedia.org/wiki/Esther_Hobart_Morris
13. www.en.wikipedia.org/wiki/Buffalo_Bill

Chapter Forty-five

SOURCES FOR UTAH

1. www.en.wikipedia.org/wiki/History_of_Utah
2. www.en.wikipedia.org/wiki/Territorial_Evolution_of_Utah
3. www.en.wikipedia.org/wiki/State_of_Deseret
4. www.en.wikipedia.org/wiki/History_of_Utah
5. White, Jean Bickmore. "Utah History Encyclopedia." www.historytogo.utah.gove/utah_chapters/statehood_and_the_progressive_era/
6. www.Womensuffrageinutah.hjtml.
7. Bringhurst, Newell G., "Utah History Encyclopedia." www.historytogo.utah.gov/people/brighamyoung.html.
8. Ibid.
9. Paul, Rodman W., (December 1974-January 1975) "The Mormons of Yesterday and Today," "Engineering and Science," California Institute of Technology & Alumni Association. Retrieved September 19, 2013. www.en.wikipedia.org/wiki/Brigham_Young.

Chapter Forty-six

SOURCES FOR OKLAHOMA

1. www.en.wikipedia.org/wiki/History_of_Oklahoma
2. www.en.wikipedia.org/wiki/Treaty_of_Fontainebleau
3. www.en.wikipedia.org/wiki/Oklahoma_Territory
4. Ibid.
5. Ibid.
6. www.en.wikipedia.org/wiki/David L._Payne
7. www.en.wikipedia.org/wiki/George_Washington_Steele
8. "Encyclopedia of Oklahoma History and Culture." www.geneologytrails.com/oklahoma/couch.html

Chapter Forty-seven

SOURCES FOR NEW MEXICO

1. www.en.wikipedia.org/wiki/History_of_New_Mexico
2. Ibid.
3. Ibid.
4. www.history.com/this-day-in-history/spain-accepts-mexican-independence
5. www.en.wikipedia.org/wiki/History_of_New_Mexico
6. Ibid.
7. www.en.wikipedia.org/wiki/Gadsden_Purchase
8. www.en.wikipedia.org/wiki/New_Mexico_Territory
9. Linthicum, Leslie. Albuquerque Journal, October 23, 2013. www.abqjournal.com/Y286241/new-mexicos-path-to-statehood-often-faltered
10. www.en.wikipedia.org/wiki/Pope

11. Sides, Hampton, "Blood and Thunder," Doubleday, 2006.
12. www.en.wikipedia.org/wiki/Kit_Carson
13. Ibid.

Chapter Forty-eight

SOURCES FOR ARIZONA

1. www.arizonaexperience.org/member/early-conquistadors-explore-southwest
2. www.reference.com/history/did-arizona-become-state-83b5d527f2dd6648
3. www.en.wikipedia.org/wiki/James_Gadsden
4. www.en.wikipedia.org/wiki/History_of_arizona
5. Boomersbach, Jana. "The Arizona Republic." November 27, 2010. www.archiveazcentral.Com/arizonarepublic/Viewpoints/articles/20101127/Arizona-statehood-boomersbach
6. www.en.wikipedia.org/wiki/Charles_Debrille_Poston
7. www.en.wikipedia.org/wiki/George_W._P._Hunt
8. Goff, John S. (1989), "George W. P. Hunt." In Myers, John L. (ed.) "The Arizona Governors1912-1990." Phoenix: Heritage Publishers (pp. 7-17). www.en.wikipedia.org/wiki/George_W._P._Hunt

Chapter Forty-nine

SOURCES FOR ALASKA

1. www.en.wikipedia.org/wiki/History_of_Alaska
2. Ibid.
3. www.en.wikipedia.org/wiki/William_H._Seward
4. www.en.wikipedia.org/wiki/History_of_Alaska
5. www.en.wikipedia.org/wiki/Alexander_Andreevich_Baranov
6. www.en.wikipedia.org/wiki/William_H._Seward
7. Ibid.
8. www.en.wikipedia.org/wiki/James_Wickersham

Chapter Fifty

SOURCES FOR HAWAII

1. www.en.wikipedia.org/wiki/Overthrow_of_the_Kingdom_of_Hawaii
2. www.en.wikipedia.org/wiki/Great_Mahele
3. www.en.wikipedia.org/wiki/History_of_Hawaii
4. Ibid.
5. Ibid.
6. www.en.wikipedia.org/wiki/Territory_of_Hawaii
7. Ibid.
8. www.en.wikipedia.org/wiki/History_of_Hawaii
9. www.en.wikipesia.org/wiki/Territory_of_Hawaii
10. Ibid.
11. Ibid.
12. www.en.wikipedia.org/wiki/Lorrin_A._Thurston
13. www.en.wikipedia.org/wiki/Sanford_B._Dole
14. www.en.wikipedia.org/wiki/John_A._Burns
15. Sources for Maps
16. Maps 2-15: "The National Atlas of the United States of America" 1970 edition. "U.S. Territorial Maps for 1775-1959". United States Department of Interior. Library of Congress (pp. 140-141).

17. Maps 1, 16-17: www.dsl.richmond.edu/historicalatlas/46/c/. With permission from The Carnegie Institute.
18. Additional maps for viewer retrieval:
19. www.xroads.virginia.edu~MAP/terr. American Studies Project at University of Virginia, 1992-2006, www.usterritorialmaps1775-1920. Prof. Alan B. Howard.

M·J
Morgan James
Speakers Group

FOR THE
DEVELOPING WORLD
LIBRARY
FOR ALL
DIGITAL LIBRARY

CPSIA information can be obtained
at www.ICGtesting.com
Printed in the USA
BVHW03s0143200918
528018BV00001B/4/P